AF477090

INTERNATIONAL GARDEN PHOTOGRAPHER OF THE YEAR

CELEBRATING FIVE YEARS OF AWARD-WINNING IMAGES

MURDOCH BOOKS

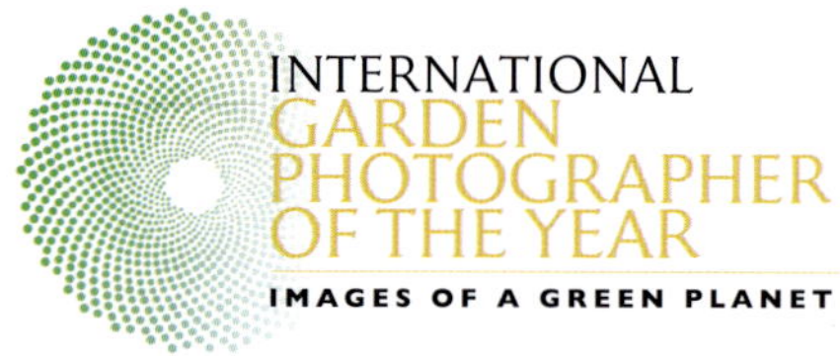

Published in 2012 by Murdoch Books Pty Limited

Murdoch Books Australia
Pier 8/9
23 Hickson Road
Millers Point NSW 2000
Phone: +61 (0) 2 8220 2000
Fax: +61 (0) 2 8220 2558
www.murdochbooks.com.au
info@murdochbooks.com.au

Murdoch Books UK Limited
Erico House, 6th Floor
93–99 Upper Richmond Road
Putney, London SW15 2TG
Phone: +44 (0) 20 8785 5995
Fax: +44 (0) 20 8785 5985
www.murdochbooks.co.uk
info@murdochbooks.co.uk

For Corporate Orders & Custom Publishing contact Noel Hammond,
National Business Development Manager, Murdoch Books Australia

Publisher: Paul Mitchell
Designer: Nick Otway
Project Editor: Claire Grady
Production: Mike Crowton

A cataloguing-in-publication entry is available from the catalogue of the National Library of Australia at www.nla.gov.au.

A catalogue record for this book is available from the British Library.

Printed by 1010 Printing International Limited, China

Contents

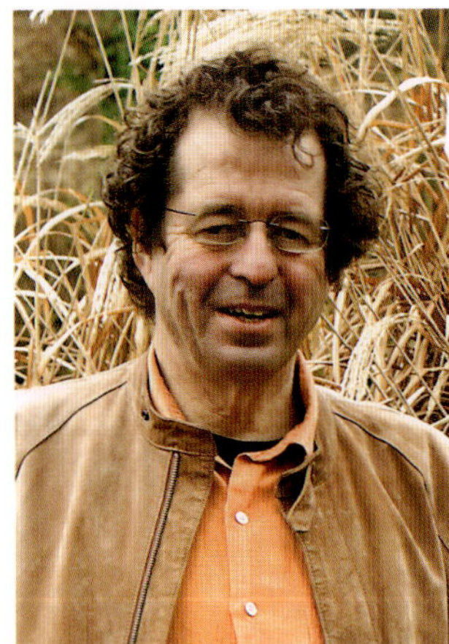

Introduction *Philip Smith*

With the publication of this book we are marking five years of International Garden Photographer of the Year. In that time the project has inspired and delighted thousands, if not millions, of people who have entered the competition, seen the exhibitions or bought the books – or who have just come across it on the internet, magazine or newspaper.

The project started in 2007. The UK Professional Garden Photographers' Association, part of the Garden Media Guild, had created a series of exhibitions in London and at the Royal Botanic Gardens, Kew. As a result, a few of the committee members, Andrew Lawson, Clive Nichols, Jane Nichols, Derek Harris and myself, created International Garden Photographer of the Year as a global competition that would attract interest from photographers, professional and amateur, from around the world.

As the competition opened, we were amazed by the level of interest and tremendous commitment both to photography and the natural world that our competing photographers were showing.

The Royal Botanic Gardens, Kew was our key partner from the outset. The first exhibition was held there in 2008 in a purpose-built outdoor gallery and we toured the show to a few other locations in the UK, including Wakehurst Place. In 2010, we started to create traditional indoor exhibitions. This has greatly increased the breadth and depth of the project and continues to do so. In 2011, we expanded overseas and held exhibitions in Portugal, New York and Sydney.

Photographers enter their pictures through the project website – igpoty.com. There is a range of categories that will excite any serious photographer – from luscious close-ups of plants to stunning wildflower landscapes. There is a special category for people under 16 years of age.

International Garden Photographer of the Year is now run by me with great assistance from Mary Denton and my wife, Eileen Powell. Many people have helped us along the way – there is no room here to list them all but we could not have come so far without them.

Many at Kew have been involved from the outset, including Tina Houlton and the festivals and marketing teams, Anna Quenby and the Press teams, the Digital Media team, who support our Blog on the Kew website, and Kew Publishing. And not forgetting the competition judges, all of whom have contributed essays to this book.

This is also an opportunity to send personal thanks to Liz Williams of the Royal Photographic Society and to Nick Otway, the designer of all of our associated books which have been enjoyed by so many people. Thanks also to Andrew and Briony Lawson who host our judging process each year with such charm and generosity.

This book represents the fruits of our labours over five years – but of course it is really about the labours of the photographers. It's their love of nature and plants that we present here. Our vision is to create a body of work that is not just a meditation on the world of plants and gardens – but also a thrilling inspiration to photographers, gardeners and anyone who respects and loves the wonders of the natural world.

There is no more vital task ahead of us than to help, through the art of photography, to bring the world's attention to the imperative need to understand, preserve and cherish the natural world – and the plants upon which all life depends.

Philip Smith is Chief Executive and co-founder of International Garden Photographer of the Year.

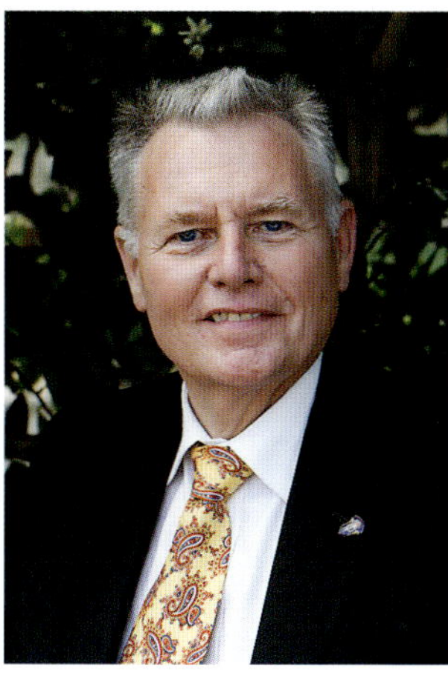

Foreword *Professor David J. Mabberley*

Looking over five years' worth of remarkable images from the International Garden Photographer of the Year competitions, is a timely reminder of the beauty yet fragility of our natural world, and the overwhelming and very serious need to protect our global biodiversity.

For all life depends on plants, as they are the providers of materials for most aspects of our lives. From the air we breathe, the food on our plates, the health of our lands and waterways, our medicines, our clothes and our shelter.

With estimates that up to 50% of our world's plant species are under threat of extinction, botanic gardens across the world are coming together to lead internationally significant science and conservation programs.

Behind the beauty and tranquillity of the green expanses of botanic gardens such as Royal Botanic Gardens, Kew and Royal Botanic Garden, Sydney some of the world's principal scientists and botanists are working together to understand and ultimately conserve our flora as climate change and habitat destruction threaten to take them from us forever.

Programs such as the New South Wales Seedbank, as part of the Millennium Seed Bank Project, described by Sir David Attenborough as 'perhaps the most important conservation initiative ever' have brought about a collaboration of leading botanic gardens collecting and storing millions of seeds to ensure the survival of species well into the future.

At a more public level, an international celebration of our natural world occurs through exhibitions such as International Garden Photographer of the Year and specifically for photos taken within botanic gardens in our own *Gardens in Focus* photography competition. Together they are the catalysts for thousands of people around the world to capture through their cameras the precious beauty and fragility of plants.

The International Garden Photographer of the Year exhibitions provide a lasting testament to the life-affirming beauty of plants – be it in the folds of a delicate bud, a robust towering tree, a tenacious wildflower on a windswept cliff or fields of flowers as far as the eye can see – with these images comes a deeper appreciation of plants in all their splendour.

We have no greater treasure than our plant life, so that if we are to continue to thrive on this earth, we must not only celebrate and cherish, but also ensure a healthy future for our sustaining plants. Capturing and appreciating their exquisite beauty, be it in a botanic garden or beyond, afford us a reminder of what we all have a duty to protect.

Professor David Mabberley (MA (Oxon) PhD (Cantab) is Executive Director of the Royal Botanic Garden and Domain Trust, Sydney.

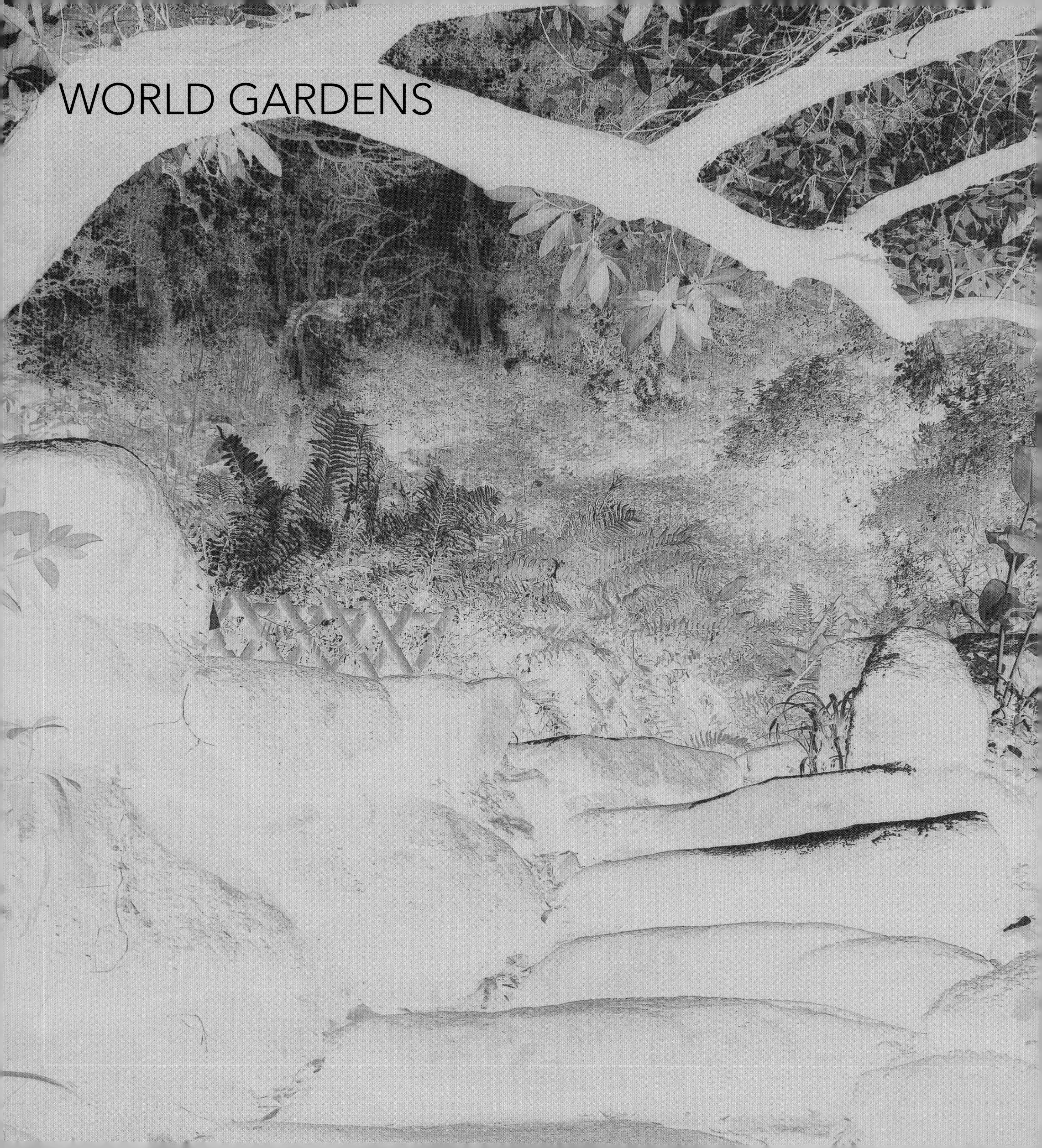

WORLD GARDENS

Photographing Gardens

Every one of the photographs in this book is conceived with passion. The starting point with any successful garden or plant photograph is a love of the subject. Then comes patience – being at the right place at the right time – and getting the moment right. Technical prowess on the camera and the computer is important too, but serves best when it is understated, even invisible.

As a judge, I have found it thrilling to encounter talented photographers from around the world and to discover the gardens that have inspired them. Through the International Garden Photographer of the Year project, there is a wonderful transmission of garden-related themes from around the globe.

Professional garden photographers, like myself, seek out the light and weather that can show gardens at their best. The least we can do for the owners and creators of the gardens is to go that extra mile to show their work in the most atmospheric conditions. If this is at dawn, as it often is, so be it. I appreciate that it is a tremendous privilege to see gardens and wild places at times when the rest of the world is still asleep. But our photographs should enable anyone to experience the pleasure that has gone into the making of them.

That said, there are limits to what a photograph can achieve. Any photograph, however good, is no more than a 'snapshot', a moment in time. It can never fully convey the full continuum of experience that comes from being in a garden or a landscape. There is no birdsong in a photograph, no sound of the wind in the trees, no smells, no touch. But the best photographs manage to give hints of these additional senses. I also enjoy the photographer's descriptions that accompany many of the pictures, especially when the words add further depth to the poetry already present in the pictures.

Andrew Lawson
Garden photographer, artist and International Garden Photographer of the Year judge.

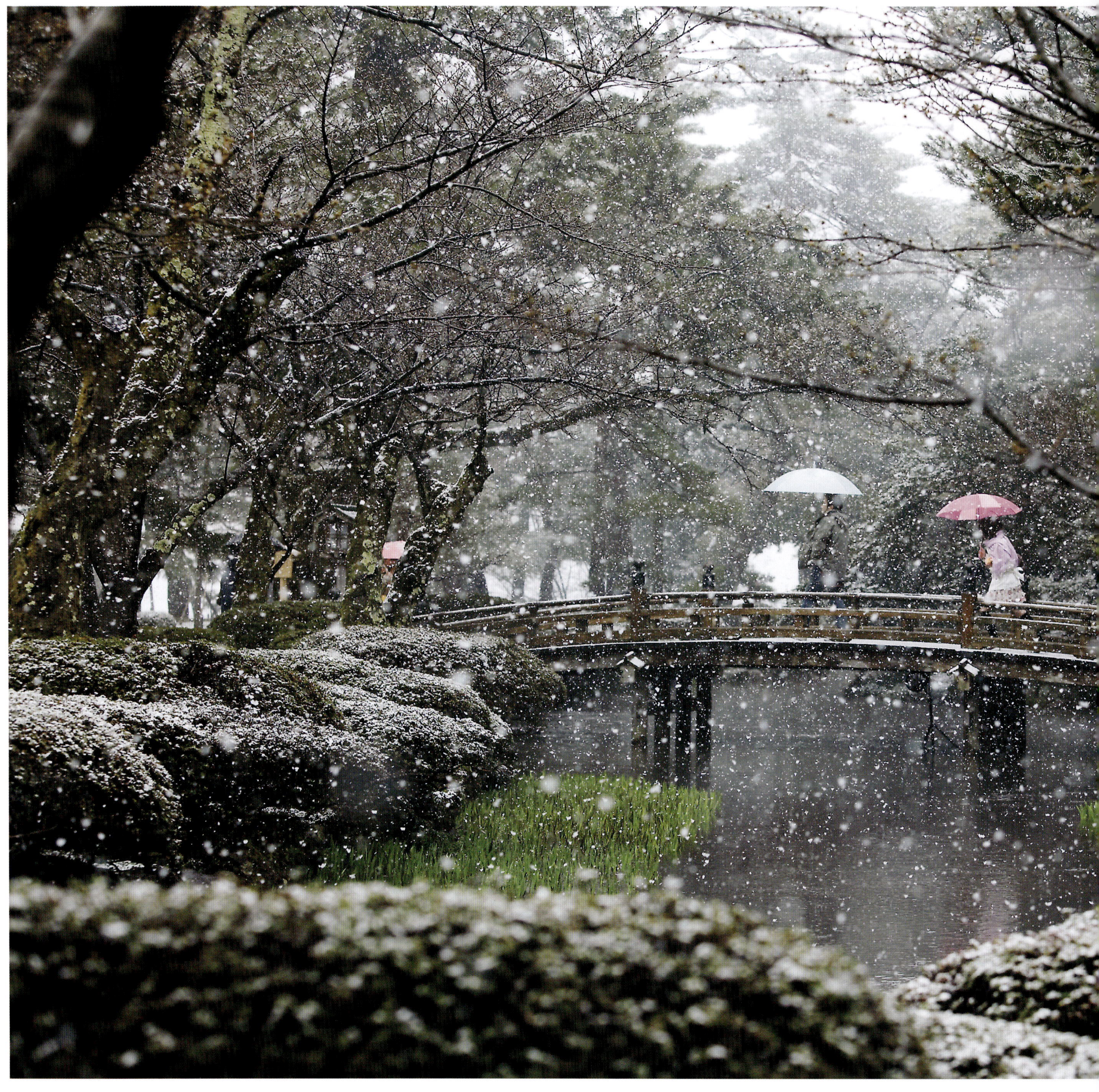

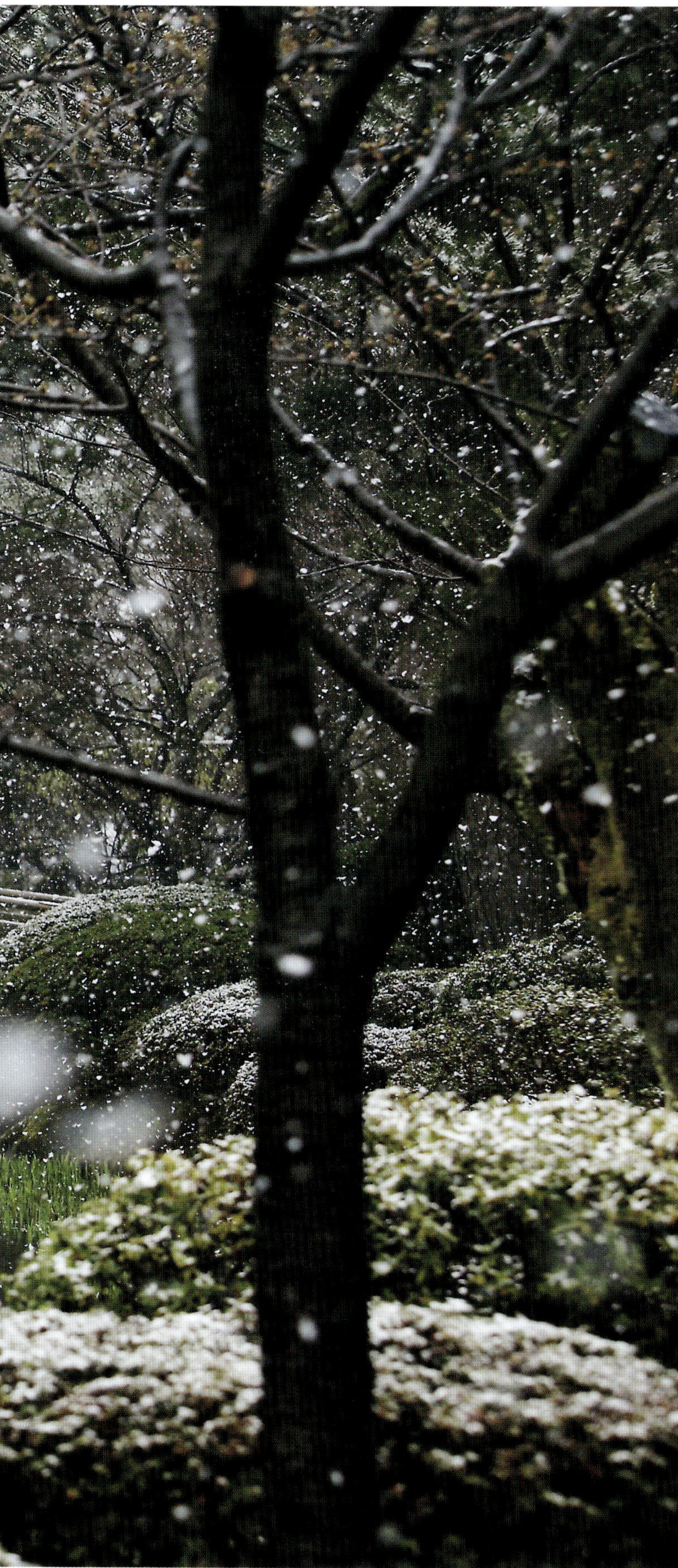

KANAZAWA, ISHIKAWA
KENROKUEN

CLAIRE TAKACS

Canon EOS-1Ds, 70–200mm lens, f/4. Adjusted levels and curves in Photoshop. A large aperture and fast shutter speed were necessary to capture the falling snow. I photographed for as long as my fingers could withstand the cold!
INTERNATIONAL GARDEN PHOTOGRAPHER OF THE YEAR, 2008

I went to Japan specifically to photograph the gardens during cherry blossom season. Visiting Kenrokuen while it was snowing was like being in a painting, but the visitors weren't deterred by it. It was such a sight to see the colourful umbrellas passing through the gardens and over the bridges, and definitely added a whole new dimension to the visit.

Thomas Jefferson was one of the founding fathers of North America. His garden is a botanic showpiece, a source of food and an experimental laboratory of ornamental and useful plants from around the world.

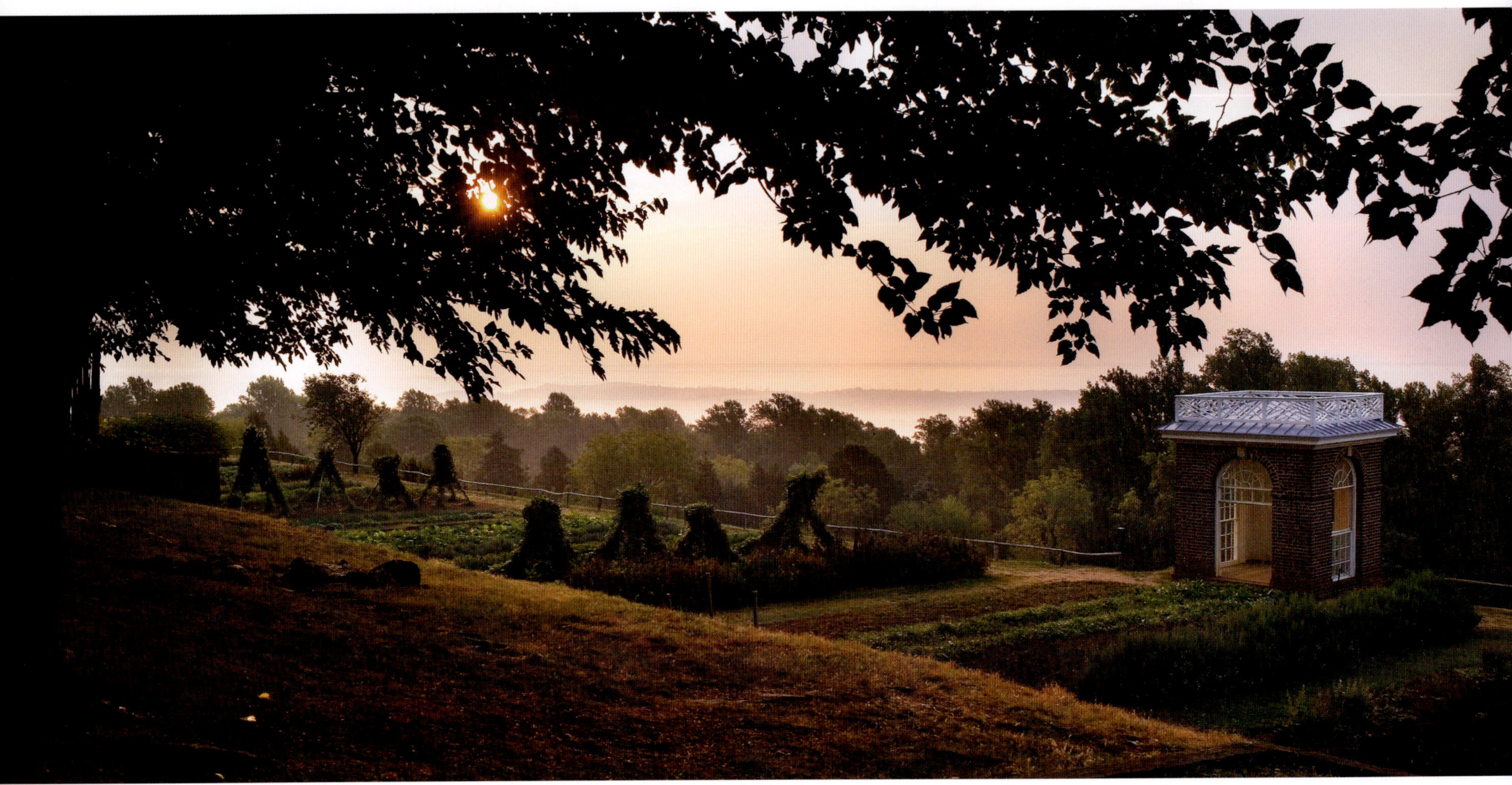

CHARLOTTESVILLE, VIRGINIA
THOMAS JEFFERSON'S MONTICELLO GARDENS

ANDREA JONES

Kodak Pro SLR/n. I arrived before dawn and waited for the sun to rise. When the light appeared through the mist it created a magical glow of colour. I removed an unsightly light fitting beneath the tree and enhanced the image using curves in Photoshop.
FINALIST, 2009

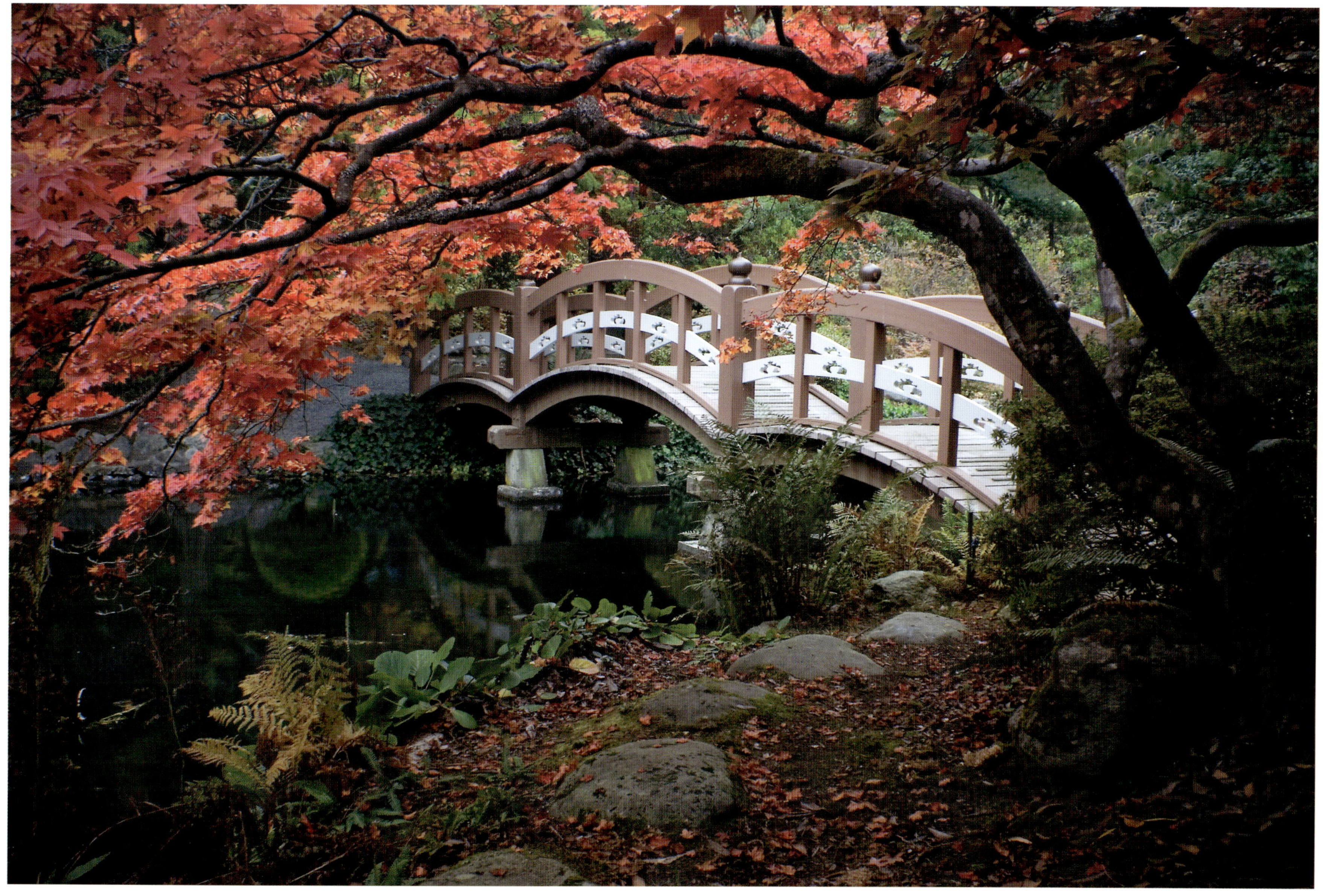

I live in a very short growing-season area at a high elevation and this was my first visit to the west coast in the autumn. I was astounded by the colours on this damp and misty day.

HATLEY PARK, BRITISH COLUMBIA
JAPANESE BRIDGE AND MAPLE

DAVID BALLANTYNE

Canon EOS 20D, Takumar 24mm lens. When I saw this view from a tiny wooded island looking back at the bridge I knew I'd found something special. I liked the feeling of being sheltered and the arch of the branches over the arches of the bridge.

FINALIST, 2008

TRESCO, ISLES OF SCILLY, ENGLAND

IN TRESCO ABBEY GARDEN

JONATHAN BERMAN

Canon D60, DIY infrared sensor conversion. I used a sensor filter that was sensitive to infrared (from Life Pixel). Digital infrared images often lack contrast so I undertook contrast enhancements using Photomatix Pro for general tone control and Photoshop CS3 for local control using layers and masks. The image was desaturated then toned.

INTERNATIONAL GARDEN PHOTOGRAPHER OF THE YEAR, 2009

This is an early-afternoon infrared view over Tresco Abbey Garden, looking south, with my daughter viewing the scene. A tiny, four-day-old crescent moon is just visible. I first visited Tresco and its gardens as a child, and I remembered it as a magical place. I did not return for many years until I came for holidays with my own children. I wanted to capture in this photograph my undiminished wonder at this special place. I used infrared – with its ability to darken skies and lighten foliage – to create the fairytale atmosphere. The inclusion of my daughter added depth. I had photographed this scene on several occasions but on this occasion the cloud patterns and presence of the moon lifted it out of the ordinary.

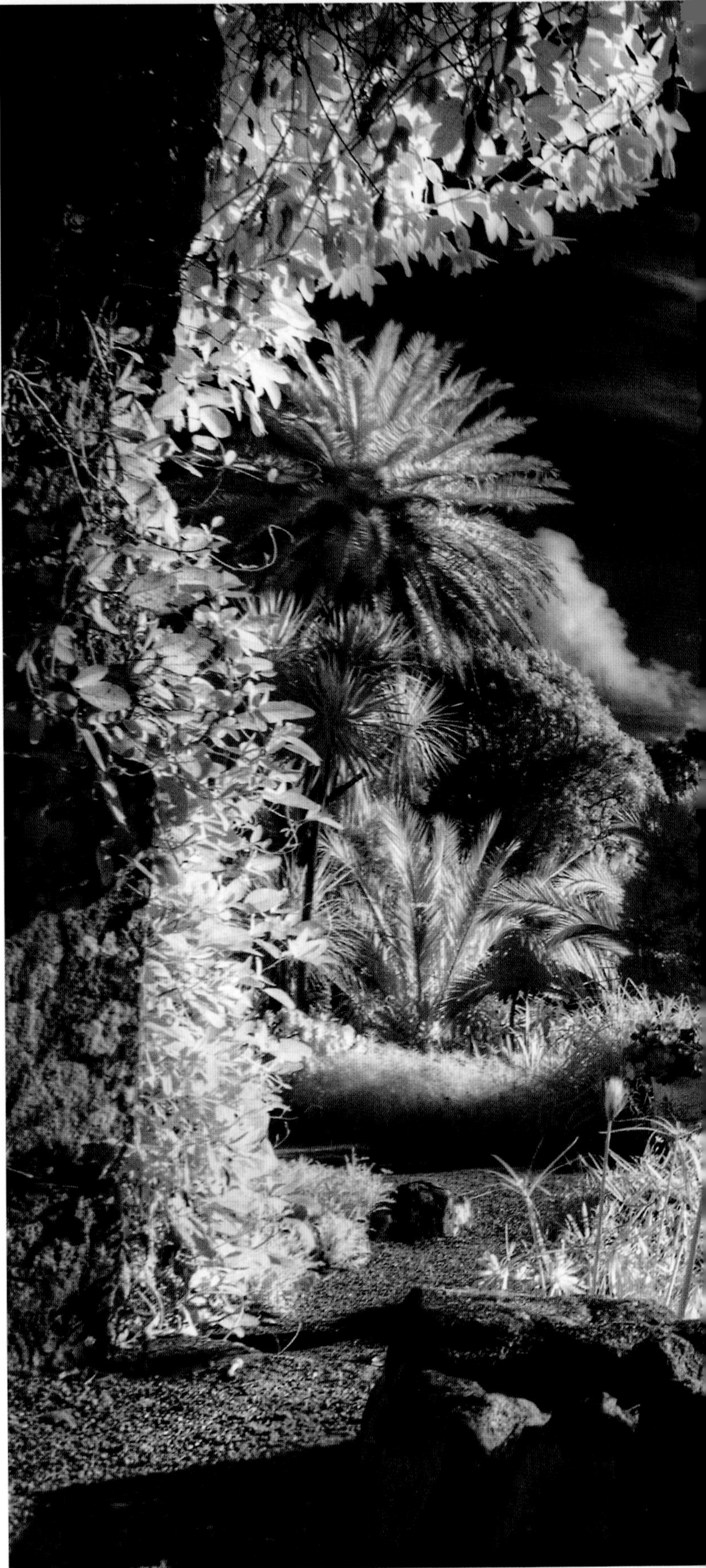

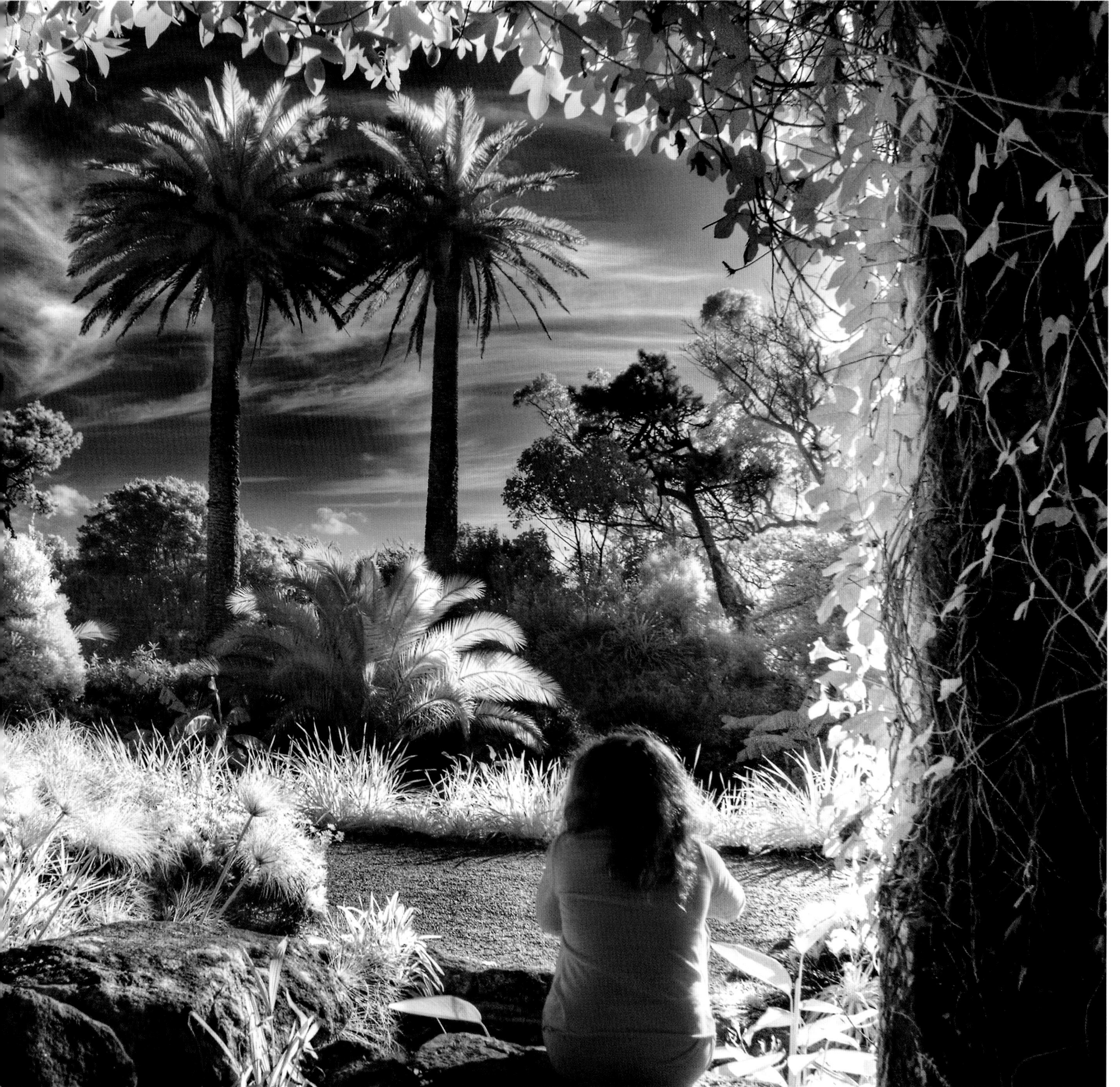

ARDENTINNY, LOCH LONG, SCOTLAND
BREAK IN THE CLOUDS

ANDREA JONES

Kodak DCS Pro SLR/n, Nikkor 28-70mm, 1/60sec at f/6.7. Post-capture: I enhanced the streams of light.
SECOND, 2011

Sunlight breaks through dark clouds illuminating the garden belonging to one of the Swedish Houses. The light was my inspiration! I loved the simplicity and style of this artist's garden and the colours of the gate, furnishings and summer house. Knowing Scottish weather, I thought if I waited long enough the clouds might eventually break. Luckily the hospitable garden owners allowed me to stay until I got the result I wanted. At the first sign of light I ran upstairs to shoot from my tripod-mounted camera, which was ready by the window.

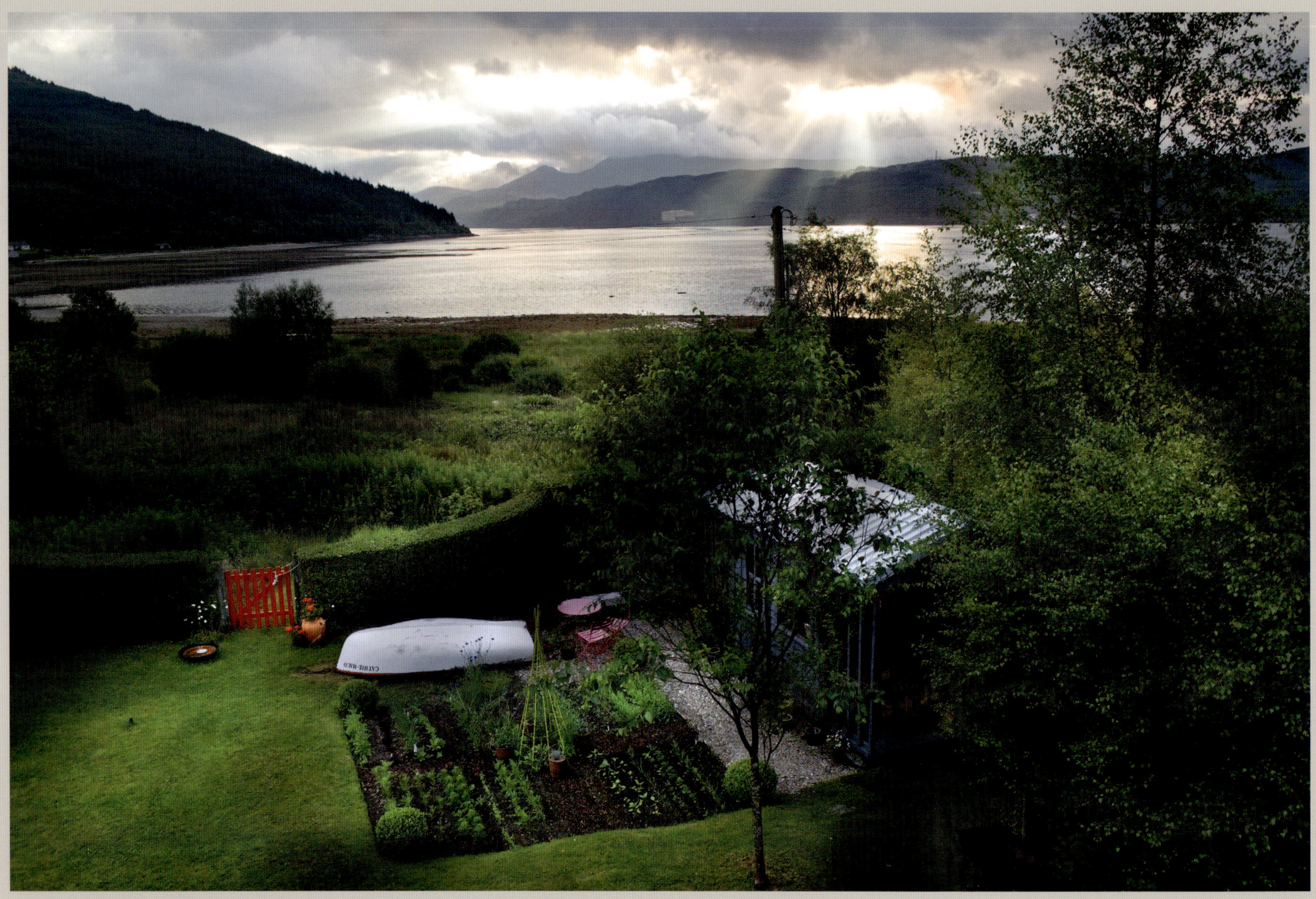

RICHLAND WILDFLOWER PROJECT, OREGON

DESERT GARDEN

DENNIS FRATES

Canon EOS-1Ds Mark II, Canon 24–105mm IS lens, polariser. I used a moderate telephoto lens to compress the elements of the hills and garden.

FIRST, 2008

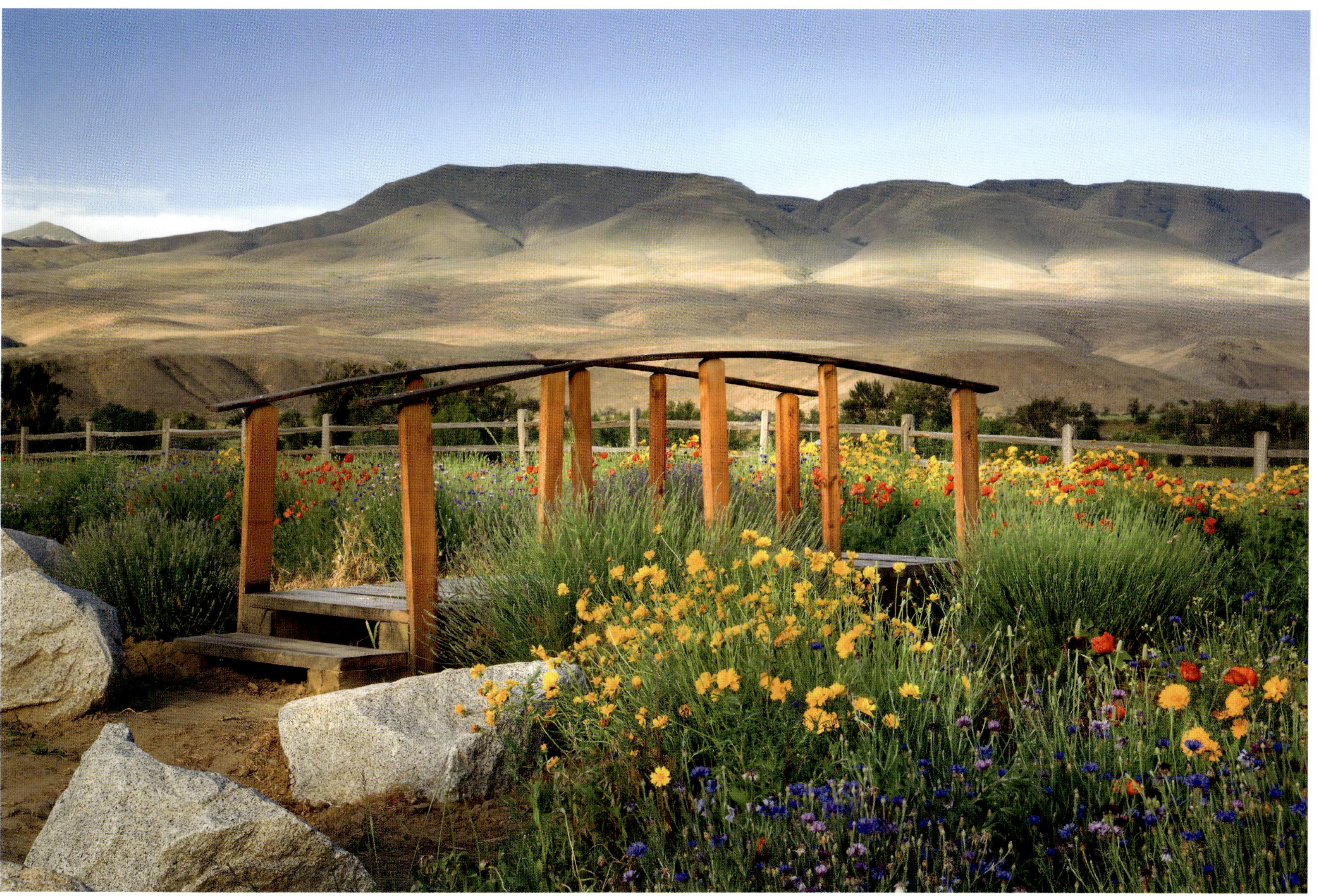

I wanted to show the stark contrast between this lush garden and the backdrop of the dry, barren desert hills of eastern Oregon. It was partly cloudy and I waited until the light was filtered and less direct on the flowers, otherwise it would have had too much contrast.

CAMBRIDGE UNIVERSITY BOTANIC GARDEN, CAMBRIDGE, ENGLAND
BIRD OF PARADISE FLOWER (*STRELITZIA REGINAE*)

DAMIAN GILLIE

Canon EOS 5D Mark II, 28mm lens, f/9.5.
COMMENDED, 2009

This bird of paradise flower was found in front of the new 'Continents Apart' glasshouse. Here we can see plants from southwest Australia and the cape of South Africa, which were once joined as the ancient landmass of Gondwanaland. Most of these plants are unique to these two areas of the world. A world away from the freezing January conditions outside, this image illustrates the haven of warmth and colour on the inside. I visit this place often in the winter months, and it feels different each time I visit. It is usually empty of people. This is just next to the entrance and so is the first and last thing I see as I arrive and leave.

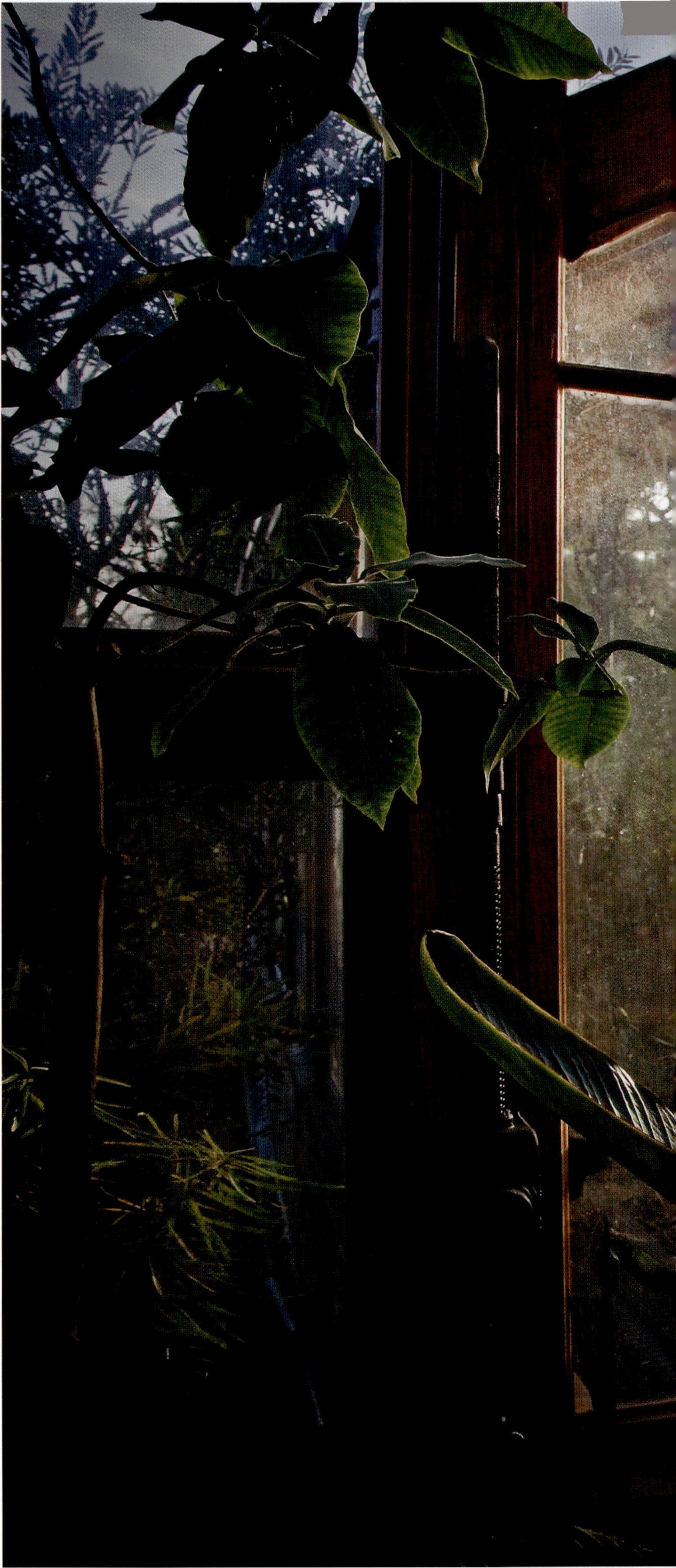

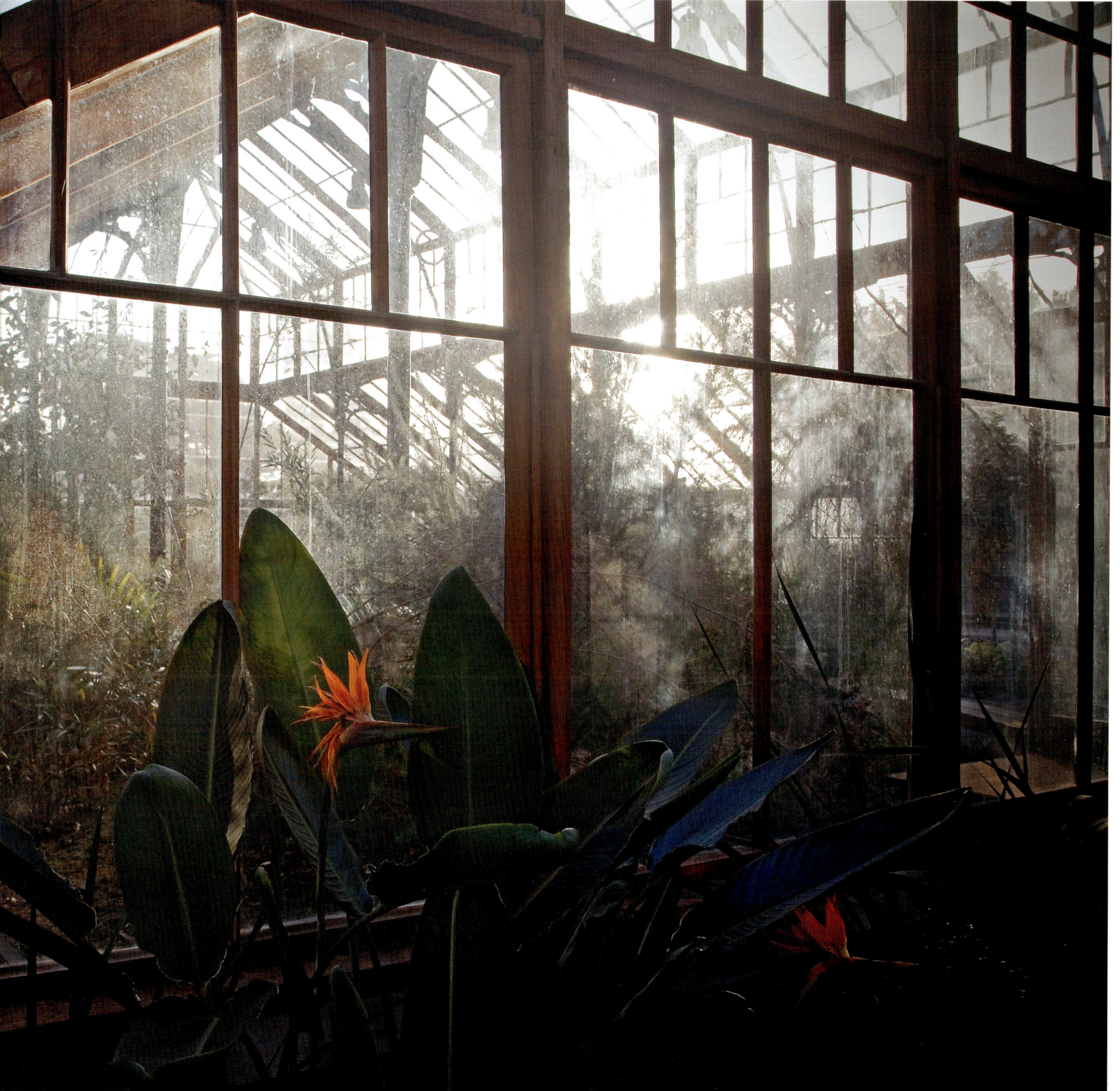

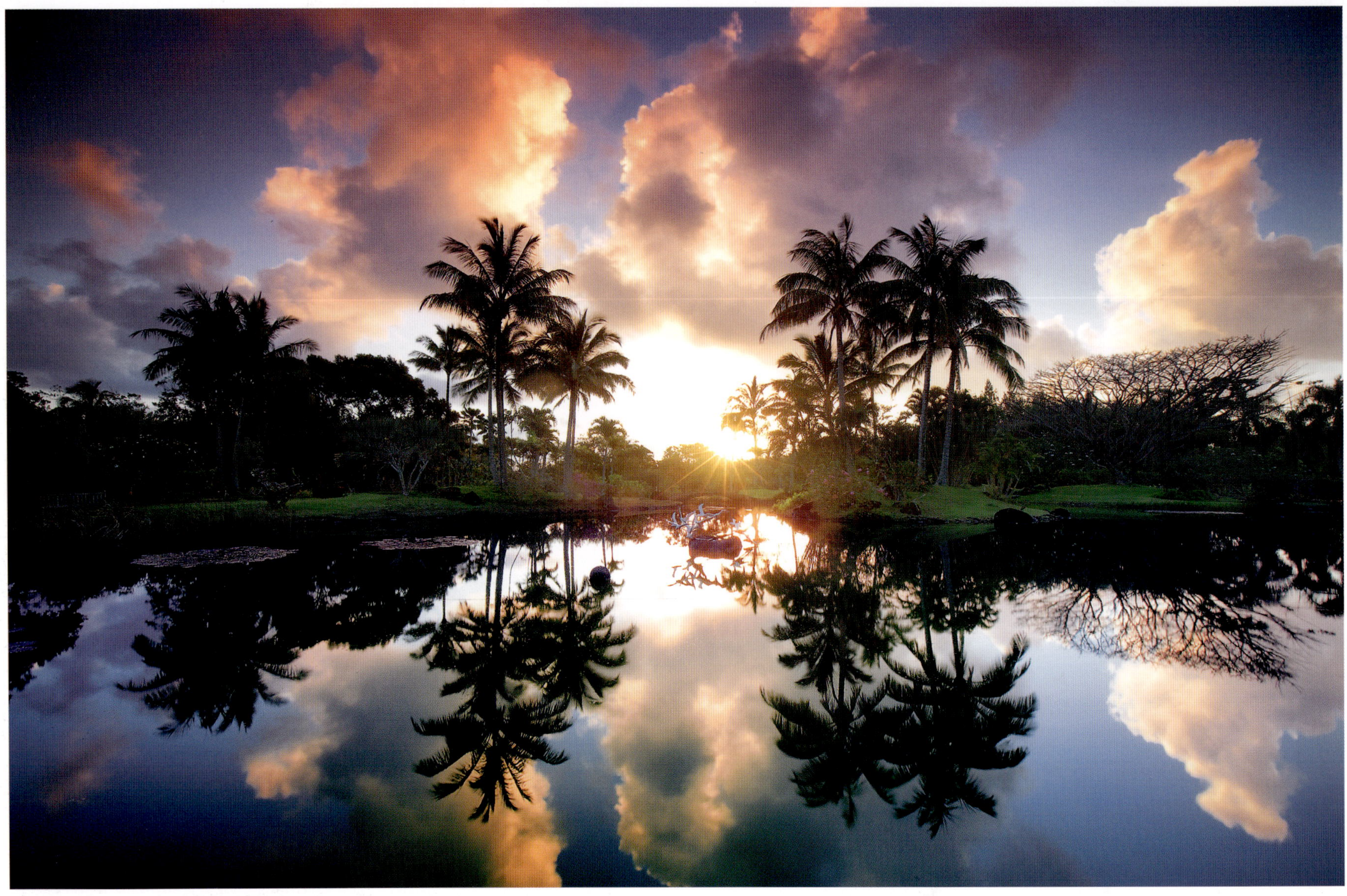

NA AINA KAI BOTANICAL GARDENS, KAUAI, HAWAII
TROPICAL GARDEN SUNRISE

DENNIS FRATES

Canon 1DS Mark III, Canon 16-35mm lens. 1.3sec at f/14.
Post-capture: tone and colour correction.
FINALIST, 2012

This shot was taken at sunrise. The shot was made before the gardens opened to the public, so all was peaceful and calm. This type of morning cloud is not uncommon in tropical environments, but they especially lit up this morning.

I like how there is something of interest in every part of the image. I contacted the nursery months in advance and arranged a sunrise visit: it normally doesn't open, even for guided tours, until way after sunrise.

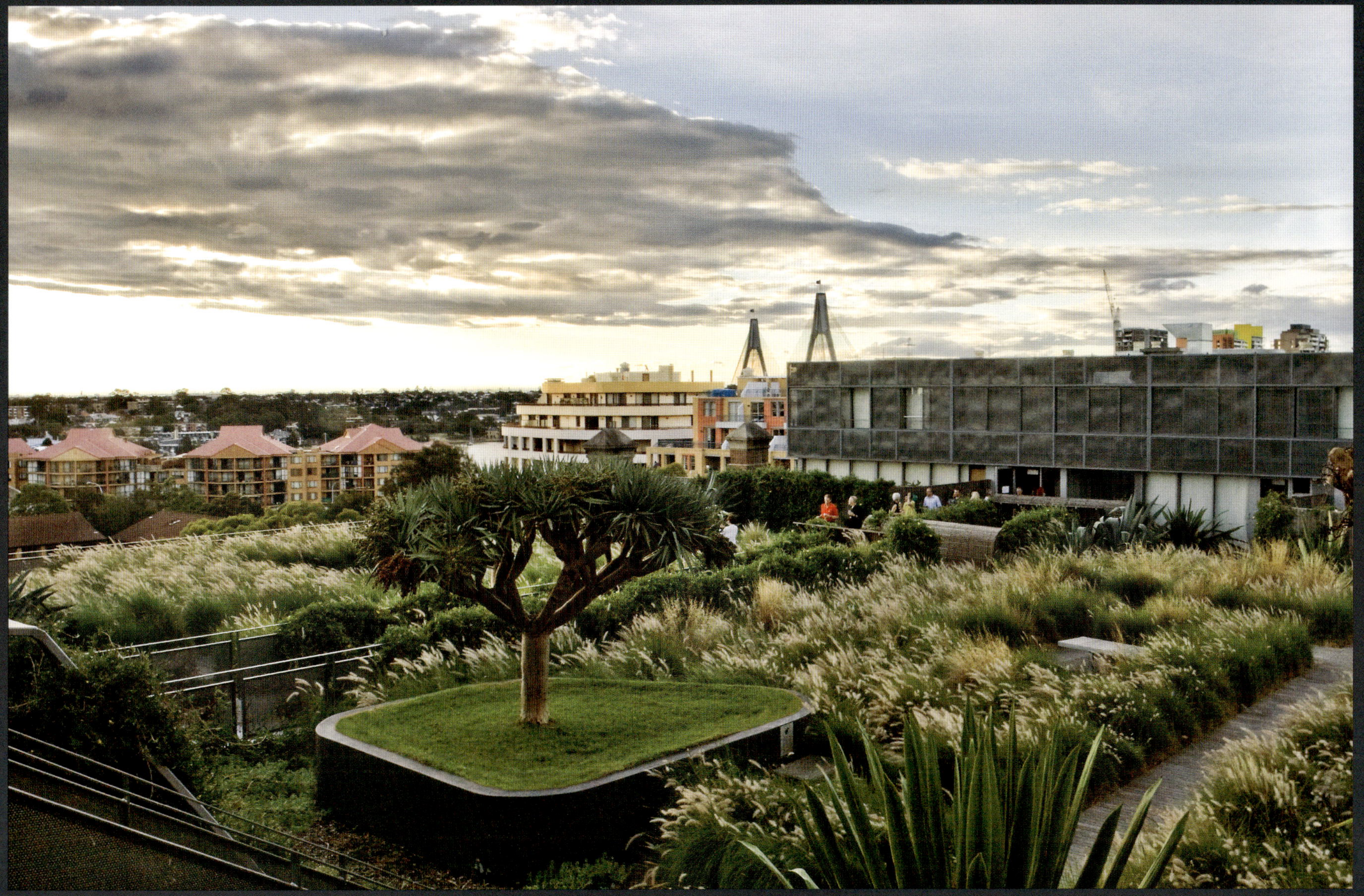

The rooftop garden at M Central is an urban oasis of grasses and small, secluded havens with a stunning view. The building has been converted into apartments from a wool store, but much of the original building and its character has been retained. Its dramatic architectural elements contrast with the flowing softness of the grasses, and those who live in the apartments fully appreciate and love the garden. The building fronts a main road but, once you are in the garden, the busy city seems far away. It is a little slice of heaven.

M CENTRAL, SYDNEY, NEW SOUTH WALES
GARDENS ARE FOR PLEASURE

SUE STUBBS

Canon EOS-1D Mark III, Canon EF 24-70mm f/2.8 lens, f/22. I was on top of the stairs, looking out over the garden to the sunset. I wanted depth of field and a fast shutter speed, and the light was getting low. Changing to a faster ISO allowed me to capture the flowing grasses and retain the depth of field.

FINALIST, 2009

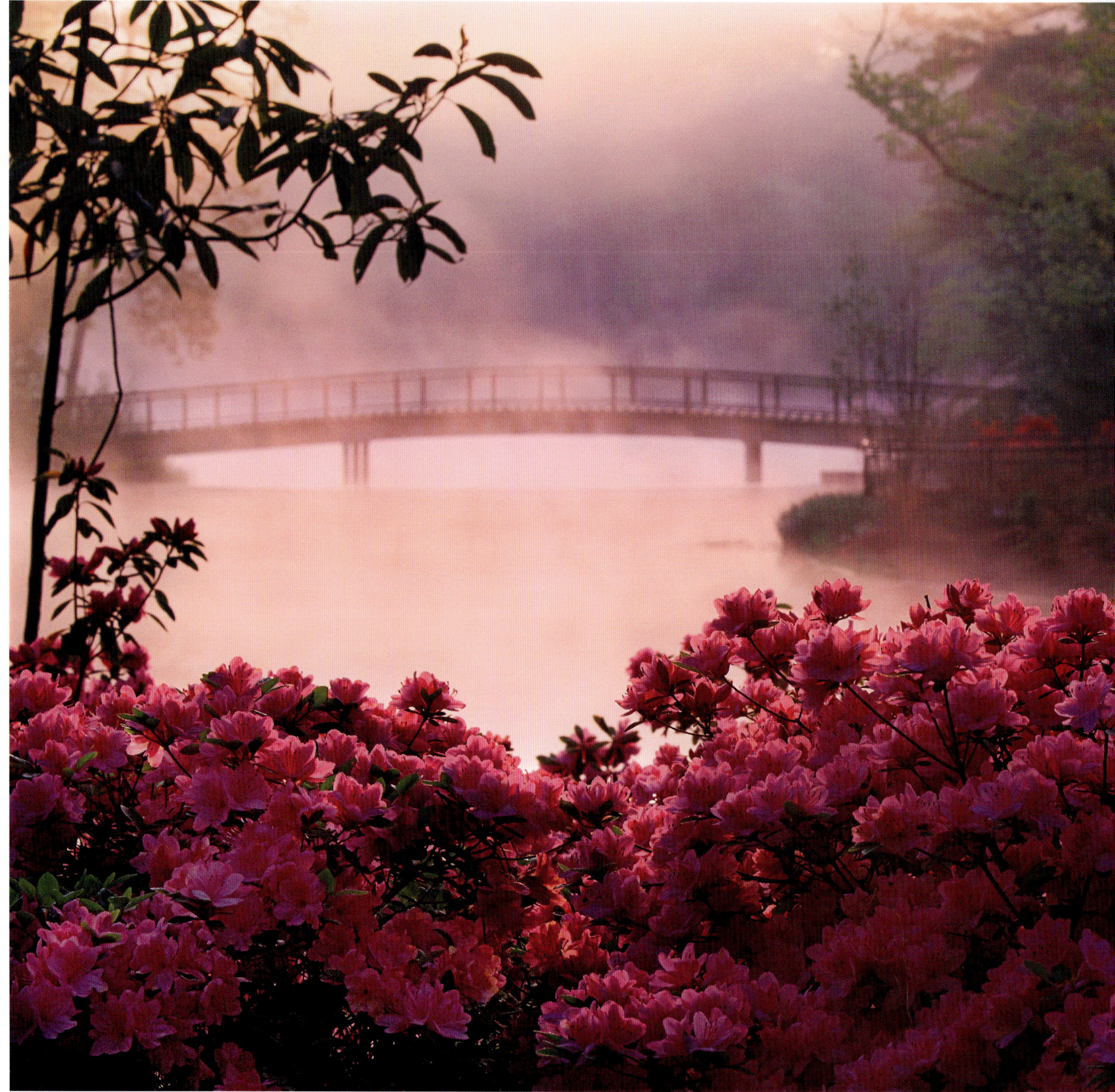

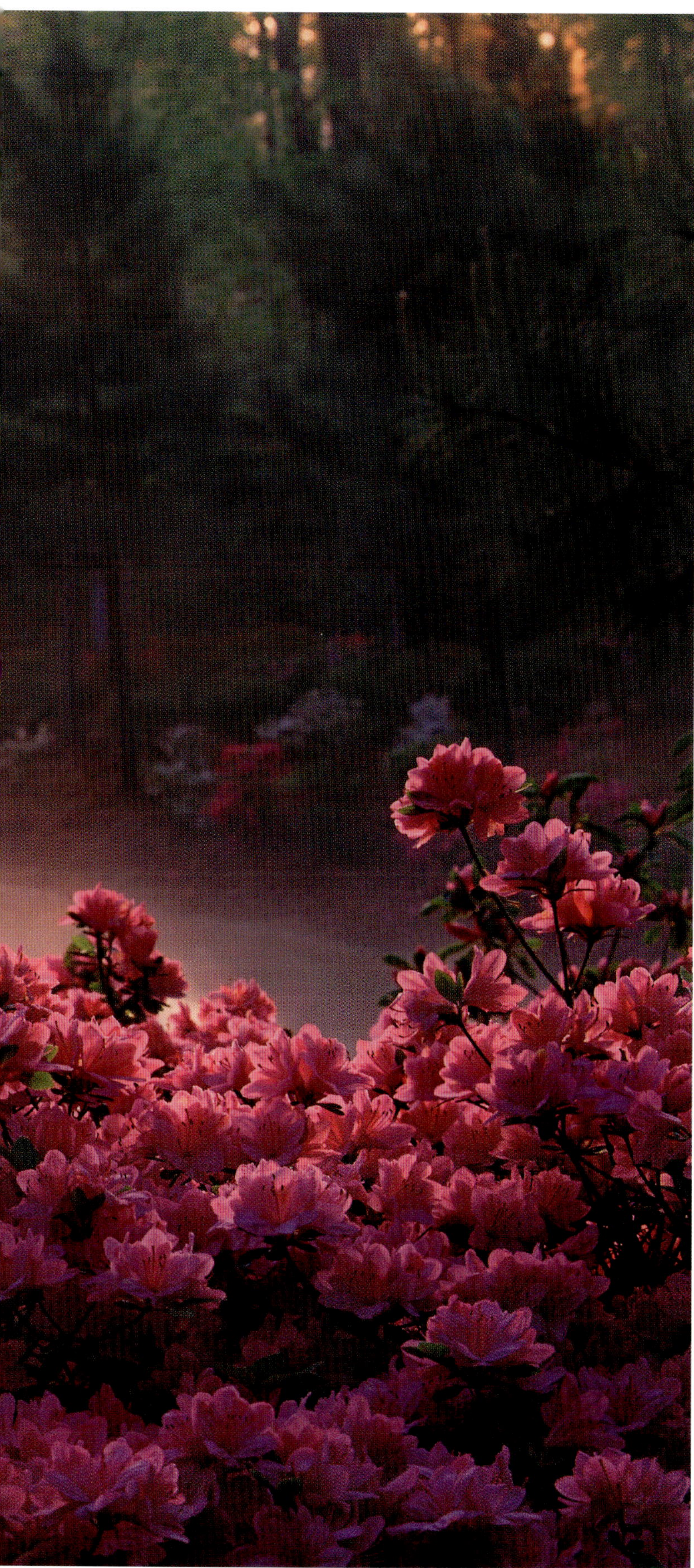

CALLAWAY GARDENS; PINE MOUNTAIN, GEORGIA
MORNING SPLENDOUR

CHARLES NEEDLE

Nikon F4, Nikkor 24-50mm lens, 1/4sec at f/16, Fujifilm Velvia. I also used a filter to warm the scene slightly and enhance the pink colour of the azaleas. Post-capture: no digital alterations, other than cleaning and basic colour management.
FINALIST, 2011

The Callaway Brothers Azalea Bowl is a 12-year-old, 40-acre public garden that contains more than 3,400 hybrid azaleas (*Rhododendron* spp.). Each spring, the garden erupts with a colourful palette of pinks, reds, purples and whites. Additional plantings include 2,000 trees and shrubs. I was inspired by all the elements coming together at just the right moment when making this photograph; the warm, pink sunlight, dancing fog on the lake, and hundreds of vibrant, pink azaleas in the foreground all erupting in peak bloom.

I had attempted to photograph this same scene several mornings in a row, but was unsuccessful because there was no fog on the lake. When I returned on this particular morning, all the right conditions came together to create a magical moment. Camera angle and careful composition were key here. I positioned my tripod low and used a wide angle lens to capture the vast expanse of picture space. I carefully considered aspects such as leading the eye back using the natural 'v notch' in the azaleas and making sure the pink blossoms did not merge with the opposite bank.

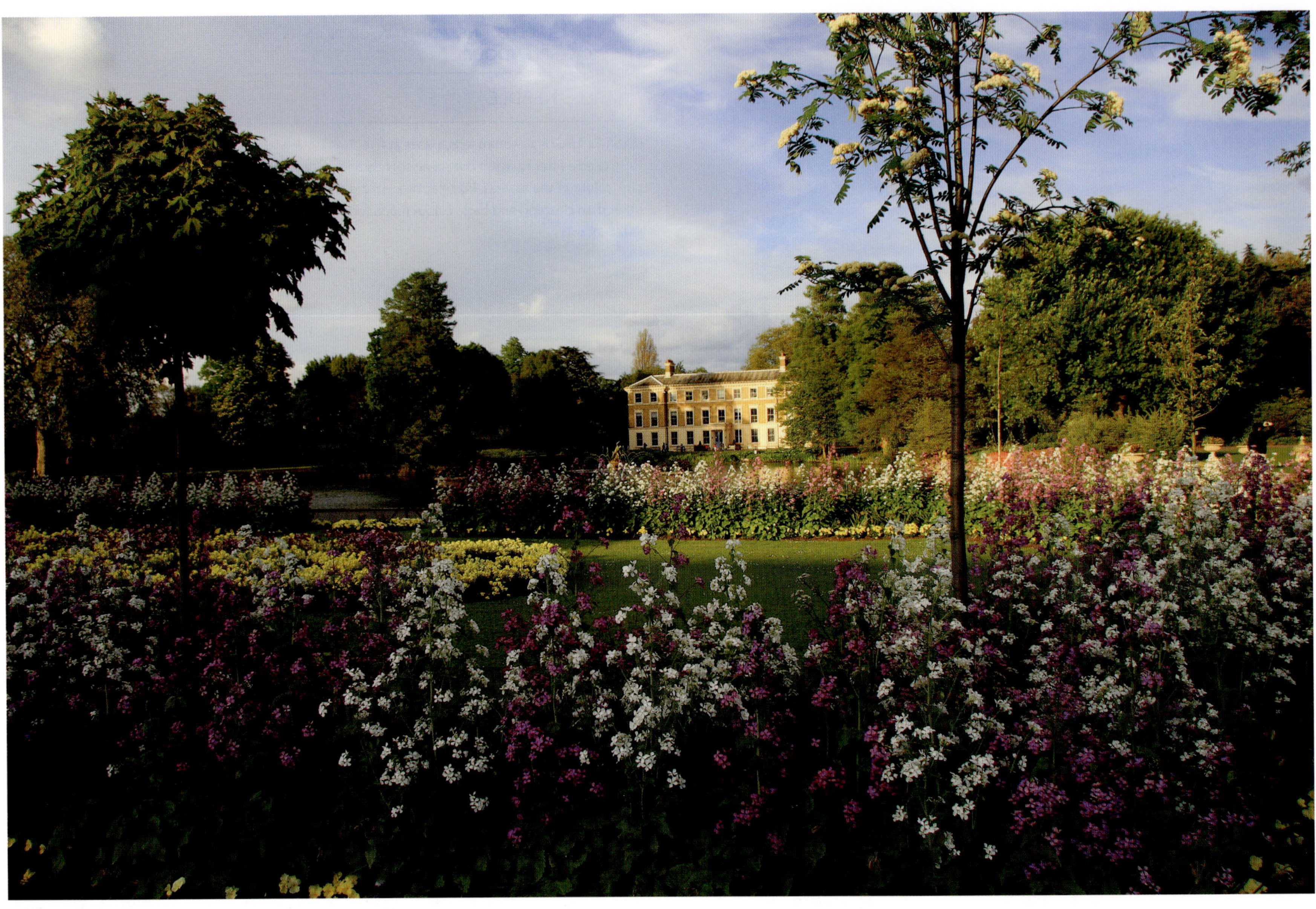

ROYAL BOTANIC GARDENS,
KEW, SURREY, ENGLAND
EARLY EVENING LIGHT

DEBRA DE SOUZA

Canon EOS 40D, Canon 17-85mm lens, 1/125sec at f/8. Post-capture: no manipulation.
HIGHLY COMMENDED, 2011

I took this photograph as I was heading for the exit, as the gardens were about to close. I was standing with my back to the Palm House, with a view across the purple and white planting and lake, to the building beyond. The early evening light produced softened tones, and bathed the scene in a warm glow, imparting a feeling of warmth and tranquility. What I found inspiring was the way the early evening light infused the scene with a softness and warmth, absent earlier in the day. I was also attracted by the wonderful contrast in the colours of the planting and the opportunity to frame the building between the trees. I chose my vantage point to make the most of the layering effect of the horizontal planes to achieve a sense of depth, as well as the framing vertical divisions and the subtle contrasts of light and shade.

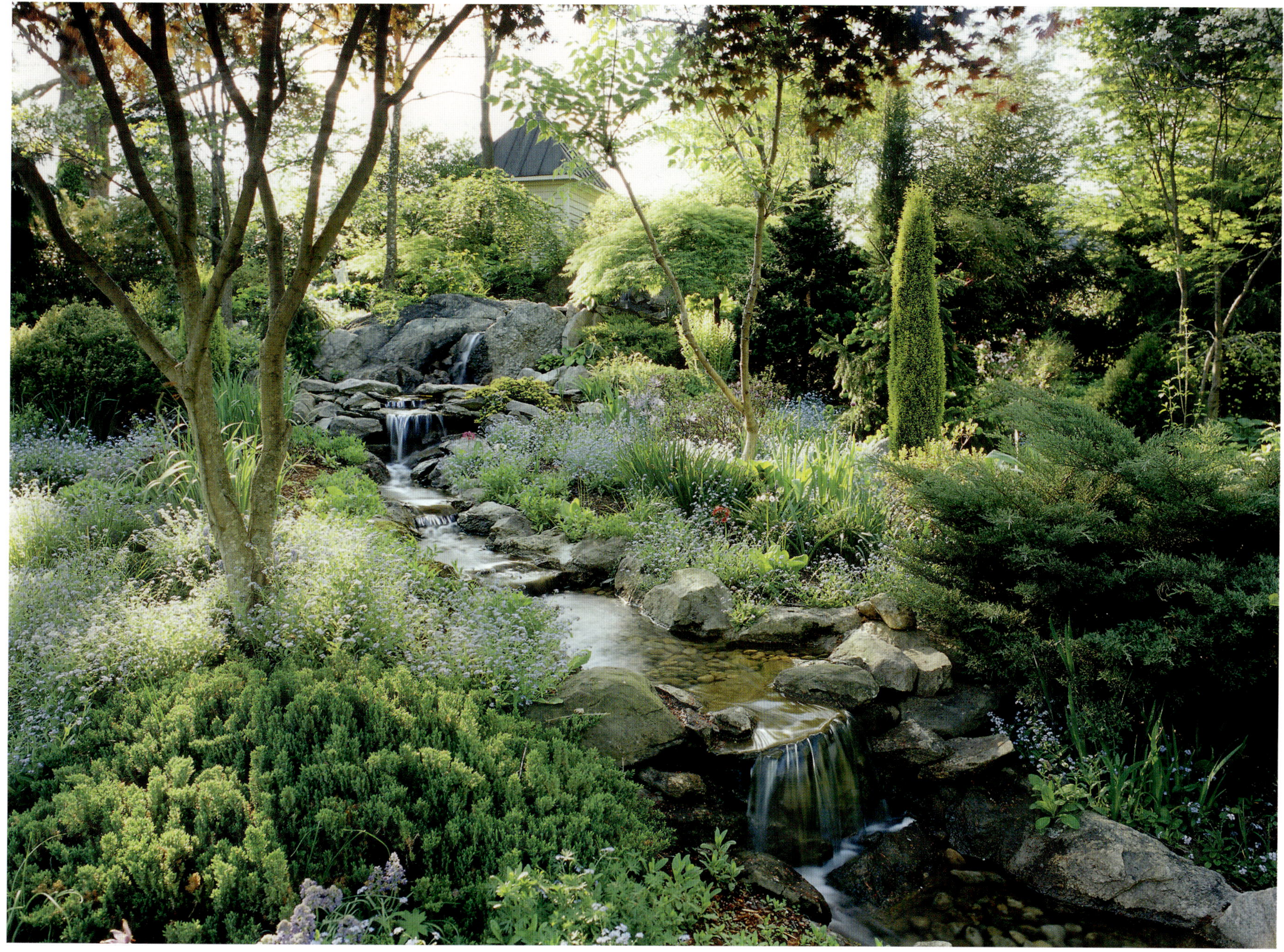

HIGHLAND SPRING, MIDDLEBURG, VIRGINIA
HIGHLAND SPRING

ROGER FOLEY

Fuji Velvia 100 film. Contax 645 film camera, 45mm lens. 1sec at f/11. Post-capture: scanned with a Nikon Coolscan 8000.
HIGHLY COMMENDED, 2012

Highland Spring is a three-acre garden designed and maintained by its owner, Donna Hackman. The design takes inspiration from a rock outcropping at the top of a hill on the property. There was just enough sunlight at the scene to create a sense of a three-dimensional space. I wanted the viewer to feel they were within the picture and almost hear the stream.

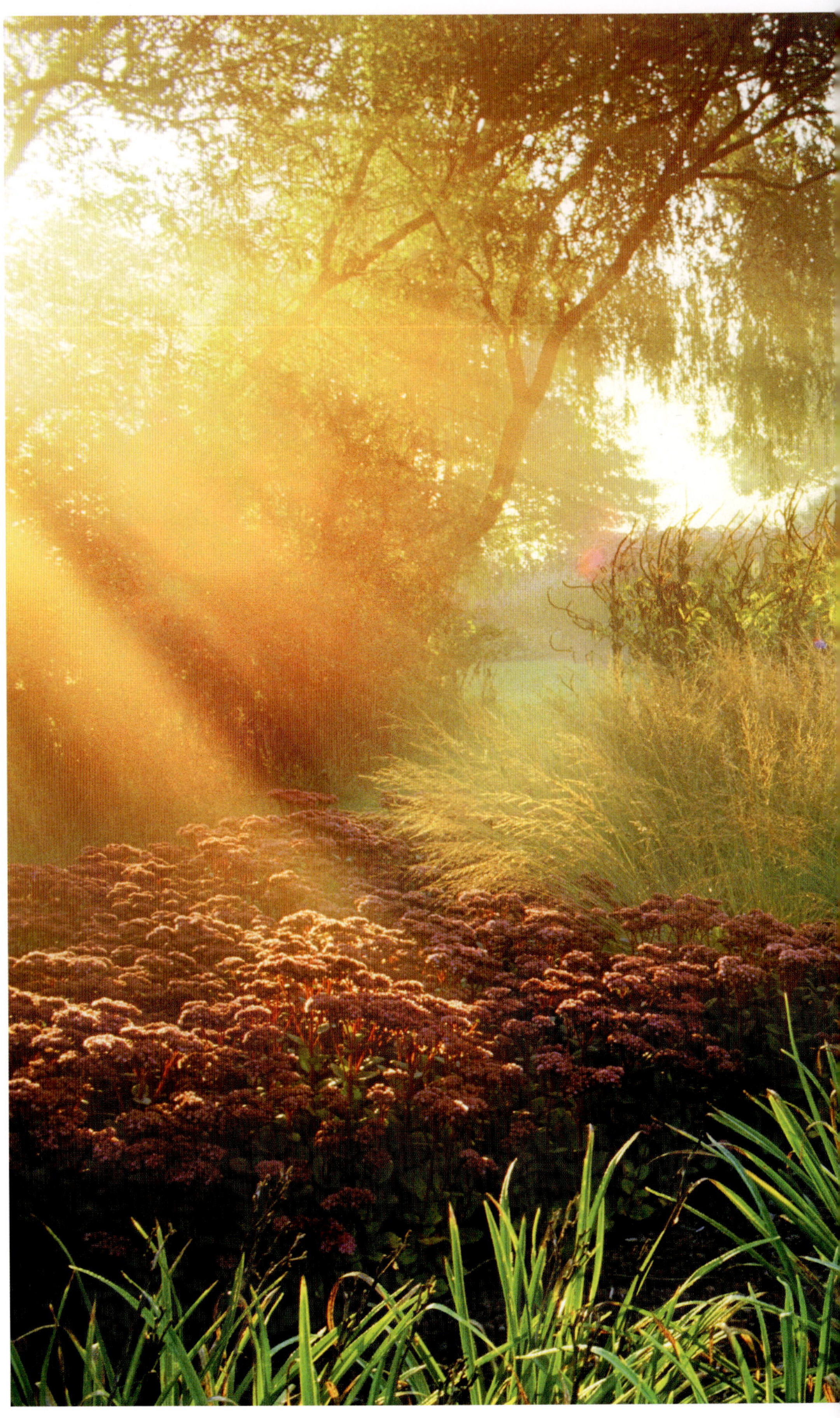

Sunlight streams through the trees to baneberry (*Actaea simplex*) (*Atropurpurea group*) and ice plant (*Sedum spectabile*), and the layering of the mist over the fields in the distance provides a stage on which the plants perform their morning dance. The scene was utterly irresistible as the early morning light broke through the tree canopy and tickled the *Actaea*.

PRIVATE GARDEN
LAYERED LANDSCAPE: A MOMENT CAPTURED

MARIANNE MAJERUS

Fuji Velvia 50, Leica R9
INTERNATIONAL GARDEN PHOTOGRAPHER OF THE YEAR, 2010

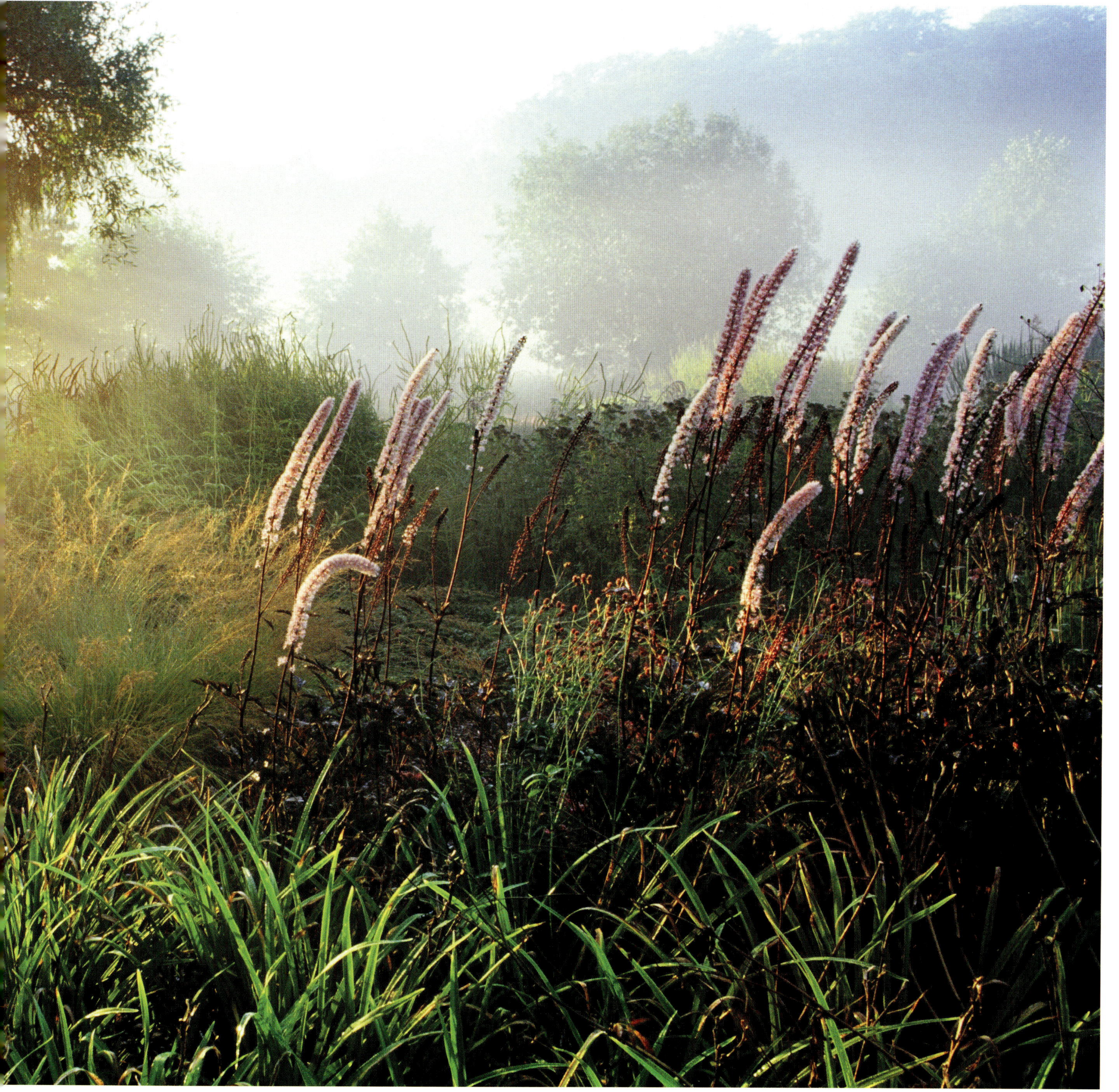

It was a softly sunny May afternoon – one of those magical times that occur only two or three times a year – and the blossom was *au point*. The light and shade provided so many different tones, so much depth, all that was needed was to find the best views.

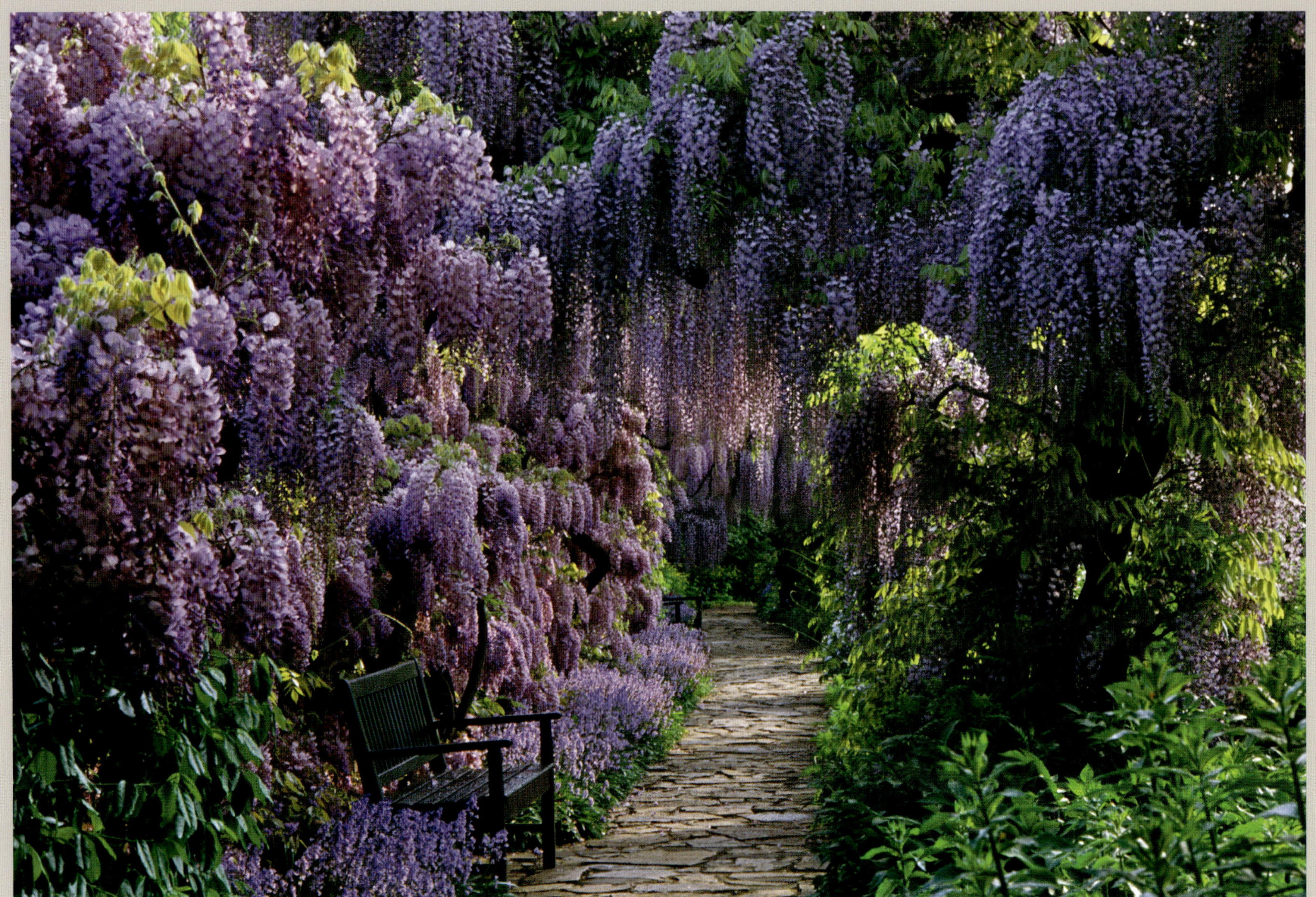

JAPANESE WISTERIA (*WISTERIA FLORIBUNDA* 'MACROBOTRYS'), HERMANNSHOF
WISTERIA WALK

JERRY HARPUR

Nikon F3, Nikkor 28mm lens, Velvia 50, f/22, polariser. It was important to record the disappearing curve of path and the depth of the wisteria tunnel, so a moderately wide-angle lens was chosen. The varying sizes of the seats, by comparison, emphasise the effect.
THIRD, 2008

LOSELEY PARK, NEAR GUILDFORD, SURREY, ENGLAND

THE WHITE GARDEN

FLEUR ROBERTSON

Canon Power Shot S95, 28-105mm lens, 1/500sec at f/8, ISO 320.
FINALIST, 2011

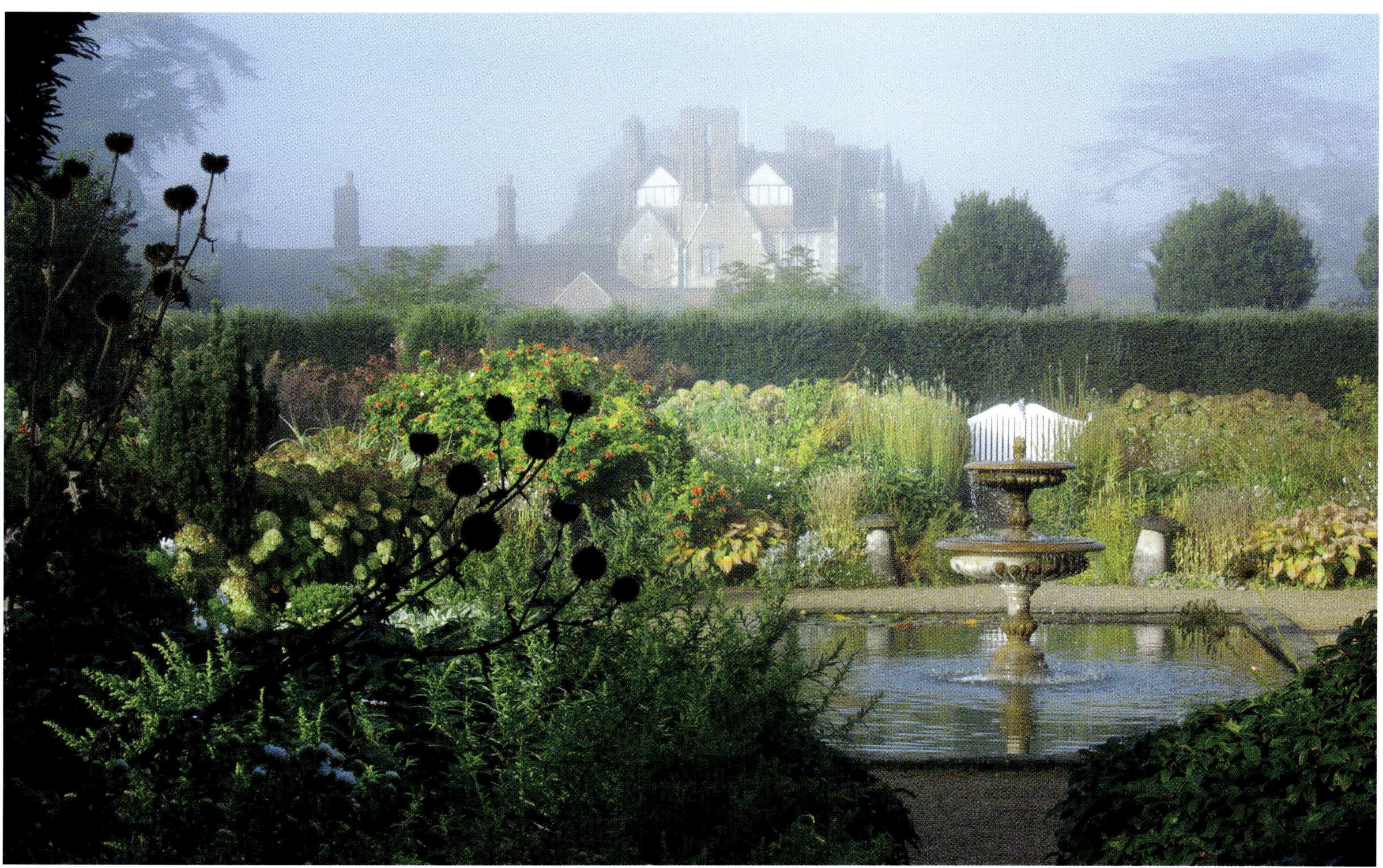

Of the six Loseley gardens, this is my favourite because I feel its softened symmetry lends itself to the view. This sunny September morning felt like one last joyous 'hurrah!' before winter. I was hoping to pull together the formal/informal quality of the garden. Perhaps something like that happens here, in the echo of the thistle's (*Echinops* spp.) seed heads, with their rounded forms and straight tops, in the curved fountain bowl, and then again in the rotund trees against the hedge line. This was a morning when I was meant to be somewhere else, and my 'back pocket' camera was all I had with me. But I was tempted by the light and detoured, reaching Loseley just as the mists of morning were fading. Ironically, after a season of photographing this garden with my 'proper' camera, it's this morning and this image I will best remember.

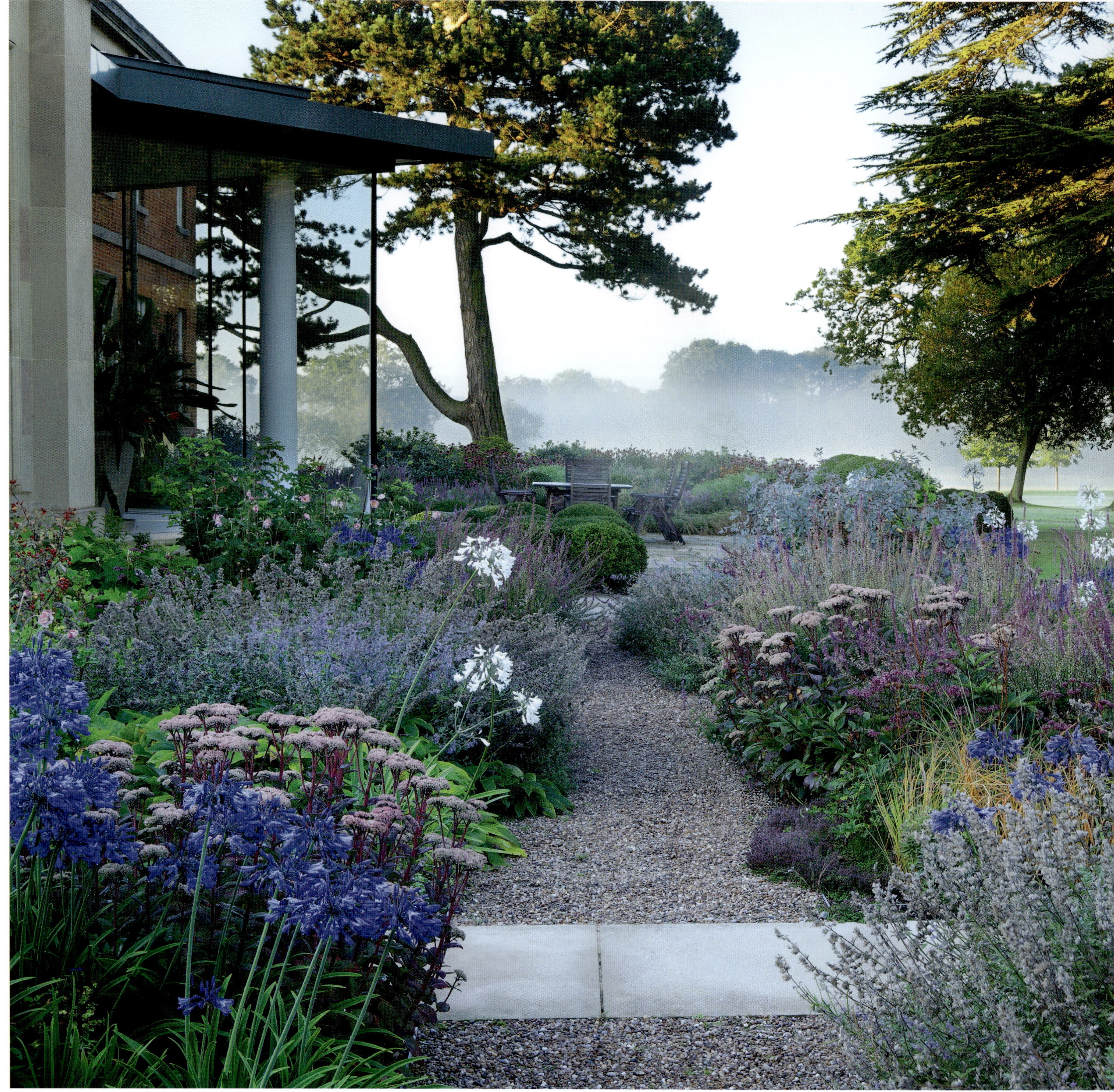

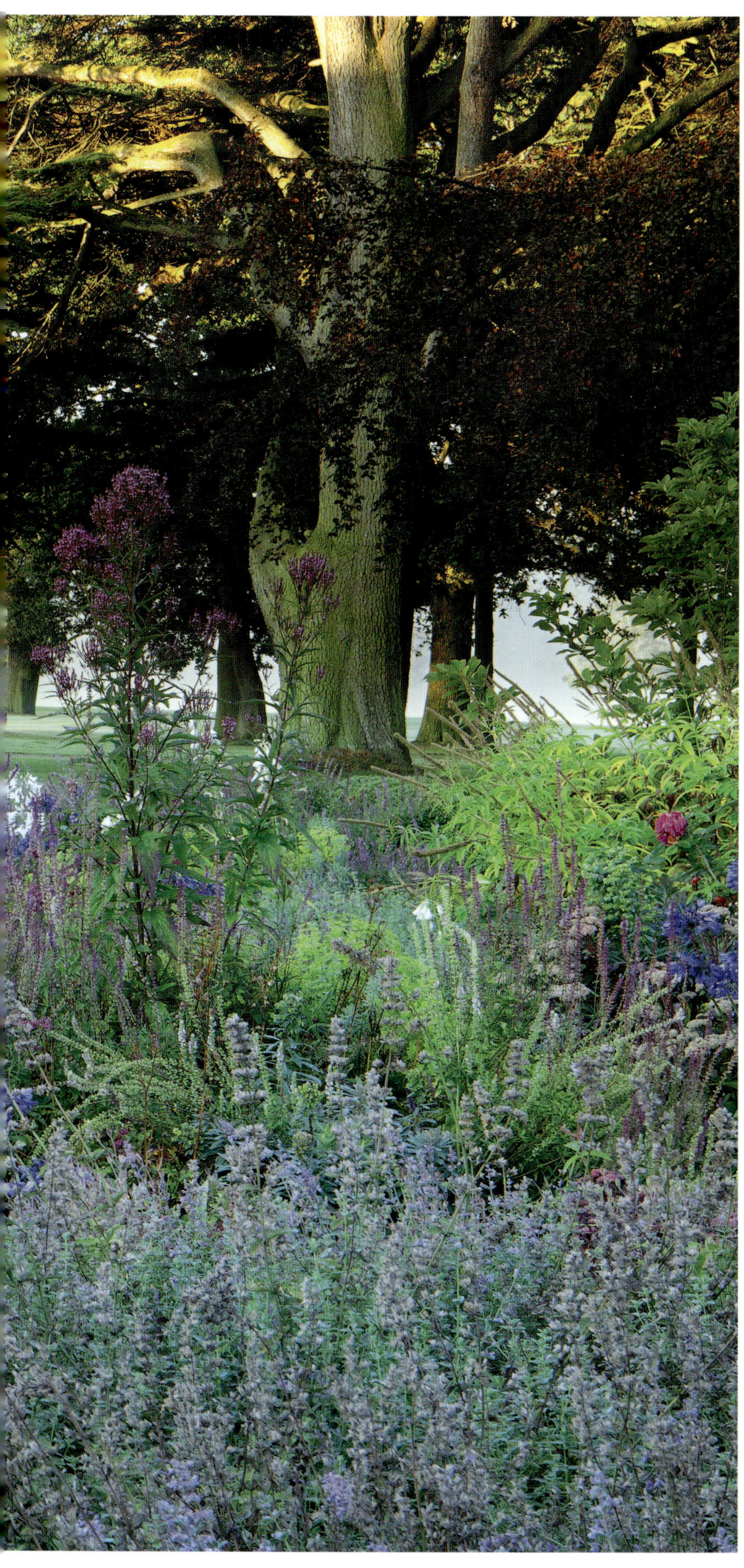

The morning holds its breath for a fleeting moment before the sun rises. The photograph is about anticipation: the meeting of night and day. It was taken a few moments before the garden is transformed by sunshine and the distant mist has disappeared. This delicate balance is echoed in the interaction between the contemporary architecture and planting and the traditional parkland beyond.

PRIVATE GARDEN, CHESHIRE, ENGLAND
BLUE DAWN

MARIANNE MAJERUS

Canon EOS 5D Mark II, 24-70mm lens. 1/10sec at f/16. Post-capture: no digital alterations.
THIRD, 2012

WINDMILL PALM (*TRACHYCARPUS FORTUNEI*) GARDEN OF EDEN BOTANICAL GARDENS, MAUI, HAWAII

OCEAN VIEW GARDEN

DENNIS FRATES

Canon EOS-1Ds Mark II, Canon 70–200mm L IS lens, f/9, polariser. There were many similar plants at this location but I narrowed it down to a small portion of the scene by using a telephoto lens. I also worked to include a portion of the ocean and clouds in the background.

COMMENDED, 2008

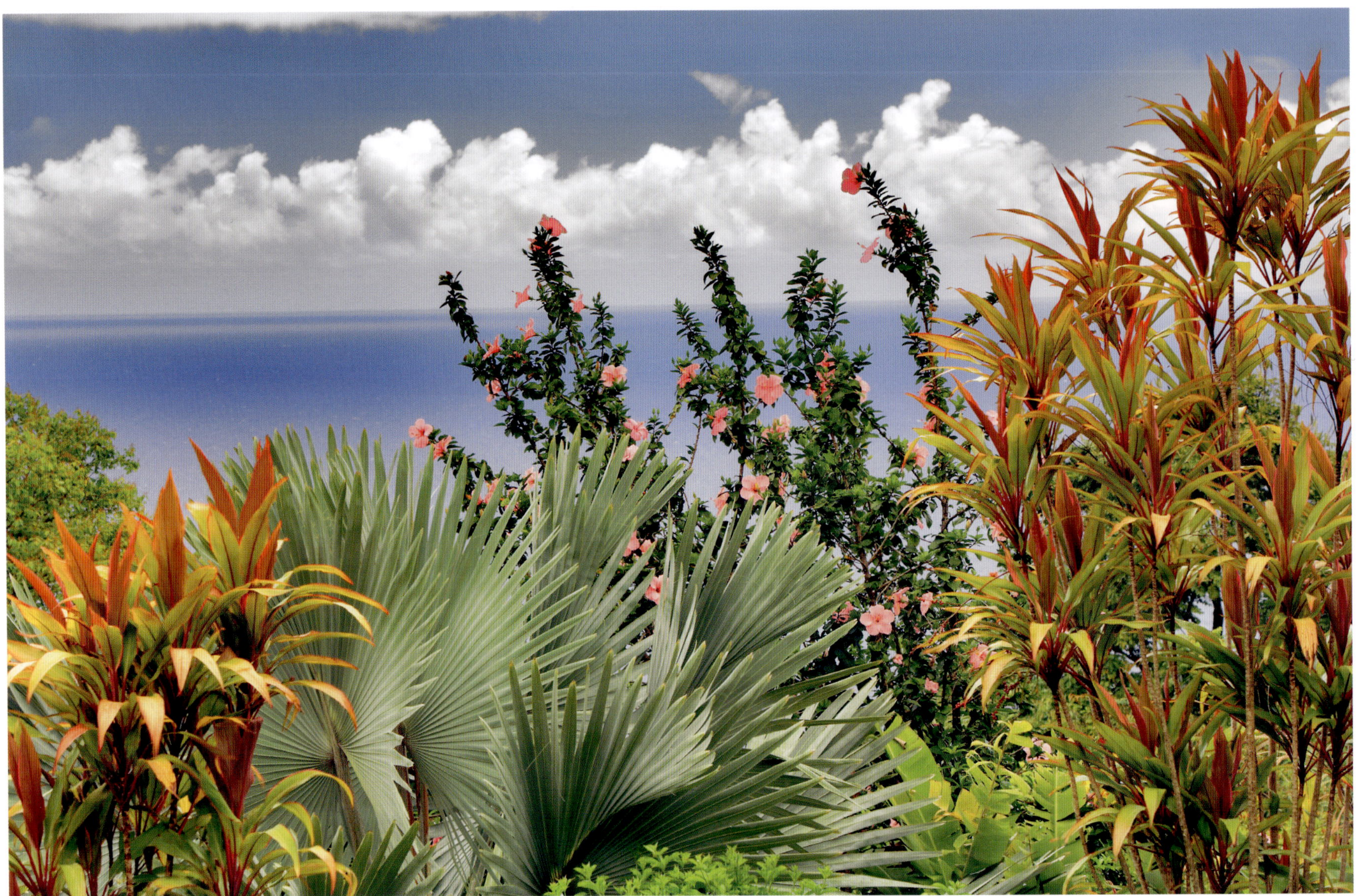

I love the textures of tropical plants. In this picture, the hibiscus flowers are the focal point, and I was also attracted by the full spectrum of red, green and blue – a powerful compositional element.

PORTLAND JAPANESE GARDEN, PORTLAND, OREGON

GARDEN BRIDGE

DENNIS FRATES

Canon EOS-1Ds Mark II, Canon 16–35mm lens, f/13. The fog and sun lasted only a few moments so I had to react quickly. Within a minute of making the image, the sun started hitting the trees, which made it too contrasty, and the fog was gone.

COMMENDED, 2008

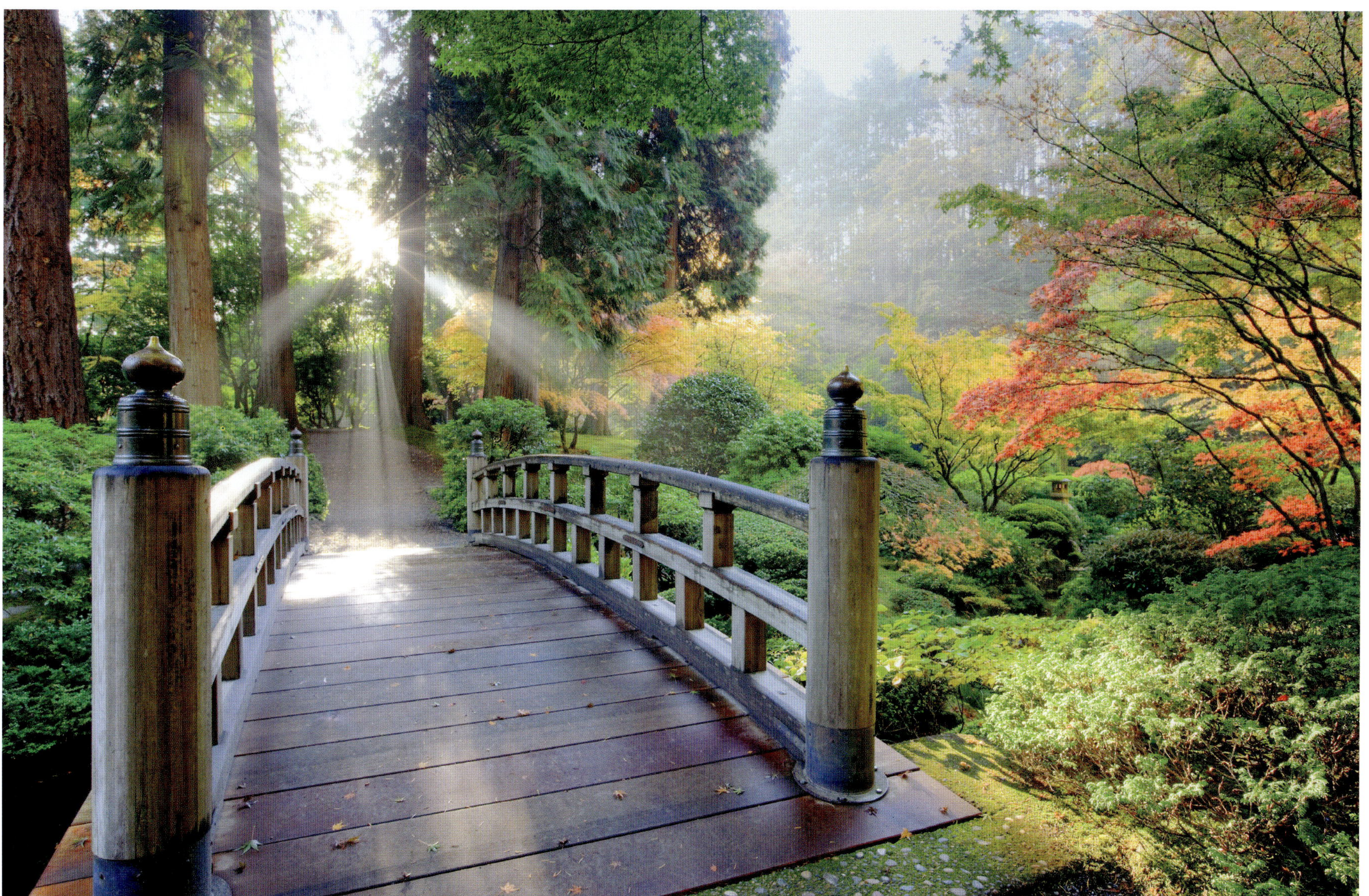

I have photographed this composition many times, but the combination of autumn colour, fog and sunrays made it unique.

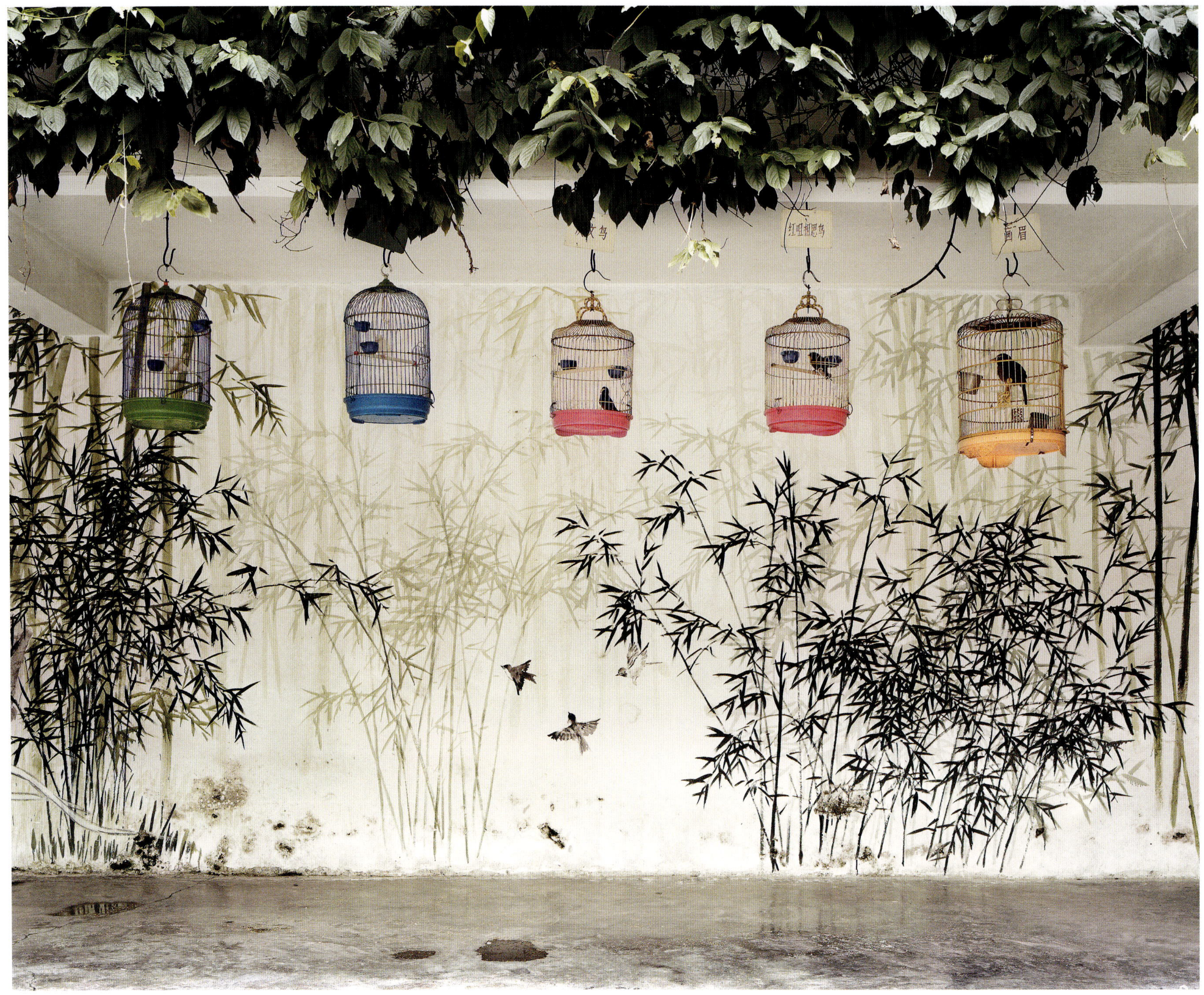

The image is taken from the series 'People's Park', which documents the current state of public parks in China, once important cultural and societal spaces that have gone through great changes as China progresses. It was taken in the 'Chinese Garden' section within Guangzhou Zoo, which also houses the avian species.

GUANGZHOU ZOO, GUANGZHOU, GUANGDONG SHENG
BIRDCAGES

KURT TONG

Linhof Master Technika, Kodak Portra 160NC. The juxtaposition of the real trees with the caged birds against the fake bamboo and free birds appealed to me. The colours were quite muted except for the plastic cages.

FINALIST, 2009

I was inspired by the golden orange colour of the bridge against the background greenery.

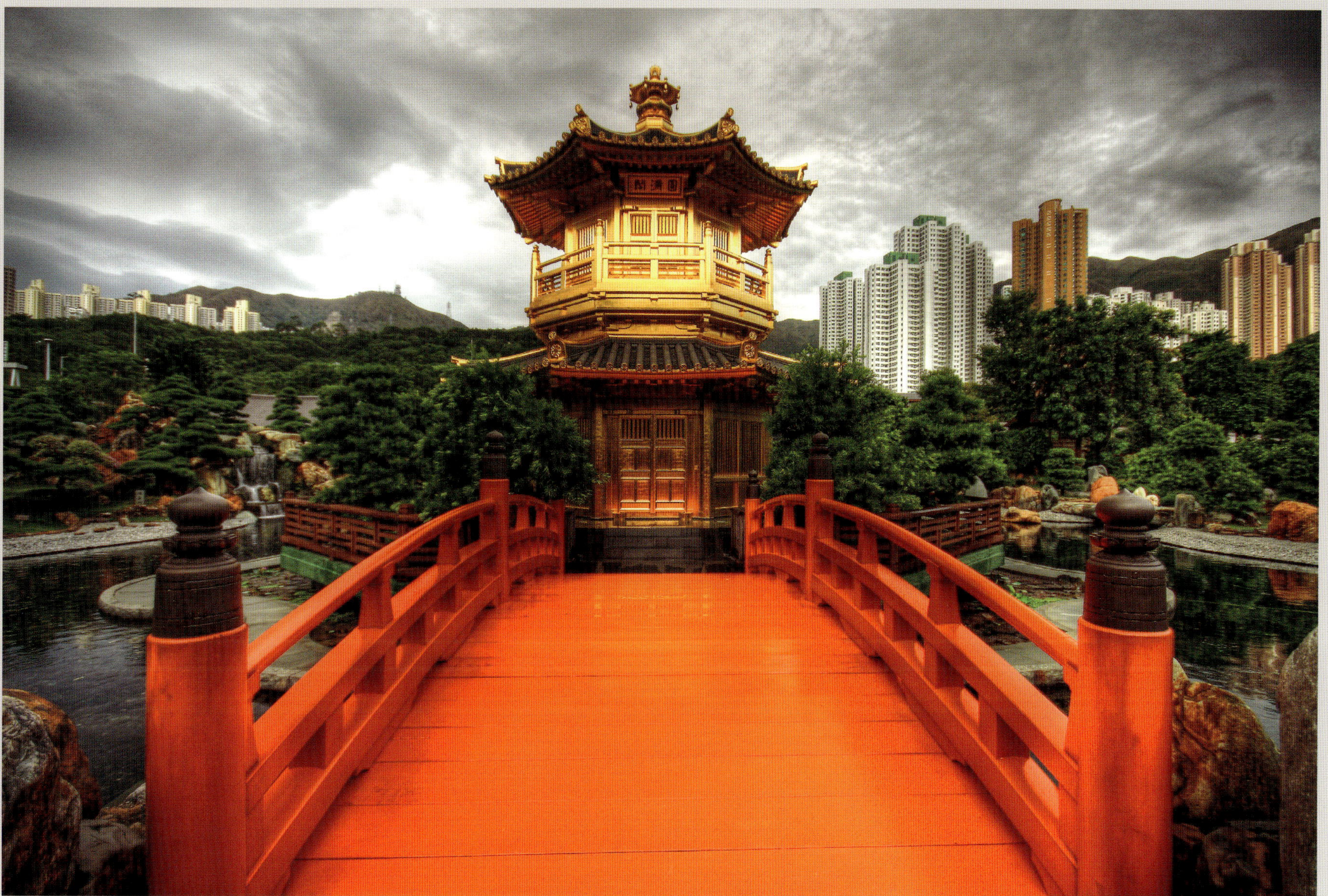

NAN LIAN GARDEN, HONG KONG
NAN LIAN GARDEN BRIDGE

THAMER AL-TASSAN

Canon EOS 450D, Sigma 10-20mm lens, f/4. I used a wide-angle lens in order to get more perspective on the bridge.

FINALIST, 2009

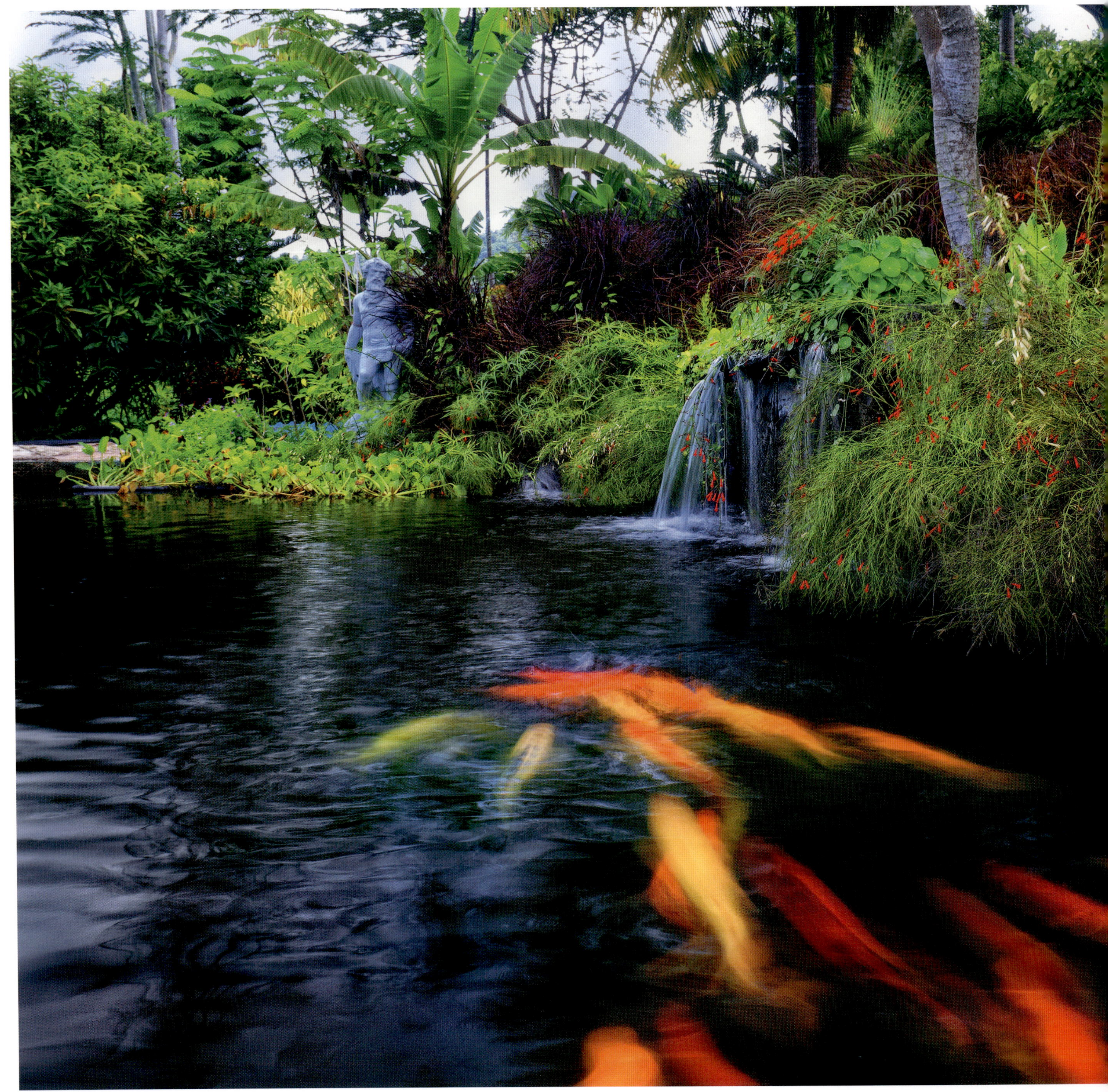

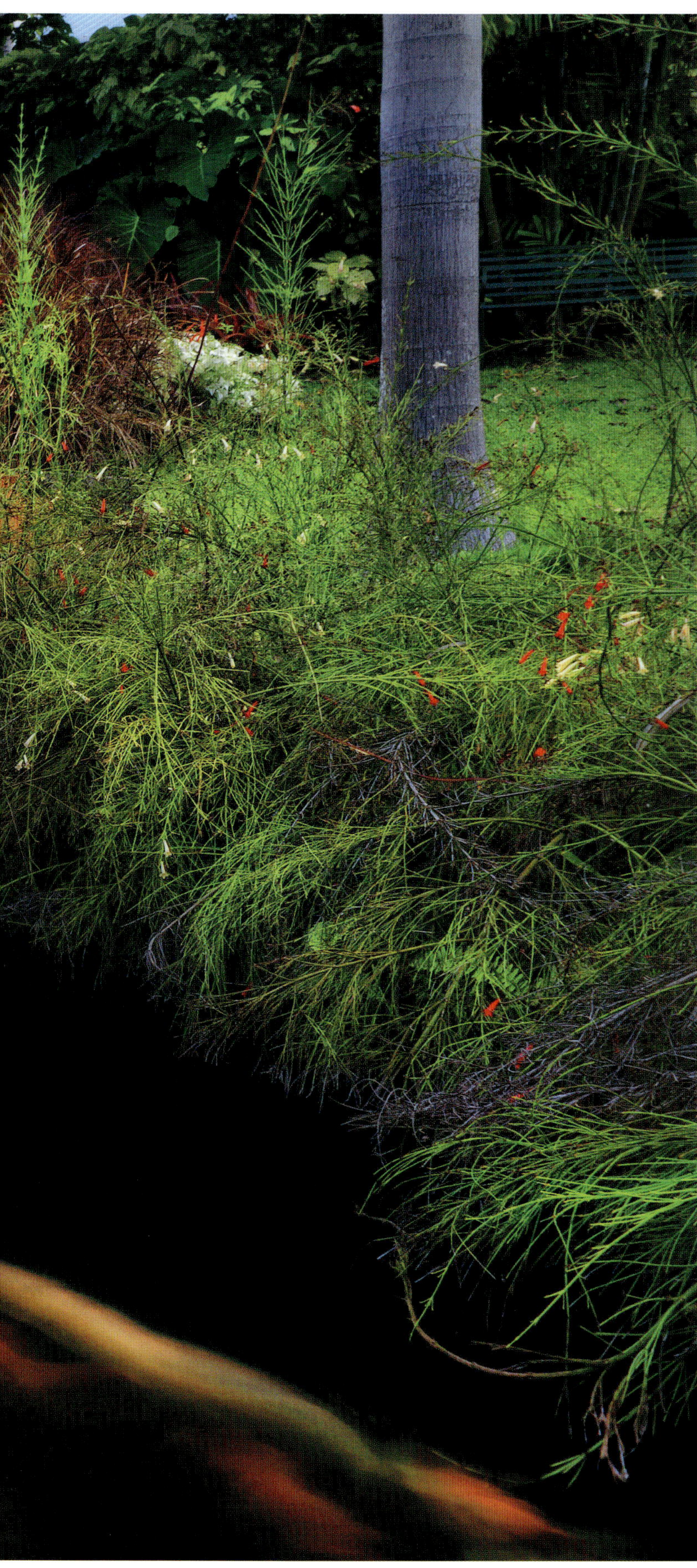

GRENADA
SUNNYSIDE GARDEN

DEREK GALON

Nikon D90, 20mm lens, 1/5sec at f/18, ISO 100, polarising filter. Shot on a tripod with infrared remote. Post-capture: parts of image saturated and darkened, image sharpened.
HIGHLY COMMENDED, 2011

Sunnyside Garden is a private garden in Grenada, open for tours and special appointments only. It features an artificial pond created especially for Koi carp approximately 15 years ago. I dropped fish food several times in various spots, then photographed using a long exposure, to allow fish movement to register. They created long colour smudges like wet brush strokes.

GEORGENGARTEN, DESSAU

SEBASTIAN KAPS

Fuji FinePix S3 Pro, 10mm to 70mm zoom lens settings.
WINNING PORTFOLIO, GARDEN VIEWS, 2009

The Georgengarten is one of the biggest parks in the Dessau-Wörlitz Garden Realm, a UNESCO World Heritage site. Prince Johann Georg von Anhalt (1748-1811), brother of Prince Franz, built the palace and its surroundings with the help of the architects JF Eyserbeck and JG Schoch – to complement the Wörlitz Park. A 50-acre garden surrounds the Georgium Castle and stretches as far as the River Elbe. Within the park, many classical buildings, smaller examples of architecture and sculptures, can be found working in harmony with their surroundings.

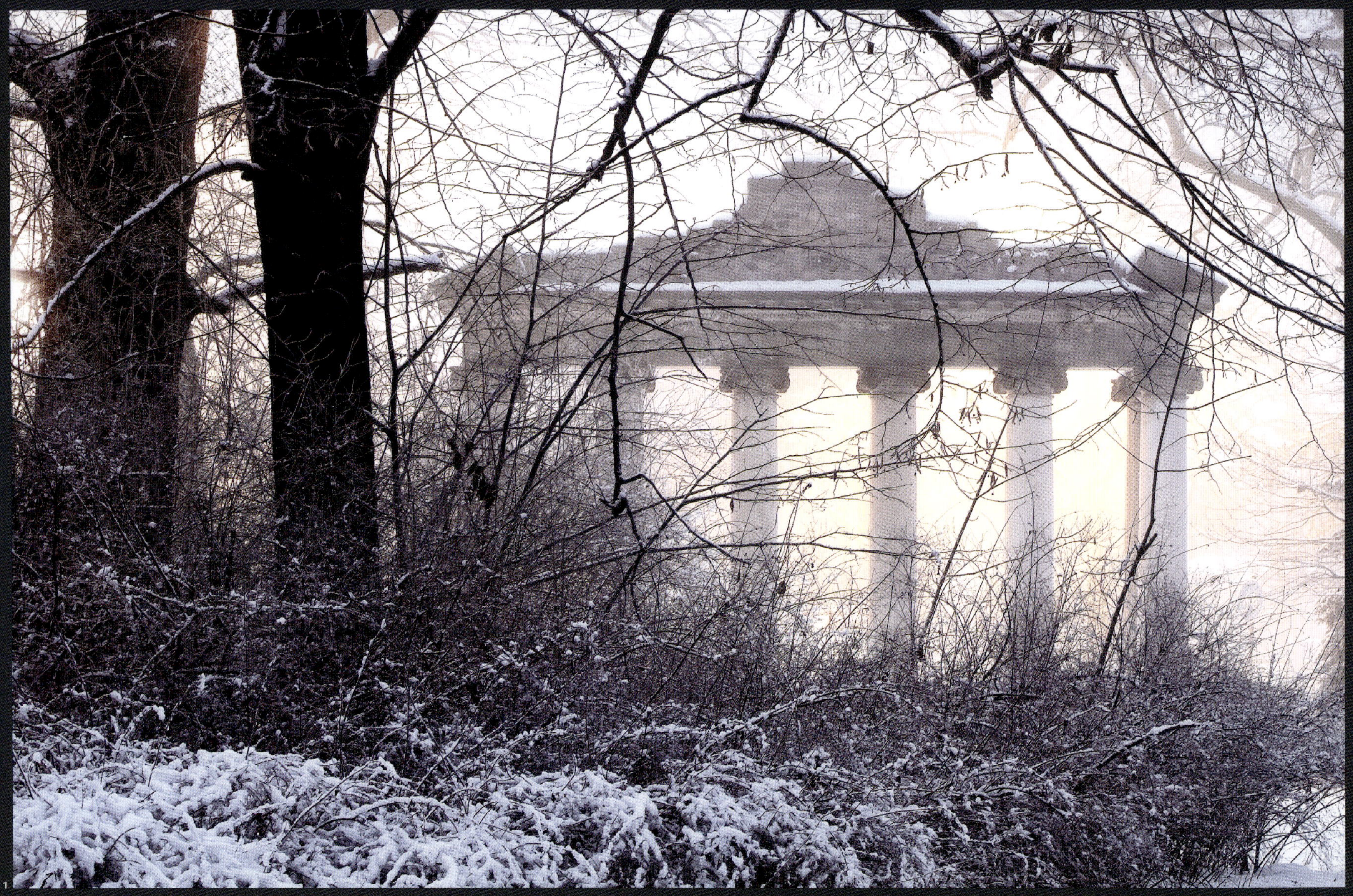

1

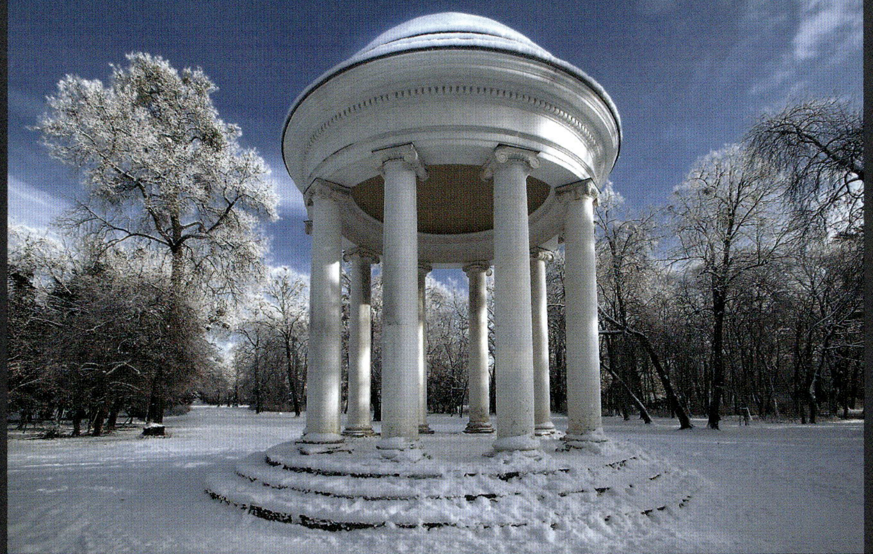
2

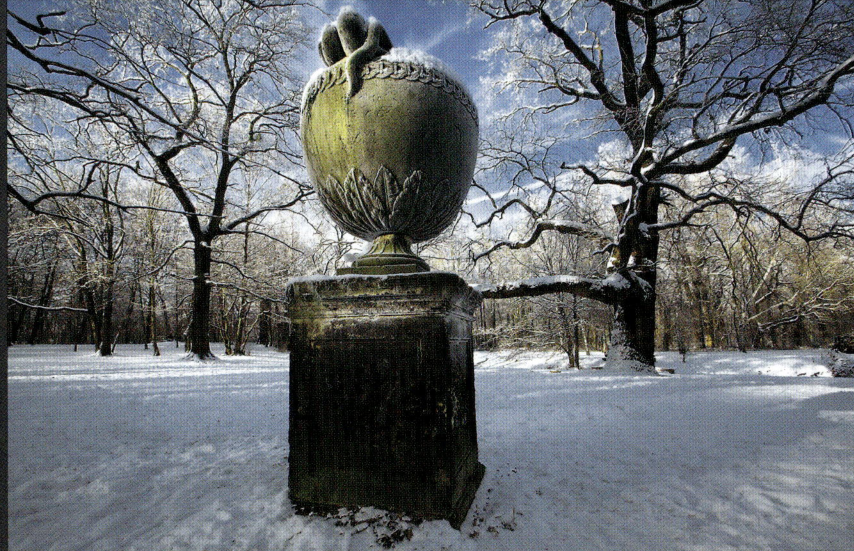
3

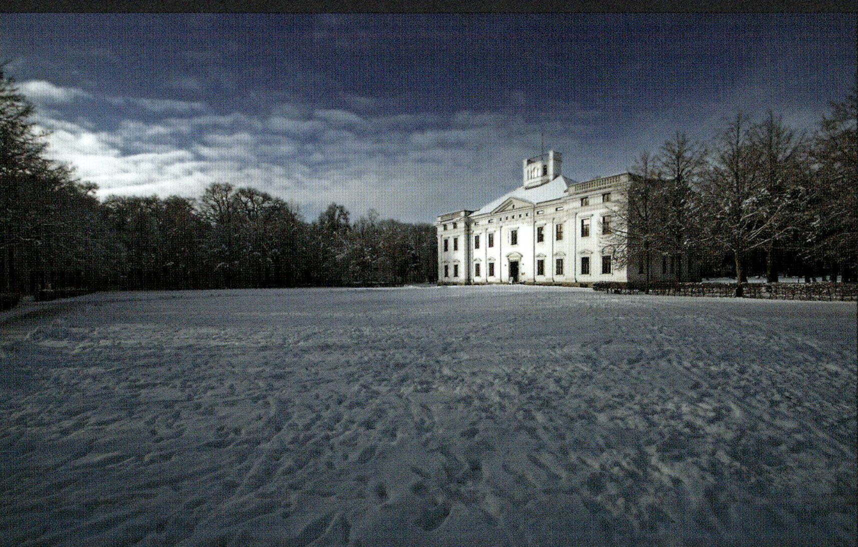
4

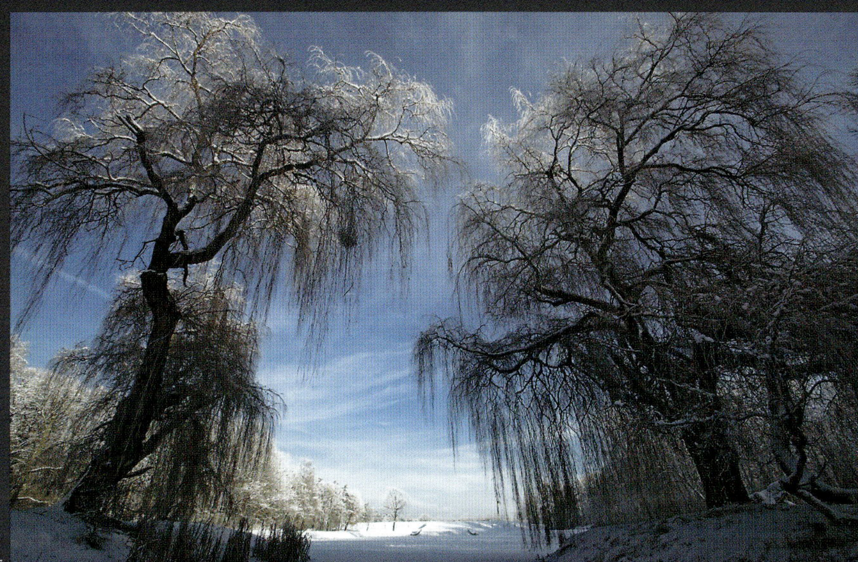
5

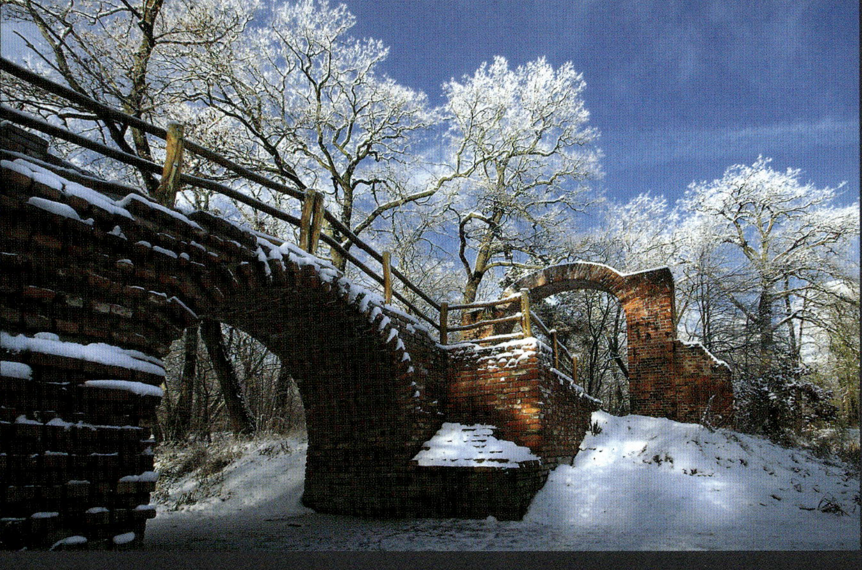
6

1–*The Seven Columns* The seven Columns in morning fog (-15°C).

2–*Monopterus* The Ionic Temple (or Monopterus) at Georgengarten.

3–*The Bevernvase* The Bevernvase at Beckerbruch (a part of the Georgengarten).

4–*Georgium Palace in the evening* Georgium Palace was built in 1782 in the classical style by Friedrich Wilhelm von Erdmannsdorff. The palace is surrounded by Georgengarten park with numerous early classical-style buildings. Georgium Palace is a UNESCO World Heritage site.

5–*Two Willows* Snow-covered willows at the entrance to the so-called Viereckteich.

6–*The Ruined Bridge* The so-called Ruined Bridge at the Beckerbruch (part of the Georgengarten).

Various fall-coloured Japanese maple trees (*Acer palmatum*) came into peak autumn colour at the same time. I had been to these gardens dozens of times over a period of 20 years, but had never been able to capture the trees at their absolute peak.

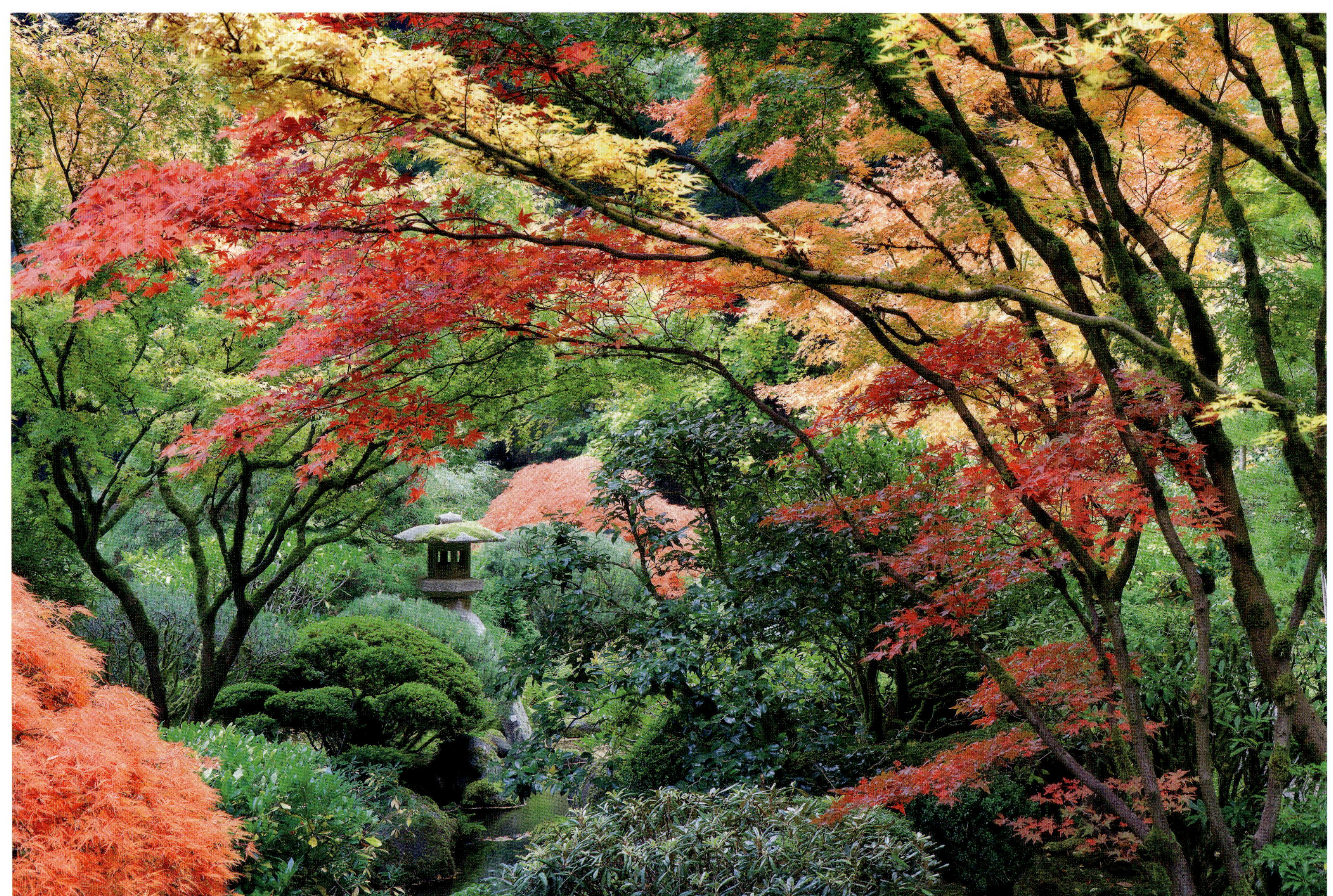

PORTLAND JAPANESE GARDEN, PORTLAND, OREGON
JAPANESE GARDENS IN FALL

DENNIS FRATES

Canon EOS-1Ds Mark III, Canon 24-105mm f/4 IS lens, f/14. The lack of wind allowed me to make the long exposure needed. I took three vertical images of this scene and then stitched them in Photoshop. I also used a polariser to saturate the colours.
FINALIST, 2009

The Leeming garden uses a lot of native planting materials indigenous to Victoria's Mornington Peninsula. This was a commissioned photograph for *Belle* magazine.

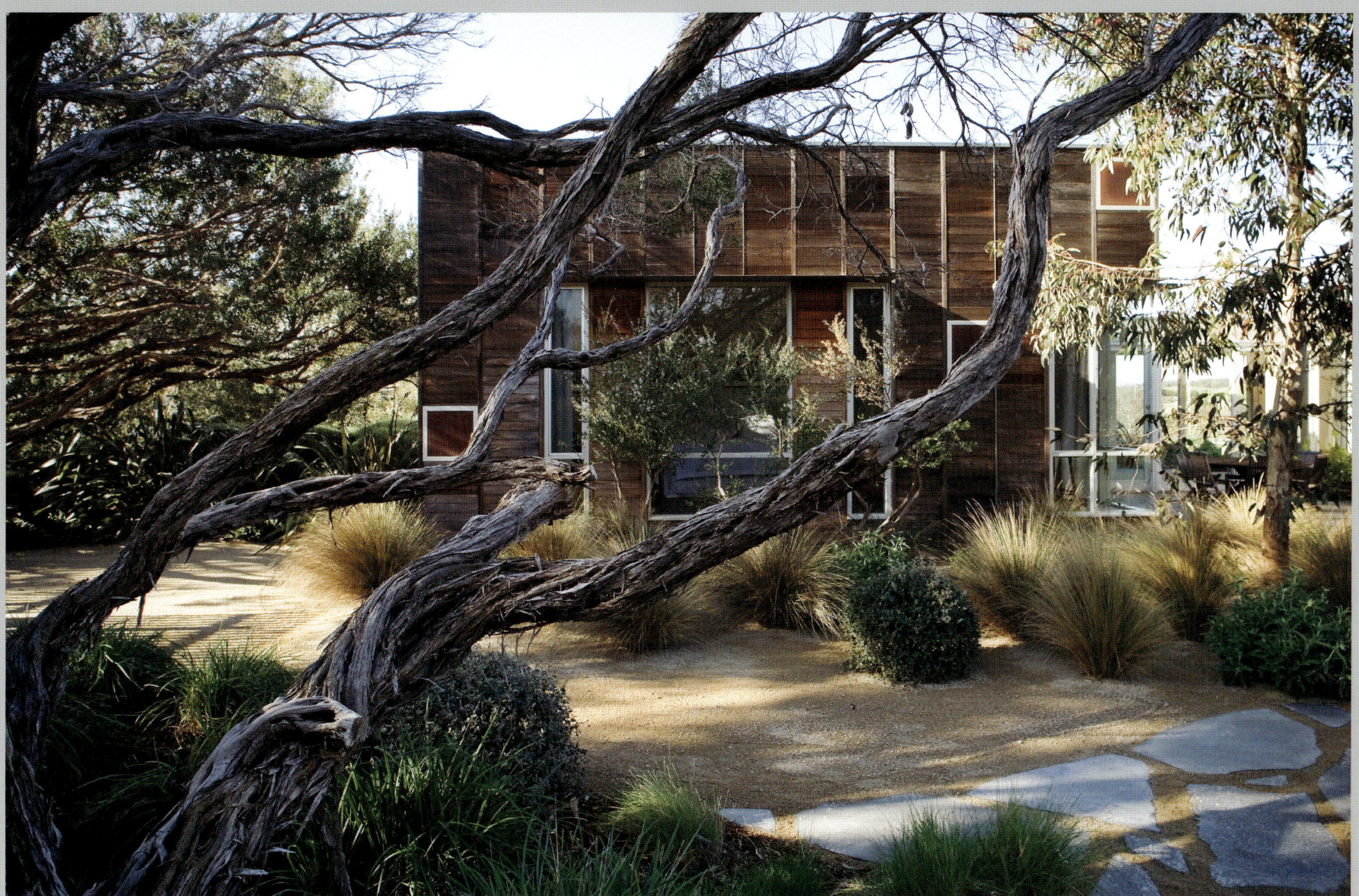

MORNINGTON PENINSULA, VICTORIA
THE LEEMING GARDEN

SIMON GRIFFITHS

Canon EOS-1D Mark II, 24-70mm lens, f/10. I had photographed this garden before, so was familiar with it and knew I wanted to achieve some more unusual views of the house and garden.
FINALIST, 2009

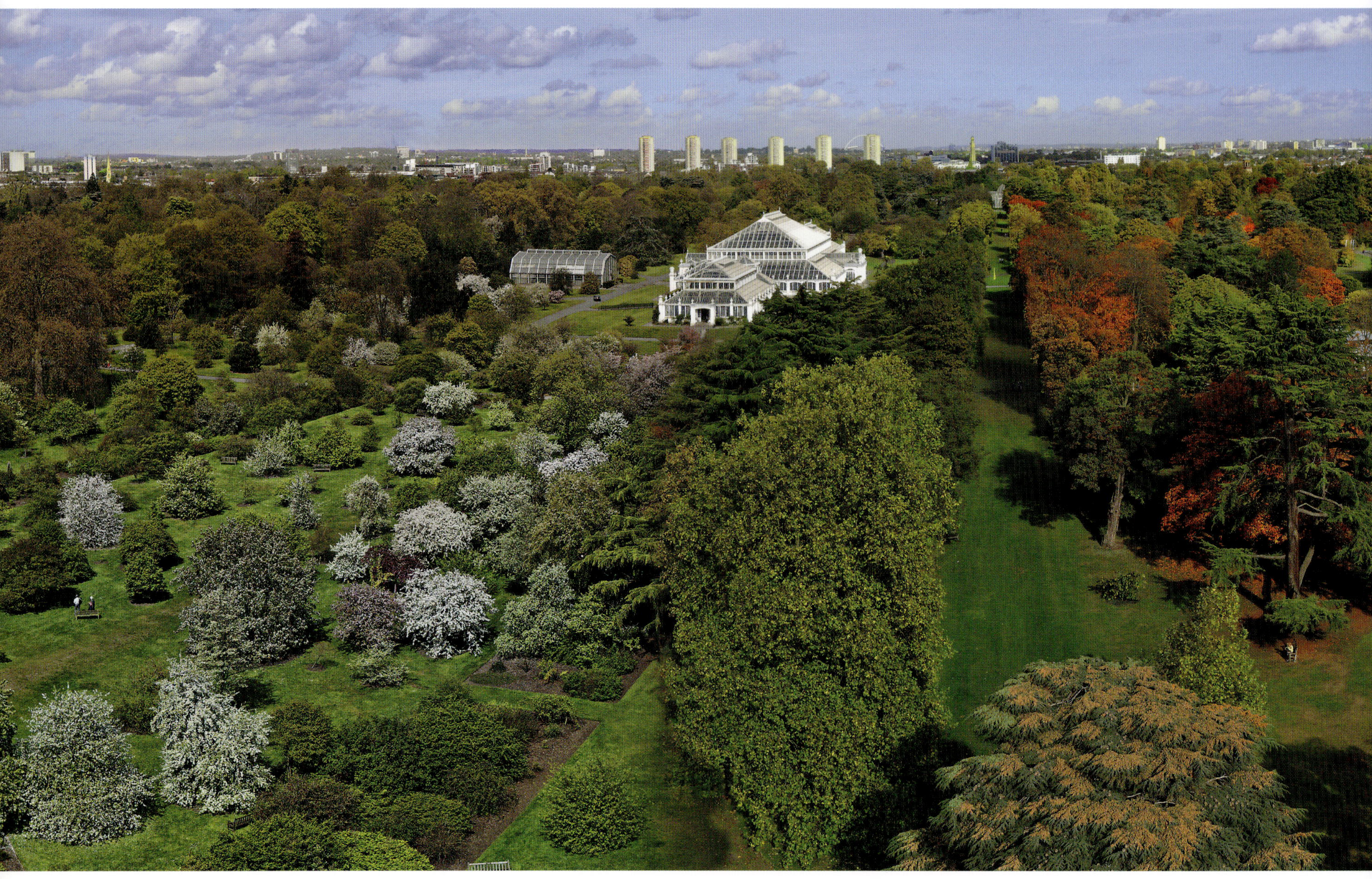

ROYAL BOTANIC GARDENS, KEW, SURREY, ENGLAND

ACROSS THE SEASONS AT KEW

JAMES MORLEY

Nikon D300, Nikkor 17-55mm lens, multiple exposures (each was typically 1/125sec at f/16). Post-capture: The images were 'stitched' together, initially automatically, then fine-tuned by hand. Each layer was subsequently aligned with pixel precision, and then they were painstakingly blended to create the continual change across the seasons. A single sky was then chosen, enhancing the sense of unity in the image.

FINALIST, 2011

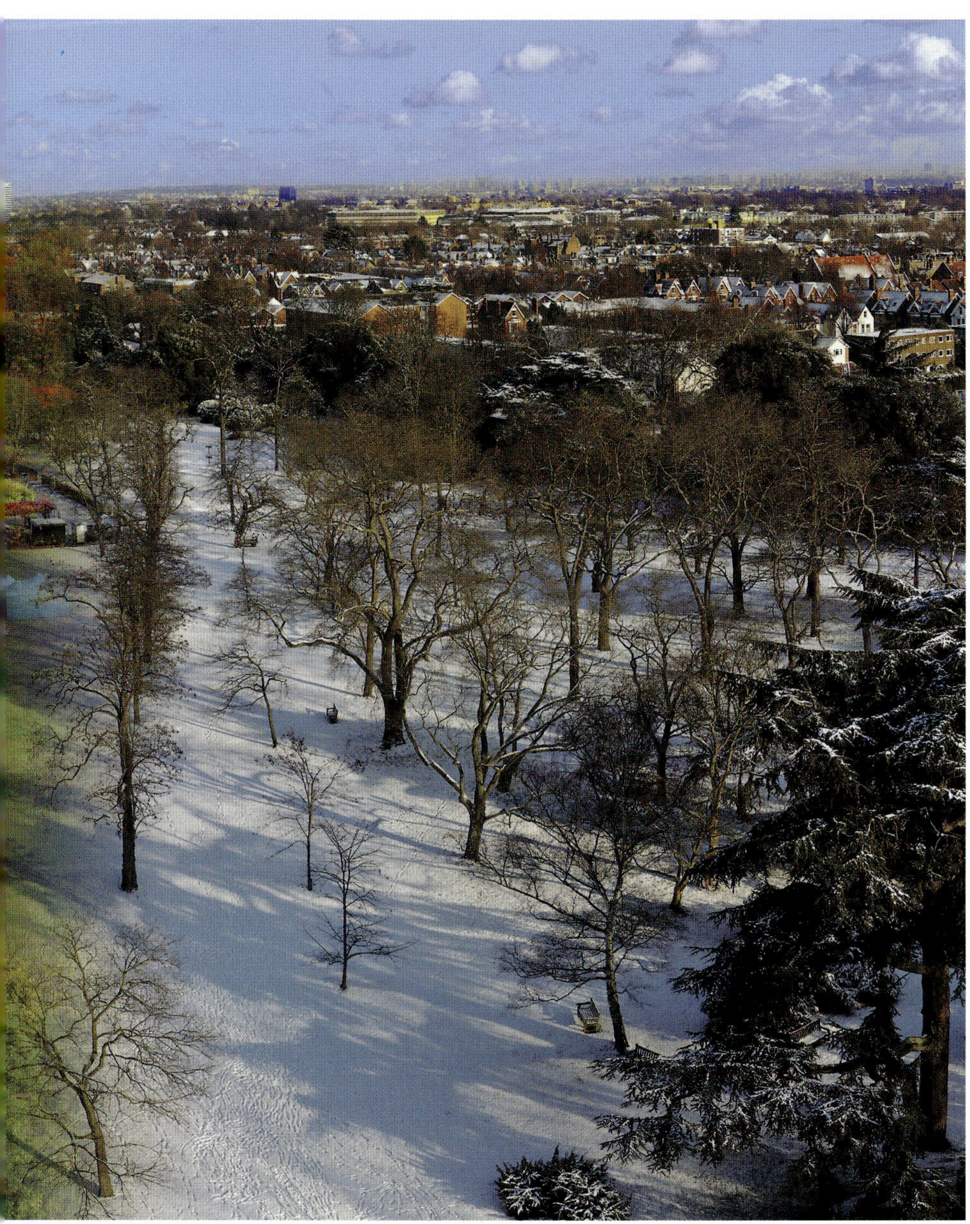

This composite panorama shows Kew's historic landscape with Nesfield's Pagoda Vista, stretching to the distant Palm House which takes centre stage. Features include the Temperate House, Evolution House and the extensive Arboretum, plus panoramic views across the London skyline, plus cherry blossom (*Prunus* spp.) verdant lawns, fiery autumn leaves and snow-laden branches. It is made up of multiple, carefully blended images to create a seamless transition across a year in the gardens.

The main inspiration was the view itself, but having photographed it on numerous occasions what struck me is how, even with so many constants, every time it has a completely different feel. The aim was to capture all that in one view! High-quality, high-resolution panoramas present a technical challenge. Multiple shots were taken using a panoramic tripod head. Presenting them as one image just enhances that challenge, as great care was needed to get exactly the same view, and to match the lighting conditions as closely as possible. Each layer (season) of the final image consists of multiple, high-resolution segments, typically three rows of 11 images. They were taken at fixed angles using a panoramic tripod head, carefully ensuring a significant overlap in both horizontal and vertical planes. The resulting image measures over 11,000 pixels across.

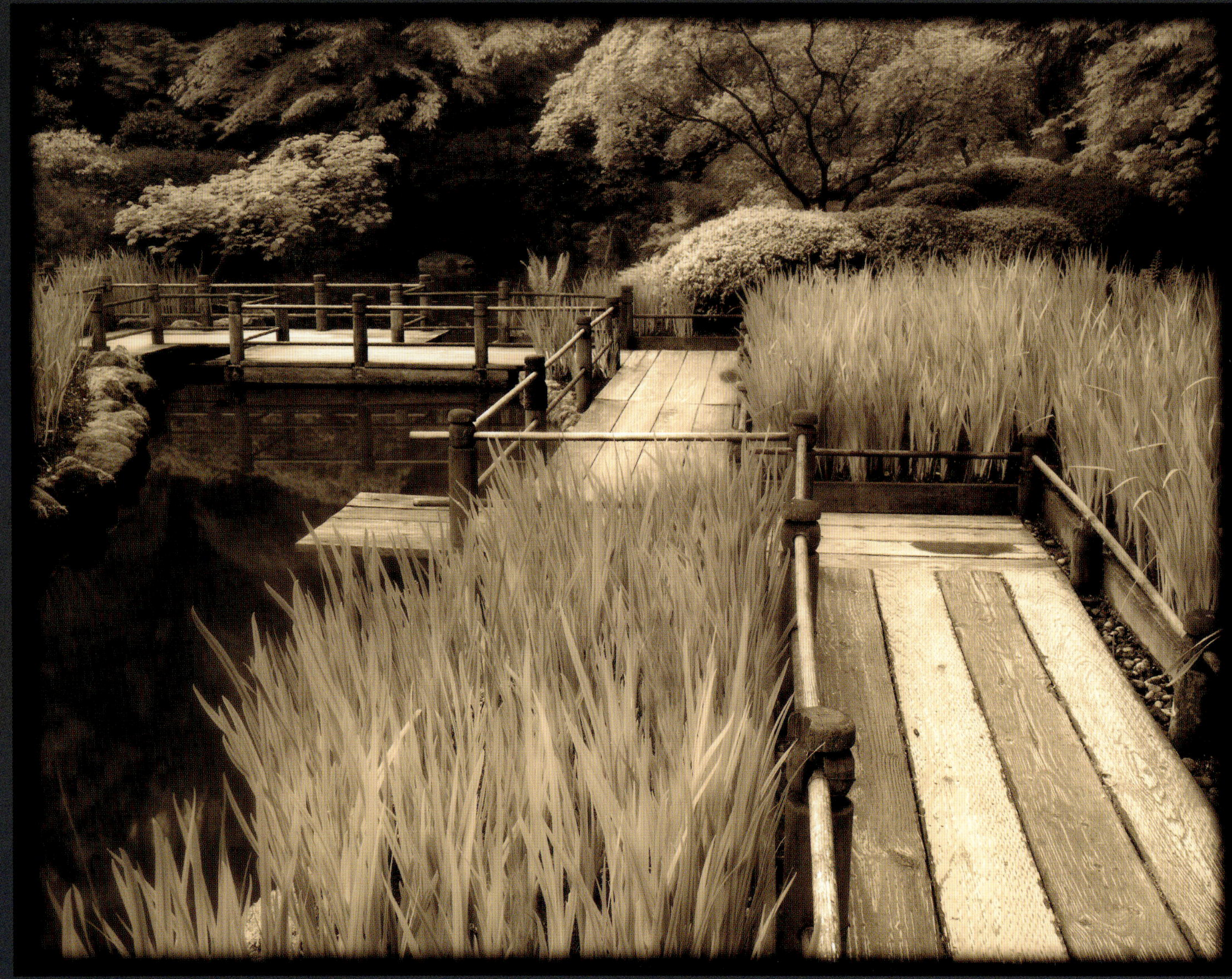

PORTLAND JAPANESE GARDEN, PORTLAND, OREGON
THE HIDDEN BRIDGE

JEFF FRIESEN

Canon EOS 5D, 24–105mm, f/14.
THIRD, 2010

In Japanese tradition it is thought that crossing a zig-zag (or *yatsuhashi*) bridge helps one to avoid evil spirits, which flow in straight lines. I love Japanese gardens and would happily photograph nothing else. I am inspired by the miniature, self-contained world formed by a Japanese garden. My approach was to frame the bridge so that it led the viewer through the photograph like a virtual garden stroll.

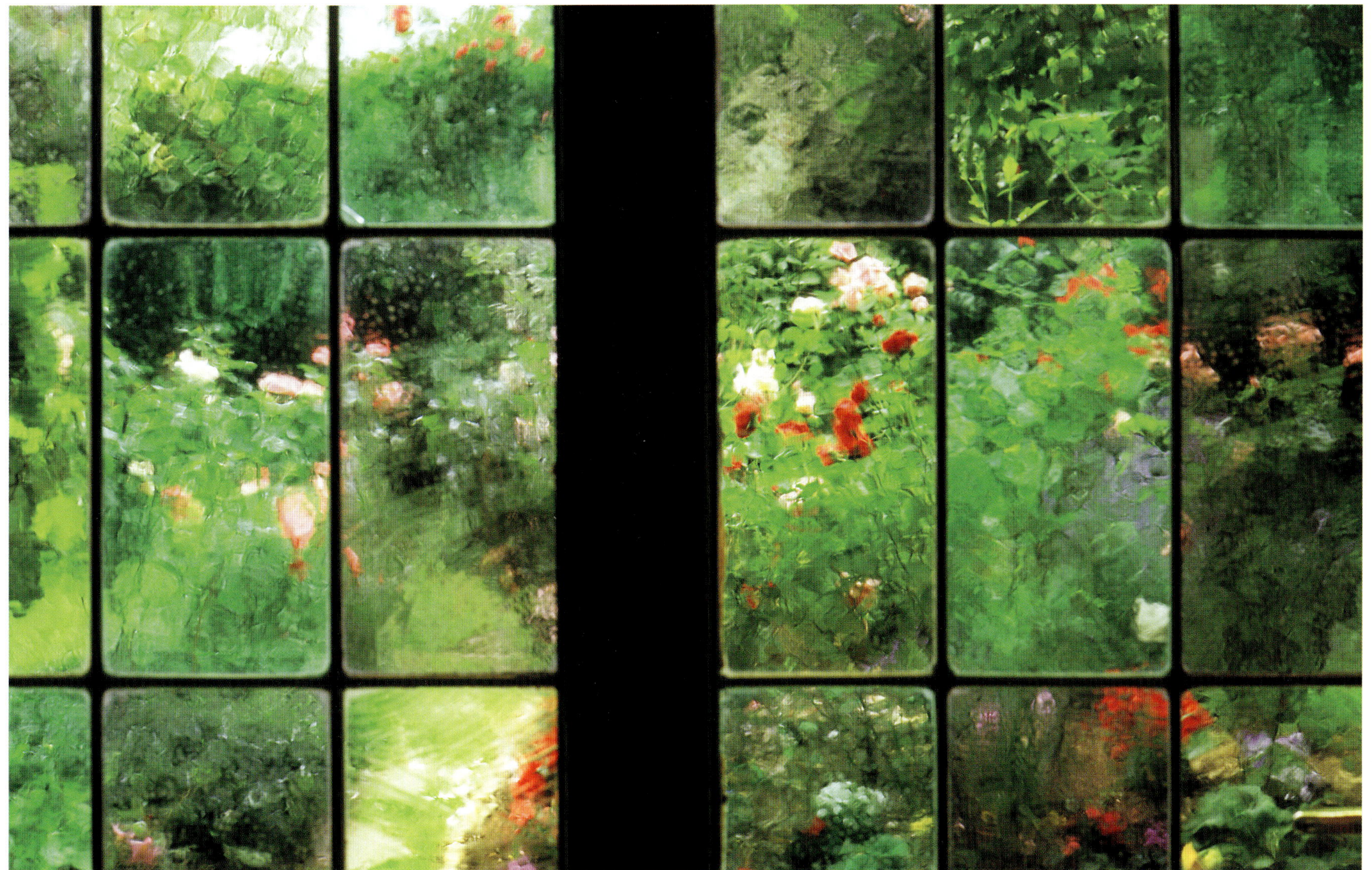

An image of images: the panes of glass, framed in lead, playfully distort the secret garden outside and create an Impressionist collage, each pane with its own unique character and hue. The nostalgic feeling is enhanced by the promise of the scented rose garden beyond. I really liked the way the garden had transformed the glass into a wonderfully intricate stained glass window, and I wanted to capture an image composed of many smaller images.

NELLY'S GARDEN, ESCH-SUR-ALZETTE
ABSTRACT IMPRESSIONS OF A SECRET GARDEN

MARIANNE MAJERUS

Leica R9, Fujifilm Velvia. Post-capture: no manipulation.
FIRST, 2011

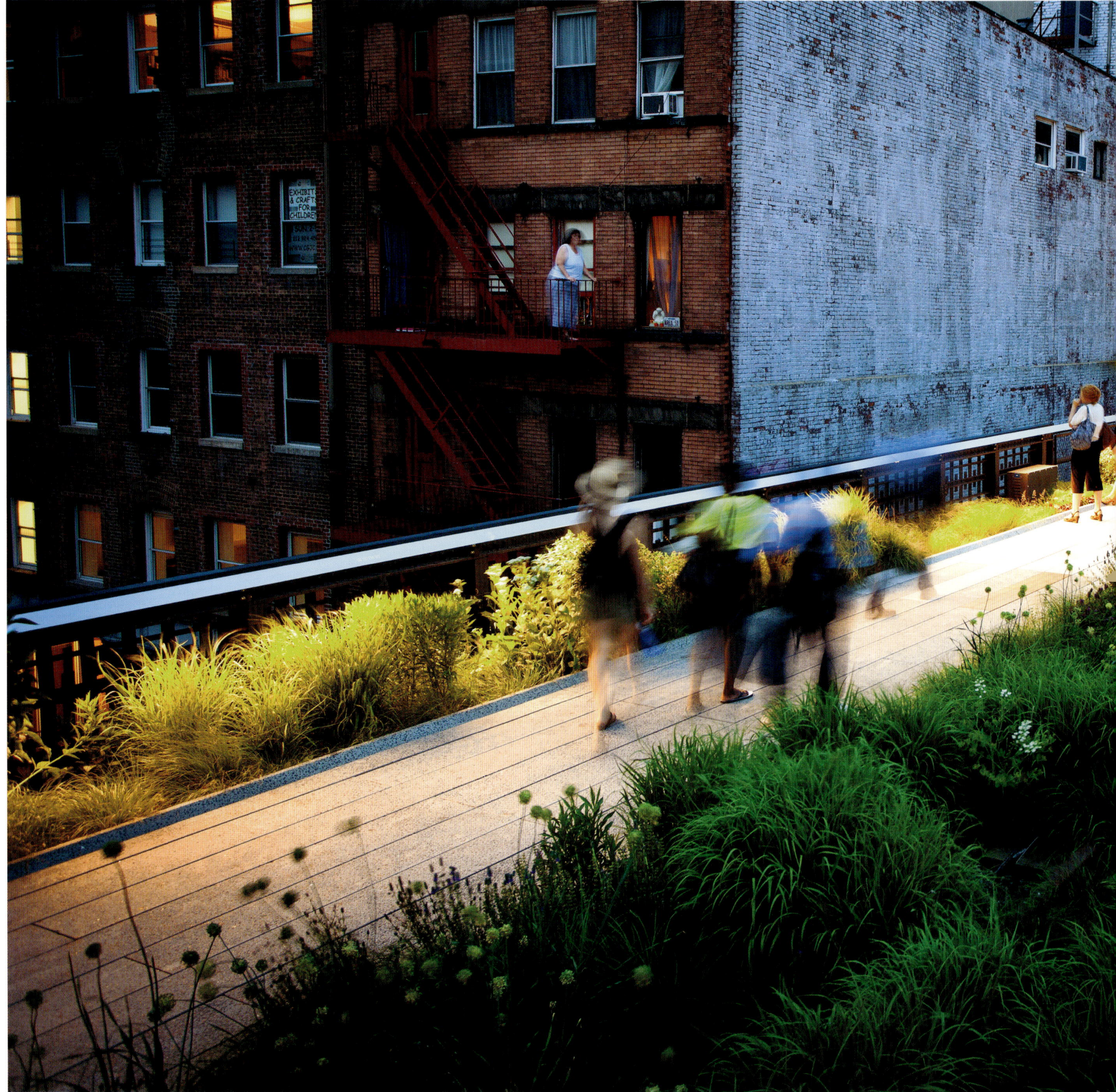
EXHIBIT
& CRAFT
FOR
CHILDRE

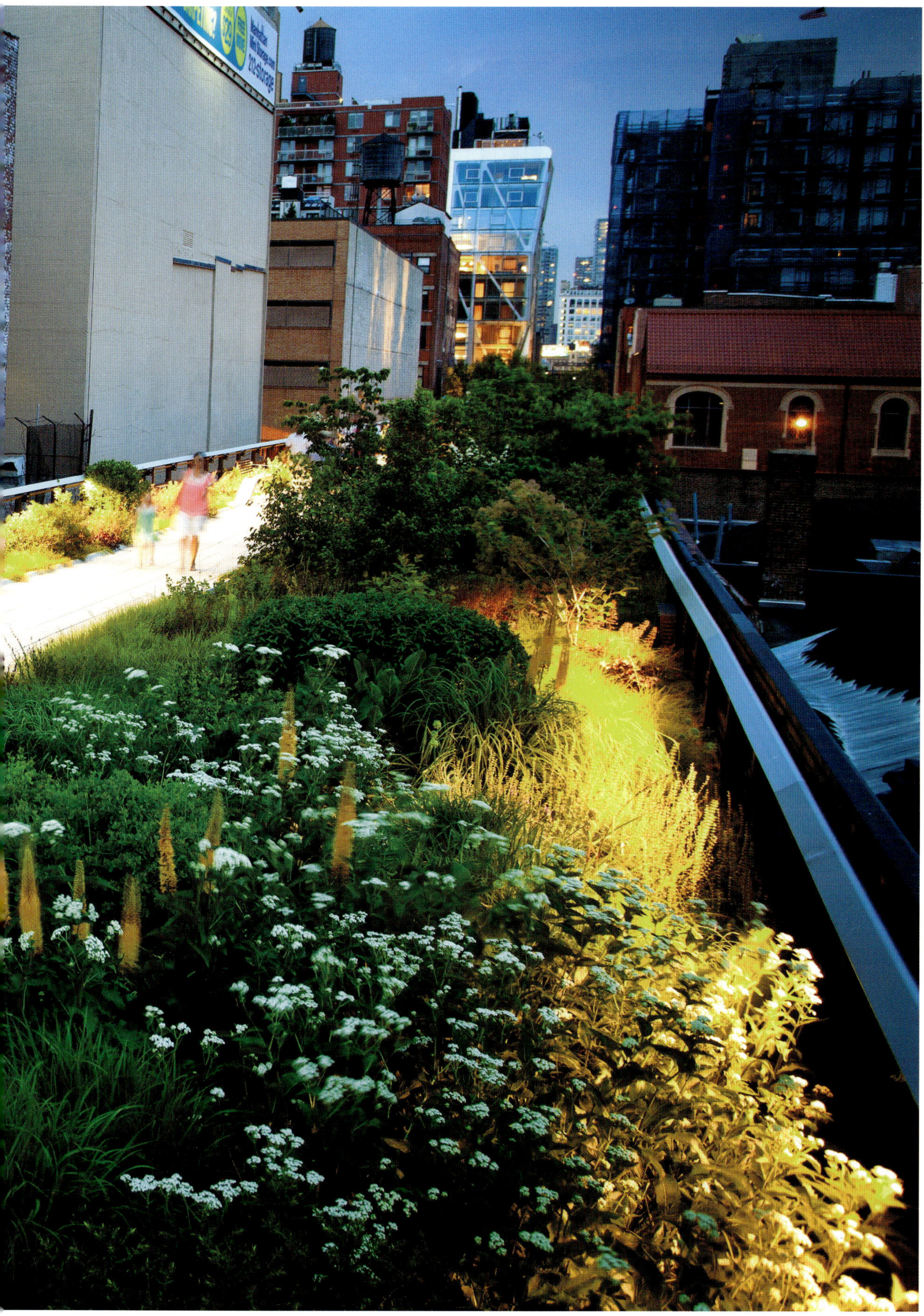

I was photographing the High Line for a magazine. This was my first visit and I absolutely loved it, especially at dusk when this was taken. The human interaction was something I wanted to capture. I think there is something really special about this wonderful green space: I am sure it means so many things to so many people and results in so many daily exchanges.

THE HIGH LINE, NEW YORK CITY, NEW YORK
CONVERSATIONS FROM A BALCONY AT DUSK ALONG THE HIGH LINE

CLAIRE TAKACS

Canon EOS 5D Mark II, 17-40mm lens. 0.8sec at f/5.6. Tripod, remote shutter release. Post-capture: no digital alterations.

FIRST, 2012

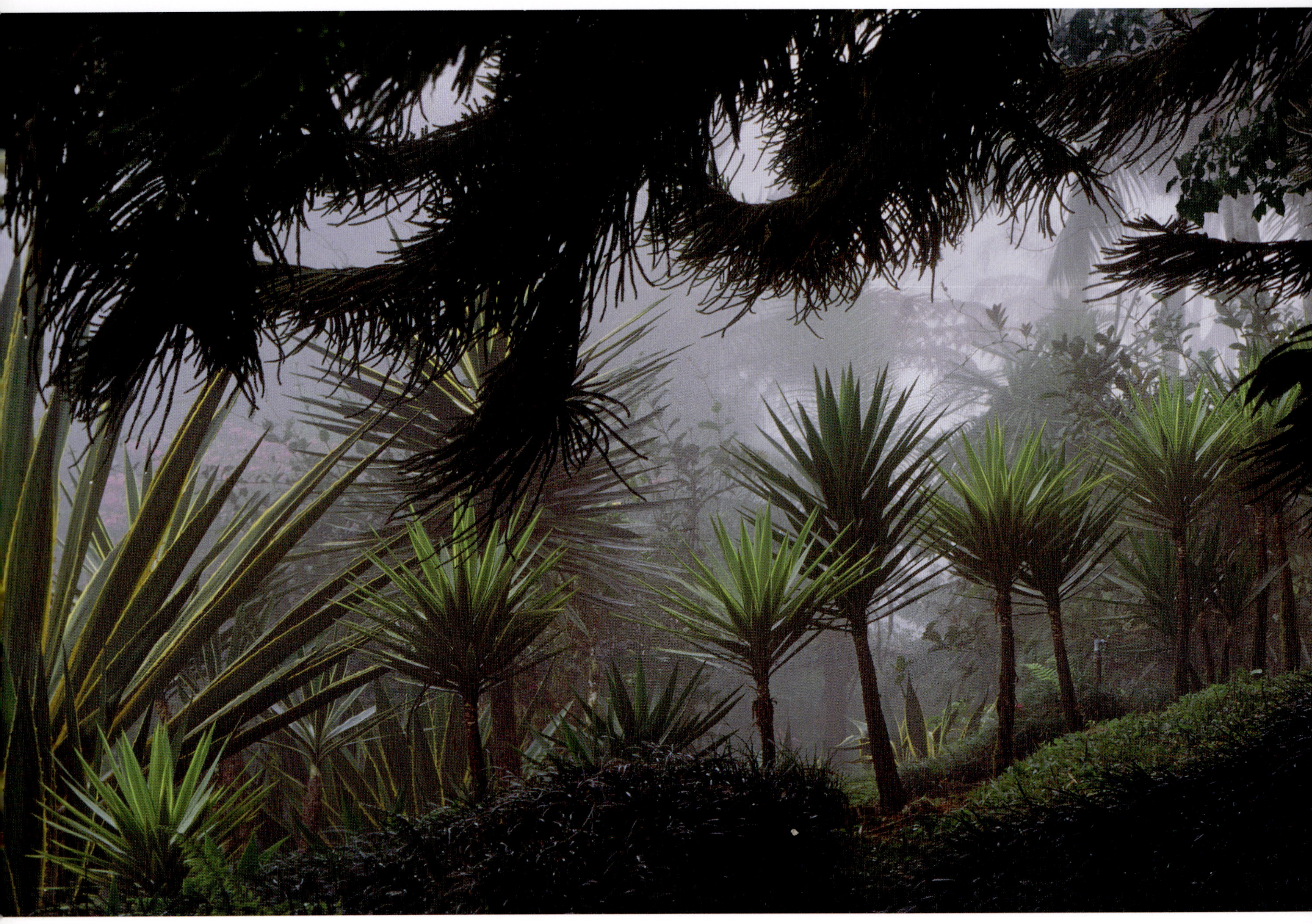

THE MONOCOT GARDEN, JARDÍN BOTÁNICO WILSON
JARDÍN BOTÁNICO WILSON

DANNY BEATH

Fuji Velvia 50, Nikon FE2, Nikkor 55mm, f/5.6
HIGHLY COMMENDED, 2010

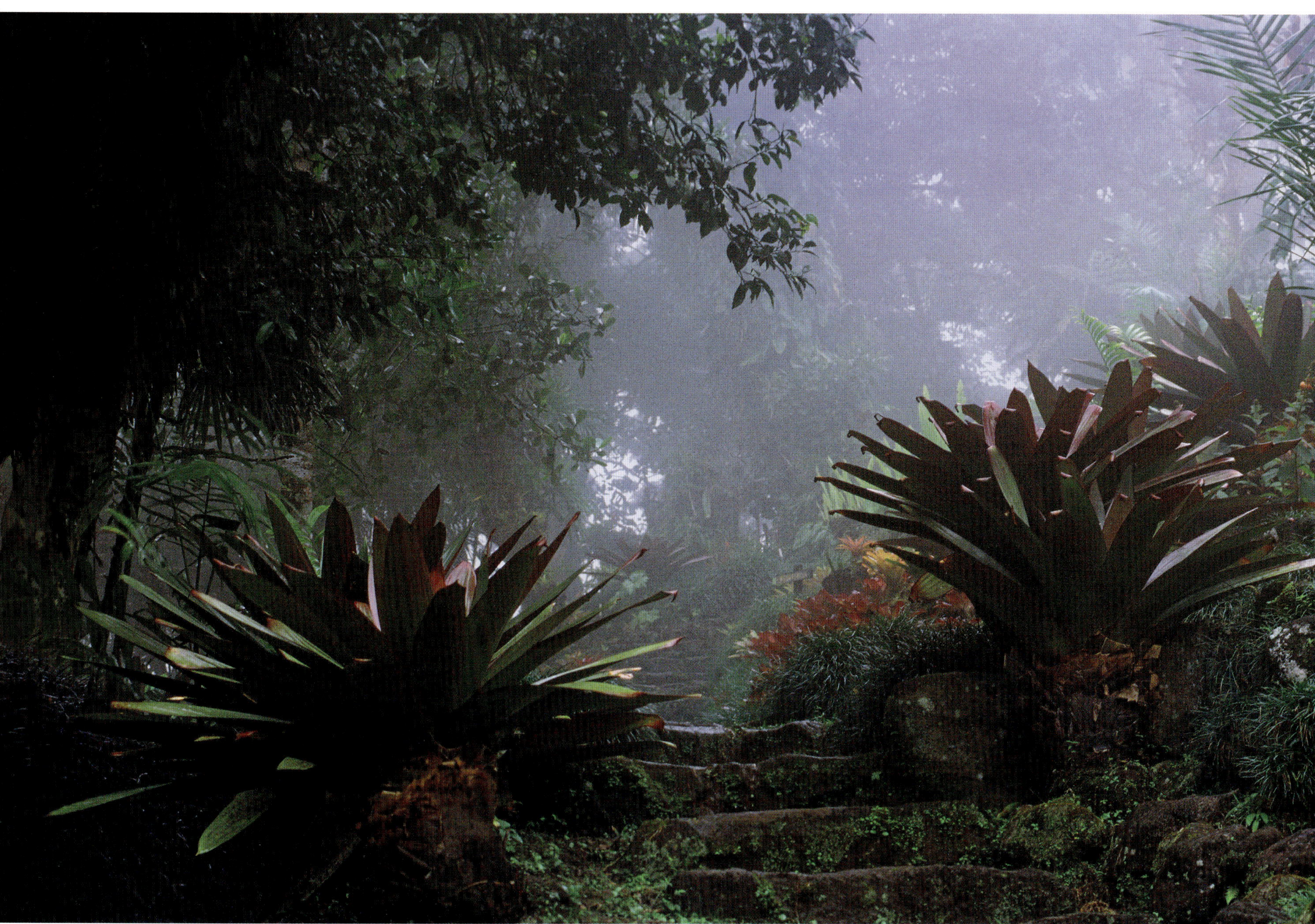

This photograph shows the rare, specialist collection of monocots and bromeliads half-hidden in the morning mists and dripping with the abundant moisture of its cloud-forest habitat. I was inspired by images of the cloud forest around the gardens and wanted to create an almost Tolkien-like feel to my final shot, with moody silhouettes in the mist. I waited for a good fog to descend on the gardens before choosing my vantage point and using a tripod and two shots to create a distortion-free panorama of the misty gardens.

GOL, BUSKERUD

ROOF GARDEN

RENATA GIERLACH

Canon EOS 300, Canon EF 28–80mm lens, Kodak GC 400. I waited for 20 minutes hoping for the rain to stop. As it kept on pouring I had to cover the camera with a blanket and use flash to take the picture.

COMMENDED, 2008

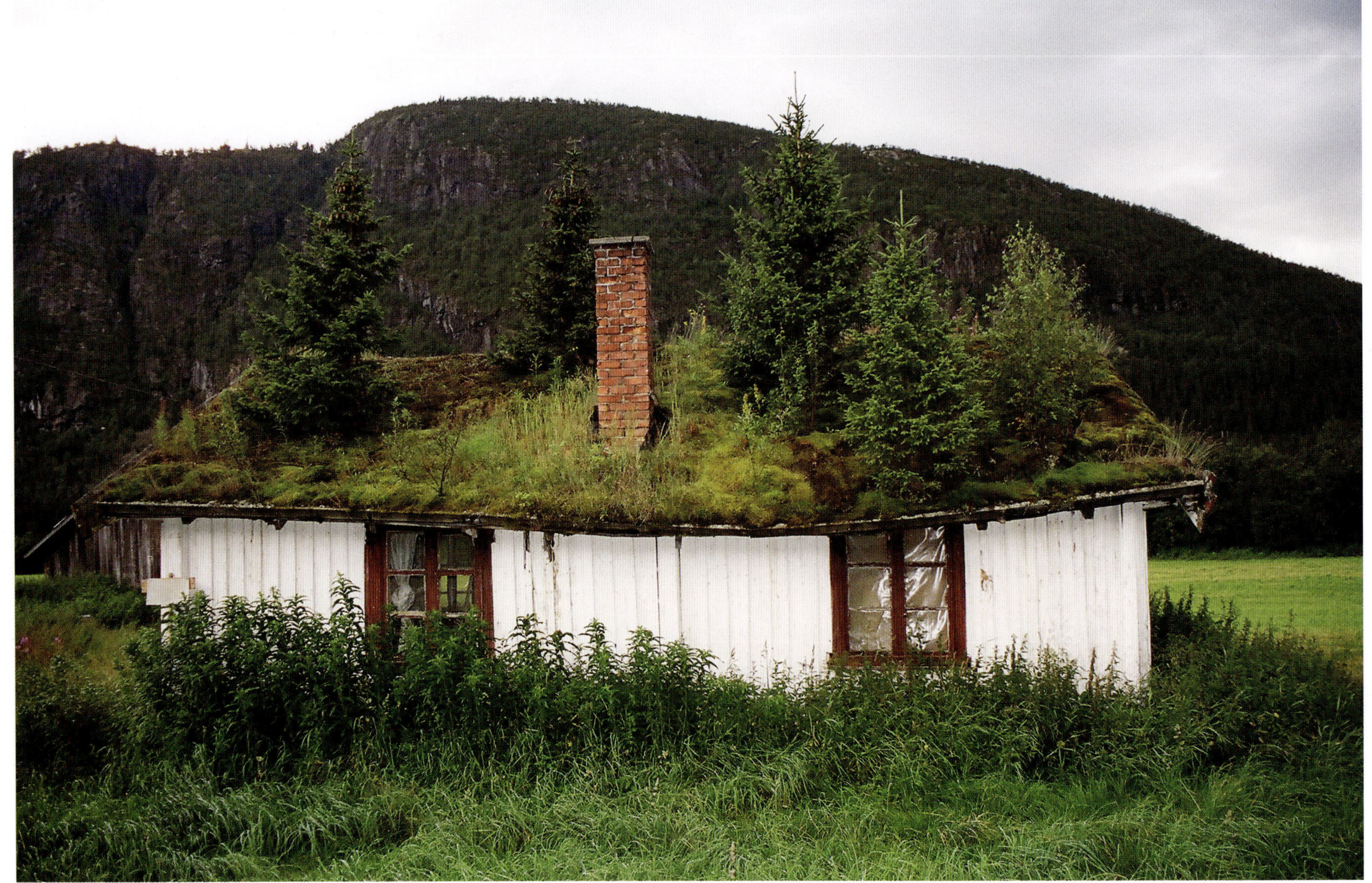

Before this moment, I had never seen real trees growing on a building. It was as if someone had started a wild garden on the roof of their house, and then abandoned it.

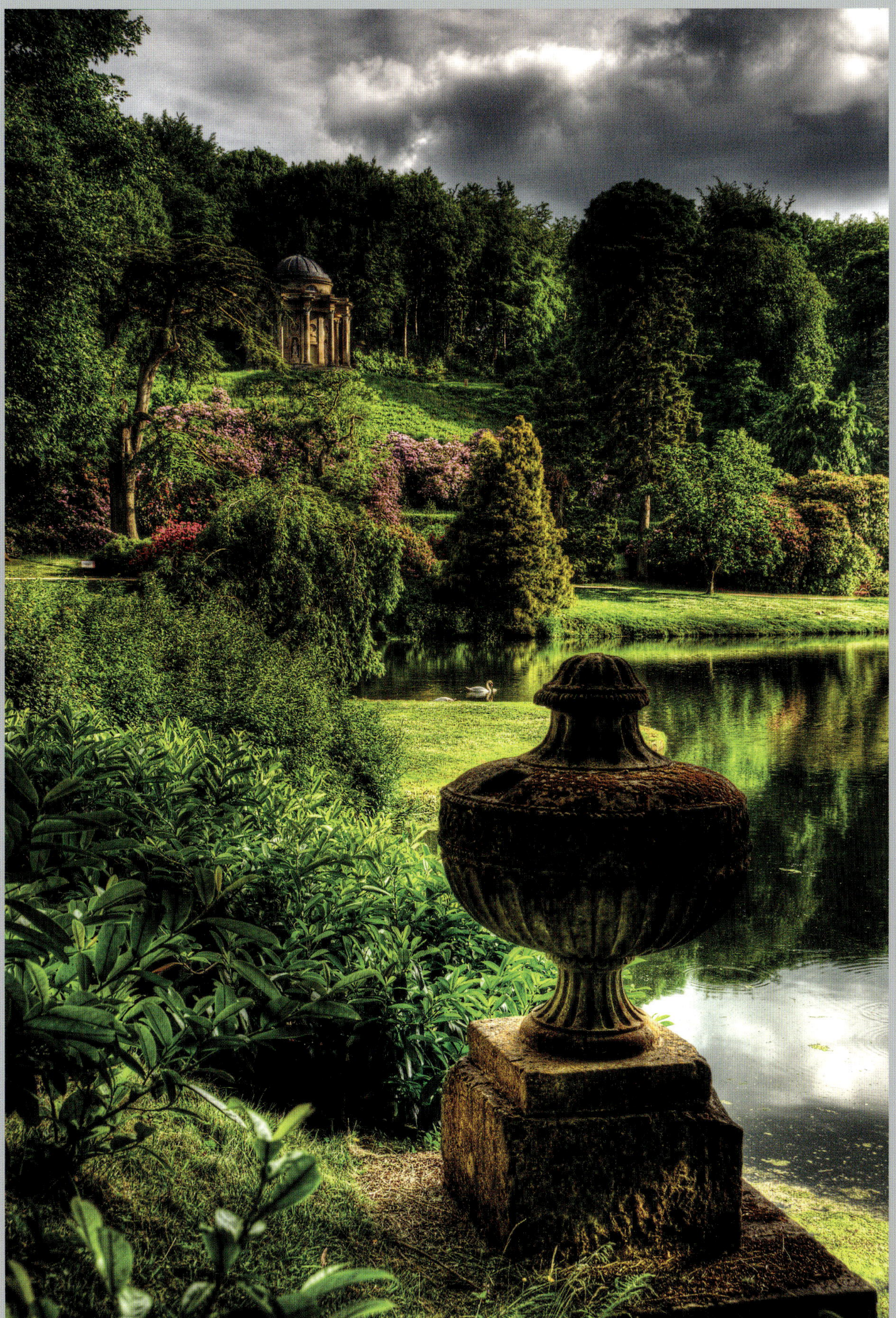

STOURHEAD GARDENS, WILTSHIRE, ENGLAND

By kind permission of the National Trust

URN AND TEMPLE

ANTHONY WORSDELL

Nikon D90, Nikkor 18-200mm lens. I shot three images at the following exposures: 1/800sec at f/8, 1/200sec at f/8 and 1/50sec at f/8. Post-capture: the three RAW images were combined and tone mapped, saved as a 16-bit TIFF, and then further processed (levels, noise reduction, slight sharpening and contrast enhancement in curves).

HIGHLY COMMENDED, 2011

This is a view of the Temple of Apollo, Stourhead, showing the lake with a decorative stone ornament in the foreground. I was attracted to the beauty of the scene, the contrast of sunlight and cloudy sky, the interesting combination of the foreground ornament with the background temple and the sunlight reflecting off the water to the underside of the ornament. I was experimenting with HDR imaging and a late afternoon stroll round Stourhead was a good opportunity to capture some images with good contrast. I wanted to get a slightly dreamy quality to the image.

Photograph taken in autumn morning in the gardens of Monserrate, Sintra, Portugal. This is the granite ladder marking the beginning of the Valley of Ferns. I enjoy shooting against the sun and I liked the arrangement of the elements. The photo was taken at ground level and I used the articulated screen to get my camera close to the ground to achieve the composition I wanted.

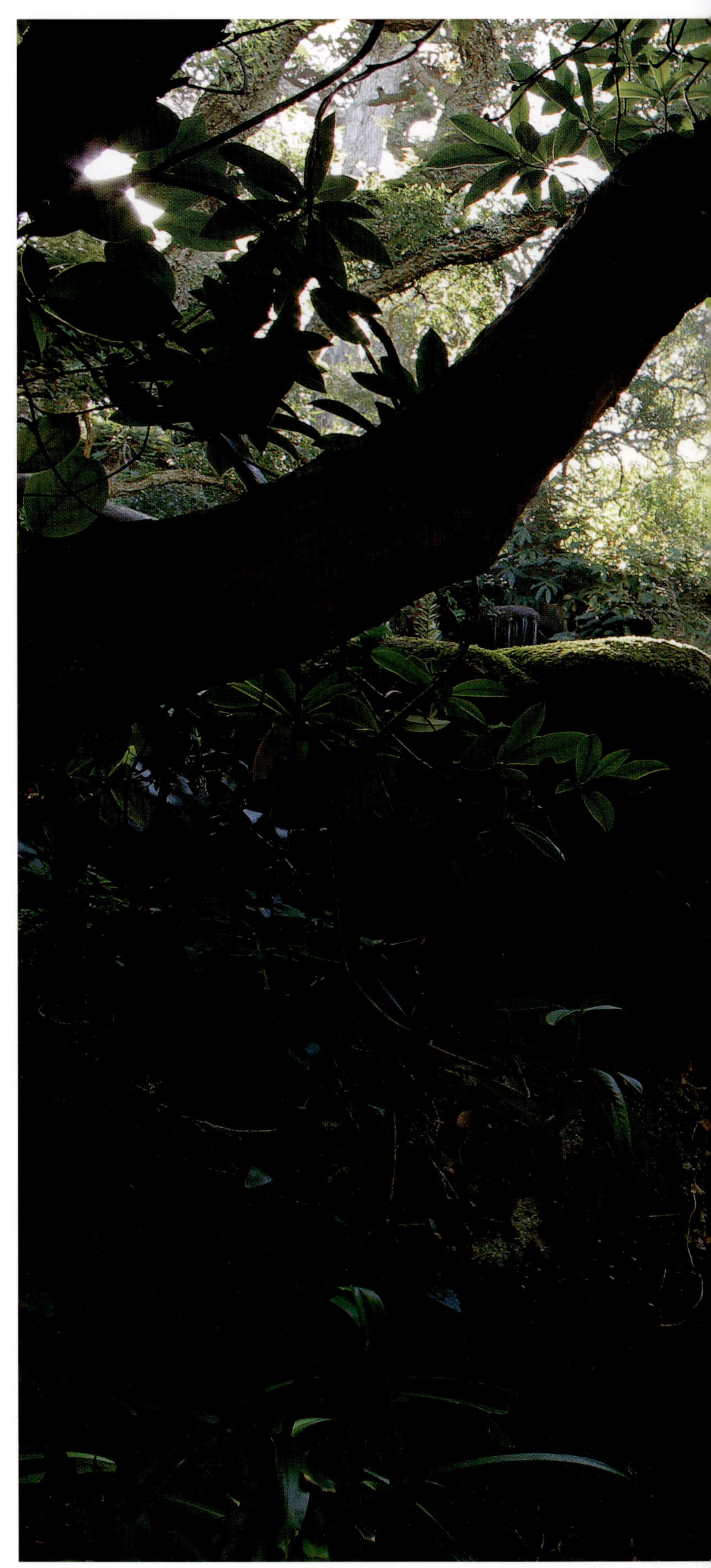

PARQUE DE MONSERRATE, SINTRA
MORNING IN THE GARDEN

FÁBIO CLAUDINO

Canon 600D, 18-55mm lens. 1/10sec at f/11. Post-capture: basic adjustments to tone and colour balance, saturation, brightness and contrast.
HIGHLY COMMENDED, 2012

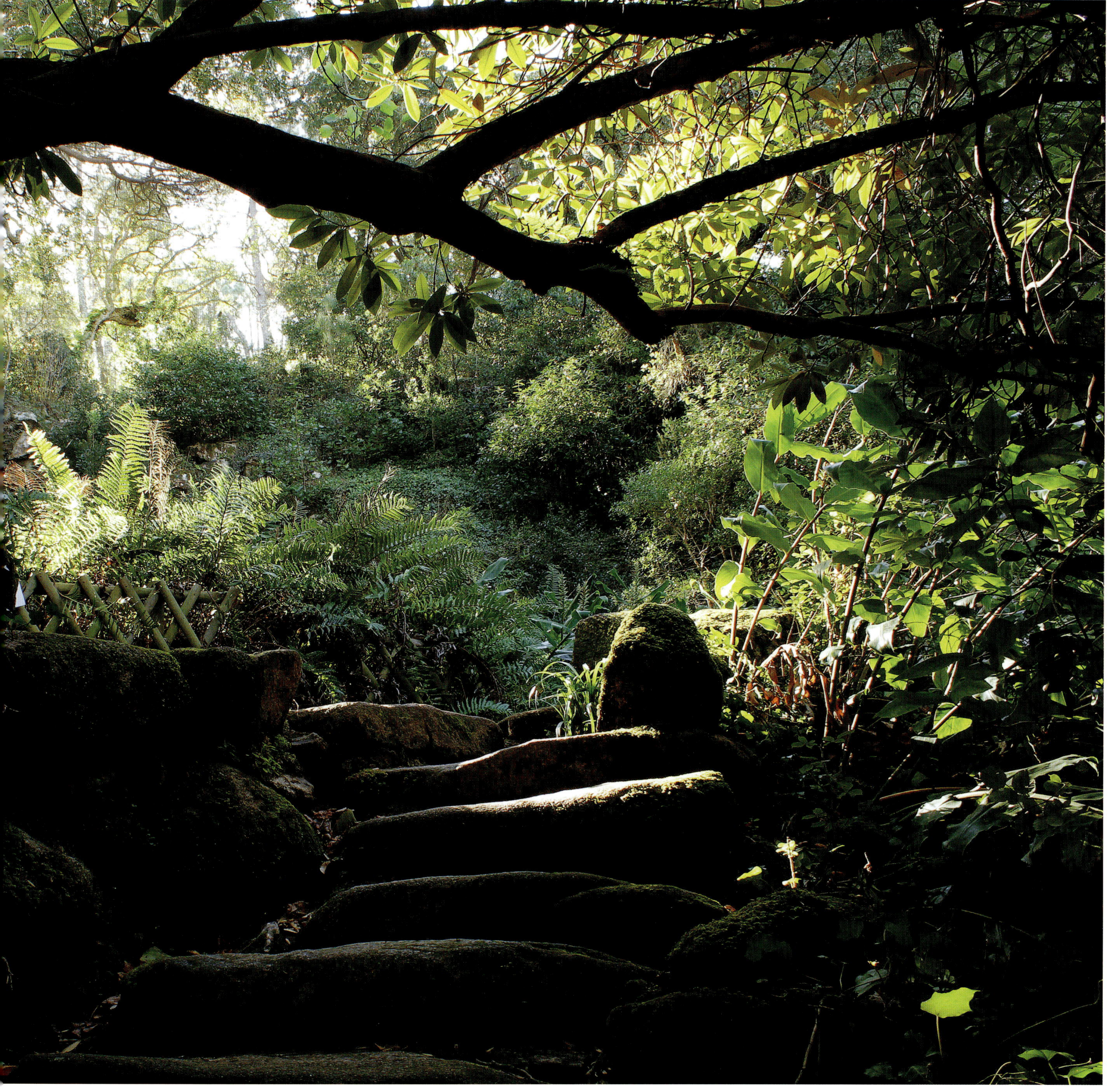

I have spent several years experimenting with infrared film, and in this case knew that the topiary and leaves would appear as if covered with snow, despite it being summer. The shapes created by the topiary, the weather conditions and the position of the sun were all favourable for the technique I used.

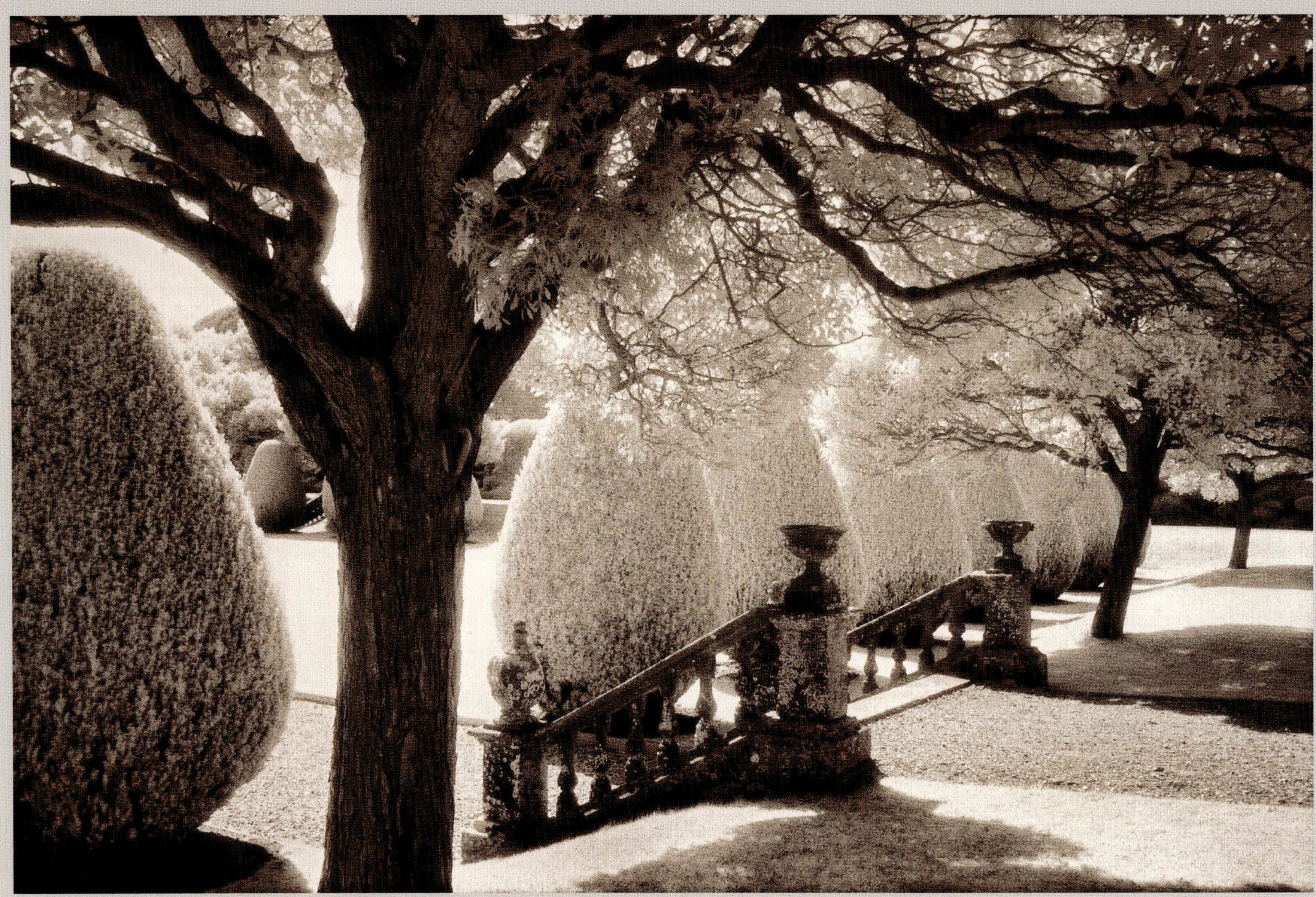

MONTACUTE HOUSE NEAR YEOVIL, SOMERSET, ENGLAND
By kind permission of the National Trust
AN ENGLISH COUNTRY GARDEN

COLIN HOSKINS

Canon F-1N, Canon FD 35mm lens, f/11, Kodak HIE. I waited two and a half years to be able to make this image. It was a case of being able to visit the garden when the lighting conditions were favourable.
COMMENDED, 2008

THE ROYAL BOTANIC GARDENS, KEW, SURREY, ENGLAND

MORNING WALK

YOSHKO PALENIK

Olympus E-500, Olympus 14-45mm lens at 25mm setting, f/6.3.
FINALIST, 2009

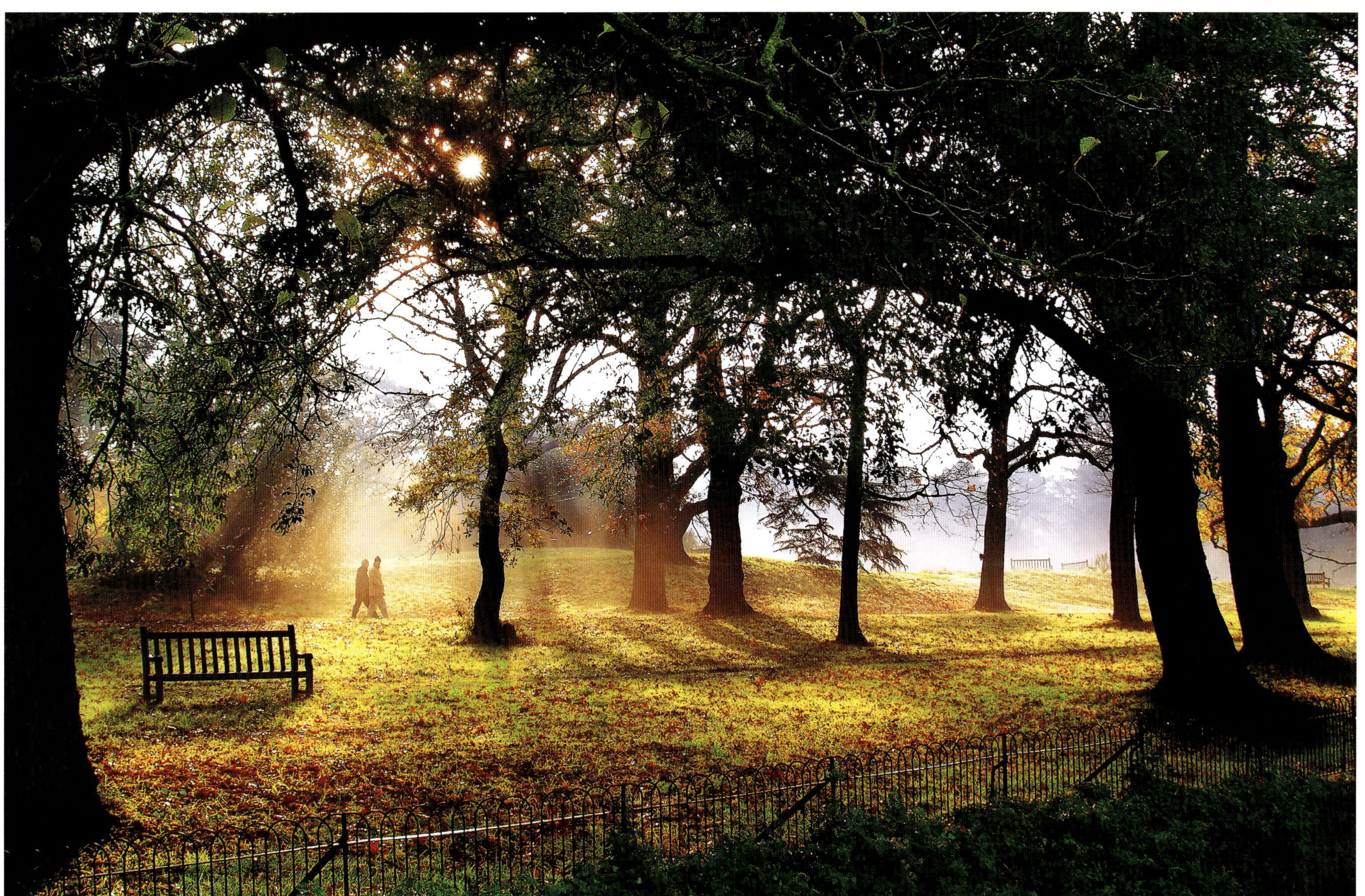

The silhouettes of two figures are captured walking through the gardens at Kew in the misty sunshine early one morning. The misty atmosphere, full of sunshine and beautiful autumnal colours, amazed me.

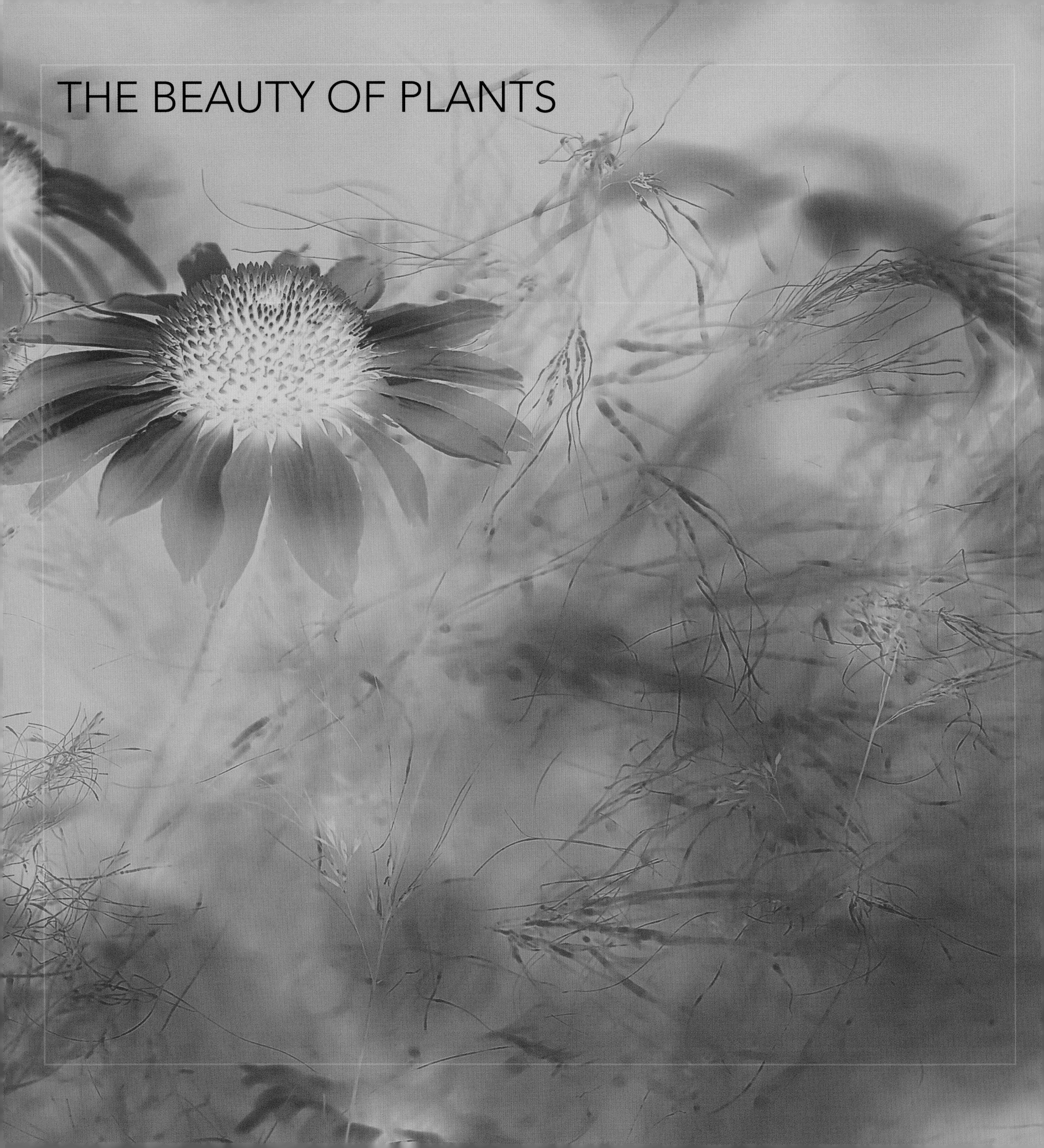
THE BEAUTY OF PLANTS

Plant Portraits

Plants have featured in photography since the early 1800s, from Fox Talbot's first images, Carl Blossfeld's influential plant photographs (*Art Forms in Nature 1928*), through to contemporary artists such as Rob Kesseler, who currently uses photography and scanning electron microscope to create images that reveal the amazing beauty of minute pollen grains and seeds – photographic images that continue the tradition of this medium to inspire interest in the plant world.

Photography is part science and part art and, alongside botanical illustration, it encompasses both disciplines. Botanical art has a much longer history – images of plants captured in paint date back to AD 512, and are featured in herbals as early as the first century BC. Botanists still primarily use drawing and painting to illustrate their scientific work and, in the hands of skilled recorders and artists, many of these works are not only accurate but beautiful, and considered as fine art. Today, with the popular use of digital technology, from the phone to more sophisticated photographic equipment, there is clearly an extraordinary desire to capture images. For those wanting to grasp the ephemeral nature of a flower or a garden, photography has real immediacy and appeal. From images that capture a moment through to carefully considered compositions, photographs can also reach the status of art.

Since 2000, photographic exhibitions of plants and related subjects have featured as part of Kew's themed Festival program. These exhibitions have included the work of many of today's finest plant and environmental photographers. The International Garden Photographer of the Year competition has inspired a huge response and a wide variety of superb submissions. This annual competition has become acknowledged as a major showcase for inspirational plant, garden and landscape photographs from around the world.

I have been involved with the relationship between International Garden Photographer of the Year and Kew since its inception and, for the past five years, have had the privilege to be part of the competition selection process. From the start it has been a revelation and real joy to see, analyse and select images from the wonderful variety of submissions.

The process is stimulating, challenging and great fun. First, short-listing on-line, then to the debate and final selections with fellow judges. It also provides a continuing learning process, where we have the opportunity to gain some new insight into the technical and the aesthetic knowledge and opinions of our colleagues. Throughout this process I have been continually impressed by the clear passion for plants that shines through the images. The list of adjectives to describe many of the photographs is extensive including: elegant, beautiful, witty, humorous, light/dark, colourful, considered, spontaneous, technically brilliant, atmospheric, painterly and so on... International Garden Photographer of the Year has clearly inspired people of all ages to use the medium of photography to examine and capture the world around them.

Together with Kew's changing program, International Garden Photographer of the Year continues to provide visitors to the gardens with an unprecedented opportunity to experience some of the best examples of contemporary photography, alongside our exhibitions of historic and contemporary botanical art. Through access to this astonishing resource, I hope that the significance of biodiversity and the need to protect and conserve the fragile beauty of the natural world will continue to be revealed.

Laura Giuffrida
Galleries and Exhibitions Leader, Royal Botanic Gardens, Kew

WILDFLOWER GARDEN, UNIVERSITY OF OREGON
CALIFORNIAN POPPIES

DENNIS FRATES

Canon EOS-1Ds, Canon 20–200mm f/2.8 lens, f/4.
COMMENDED, 2008

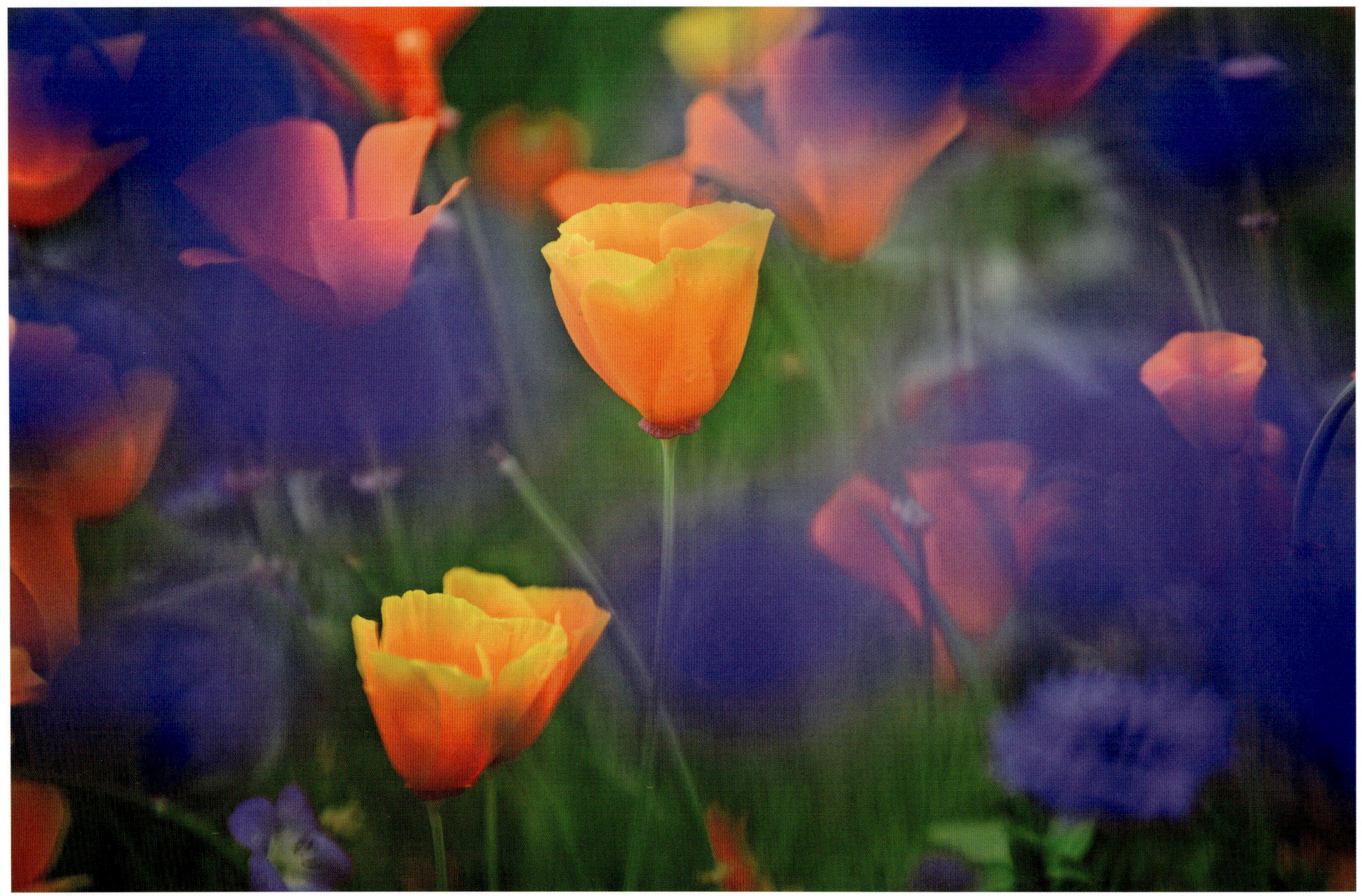

I loved the complementary colours of blue and orange in this scene. I also saw that, because of the arrangement, I could blur the blue Bachelor's Buttons (*Centaurea cyanus*) while keeping a poppy (*Eschscholzia* spp.) or two in focus.

I had just recently bought a new camera and was experimenting with it. I took quite a number of shots of these flowers but this was my favourite. I was trying to show my 10-year-old daughter how to take flower pictures.

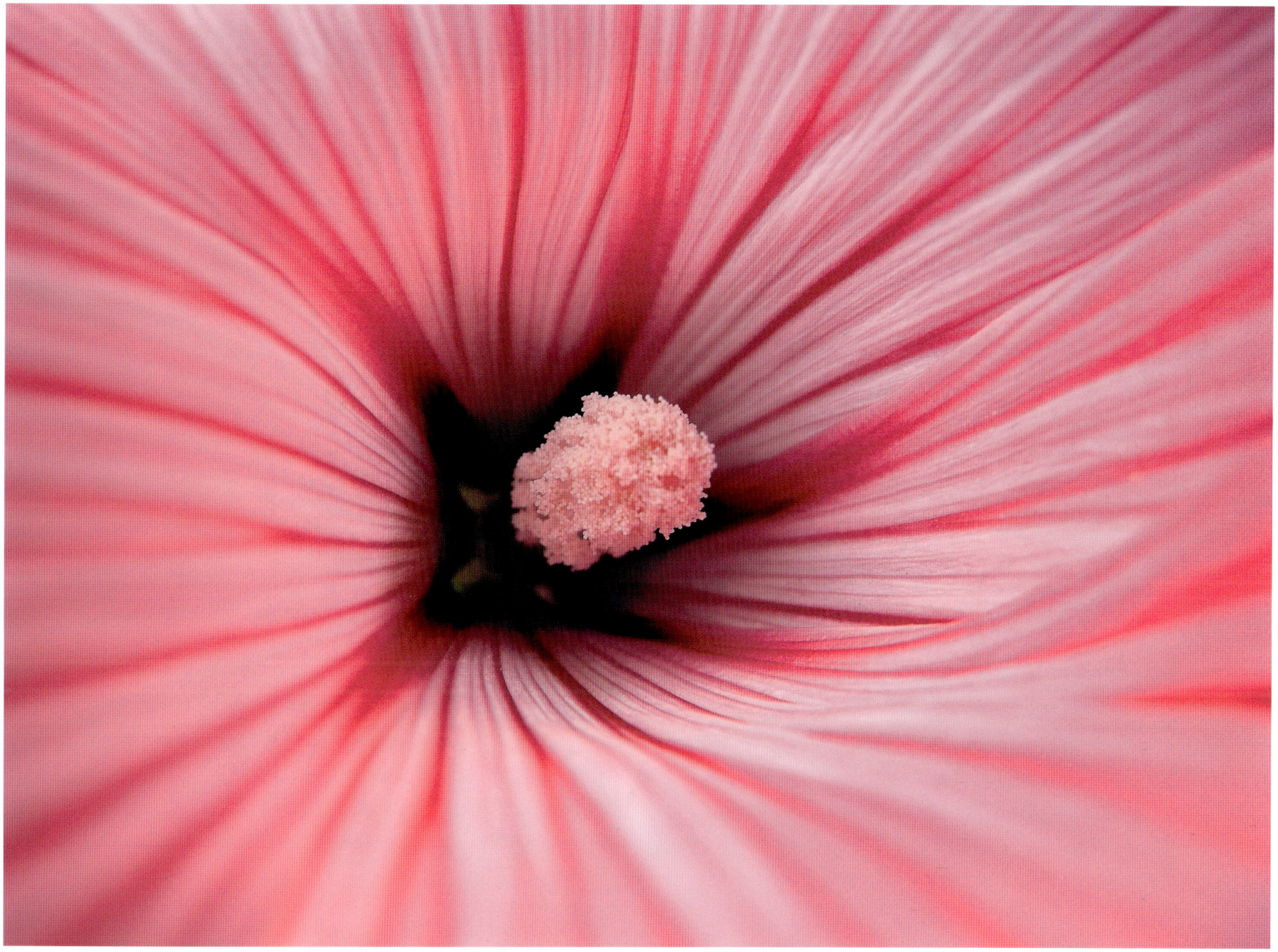

NEW GLASGOW, NOVA SCOTIA
PINK LAVATERA

JOHN PETTIGREW

Nikon Coolpix P5000, f/3.4. Adjusted brightness and boosted colour slightly. I took several pictures but this one stood out from the rest. I like the way the markings lead you into the photograph.
COMMENDED, 2008

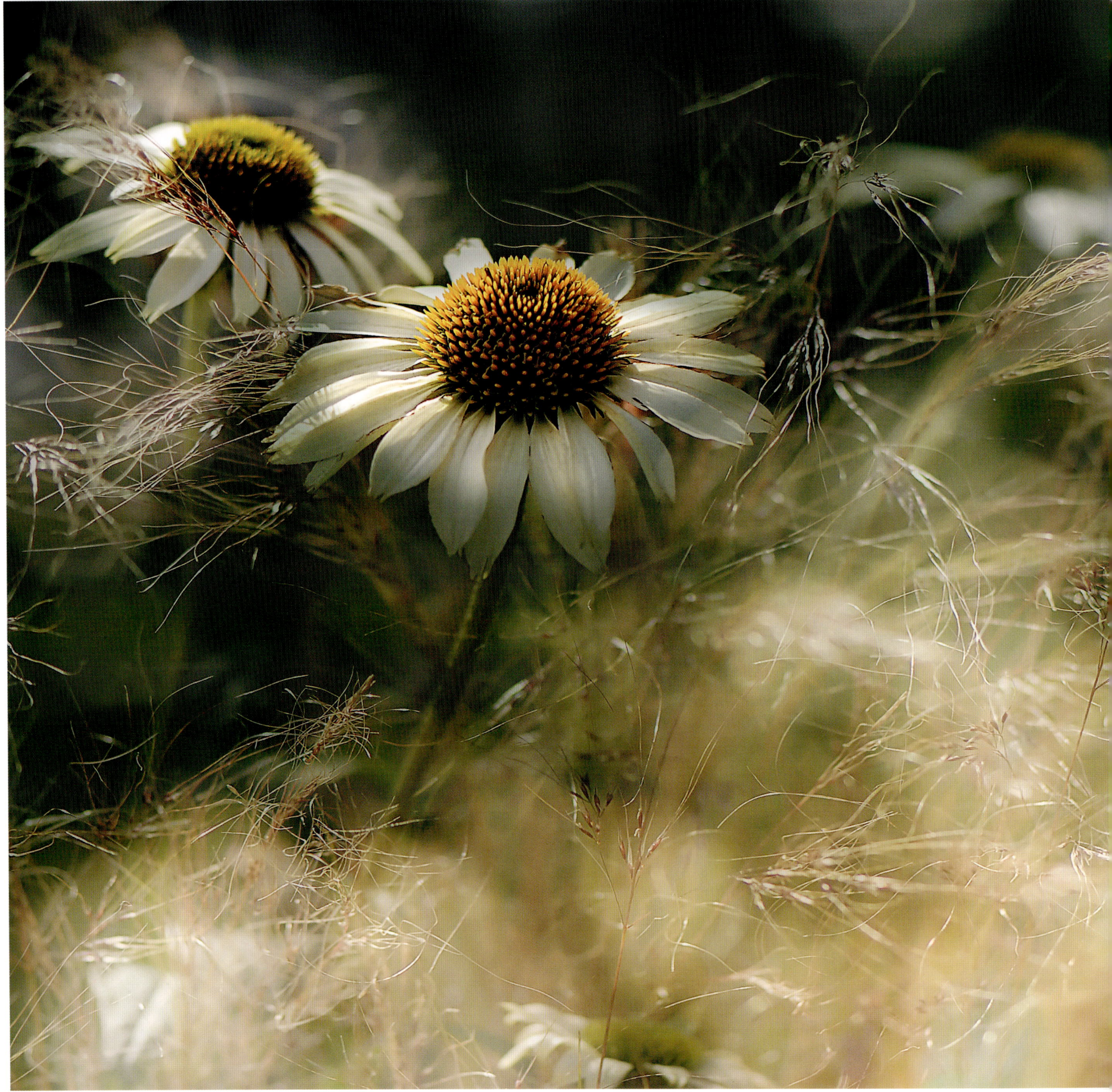

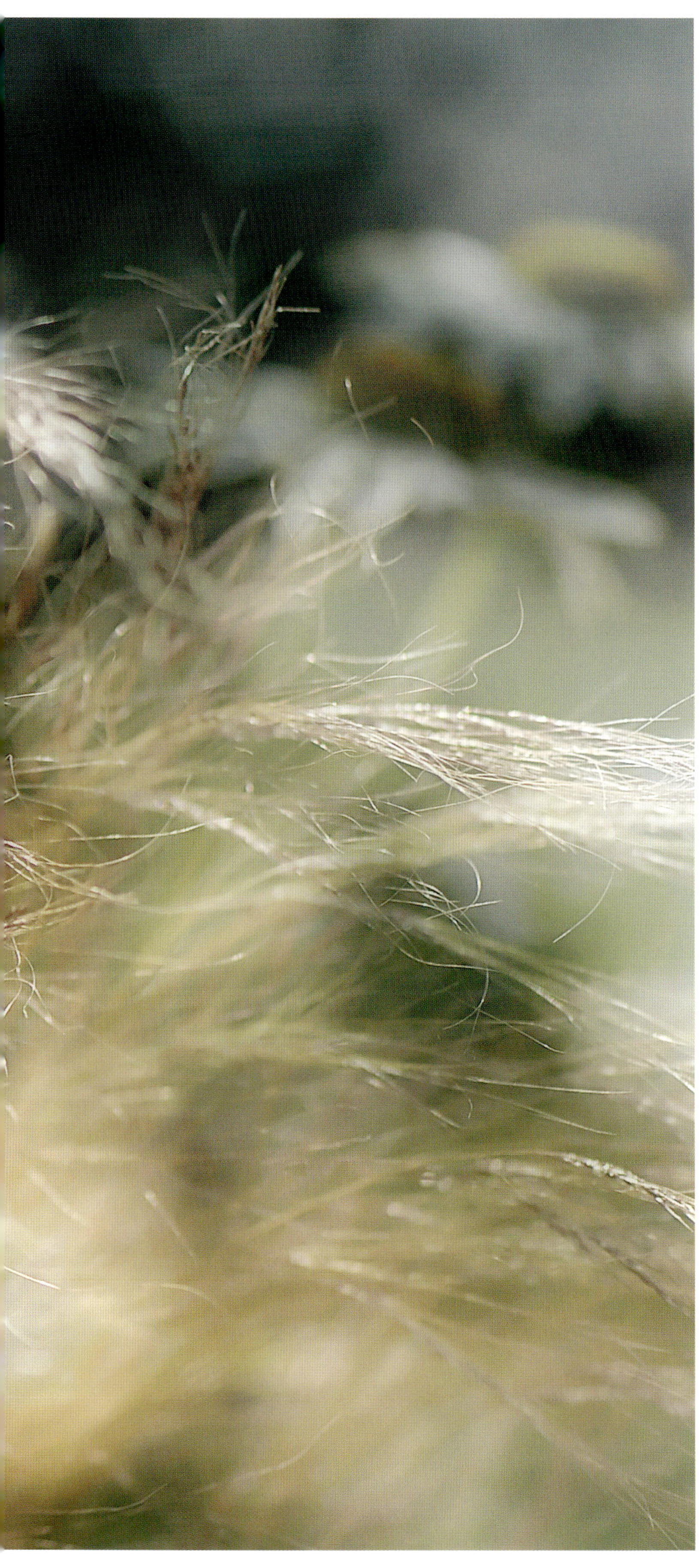

The soft white coneflowers (*Echinacea purpurea* 'White Lustre') in amongst the delicate soft grasses of feather grass (*Stipa tenuissima*). I liked the way the soft grasses seemed to wrap themselves around the white coneflowers, gently swaying in the breeze.

BUCKINGHAMSHIRE, ENGLAND
SOFT TONES OF AUTUMN

JACKY PARKER

Nikon D200, Nikkor 105 micro VR.
HIGHLY COMMENDED, 2010

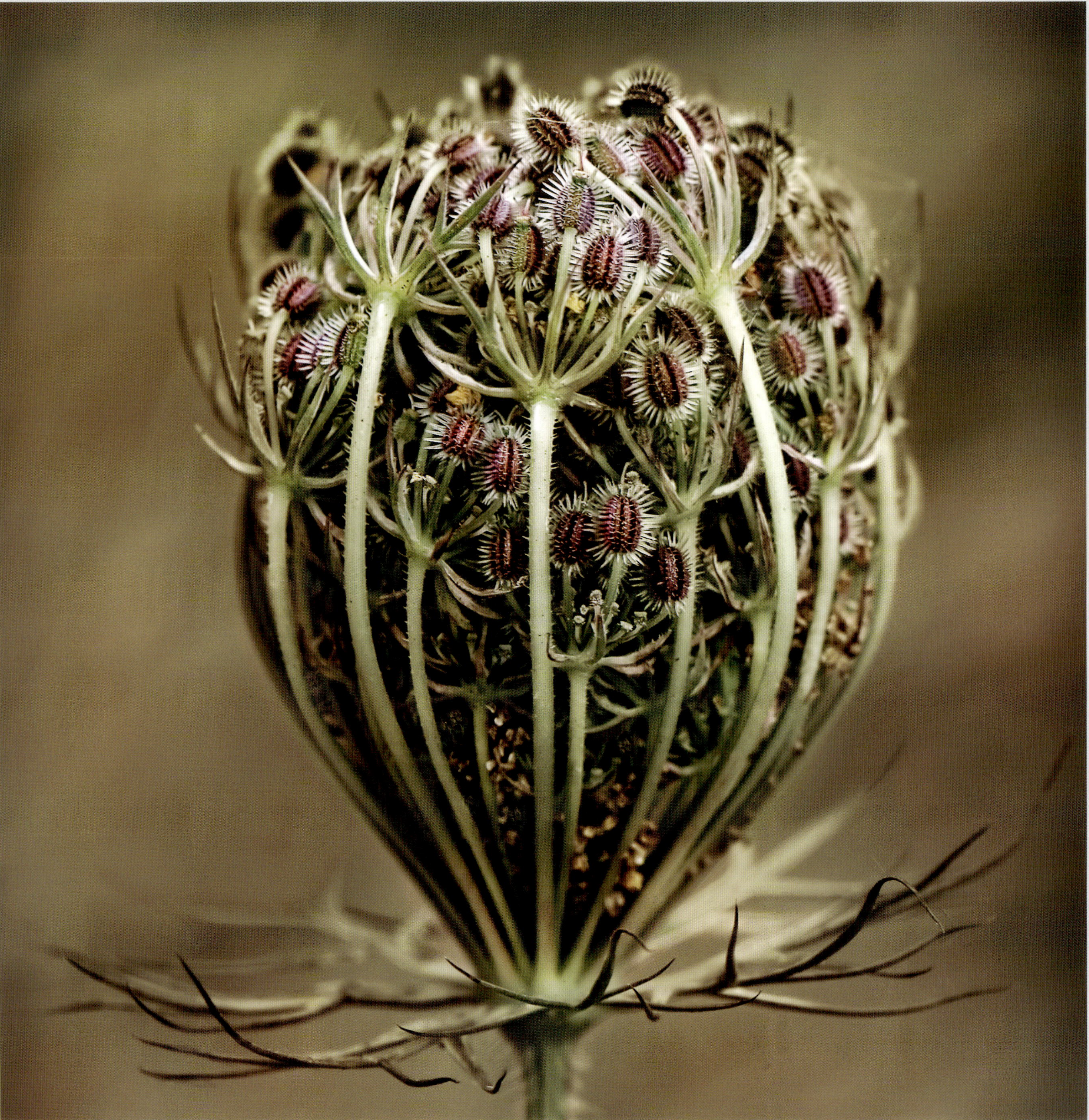

I was drawn to this plant for its graceful beauty, its attention to detail with its hundreds of jewel-like seeds and its ability to protect itself by compressing into a tightly woven nest. It spoke volumes about the universal aspect of new beginnings, accompanied with hope.

MONTARA, CALIFORNIA
BOUND TO PROSPER

DIANE VARNER

Canon EOS Digital Rebel XT, 100mm macro lens, f/7.1. Curves adjusted, colour fill overlay, dodge and burn, contrast adjustment and noise reduction. All my images are taken on my daily walks with my handheld camera. I find myself noticing nuances of light and detail; hence this particular shot.
SECOND, 2008

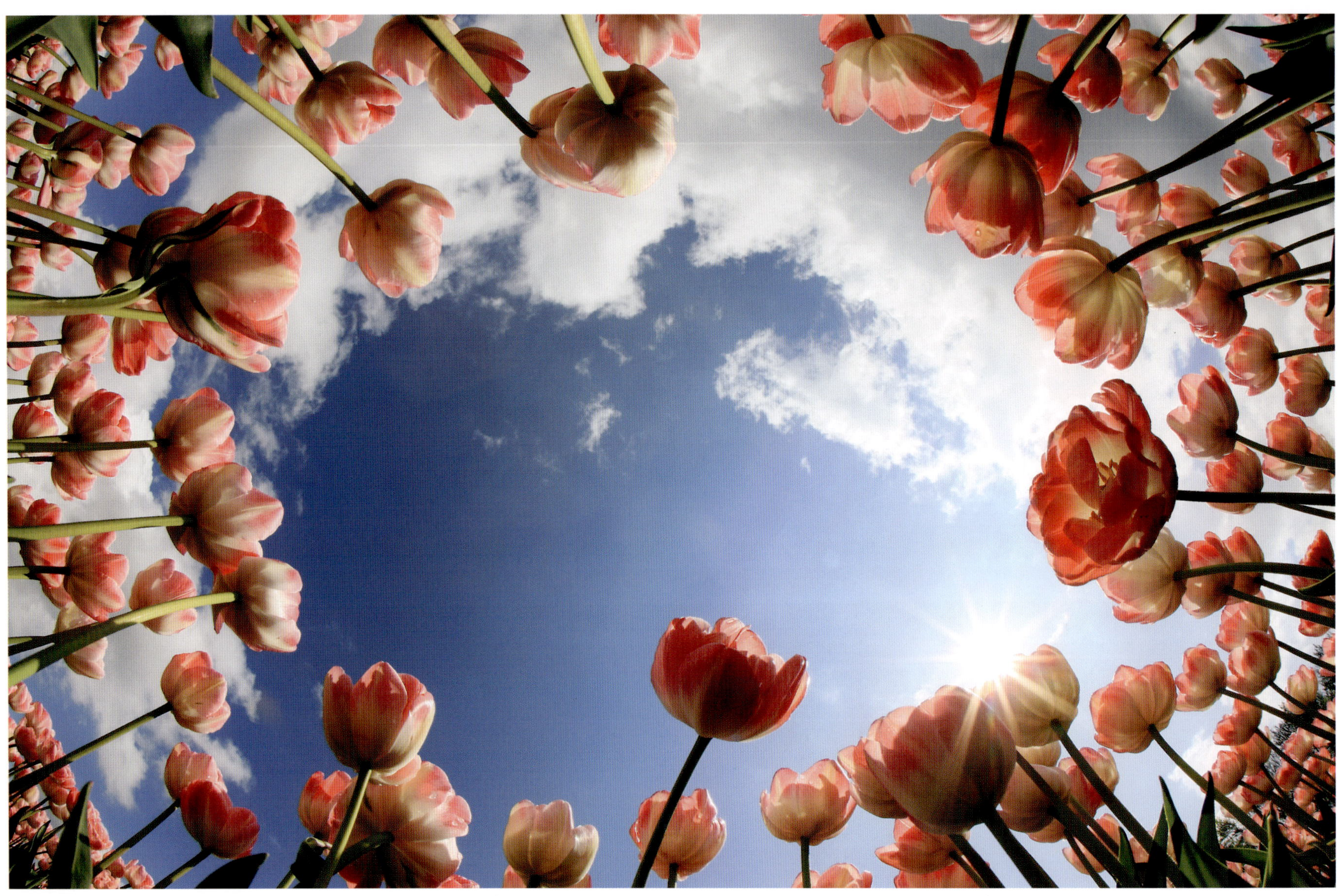

THE NETHERLANDS
TULIPA – UNIVERSE OF FLOWERS

SERGEY KAREPANOV

Canon EOS 1 Ds Mark III, Canon EF 15mm, f/2.8.
THIRD, 2010

I grow tulips (*Tulipa* spp.) at home, but had never seen such an enormous amount of flowers as I found when I visited a Dutch polder full of tulips last spring. The sky is the only possible backdrop for a scene of such magnificence.

These beautifully coloured rudbeckias caught my eye across the large garden I visited in late October – mainly because the orange was so intense. As I went closer, I noticed they had been shaped by the wind and rain. It was a quite extraordinary sight.

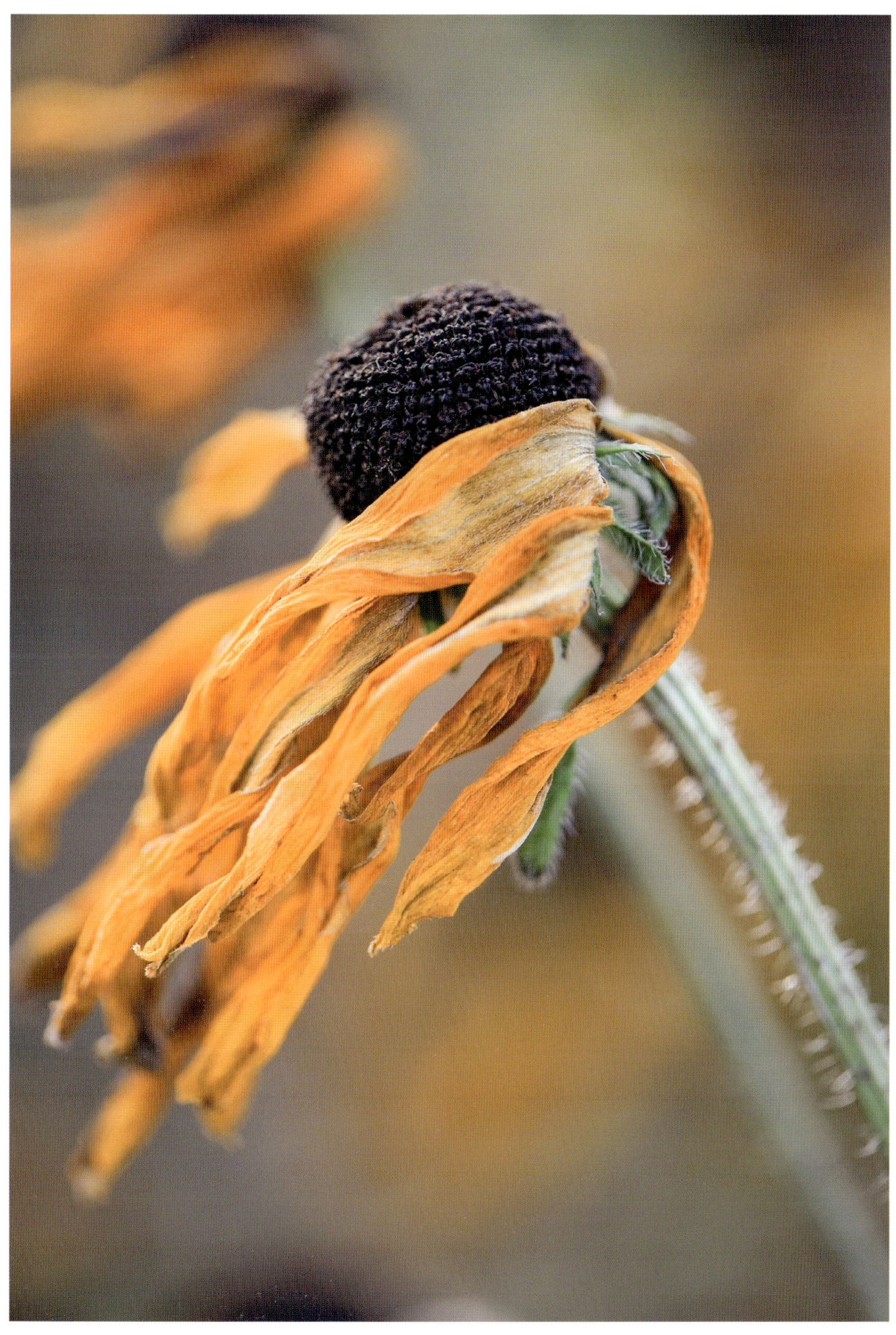

SWEDEN
WINDSWEPT RUDBECKIAS

PERNILLA BERGDAHL

Canon EOS 5D, Canon 180mm macro lens. I had to lower my tripod so my camera was facing the flower straight on, but I also made sure I included some more of the orange rudbeckias in the background.
FINALIST, 2008

SAN BERNARDINO NATIONAL FOREST, CALIFORNIA

WATER PLANT

SEISHI NAGATSUKA

Handmade 8 x 10 inch camera, 420mm Fujinon lens, f/22, flash.

COMMENDED, 2009

I was enjoying a quiet walk in San Bernardino National Forest, having travelled through the desert in Arizona and California for almost two weeks. It was around 6 o'clock on the warm summer evening when I found a small stream running through the forest. It was so beautiful that I started shooting water plants flowing along the stream using the flash bulb for more interesting light.

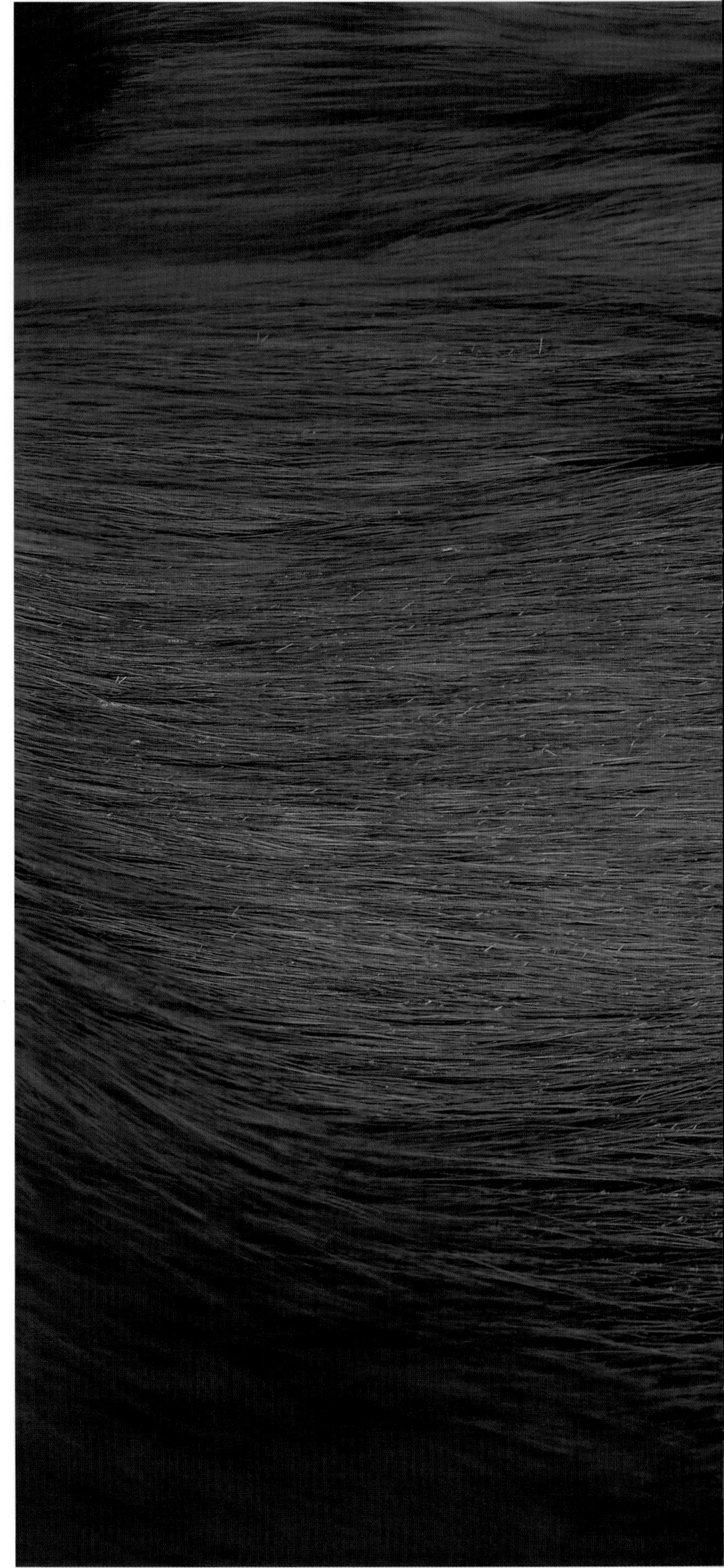

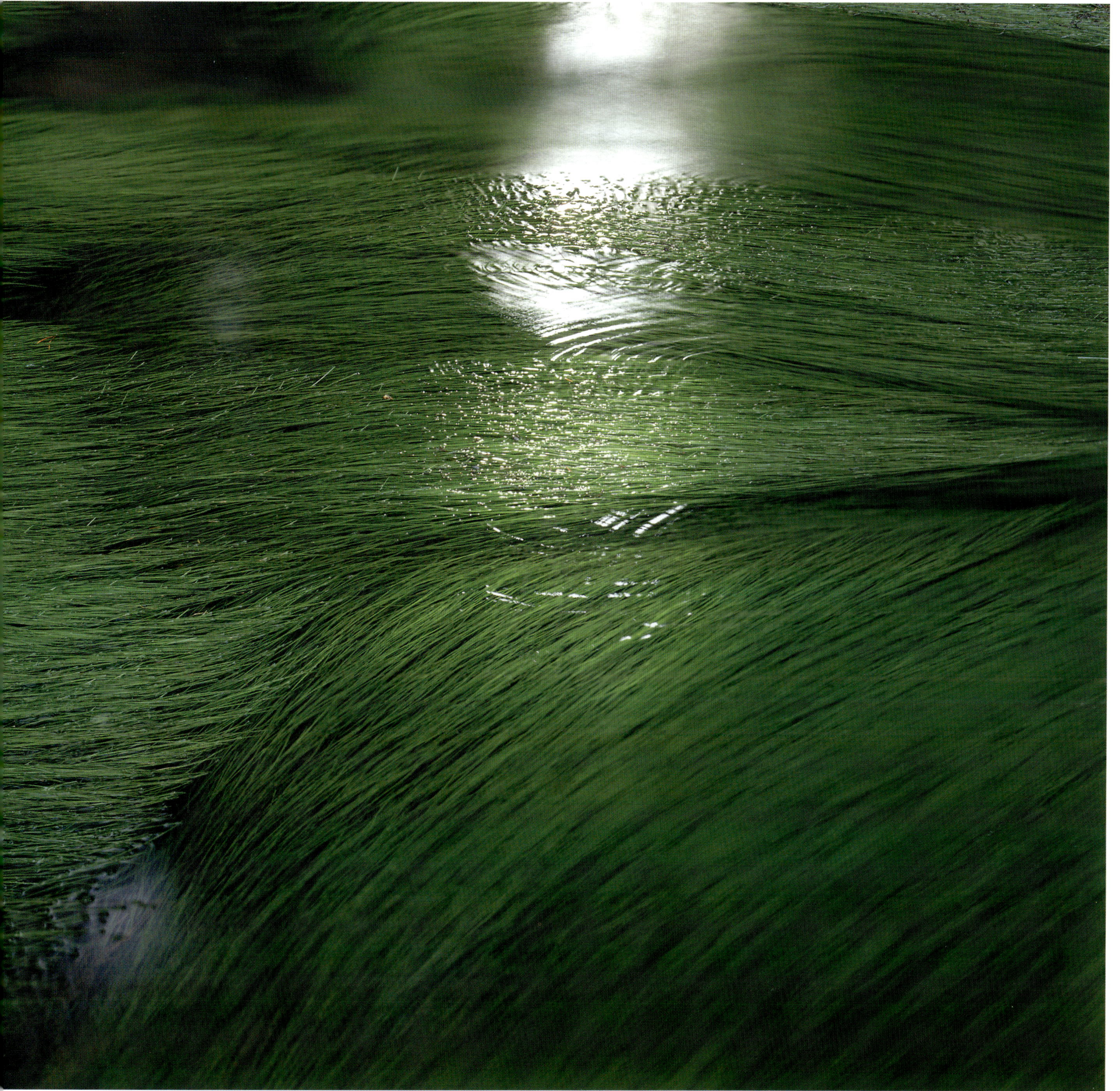

CAMBRIDGESHIRE, ENGLAND

WINDOW DRESSING

MANDY DISHER

Canon EOS 7D and Canon EOS 450D, Canon 50mm lens, Tamron 60mm and Tamron 90mm lenses. Post-capture: I combined the three shots I had taken together. I also photographed a variety of fine net fabrics and merged them into the floral image to add more interest and create a feeling of movement.

FINALIST, 2012

1–Cherish
2–Pure
3–Romance
4–Joy
5–Celebration
6–Cheer

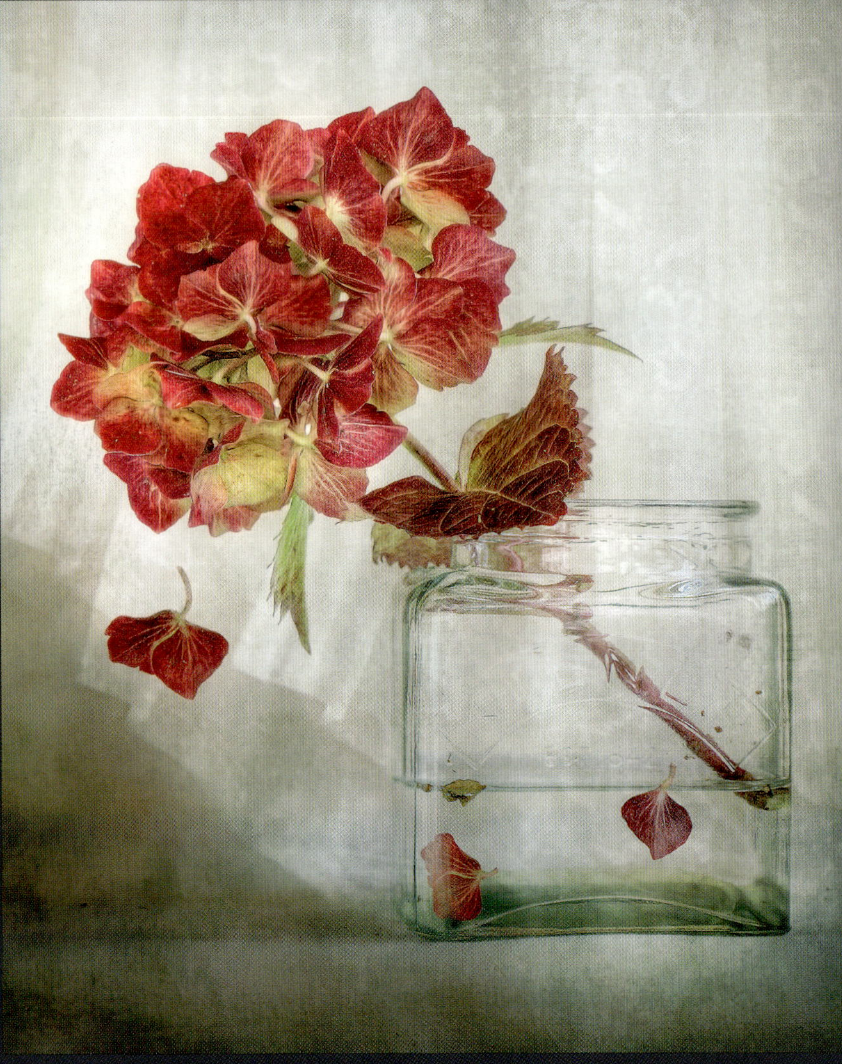

1

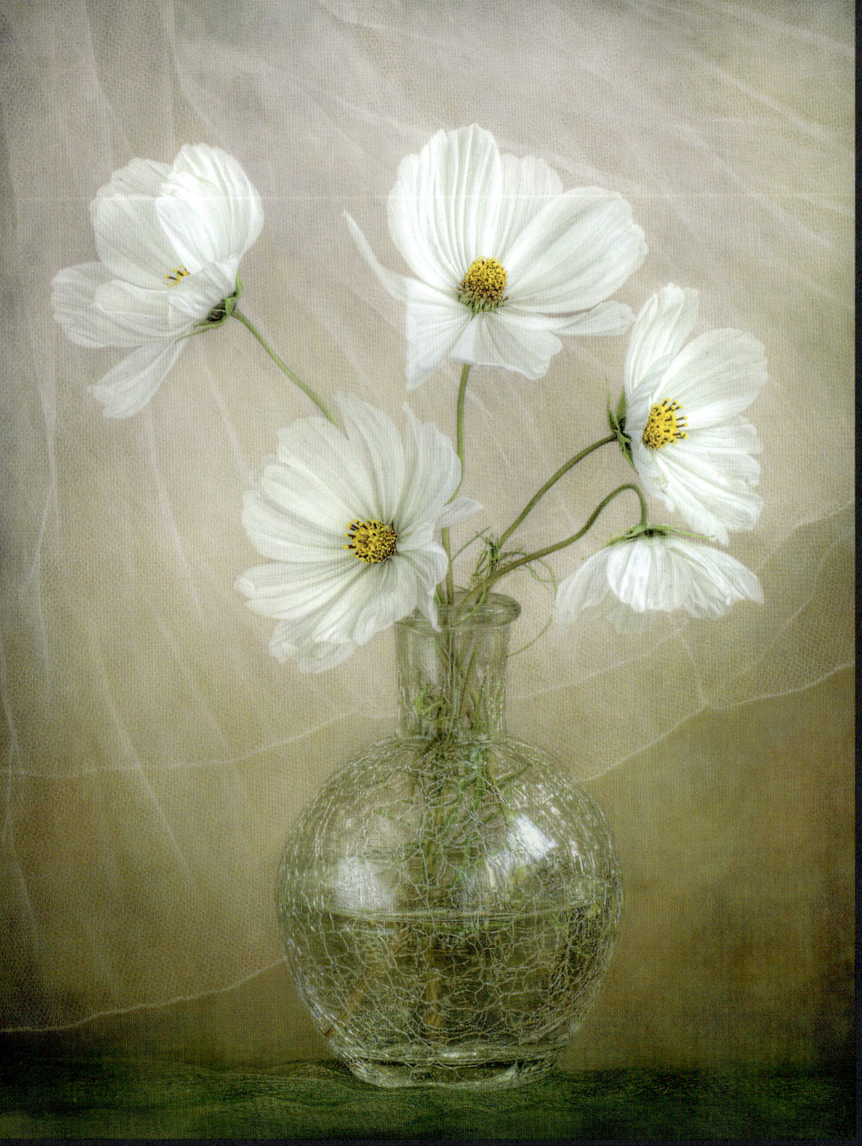

2

My aim was to create a series of floral studies with a warm and nostalgic feel. Fresh-cut flowers taken from the borders of my garden during the summer months are arranged in glass containers ranging from jam jars to fine crystal vases, with the inclusion of a fine net draped behind or over the flowers to create an informal scene. I chose subjects that were different in colour and flower shape but that worked well together. My inspiration is drawn from the beautiful natural colours, textures and diverse forms of flowers that give such wonderful scope for photography. Three bracketed shots were taken for each image to capture a high dynamic range of the tonal values. Using three exposures at a stop apart allowed me to see a greater dynamic range between the lightest and darkest areas than if I had used just a single photograph.

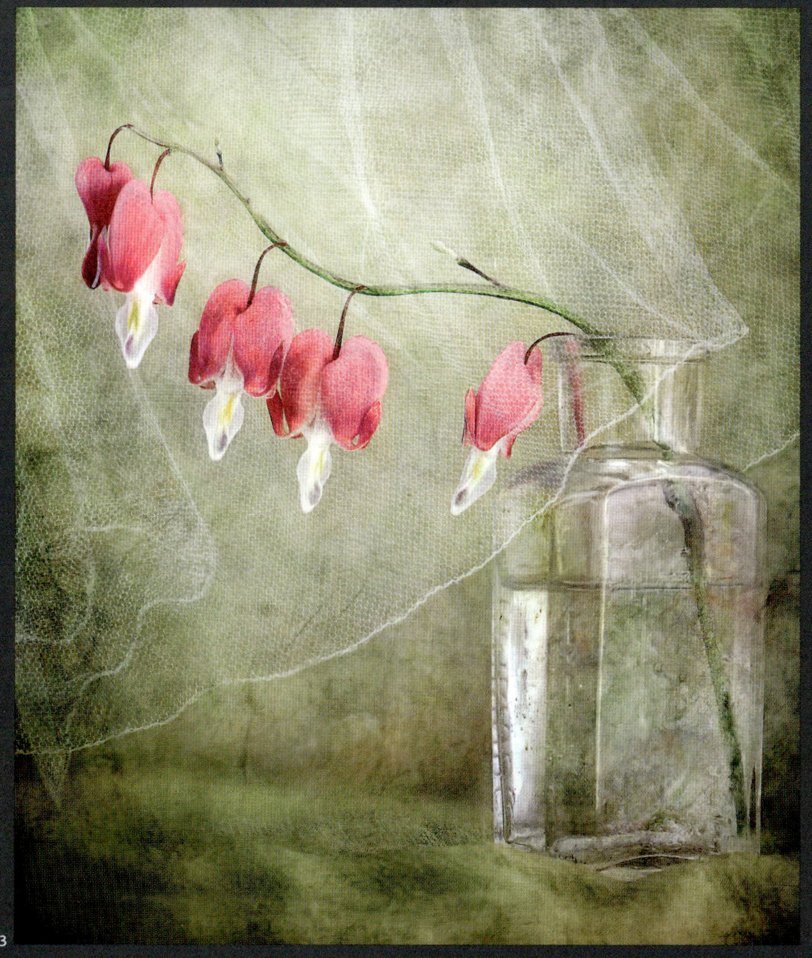
3

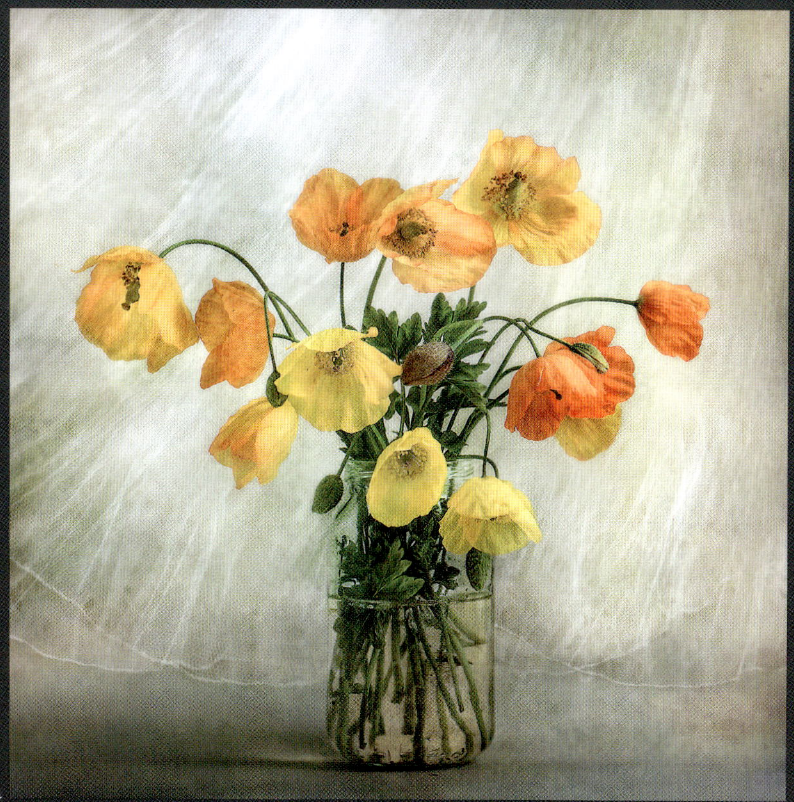
4

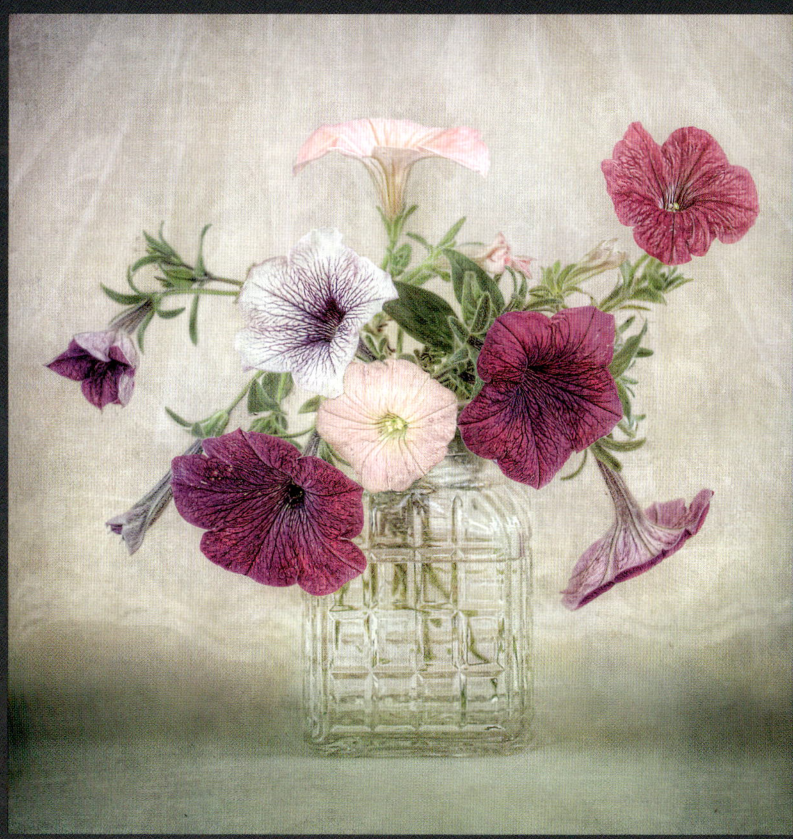
5

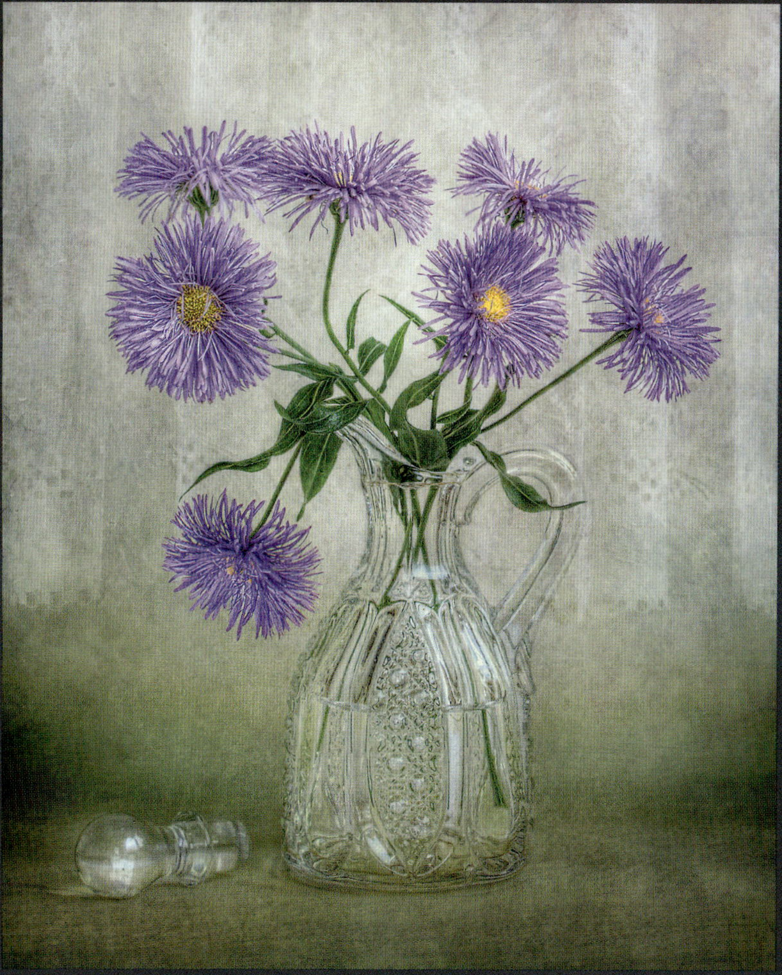
6

LOS ABRIGOS, TENERIFE, CANARY ISLANDS
HEAT

KATHRYN WEST

Canon EOS 450D, Canon EF 18-55mm lens. 1/320sec at f/8. Post-capture: no digital alterations.
HIGHLY COMMENDED, 2012

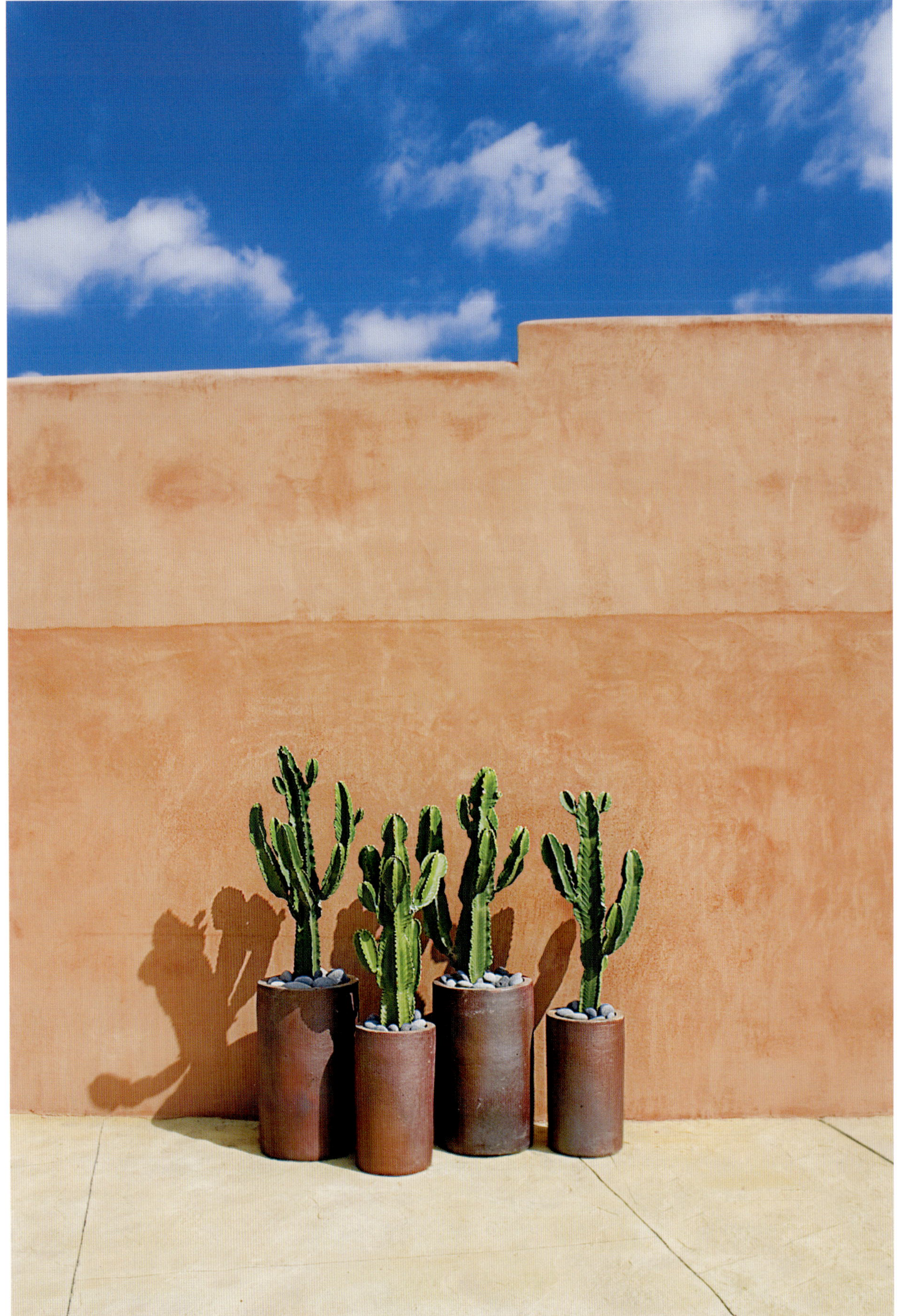

These four potted cacti are typical examples of the cacti and succulents that flourish in Tenerife's sub-tropical climate. I wanted to capture the feeling of heat by showcasing the ornamental beauty potted cacti offer, as opposed to shooting them in their wild environment. I decided to include background details, especially the bright sky, and I lined my subject at a point where I could frame it in a portrait format.

This Japanese hibiscus (*Hibiscus rosa-sinensis*) is called 'Fifth Dimension' – what an apt description. Due to distracting background elements a 180mm macro lens was used to isolate a pleasing composition. The metallic look and colour were what initially attracted me to this flower, and the combination of the inorganic and organic makes this one of the most striking flowers in my opinion.

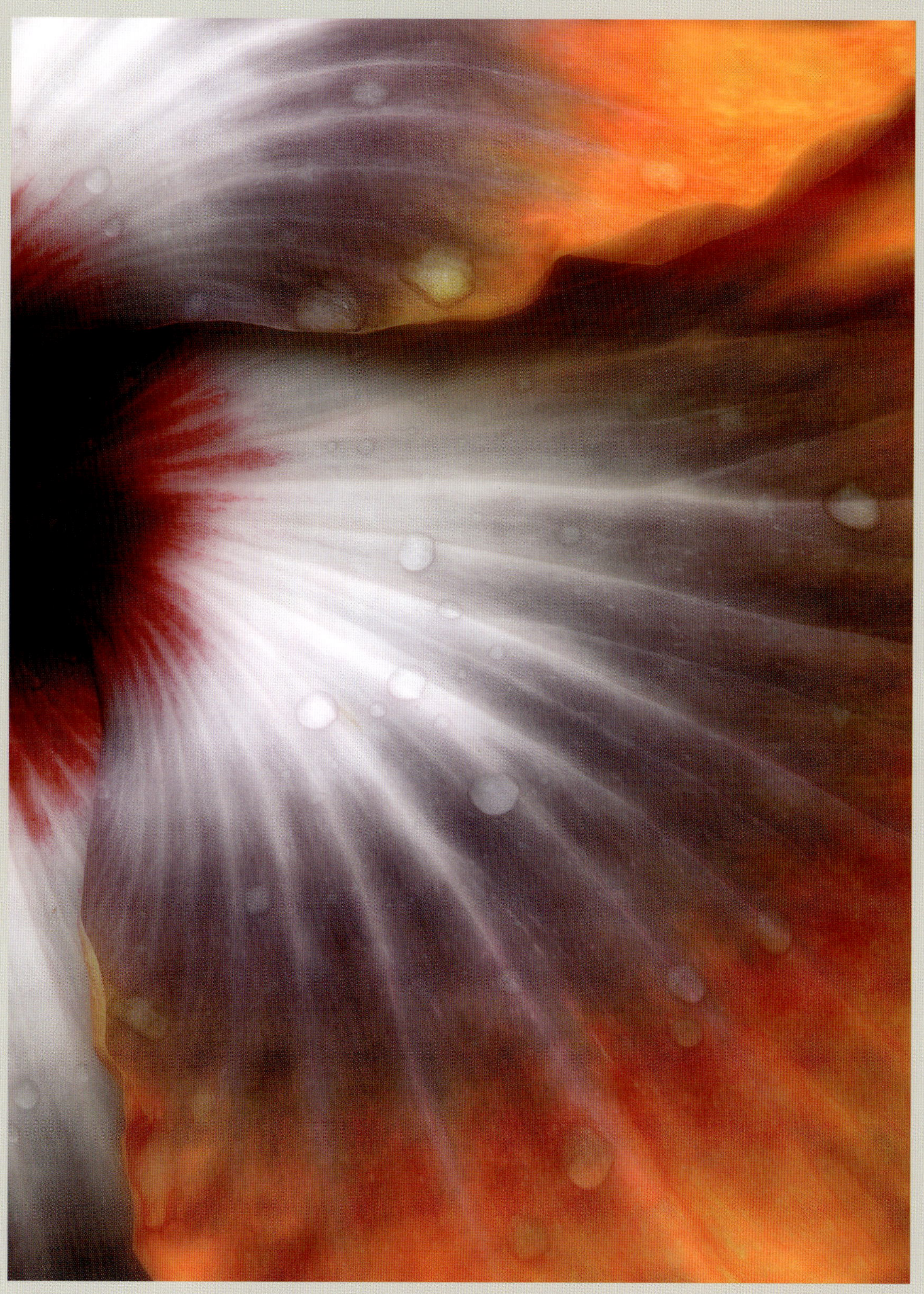

LONGWOOD GARDENS, PENNSYLVANIA
HEAVY METAL HIBISCUS

MICHAEL LOWE

Canon EOS 5D.
FINALIST, 2010

UMBRIA

MAGICAL UMBELLIFER

CAROL SHARP

Nikon 200, Nikkor 70–300, f/5.

FINALIST, 2010

This beautiful wild umbellifer was growing in profusion on a rough bit of land in Italy. I was entranced by the delicate, graceful and demure stance of the plant, beautifully demonstrating the network of tiny umbels.

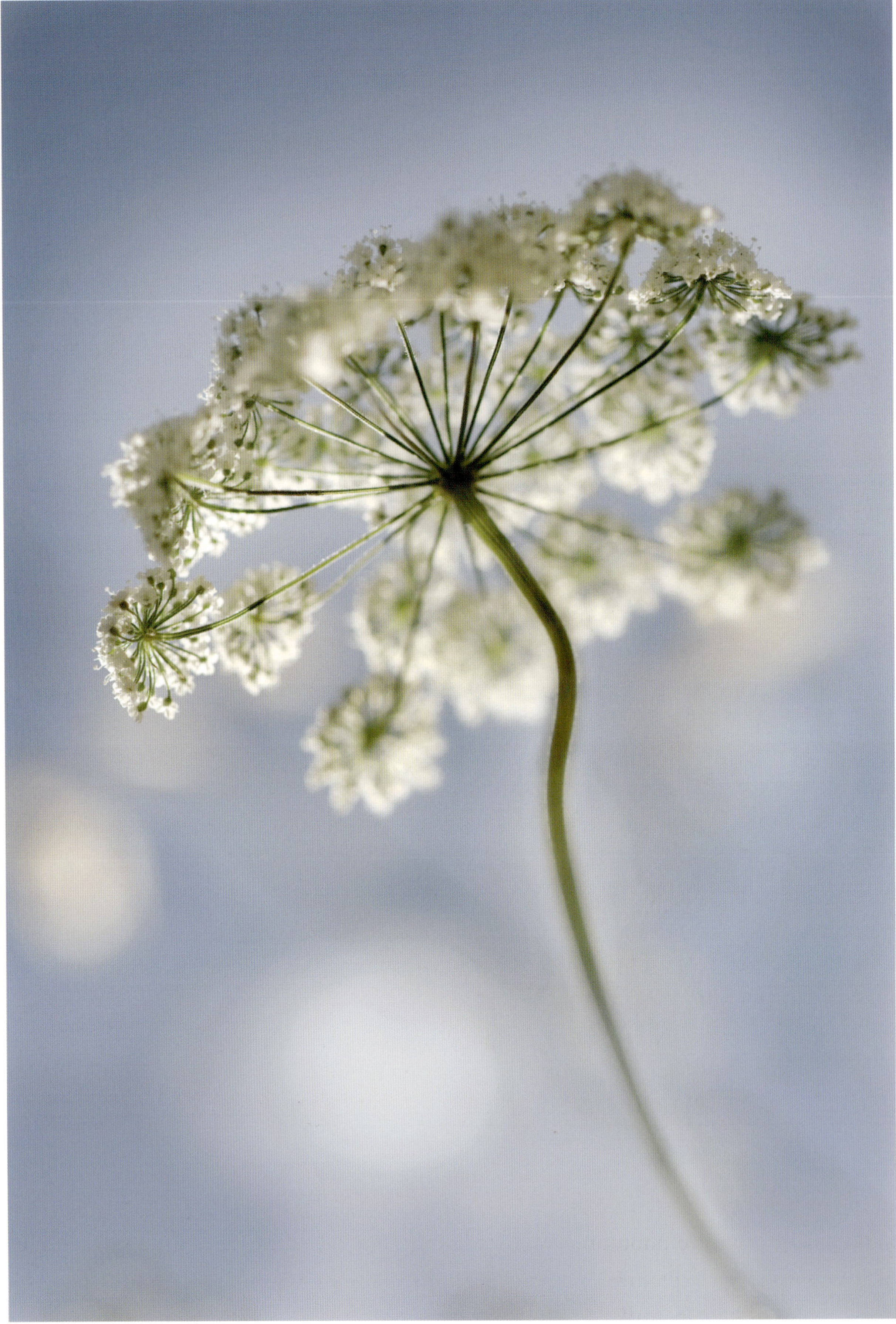

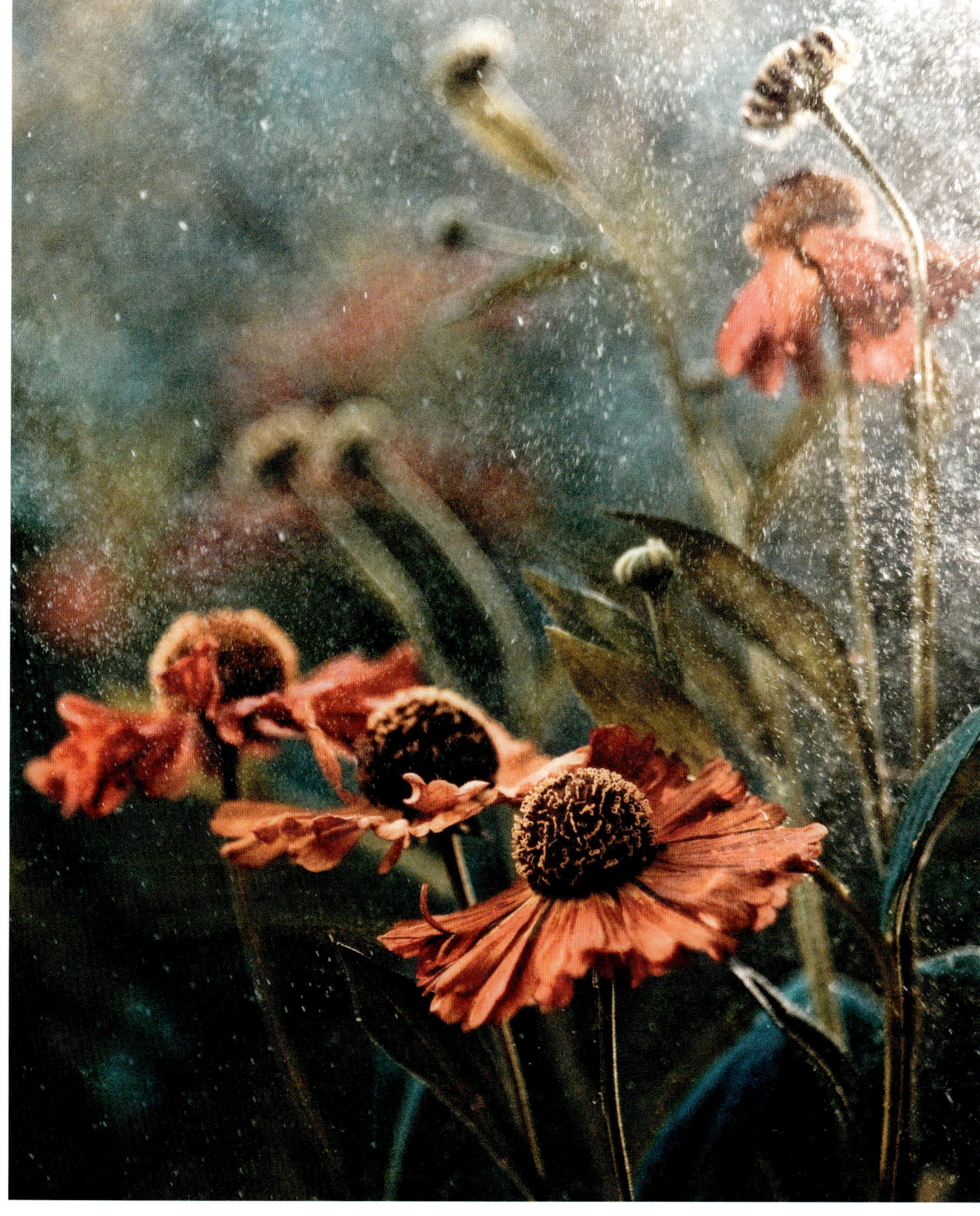

GLICHÓW, MALOPOLSKA REGION
SUMMER IN RAIN

MAGDALENA WASICZEK

Nikon D300, Pentacon 50 manual lens. 1/250sec at f/2. Post-capture: basic contrast and colour management, some desaturation.
FIRST, 2012

Every year we spend part of the holidays in Glichów. Because of the abundance and diversity of fauna and flora, it is a true photographic paradise for me. *Dzielzan* (*Helenium* spp.) is one of my favourite plants of late summer. My pictures are a record of impression, colours and light effects rather than encyclopaedic documentation. I can walk for hours in the garden and observe the change of lights, shadows and colours.

HOME STUDIO, CAMBRIDGESHIRE, ENGLAND

THE BEACON

MANDY DISHER

Canon EOS 450D, Tamron 90mm Di Macro, f/11.

FIRST, 2010

My love of nature, especially flowers, has inspired me to strive to capture and share my view of its beauty. *Cosmos bipinnatus* Sonata Series is such an elegant and beautiful flower, so I wanted to try to capture its wonderful ethereal qualities – its pure white flowing petals reaching up from the slender stem reminded me of a bright light in the dark.

These half-hardy annual plants are very easy to grow from seed. Ideal for the garden border, they can be arranged in groups for height and colour among other tall plants. They are also ideal for cutting, lasting well in water, and are appreciated for their long stems. They are undemanding plants and will flourish in warm sun and poor soils. The 'Sonata Series' produces compact plants with large red, pink and white flowers. The word *Cosmos* is derived from the Greek, meaning 'a balanced universe'.

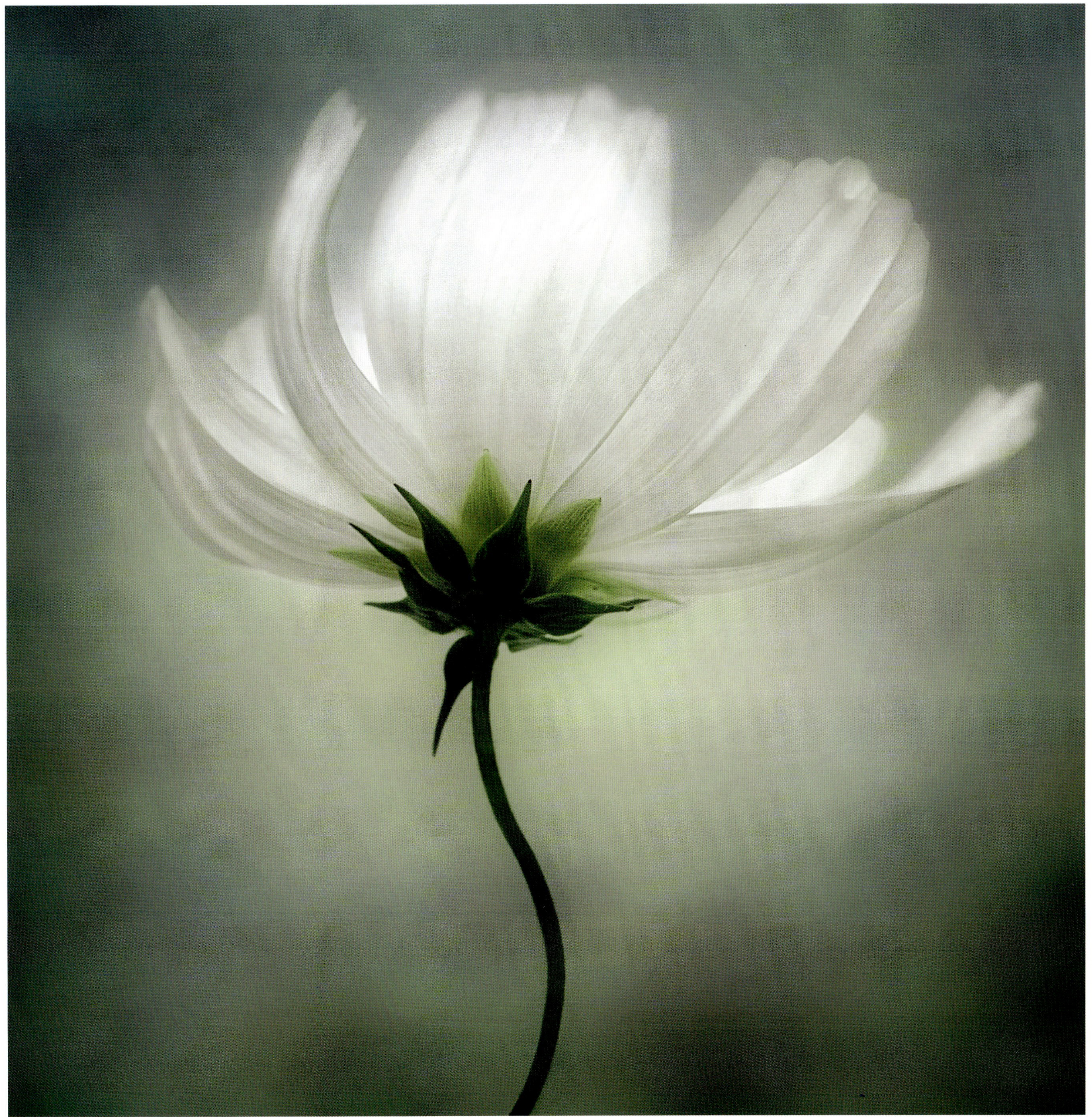

The white bat flower (*Tacca integrifolia*), commonly known as white bat plant, is native to India and Malaysia. The plant is large and the batflower is particularly striking with long 'whiskers' that are actually filiform bracteoles (small leaves) that can grow up to 30cm. This is the most amazing flower I have seen. I was absolutely transfixed. It is perfection. I kept finding new aspects and nuances, and was especially taken by the symmetry and the 'whiskers'. I intended to take many photos in the gardens but I could not leave this flower. My photography is intimate, bold and personal. That is my experience with *Tacca*, and I want you to be surprised, to look more, to explore every detail, look at every aspect, find the secrets.

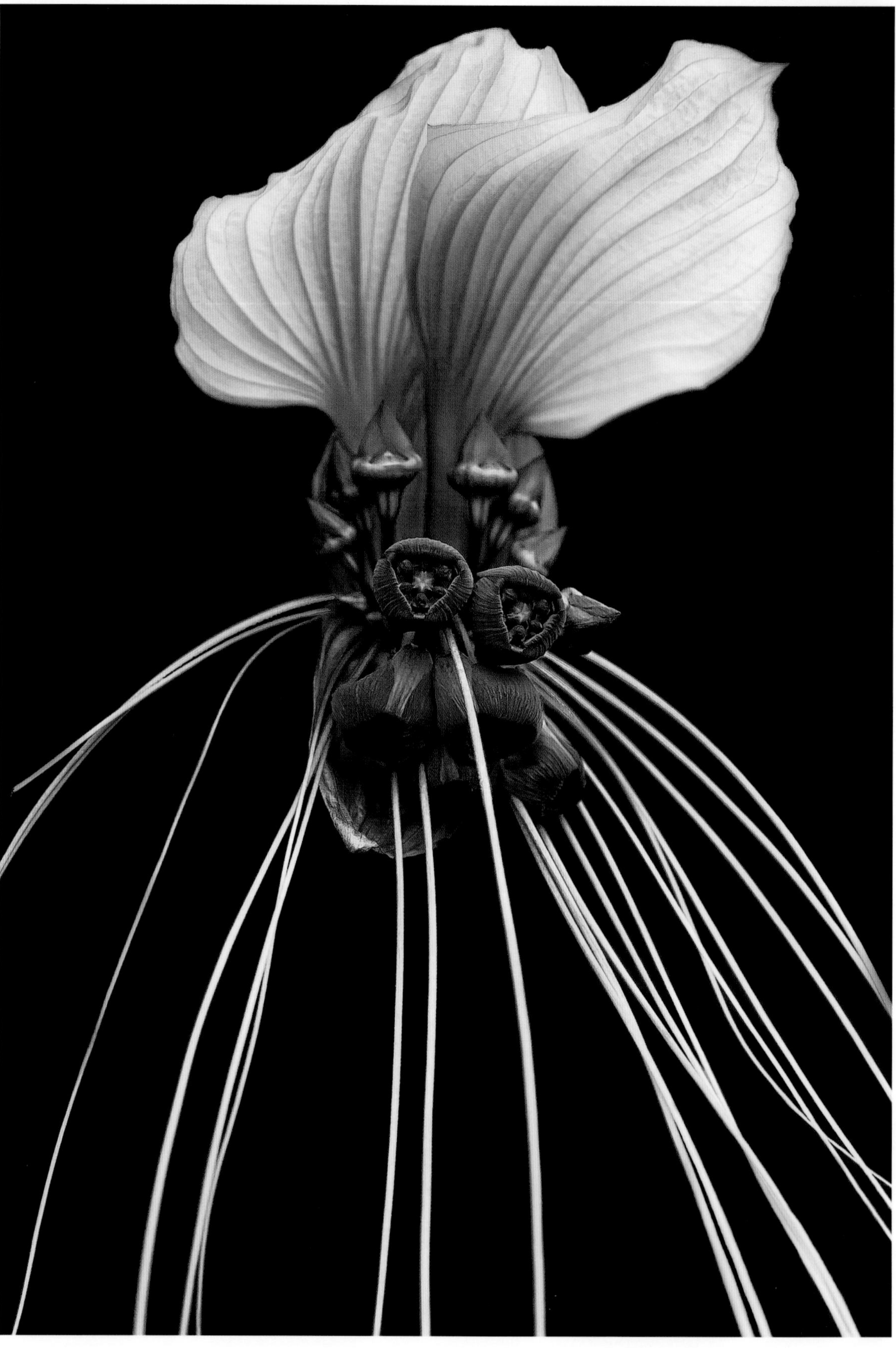

ROYAL BOTANIC GARDENS, MELBOURNE, VICTORIA
BAT PLANT 1

NANCY JOHNSON

Canon EOS 5D Mark II, Canon EF 70-200 lens. 1/160sec at f/2.8 ISO 100. Tripod. Post-capture: original colour image converted to black and white in software. Some foliage removed in software to emphasise the drama of the flower.
FINALIST, 2012

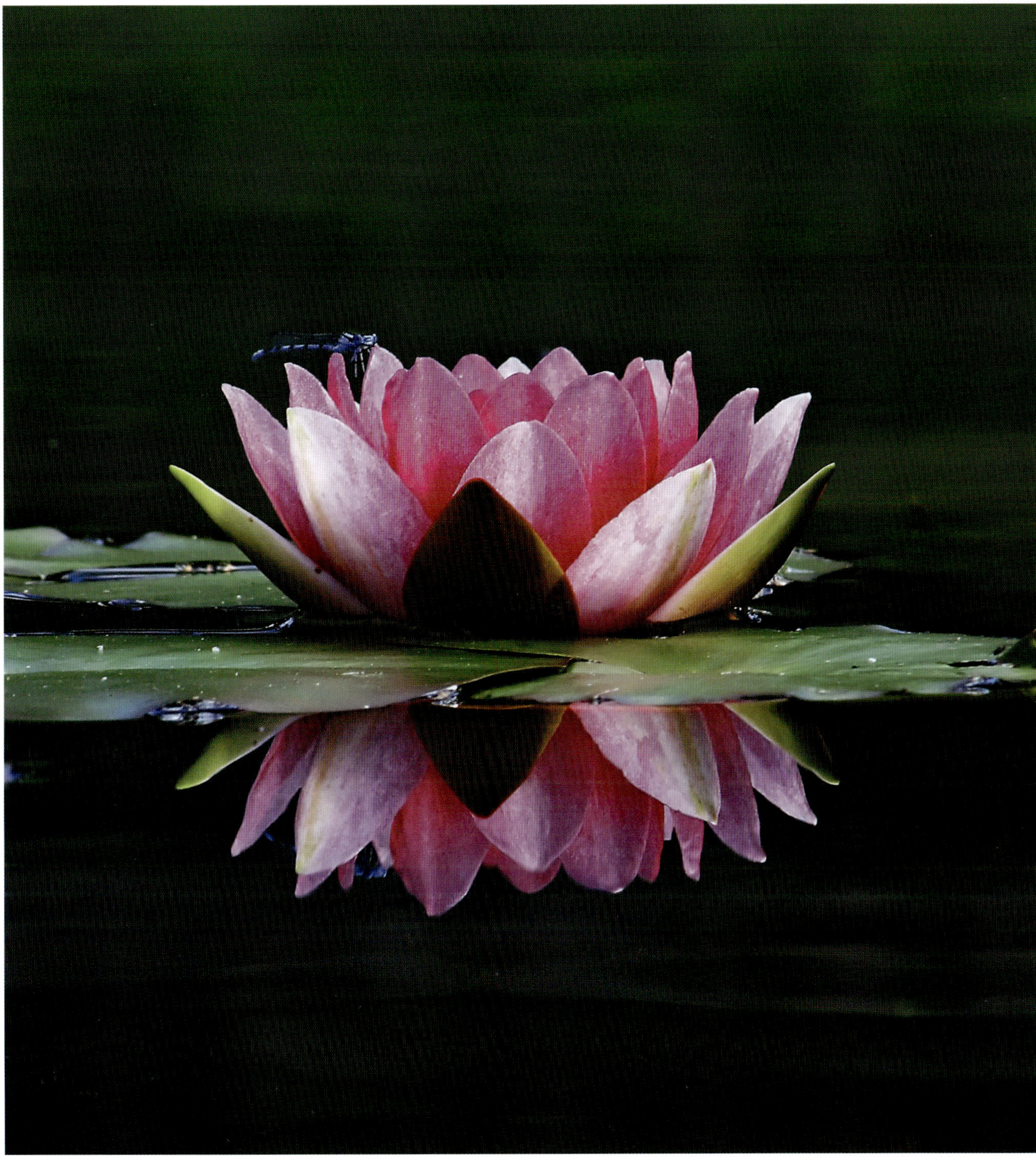

PHOTOGRAPHER'S GARDEN, SOMERSET, ENGLAND
WATER LILY

TONY KEENE

Canon EOS 20D, Sigma 200mm f/2.8 lens, f/8. Inspired by the contrasting colours, I could only get all the reflected information right with the camera just above water level. This meant putting a tripod in the water, shielding the screen and leaning precariously out from the bank.

COMMENDED, 2008

The pink of this first water lily (*Nymphaea* spp.) to appear in our new pond sang out in the soft light against the black of the pond liner and the cool greens of the reflected trees. The sharp blue damselfly was a bonus.

MY KITCHEN TABLE, CANBERRA

FROZEN FLORA

DEBBIE HARTLEY

Canon EOS 7D, 100mm macro lens. Post-capture: basic colour management, cropped to a square frame. I like to keep the images as close to straight from the camera as possible.

FINALIST, 2011

I am constantly looking for new ways to photograph things. One thing I like to do is to freeze the subject and let the ice create a unique and sometimes 'kaleidoscope' effect. Except for the wild rose, all of the subjects are from my backyard. I selected subjects that were colourful and transparent. When frozen, the plant ice blocks were placed on a light box for backlighting to bring out the detail and colour of each subject. I had to work quickly as the heat from the lightbox melted my subjects! I wanted to make a portfolio that was colourful, interesting and different.

The ice adds a new dimension, but does not distract from the beauty of each plant. I think it enhances it.

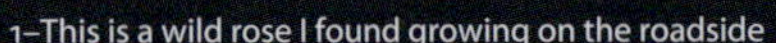

1–This is a wild rose I found growing on the roadside
2–Autumn leaves from my backyard
3–Wallflower (*Erysimum* spp.)
4–Flowers, buds and leaves from begonia (*Begonia* spp.) plants in my backyard
5–These callistemon (*Callistemon* spp.) flowers are from my backyard
6–Geranium (*Geranium* spp.) flowers from my backyard

1

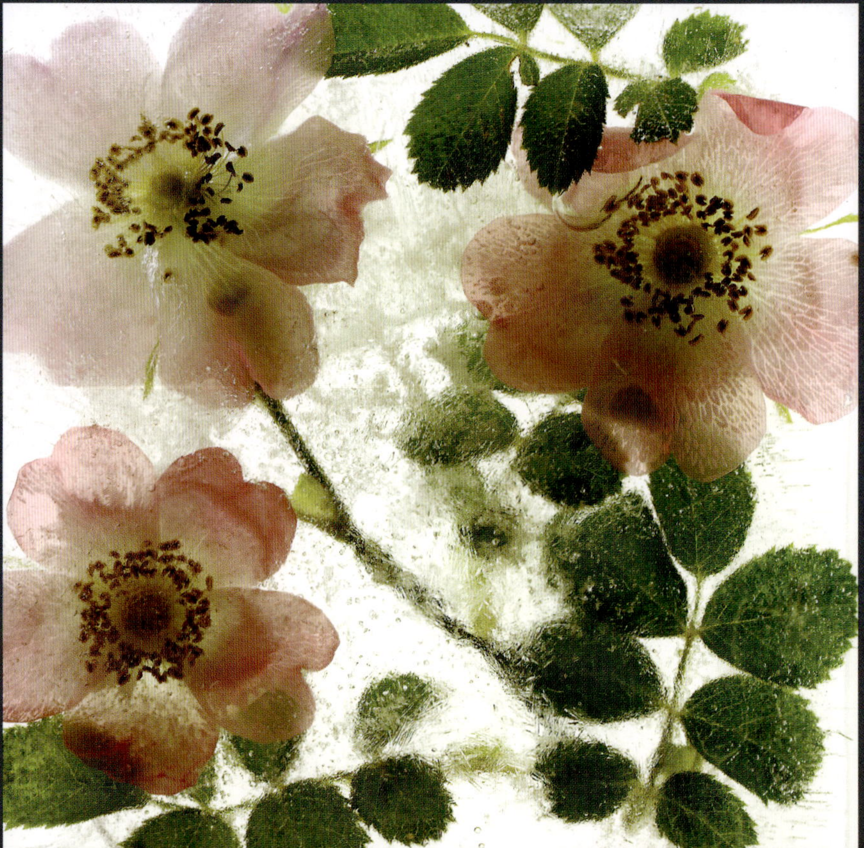

2

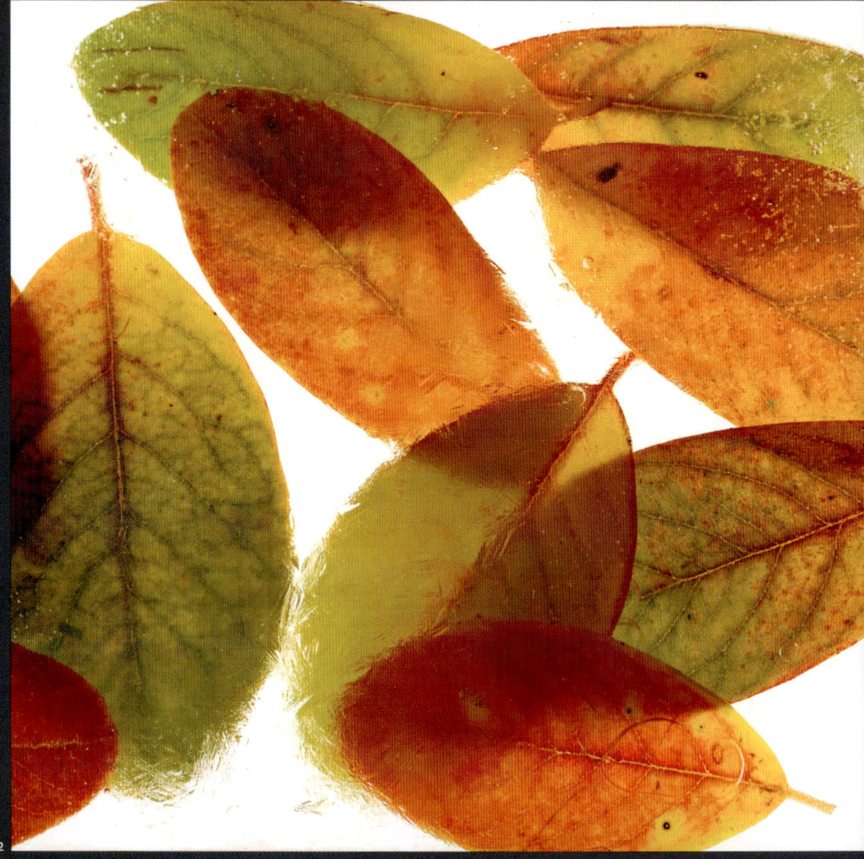

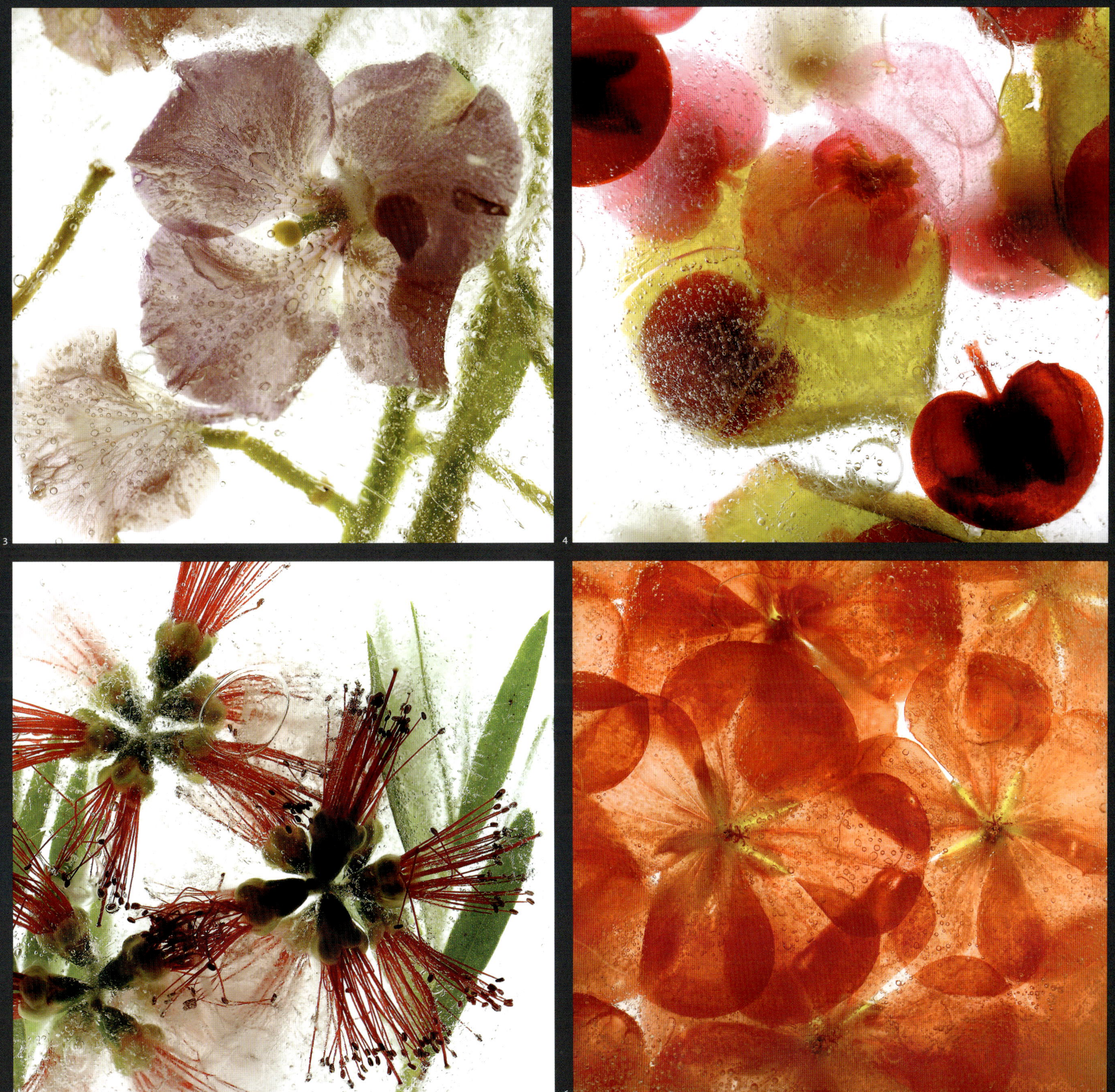

3 4 5 6

The flower stem of the cyclamen (*Cyclamen* spp.) coils up when the fruit begins to form. The fruit is a pod that contains the seeds. When it is mature, the flaps of the pod open to release the seeds. As usual, I was patrolling the garden, looking for interesting things that might be happening. I saw all the coiled stems of the cyclamen looking like little springs and was fascinated. I wanted to show the coils and needed to be on a level with the subject. It made me think of a snake that was ready to attack and I wanted to convey this poised energy. I cut the stem and took the cyclamen inside to photograph as the plant is so low on the ground it would have been impossible to shoot in situ. I put it against a previously printed, out-of-focus picture of foliage to take the picture.

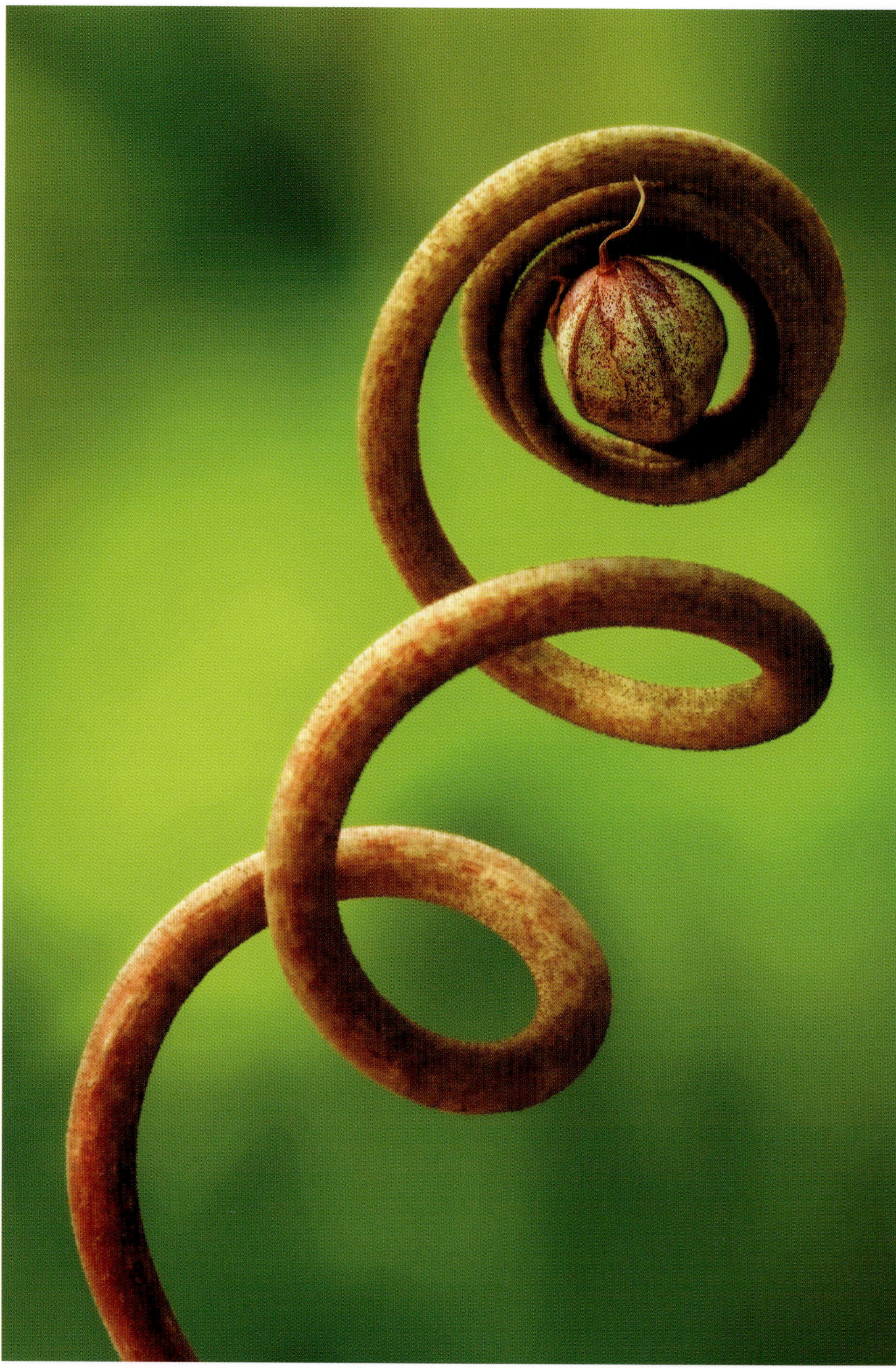

MY GARDEN, CHESHIRE, ENGLAND
CYCLAMEN

LIZ EVERY

Canon EOS 40D, 60mm macro lens, 1/8sec at f/32. Post-capture: no digital alterations.
HIGHLY COMMENDED, 2012

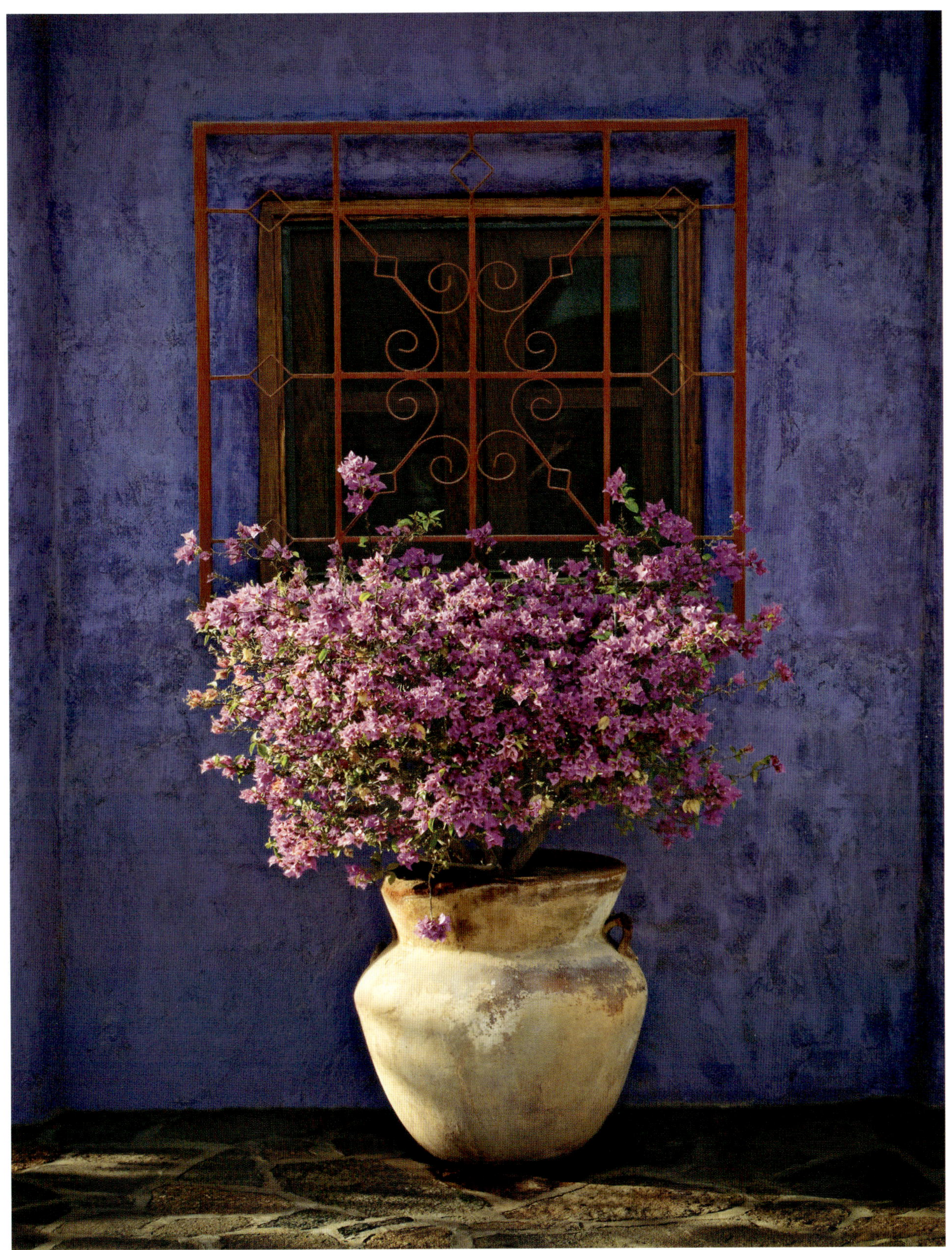

TODOS SANTOS, BAJA SUR
BOUGAINVILLEA WITH BLUE WALL

WILLIAM PIERSON

Canon G10. Once I saw the image, I moved quickly so as not to lose the light. Once on the scene, I went down on one knee to frame the bougainvillea in the window with the metal framework, to complete the composition.
COMMENDED, 2009

This photograph is about the magic of the relationship between colours. I first saw the image from a distance, looking down a dusty Mexican street. The deep pink bougainvillea (*Bougainvillea* spp.), illuminated from the side by the intense Mexican light, with the background of blue stucco, was stunning. This flowering shrub, highlighted by the metal-framed window, completed a beautiful composition in colour and form.

MY STUDIO, VIRGINIA
DANCE

JOHN GRANT

Canon EOS 5D Mark II, 100mm lens. 1/60sec at f/8. Post-capture: no digital alterations.
SECOND, 2012

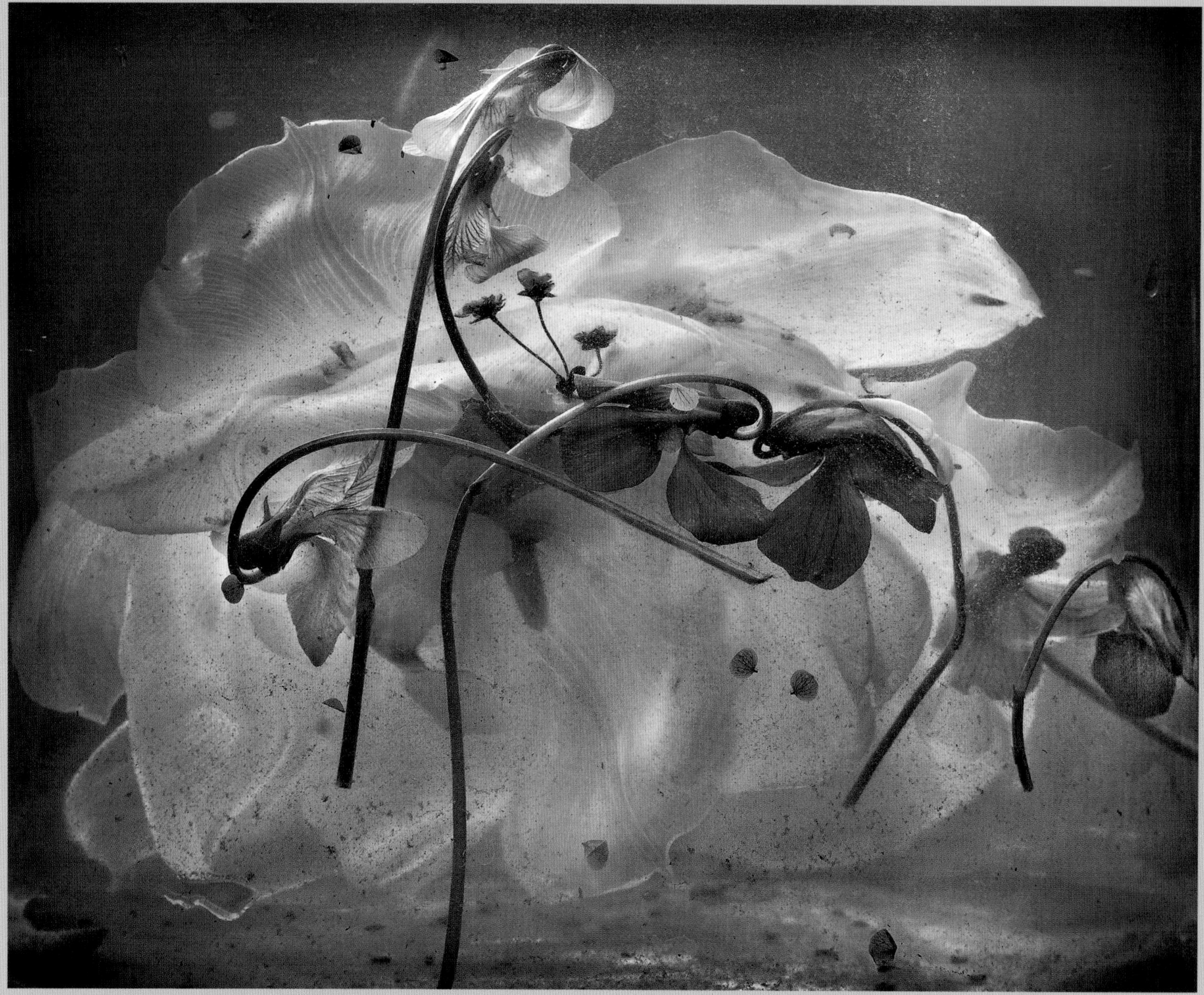

This is an image of decayed white tulips (*Tulipa* spp.) along with fresh violets (*Viola* spp.) under water. The flowers were allowed to float in the water for several weeks, making them very delicate. The results of the work can never be predicted; it requires patience and steady observation, along with just the right natural light. All the specimens were grown in my own garden.

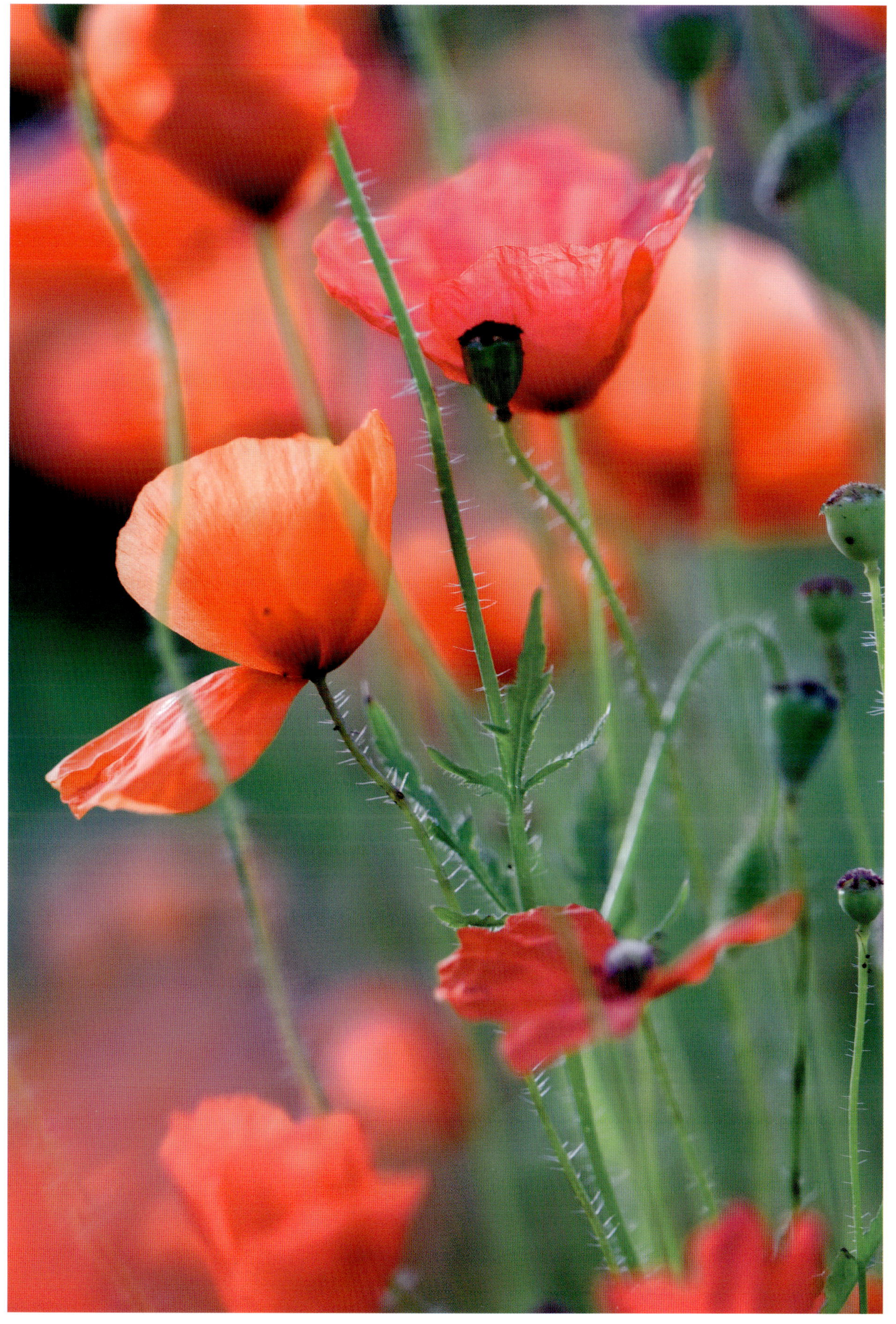

This picture was taken in a botanical garden in southern Sweden, and I just love these colourful flowers. The more colours in a flower, the more I love them. Bees also adore the poppy (*Papaver* spp.) and use them as an excellent pollen source. I wanted to capture the last, late summer colours and I found these poppies dancing in the wind – as if they were waving goodbye to the summer.

UPPSALA
COLOURFUL

LENA PESULA

Canon EOS 30D, Canon 100mm macro.
HIGHLY COMMENDED, 2010

ROYAL BOTANIC GARDENS,
KEW, SURREY, ENGLAND
BERBERIS ANTONIANA

JOHN BARBER

Canon EOS-1D Mark III, Prinzflex wide angle manual lens with extra element attached, 1/400sec at f/2.8. Post-capture: no digital alterations.
FINALIST, 2010

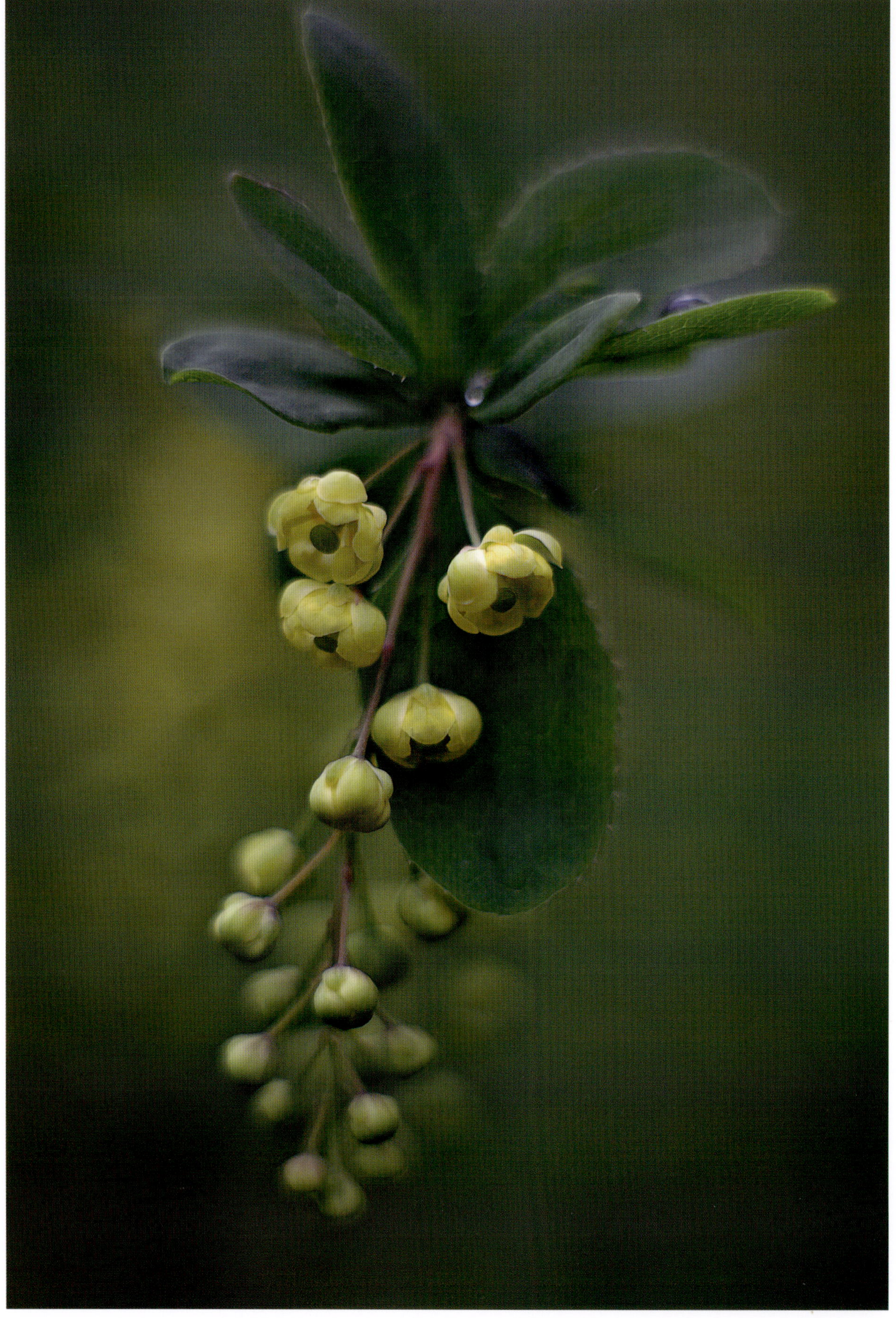

In my flower portraits, the background is as important as the main subject. In this picture, green and yellow colours blend while the small barberry (*Berberis* spp.) flowers unobtrusively come to the front of the image. I prefer to get as close as possible to the plants for these portraits.

The shape and translucency of these beautiful seeds evoke the energy of life, while the larger seed's wing protects the smaller ones. Using a combination of shadow and light, I wanted to create the illusion that the light was coming from the heart of the seed.

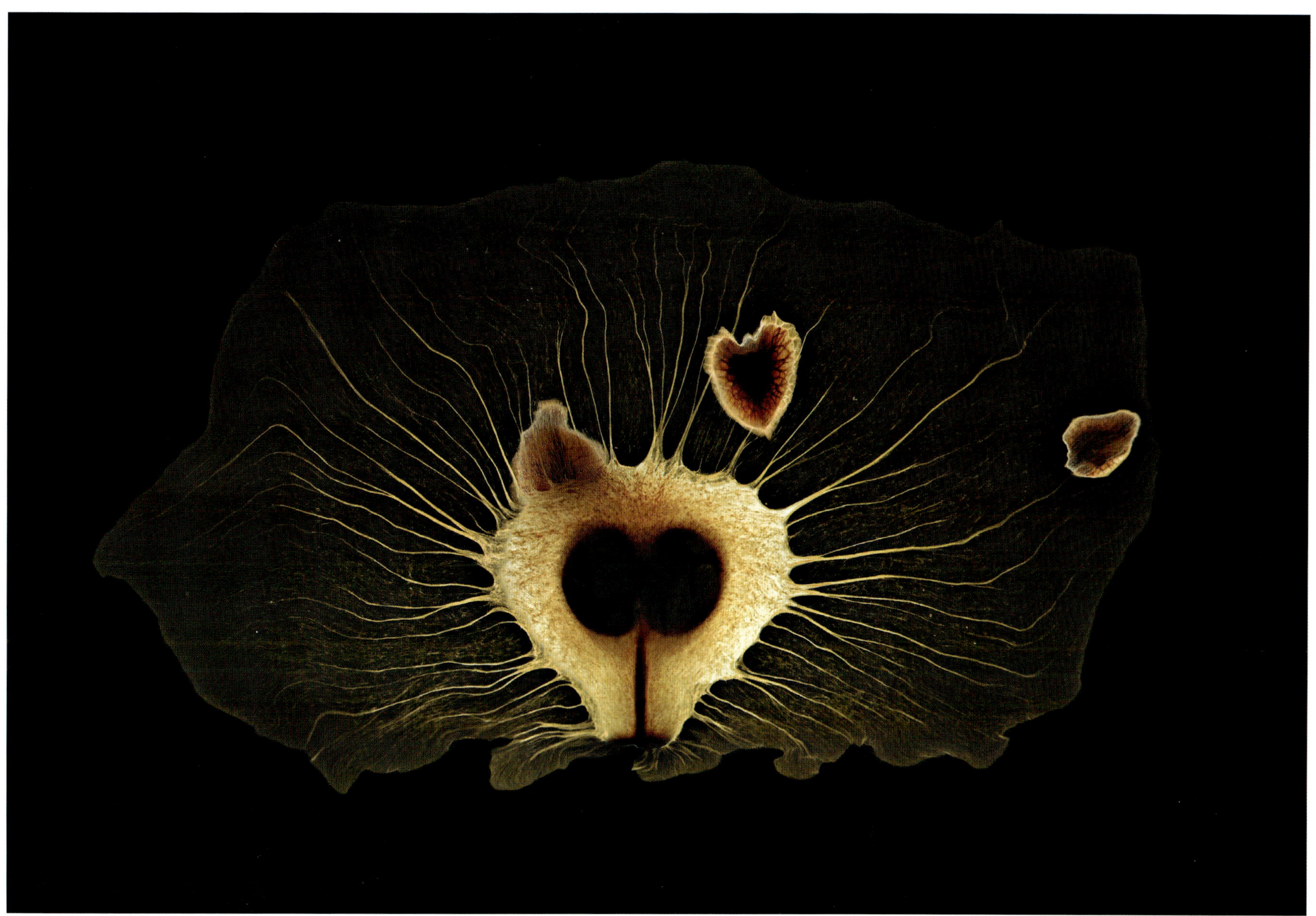

GENEVA BOTANICAL GARDENS
SORREL AND MONKEY'S-COMB SEEDS

CEDRIC BREGNARD

Phase One P45+, Mamiya 80mm lens, f/22. I created a combination of positive and negative images of the seed in order to give the illusion of light passing through the grain of the wing.
THIRD, 2009

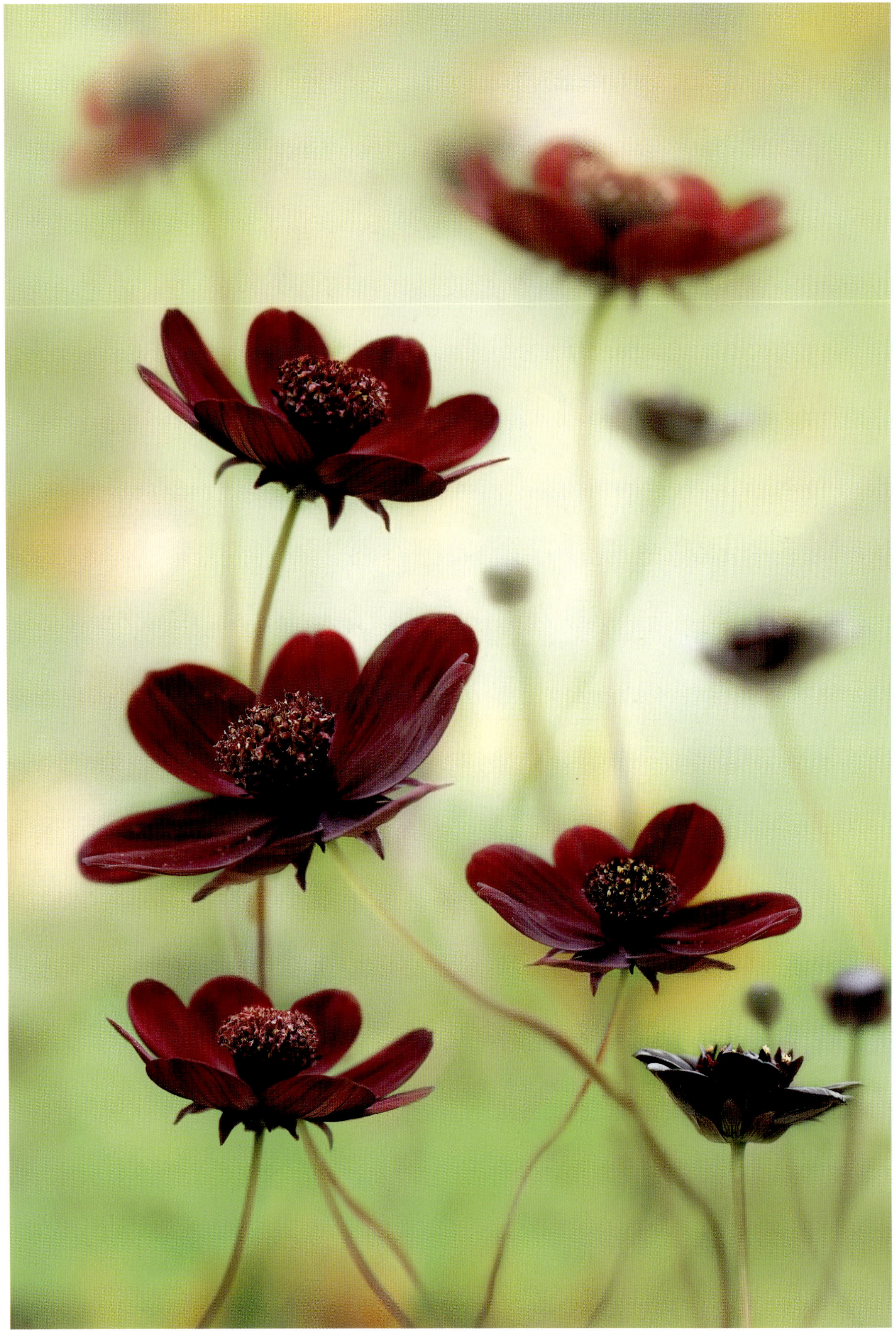

A SUNNY SPOT IN MY GARDEN IN SOUTHEAST ENGLAND
COSMOS ATROSANGUINEUS 'CHOCA MOCHA'

MANDY DISHER

Canon EOS 450D, Tamron 60mm macro lens, 1/125sec at f/3.2.
Post-capture: basic colour and contrast adjustments and lightened areas of the background to give emphasis to the flowers.
FIRST, 2011

Chocolate Cosmos (*Cosmos atrosanguineus* 'Choca mocha') flowers fill the late afternoon air with a delicious vanilla chocolaty scent, attracting pollinators such as butterflies and bees. It's an easy-to-grow, half-hardy tuberous rooted perennial, native to Mexico. The cosmos obtained its name from the Greek 'ordered universe' because of the symmetrical petals of the flower. I was inspired to capture the cosmos because of its beautiful rich burgundy tones and its velvety textured petals. I also liked the lyrical flow of the flowers and the way the thin stems twisted and turned. I waited for a calm and bright day and arranged the flowers into an attractive composition, removing stray leaves, small debris and imperfect flowers to create flowing lines and gentle curves. I found the cosmos quite a challenge to photograph because of its very dark colour; getting the exposure correct to reveal the detail in the dark tones proved quite difficult. I experimented with different settings and found that over-exposing the shot gave me the best result. I used a large aperture of f/3.2 to give a shallow depth of field. The flowers were shot against a light, sunny garden backdrop which made a good contrasting colour for the dark flowers.

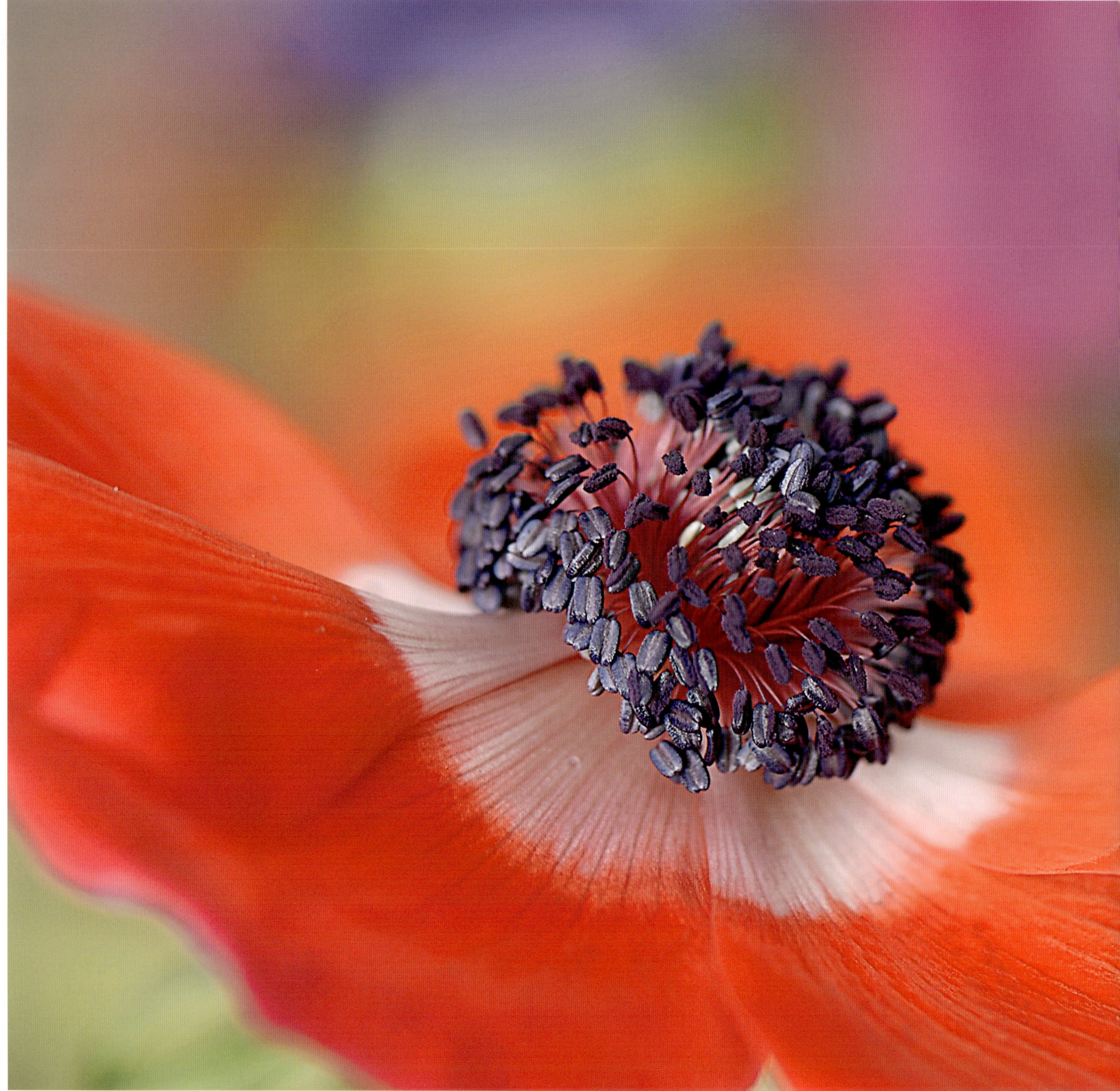

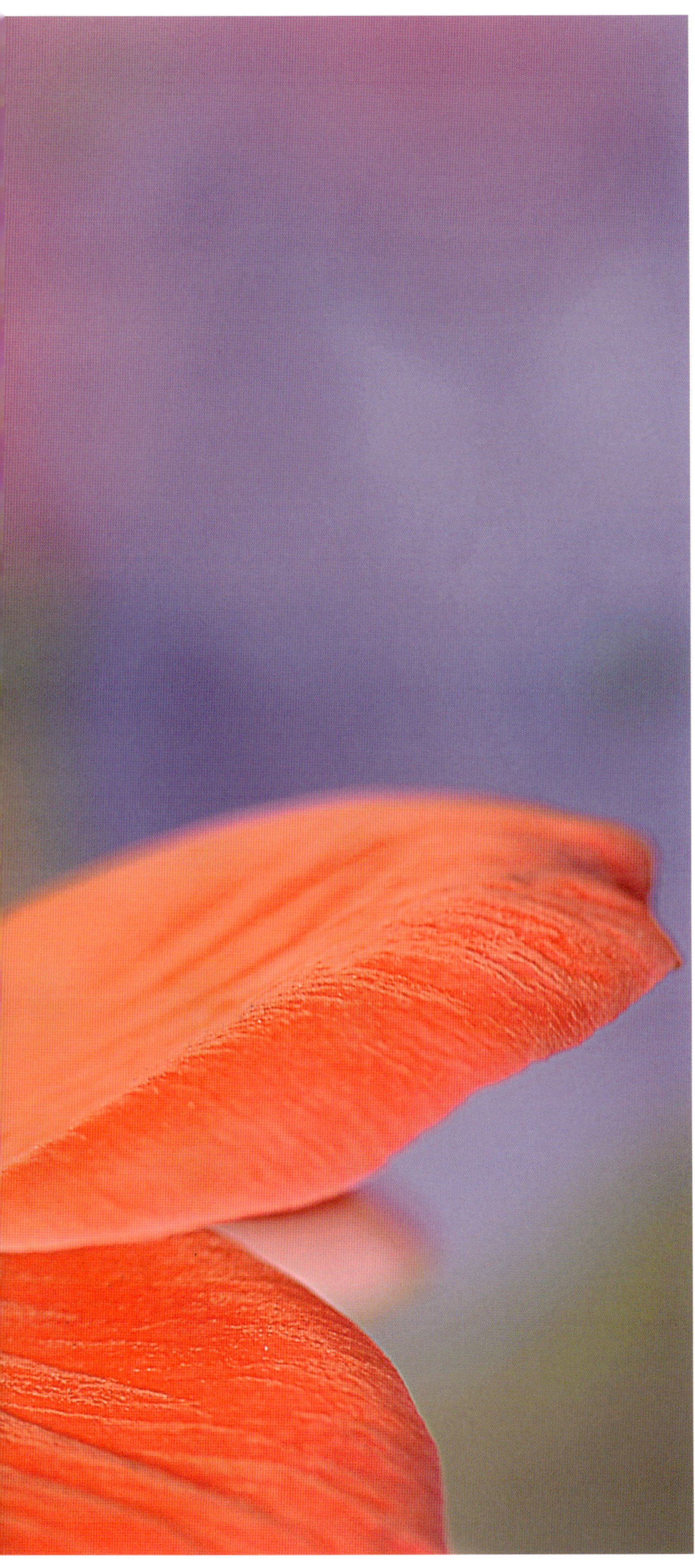

A single red anemone flower of the De Caen strain (*Anemone coronaria*). This group is a collective name for a race of single-flowered cultivars with five to eight petals in red, blue or white, which flower in spring. I loved the bright and vibrant colours of these little poppy-like flowers, which, after the long winter months, seemed so welcome in the spring. As a result, I aimed to capture the vibrant colour of this little red flower while using the other coloured anemones as a background.

IVER, BUCKINGHAMSHIRE, ENGLAND

A SPLASH OF SPRING COLOUR

JACKY PARKER

Nikon D200, Nikkor 105mm micro VR lens, f/4. I wanted to focus on the delicate little stamens of this flower while blurring the colourful background. I set the camera to Aperture Priority and used natural light.
FINALIST, 2009

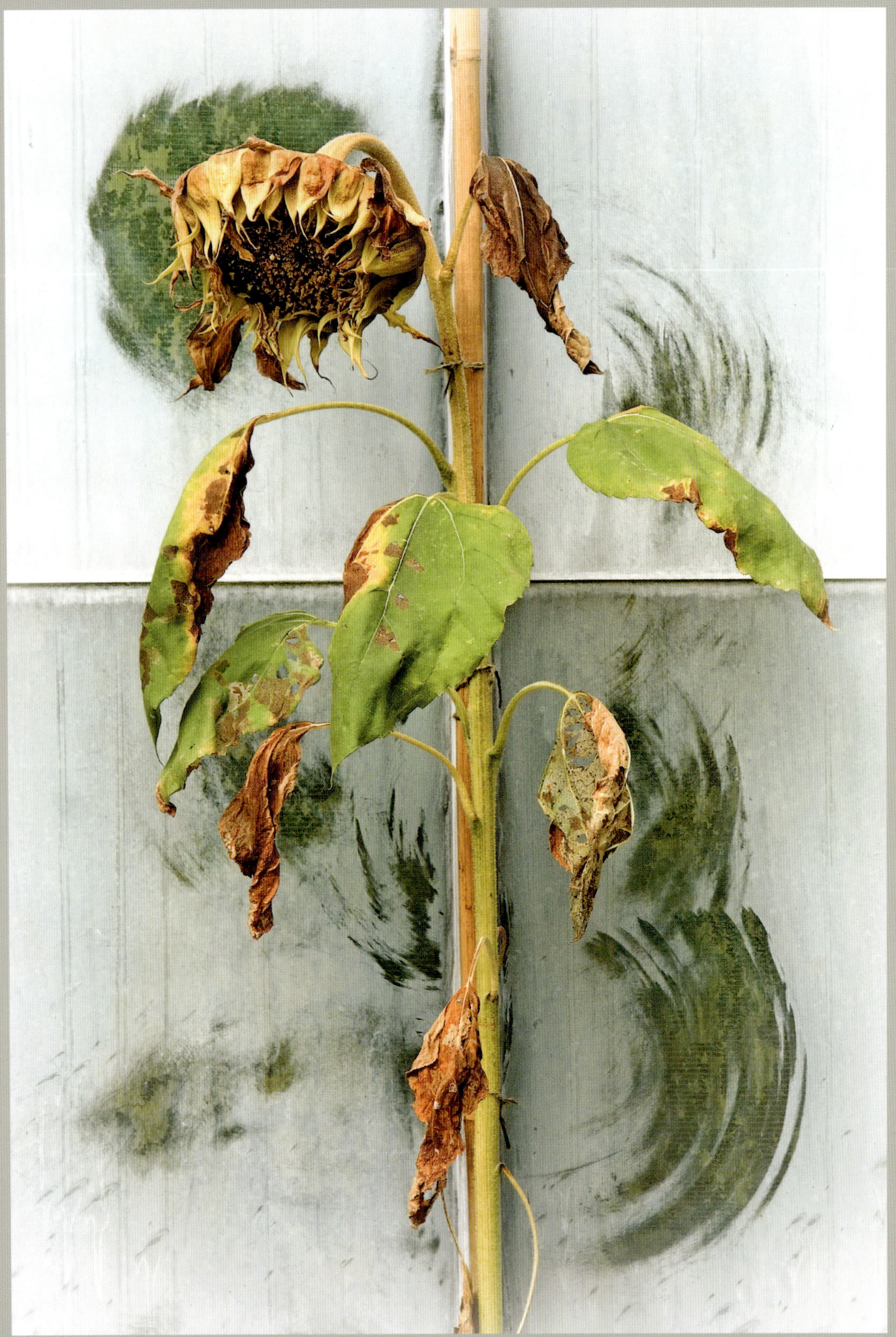

CHATSWORTH HOUSE, DERBYSHIRE, ENGLAND

SUMMER'S END

REBECCA NEX

Canon EOS 30D, Canon 17-85mm lens, 1/100sec at f/8, ISO 200. This picture was mainly created in-camera, with little digital enhancement required afterwards. I slightly cropped the image and increased the contrast as well as slightly sharpening the sunflower and lightening the glass. I also added a subtle vignette to further fade the edges.

FINALIST, 2011

I was drawn by the elegance of this sunflower (*Helianthus* spp), even in its decayed state. There was enough colour and height in it to convey its original grandeur, especially against the simplicity of the white-washed background. To me, it perfectly conveyed the end of summer and the transition into autumn. My main approach to making this picture was to ensure that I had isolated the sunflower from any other distractions, in order to focus all the attention on its faded beauty. I included enough of the flower to convey its height but made sure that nothing else was in the frame. My main aim was to create a simple portrait of the sunflower. The plain, pastel background provided by the white-washed glass helped me to achieve this without the need to significantly simplify the picture in post-production software.

Giant water lily (*Victoria amazonica*) is native to the Amazon River, and is the largest of the Nymphaeaceae family. The giant pads can reach diameters of three metres and can support the weight of small mammals. The huge flowers start life almost white, before maturing into a delicate pink. I have always been fascinated by giant water lilies, their relationship to each other and to the surface tension of the water which supports their great weight. With this shot I wanted to explore the wonderful symmetries and slightly abstract nature of the capillaries as the sun filtered through them.

TROPICAL GLASSHOUSE, ROYAL BOTANIC GARDEN EDINBURGH, SCOTLAND
VICTORIA AMAZONICA

ANDY PHILLIPSON

Canon EOS 5D, Canon 180mm Macro f/3.5 lens, ISO 200, 1/50sec at f/9. The constraints of the water's edge and the low position of the pad meant that the photograph had to be taken handheld while I leant out over the water partly unsupported.

COMMENDED, 2009

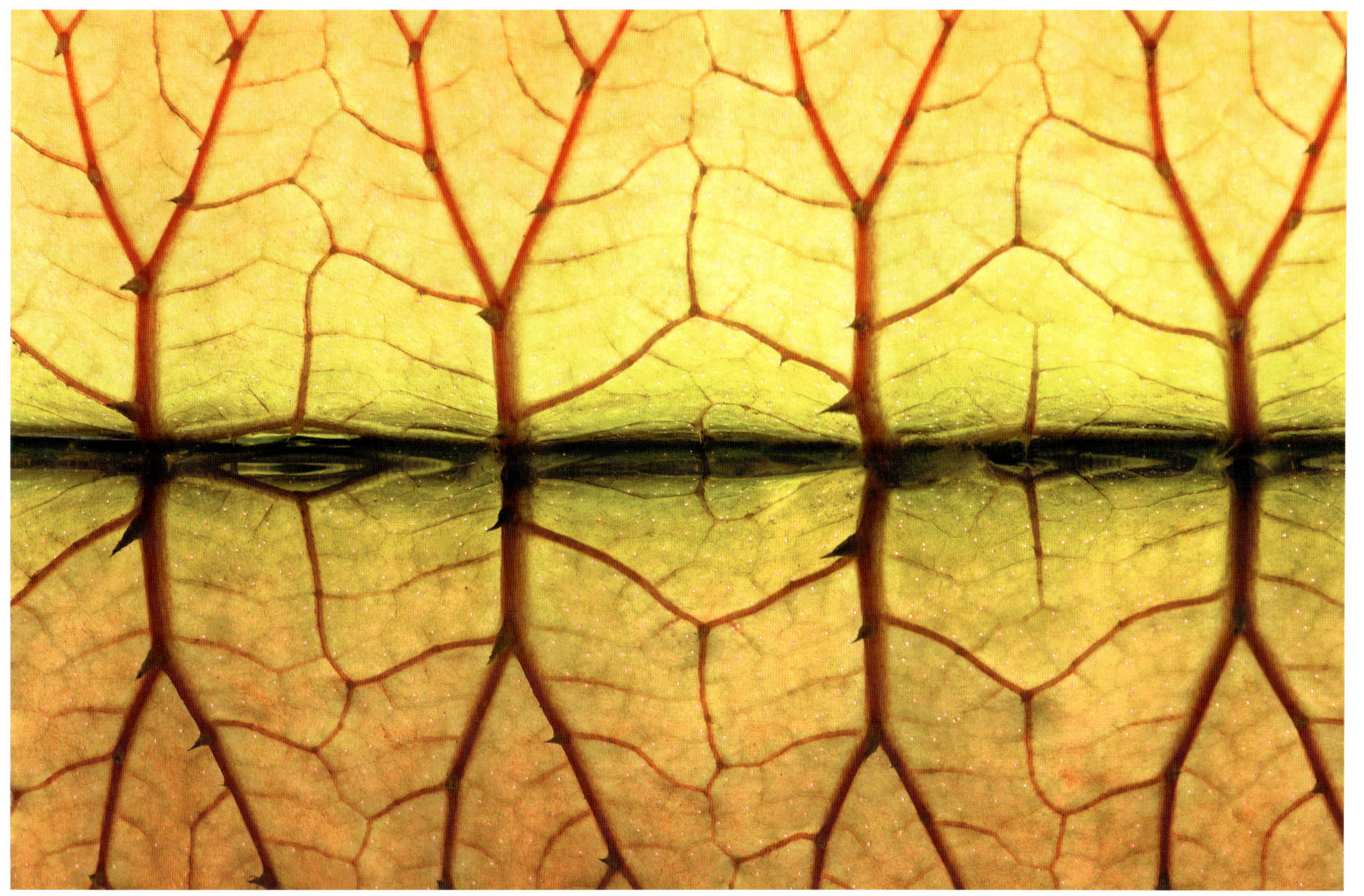

AMBALAPUZHA, KERALA
WATER LILIES

NIGEL SYMINGTON

Nikon D700, Nikkor AF-S VR 70–200mm f/2.8G at 200mm, f/11.
HIGHLY COMMENDED, 2010

As the sun comes up a single water lily (*Nymphaea* spp.) reaches above the surface of a mirror-smooth pond. Its leaves form flat plates on the surface of the water. A large drop of dew has gathered in the centre of one leaf, giving an impression of coolness before the heat of the day builds up. A solitary green blade of grass provides a splash of contrast in an otherwise largely two-tone image. I used a low camera angle to capitalise on the low rays of the rising sun. I explored the best camera position to give a pleasing composition to the leaves, and bracketed the exposure to achieve an optimum balance between the leaves, the water surface and the bloom.

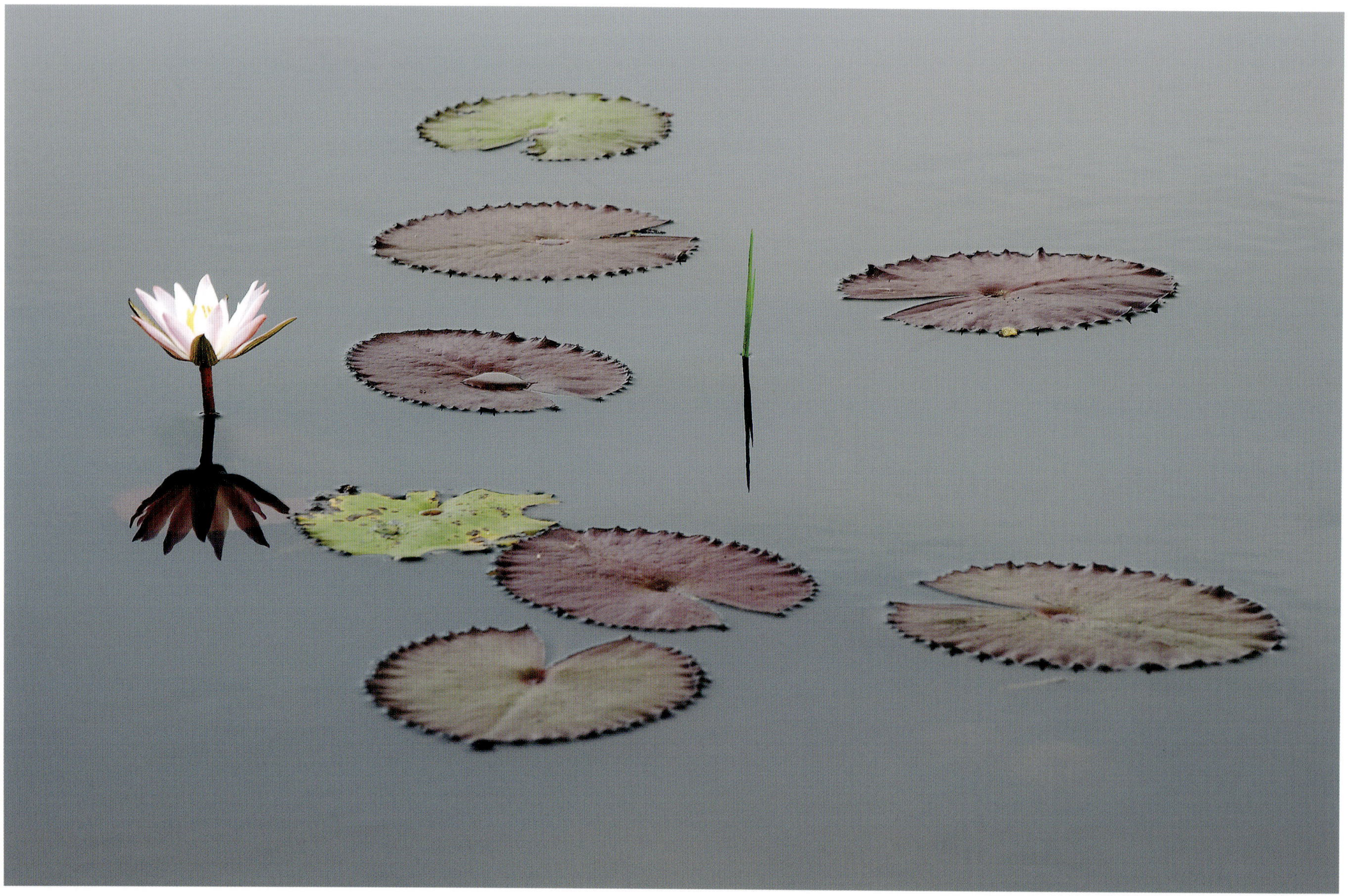

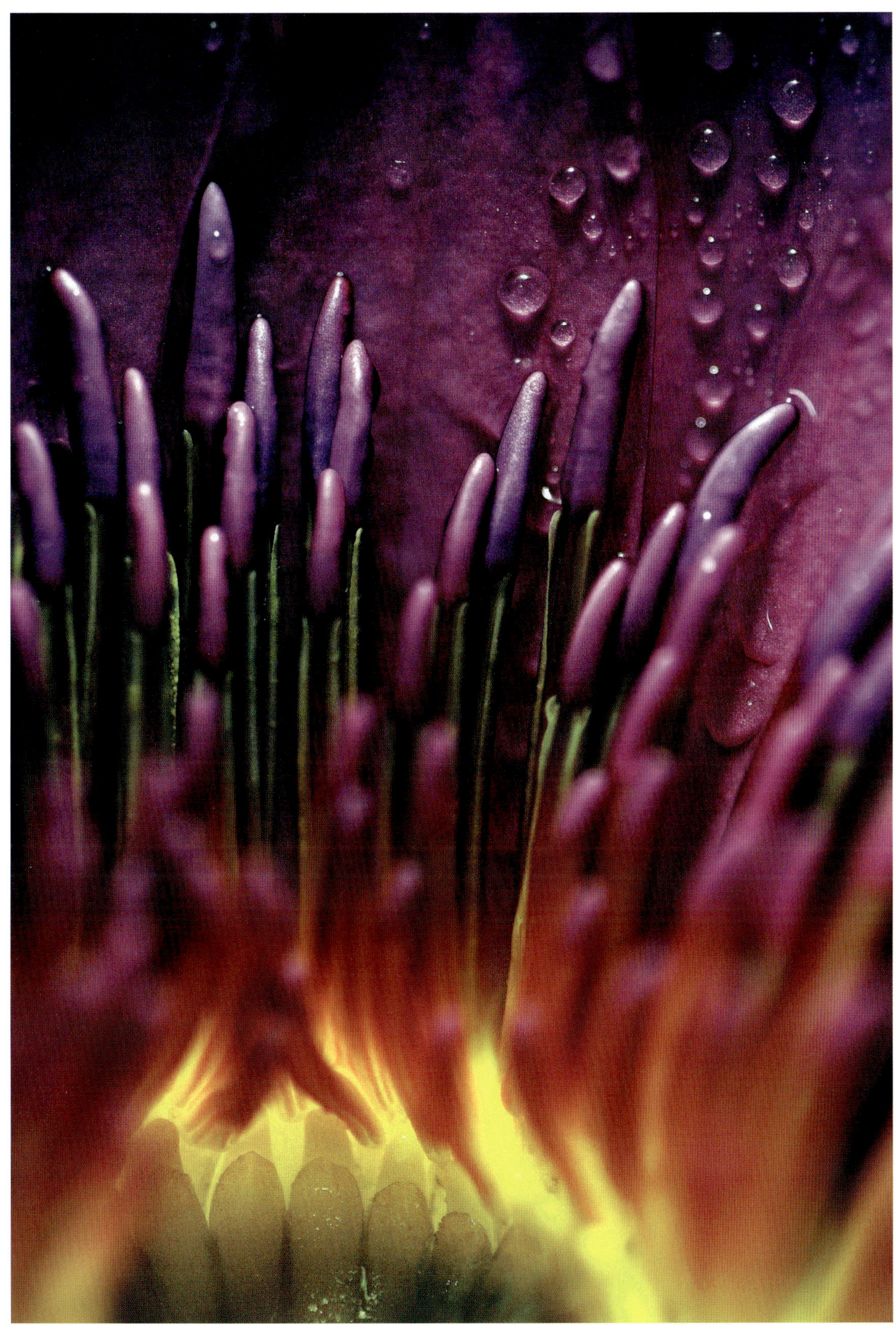

I saw this beautiful flower in the supermarket and could not resist buying it. Winter is such a dark time, and this flower made life beautiful again. I had to pull the flower apart to capture all the colours. The light was not the best, but with a tripod I could photograph even at night, indoors and in the middle of winter.

MY HOUSE, GOTHENBURG
PINK NAILS

ANNA ULMESTRAND

Canon EOS 350D, Tamron 90mm lens. 1/40sec at f/2.8.
Post-capture: contrast and tonal manipulation.
HIGHLY COMMENDED, 2012

SAN MATEO COAST, CALIFORNIA
SWEET DAWN

DIANE VARNER

Canon EOS 5D Mark II, 70-200mm lens. 1/800sec at f/4.0. Post-capture: tonal adjustment.
THIRD, 2012

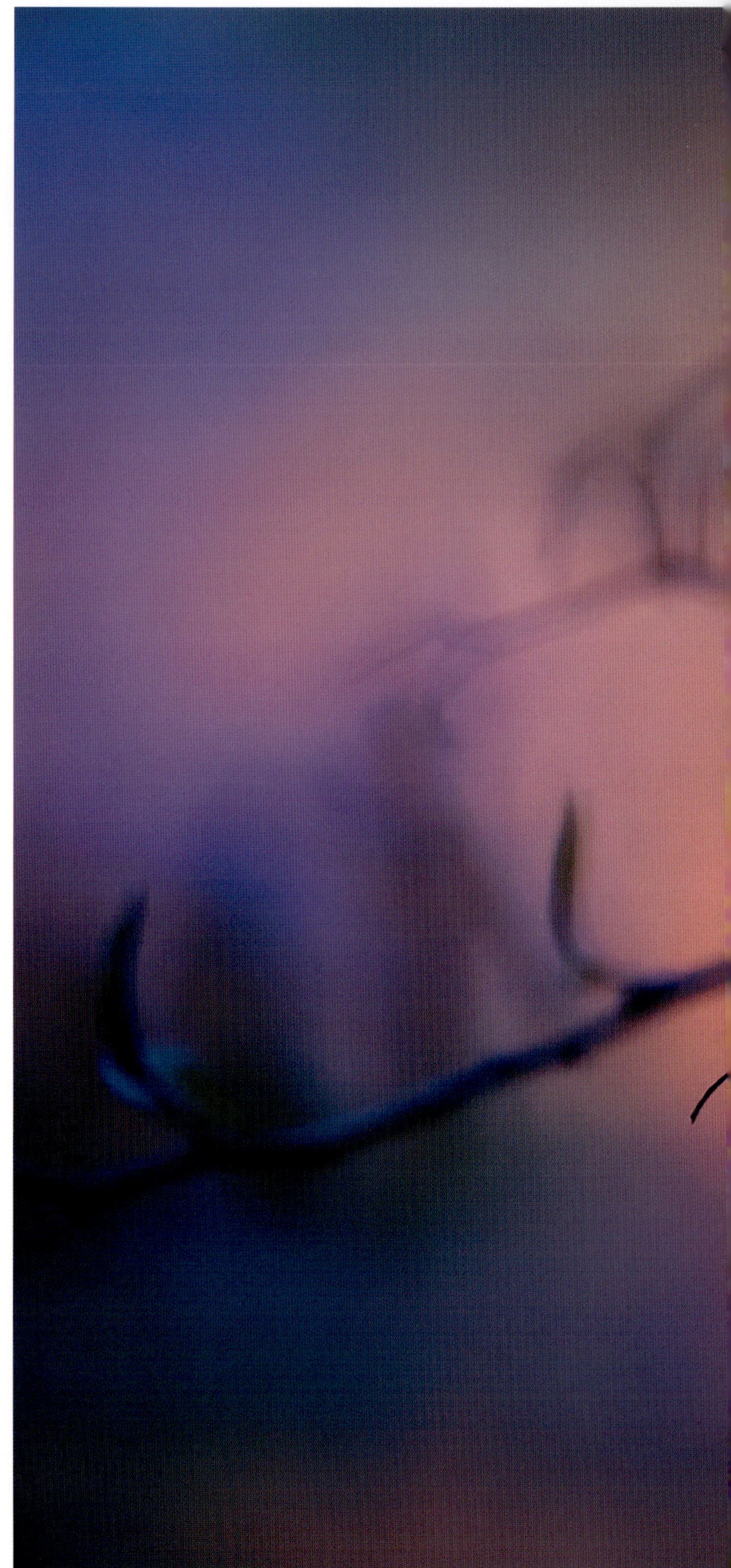

On this particularly brisk November morning, these fragrant potato vine flowers (*Solanum jasminoides*) seemed to have a presence that invited me to look closer and photograph their beauty. The image was taken with a hand-held camera.

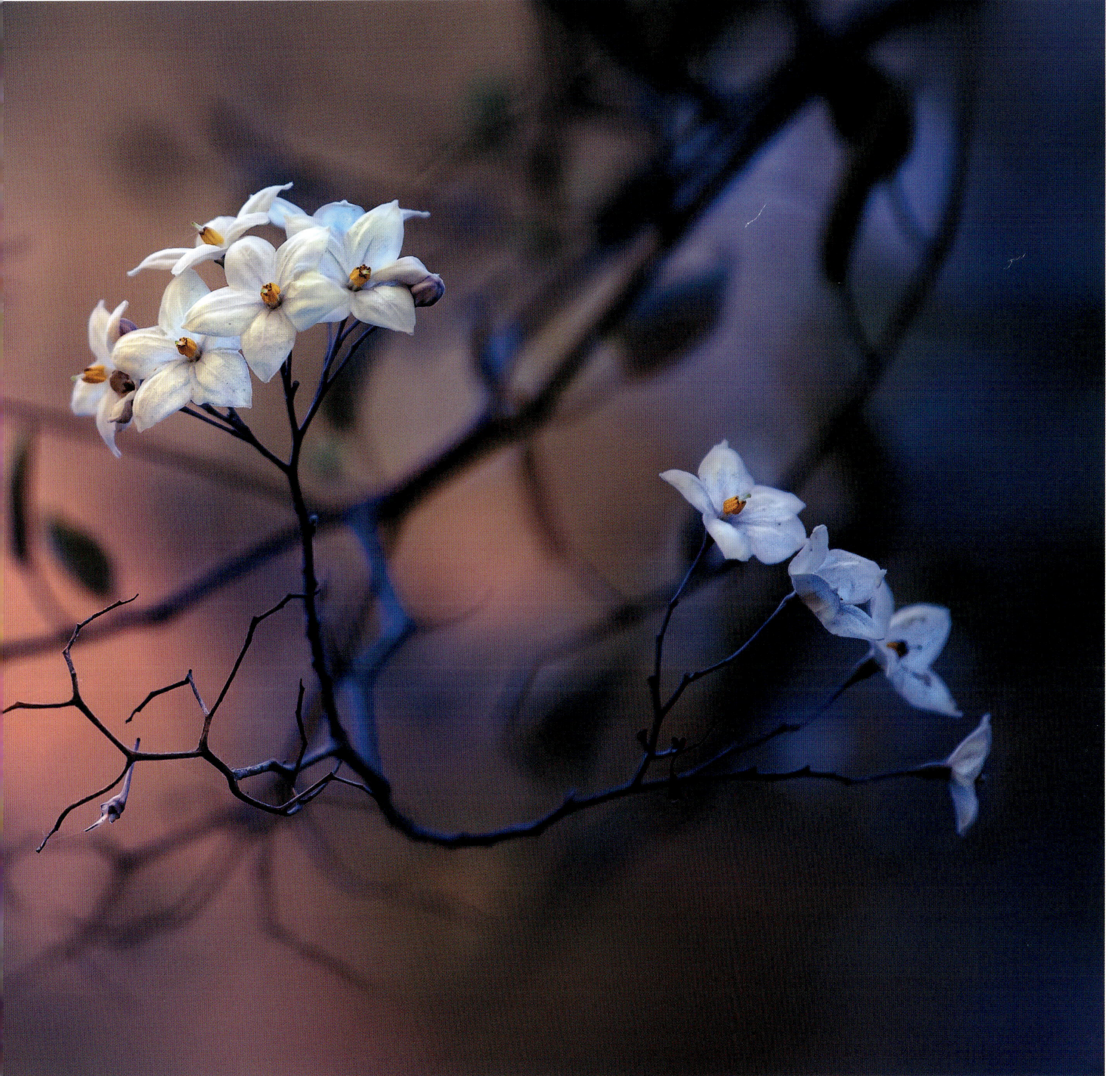

WASHINGTON PARK ARBORETUM, SEATTLE, WASHINGTON STATE

LONE LILY PAD

DEBORAH CASSO

Nikon D200, Nikkor 80-200mm f/2.8 lens, f/5. I used a circular polarising filter with a modest degree of polarisation to cut down on the glare but still leave a silvery sheen on the water.

FIRST, 2009

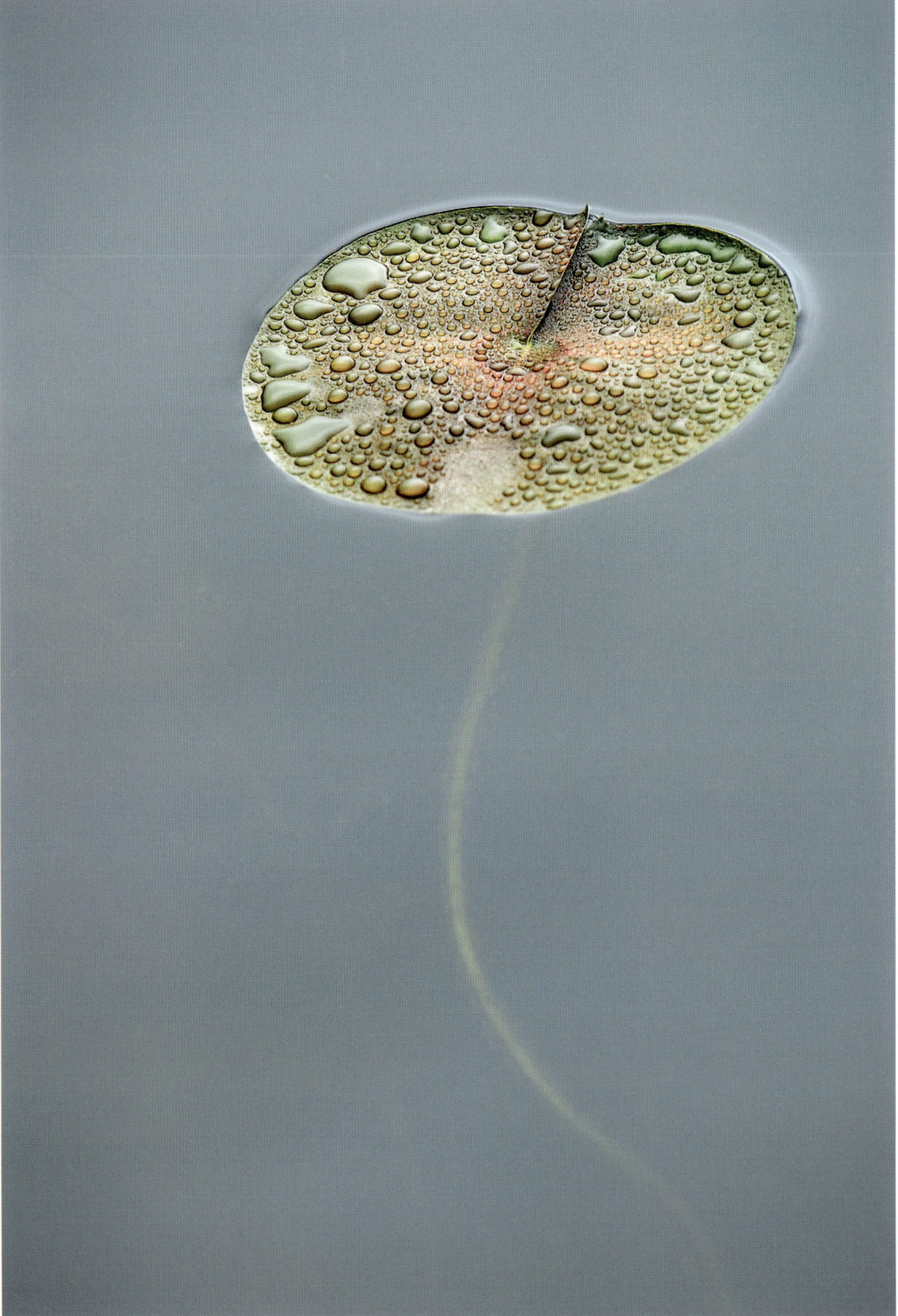

A single lily (*Nymphaea* spp.) pad with iridescent tones floats gracefully on the water of Union Bay in the Washington Park Arboretum. The simplicity of the subject, the interesting colours and the grace of the lines in the image all inspired me to take this photograph.

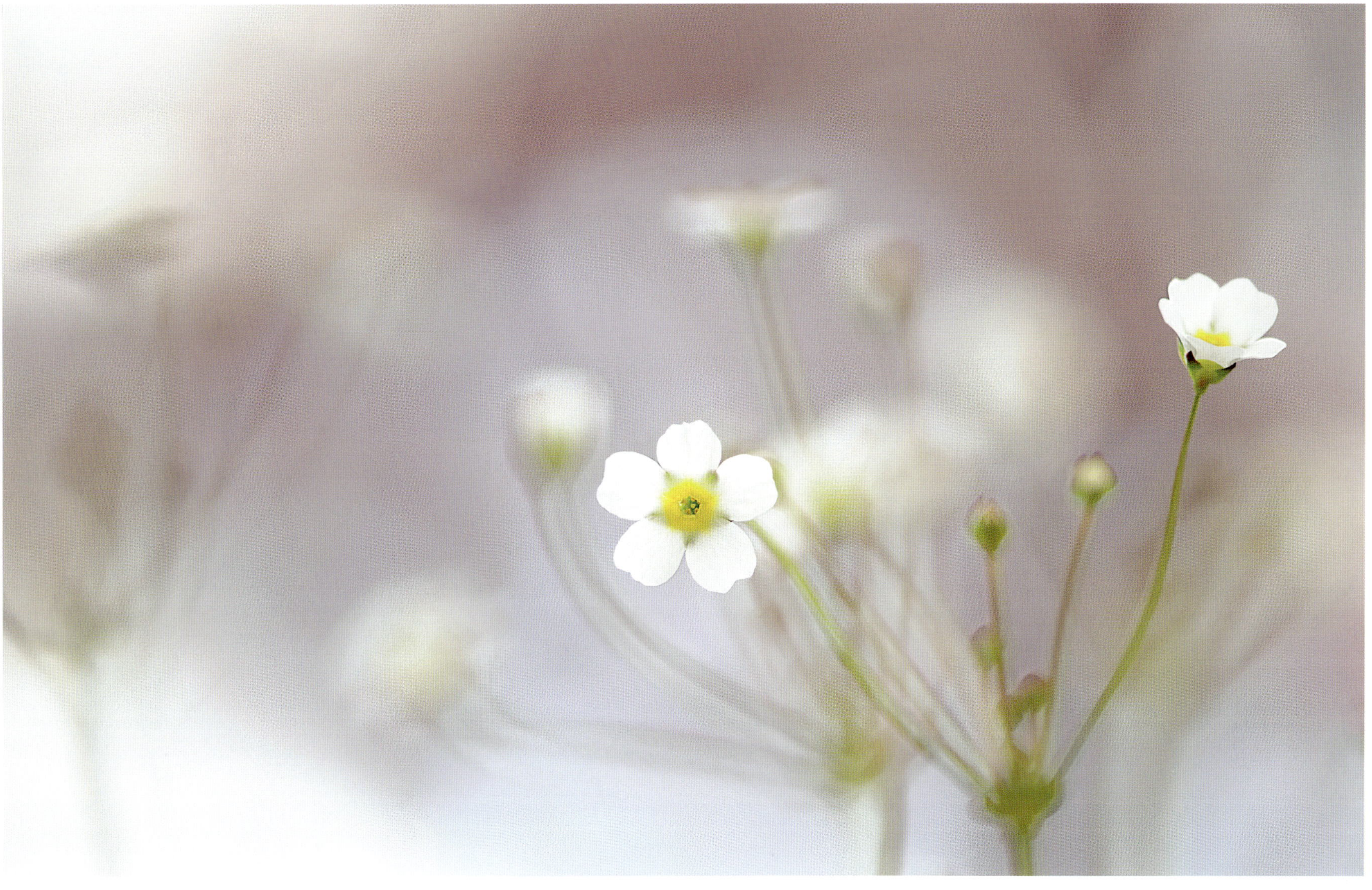

IVER, BUCKINGHAMSHIRE, ENGLAND
SPRING STARBURST

JACKY PARKER

Nikon D300, Micro-Nikkor 105mm lens, 1/640sec. Post-capture: no digital alterations.
FINALIST, 2011

This is a macro image of rock jasmine (*Androsace septentrionalis* 'Starburst'). I feel that often these tiny alpine flowers go unnoticed in a garden and I was drawn to the simplicity of these pure white rock plants in the spring. I wanted to capture their delicate form in a soft and creative image.

LONDON, ENGLAND
AUTUMN STUDY

RACHEL WARNE

Scanner. I experimented with the colours and reversed the image, using the negative instead of the positive image.
SECOND AND GPA BEST PORTFOLIO, 2009

I wanted to make a study of plants outside their usual environment. The plants were all gathered from my neighbourhood – from the forest, the sides of roads and even someone's front garden. Although they are all dead, photographing them is a way of bringing them back to life. I used a technique that allowed me to get really close to the fine detail found in a plant's skeleton.

1–Sycamore (*Plantanus* spp.) seedling.
2–Dried fern.
3–Grasses.
4–Beech (*Fagus* spp.) .
5–Aster.
6–Cow parsley (*Anthriscus sylvestris*).

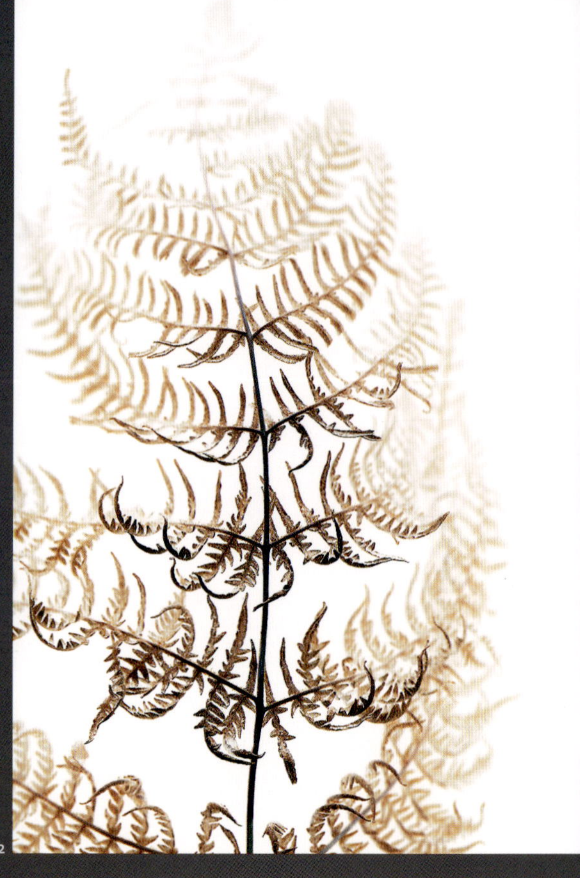

2

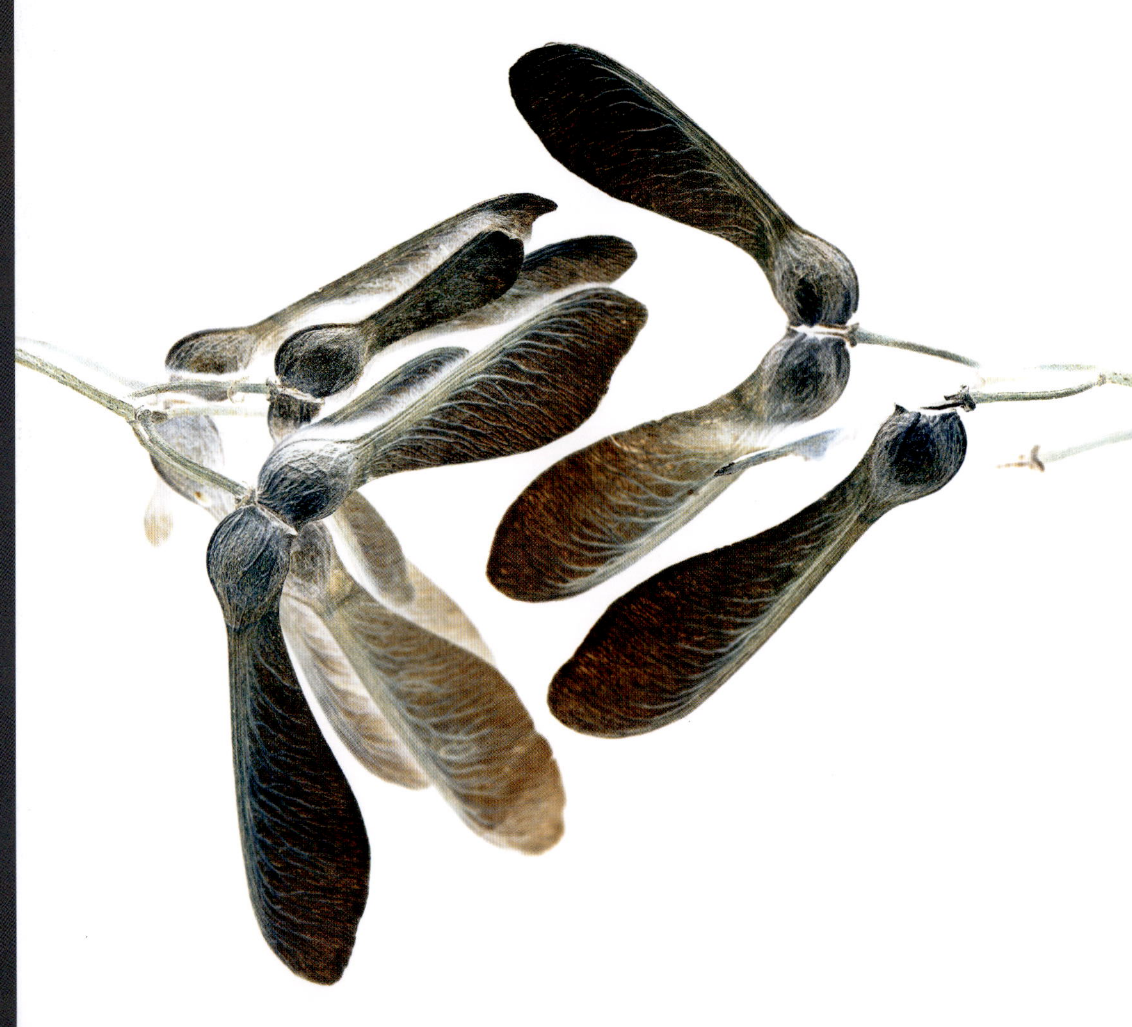

1

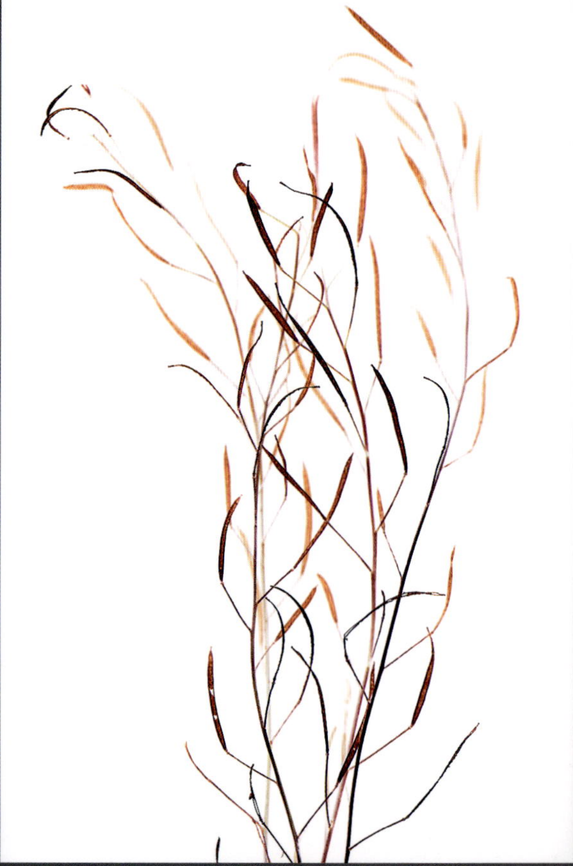

3

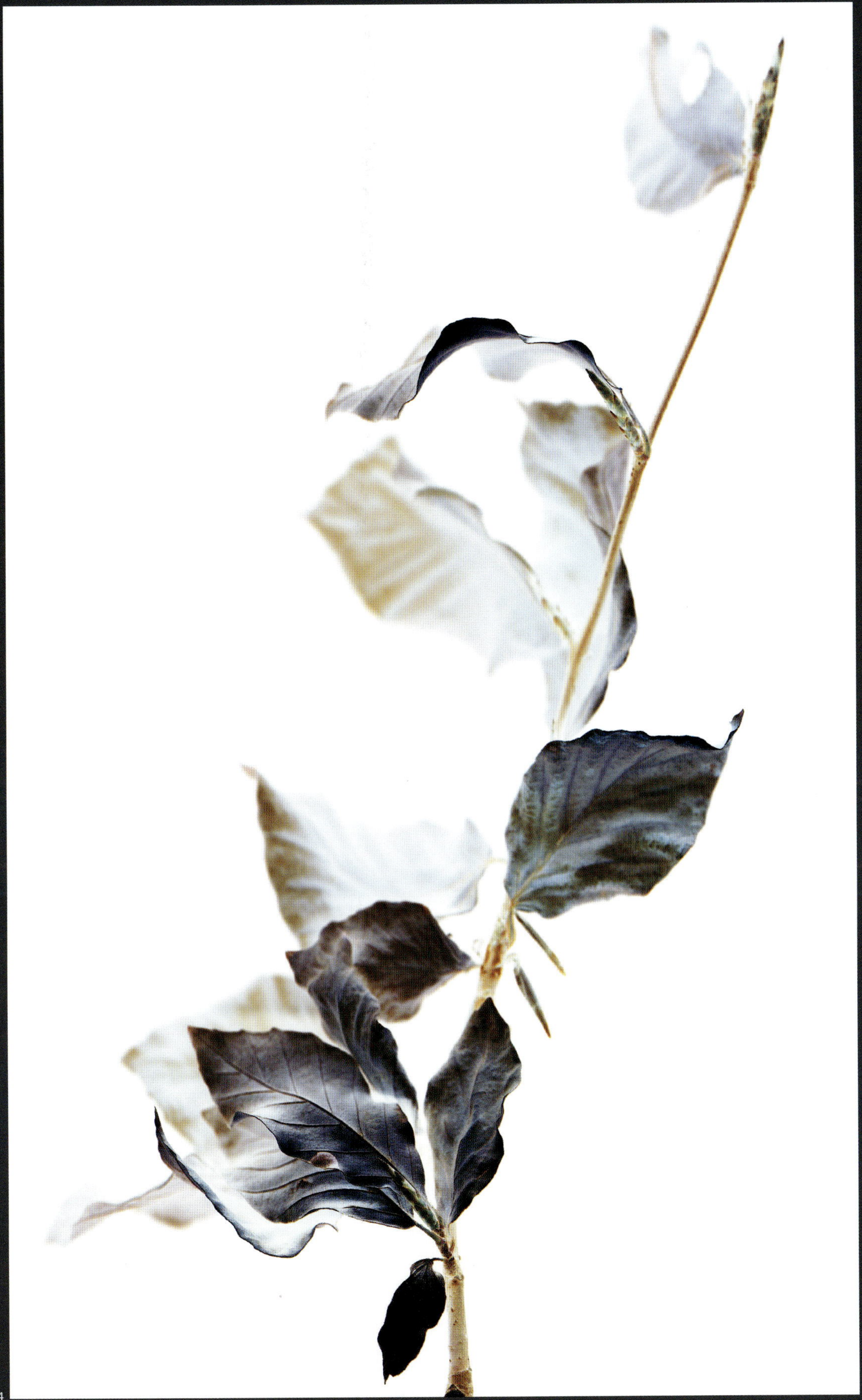

4

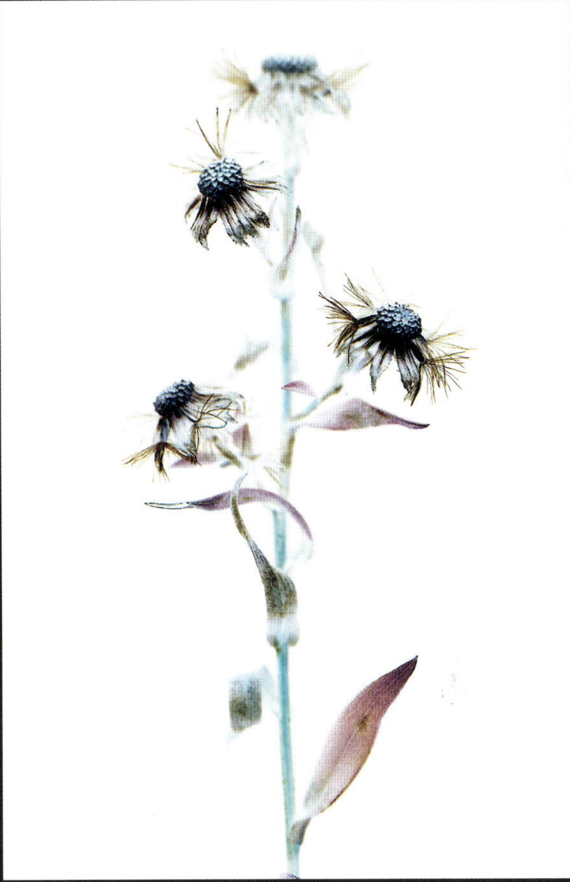

5

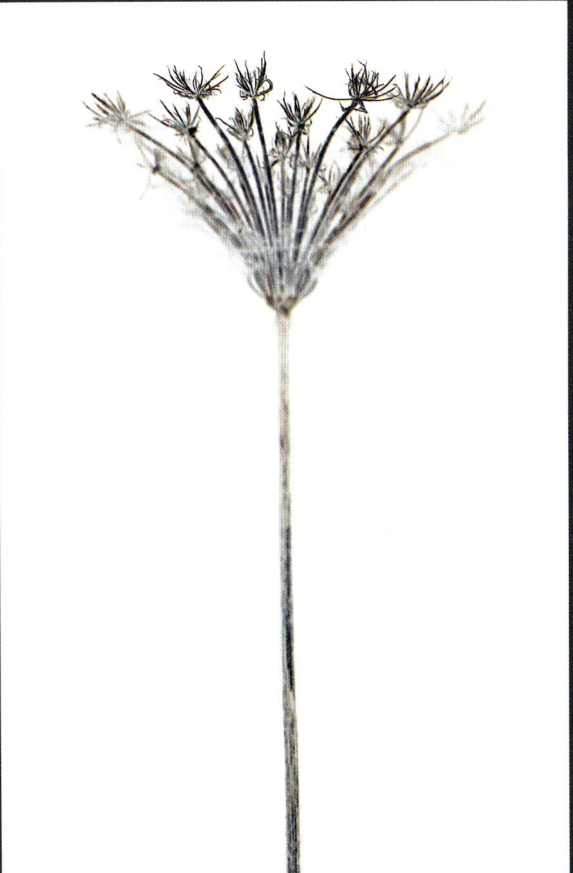

6

I was in New Zealand to shoot landscapes and wildlife. Interested in gardens and plants, I had heard about the Mount Cook lily (*Ranunculus lyallii*) (it's actually a giant alpine buttercup, not a lily!) and was eagerly anticipating finding it. Walking up the Hooker Valley towards Mount Cook, I found the flower in bloom and growing in profusion. The mountain itself made an appropriate backdrop for the shot.

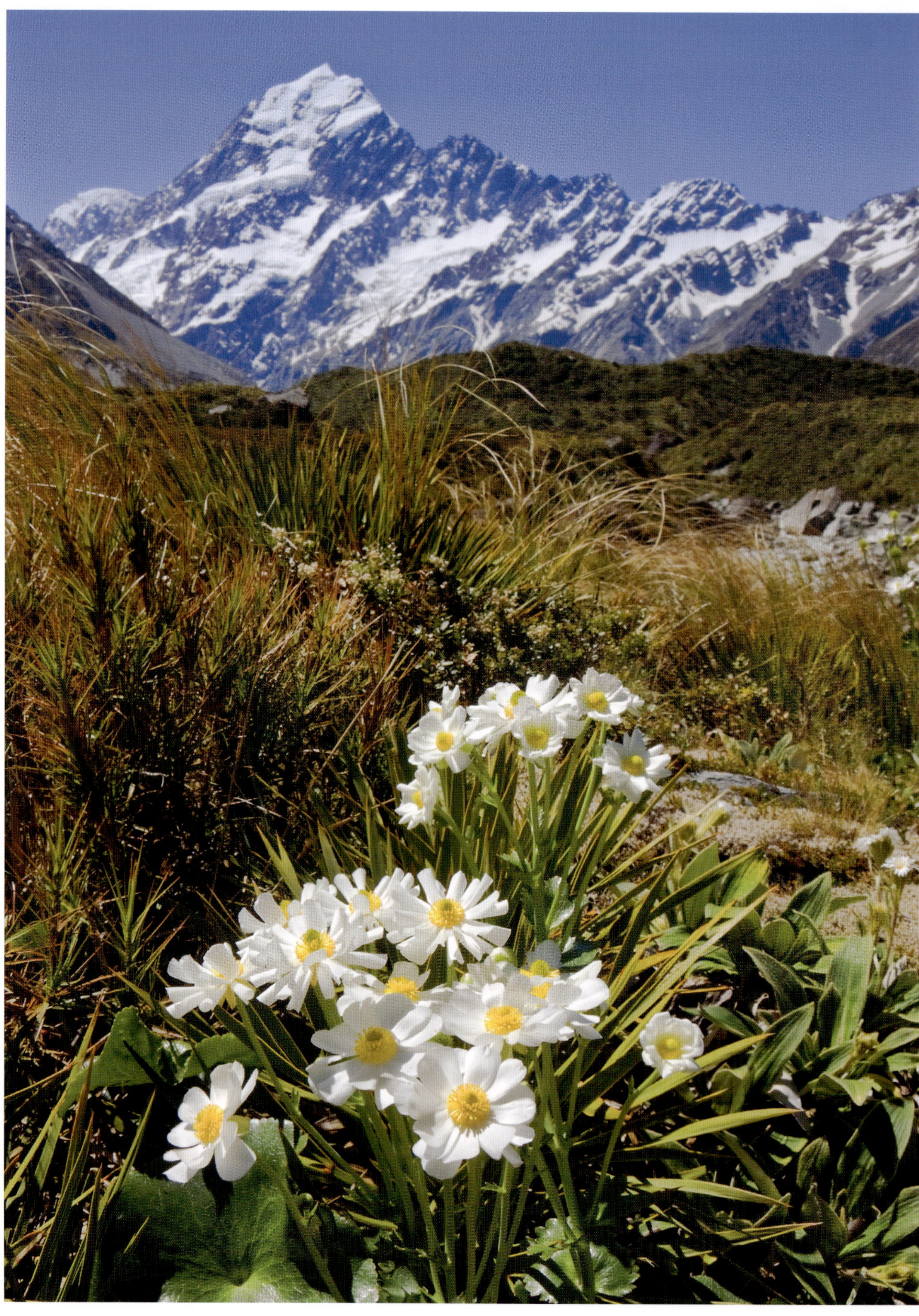

HOOKER VALLEY, AORAKI/MOUNT COOK NATIONAL PARK
MOUNT COOK LILY

NIGEL BURKITT

Canon EOS 40D, Canon EF-S 17-85mm lens, f/13, circular polariser. I just had to include this stunning view of Mount Cook as a backdrop to my shot of the plant. I stopped down to f/13 so as to make the mountain itself out of focus but still recognisable.
FINALIST, 2009

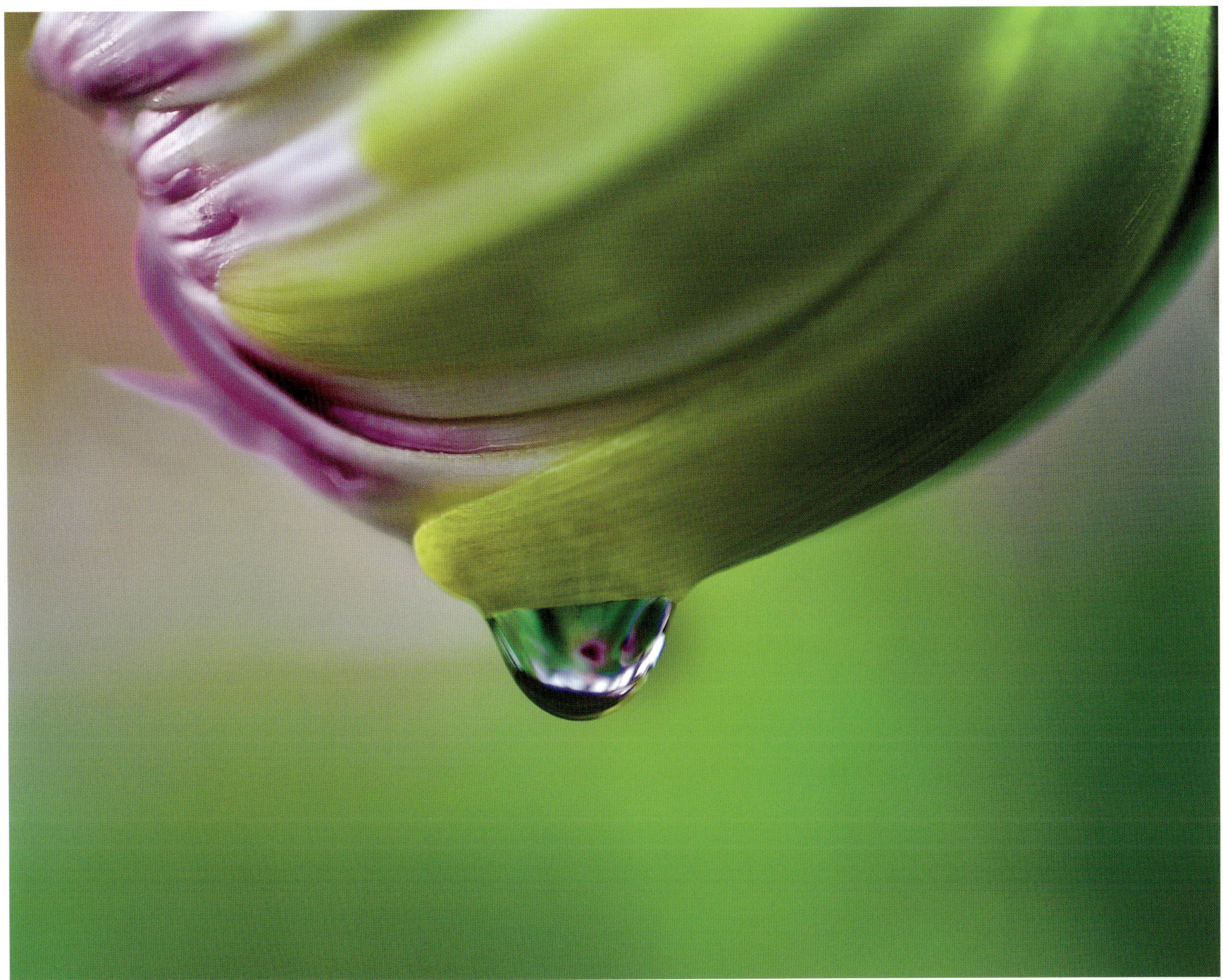

PLYMOUTH, DEVON, ENGLAND
CHRYSANTHEMUM RAINDROP

DIANE FIFIELD

Canon EOS 400D, Tamron 90mm lens. 1/100sec at f/3.2. Post-capture: some tonal adjustment.
HIGHLY COMMENDED, 2012

The rain had just stopped so I ventured out into the garden with my camera and macro lens. I wanted to capture raindrops and saw this chrysanthemum (*Chrysathemum* spp.) bud with one little raindrop about to fall. I quickly set up, focused with a manual setting to give me control, and took the shot. Macro photography shows up all the wonderful details and textures in the flower which normally go unnoticed by the human eye. I edged my way between the dripping wet chrysanthemums until I found just the shot I was looking for.

The image shows a cut stem of spring blossom resting across a weathered wooden bowl which holds a single large beach pebble and a small contorted piece of collected driftwood. These are arranged upon a weathered wooden rustic table and viewed from above. Spring blossom always reminds me of the Orient which in turn makes me admire the simplicity of the Japanese style of garden art. This inspired me to try to bring an element of that simplicity into a still life image inspired by the beauty of the spring blossom. I used natural diffused sunlight with the camera mounted on a tripod and a remote shutter release.

MY GARDEN, LANCASHIRE, ENGLAND
ALMOND BLOSSOM

JAMES GUILLIAM

Canon EOS-1Ds Mark III, Canon 70-200mm lens, 1/5sec at f/16. Post-capture: this image was created from four separate exposures, which were blended together to create a single image. The edges have been darkened to help focus the attention on the centre and the overall image has been desaturated slightly to mute the colours.
FINALIST, 2011

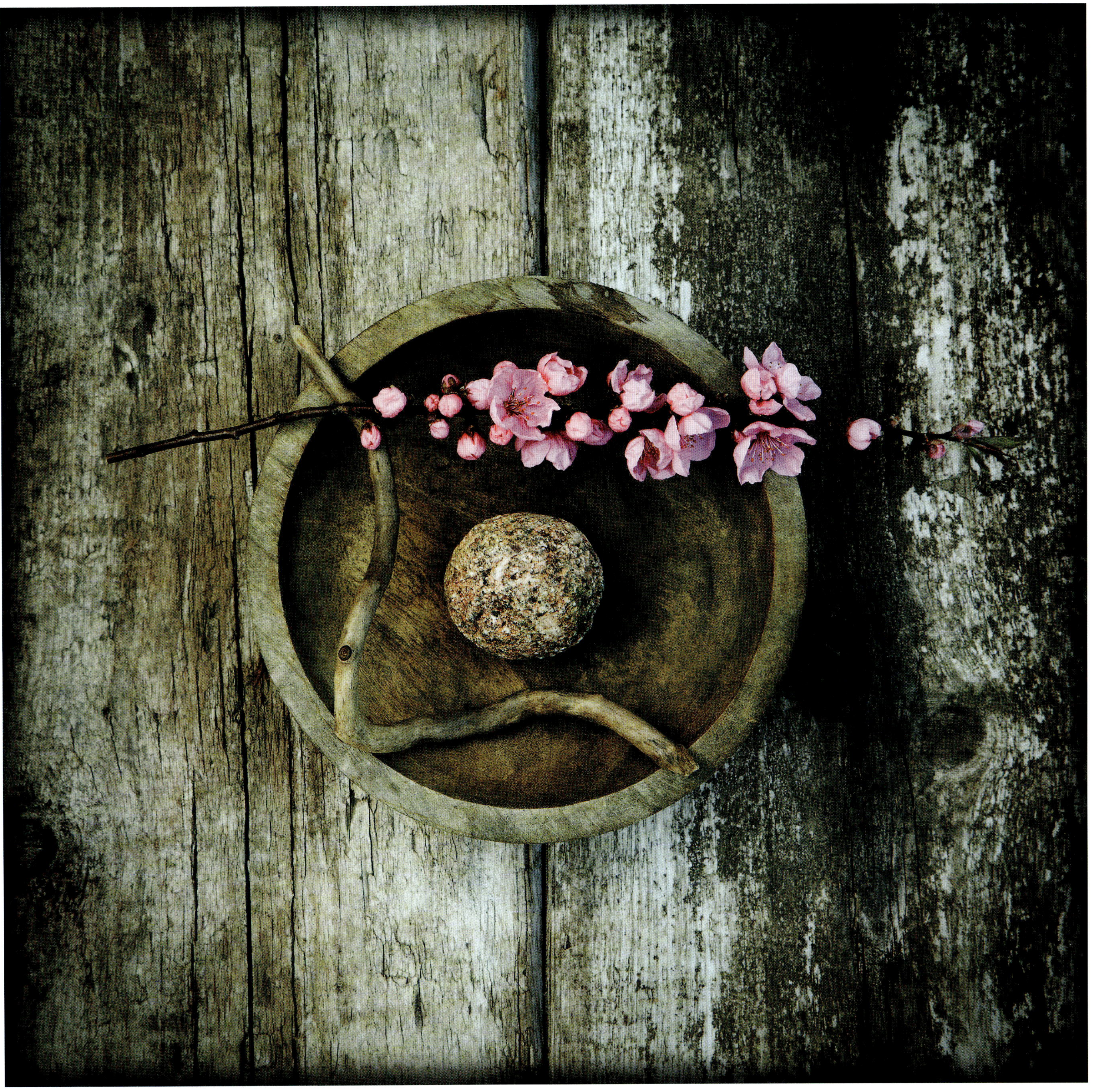

CORNWALL, ENGLAND
MAGNOLIA CAMPBELLII VAR. 'ALBA'

BRIAN HASLAM

Canon EOS 5D, Canon EF 24–105mm, f/9.
SECOND, 2010

The tree was stunning – full of perfect flowers and conveniently situated at eye level. I held the front petal down with one hand to show the central pistil and stamens.

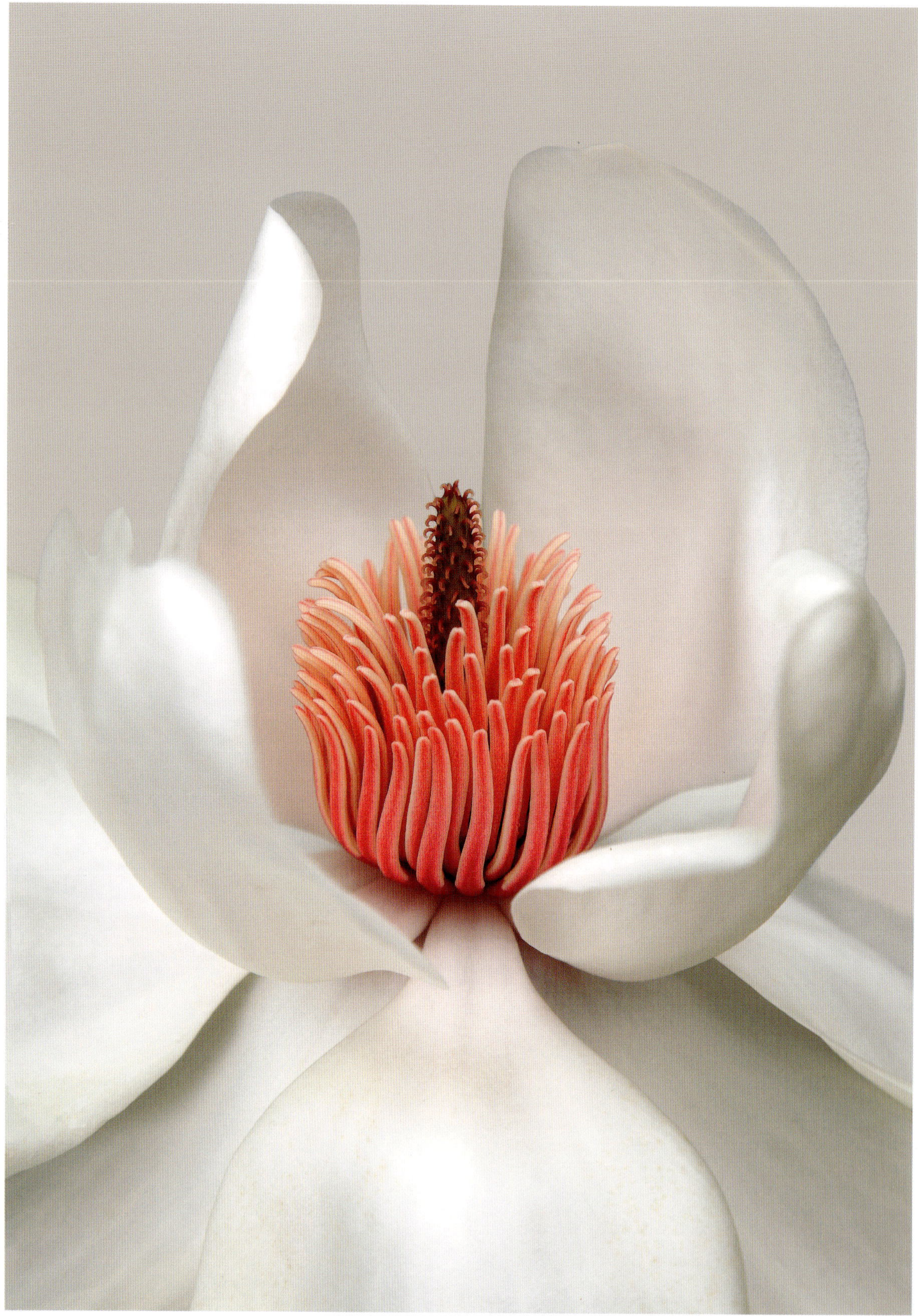

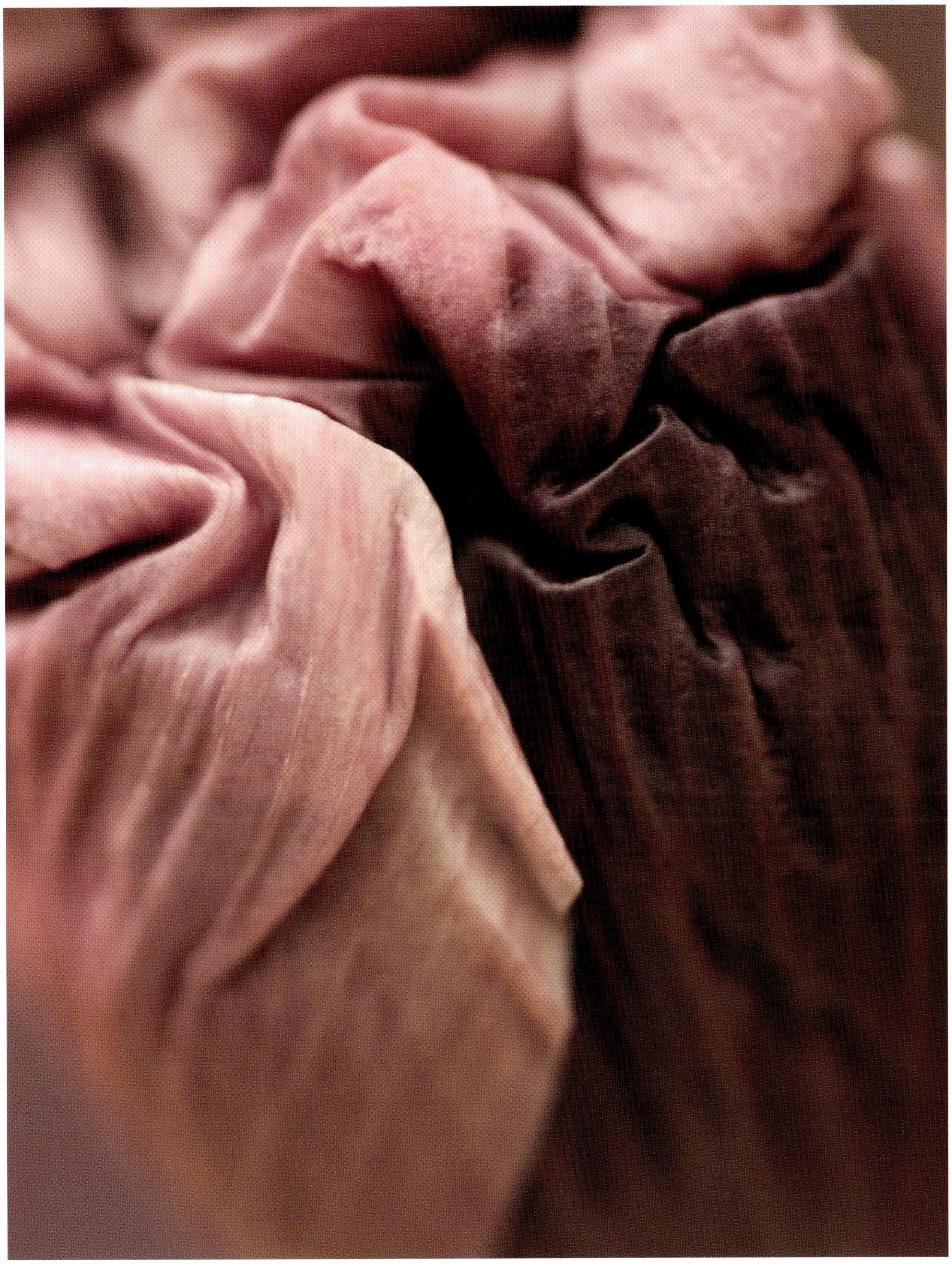

The colours and textures of this opium poppy (*Papaver somniferum*) were extremely sensuous. I wanted to create the feeling of crumpled velvet and the variety of shades one would see in the pile of the cloth. I often spend time photographing poppy petals because I love their tissue-like quality. On this occasion I gently peeled back the outer casing of the bud and enjoyed working with the crumpled petals. I could see the possibility of creating a beautiful image that would leave the observer wondering what it was.

ENGLAND
POPPY UNFOLDING

MARY SUTTON

Olympus E3, Sigma 150mm macro lens, f/2.8. The poppy moved a little, so I used a clamp attached to my tripod to hold it steady. A reflector created shade in order to maximise the tonal variation. By using a wide aperture I was able to achieve softness, yet retain some essential detail.
FINALIST, 2009

THE BOUNTIFUL EARTH

The Bountiful Earth

When we ask visitors their reason for visiting the Gardens, the most common answer is to experience the beauty and tranquillity that we all need to salve our souls amidst the hassle and bustle of our 21st-century lives. That reconnection with the natural world remains a vital part of being human, perhaps even more so as we are increasingly immersed in a world of human artefacts that intervene in and mediate our interactions with one another, as well as the rest of the living world. It is perhaps the defining characteristic of any garden that it affords us an opportunity to make that reconnection – even if only for a moment as we pass.

The sheer joy of the International Garden Photographer of the Year exhibition is that it captures those moments as framed by the gifted eye of both the practised professional artist and the talented individuals who take their inspiration from the gardens of the world. In these days of digital photography, where nearly everyone has a camera of sorts in their pocket at all times, it is easy to dismiss the skill, patience and creativity of truly inspired photography. The range of images that make it through into the exhibition is breathtaking. My particular favourites include those images, often of a single bloom, that have a painterly or sculptural quality.

The collection of images that results from International Garden Photographer of the Year also serves as a reminder that the spaces that inspire are not just the great gardens of the world – although these feature heavily and I am always intrigued to see new angles on Kew. But some of the most touching images come from the photographer's own backyard, or even window box! The behind the scenes shots, of abandoned tools and the potting shed, celebrate and remind us of the long hours of backbreaking work that have gone into producing the beauty and apparent spontaneity of the garden scene in most cases. The category of Breathing Spaces underlines this as we see ravaged hands and bent backs. It also showcases both the exuberant and more contemplative activities we all like to indulge in when we get time to ourselves in a garden.

Gardens are many things to many people – a source of food where is it otherwise scarce, a place to exercise or rest, a place to show off our wealth or cherish the living things we share this planet with. Some gardens are all these things at once. The magic of International Garden Photographer of the Year is that it reminds us of the many dimensions of gardens, gardeners and our endless love affair with the world of plants.

Professor Angela McFarlane
Director of Public Engagement and Learning, Royal Botanic Gardens, Kew

LONDON, ENGLAND
RUNNER BEANS

JOHANNA PARKIN

Sinar, 150mm Sinaron lens, Fuji Velvia 100. The contours of the beans' edges shone beautifully in the light, so I wanted to make a graphic and linear shot that was slightly abstract, while retaining the honest organic naturalness inherent to these long, striking vegetables.
COMMENDED, 2009

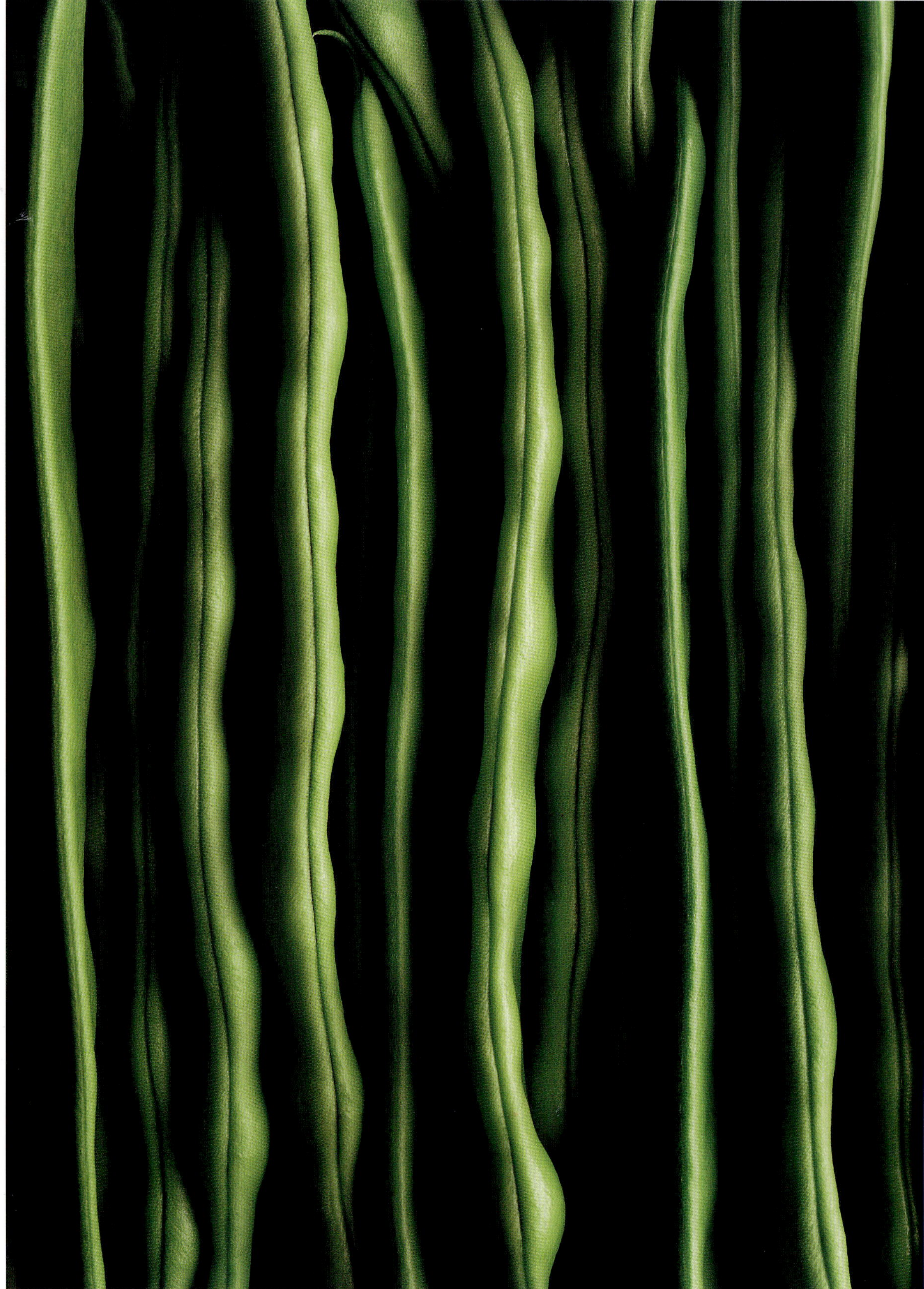

I love the bold, natural, healthy green of runner beans (*Phaseolus coccineus*), and the graphic yet imperfectly wobbly lines their sides form when clustered together. This gives them character as a group of vegetables. I photographed this group of scarlet runner beans, grown organically in my friend's vegetable garden, from overhead and against a black background, so the edges would gleam out of the darkness.

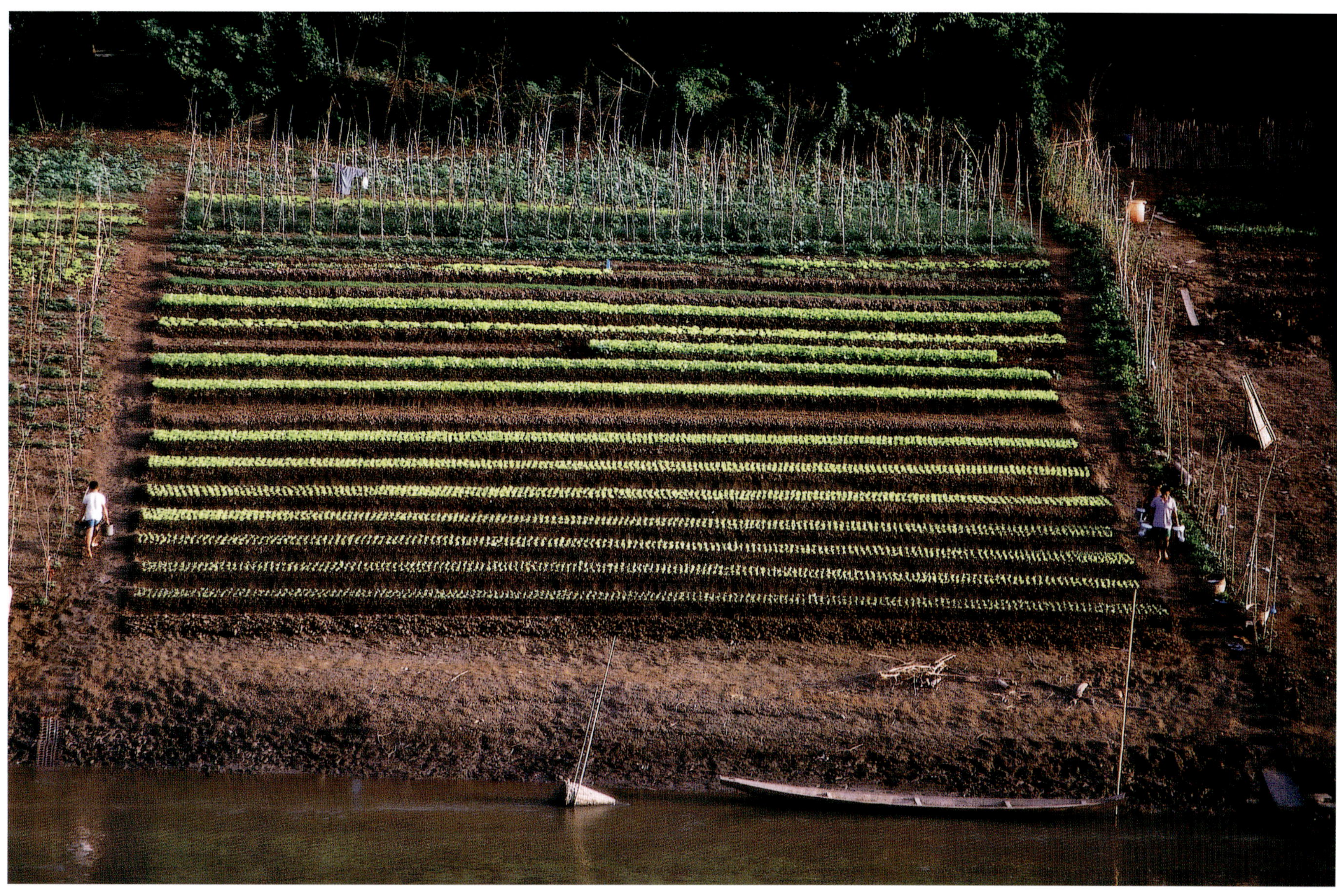

MEKONG RIVER, LUANG PRABANG
MEKONG GARDEN

DAVID THURSTON

Fuji Provia film. Canon EOS 5, 70-200mm lens, 1/125sec at f/11. Post-capture: no digital alterations.
SECOND, 2012

When the river level begins to recede in late summer, slow-growing crops such as legumes are planted. A succession of salad crops follow as the water level continues to fall. They grow quickly and are harvested. There is still time before the upriver snow melts for a second crop, aided by the warmth and fertility of the riverbank soil.

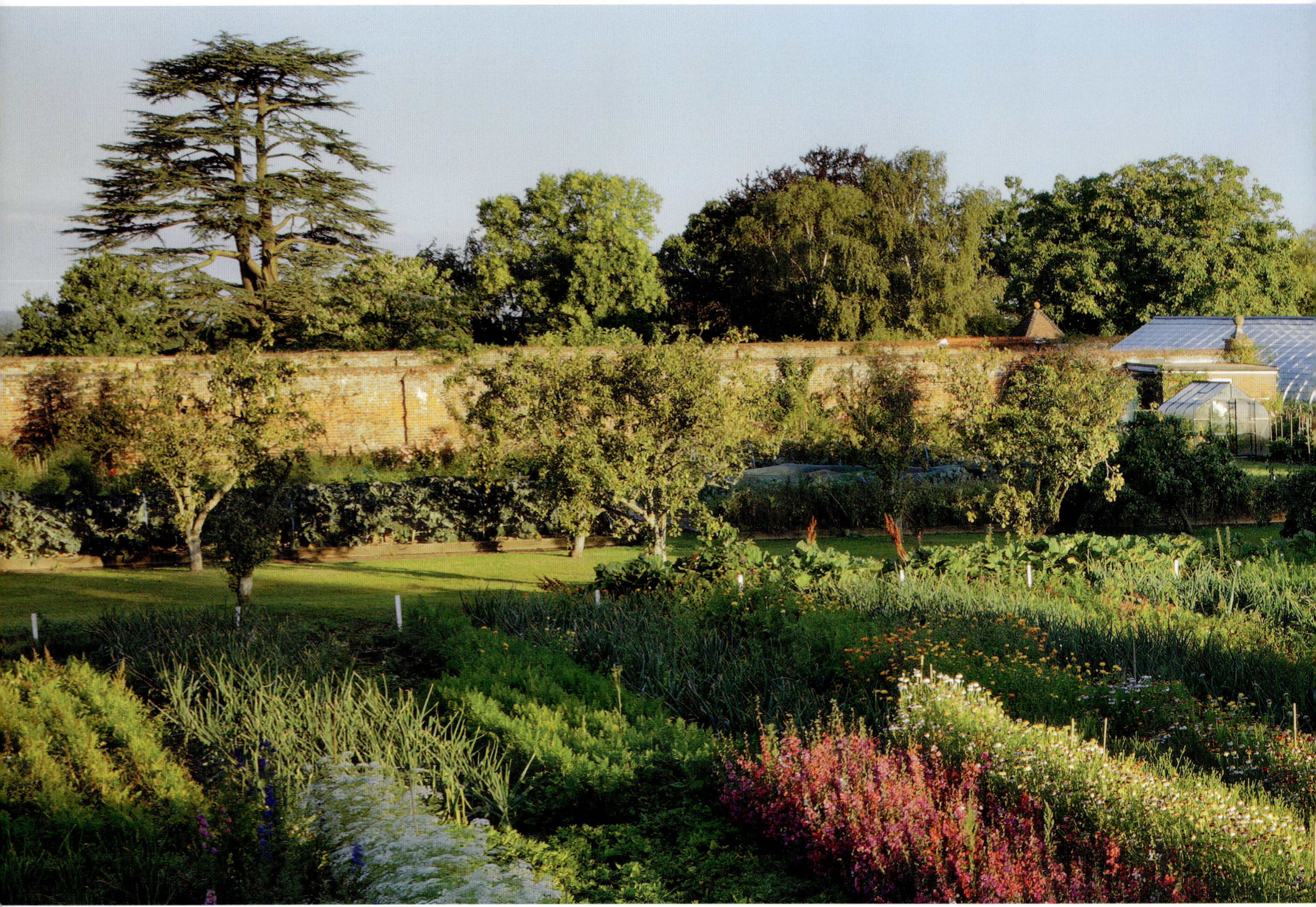

CLAYDON ESTATE GARDENS, MIDDLE CLAYDON, BUCKINGHAMSHIRE, ENGLAND
THE WALLED KITCHEN GARDEN AT CLAYDON

NIGEL BURKITT

Canon 5D Mark II, Canon EF 24-105mm lens, 0.6sec at f/20.
Post-capture: basic adjustments.
HIGHLY COMMENDED, 2012

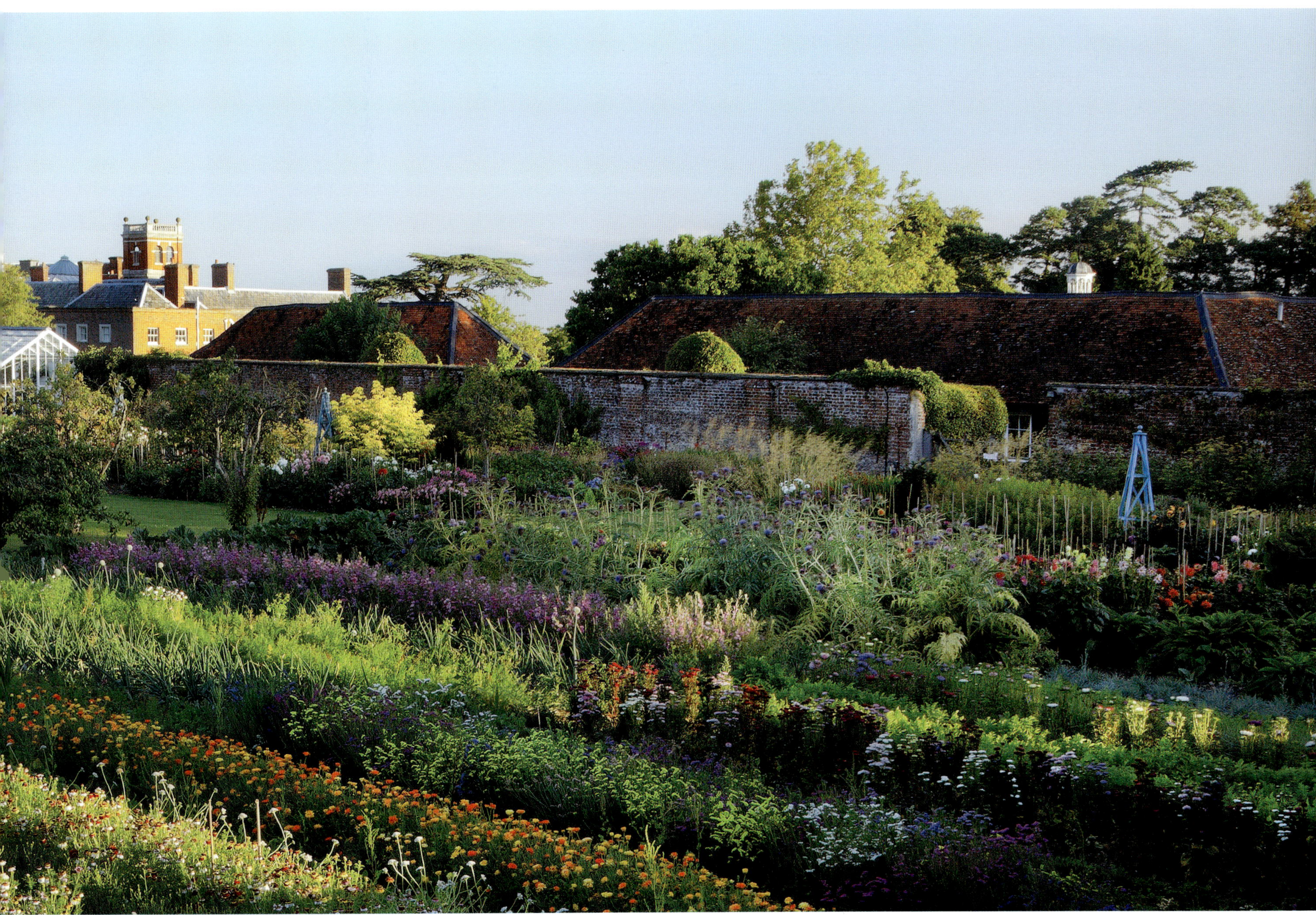

In the last six years, this two-acre kitchen garden has been returned to full productivity, growing organic vegetables, fruit from heritage trees and exquisite flowers, including many unusual varieties not seen on supermarket shelves. This view across the kitchen garden is top of my favourites and I can imagine it was not so different in Victorian times. I know the position where the sun rises and sought to catch the early morning light coming through surrounding trees. A ladder against the wall gave me convenient elevation.

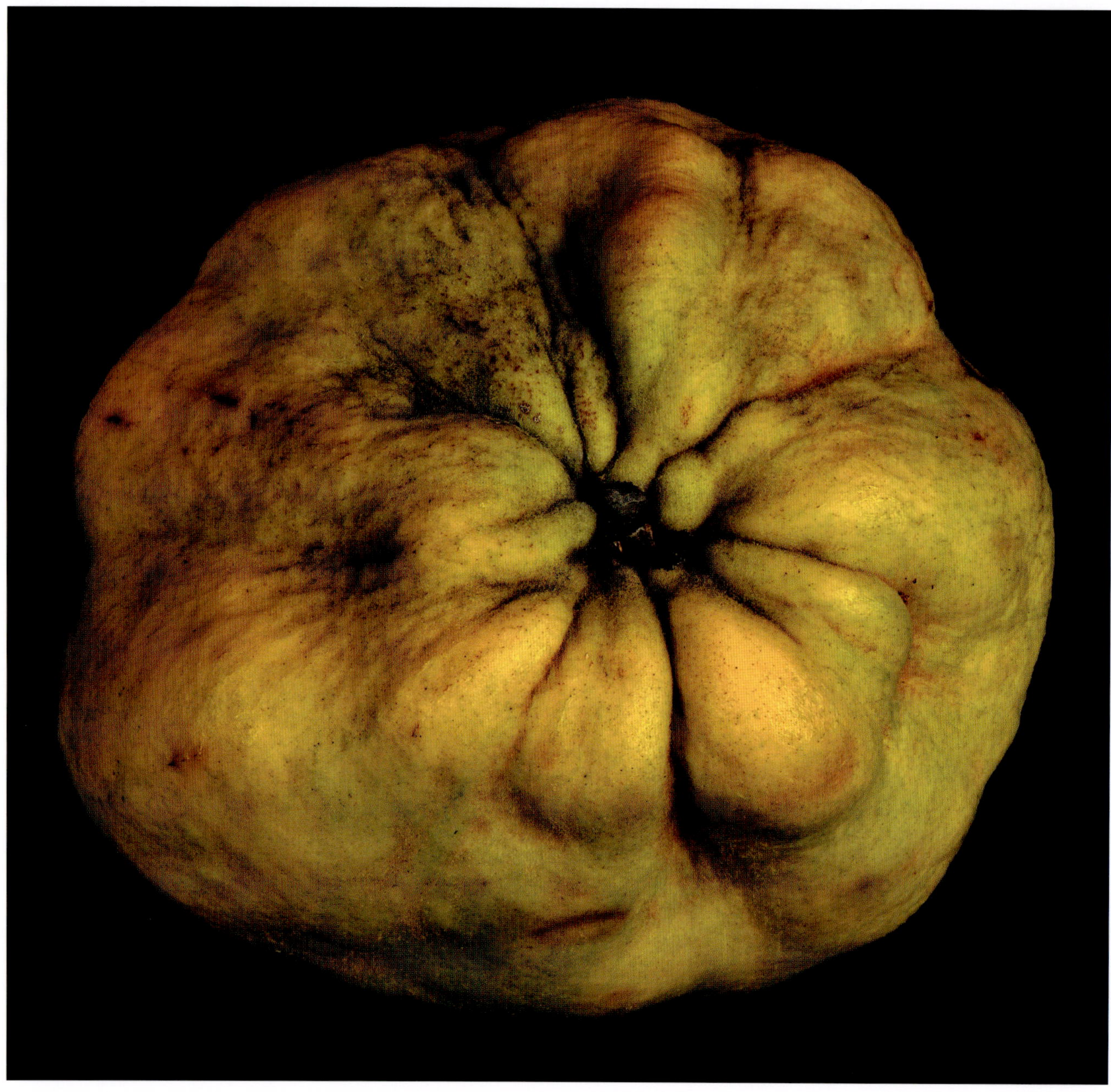

STUDIO, LISBON
QUINCE

HENRIQUE SOUTO

Nikon D300, Nikkor 60mm lens, 1/125sec at f/20. Post-capture: image cropped to a square format. Adjustments to colour and contrast.
FIRST, 2012

I have been photographing fruits and vegetables especially for the aesthetic value that some of them have. I wanted to bring out the roughness of the fruit, and I used two flash units positioned on opposite sides of the fruit, with a slight underexposure to bring out the colour. This photo is part of an ongoing series.

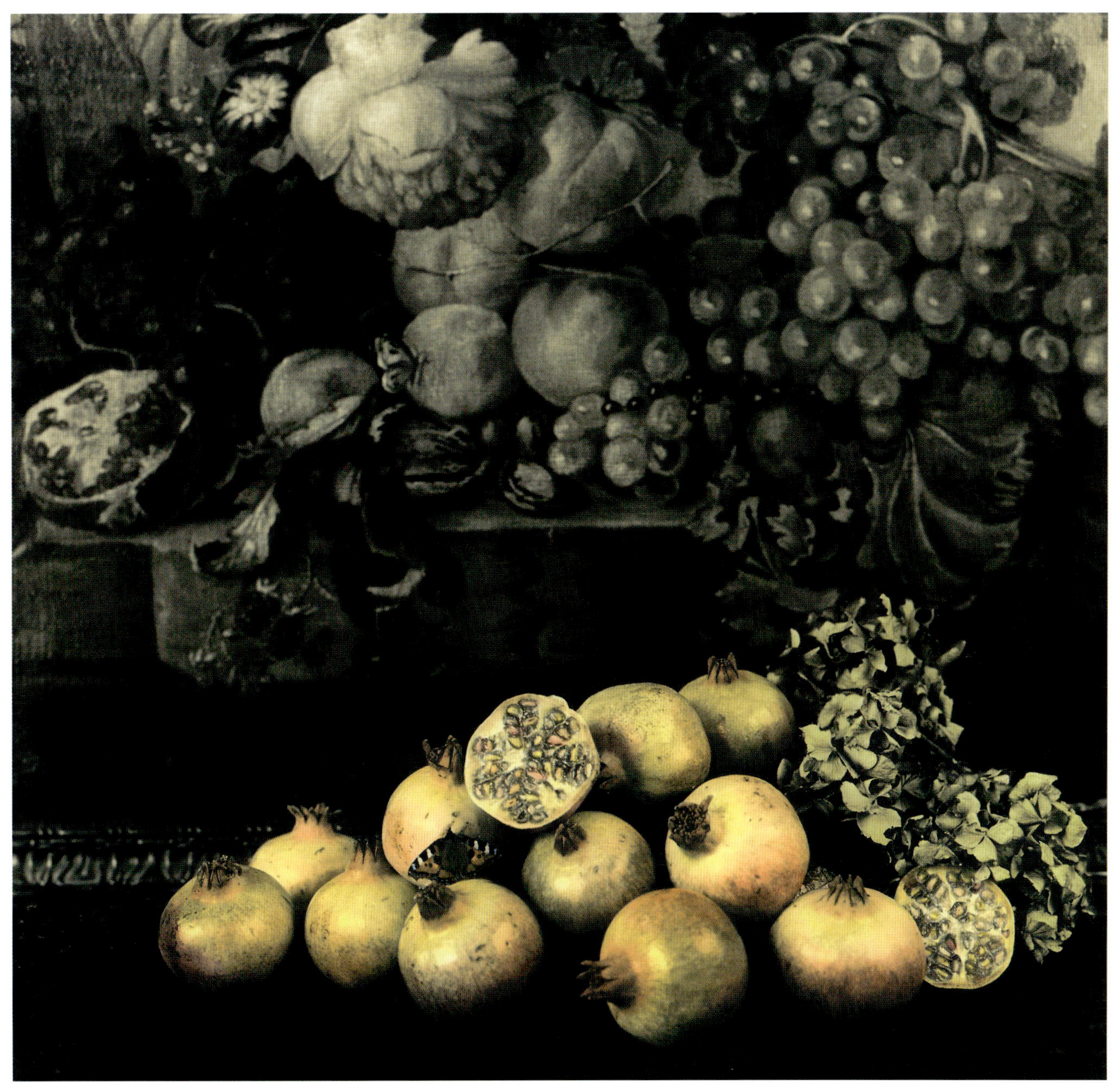

HOME STUDIO, OXFORDSHIRE, ENGLAND
POMEGRANATES

CAROLINE HYMAN

Ilford HP5, Hasselblad 501C, Planar f/2.8 80mm. Sepia-toned and hand-coloured silver bromide print.
FINALIST, 2010

This image forms part of a series of still lifes featuring fruit and vegetables. The colour and shape of pomegranates (*Punica granatum*) has always intrigued me, and I had always wanted to photograph them.

These tomatoes (*Lycopersicon esculentum*) not only had attitude, but also possessed powerful sculptural qualities. I never realised tomatoes could be this sexy...

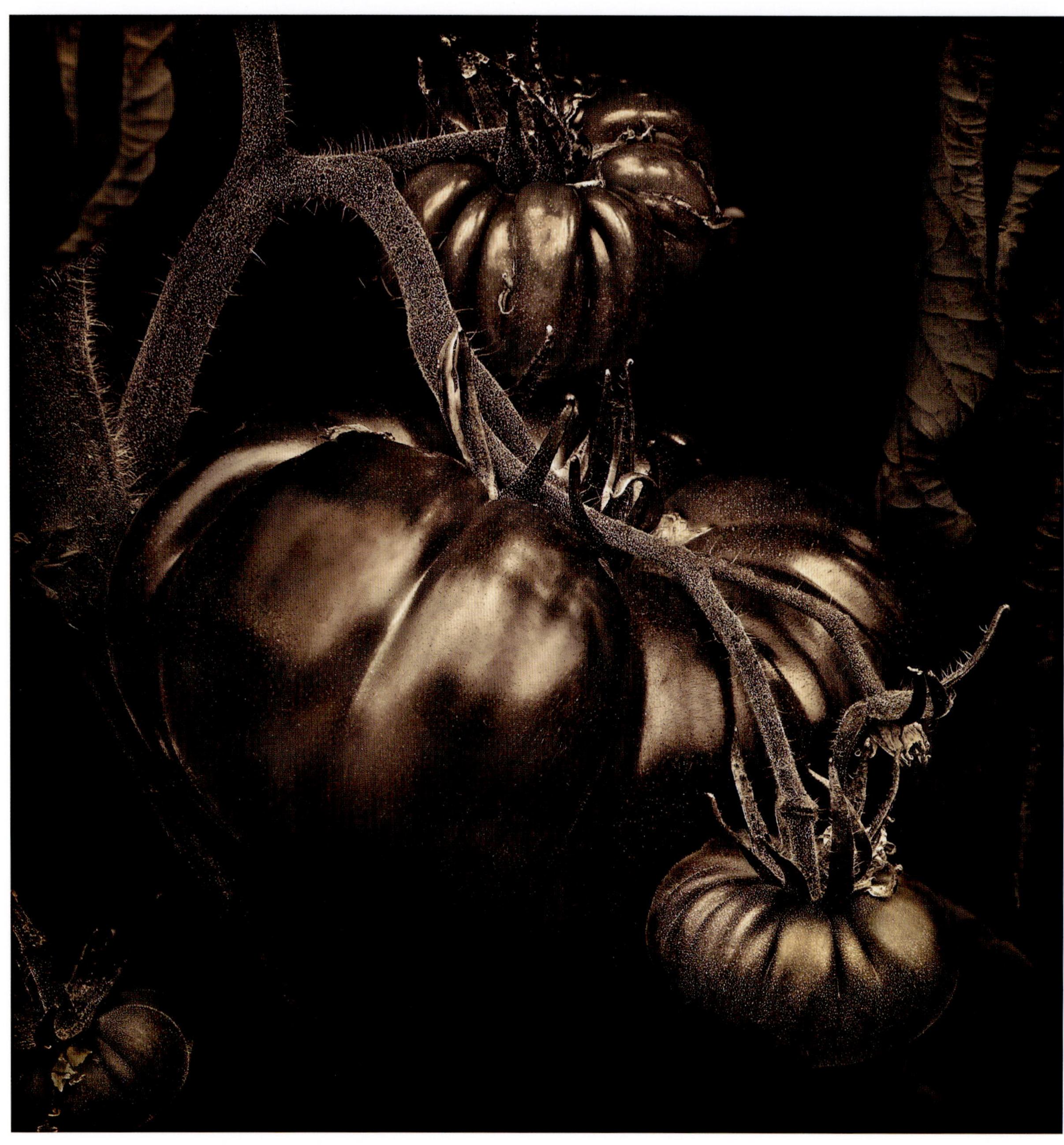

VANCOUVER
TOMATOES WITH ATTITUDE

BAPI CHAKRABORTY

Canon EOS 40D. This is heavily altered in terms of tone, but not shape; nothing needed to be plumped up. Dodging and burning was carried out in Photoshop to emphasise shape and texture.
FIRST, 2009

WALLED GARDEN OF NEWBOLD HOUSE, FORRES, SCOTLAND

FROM SMALL BEGINNINGS, GREAT THINGS GROW

MARIA SANTOS

Olympus E 500, 14-45mm lens, 1/30sec at f/5.6. Post-capture: no digital alterations.

HIGHLY COMMENDED, 2012

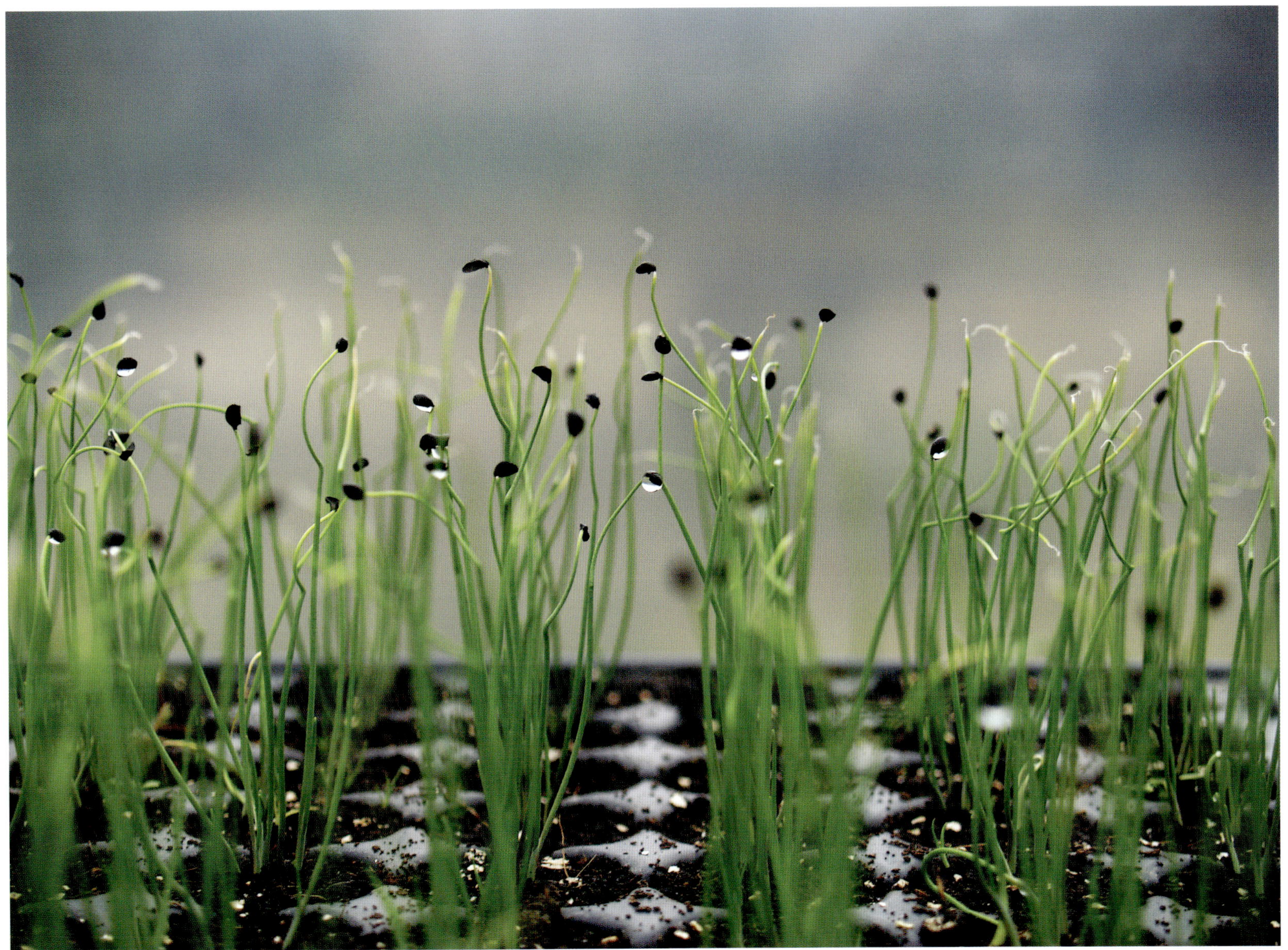

The inspiration for this photograph comes from the beauty and vulnerability of the tiny green onion (*Allium cepa*) shoots. The tray was sitting on a table inside the polytunnel. I held the camera in my hands and positioned it at the same level as the table and got as close as I could to the seedlings for the close-up shot.

This photograph was taken on an autumn morning, complete with mists and a lot of 'mellow fruitfulness'. The location was on the allotments in the centre of Bristol, and I was probably walking towards my own site thinking about what I was about to pick!

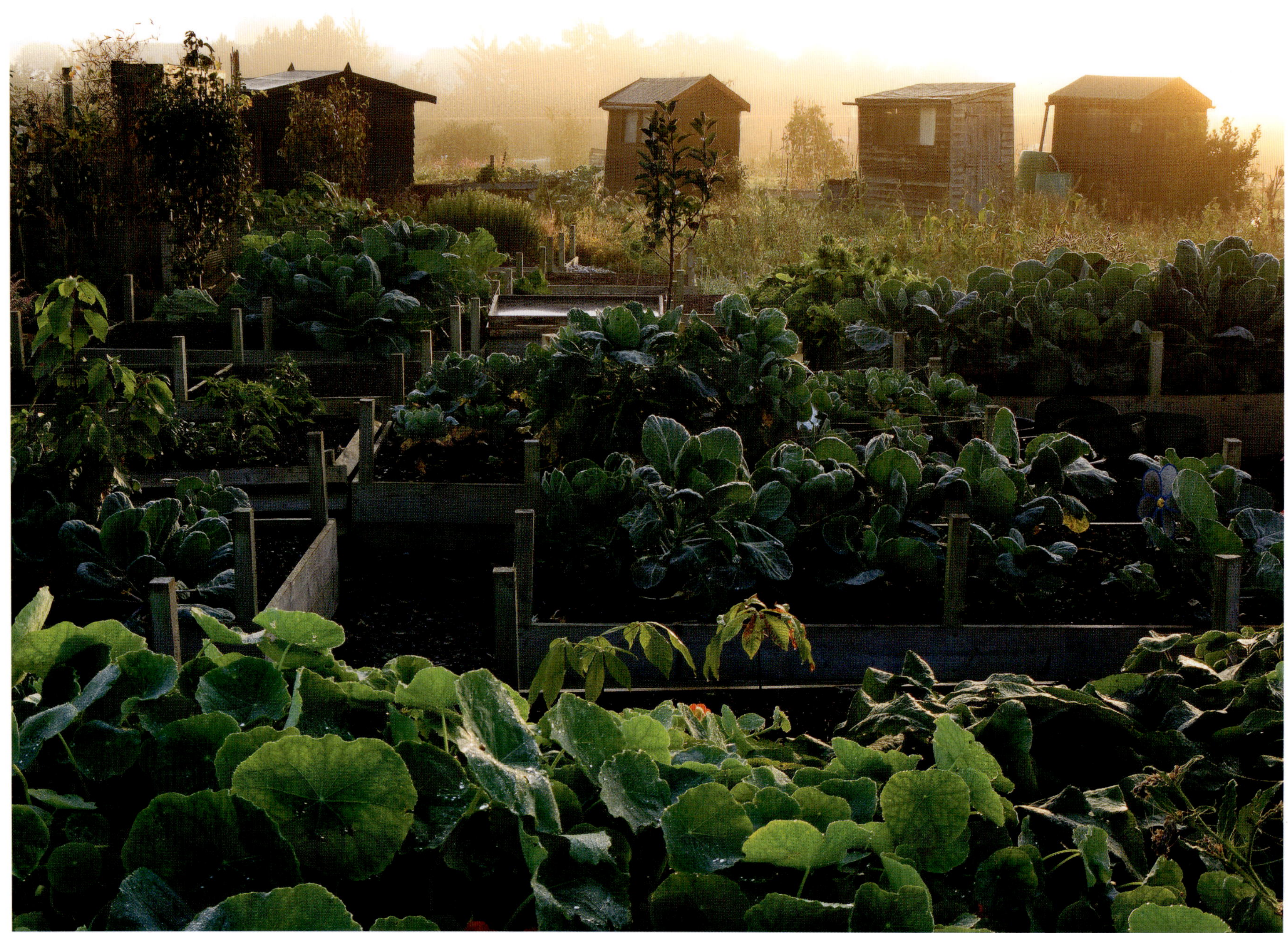

ALDERMAN MOORE'S ALLOTMENTS, BRISTOL, ENGLAND
AUTUMN MORNING DOWN ON THE ALLOTMENTS

MARK BOLTON

Canon G9 handheld, probably used my hand to screen the lens from flare.
FIRST, 2010

LONDON, ENGLAND

AUBERGINES 'FARMER'S LONG' WITH BORLOTTO BEAN 'FIRETONGUE'

JO WHITWORTH

Nikon D200, 105mm macro lens, f/5.6.
FINALIST, 2009

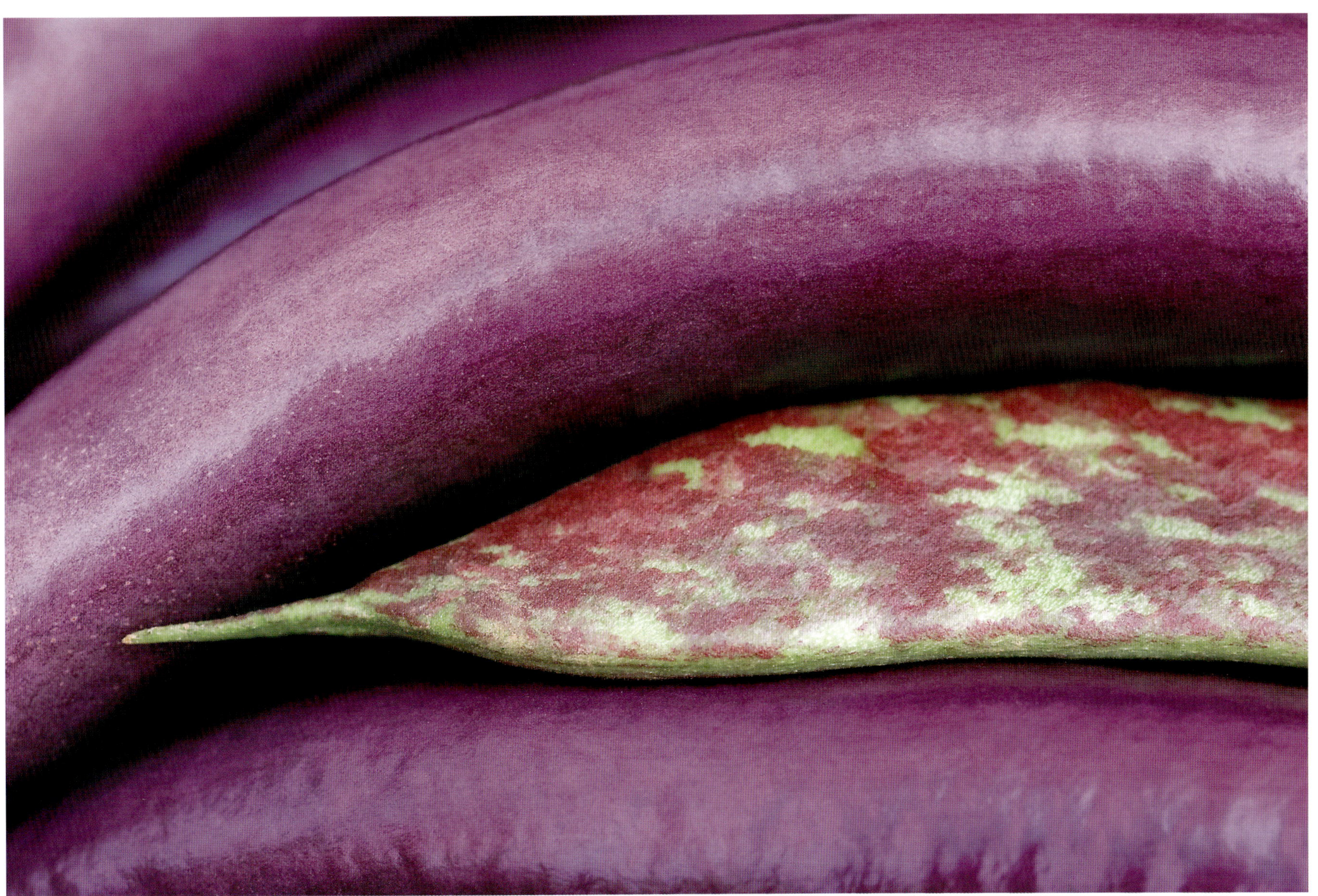

The strips of vibrant colour, broken up by the speckled bean, create an almost abstract image.

LOMBARDY
MELONE MODIGLIANI

CARLO SILVA

Nikon D200, Nikkor 18–200 VR, f/13.
THIRD, 2010

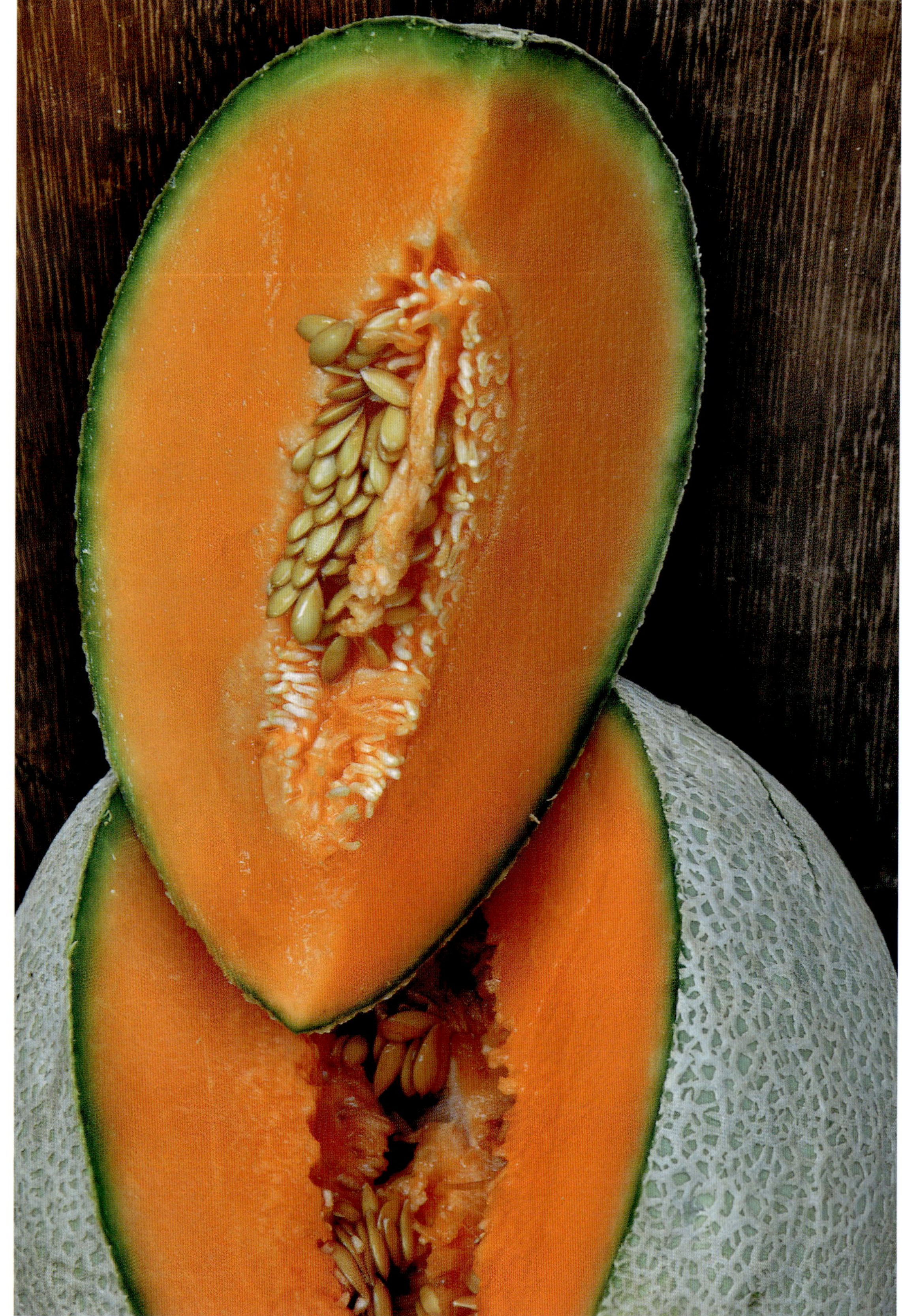

This is an interpretation of a natural product – an example of one of many original and particular gifts of the earth. The shot is inspired by Jeanne Hébuterne in a painting of Amedeo Modigliani.

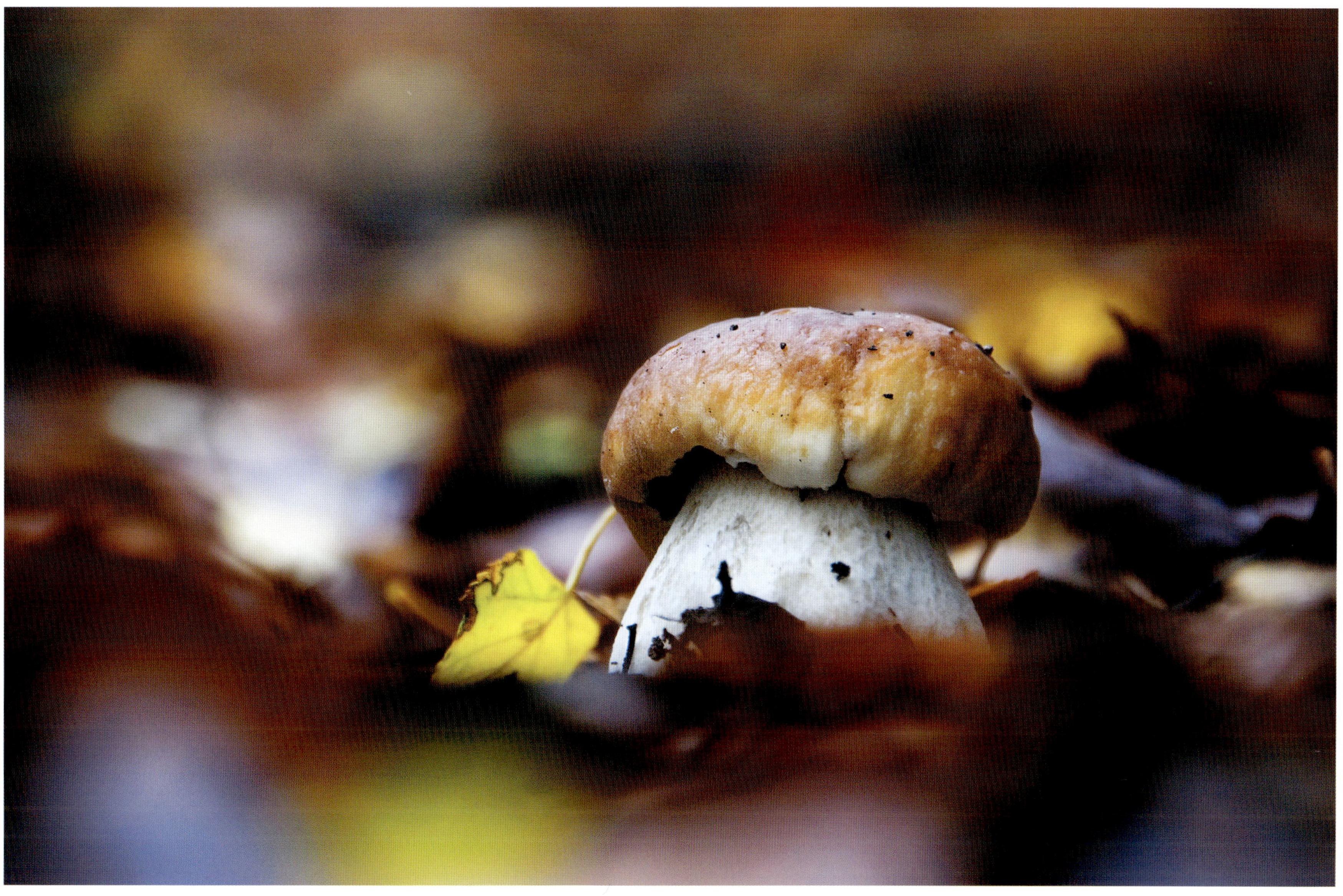

KENT, ENGLAND
DELICIOUS PORCINO

MAGDALENA KNIECKA

Nikon D80, Tamron 18-270mm lens, 1/13sec at f/6.2. Post-capture: I merged two shots to improve depth of field and sharpness.
THIRD, 2012

Boletus edulis, or porcino, is the king of edible mushrooms because of its aromatic, earthy-chestnut flavour. They are the colour of fallen leaves and are easy to overlook, so finding one is an exciting moment. This particular porcino was just a few hours old, untouched by snails. I love its distinctive texture, shape and colour. I gathered leaves to create a stable base for my camera to minimise any movement, and used very shallow depth of field to make the porcino stand out.

ERIC'S ALLOTMENT, KENT, ENGLAND

EL BONANZA

SUZIE GIBBONS

Pentax 645N, 70mm lens, Velvia 50, f/8. I just wanted Eric to be himself, so we chatted and joked and I snapped away. I only wanted to focus on Eric and the name of his allotment so used an aperture of f/8 and handheld the camera to keep it informal.

SECOND, 2008

Eric simply radiates with the joy of growing his own produce. He comes here to relax, too, and enjoy the camaraderie of the allotments. Eric's big personality inspired me – he was a natural in front of the camera and we had great fun shooting this portrait.

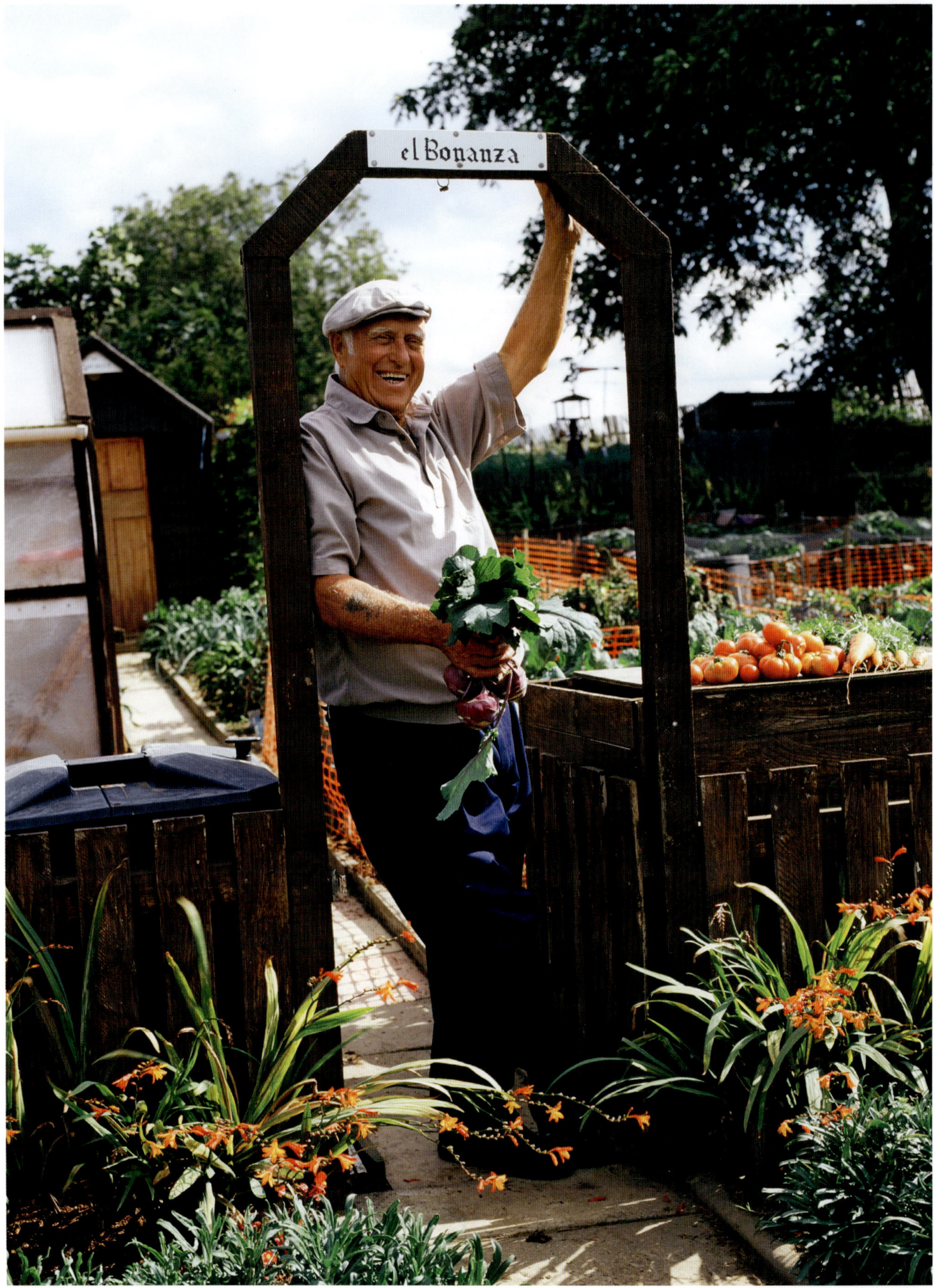

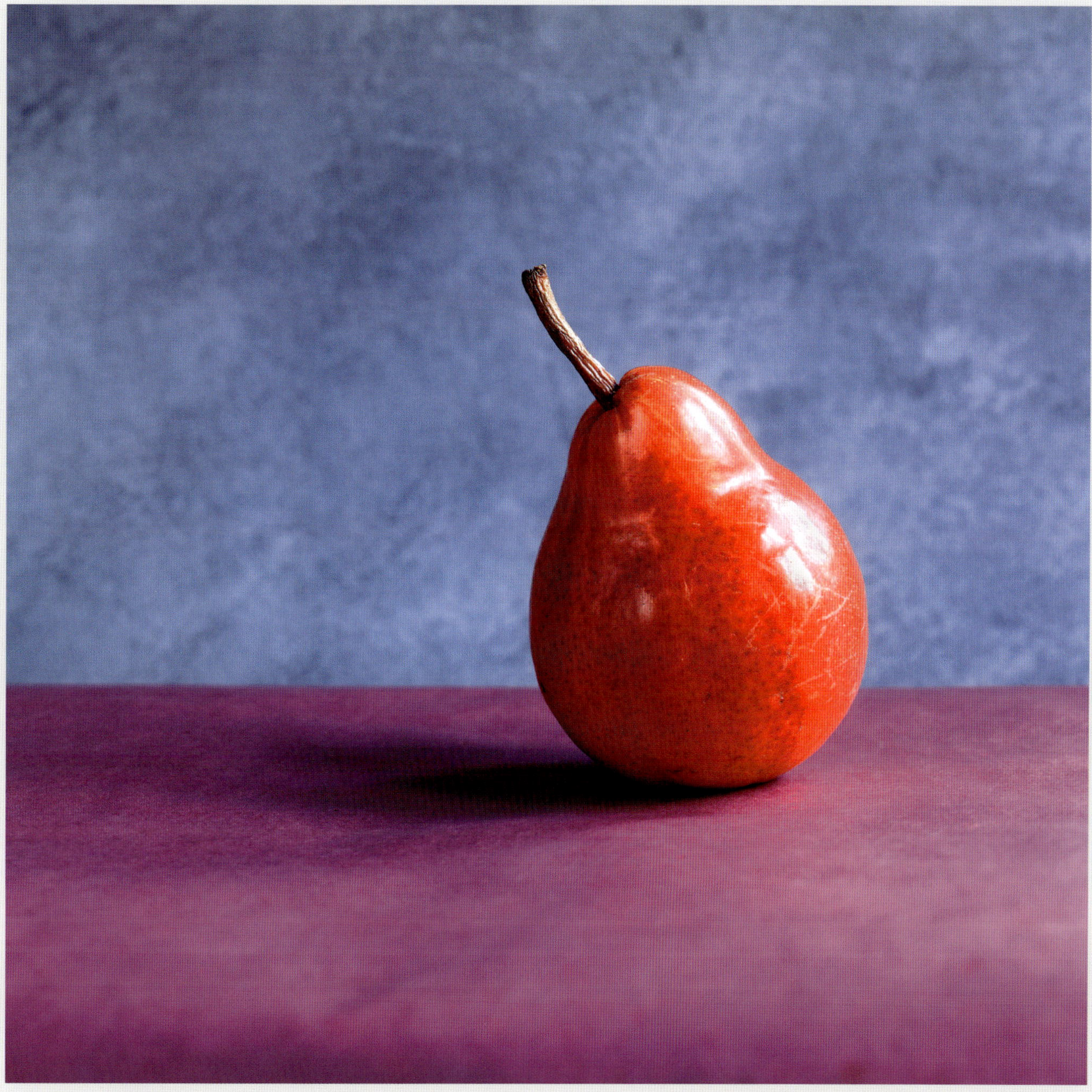

MY HOME, CALGARY, ALBERTA
RED PEAR SQUARE

DAVID BALLANTYNE

Fujifilm Velvia 50. 4x5 Cambo SC 135mm.
Post-capture: cropped to square format.
HIGHLY COMMENDED, 2012

I had purchased a few red pears (*Pyrus communis*) with the intention of photographing them indoors as it was early winter and not much was happening in the snow-covered garden. I liked the colour of the pear against the blue wall and added the wrapping paper as a third colour to the composition. I placed the pear near a window and used the north light to light the pear. I felt a square crop created better balance in the final composition.

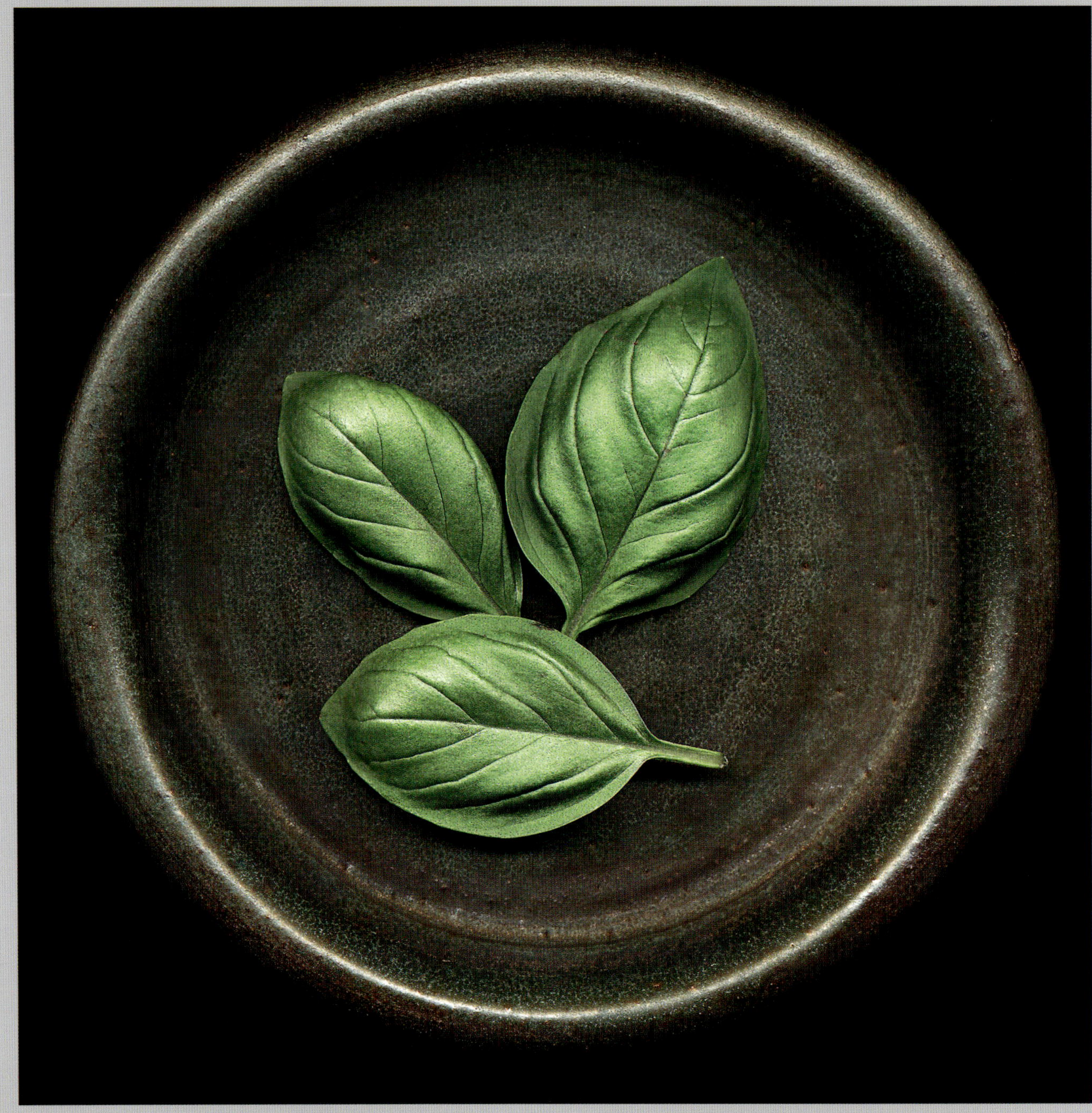

I love the smell of basil, and wanted somehow to evoke this in my image, so emphasised the deep, saturated green of the leaves.

BASILDON, ESSEX, ENGLAND
FRESHLY PICKED SWEET BASIL LEAVES (*BASILICUM*)

DEE FISH

Epson Perfection 2480 Photo flatbed scanner.
SECOND, 2009

In this picture, a young gardener is shown harvesting her first carrot. I was touched by the closeness between mother and daughter as they explored the plants and insects in their community garden plot. The mother was a very gentle and intuitive teacher, guiding her daughter while allowing her to explore at her own pace. I crouched at plant-height to be unobtrusive. Mother and child were completely involved in their activity so I was able to capture their natural exploration of the garden. When the child held up the carrot, it was the result of her excitement, not my direction.

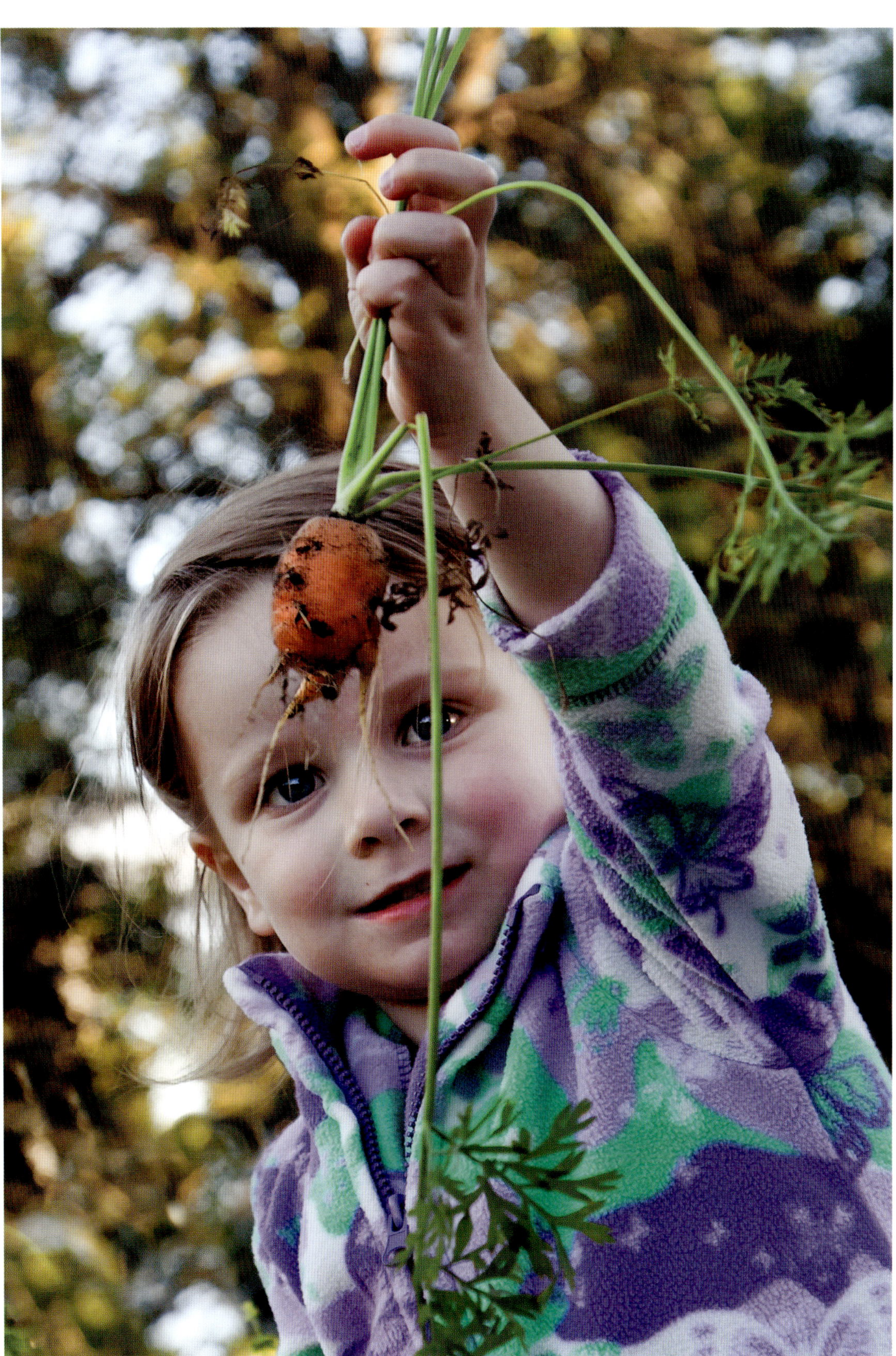

A COMMUNITY GARDEN IN TORONTO, ONTARIO
FIRST HARVEST

LAURA BERMAN

Canon EOS 5D Mark II, 24-105mm lens, 1/200sec at f/5.6. Post-capture: basic RAW processing, colour management, selective sharpening and noise reduction. It was cropped from a horizontal format to a vertical one, to exclude the mother and distracting elements and to concentrate attention on the child's face.
HIGHLY COMMENDED, 2011

I made the shape of a wine glass out of rosemary (*Rosmarinus officinalis*), dill (*Anethum graveolens*), chervil (*Anthriscus cerefolium*), white and purple lavender (*Lavandula* spp.) and strawberries (*Fragaria* x *ananassa*)– the bouquet of flavours found in certain white wines.

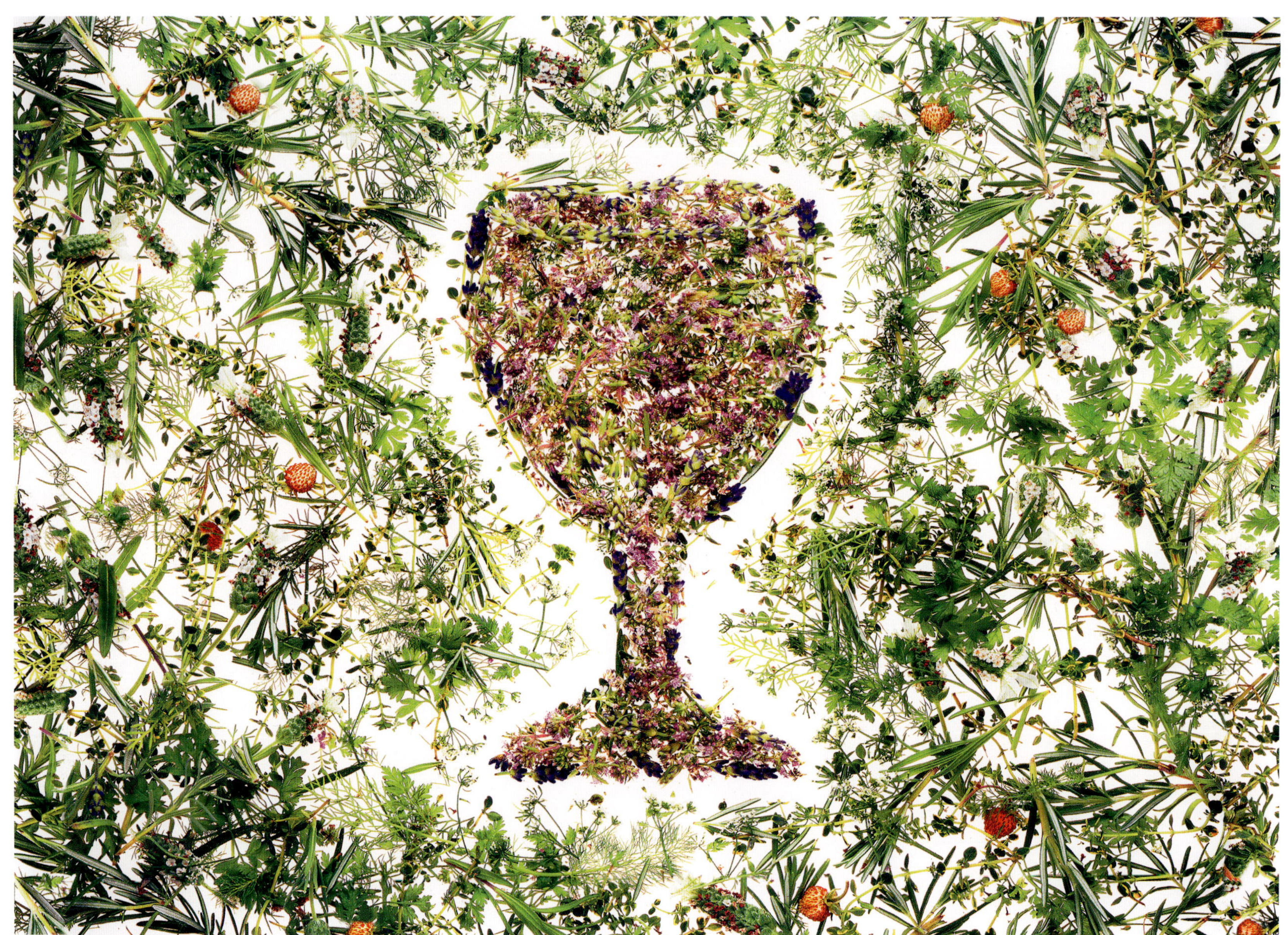

LONDON, ENGLAND

WINE BOUQUET

JOHANNA PARKIN

Sinar F2, Fuji Velvia 100. I love to create shapes out of shapes, objects created out of their own essence, making an image that has more than one facet to it. In this case I wanted to make a fresh, bold, vivid image which is as full of summer, vitality and crisp colourful delicacy as the essence of what makes the image up.

FINALIST, 2009

STUDIO, NORFOLK, ENGLAND
HERITAGE PURPLE PODDED PEA

CAROL SHARP

Leaf Aptus 65 back on a Sinar 5x4 camera, 150mm
SECOND, 2010

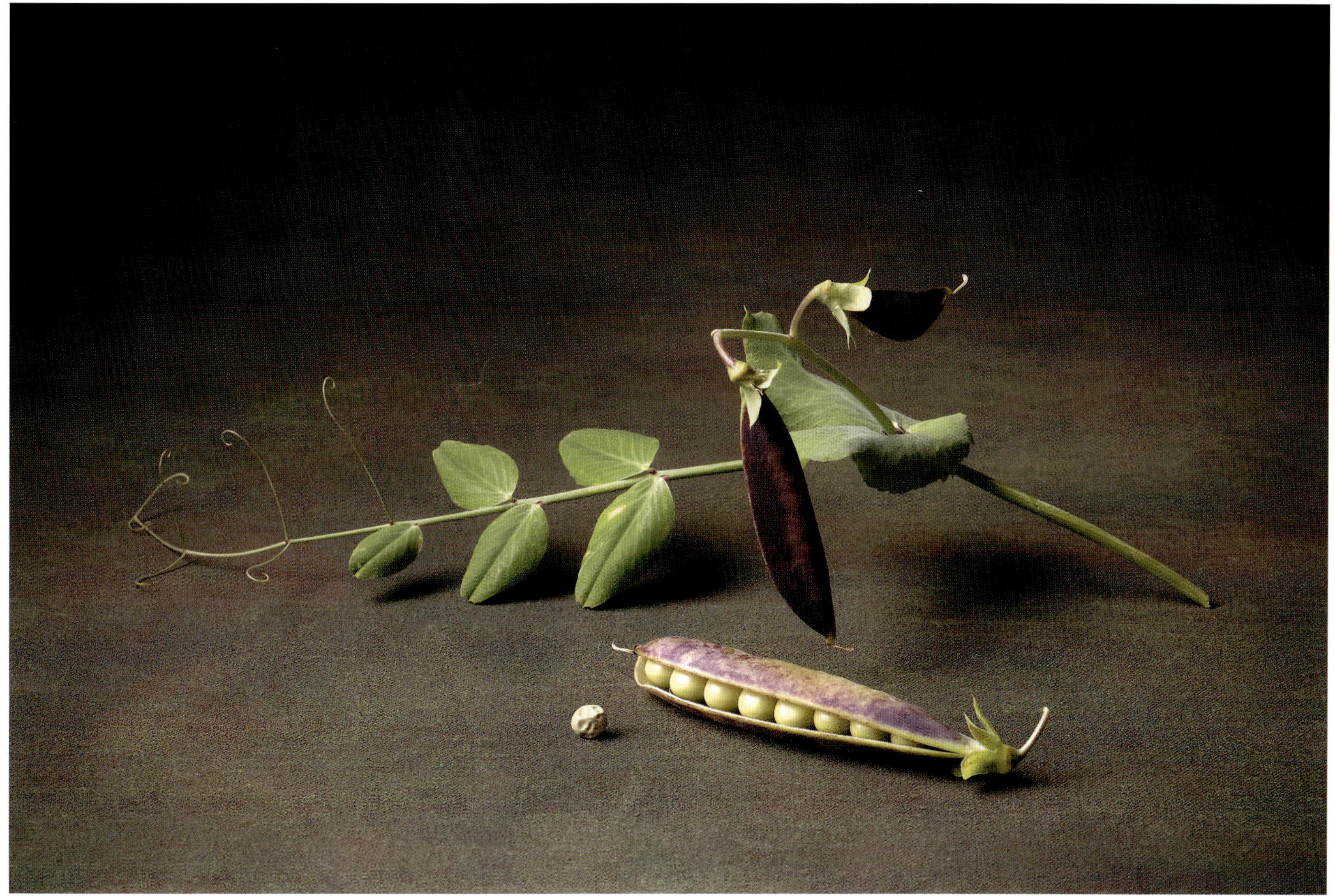

I grew these purple podded peas (*Pisum sativa*) from seeds from Garden Organic's Heritage Seed Library, as part of a self-initiated project to find beautiful and garden-worthy heritage vegetable varieties from their library. The seeds are being saved for our future biodiversity – they are our heirlooms. This was my favourite. I painted the background and composed the shot to evoke the mood of an old master's still life painting. *Pisum sativum* 'purple podded' is a heritage variety supplied by Garden Organic. This is a great garden worthy plant with beautiful bicolour burgundy and pink flowers, followed by the rich burgundy pods, mottling with green as they ripen.

THE EDIBLE GARDEN

SUE STUBBS

Canon EOS-1D Mark III, Canon EF 24-70mm f/2.8 lens. The idea was to use these simple shapes in natural light to create a still life study with softness and depth that would draw you into the image. The backgrounds were layered with paint to add rich colour and texture, creating a painterly mood.
COMMENDED, 2009

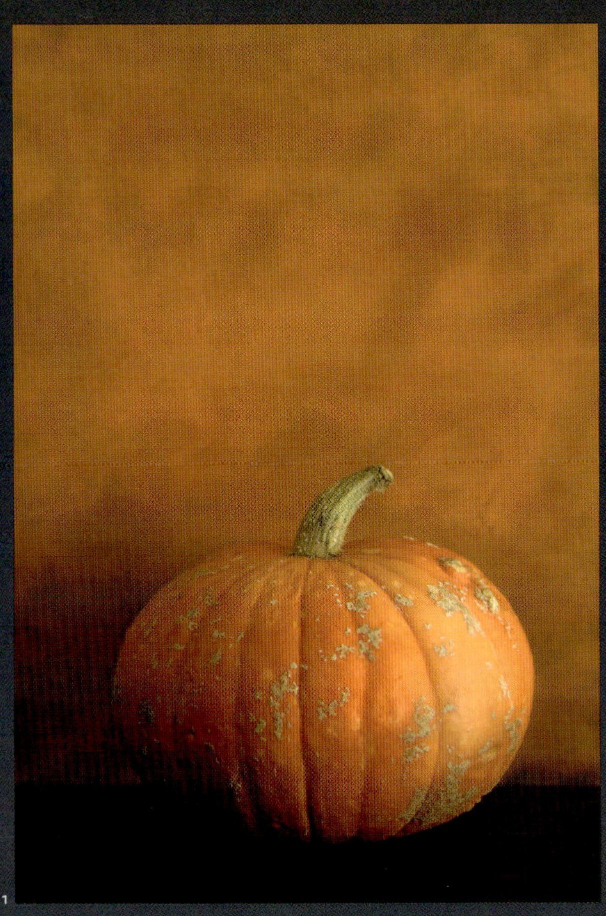

1

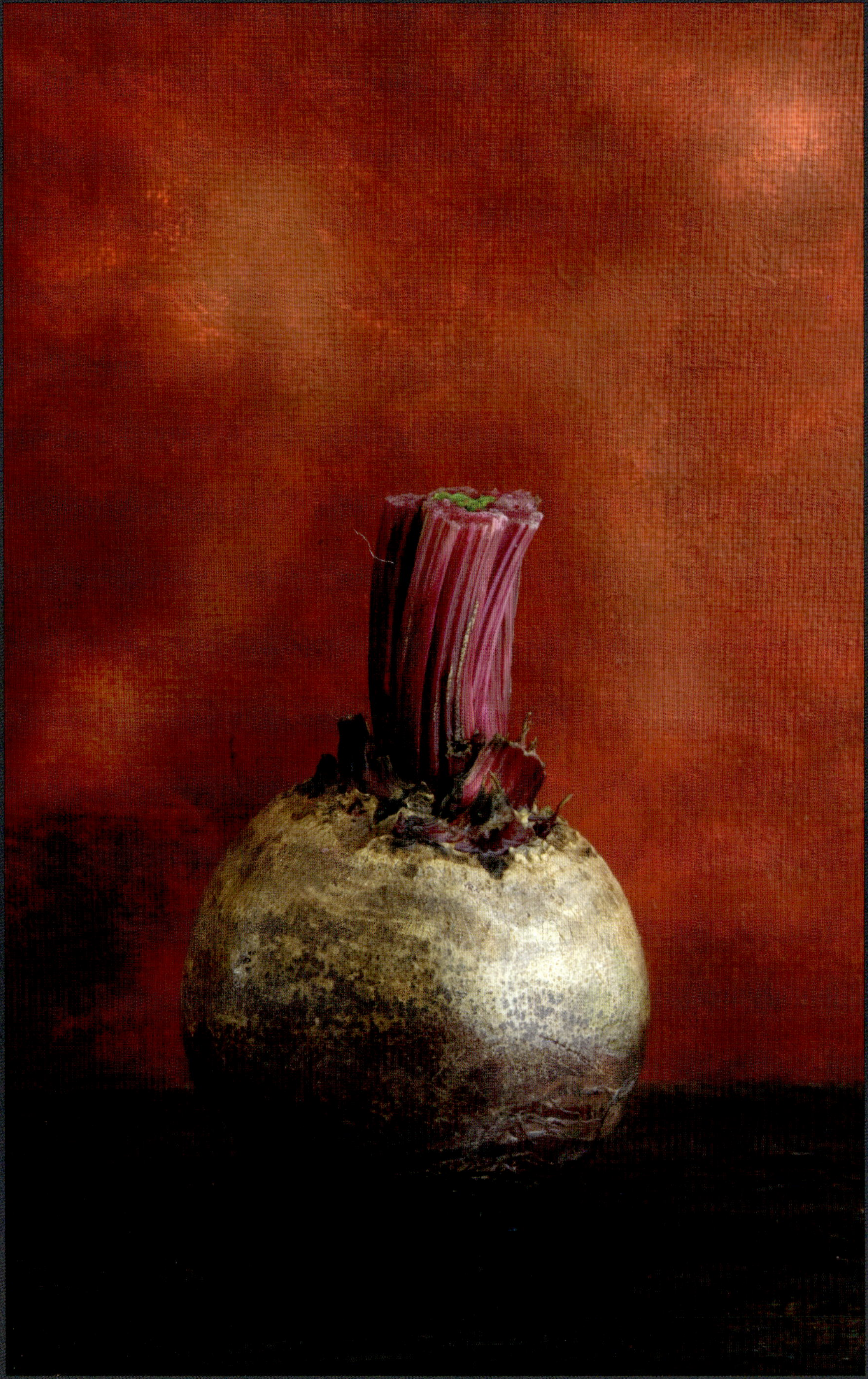

2

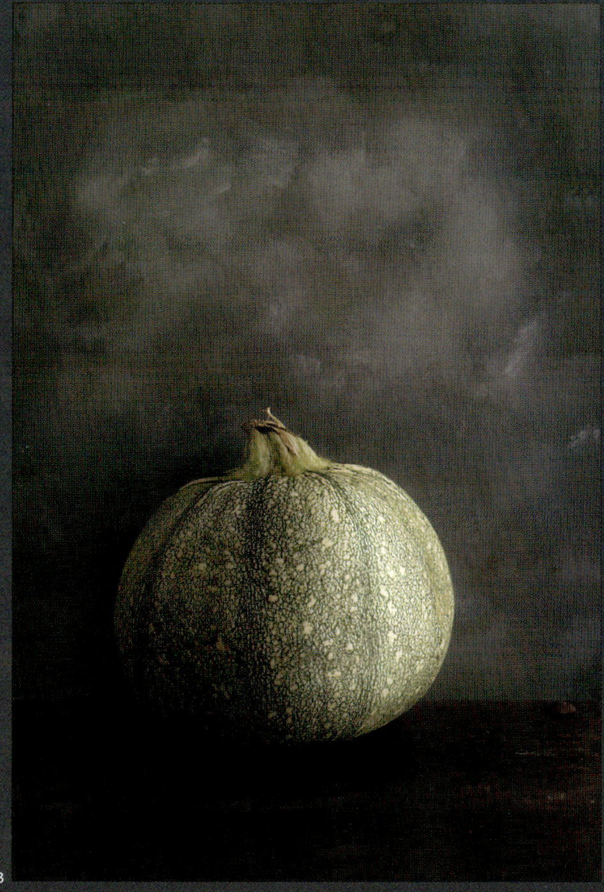
3

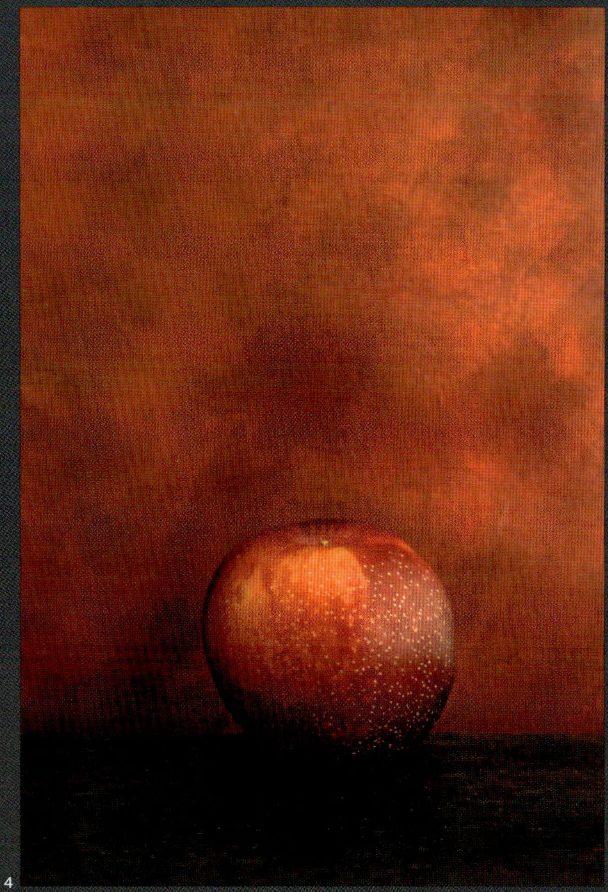
4

With this portfolio I wanted to convey the sheer beauty of both everyday and exotic edibles. Their shape, colour and texture is shown in its simplest and purest form, each against a background painted with acrylics, while the colour and texture gives a different complexion to these fruit and vegetables, which are often taken for granted.

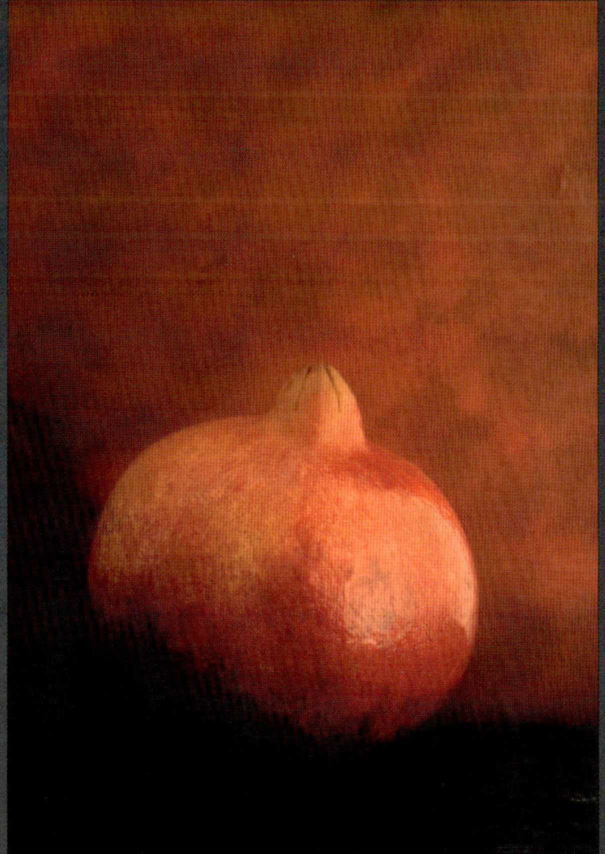
5

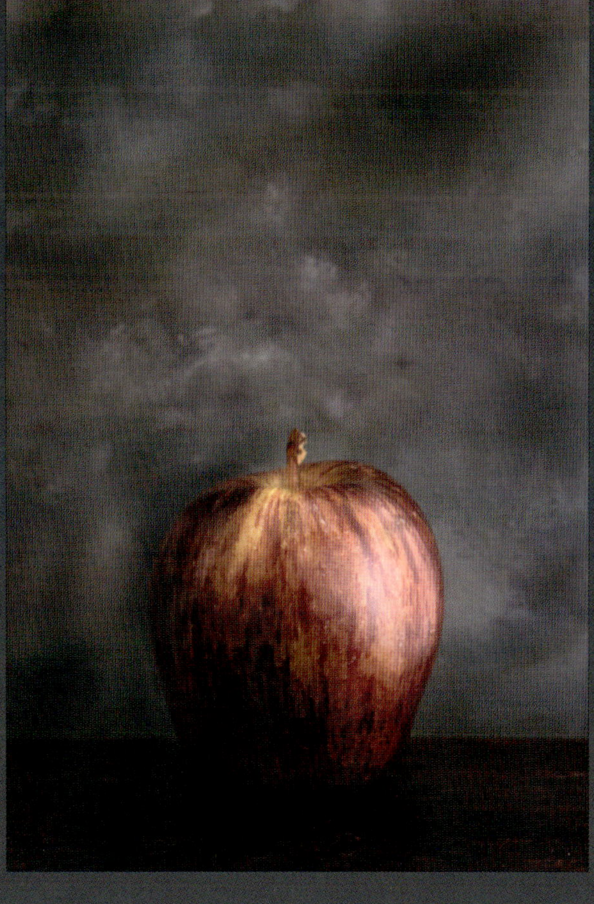
6

1–*Pumpkin* (*Cucurbita* spp.) Golden nugget pumpkin on orange background.

2–*Beetroot* (*Beta vulgaris*) Beetroot on red background.

3–*Zucchini* (*Cucurbita pepo*) Round grey zucchini on grey background.

4–*Plum* (*Prunus* spp.)Plum on red background.

5–*Pomegranate* (*Punica granatum*) Pomegranate on red background.

6–*Apple* (*Malus domestica*) Delicious apple on grey background.

CALNE, WILTSHIRE, ENGLAND

VELVET SHANK FUNGUS (*FLAMMULINA VELUTIPES*)

DAVID MAITLAND

Canon EOS-1Ds Mark II. This clump was at about chest height on the tree. I wanted an interesting angle to emphasise the gill structure, so crouched down beneath to look up into the canopy for a view from below. This also places the fungus in its habitat.

FINALIST, 2009

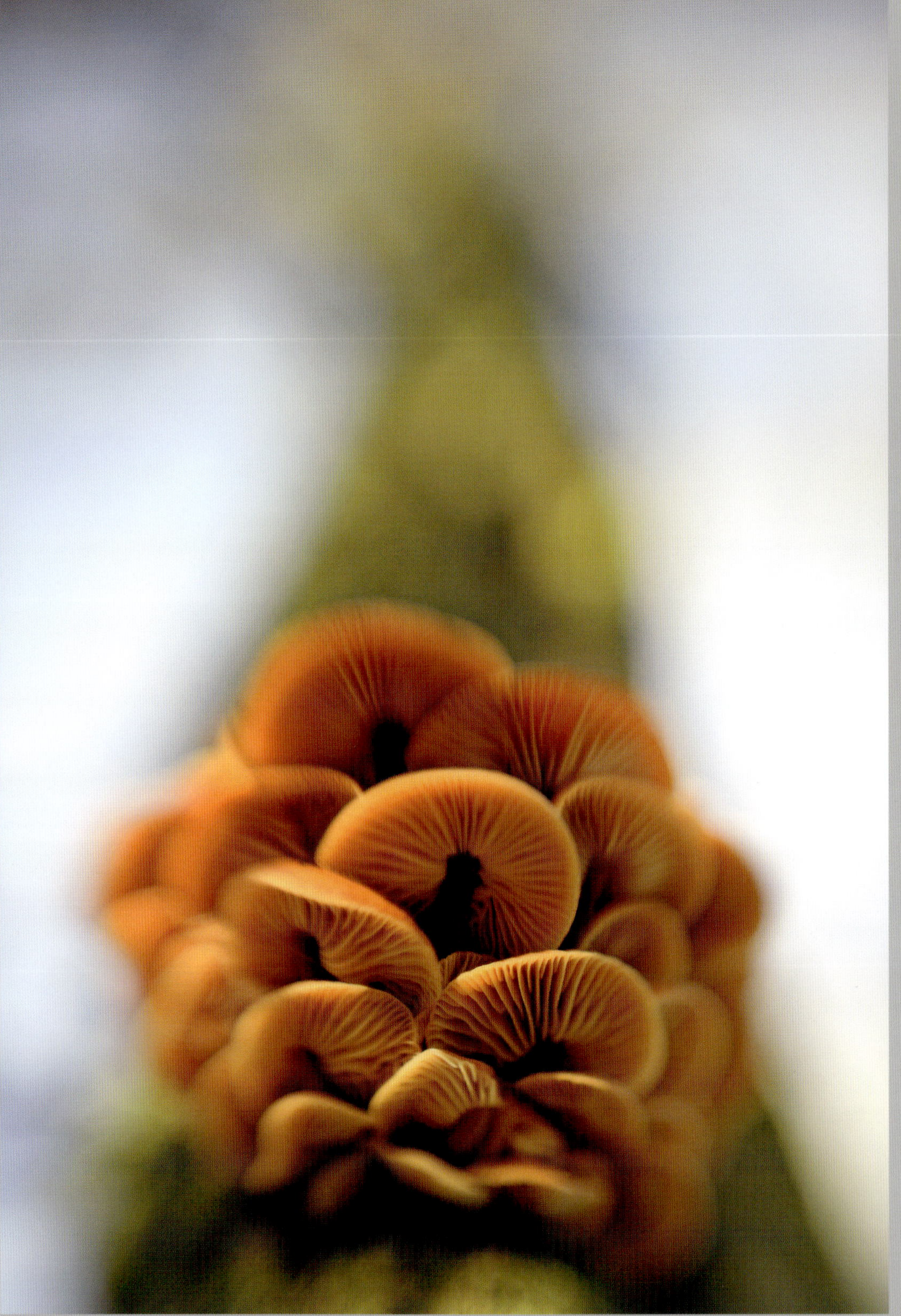

This edible fungus grows on deciduous trees – a young dead oak, in this case. I love fungi. Not only are many of them good to eat, but also they have a wonderful and beautiful architecture.

The pergola that contains the Lagenaria National Collection of gourds (fam. *Cucurbitaceae*) is a full 110 metres long, and features almost every size and form of these fascinating plants. It was just one highlight in an assignment to photograph the castle gardens of the Loire.

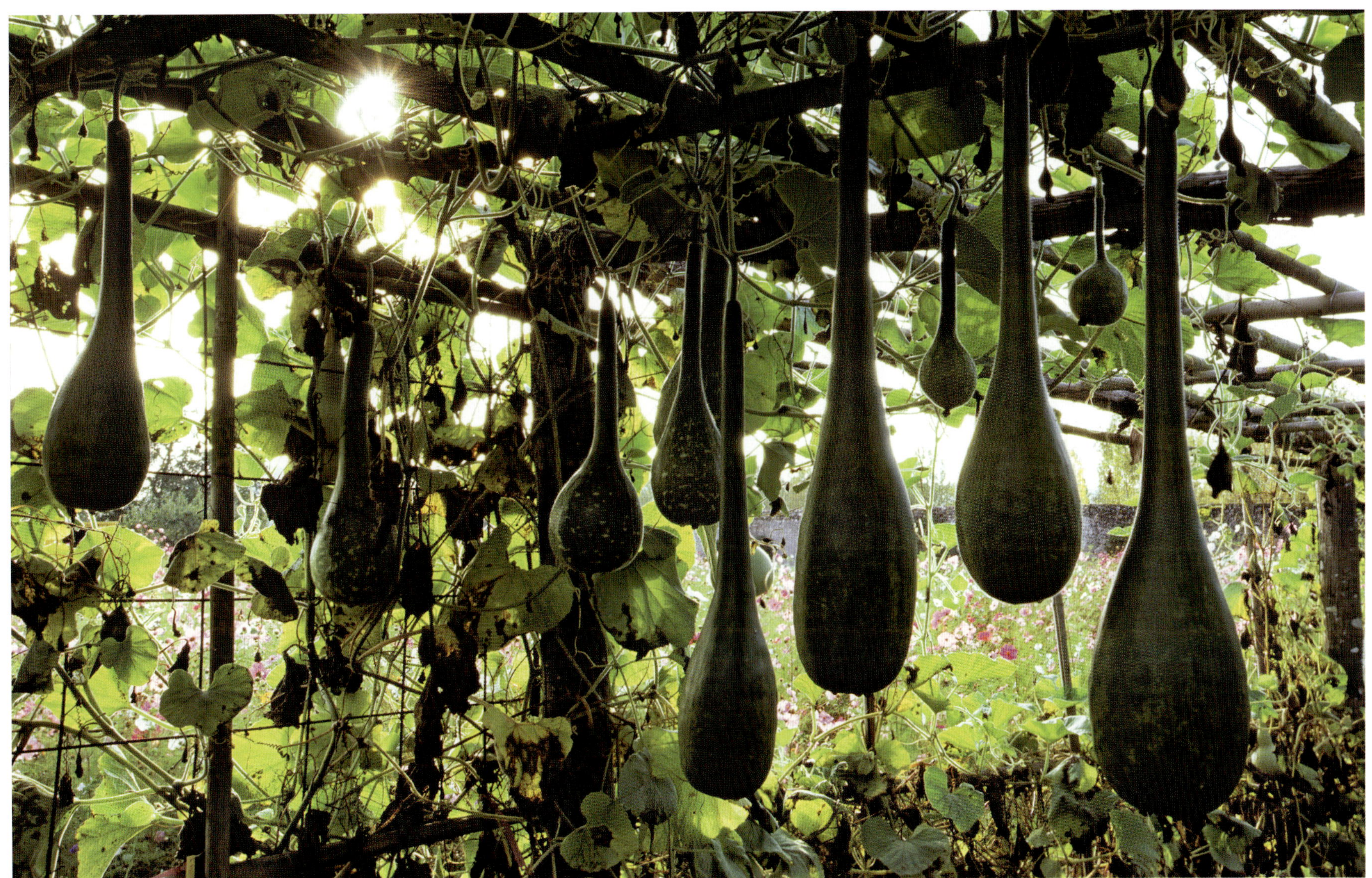

CHÂTEAU DE VALMER, VOUVRAY
THE GOURD TUNNEL

GARY ROGERS

Nikon F3, AF-S Nikkor 17-35mm zoom lens, Fuji Velvia, f/16.
FINALIST, 2009

BRISTOL, ENGLAND

THE HANDS THAT PICK THE FOOD THAT I EAT

JASON INGRAM

Nikon D2x and Nikon D3x, 60mm macro lens, approximately 1/125sec at f/4 for all the shots. Post-capture: the images were converted to black and white. I then wanted to split-tone the images to have warmth in the highlights and coolness in the shadows. This is very similar to how I used to work in the darkroom. The additional processing work was all to do with getting the mid-contrast range just how I wanted it, with sumptuous darker tones and rich detail.
RPS BRONZE MEDAL, 2011

I was very inspired by a collection of work by the great photographer Tessa Traeger, who worked closely with French peasants and the food they produced. I wanted to evoke a similar feeling by working purely with the hands, showing the freshly picked produce as an extension of the people who had grown it. This portfolio was shot after shooting something similar commercially for a chain of garden centres. I really wanted to do justice to the subject and decided to shoot it as a personal project. I wanted everything to look as real and as 'rough around the edges' as possible.

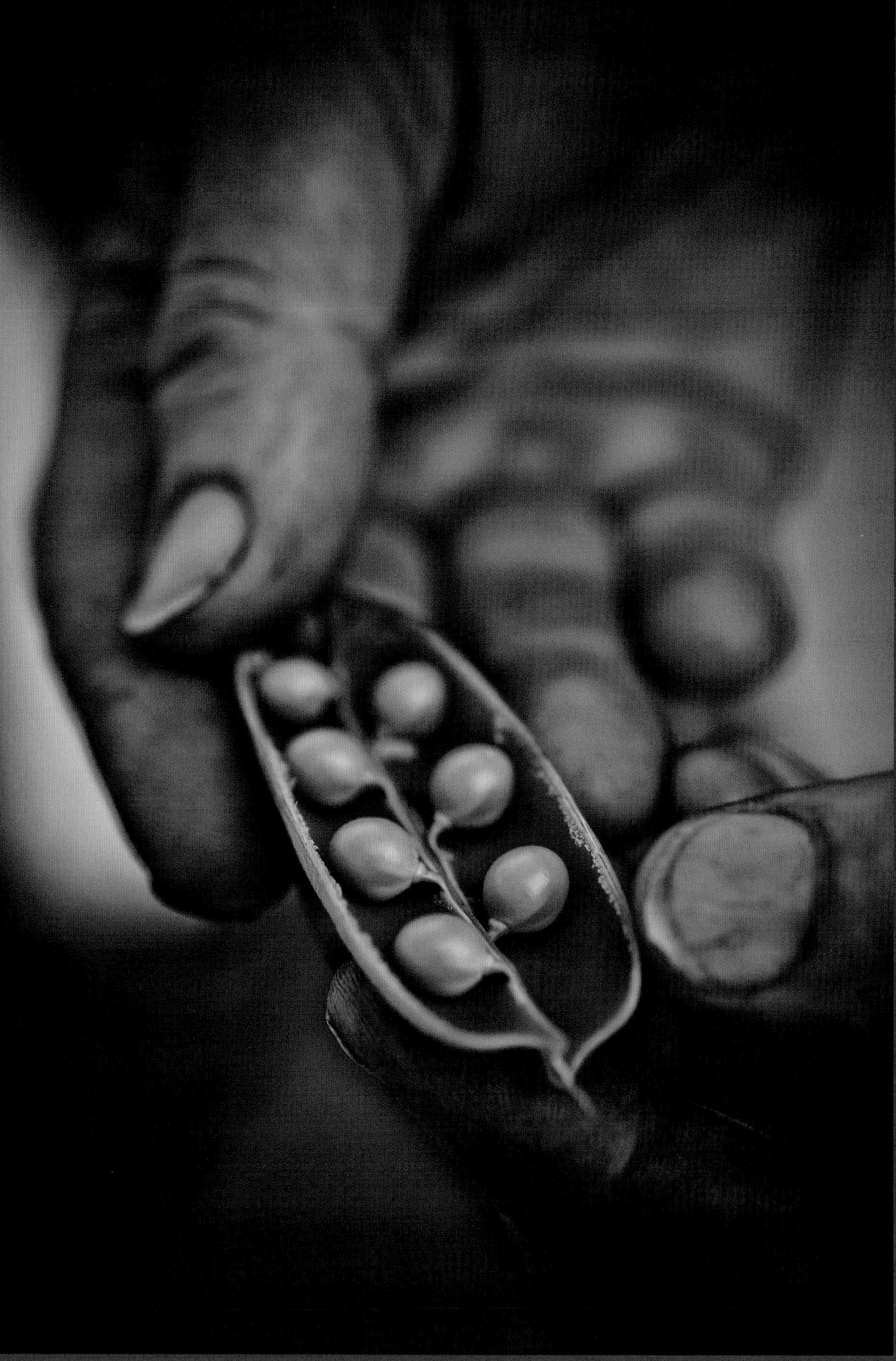

1

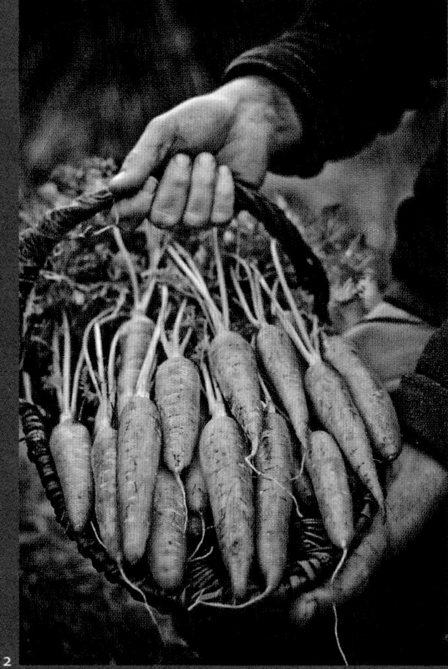
2

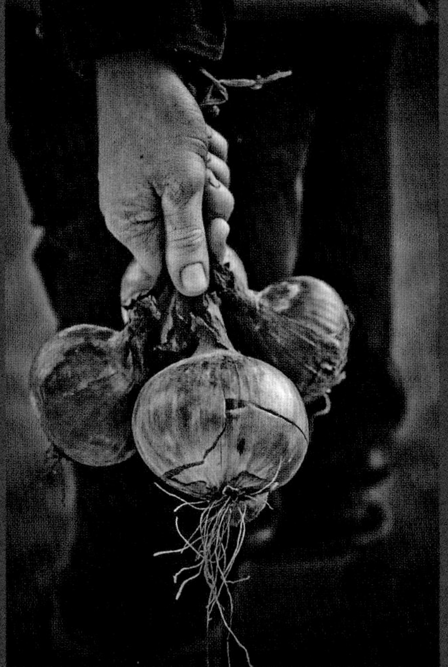
3

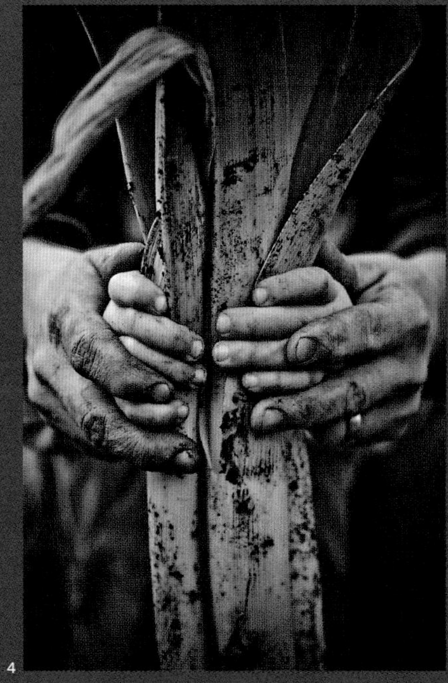
4

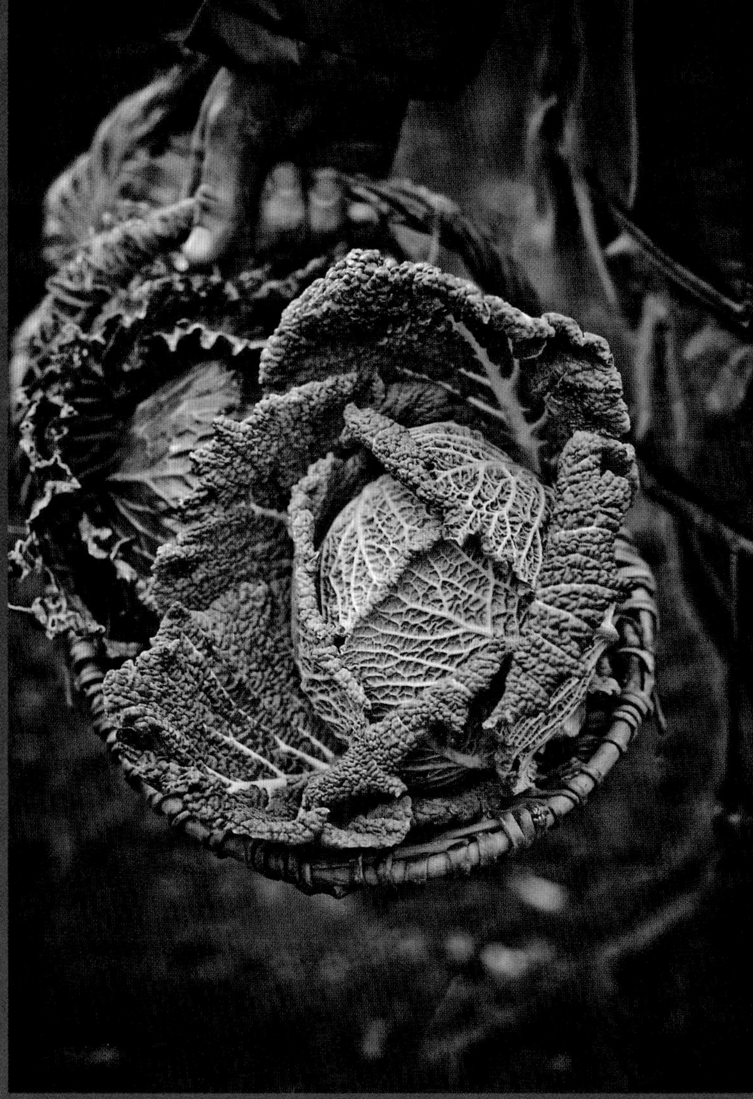
5

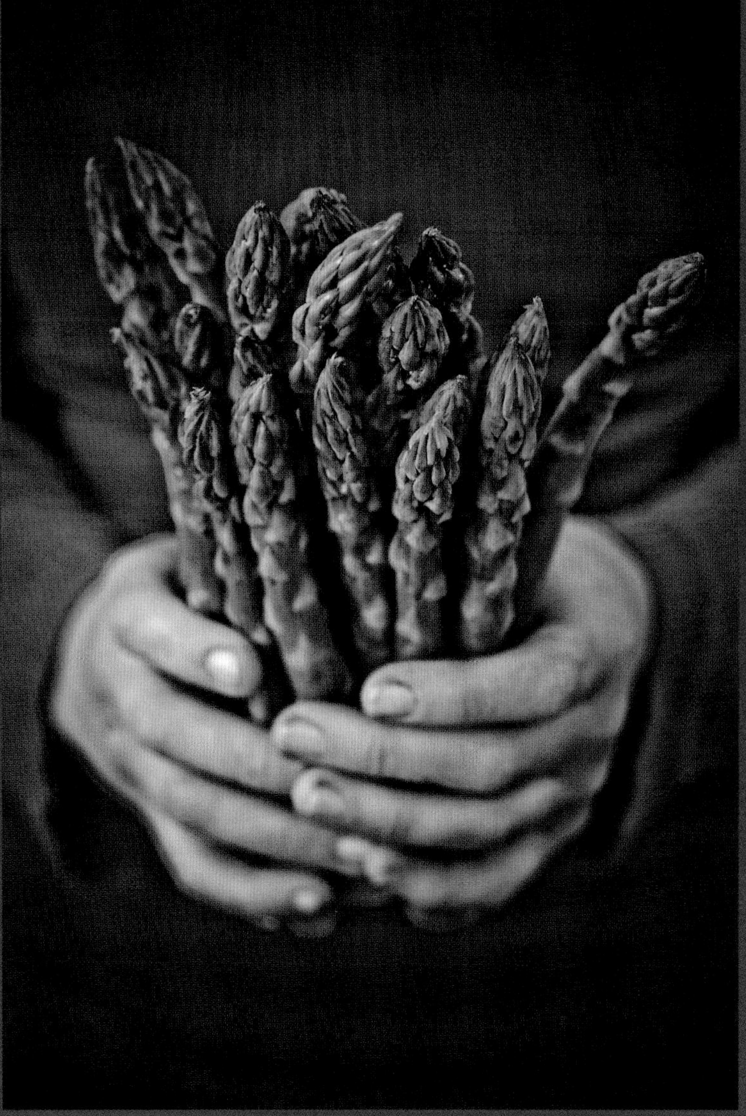
6

1–Peas (*Pisum sativum*).
2–Carrots (*Daucus carota*).
3–Onions (*Allium cepa*).
4–Leeks (*Allium porrum*).
5–Savoy Cabbage (*Brassica oleracea*).
6–Asparagus (*Asparagus officinalis*).

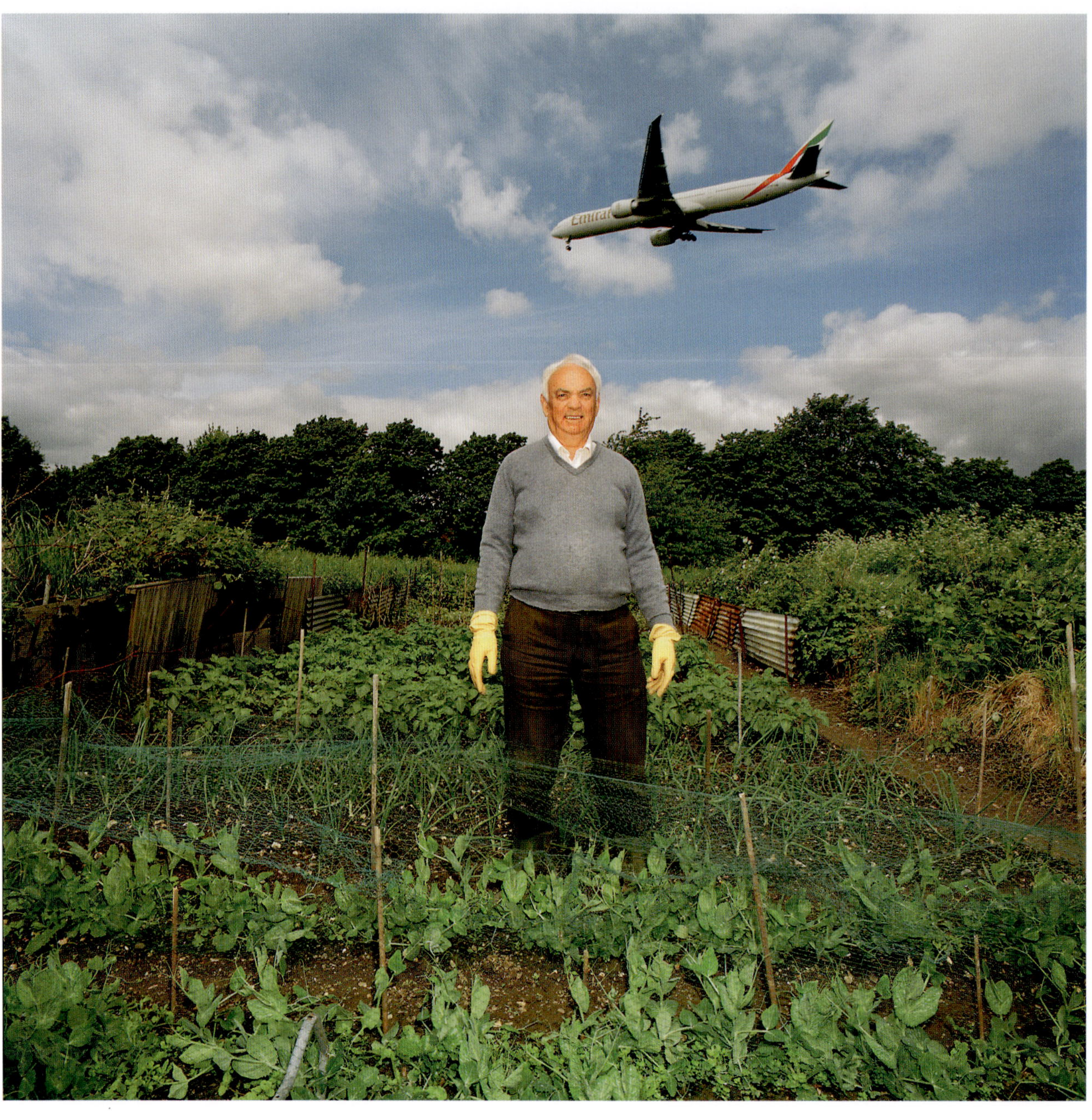

Les has been working this allotment for 40 years, so he has seen and certainly heard the changes that Heathrow Airport has gone through over this time. With this in mind, I wanted to develop and contrast the two worlds we see in the photograph. On the one hand we have an historic British pastime and a sublime and wondrous world where time stands still; on the other we have a representation and embodiment of progress and change with all its noise and negative aspects. I visited the allotment a number of times before I took my camera as it was nice to talk to Les and get to know him first. The shot presented itself early into the project as the contrast between the natural and unnatural was immediately apparent.

AN ALLOTMENT OFF THE A312, NEXT TO HEATHROW AIRPORT, ENGLAND
ENVIRONMENT VERSUS PROGRESS

MARCUS HARVEY

Bronica SQ-A, 40mm lens, Fuji Provia 400.
Post-capture: no digital alterations.
FINALIST, 2011

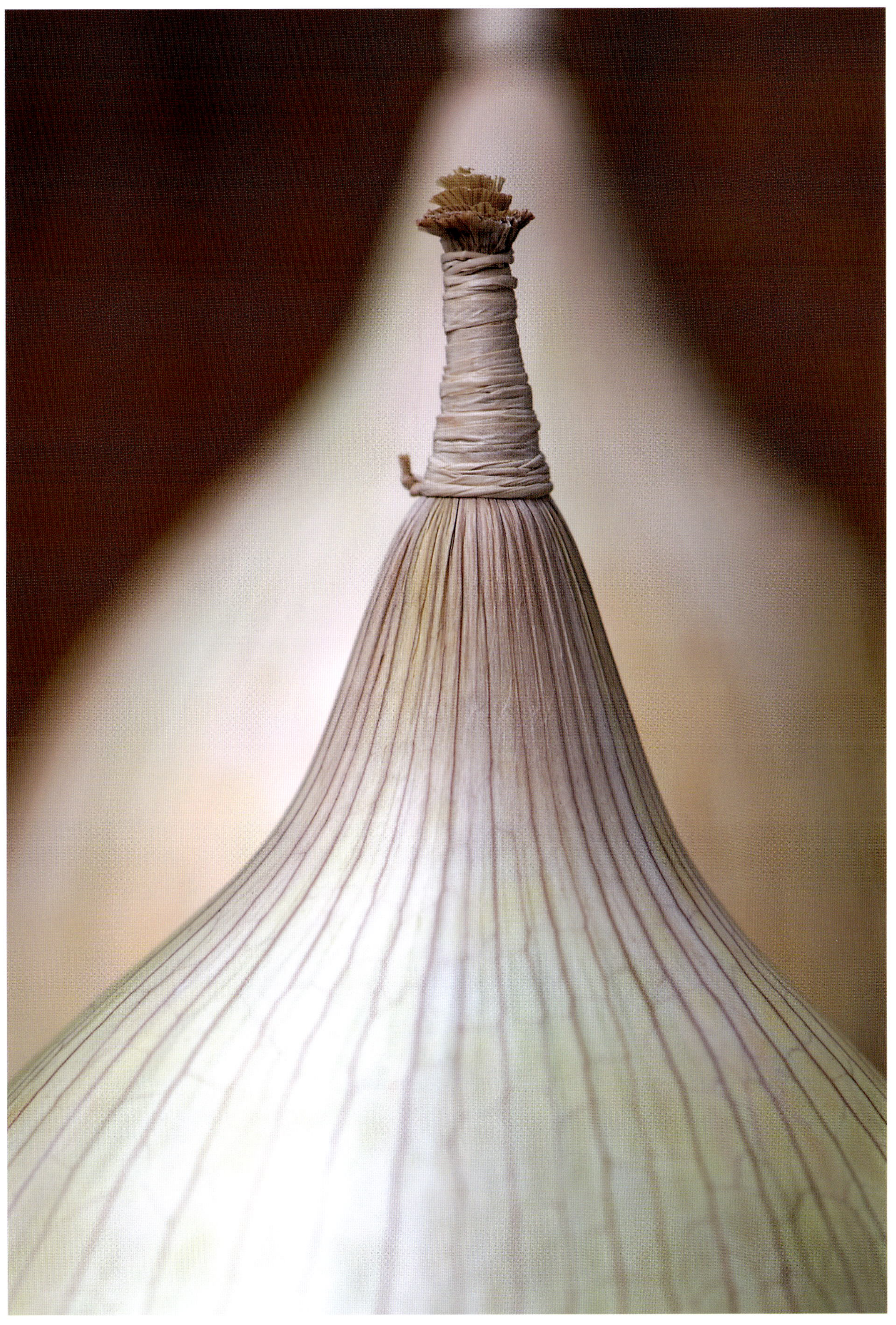

This prize-winning onion (*Allium cepa*), entered by Mr H. Thomas, was on display at the Royal Horticultural Society's annual autumn show, and just cried out for a close-up. 'Biggest vegetable' competitions still hold great appeal all over the country, and this is what attracted me to document the event.

THE ROYAL HORTICULTURAL HALLS, LONDON, ENGLAND

PRIZE-WINNING ONION 'KELSAE'

JO WHITWORTH

Nikon D200, 105mm macro lens, f/4. This particular onion stood out for its graphic simplicity, with its twine binding complementing its own stripes, and the larger onion framing it behind. I made the sepia image to link this photo, taken in the 21st century, to its history dating back for generations.

THIRD, 2009

GARDEN WILDLIFE

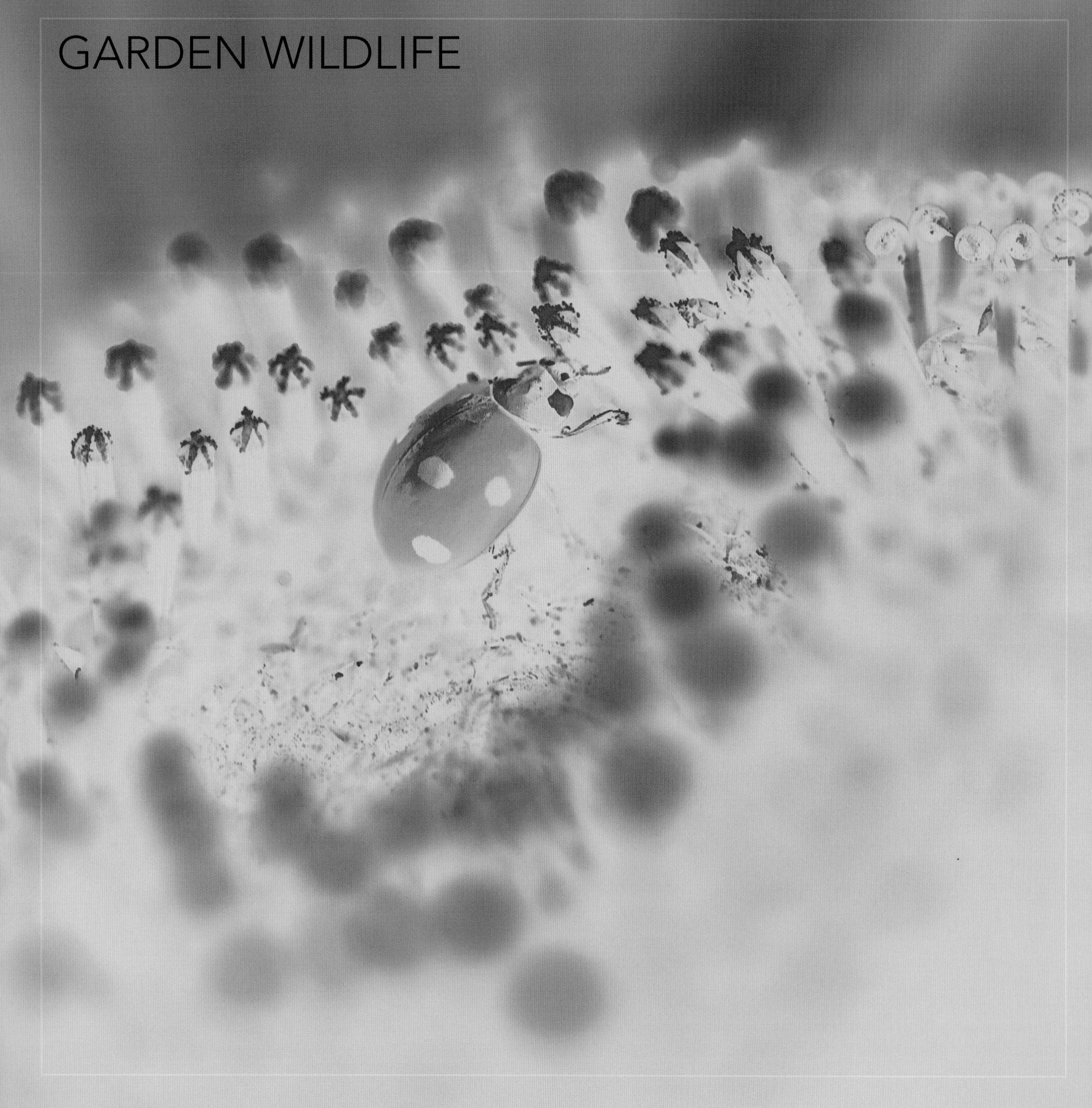

Garden Wildlife

It has been estimated that we share this planet with 13 million different living species – from microscopic viruses to the largest mammals and plants. But we have only named around 1.75 million of these species; we still know relatively little about the great web of life around us and of which we are but one part. Any disappearance of a species is a profound loss as it affects other species connected to it and the habitat it once lived in. One of the main aims of Kew's work is to find, collect, record, map and name new species of plants and discover how they fit into the habitats in which they are found; in essence, to increase the knowledge of plant life. Such knowledge is vital if we are all to conserve and restore habitats to protect the health of our planet.

You may think such high aims are far removed from your own little plot of land but every garden plays host to an amazing number of species – from insects, soil fungi and bacteria, to the wide range of birds and mammals that come to visit. They may not sound as exciting as tigers, pandas or orangutans but supporting these species is important, they are all individuals in an intricate food chain and part of our own local biodiversity – your garden is part of the wider natural world after all. Photographing these wild visitors and neighbours can be a great joy but can also fundamentally help us to understand them.

I am a keen photographer but I know there is little chance I could attain the high standards that are entered into International Garden Photographer of the Year. I always leave on judging day both enthused and envious in equal measure. Our passion for photography is significant though – for what is a photographer without their muse? Without the conservation of our wild places and the care of our own garden spaces, there would be nothing to photograph, nothing to get excited about from a photographer's point of view. The more that images such as these can inspire people about the wonder of the natural world, the more everyone will want to conserve it in its entirety.

The range and standard of images that are sent in to the International Garden Photographer of the Year is breathtaking. Apart from the heavenly garden photography there are thousands of stunning shots of birds in people's gardens, images of beautiful wildflower meadows and even macro images of creepy-looking insects. They are all deeply inspiring. I have always loved natural history and photography; I studied ecology at university and now love communicating the importance of biodiversity through words and images in my day-to-day work. I have felt very privileged to be involved in the judging of the International Garden Photographer of the Year as it has shown me how much other people love the natural world around them too, and want to portray it and share it in the most striking way. Is there a better way to put a camera to good use?

Christina Harrison
Editor, *Kew* magazine

I really wanted to show a subject that is often regarded as unappealing, in an attractive way. I had seen a toad underneath a toadstool beside our garden pond and wanted to capture the scene in a photograph, so I created an arrangement of leaves around a toadstool, introduced a toad to it, and it moved itself into the position seen.

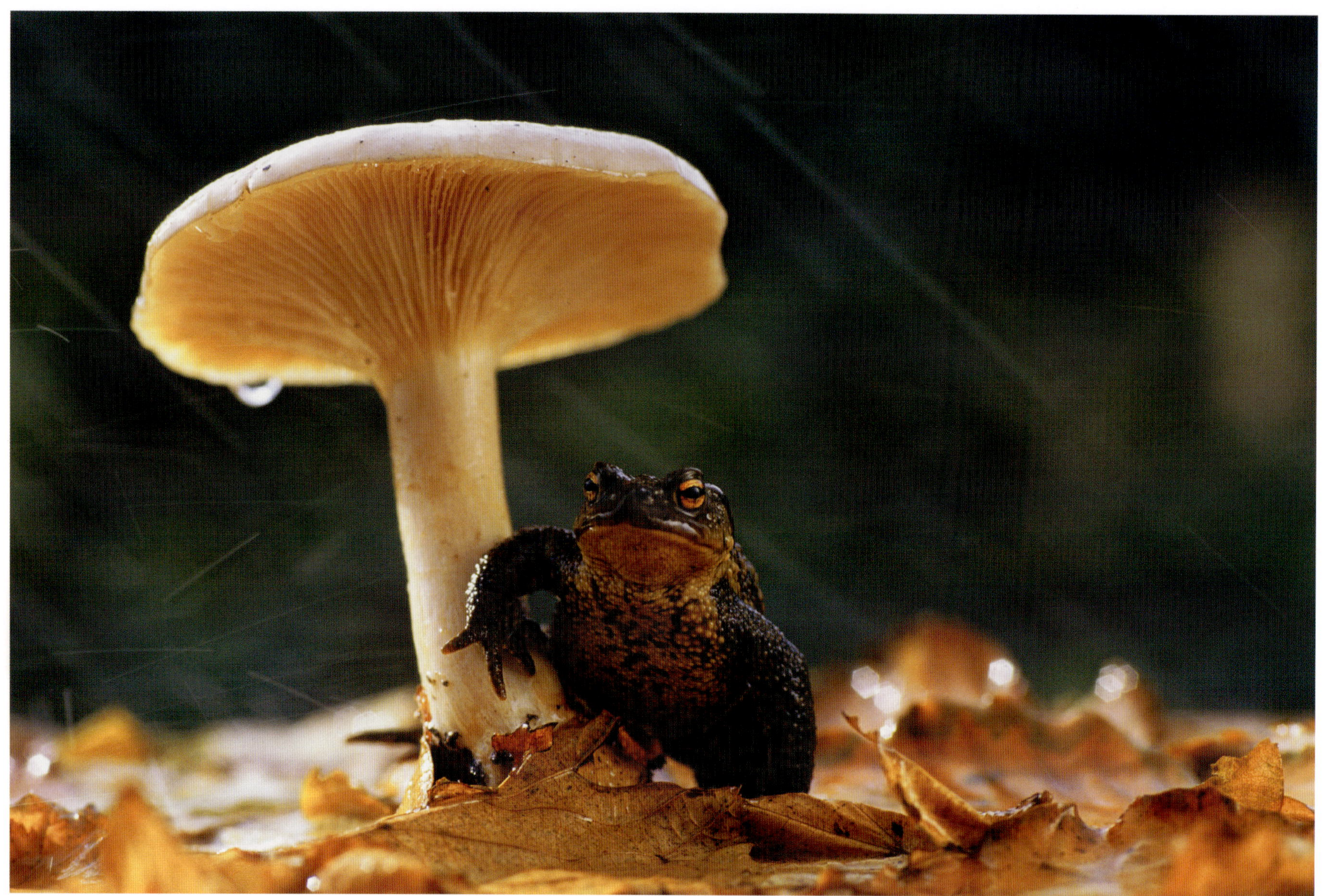

TOWNSHEND, CORNWALL, ENGLAND
TOAD IN THE RAIN

DAVID CHAPMAN

Minolta 700si, Tamron 90mm macro lens, f/8, Fuji Sensia 100. I took the photograph from a low angle facing into the sun, with a dark background, and used a golden reflector to bring more light onto the subject.
SECOND, 2008

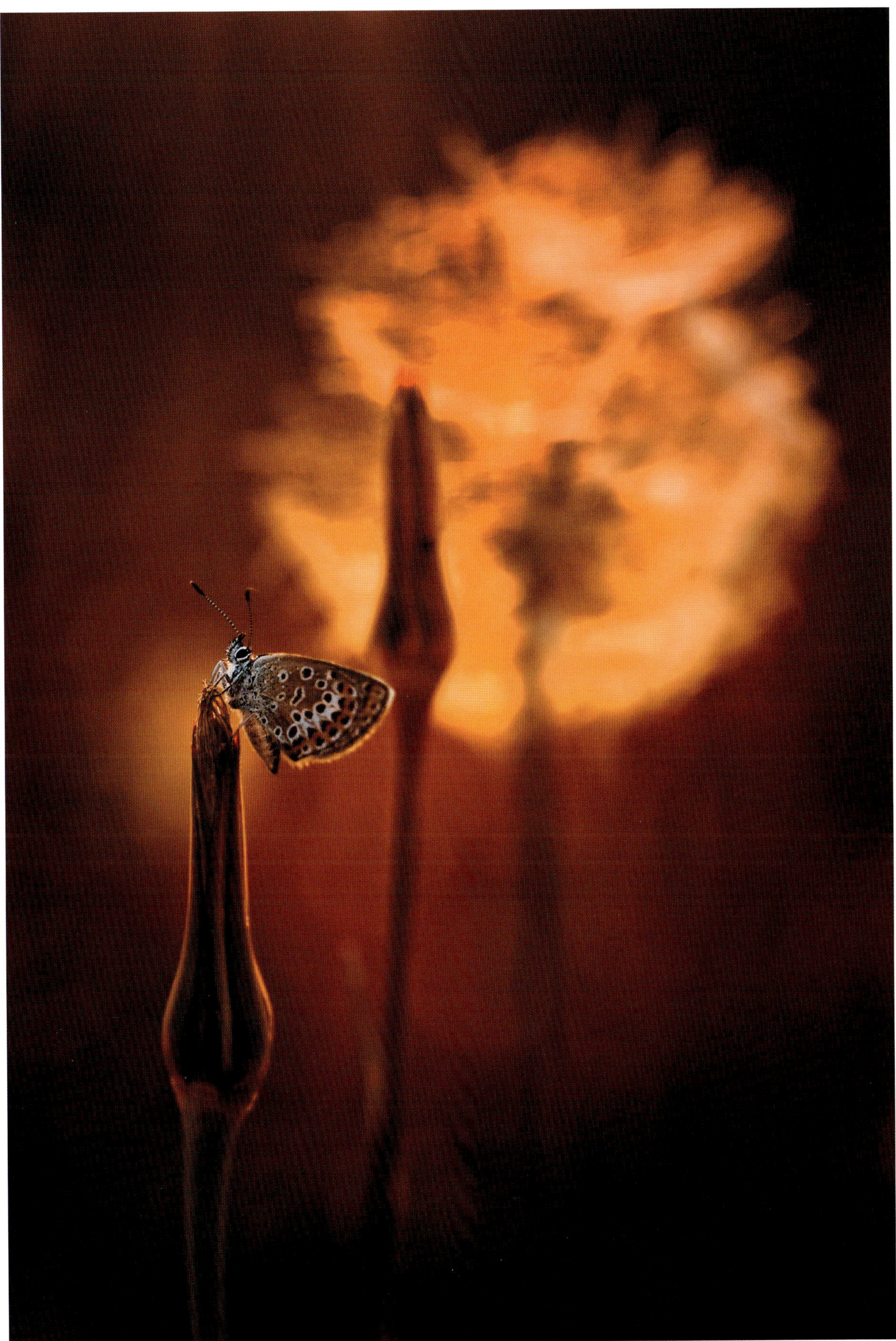

TRZEBINIA, MALOPOLSKA REGION
WHEN THE DAY ENDS

MAGDALENA WASICZEK

Nikon D300, Tessar 50/2.8, f/2.8, 1/500sec, ISO 400.
FINALIST, 2010

I love the peace and quiet of the summer evening. I long to sit and soak up the smells and sounds of the meadows. Around me are fading lanterns of dandelions, and sleeping insects on each blade of grass. It was the last picture of the day and I had to capture, out of the darkness, the tiny butterfly, a brown argus (*Aricia agestis*), against the sow thistle (*Sonchus oleraceus*).

The subject is a brightly coloured chaffinch, camouflaged amongst equally bright sycamore (*Plantanus* spp.) buds and the subtle colour of the lichen. The light, the colour, the luck – a bird landing amongst the buds I was photographing, whose colour reflected that of the buds and the lichen. What were the chances? The whole set-up had a soft focus, circular frame of branches, which draws the eye in to the subject. How could I resist this shot?

I only had seconds to take the picture as the bird landed on the tree where I was photographing the sycamore buds. I had to quickly re-frame, focus and click, and luckily I managed to take three shots before he had gone again. Right place, right time, quick thinking.

MY GARDEN, PERTHSHIRE, SCOTLAND
CAMOUFLAGE

GILLIAN HUNT

Nikon D2X, Nikon 70–200 f/2.8.
FIRST, 2010

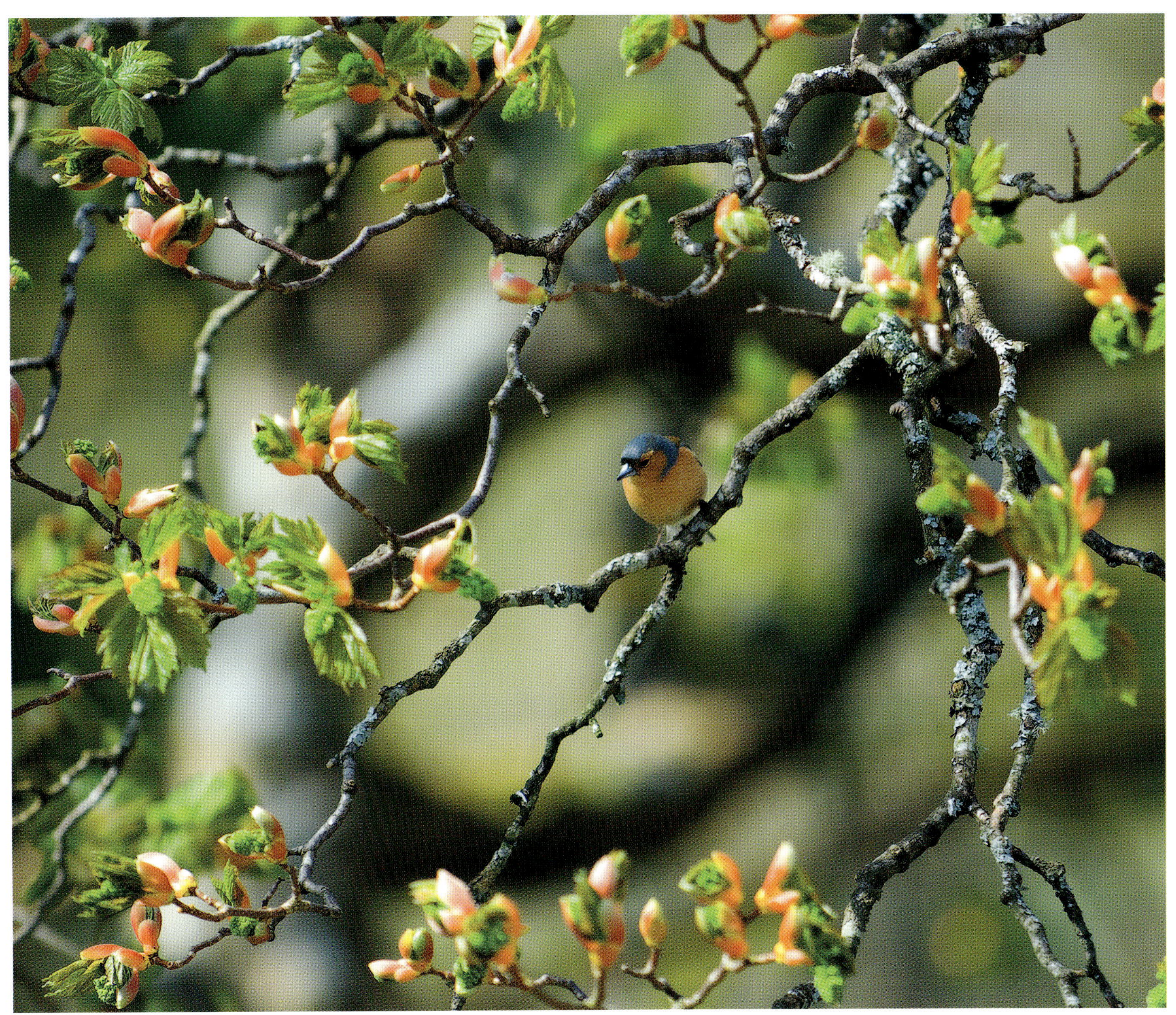

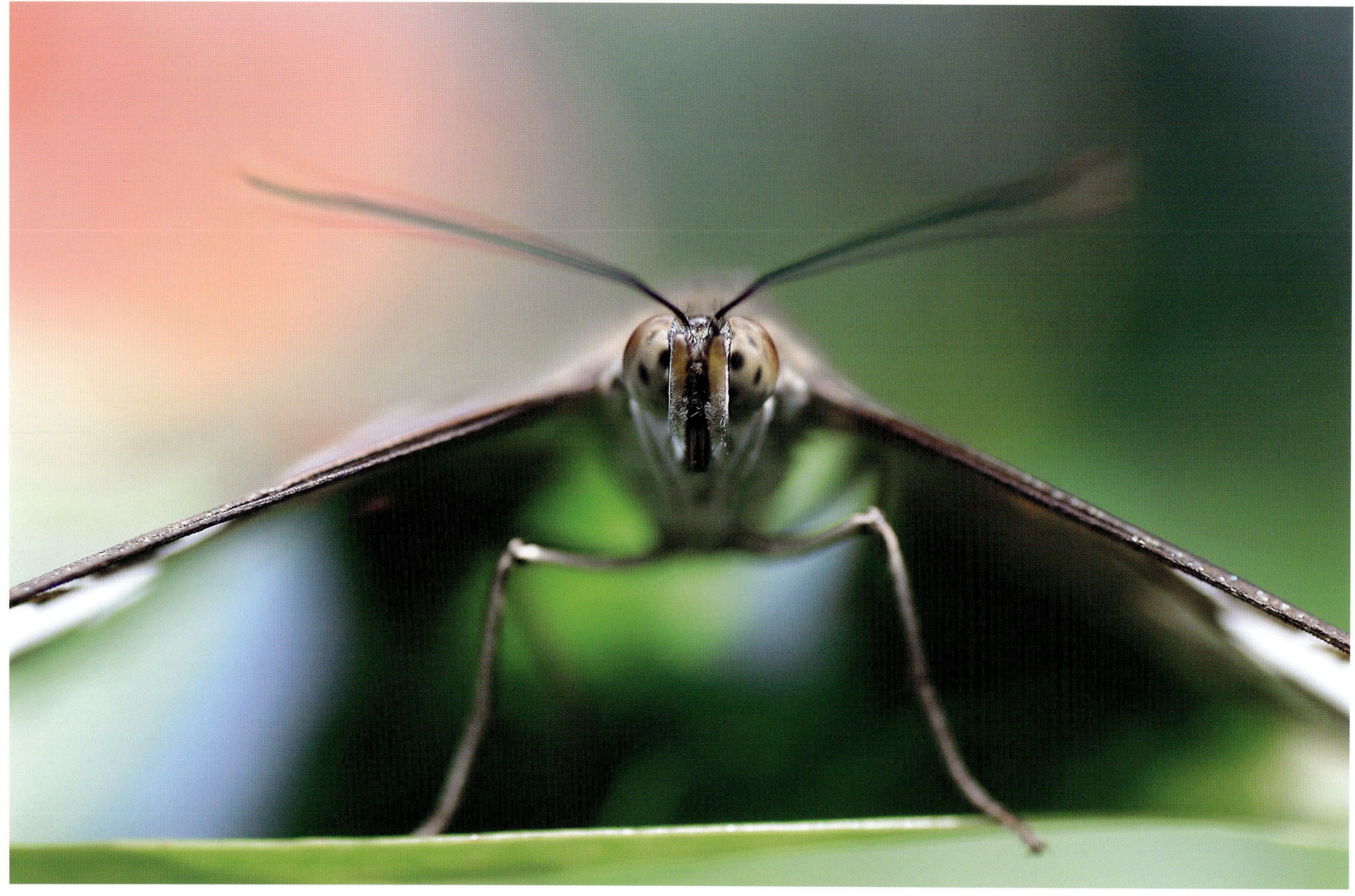

I saw this moth and approached it immediately. It was early in the morning and the light was subtle enough for me to use a wide aperture. This shot was captured handheld simply because I didn't have much time to set it up. I tried to experiment with various points of view and camera angles. This one was a lucky capture, simply because the subject landed in a spot where I could hold the camera steadily.

SEGAMAT, JOHOR

LOOKING AT YOU

SHARKAWI CHE DIN

Canon EOS 300D, Tamron 90mm macro lens, f/2.8. White balance changed in post-production. I used a wide aperture for a soft, pastel background, and manually focused on the moth's head to reveal its detail and emphasise the illusion of space.

FINALIST, 2008

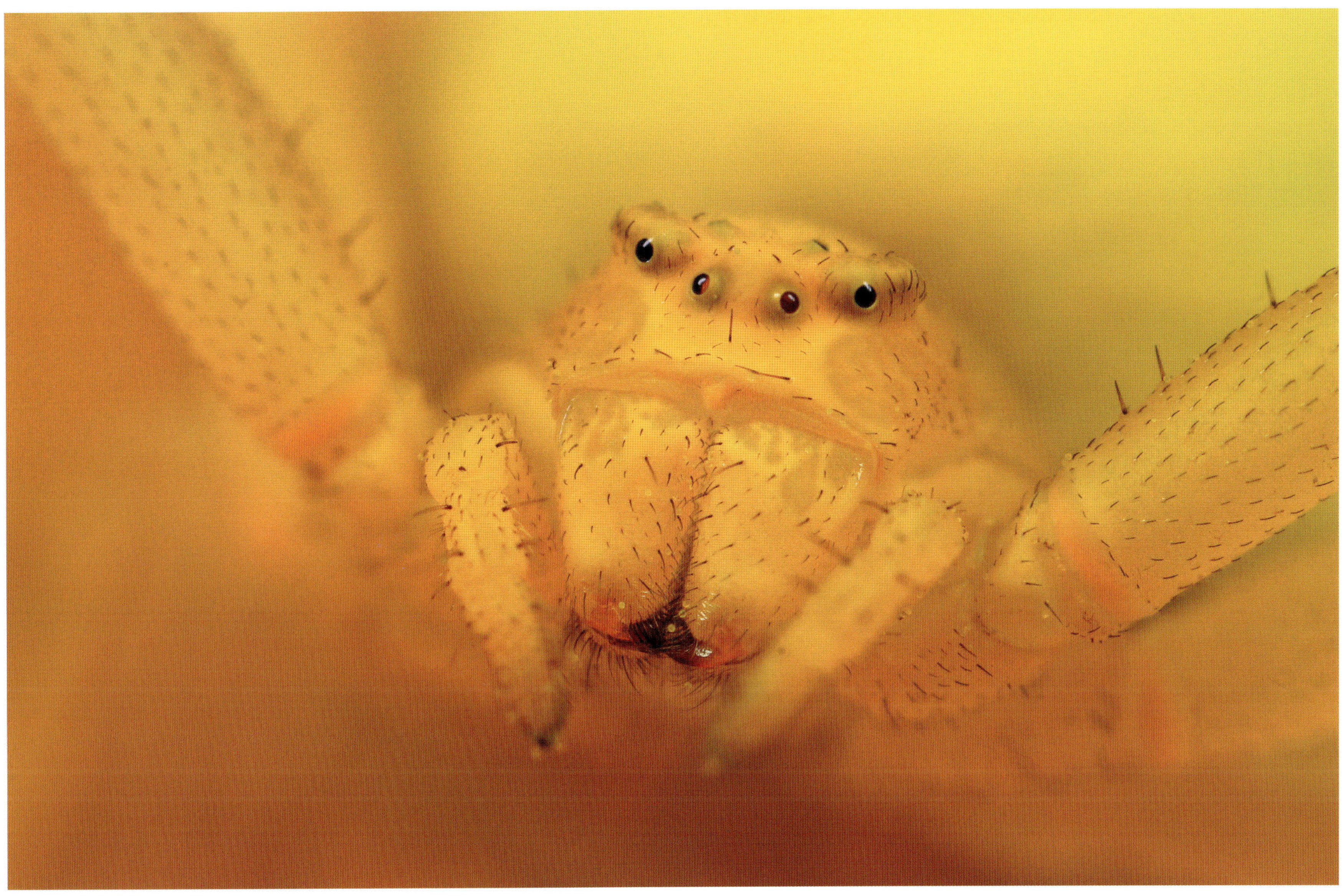

A crab spider, having taken on the colour of the flower, waits patiently for its next meal. The spider stayed on the same flower for several weeks. It took a long time for the spider to accept me and let me get this close. At x4 the end of the lens is within two inches of the subject. I was inspired by how the yellows of the flower and crab spider seem to become one, making the spider almost part of the flower and virtually invisible.

WORCESTERSHIRE, ENGLAND
PATIENCE

ALISTAIR CAMPBELL

Canon EOS 30D, Canon MPE-65 macro lens, f/6.3. This is a composite of two separate images taken at different focal points but the same point of view, that were layered together in Photoshop CS3. This technique is called focus stacking. I used this to increase depth of field without sacrificing the sharpness.
COMMENDED, 2009

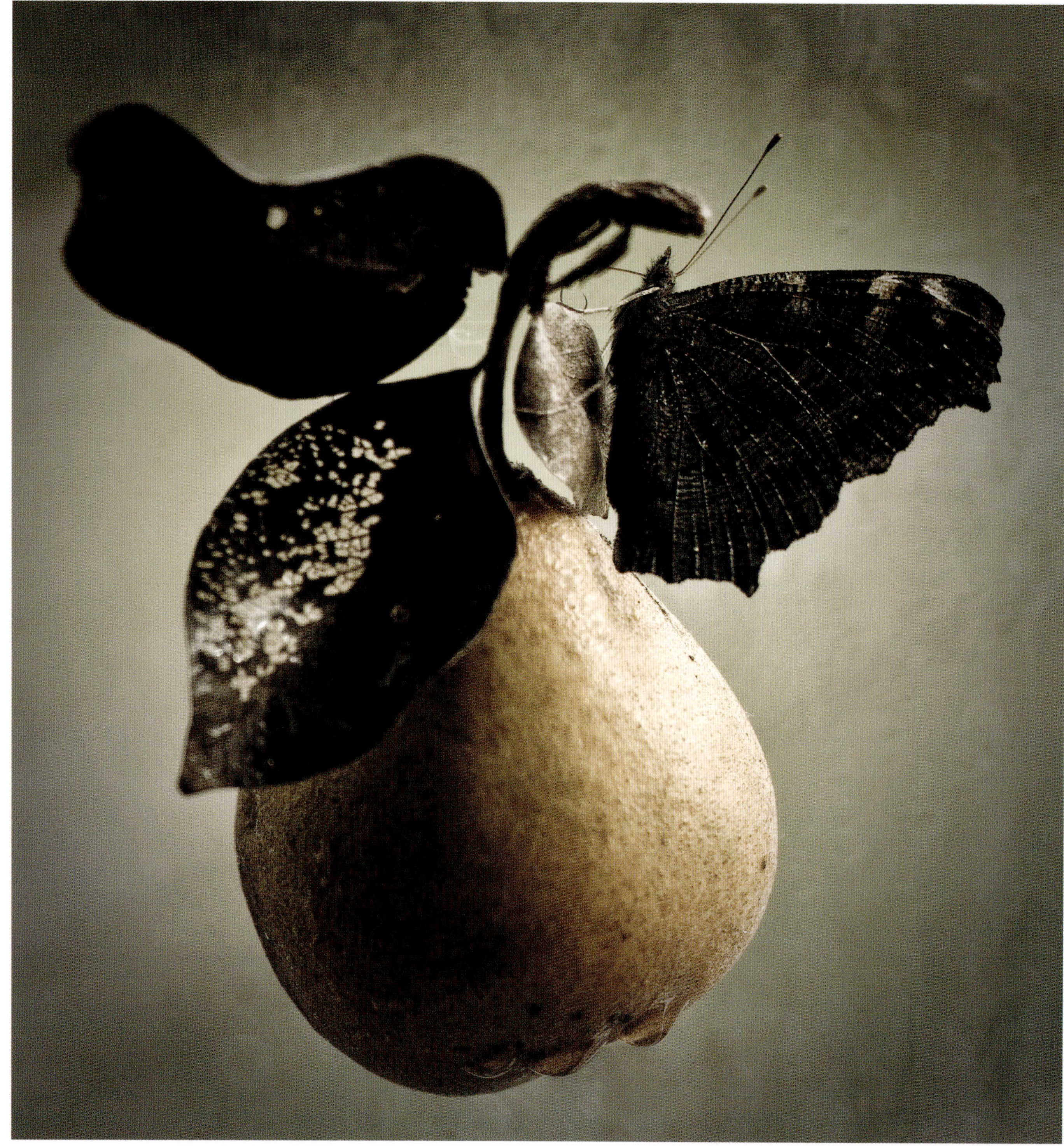

I was playing with composition of a still life with pears (*Pyrus communis*) when I saw this peacock butterfly nestling amongst the fruit. Beautiful and brightly coloured, its wings provided excellent camouflage.

TRZEBINIA, MALOPOLSKA REGION
MIMIKRA

MAGDALENA WASICZEK

Nikon D300, Tamron 90, f/6.3, 1/160sec, ISO 320, +0.3EV.
SECOND, 2010

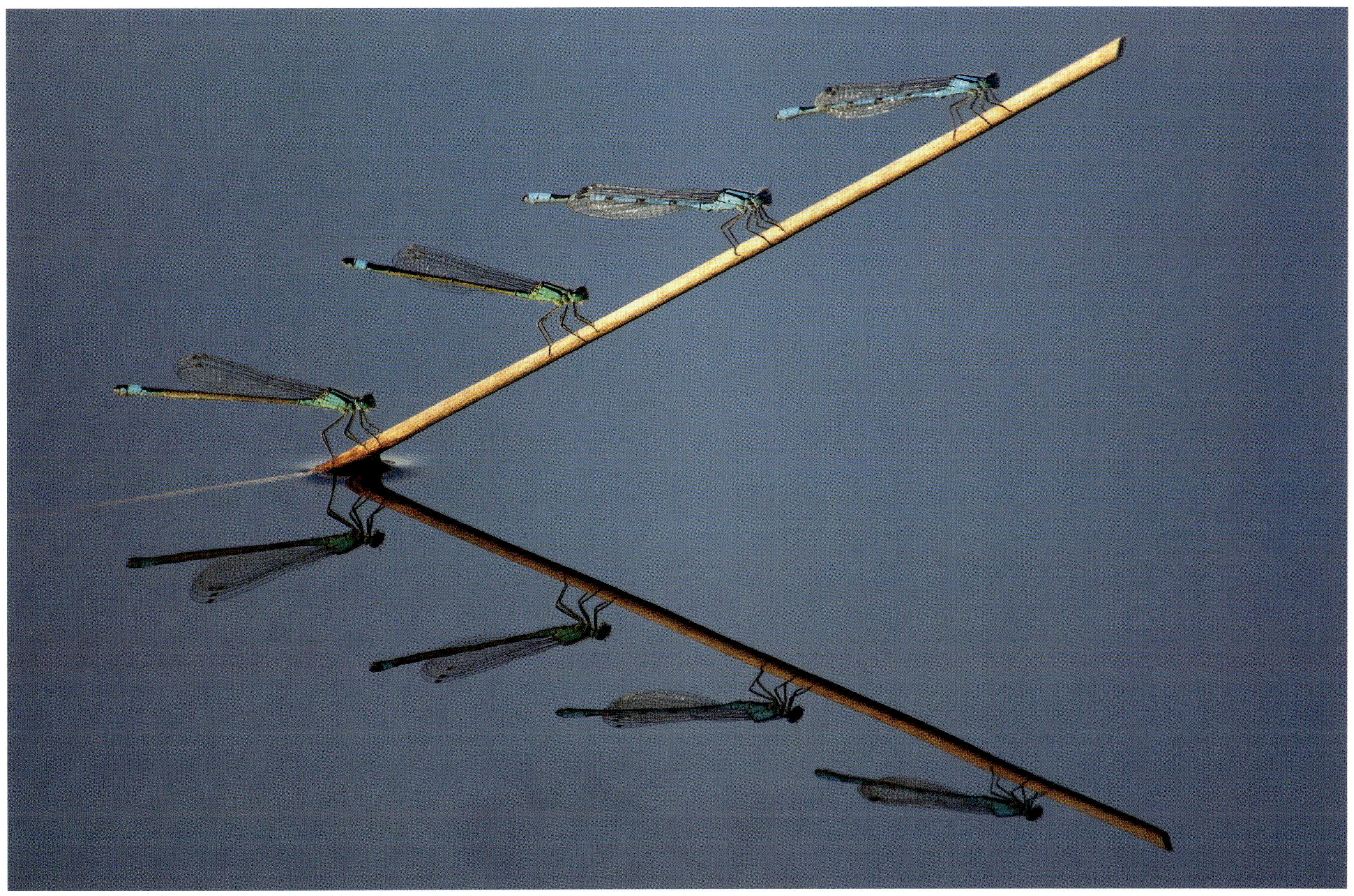

NETHERBURY, DORSET, ENGLAND
DAMSELFLIES ON GARDEN POND

COLIN VARNDELL

Nikon D2X, Nikkor 200mm macro lens, f/5.6. The wide aperture was selected to ensure the background was soft. But the resulting shallow depth of field necessitates being perfectly parallel with the subject.
FIRST, 2009

I have always been fascinated with dragonflies and damselflies and spend time photographing them every year. In this instance, I was inspired by the way they all settled on the reeds in the same direction due to the gentle breeze. I set up my tripod and seat and waited. Most of the time there were so many insects on the reeds that they looked untidy. But after a wait of a couple of hours I noticed these four, symetrically positioned on this reed. The top two damselflies are common blues (*Enallagma cyathigerum*) the lower two are blue-tailed damselflies (*Ischnura elegans*). As with many nature subjects, patience was the key with this shot. I carry a fold-up seat on my camera bag for such occasions and used this to sit and wait for the right moment.

VILNIUS

DIAMONDS ON 'FUR'

OLEGAS KURASOVAS

Canon EOS 20D, Canon 100mm f/2.8 macro lens, f/11. It was impossible to get good depth of field at high magnification, so I took nine shots with different focus plane and then combined them in Photoshop.

FINALIST, 2009

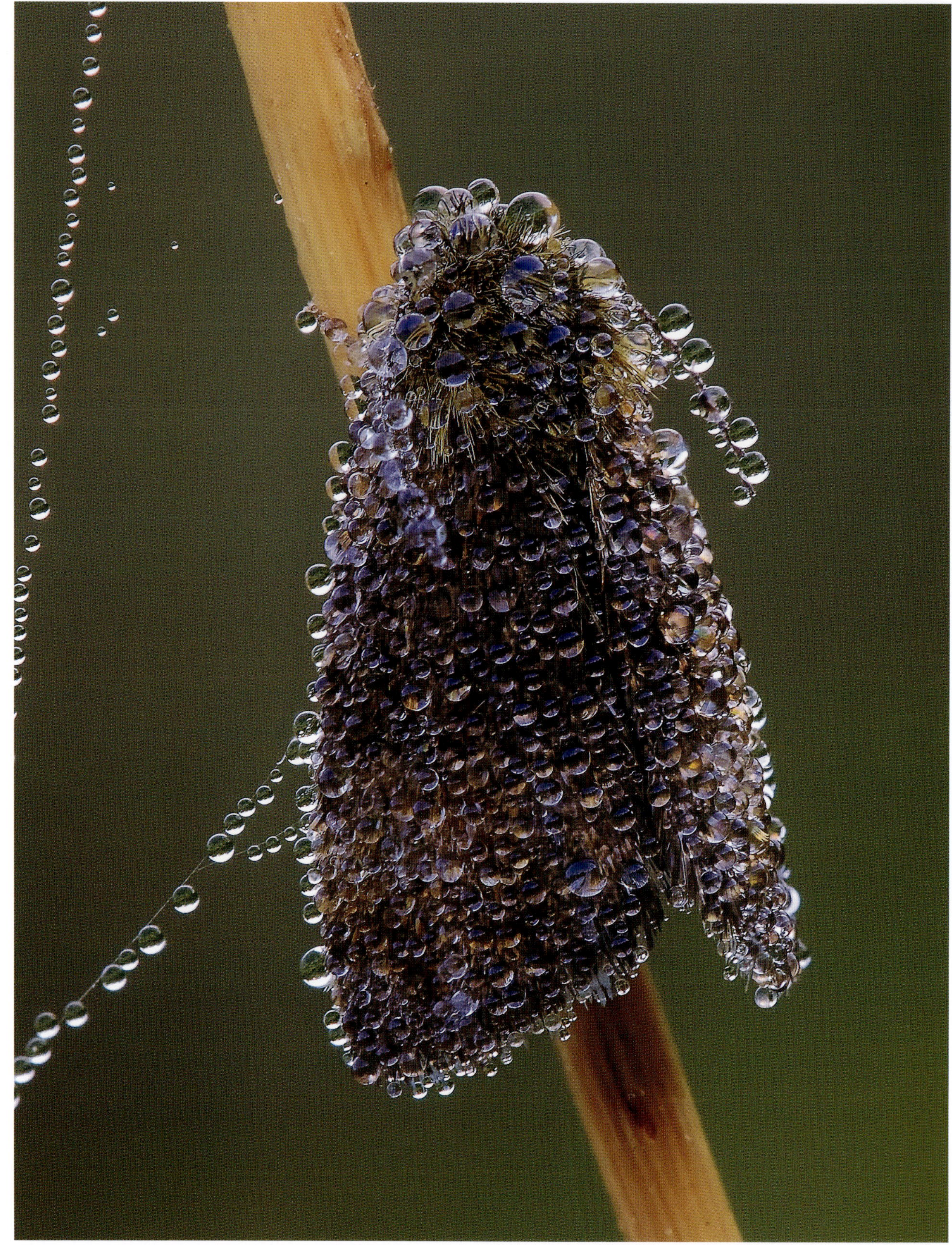

The morning light and dew sparkled on this butterfly's 'fur'.

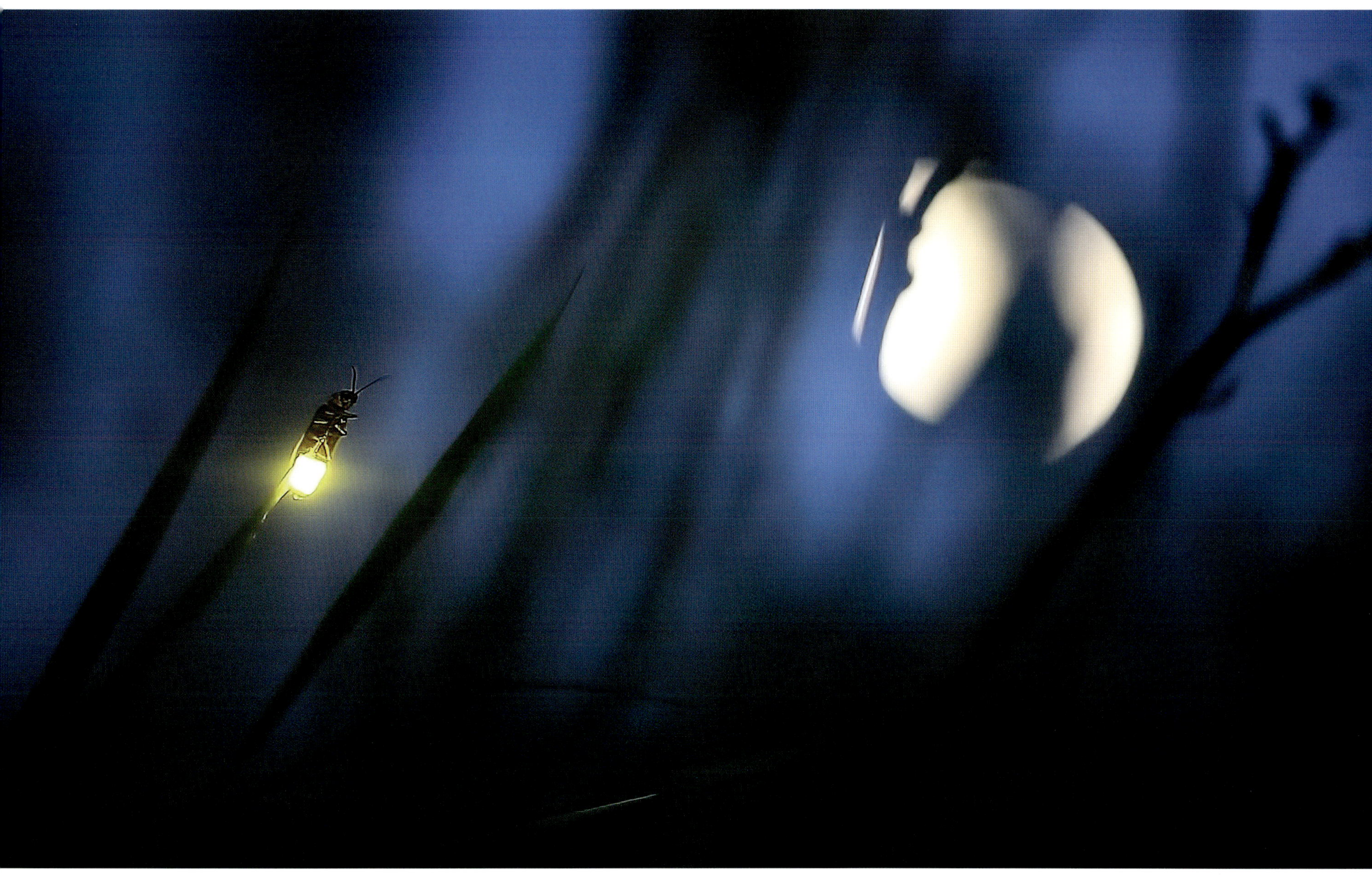

I took this photograph of a firefly a couple days before full moon. This allowed me to have enough ambient light and to have the moon placed near the horizon. The distant moon appears large and split: an effect of lens bokeh.

FAIRFIELD, IOWA
FIREFLY AND MOON

RADIM SCHREIBER

Canon EOS 5D Mark II, 100mm lens. 1/30sec at f/2.8. Post-capture: no digital alterations.
FINALIST, 2012

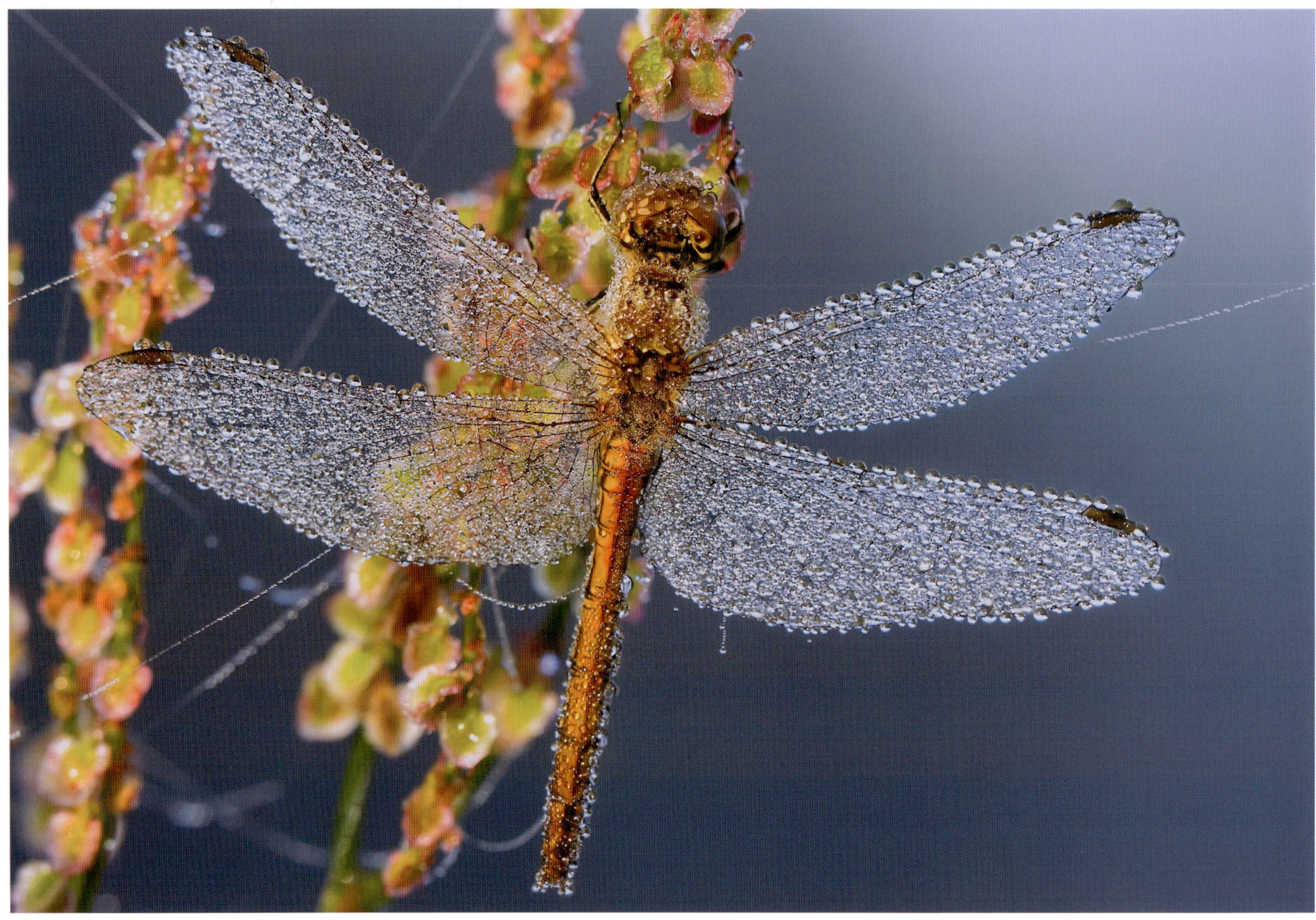

VILNIUS
WAITING FOR THE SUN

OLEGAS KURASOVAS

Canon EOS 20D, Canon 100mm f/2.8 macro lens, f/6.3. Channel blending, noise reduction and sharpening in post-production. There was a little wind, so I boosted the ISO to 1600 in order to achieve a fast enough shutter speed.
FINALIST, 2008

Such a beautiful subject, laden with dew in the misty morning light, called out to be photographed. As my tripod is short and the dragonfly was high up, I had to shoot handheld.

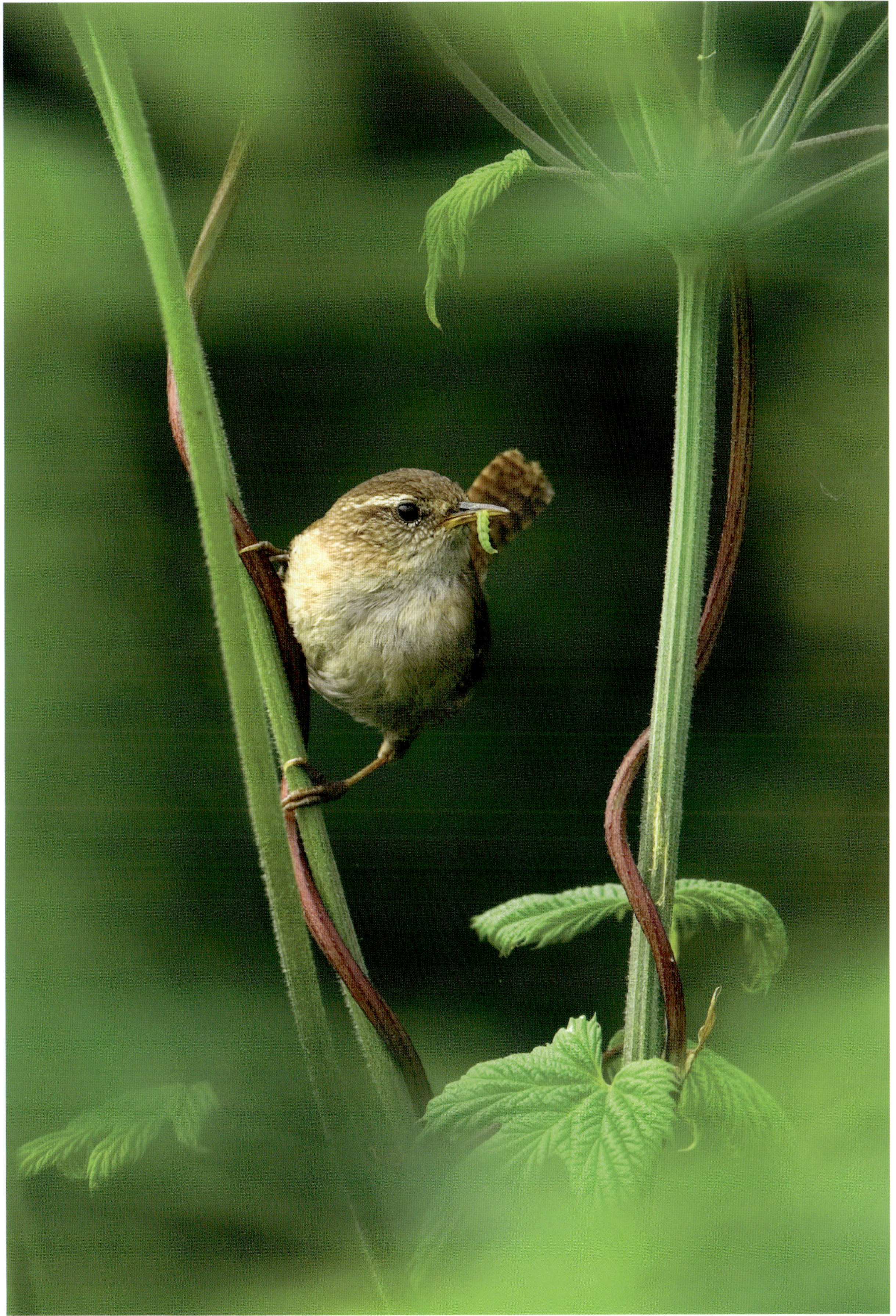

ST MARY'S, ISLES OF SCILLY, ENGLAND
WREN

DAVID CHAPMAN

Minolta 7D, Sigma 400mm lens, f/6.3. The wren had perched once on this stem and I could only just see this one point on the stem through the surrounding vegetation. I set up my camera on a tripod pointing at this spot and it returned once more.
COMMENDED, 2008

I was watching this wren feeding its young. Having left the nest, they were mobile but had rested in a patch of rough ground in this garden. I wanted to try to capture an image of the bird with food in its mouth on the way down to the young. I particularly liked the fact that the wild hops (*Humulus lupulus*) stem matches the colour of the wren and the caterpillar matches the colour of the surrounding vegetation.

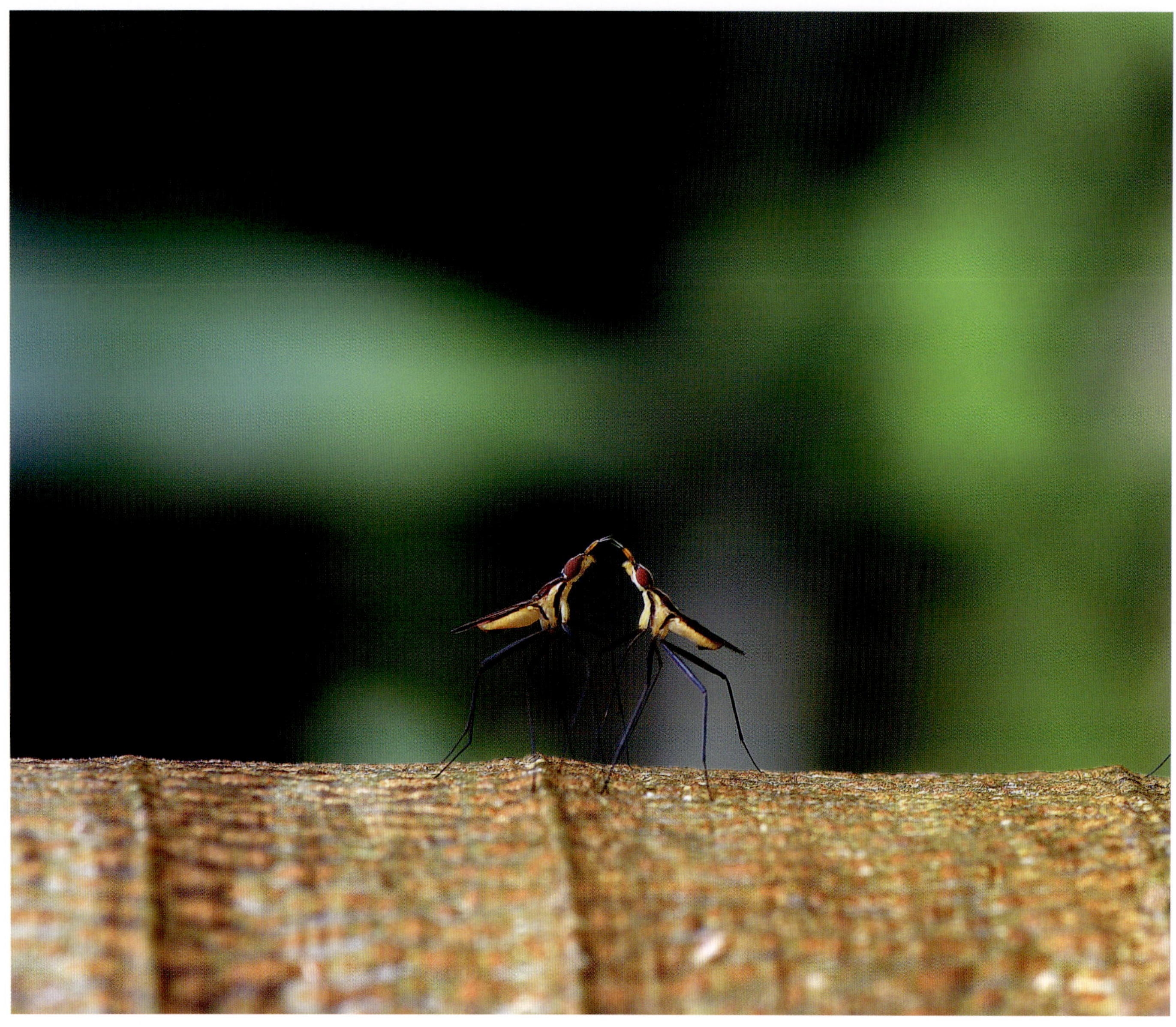

MY BACKYARD GARDEN
SWEET LOVERS

TECK PING TONG

Sony Alpha 100, Minolta Macro 100mm 2.8, f/6.3.
FINALIST, 2010

In the original image there are three insects, with two meeting each other and the other one looking on. I tried to present them from a more romantic point of view, so I cropped out the onlooker at extreme right. These insects are thin and long-legged, with yellow and black linings, and are about 10mm in height. They like decayed papayas and are very timid. Familiar with their behaviour, I prepared the necessary gear and, after some hard sweat one morning, managed to snap a few good shots.

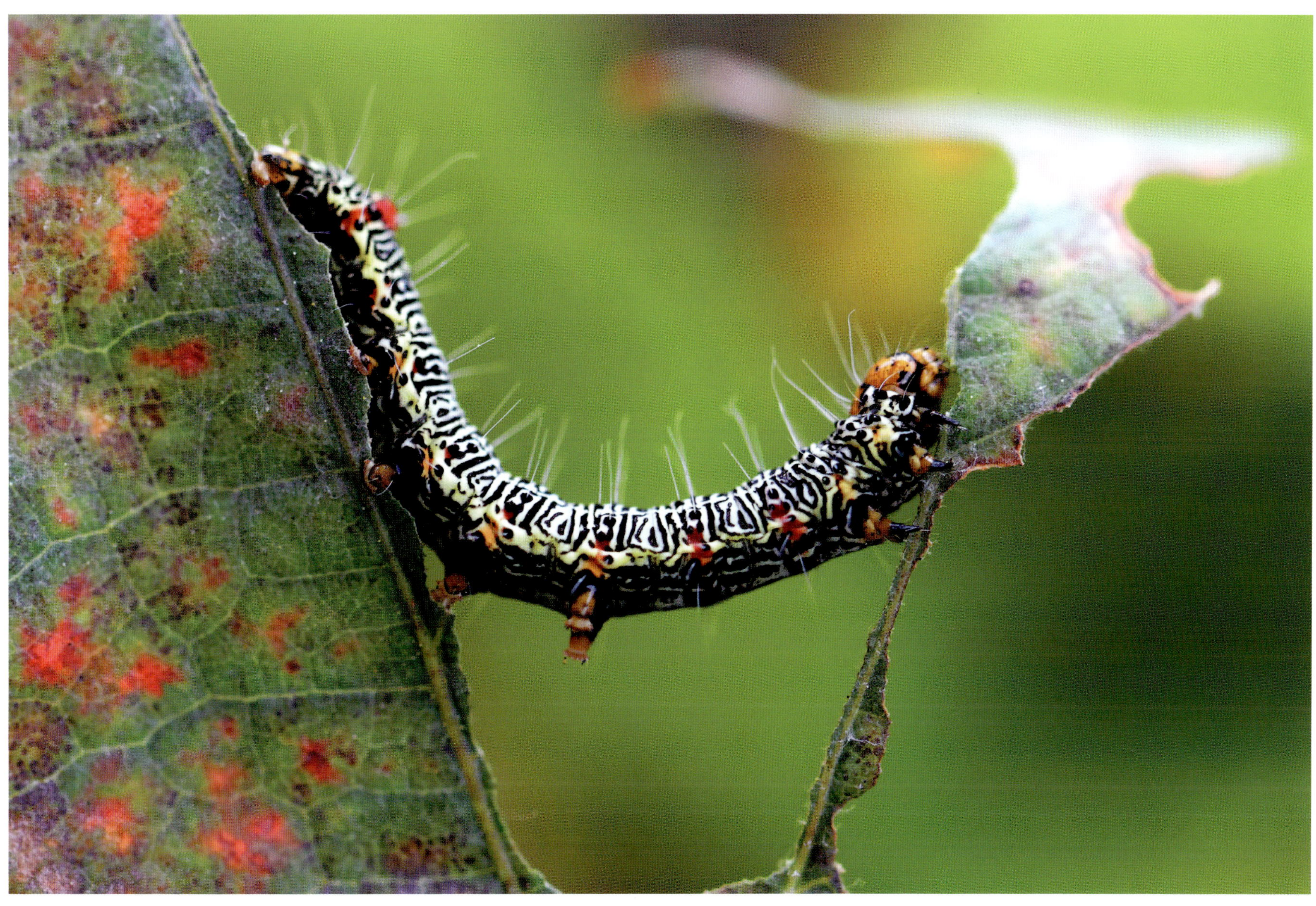

MY BACK GARDEN, CANBERRA, ACT
BACK-BREAKING

DEBBIE HARTLEY

Canon EOS 7D, Canon 100mm lens. 1/40sec at f/2.8. Post-capture: slight colour adjustment and sharpening.
HIGHLY COMMENDED, 2012

I found this grapevine moth caterpillar feeding on the grapevine (*Vitis vinifera*) leaves in my backyard. The strength and flexibility of these small creatures always amazes me: the leaf was already half gone when I found it! I am always intrigued by nature and the small world of minibeasts, and I am always wandering around my yard inspecting plants for living creatures. The camera was handheld and I used continuous shooting so I could get a sharp picture, as the caterpillar was moving slightly while it ate.

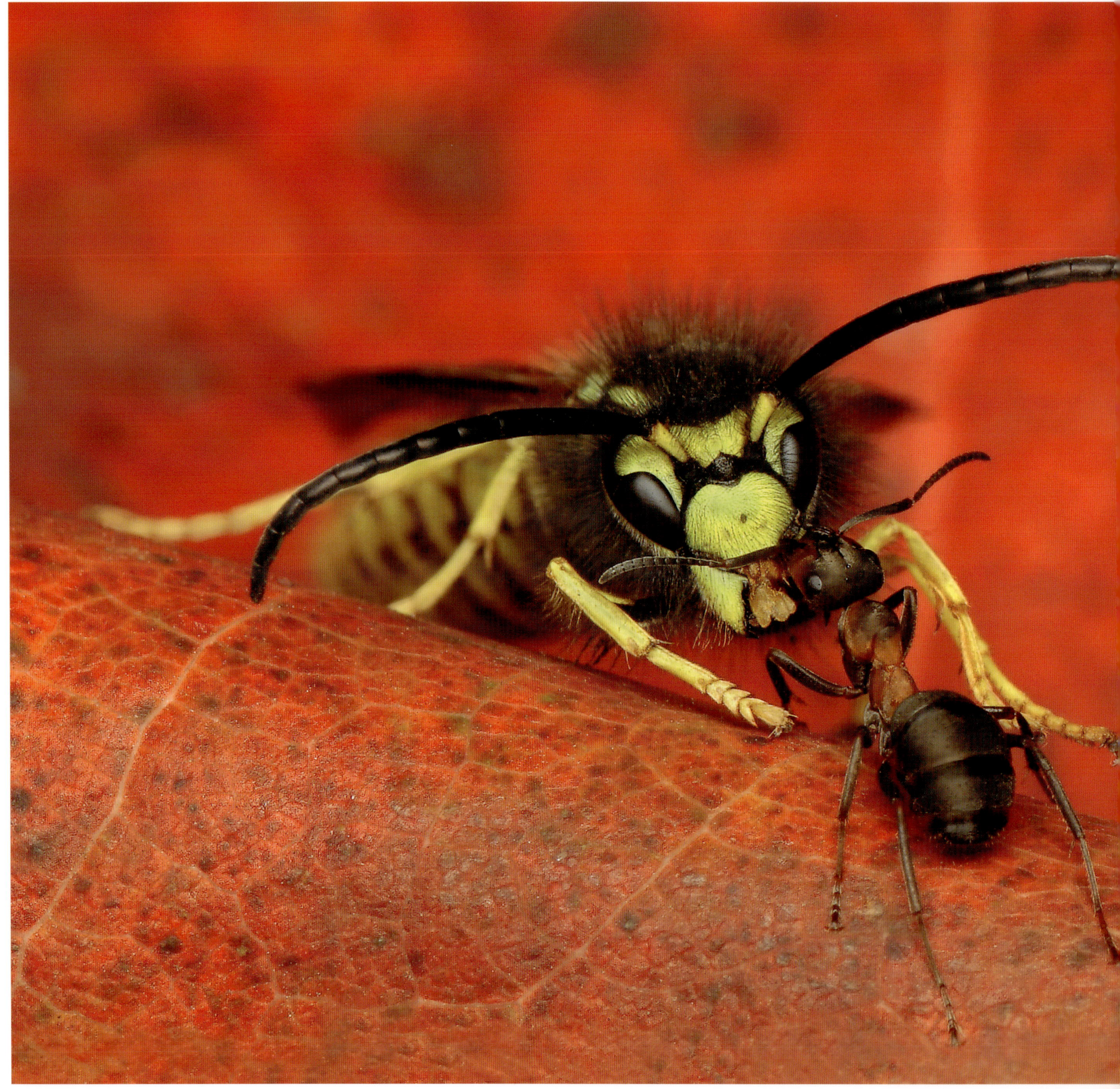

I spotted this red wood ant and common wasp engaged in a deadly struggle on this beautiful autumnal oak (*Quercus* spp.) leaf. It was an incredible sight, with the red of the leaf underlining the drama of the situation. What makes it more extraordinary is that an ant won the fight – perhaps the wasp was weakened or sick.

JABLONNA
THE KISS

PAWEL BIENIEWSKI

Sony DCS-H5, 250mm lens, f/8. Noise reduced in Neat Image; exposure tweaked in Photoshop. I had time to take a number of photographs during the fight.
FINALIST, 2008

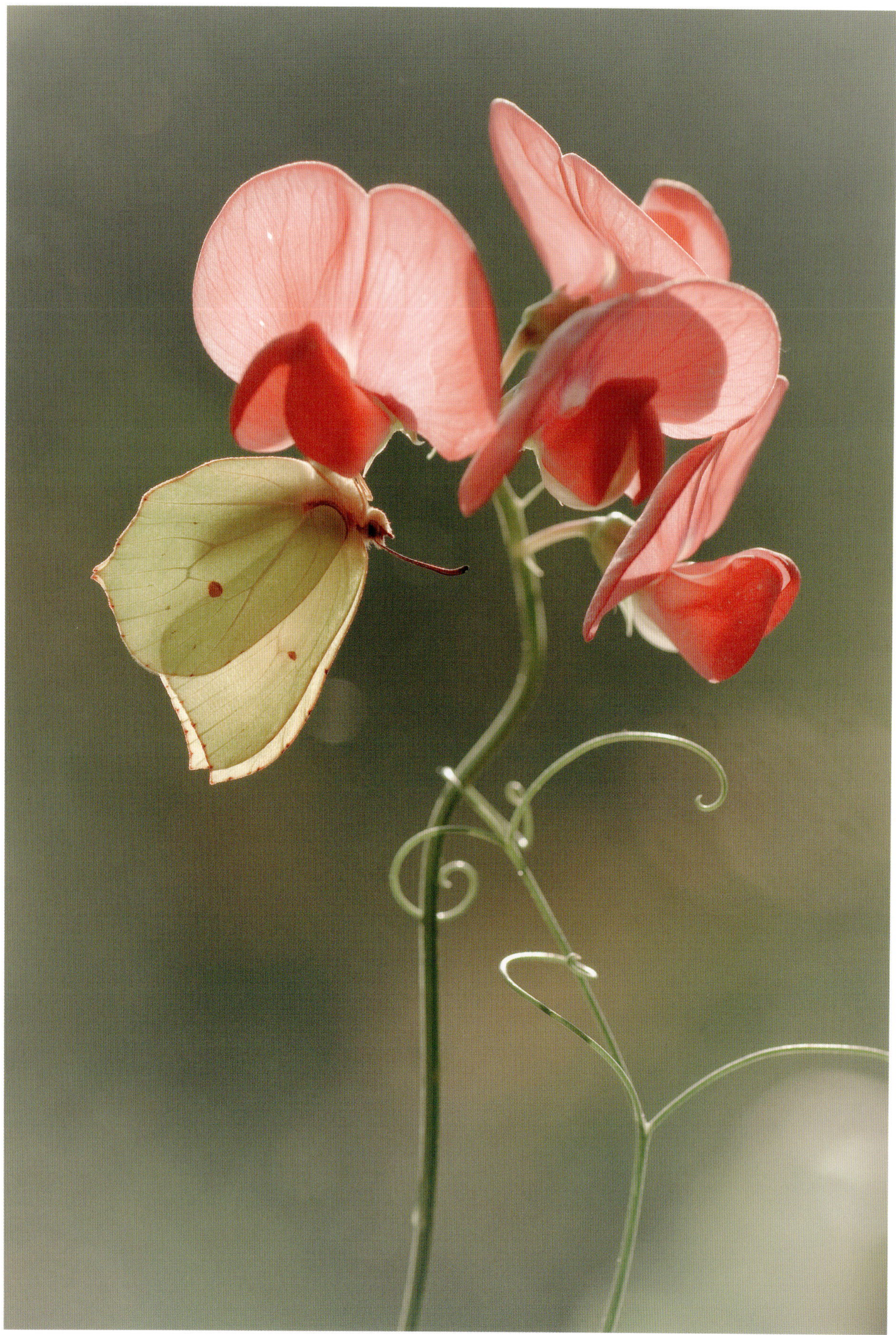

TRZEBINIA, MALOPOLSKA REGION

UPSIDE DOWN

MAGDALENA WASICZEK

Nikon D300, Tamron 90 lens. 1/640sec at f/5.6.
Post-capture: basic colour management.
INTERNATIONAL GARDEN PHOTOGRAPHER OF THE YEAR, 2012

I grow sweet peas (*Lathyrus odoratus*) to attract these brimstone butterflies (*Gonepteryx rhamni*). This butterfly's wings were beautifully illuminated by the sun. She created a delicate composition with a sprig of sweet pea.

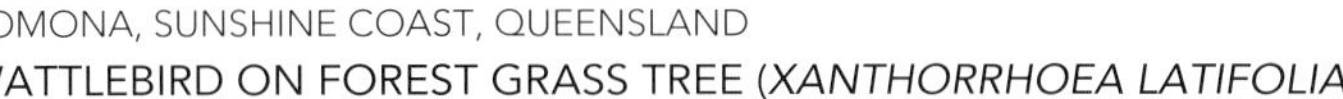

POMONA, SUNSHINE COAST, QUEENSLAND

WATTLEBIRD ON FOREST GRASS TREE (*XANTHORRHOEA LATIFOLIA*)

RAOUL SLATER

Canon EOS 30D, Canon 100-400mm 'L' lens, f/11. The photo was shot in colour. I then used the blue channel in channel mixer (Photoshop) to turn the sky pure white. A little selective burning and dodging highlighted the texture on the spikes and bird.
FINALIST, 2009

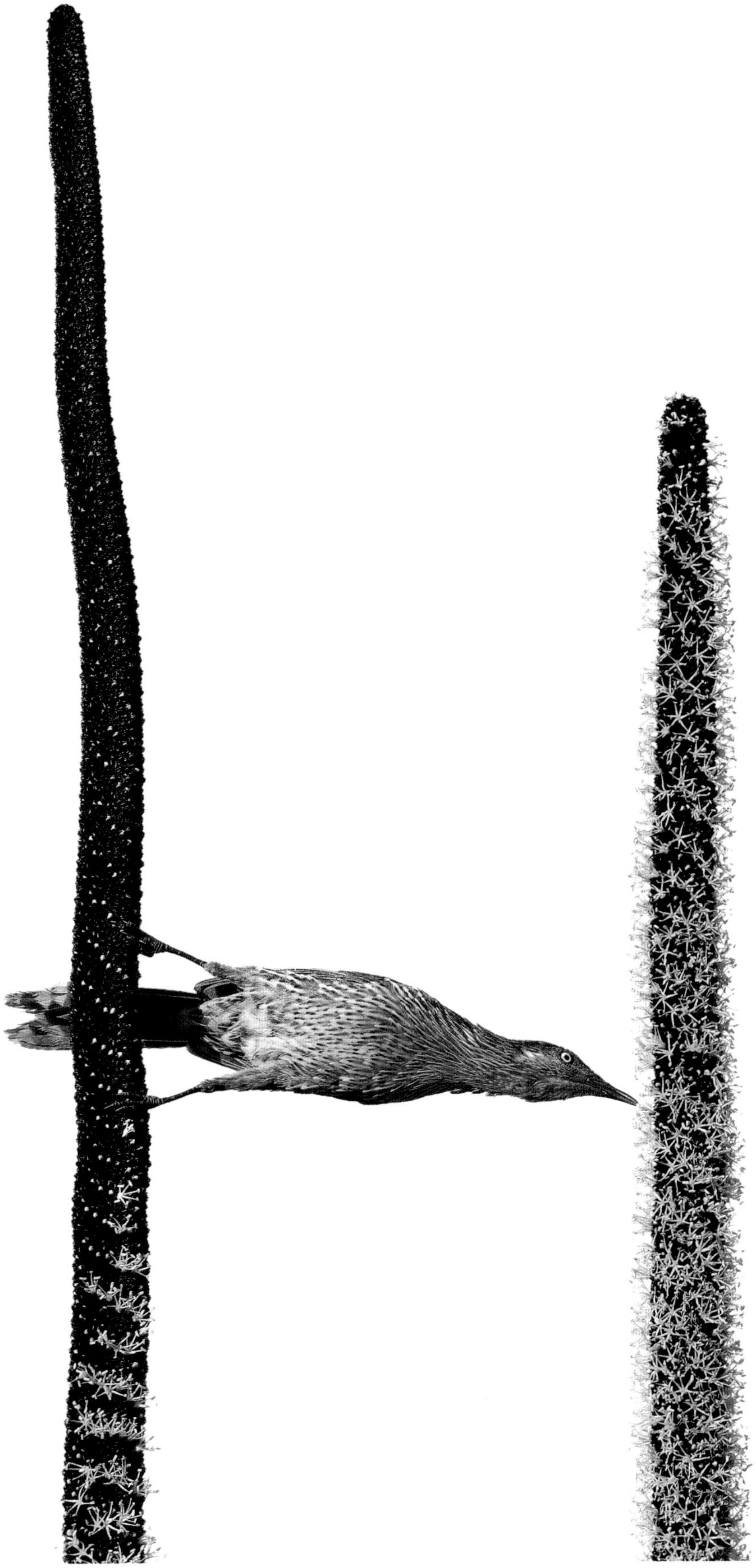

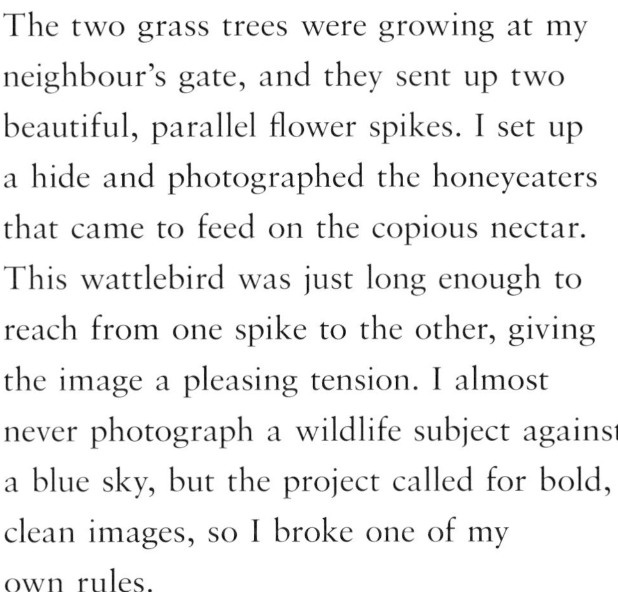

The two grass trees were growing at my neighbour's gate, and they sent up two beautiful, parallel flower spikes. I set up a hide and photographed the honeyeaters that came to feed on the copious nectar. This wattlebird was just long enough to reach from one spike to the other, giving the image a pleasing tension. I almost never photograph a wildlife subject against a blue sky, but the project called for bold, clean images, so I broke one of my own rules.

Most of the flowers in my garden I grow from seed and I choose varieties, such as this *Gazania*, that attract beneficial insects. I was drawn by the bright, bold colours and stripes of both the host and the hoverfly. I wanted to show how they complement one another, so I decided to take the shot looking down from above.

KINGFISHER COTTAGE, STONEHOUSE, SOUTH LANARKSHIRE, SCOTLAND

SUMMER STRIPES

SARAH-FIONA HELME

Canon EOS 40D, 180mm macro lens, f/4.5. I took some shots at ground level but I wanted to show the full complement of stripes, so I then decided to take the shot from directly above to create a bold and colourful image.

FINALIST, 2009

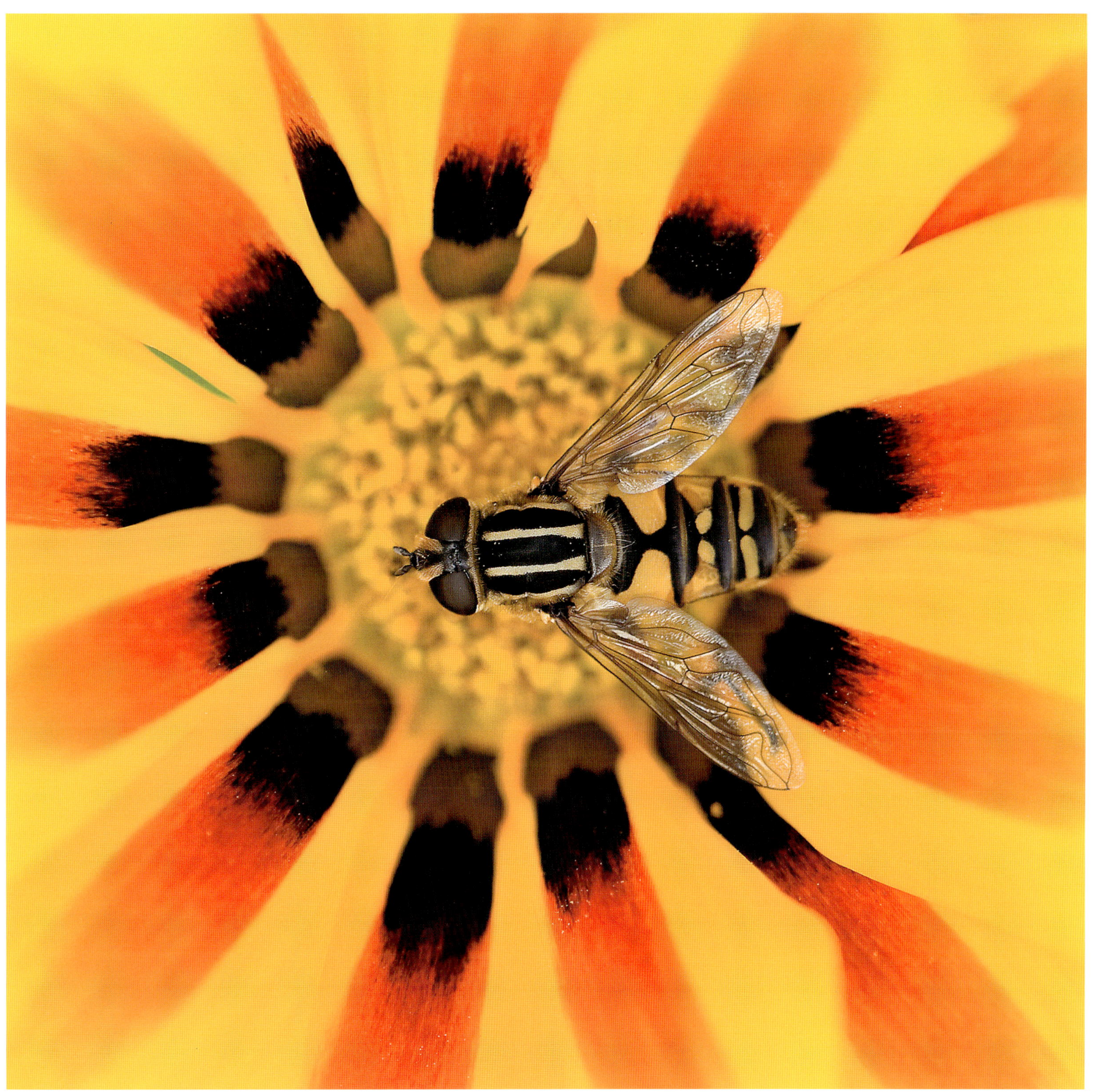

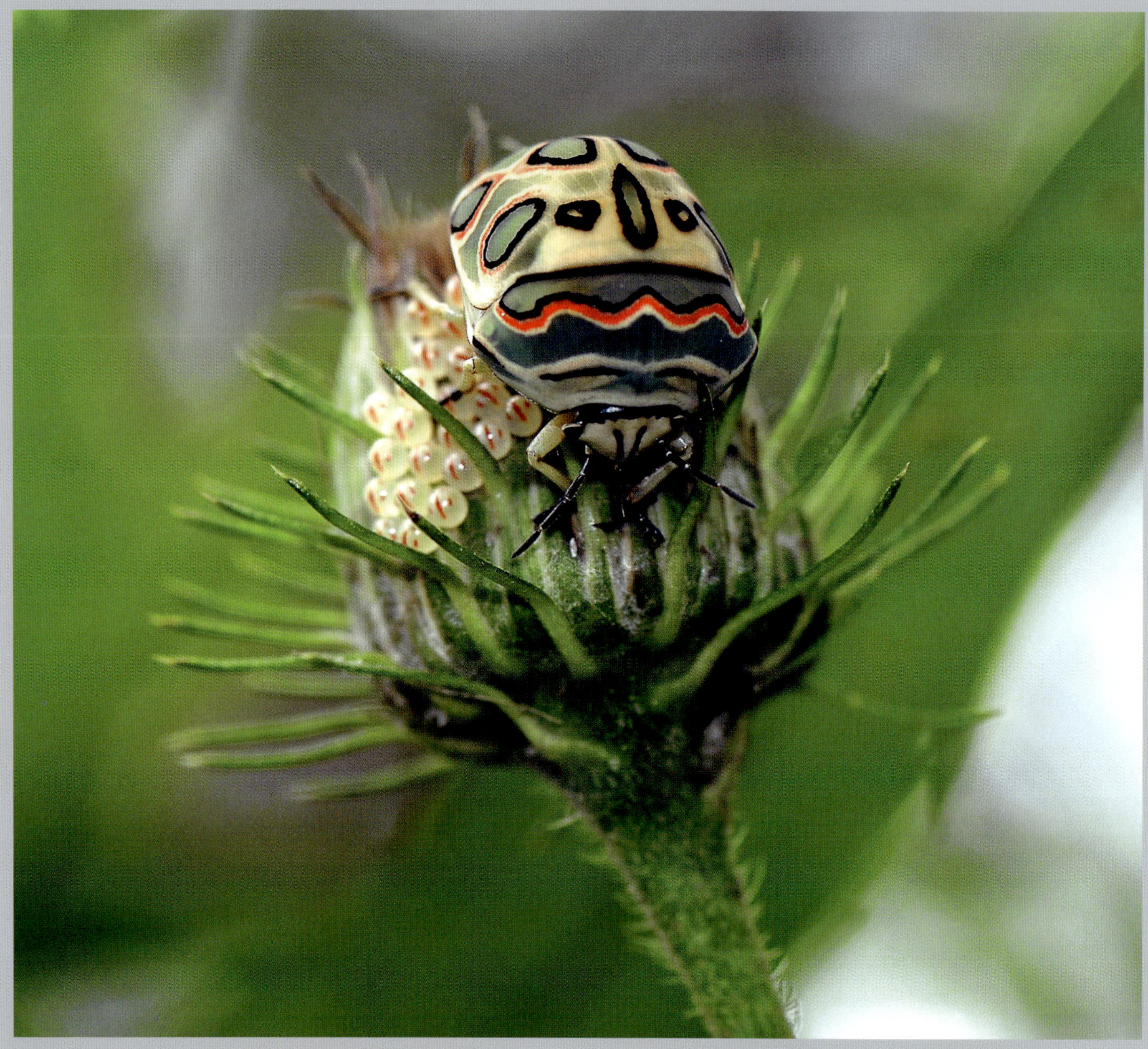

KAREN
BUG ON THISTLE BUSH

CHRIS MINIHANE

Nikon D200. This photo was taken in strong wind conditions on the top of a 1-metre-tall thistle bush.
FINALIST, 2009

This very colourful beetle was laying her eggs on a thistle bush. I took this shot because I'd never seen anything like this before, and was fascinated not only by the fact that I'd noticed this small beetle, but also by her incredible shyness. It was very difficult to get anywhere near her. I had to carefully walk up to her and simply stand for several minutes, moving bit by bit until I could get a bit of her face in the shot. It was very windy and she would turn away from me if I got too close, or if I moved an inch, so this was a lucky shot indeed.

MY GARDEN IN TOWNSHEND,
CORNWALL, ENGLAND
GREAT SPOTTED WOODPECKER
(*DENDROCOPOS MAJOR*)

DAVID CHAPMAN

Canon 5D Mark II, 800mm, f/6.3.
FINALIST, 2010

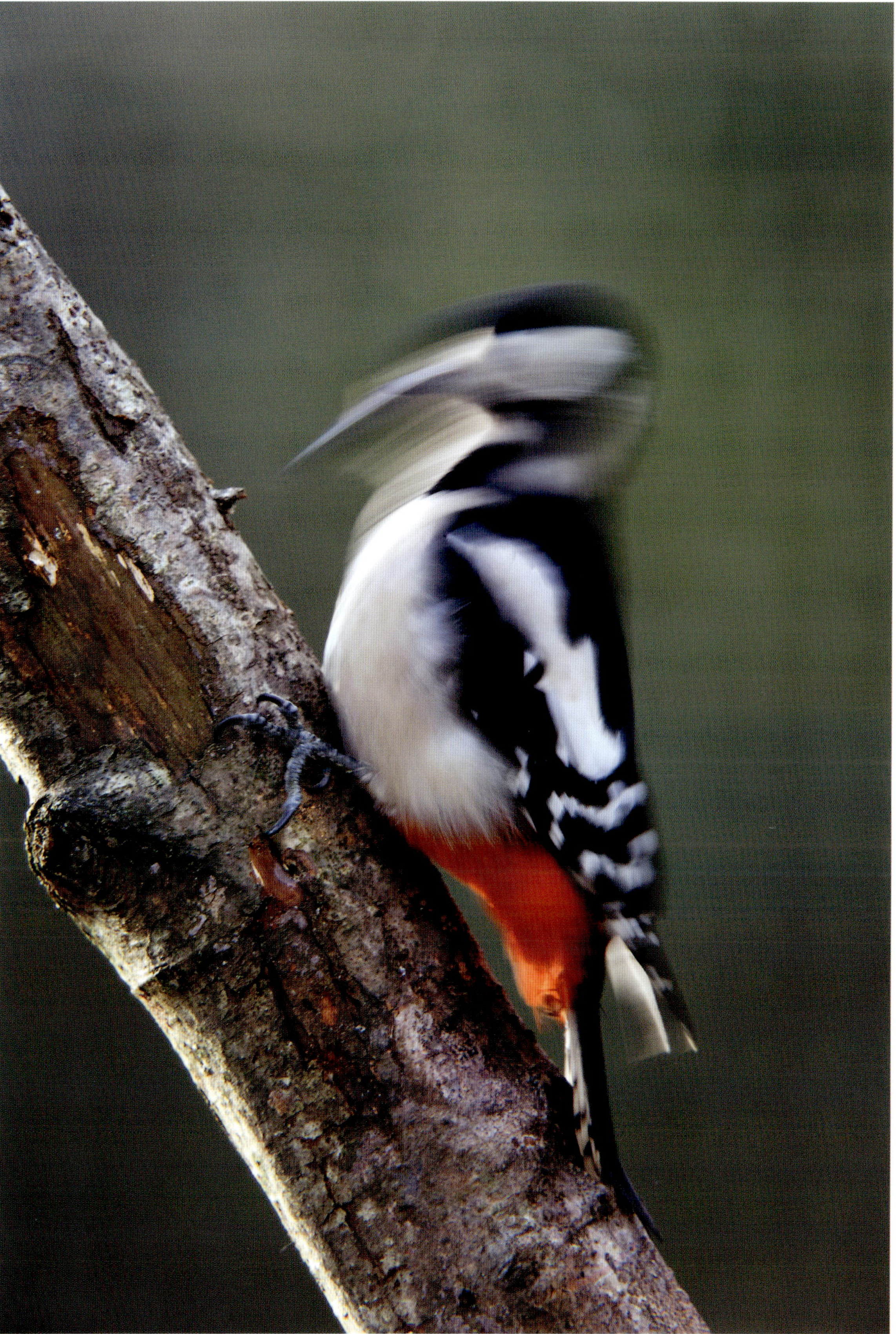

I had enjoyed watching the woodpeckers feeding on peanuts in the garden and wanted to capture a portrait of them. I particularly liked the way the backlighting created a rim-lighting on the birds. I had been feeding the birds, including the woodpeckers, in the garden. This female had eaten and hopped up the branch of the tree to drum. I used a hide to conceal myself so that I could capture the right shot.

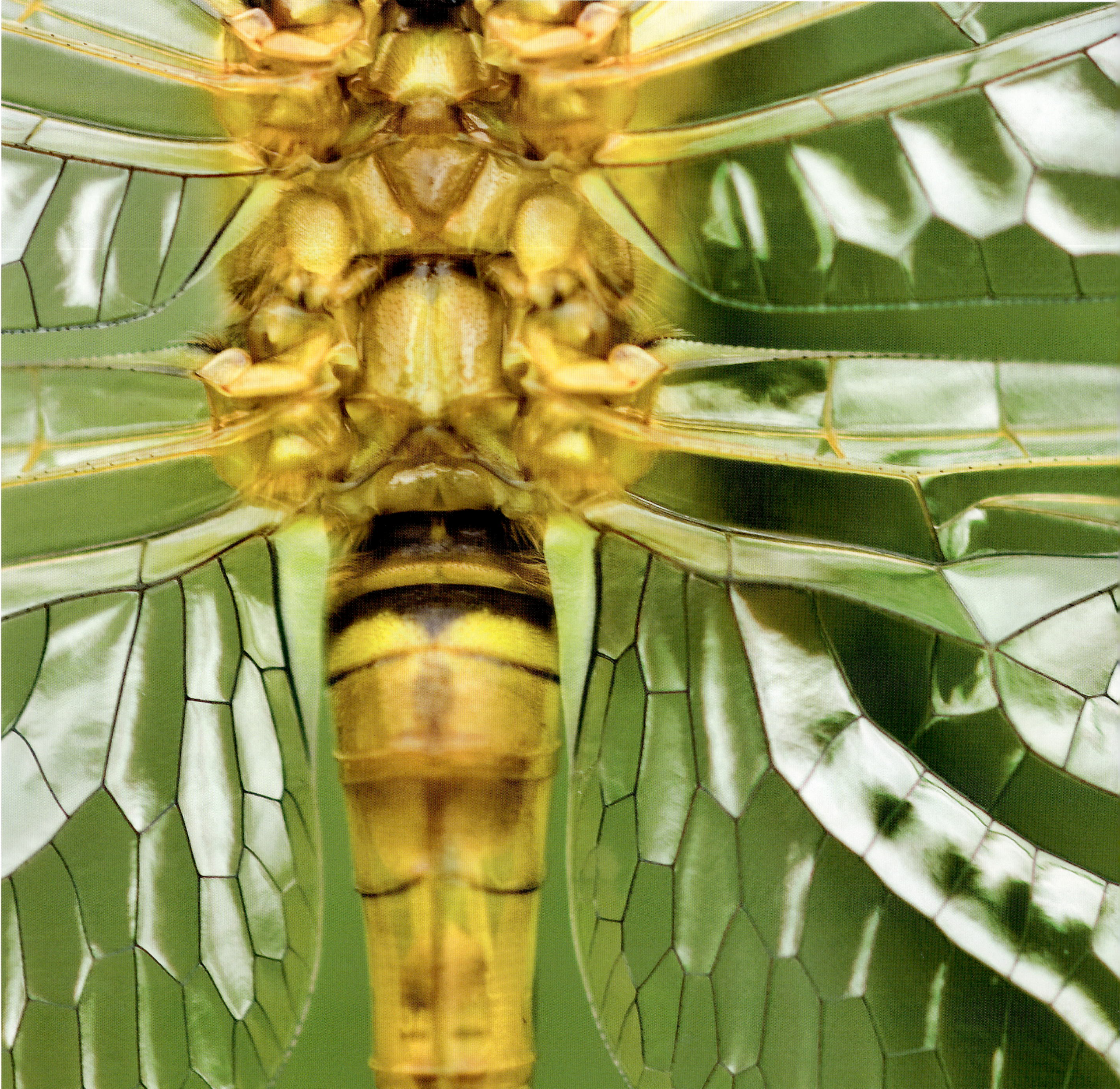

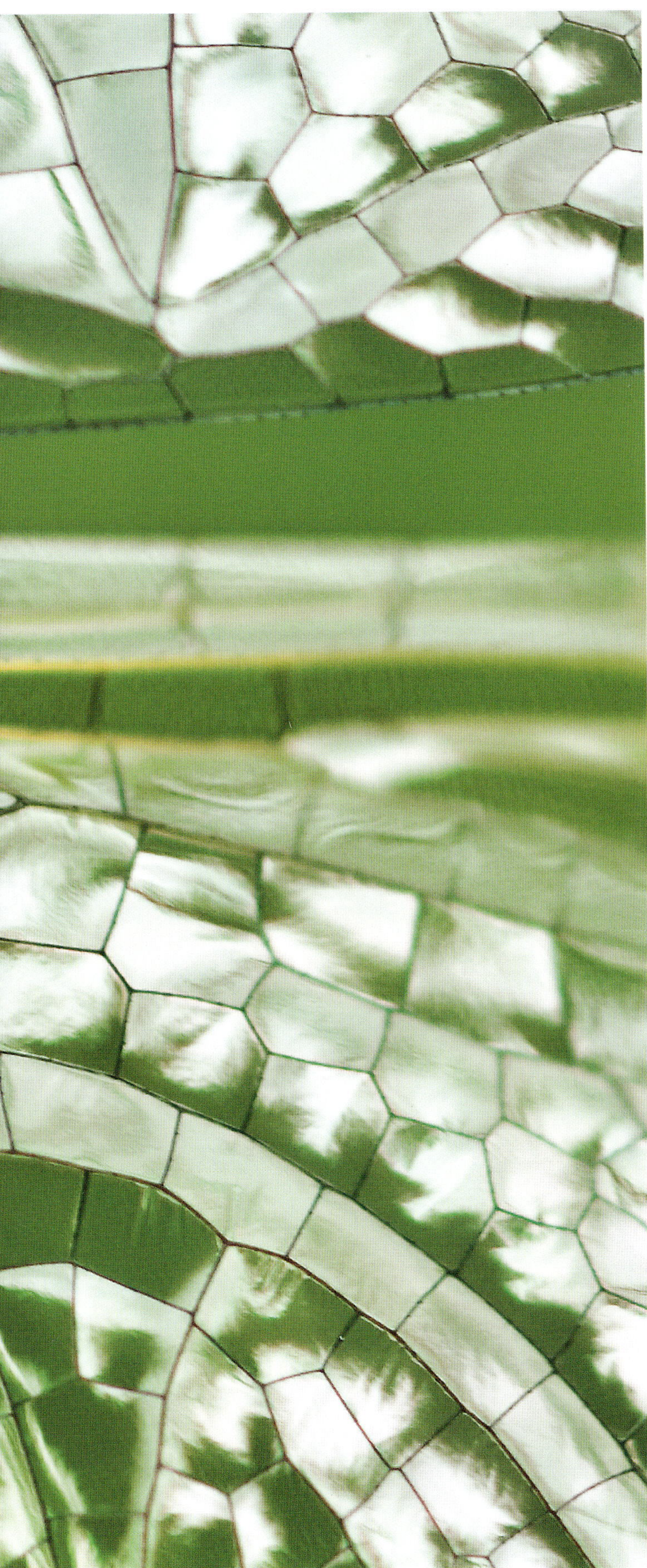

RIBBLE RIVER, PRESTON, LANCASHIRE, ENGLAND
WINGS OF NEWLY EMERGED DRAGONFLY

JASON SMALLEY

Canon EOS-1Ds Mark II, 100mm macro lens, f/4.5.
FINALIST, 2009

I was drawn to the fragility of the wings that would soon power this large insect predator. To capture the image, I had to stalk slowly through the pond-side vegetation without disturbing the dragonfly.

ROYAL BOTANIC GARDENS, KEW, SURREY, ENGLAND

GULLS ON GLASSHOUSE ROOF

JOHN PENBERTHY

Panasonic FZ20, Leica 10x zoom, 1/125sec at f/4. I laid the camera on its back and used the balustrade to steady it, making several exposures until I was happy with the exposure and balance.

THIRD, 2009

Little gulls (*Larus minutus*) are a common winter visitor to Kew. With their winter plumage and distinctive red legs and feet, they look similar to a tern. Making his first visit to Kew, my seven-year-old nephew spotted the gulls on the roof as we made our way up the stairs. He thought it was hilarious to be able to see the gulls' bottoms. I liked his laughter and the simple colour contrasts.

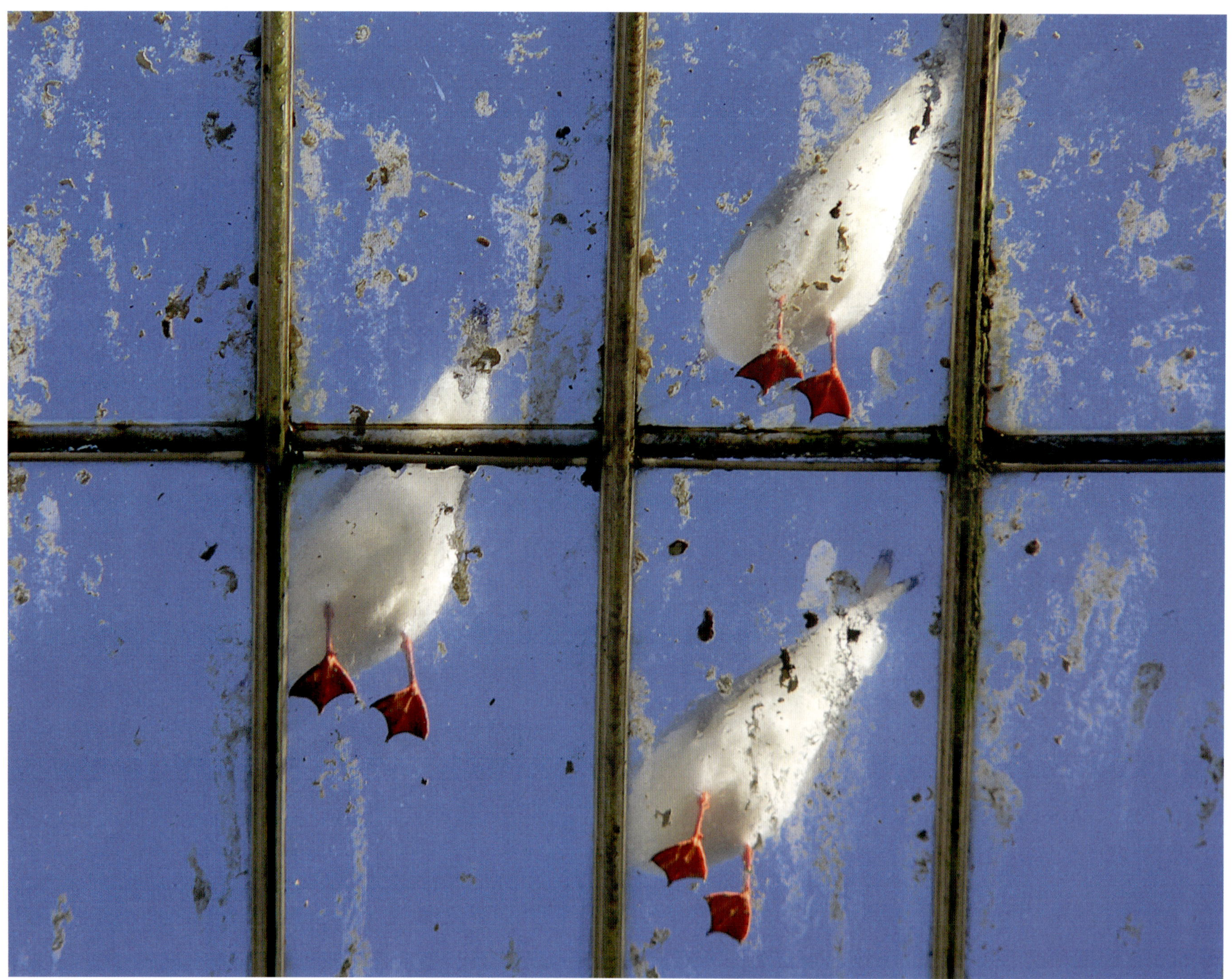

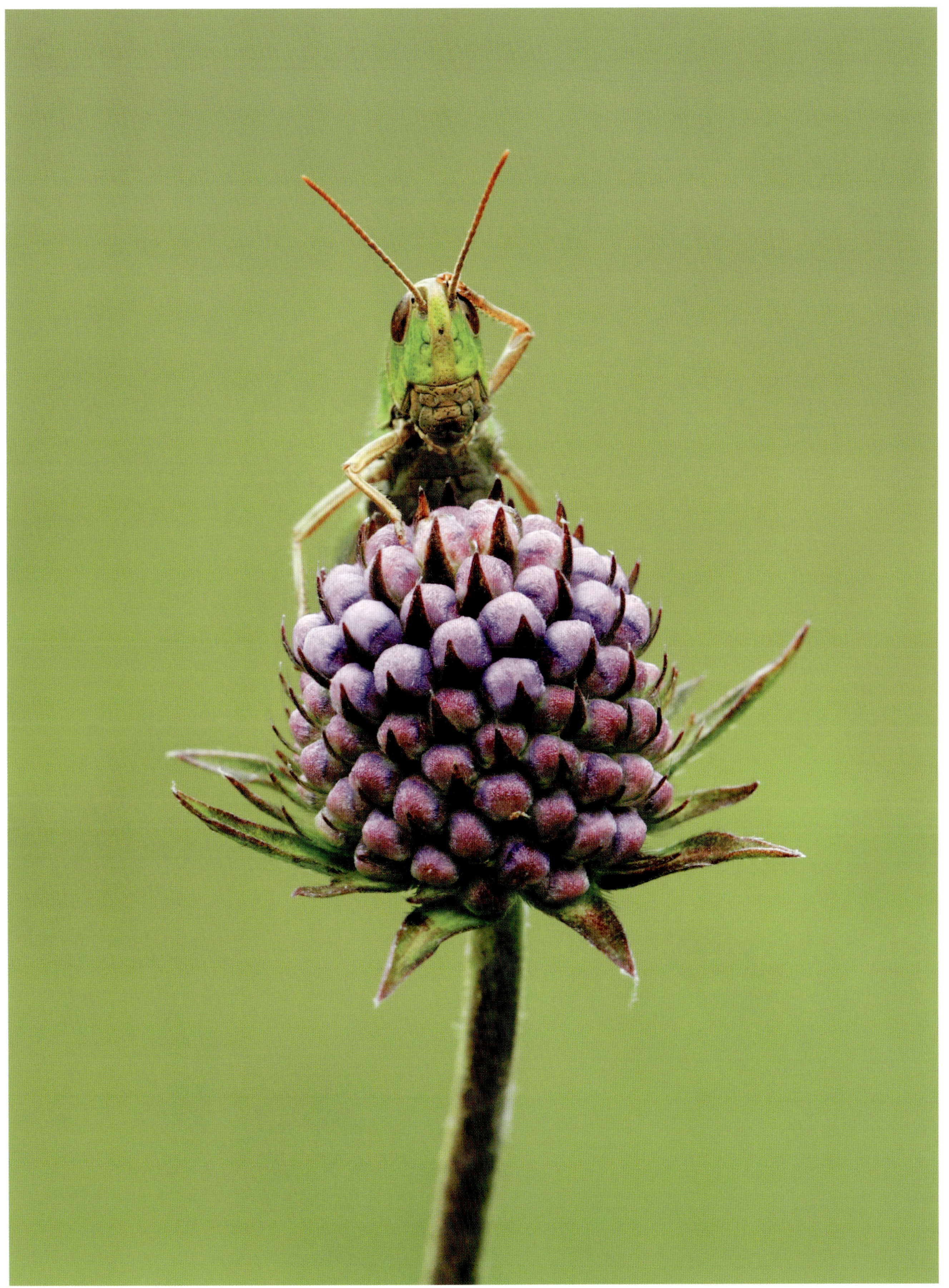

LOUNT NATURE RESERVE,
LEICESTERSHIRE, ENGLAND
CONFUSED GRASSHOPPER

MATT COLE

Canon 7D, Sigma 150mm lens. 1/100sec at f/9. Post-capture: levels, saturation and other basic adjustments.
FINALIST, 2012

A lesser marsh grasshopper (*Chorthippus albomarginatus*) perched on top of Devil's-bit scabious (*Succisa pratensis*). It was starting to rain and I think the grasshopper is wiping a raindrop from its head. I am a keen macro photographer and always on the look out for interesting insect images. This would have been a fairly standard portrait but the grasshopper's behaviour gives it that something extra. It being a cool day, the grasshopper allowed me to get quite close and to set up my tripod in front of it.

I took this photograph on Christmas morning a couple of years ago. The day was bitterly cold, with temperatures several degrees below zero. Because of this, food was very scarce and a pair of goldfinches arrived in the garden to feed on some teasels we grow every year. This image shows one of the goldfinches feeding on a frozen teasel plant, pausing momentarily to look at the camera.

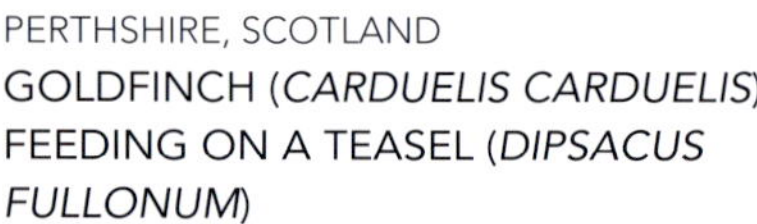

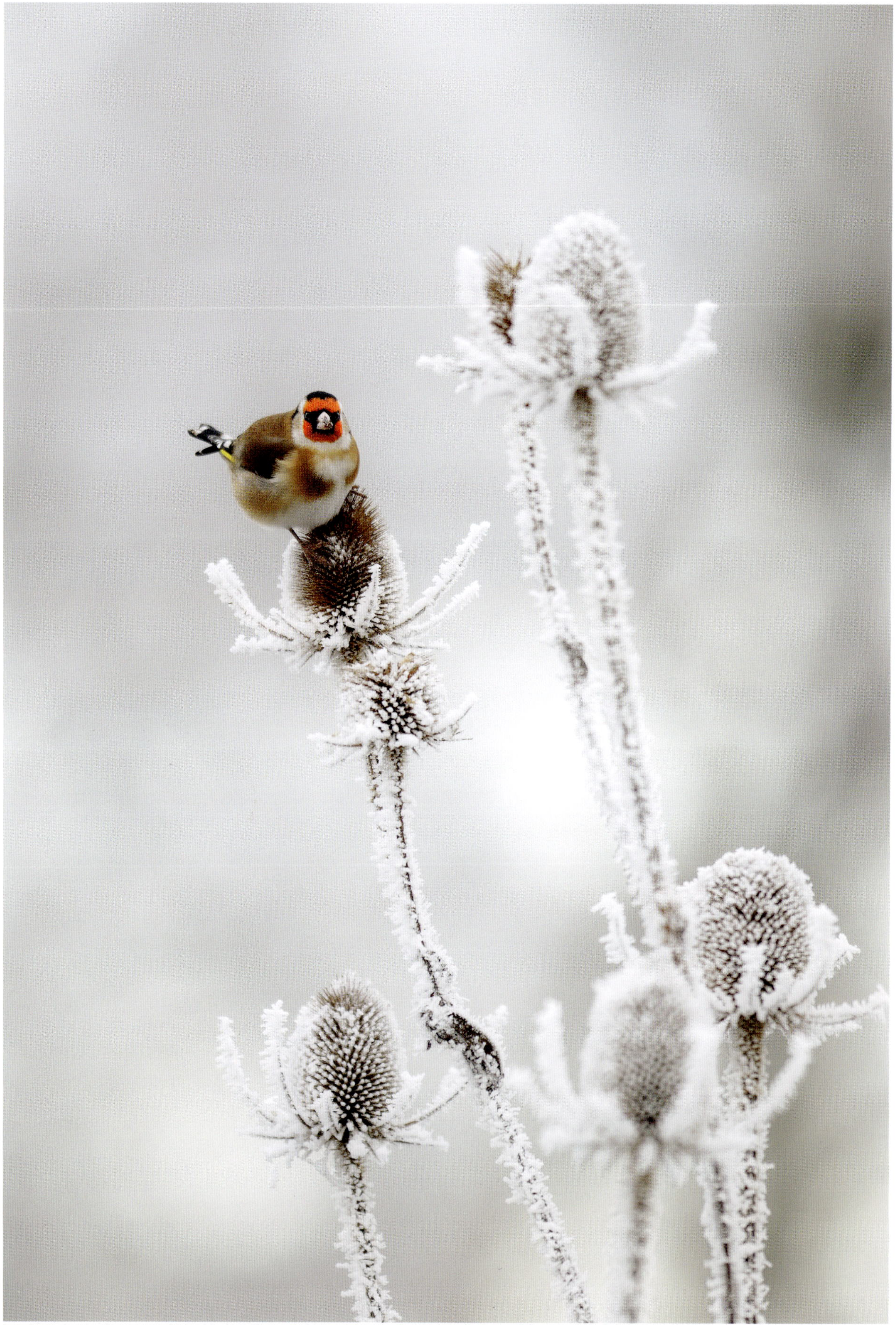

PERTHSHIRE, SCOTLAND
GOLDFINCH (*CARDUELIS CARDUELIS*) FEEDING ON A TEASEL (*DIPSACUS FULLONUM*)

FERGUS GILL

Nikon D200, 300mm f/2.8 lens, f/2.8. I rested my camera on a beanbag, which gave me a steady base and also concealed me from the goldfinches. It's critical on such cold days they aren't disturbed, as they need to eat as much as possible to survive.
FINALIST, 2009

TRZEBINIA, MALOPOLSKA REGION
SUMMER SHOWER

MAGDALENA WASICZEK

Nikon D80, Helios 77 50mm f/1.8 lens plus 0.8mm macro ring, ISO 125, 1/200sec at f/5.6.
SECOND, 2009

Polyommatus icarus is the most common butterfly in the part of Poland where I live; it's around from May until the end of September. This June day started off warm and sunny, but a summer shower caught me out while I was photographing. I managed a few shots before my 'model' escaped to find a safe place.

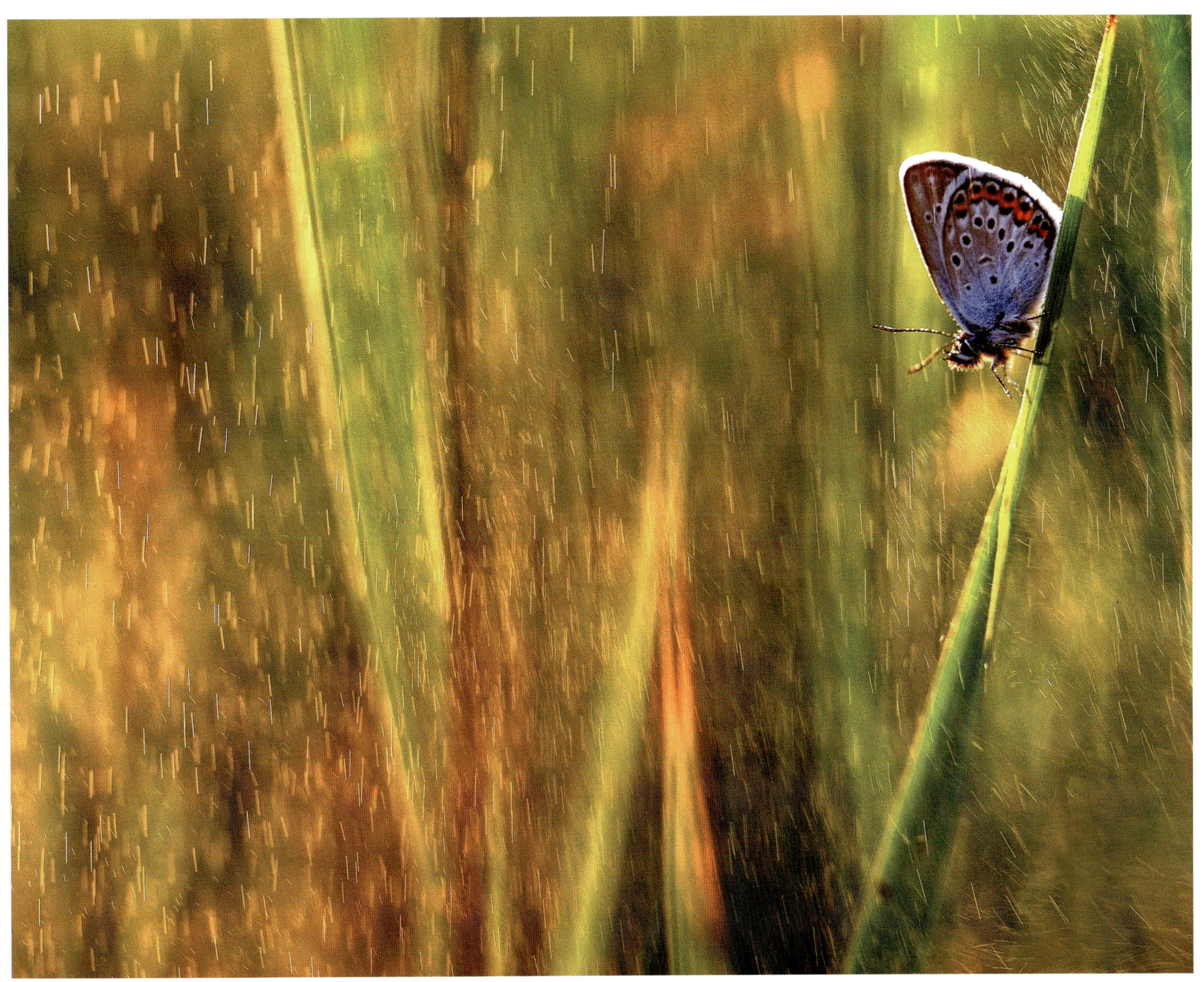

Mantises do not actively hunt their prey. They usually stay hidden or camouflaged, waiting, unmoving and virtually invisible on a leaf or stem, poised to seize any passing insect. This tiny but tenacious young mantis seems to be practising a new technique, perhaps for scaring away other predators, perched in full sight, casting a shadow much more imposing than its actual size.

There are so many layers of life in a garden. We're often inspired by the brilliance of a blossom or the graceful arc of a leaf in sunshine or in shadow. But I also like to look more deeply, finding inspiration in the small but significant life forms that are less visible at first glance.

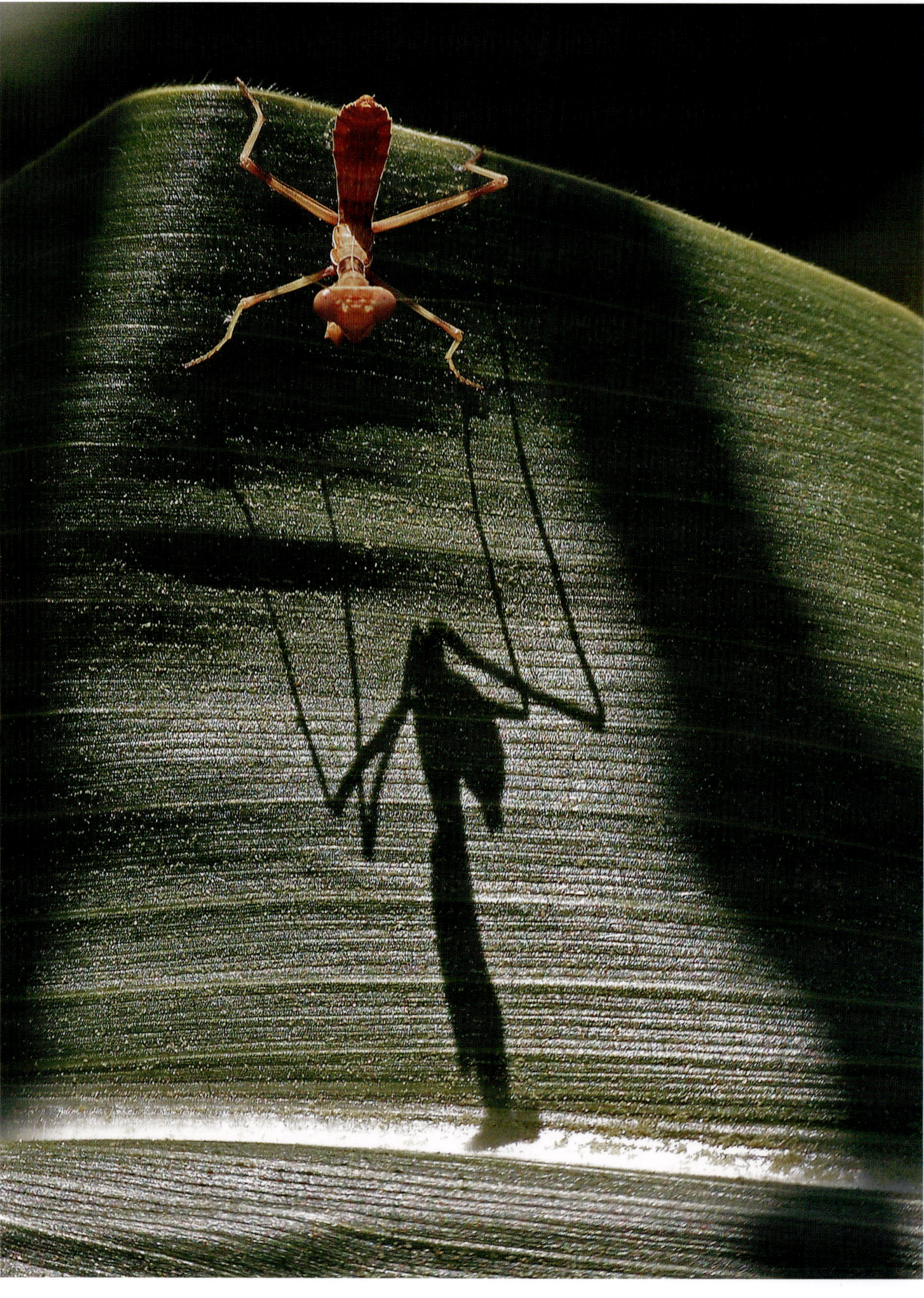

BACKYARD VEGETABLE GARDEN, SACRAMENTO, CALIFORNIA

BIGGER THAN LIFE

J. KEITH BERGER

Kodak Z712 IS.

FINALIST, 2010

MY OWN GARDEN, CORNWALL, ENGLAND
BLUE TIT (*CYANISTES CAERULEUS*)

DAVID CHAPMAN

Canon EOS 5D Mark II, 500mm lens, 1/200sec at f/5.6. Post-capture: no digital alterations.
HIGHLY COMMENDED, 2011

I wanted to show our garden birds in a typical garden environment, so that the observer could immediately understand where the scene was set. I set up a washing line and some bird feeders and sat in a hide in the garden. It took many hours and much planning to get the shots. I chose the colour of the socks to put on the washing line to try to match the colour of the blue tit which I hoped would land there.

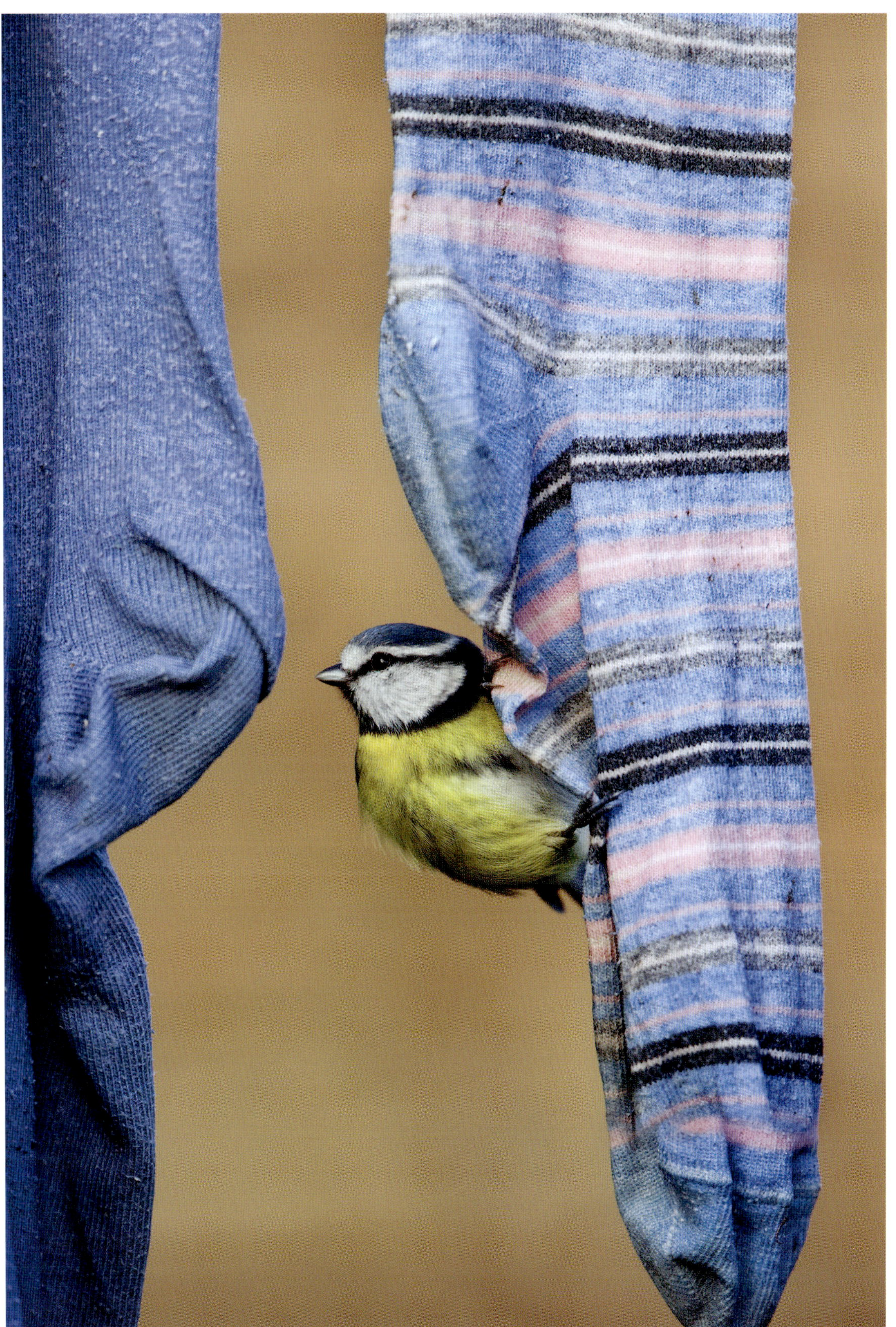

During a project for *Kew magazine* documenting the Temperate House, I noticed this single ladybird walking over the sunflower (*Helianthus* spp.) and took a couple of shots before it flew away. When I got back to the computer I realised because of the low depth-of-field in the shot, the ladybird looked like it was walking into flames. Sometimes you have to compose fast, especially when photographing insects with a tendency to fly away!

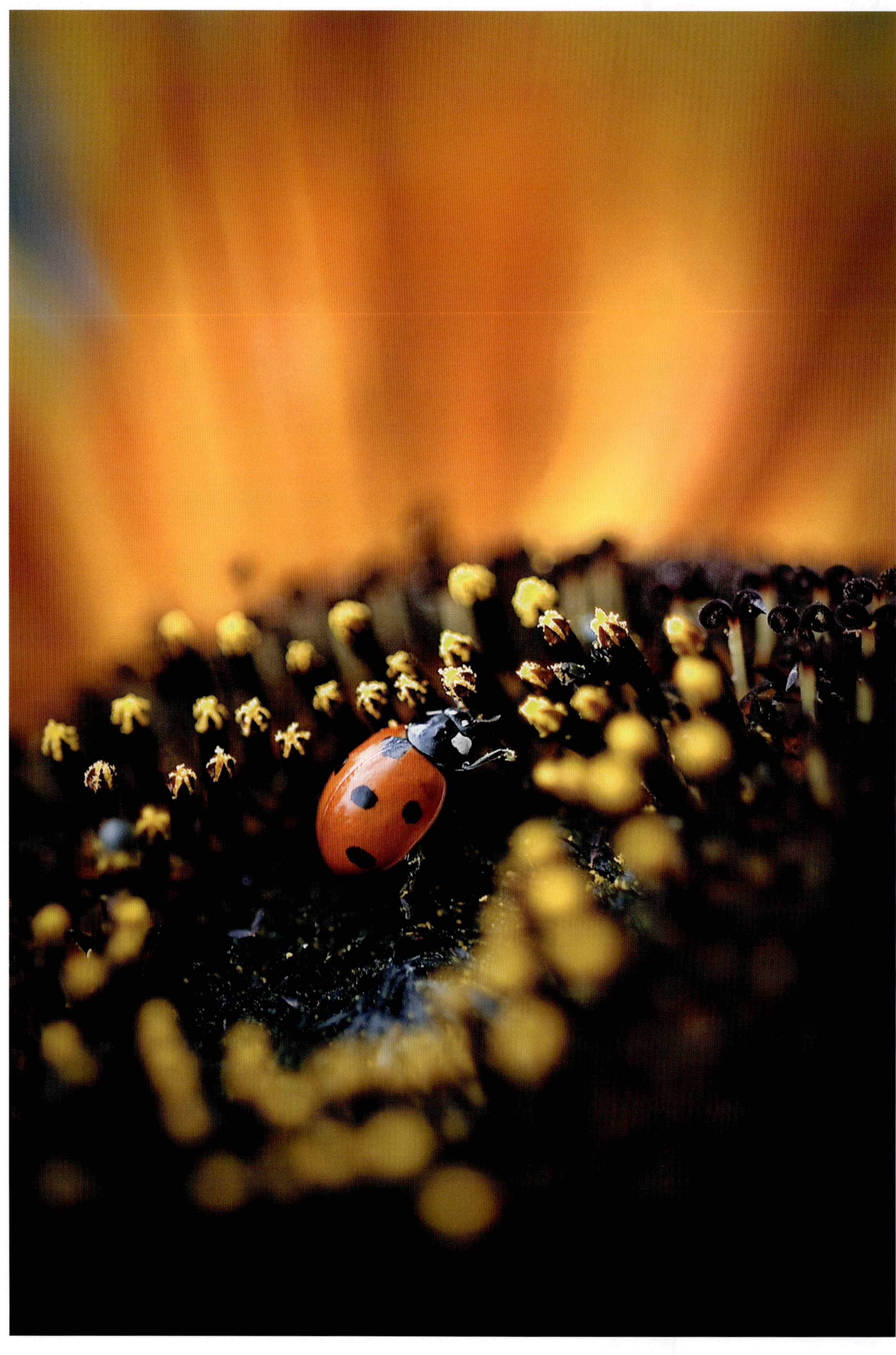

OUTSIDE THE TEMPERATE HOUSE AT ROYAL BOTANIC GARDENS, KEW, ENGLAND
FIRETRAP

JEFF EDEN

Nikon D300, 60mm lens. 1/250sec at f/4.
Post-capture: basic colour correction.
HIGHLY COMMENDED, 2012

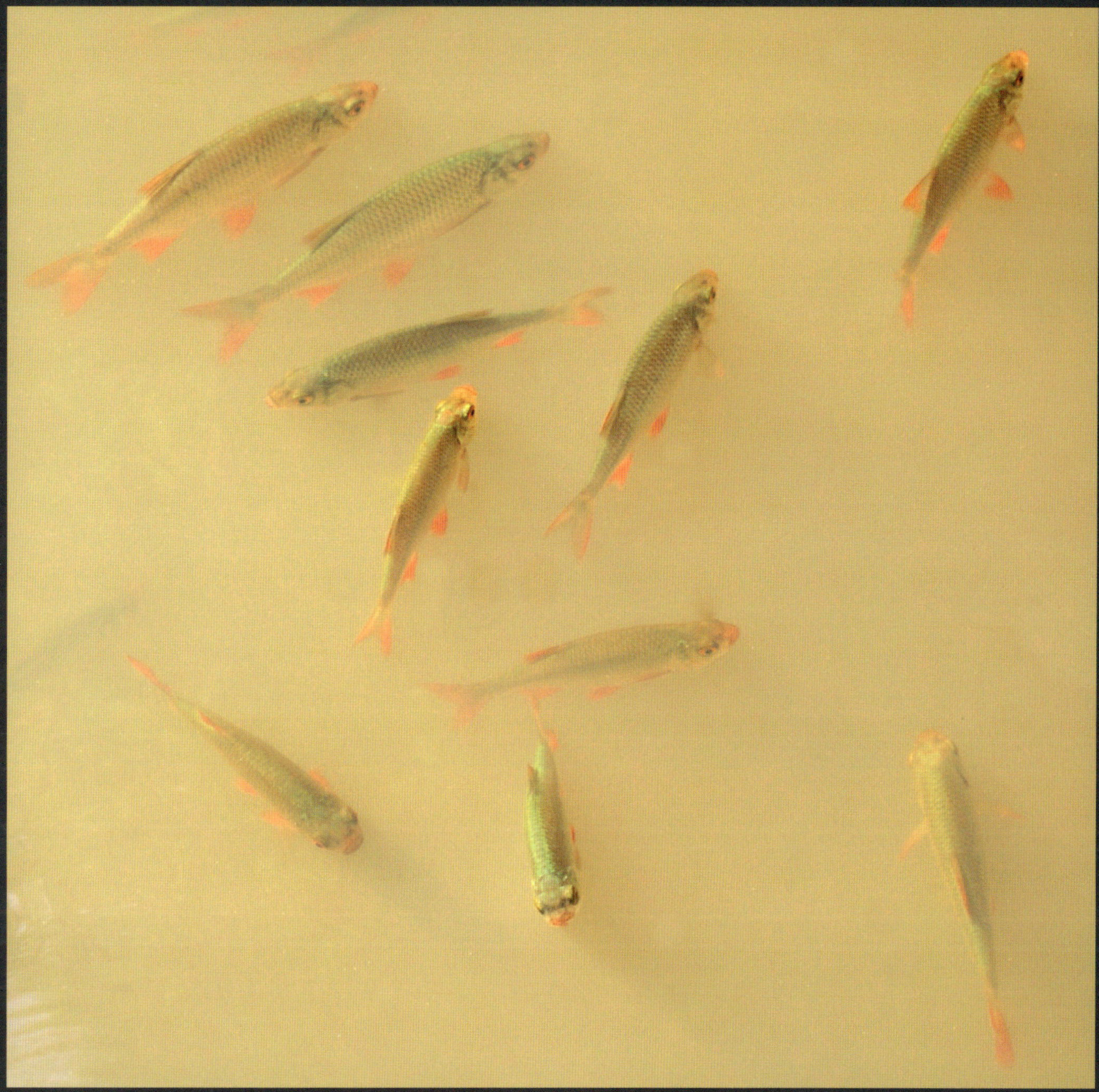

The way the sun shone through the cloudy water, casting shadows below the fish, gave the surreal impression they were floating above the water. The colour of the cloudy water complemented the colours of the fish perfectly. I chose an area where there was as little distraction as possible from shadows or ripples, to result in a very simple composition where all there is to see is the fish and their shadows on the cloudy water below.

ROMSEY, HAMPSHIRE, ENGLAND
FISH AT SIR HAROLD HILLIER GARDENS

CHRISTINE WHATLEY

Nikon Coolpix E4300, f/4.9. It was an unexpected visit without my SLR camera, which invariably results in the best photo opportunities!
FINALIST, 2009

MY GARDEN,
CORNWALL, ENGLAND
TADPOLE

DAVID CHAPMAN

Canon EOS 5D, 180mm macro lens, 0.4 sec at f/10. Post-capture: no digital alterations.
FIRST, 2011

A tadpole of a common frog (*Rana temporaria*) resting on an aquatic plant under water. I was photographing the life-cycle of the common frog and I think this was the most photogenic stage in its development. I loved the way the tadpole pushed up the meniscus of the water surface from underneath. I used a vivarium and rested the stem of an aquatic plant inside. I introduced the tadpole and waited for it to climb the stem and touch the underside of the meniscus.

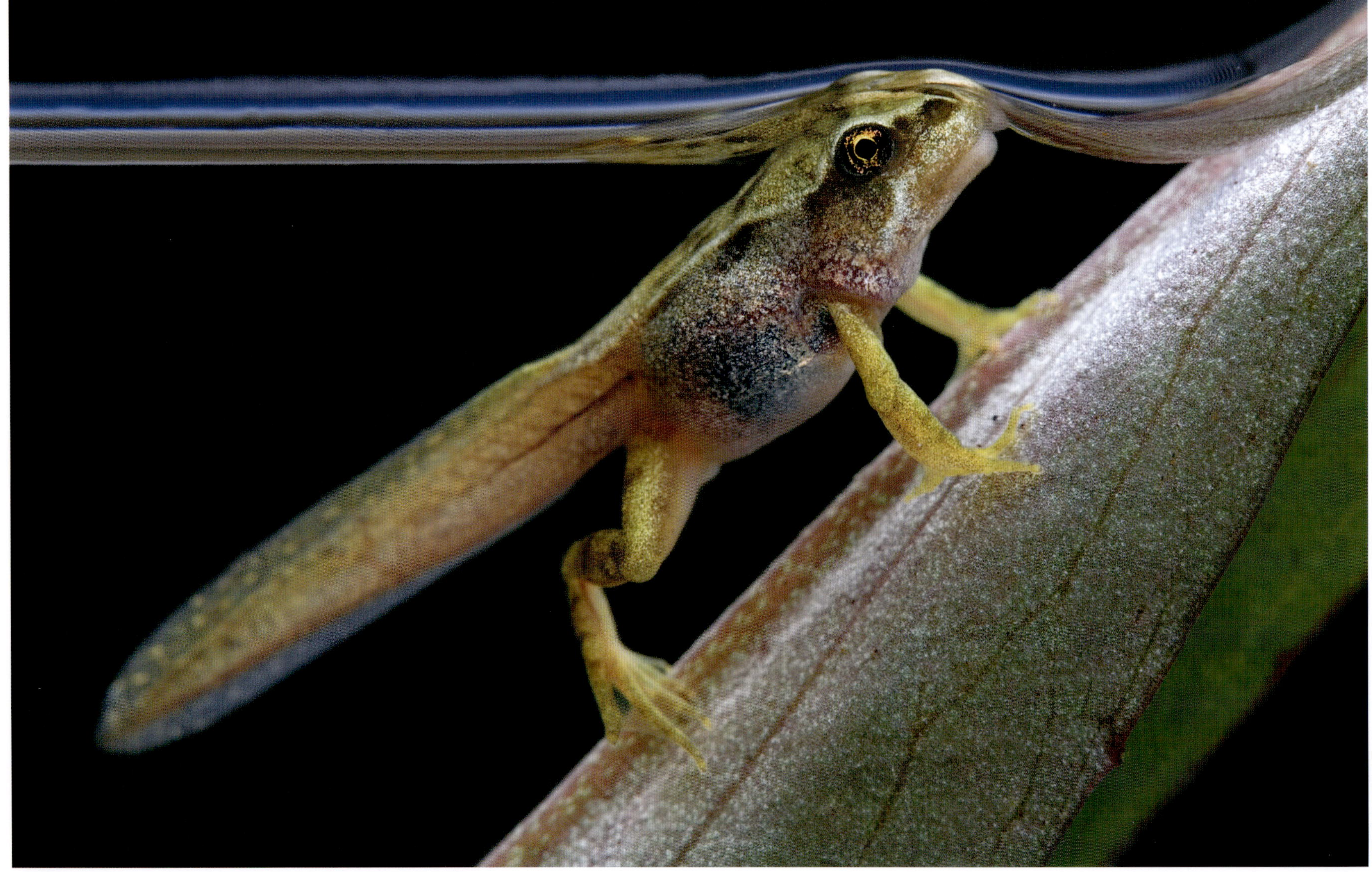

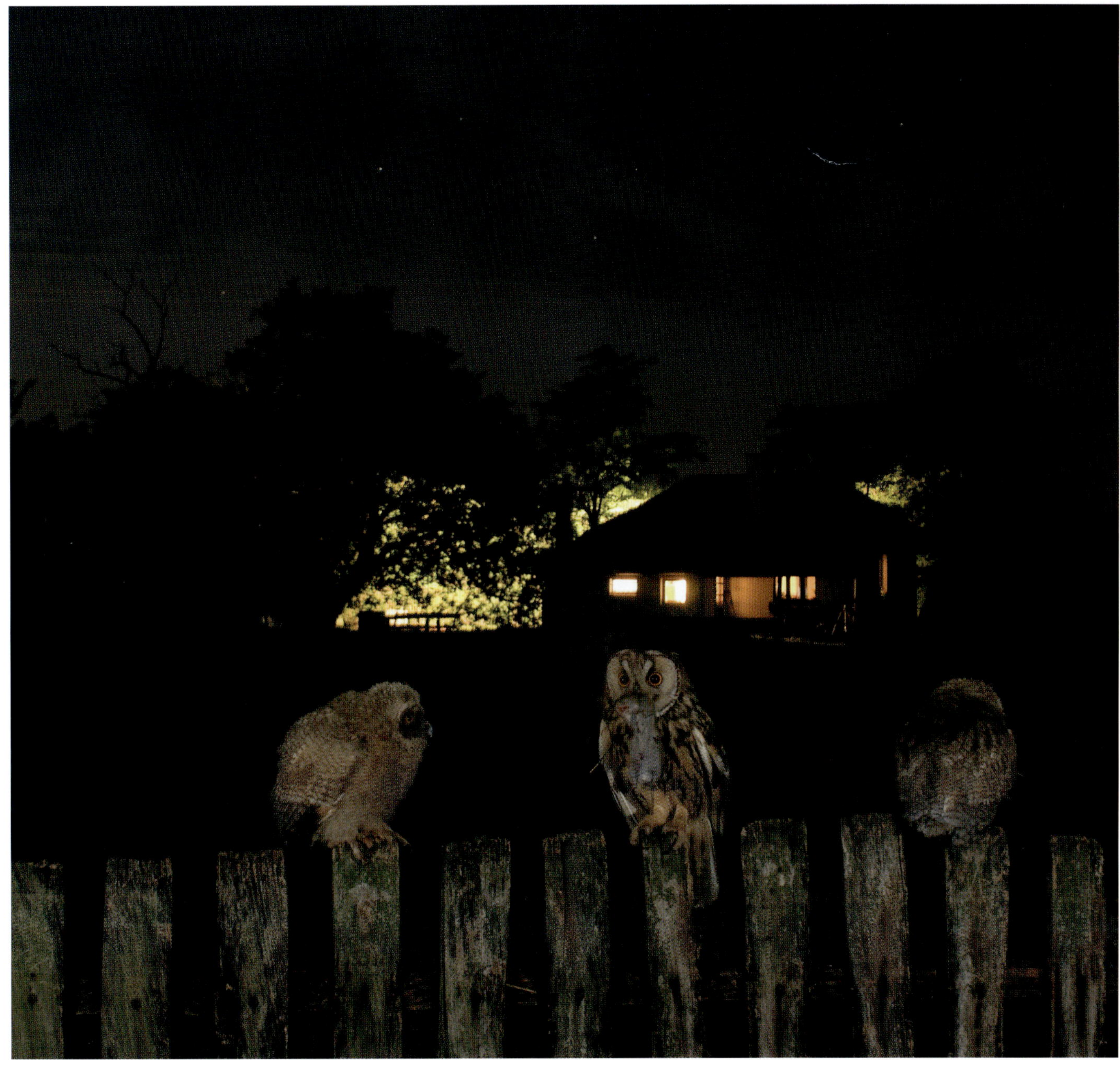

NIGHT-TIME HUNTERS

BENCE MÁTÉ

Nikon D300, 20mm, f/16, 1/10se.c
FINALIST, 2010

I live in the Hungarian *puszta* on a farm. Over the last few years I have installed a lot of bird dens in nearby trees in which rollers, kestrels, starlings and the long-eared owl family in the picture nest each year. The chicks leave the nest two weeks before they can fly and beg for food from their parents throughout the night. Sometimes their hooting is so loud that it wakes me up! These birds are used to our presence and the young ones can be photographed easily during the day. The special feature of this picture is the long, 10-second exposure, which was enough to make a few stars in the sky clearly seen. The birds were lit by torch.

INDOORS IN MY PHOTOGRAPHY STUDIO

CAST SKIN OF A LEAFHOPPER

WILLIAM FISHER

Leica S APO microscope with a Lumenera Infinity X-32 digital camera and fluorescent illumination. I took several shots using slightly different focus. Post-capture: I used Helicon Focus software to compile them into a single image. No other digital alterations.

FINALIST, 2011

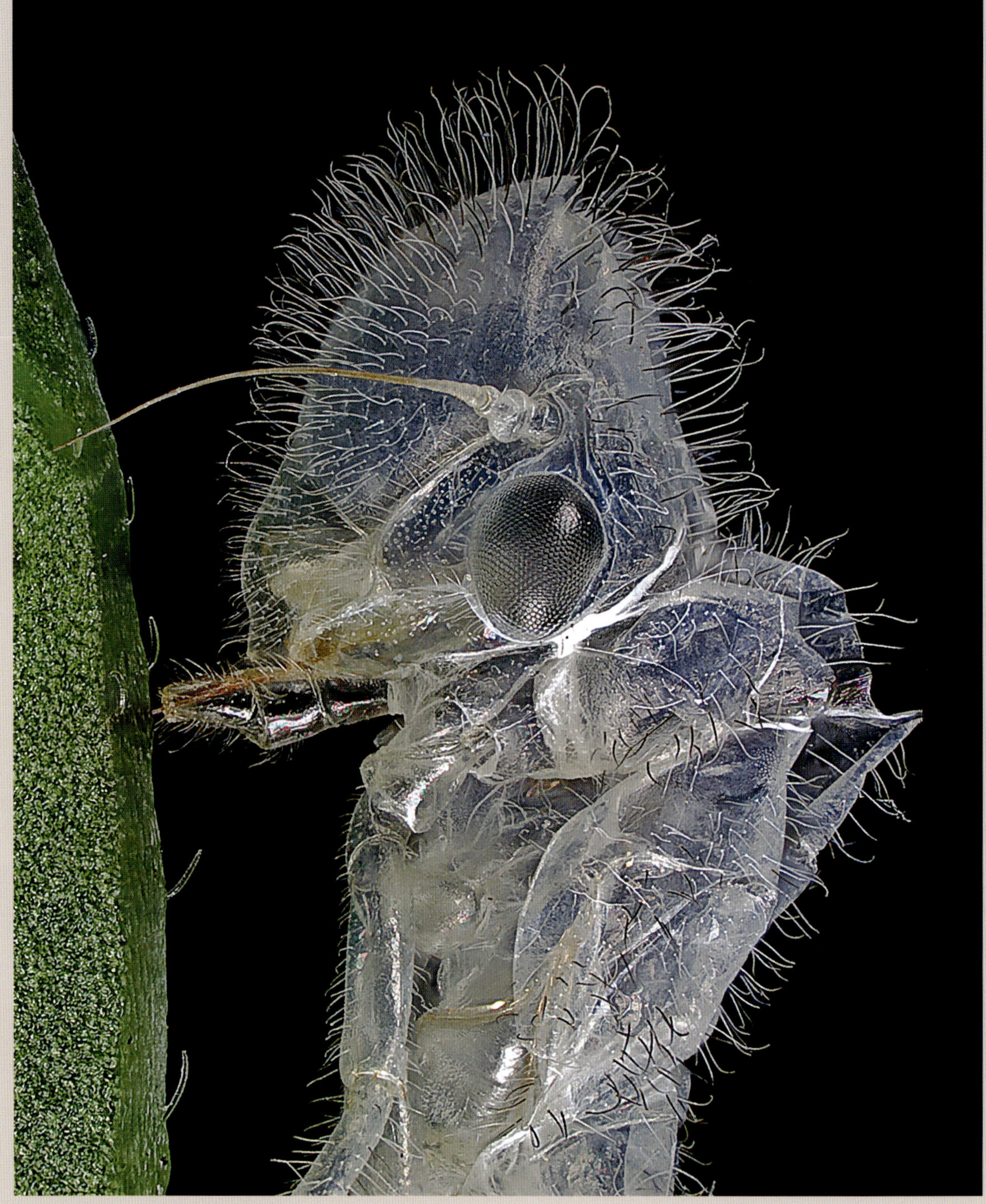

Insects have their skeleton outside their body; it's called an exoskeleton. Inflexibility of this skeleton limits their capacity to increase in size. So in order to grow, they have to molt, or shed their old skin. This can be a difficult process. To help, leafhoppers (*Paraulacizes irrorata*) anchor their exoskeleton to a main leaf vein via their mouthparts, as in this image, enabling the insect to crawl out of it more easily. Intricate details of nature such as this are rarely seen by most people. I wanted to illustrate the incredible beauty of such seemingly insignificant, overlooked creatures that play a fundamental role in supporting our ecosystems.

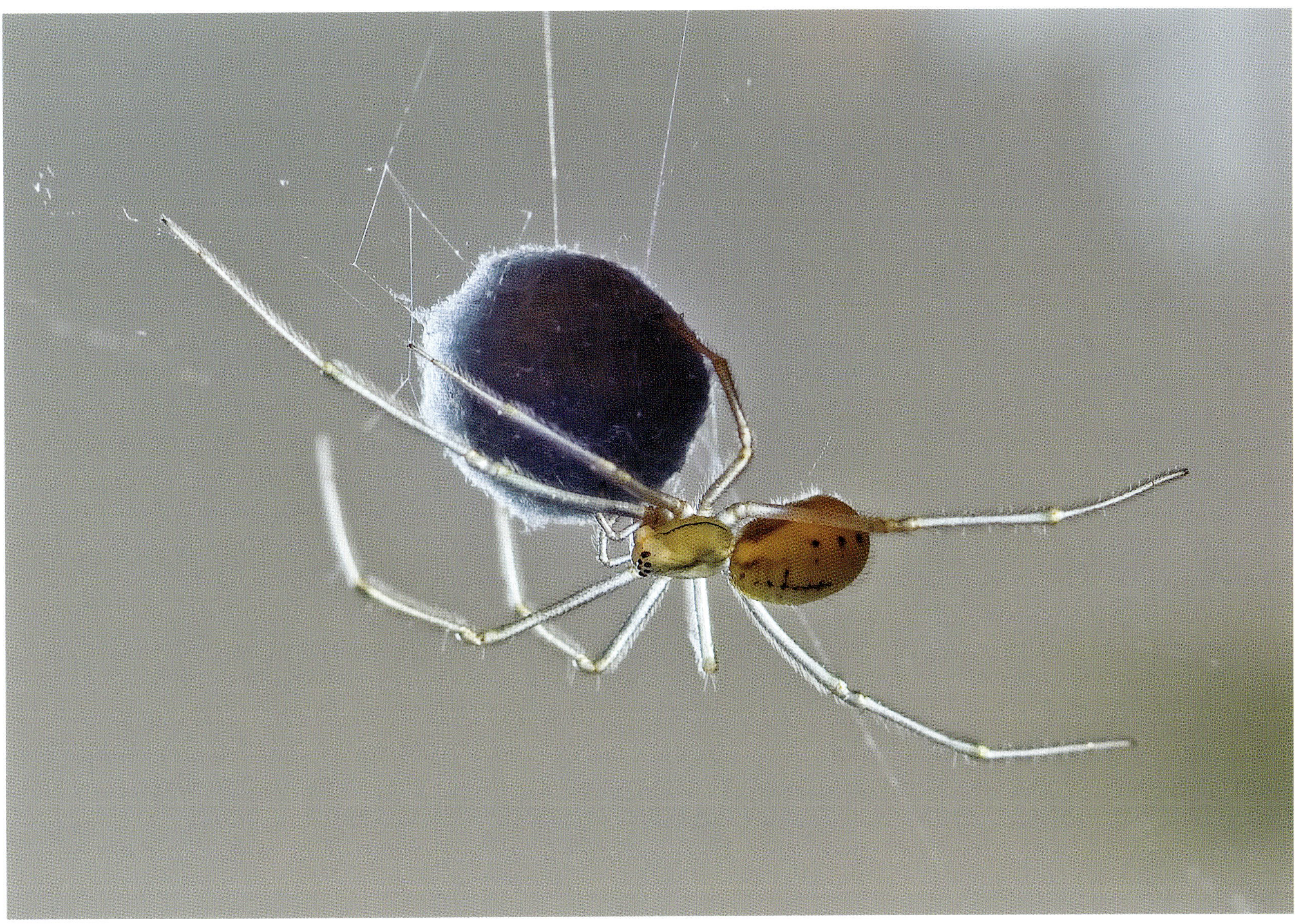

LAUDER, SCOTTISH BORDERS, SCOTLAND
COCOON

SARAH-FIONA HELME

Canon EOS 40D, 100mm macro lens, 1.3sec at f/8.0, ISO 100. Post-capture: exposure and colours tweaked, image cropped and cleaned a little. No other alterations.
HIGHLY COMMENDED, 2011

A spider carefully rolls her cocoon along the remnants of her web after accidentally being dislodged from the plant which served as her haven of protection. One of the more common species in Britain, these spiders like to spin their webs on vegetation or on structures such as garden sheds. The notable, bluish-grey cocoon caught my eye. I was in awe of the spider's behaviour after her web of protection was disturbed and torn. However, the few remaining tiny strands of silk were still strong enough to support the spider and her cocoon whilst she began to repair her web. I wanted to photograph the spider whilst she was against a light background to highlight her translucence. She was quite active and a narrow aperture was needed to create enough depth of field. I was using a slow shutter speed, so I waited until she paused. From many shots this seemed the best.

There is something quintessentially English about this image, caught as it is between ageing grandeur and the pastoral. Bathed in the late rays of a summer's day, the rabbit hopped in to steal the scene. He appears frozen in a fading shaft of light, as if on a stage for the first time. Capturing a fleeting moment celebrates the inherent nature of photography. It is serendipitous that the rabbit remained in the pool of light long enough, whilst the air of expectation created from knowing he will soon bound away is at the heart of the image.

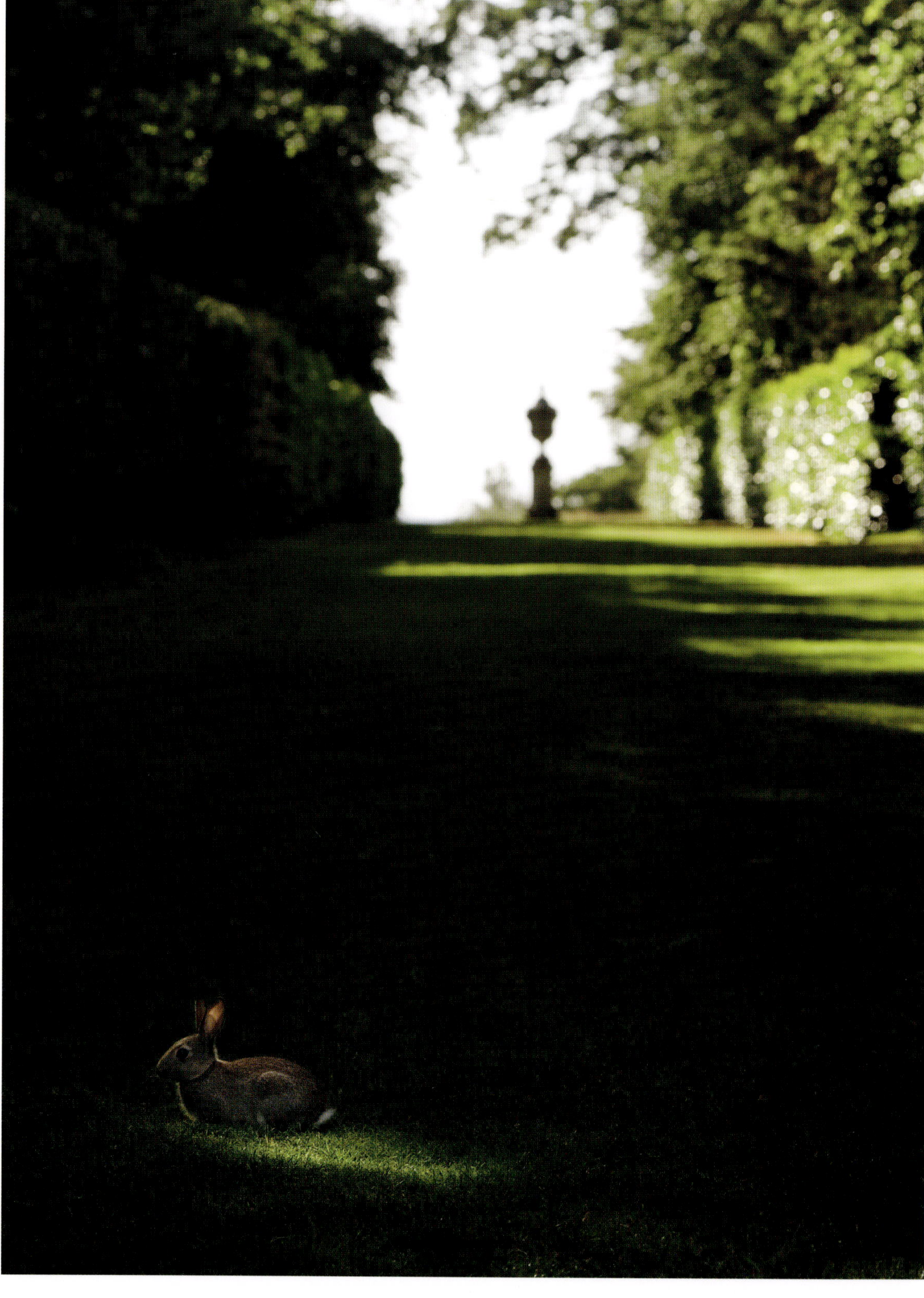

CLIVEDEN, BUCKINGHAMSHIRE, ENGLAND
THE AVENUE

NIKKI DE GRUCHY

Canon EOS 5D, 135mm lens, 1/125sec, ISO 160.
FINALIST, 2011

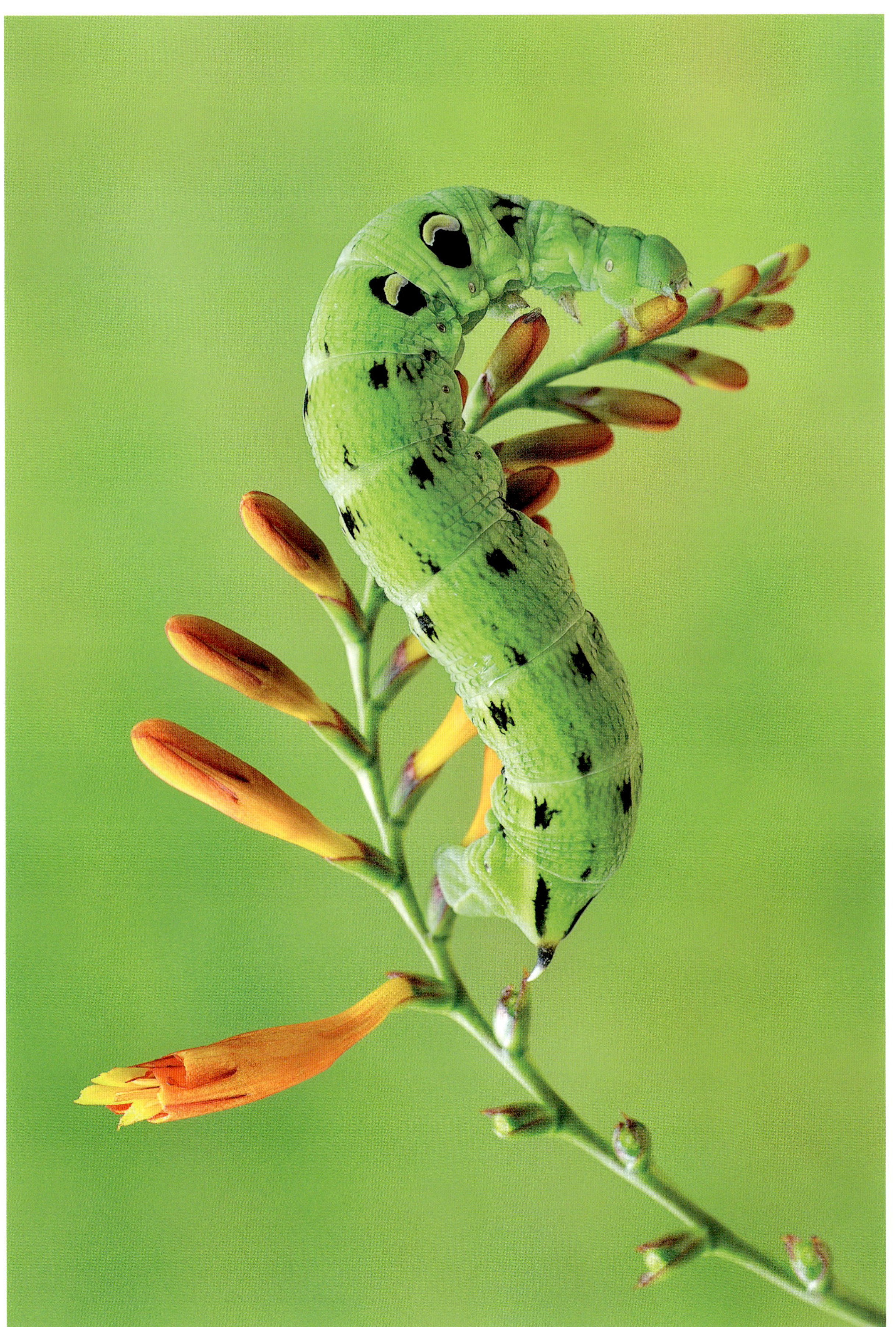

GLICHÓW, MALOPOLSKA REGION
SINUOUS

MAGDALENA WASICZEK

Nikon D300, Tamron 90 lens. 1/250sec at f/10.
Post-capture: basic colour management.
FINALIST, 2012

This is a small elephant hawk-moth caterpillar (*Deilephila porcellus*) at a young stage. I think it is one of the most beautiful caterpillars and I was amazed by its size of nearly 9cm. In this photo I like the layout of caterpillar and stem like an 'S'. This was the first time I had seen this type of caterpillar, and I could not pass up this opportunity to photograph it. I have to admit that she was a top model.

A late snowfall in March resulted in the winter thrushes desperately looking for food. The hawthorn (*Crataegus laevigata*) bush at the end of the drive held a few remaining berries and, as the snow fell, I released the shutter, hoping to catch the slow-falling flakes around the fieldfare (*Turdus pilaris*). It was a shot I had envisaged taking for a long time but a lack of snow had always prevented it. Thankfully the late winter snowfall changed that!

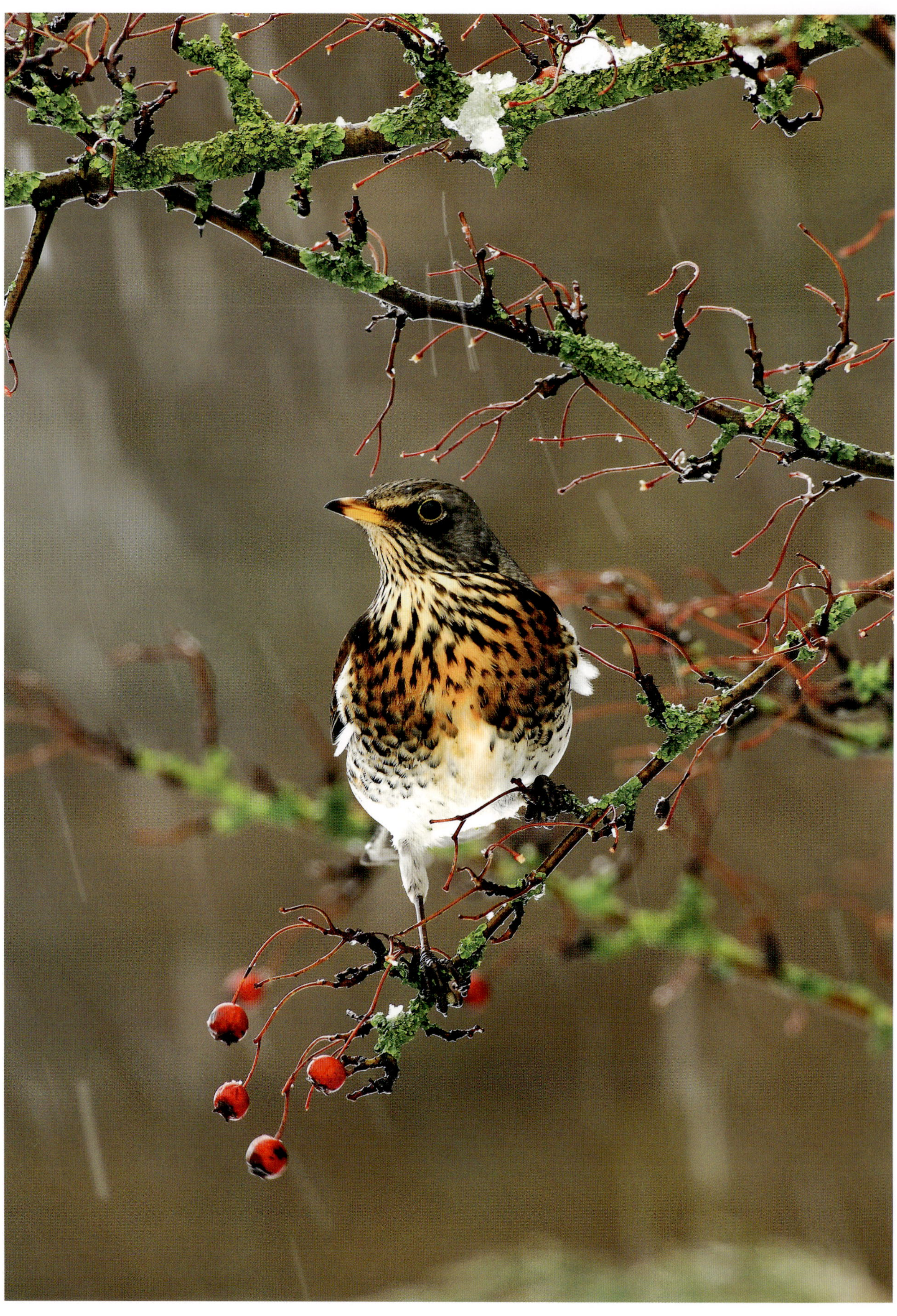

BRACKLEY, NORTHAMPTONSHIRE, ENGLAND
FIELDFARE IN THE SNOW

CRAIG CHURCHILL

Nikon D2X, Nikon 500mm f/4 AF-S II lens, f/6.7. The shot was taken from my vehicle using a beanbag for support on the window ledge. I sat and waited until the fieldfare returned and perched on an exposed branch to make the most of the falling snow.
FINALIST, 2009

TRZEBINIA, MALOPOLSKA REGION

FIND ME...

MAGDALENA WASICZEK

Nikon D300, Tamron 90 lens. 1/400sec at f/5.
Post-capture: basic colour management.
HIGHLY COMMENDED, 2011

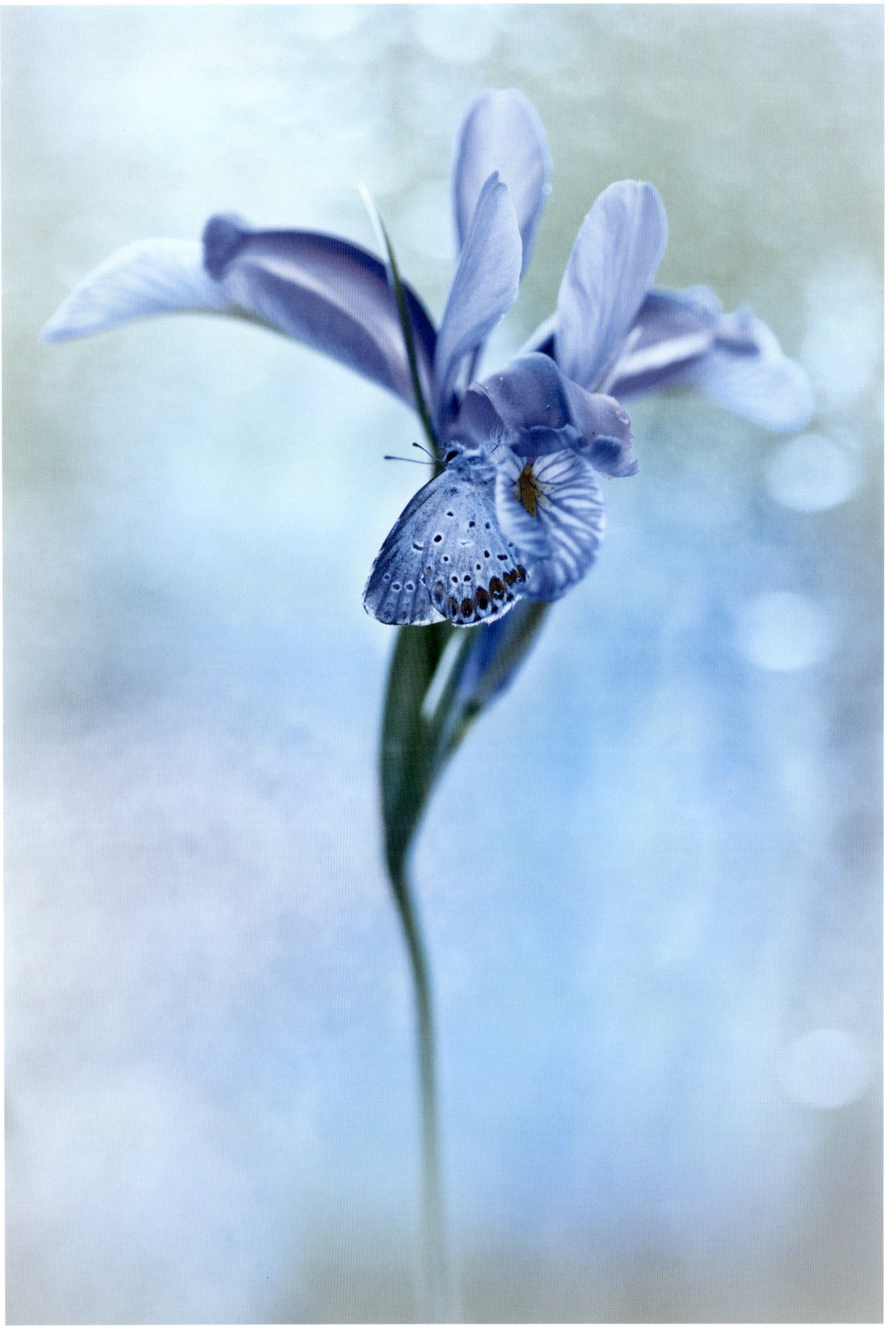

A common blue (*Polyommatus icarus*) camouflaged in iris (*Iris* spp.) petals. From a distance, this tiny butterfly looked like the petals. This photo was taken in the evening, and the butterfly did not pay attention to me. I wanted to show the gentleness of the butterfly and flower, emphasise the softness of petals and give the atmosphere of sleepiness. I fell in love with this delicate duo and with the colours of butterfly and iris in harmony.

I took hundreds of shots to capture this photo and paid a lot of attention to the behaviour of these ants. The right time to take these shots is the late afternoon, when the light is gentle enough light to produce good backlighting and a perfect reflection.

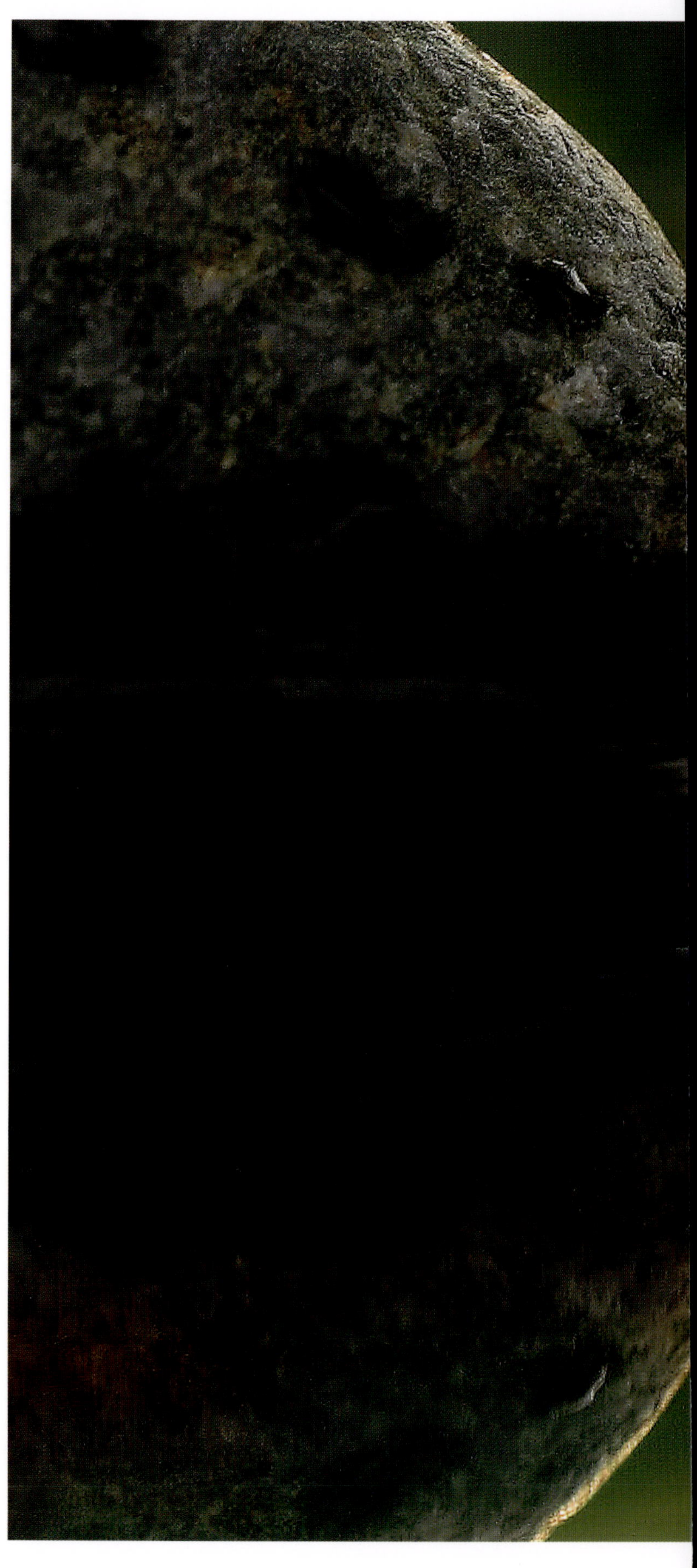

BATAM ISLAND
DRINKING II

VINCENTIUS FERDINAND

Canon 7D, 100mm lens. Post-capture: some cropping and levels adjustment.
SECOND, 2012

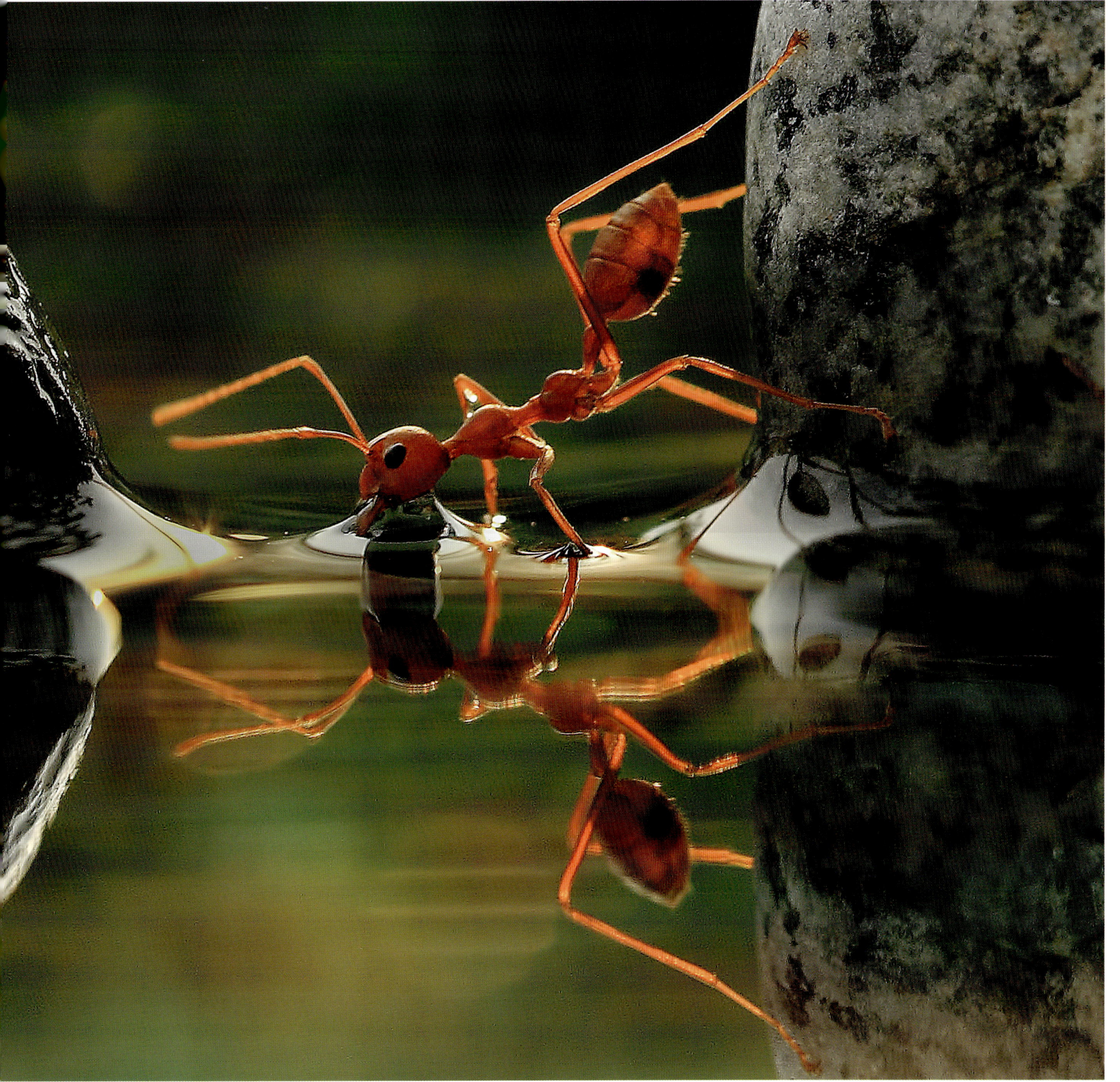

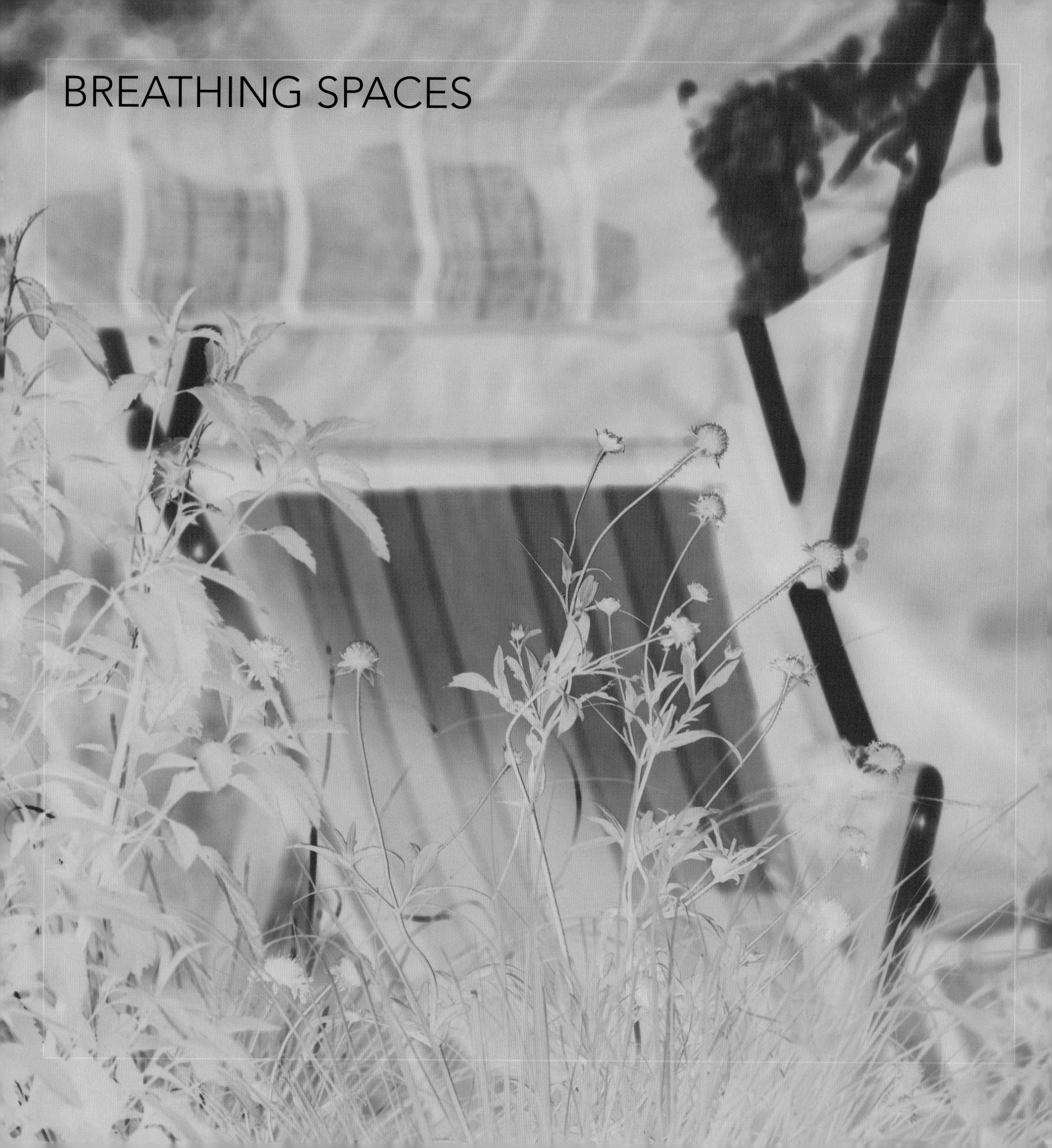

BREATHING SPACES

Breathing Spaces

Since the Industrial Revolution, we have moved away from nature in our daily lives. More and more people live in towns and cities, so that an essential connection between people and the environment has been lost. The landscape seems to be a background to our lives, rather than a part of it. We keep our eyes fixed on the tarmac ahead of us. Fewer and fewer of us tread real earth every day, walk under trees, experience growth and regeneration of plants at first hand, delight in a black, starry sky.

In this book there is plenty of evidence that the yearning for the natural, the wild, the free, is still alive. Photographers want to record and celebrate the spaces that are special to them, and to communicate to others their delight in the natural world.

Plants, gardens and natural places are essential for promoting our physical and our spiritual well-being. Photography offers us the chance to really look and appreciate these spaces at a deeper, more creative level. For many people photography is a reason in itself to get out into gardens and landscapes – sometimes at odd times of the day (and night) – to experience, record and enjoy. As an International Garden Photographer of the Year judge I am keenly aware, through the huge numbers of entries we review each year, that natural landscapes offer the photographer an infinite source of challenging inspiration. And it is highly rewarding to be able to celebrate those photographers who have risen to that challenge over the last five years.

Protecting natural spaces is an essential part of the work of organisations like the National Trust in England and Wales, and similar organisations around the world. Botanic gardens provide us with the scientific knowledge that underpins all conservation work. But it is up to all of us to support that process.

International Garden Photographer of the Year raises awareness of the importance of this work and, along the way, produces fantastic images, year after year, for the public to enjoy and savour.

Clive Nichols
Leading garden photographer, author
Acknowledgement to Lance Hattatt

Radhika and her neighbour, Saroj, on her roof garden in one of Delhi's largest slums – Kesumpur Pahari. The slum, built more than 30 years ago, has no running water or sewage facilities but, despite the residents' poverty, many have beautified their homes with plants and flowers. Radhika told me she was very proud of her plants.

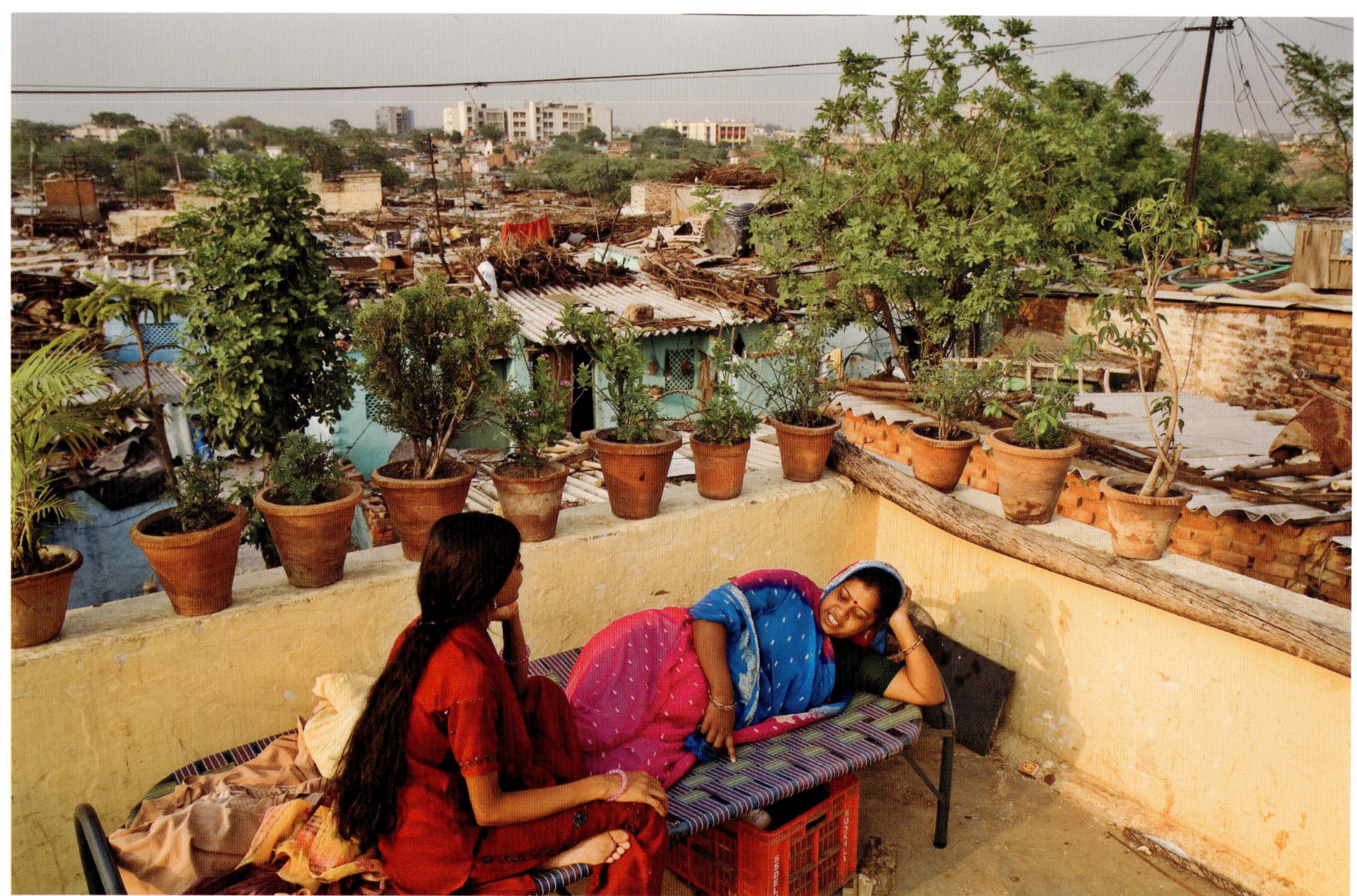

DELHI

RADHIKA AND HER NEIGHBOUR, SAROJ

STUART FREEDMAN

Canon EOS 5D, 28mm lens, f/16. I was working on a story for Channel 4 about water issues. I'd noticed the gardens and the many plant pots, so asked if I could spend an hour or so with Saroj and some of her friends.
FINALIST, 2008

This is a picture of my beautiful daughter perched on my not so beautiful feet under a tree in Ritsurin Park, Japan. This is one of the most famous parks in Japan, and is a must-see for anyone who ventures to the island of Shikoku. I shot this with a wide-angle lens while lying on a bench under the tree.

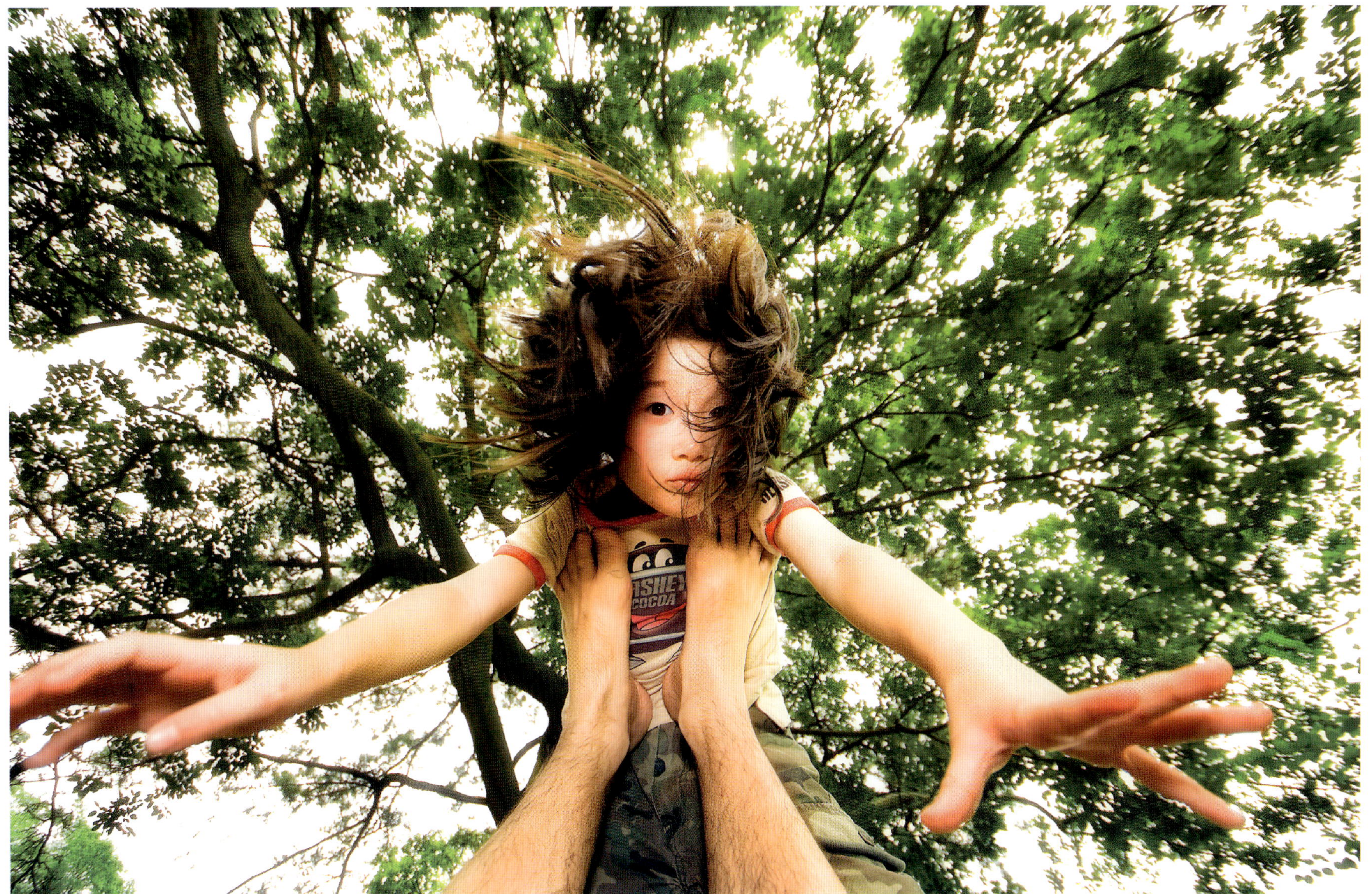

RITSURIN PARK, TAKAMATSU, KAGAWA
NATURE GIRL

KEVIN COZMA

Nikon D200, Sigma 10-20mm lens, f/5.6. I manually exposed for the bottom of the leaves as I wanted them to be bright and alive. I use a Nikon Sb800 flash on-camera with a warming gel and a mini softbox mounted on it. This exposed my daughter correctly and evenly, after I used flash value compensation exposed for her face.
FINALIST, 2009

This photograph shows my mother directing the proceedings as we cleared the garden following my daughter's wedding reception, making good for winter. My mother has a lifetime's interest in, and knowledge of, gardening and, although suffering from dementia, has retained the ability to pass on all her tips and wisdom.

The flowers in the background are cosmos (*Cosmos* spp.) and sweet peas (*Lathyrus odoratus*), which I grew from seeds especially for the wedding. I planted them in beds and containers and they flowered brilliantly all summer, making a great backdrop for the celebrations. Seeing my mother sitting peacefully and thoroughly at home in the garden inspired me to try to capture that particular moment which, to me, seemed both sad and happy.

DERBYSHIRE, ENGLAND
GARDENING BOSS

ADRIENNE BROWN

Panasonic Lumix DMC-LX2, Leica DC Vario-Elmarit lens.
I decided to take the photograph from above to record as much information as possible and create a sense of distance. I liked the way the window framed the picture, and the extra interest created by the bottles and guitar head.
FINALIST, 2009

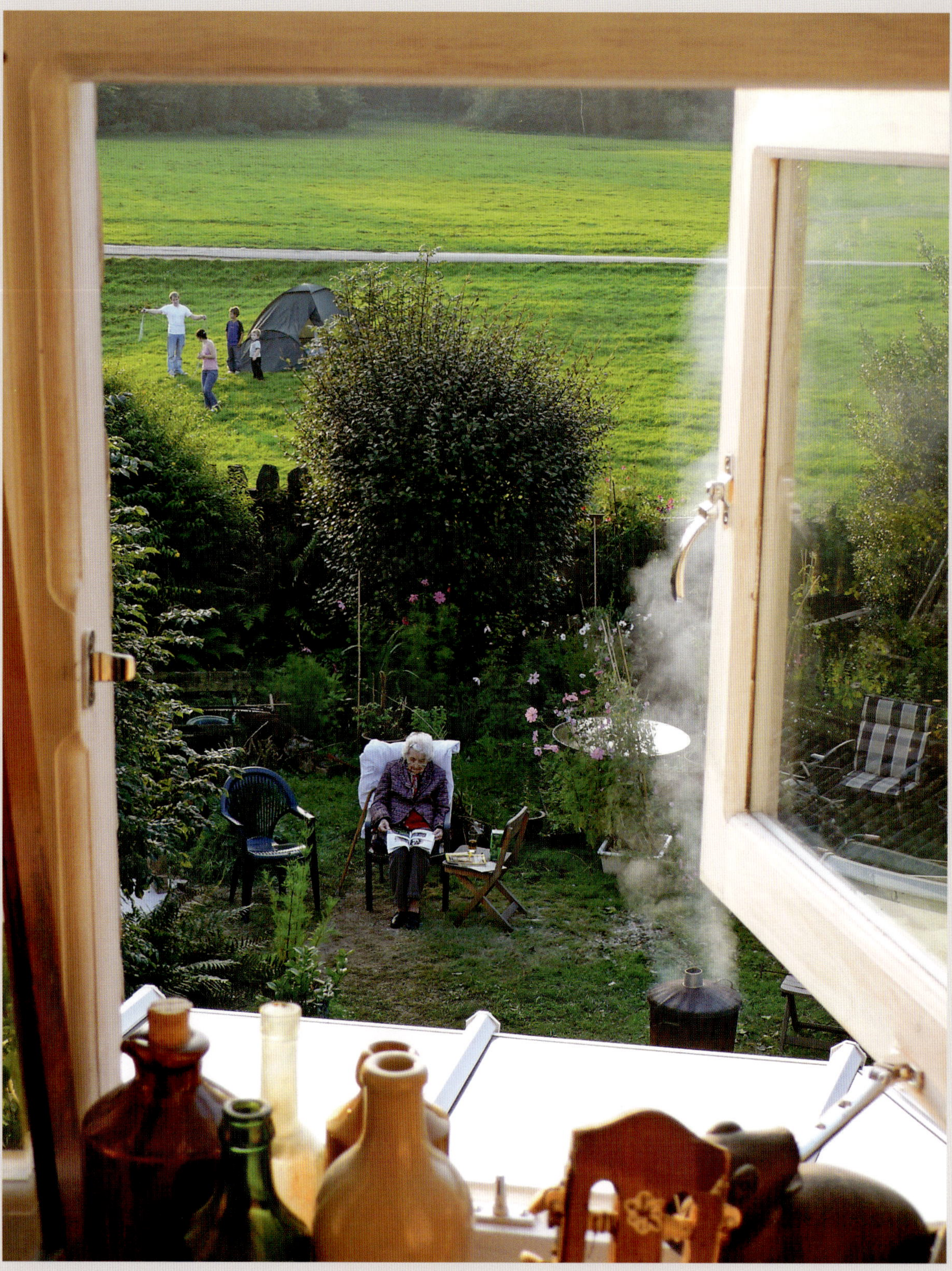

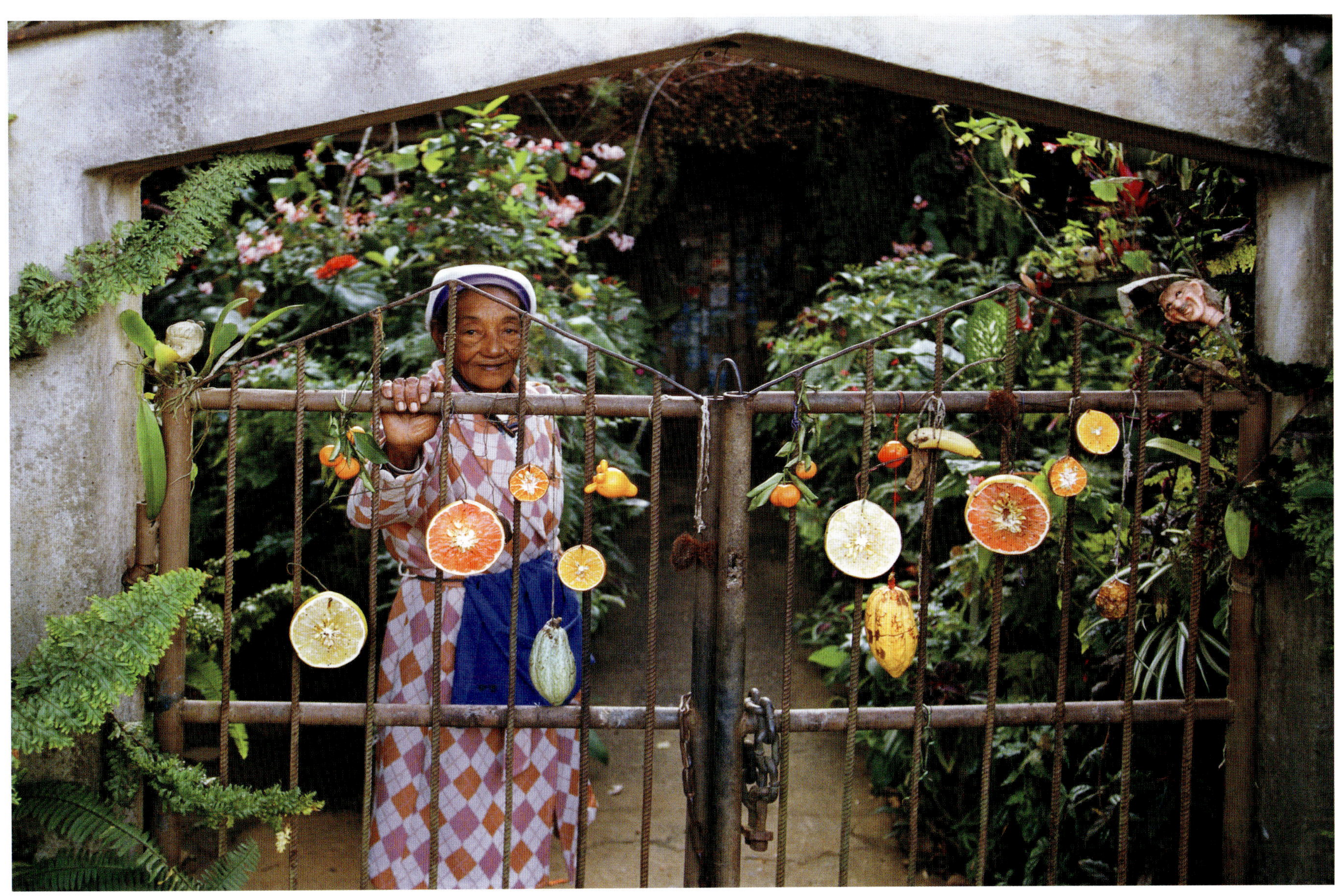

VIÑALES
GATES OF EDEN

DAVID THURSTON

Canon EOS 5, Canon 28-105mm f/3.4-4.5 EF lens, Fuji Provia, f/11. A straightforward photo opportunity. I was taking pictures when the owner appeared. She was happy to be photographed, too, although we could not communicate verbally because of the language barrier.

FINALIST, 2009

Along a street in the small town of Viñales, Cuba, is a gate into a leafy front garden which, in another owner's hands, would perhaps shelter a car. Of course, I had to make a photograph of this gate and its bizarre slices of the citrus family. Some kind of vegetarian voodoo? Out popped the woman. For a happy dollar, she showed off the tropical wonderland she and her elder sister had created out back. The fruit? No idea. The great thing about allowing the camera to lead the way is the people you meet as you go. The chance encounter and the decisive moment rate as top thrills when you let the camera do the asking.

Every morning Beihai Park is filled with dozens of people performing various forms of traditional gymnastics and playing traditional music. This brings life to the thousand-year-old imperial garden and is probably its main feature.

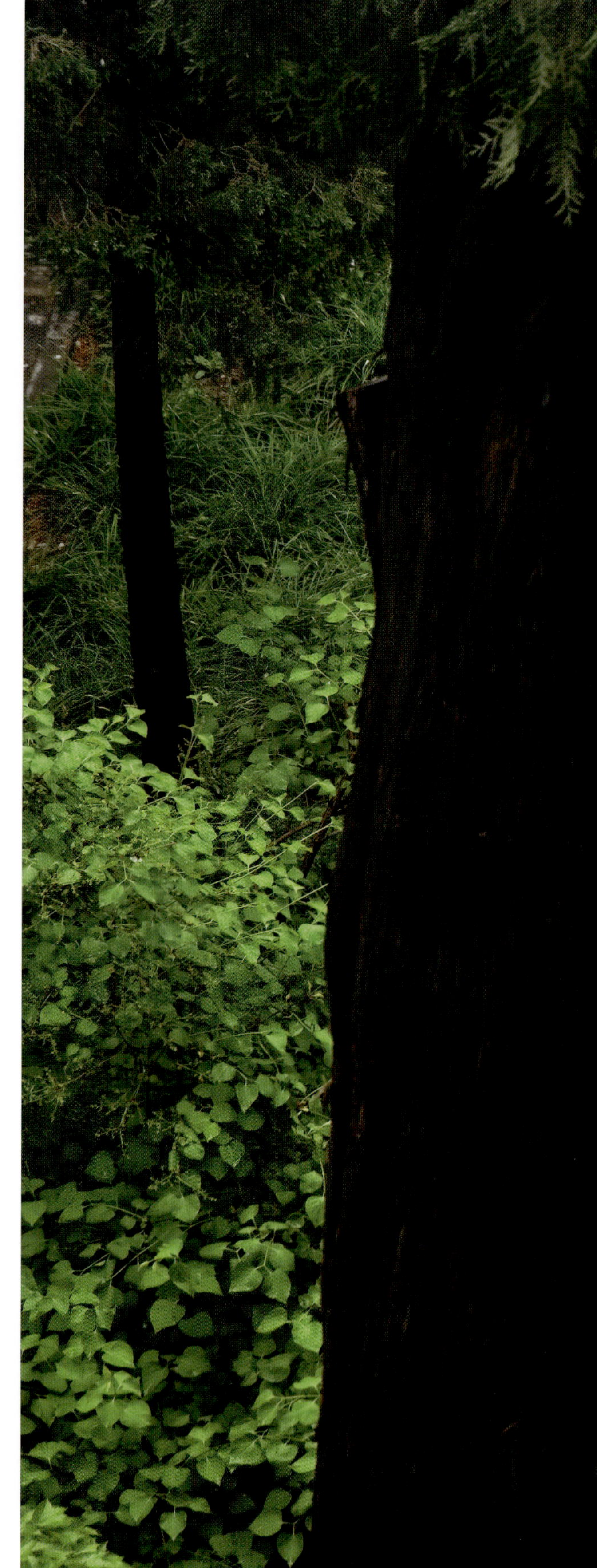

BEIHAI PARK (IMPERIAL GARDEN NEAR FORBIDDEN CITY), BEIJING
TAI CHI

VICTOR KORCHENKO

Nikon D80.
FIRST, 2010

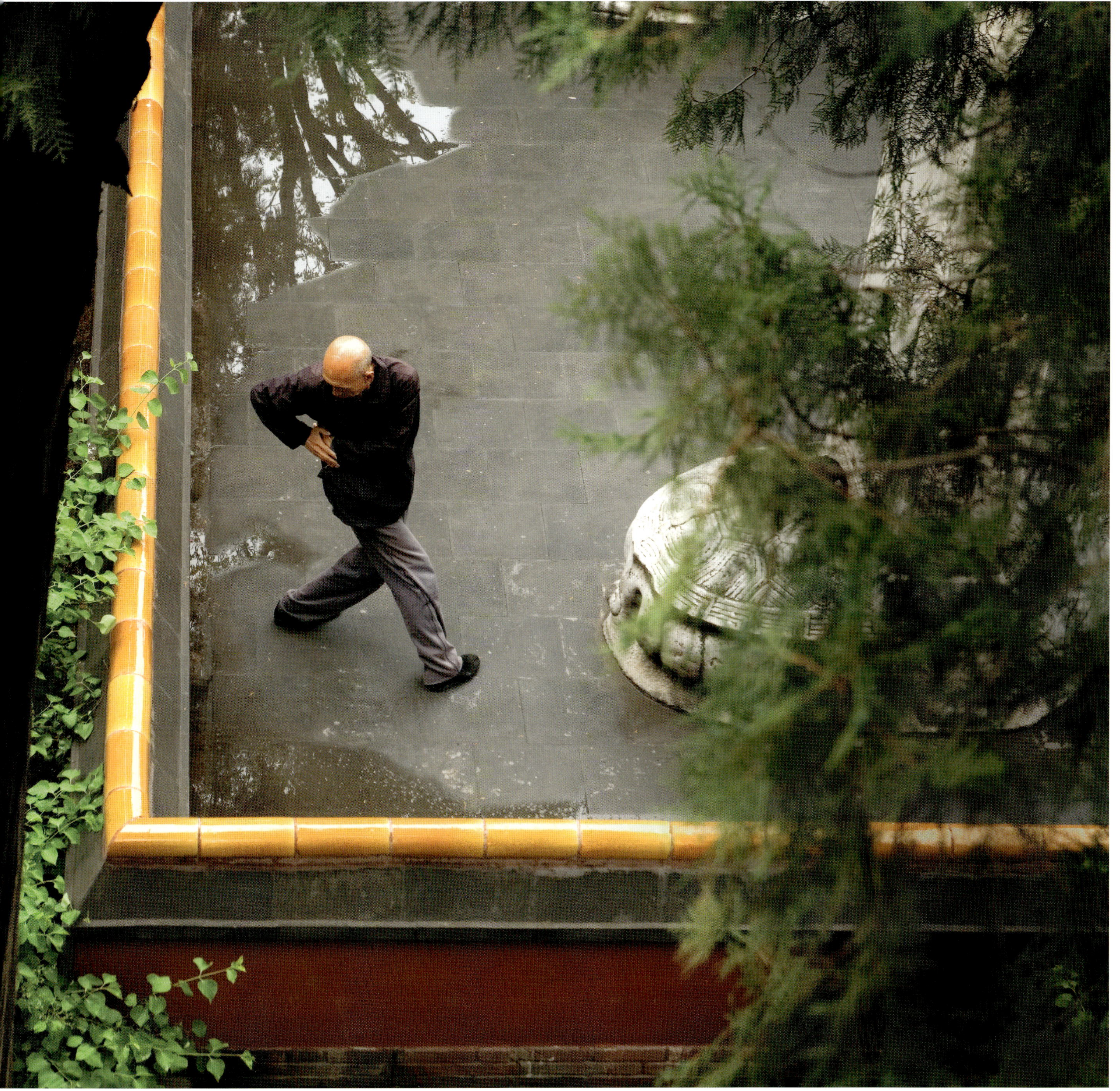

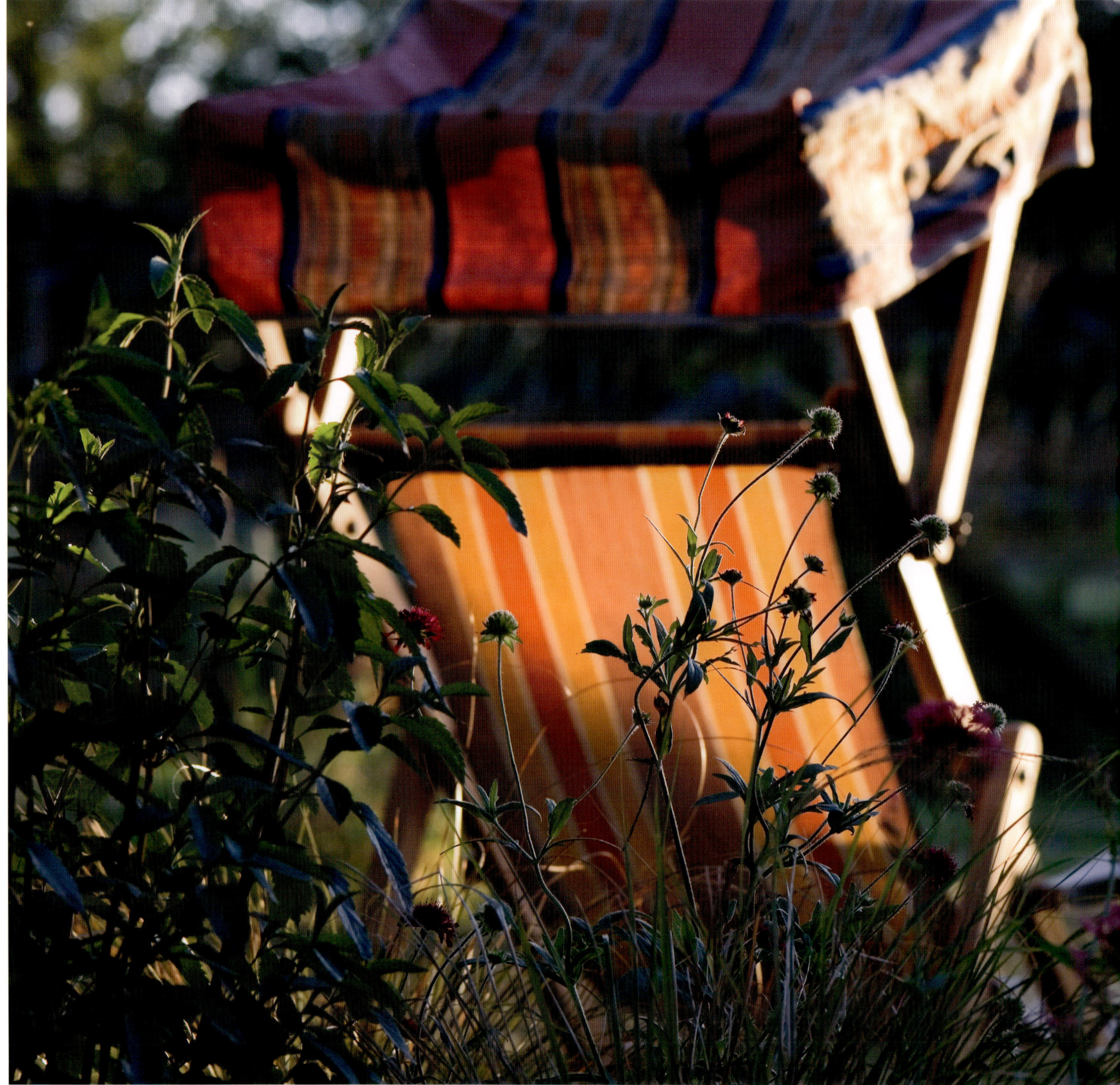

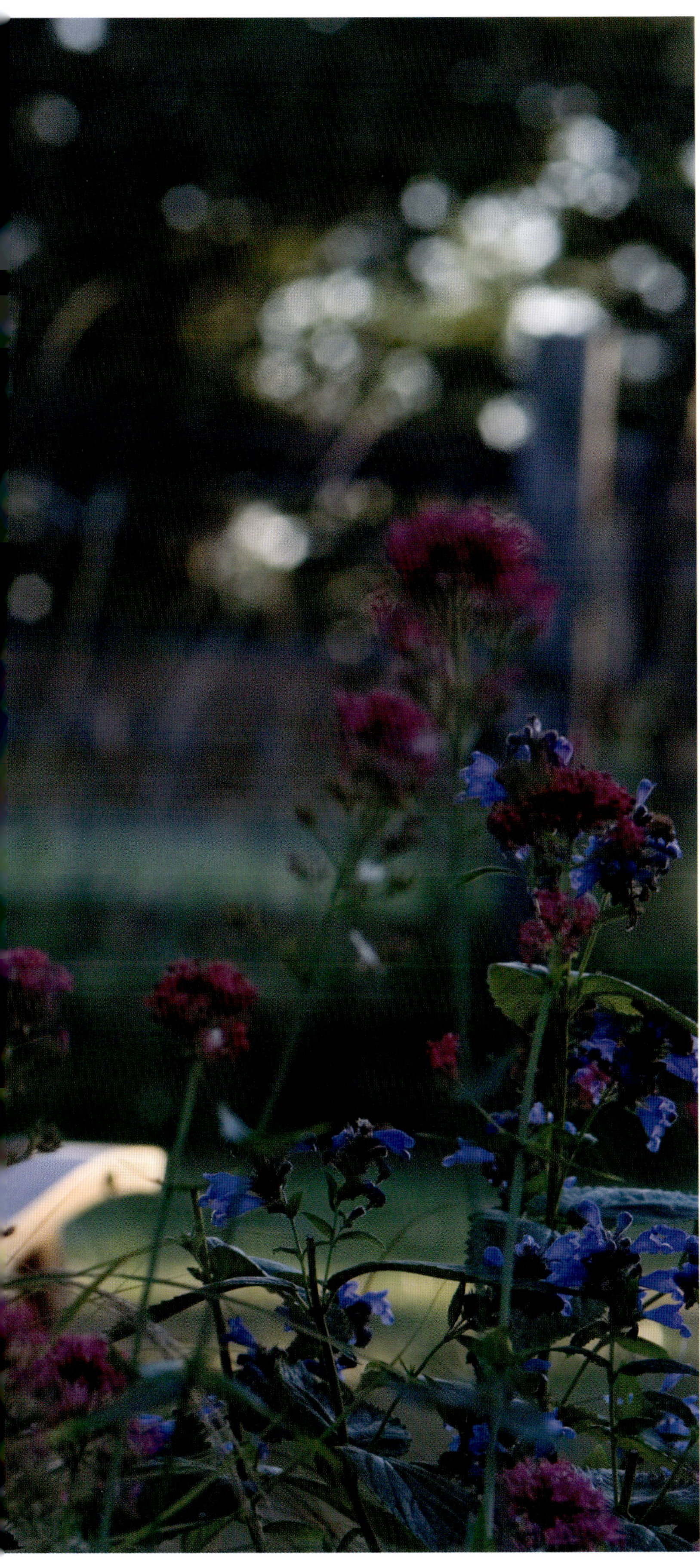

This shot was taken in our garden in Suffolk. The picture shows a stripy deckchair with a sun canopy that once belonged to my grandmother. It is seen here in the soft evening light through a group of grasses and salvias (*Salvia* spp.) that I had recently planted.

NEWMARKET, SUFFOLK, ENGLAND
DECKCHAIR IN THE EVENING LIGHT

ZARA NAPIER

Nikon D200, 105mm f/2.8 Micro Nikkor lens, f/7.1. The positioning of the camera had to be correct so that the sun hit the deckchair at the right angle, and it was important that the fence in the background was almost invisible so I used a relatively wide aperture of f/7.1.
COMMENDED, 2008

PARADISE GARDENS, CORDES-SUR-CIEL
RED CURTAIN

SERGEY KAREPANOV

Canon EOS 5D, Canon EF 24–105mm f/4 L IS lens, f/4.5. The garden is divided into several areas. The red curtain leads into the sensual garden, the yellow into the sunny garden and behind the blue one is the meditation garden.
THIRD, 2008

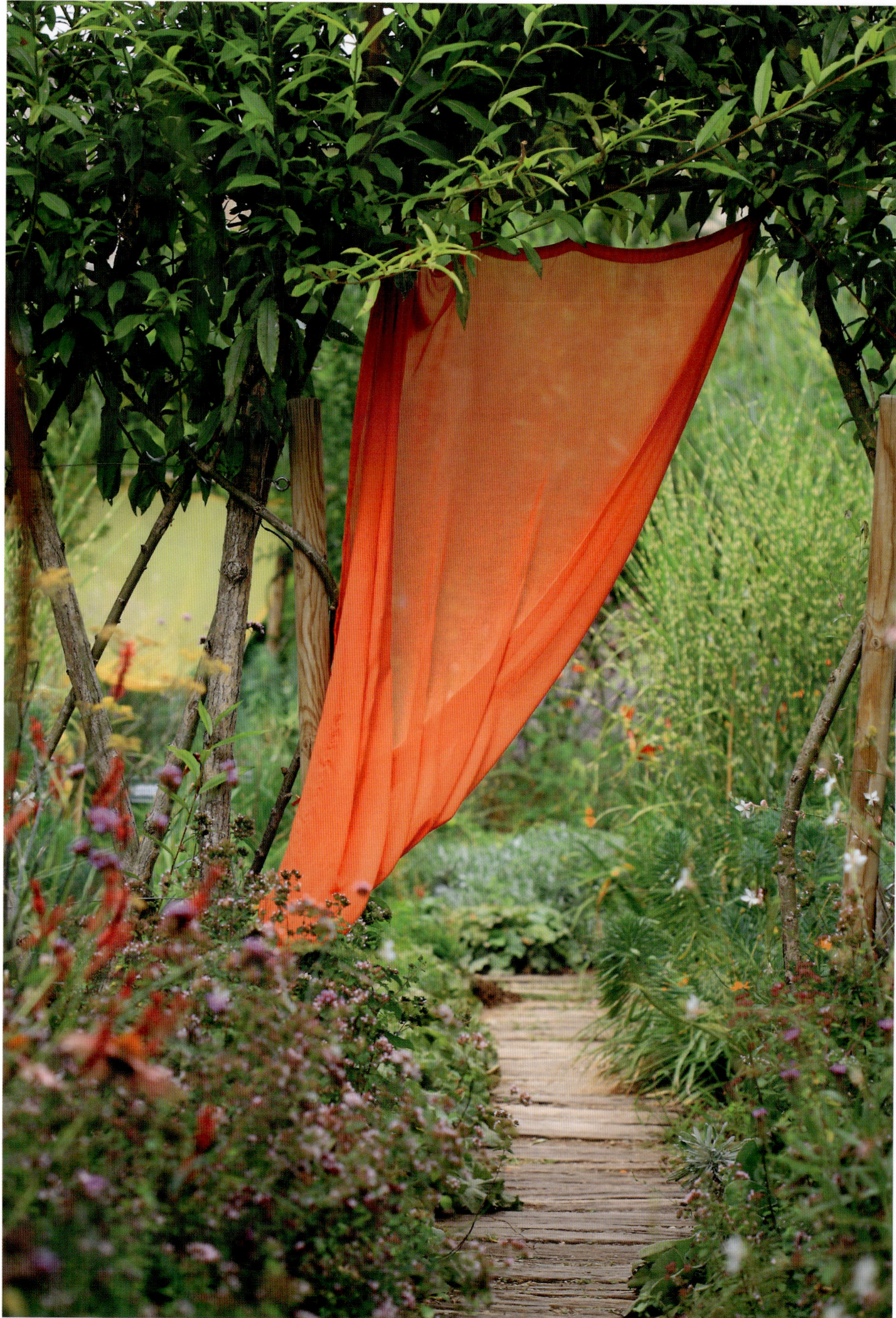

I dreamed of visiting this garden as I studied books and maps one frosty winter. I left Moscow and drove for three days; then, around a bend in the road, I saw a mountain and the medieval town of Cordes-sur-Ciel. On entering the Paradise Gardens and walking down the narrow path across the bamboo thicket, I smelled a pungent and exciting oriental aroma – and saw this red curtain luring me on.

WEST YORKSHIRE, ENGLAND
RUSTIC RETREAT

MAGGIE LAMBERT

Panasonic Lumix DMC-FZ5, f/3.2. My position had to be chosen with care so it would not be visible in the reflection. A head-on view was necessary to preserve the pattern created by the windows.
SECOND, 2009

The old summerhouse, which is situated in the shade of trees at the bottom of our garden, is a peaceful and private place (when no photographers are around) where a person can sit, read and enjoy the surroundings. The little building is now well integrated into the mature garden and birds and other wildlife felt comfortable coming near. I noticed that the reflections blended inside with outside, dissolving the walls of the building and enclosing the reader in a dreamlike world. Also I found the division into eight miniature images interesting – each surprisingly different.

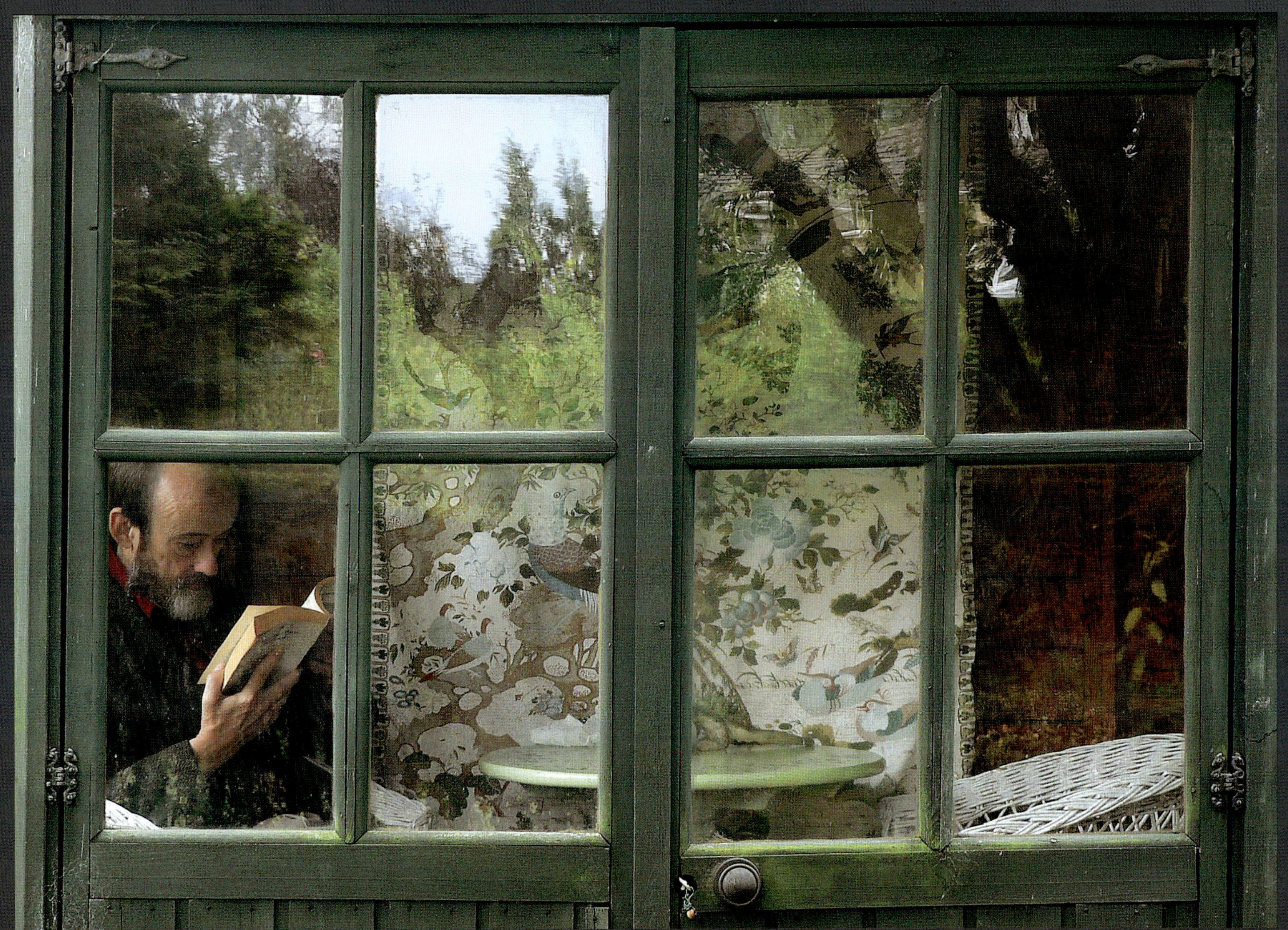

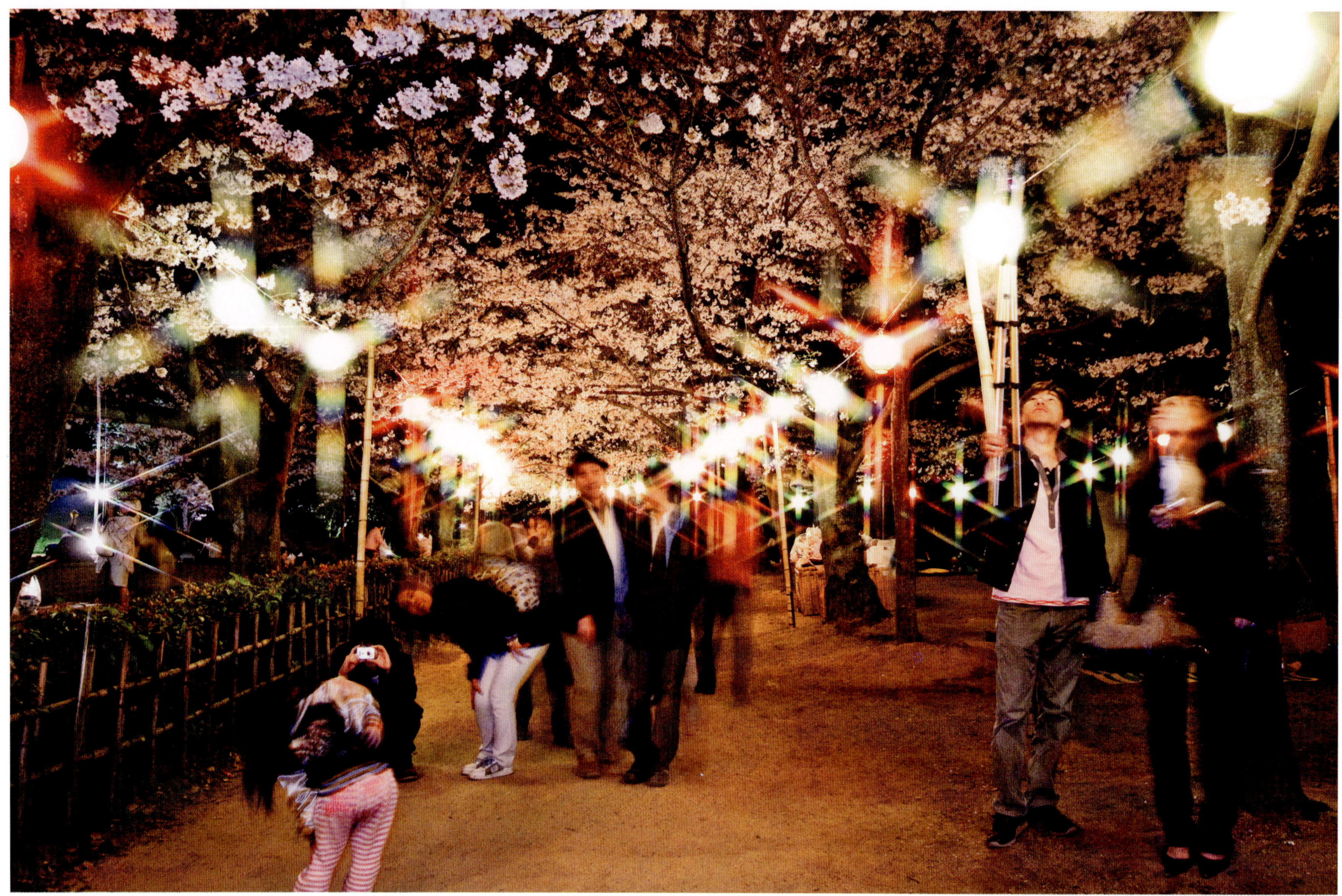

RITSURIN PARK, TAKAMATSU, KAGAWA
PROMENADE

KEVIN COZMA

Nikon D200, Sigma 10-20mm lens, f/5.6. The most important detail is the use of a star-cross filter to achieve the twinkle in the lights. I also used a tripod and a shutter speed of 0.8sec, and an off-camera flash with a small softbox in rear curtain sync mode.
THIRD, 2009

This photograph was taken during an evening illumination at Ritsurin Park. Thousands of people come here every spring to have picnics with friends and family under the canopy of cherry blossom. An off-camera flash, tripod and star-cross filter were used to help make this picture.

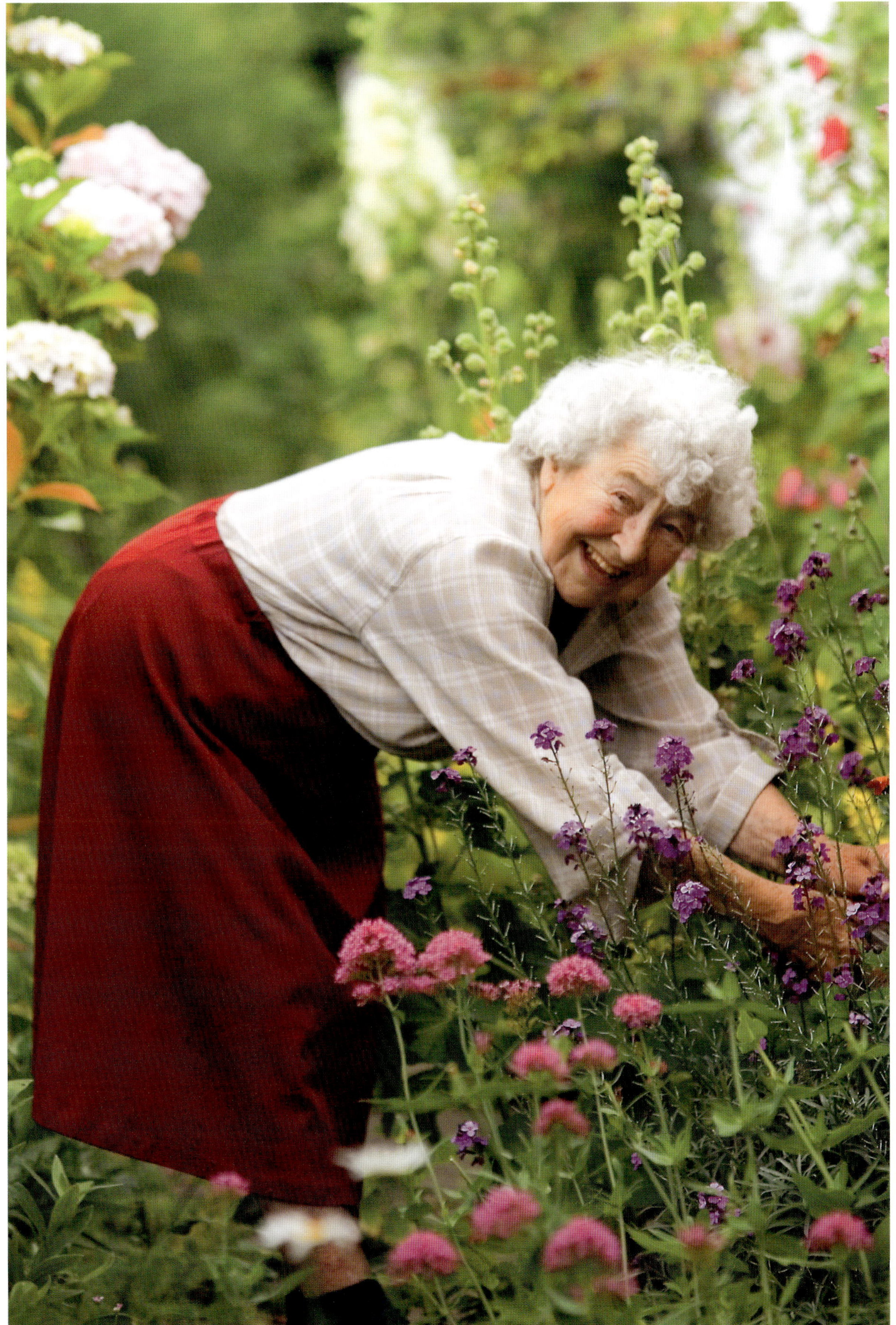

DWYGYFYLCHI, PENMAENMAWR, CONWY, WALES
ELSIE IN HER GARDEN

ANNIE WILLIAMS

Canon EOS 20D, Sigma 70-200mm DG Macro HSM lens, f/2.8. I spent a couple of hours in the garden taking photographs of flowers as Elsie was weeding, and just managed to catch this shot as she turned to me and smiled.
FINALIST, 2009

This is a photograph of my friend Elsie in her beautiful garden. Aged 88, Elsie does all the work in the garden herself, including mowing the lawns. It is an extensive garden in a classic cottage style that displays her intuitive and creative sense of colour and design. Cultivated plants sit alongside wild flowers, giving a vibrant and unique quality to the garden. I wanted to celebrate Elsie's achievements as an amateur gardener who has exceptional creative skills and has spent her life creating this beautiful environment. I also wanted to express my admiration for her keeping so fit, healthy and independent.

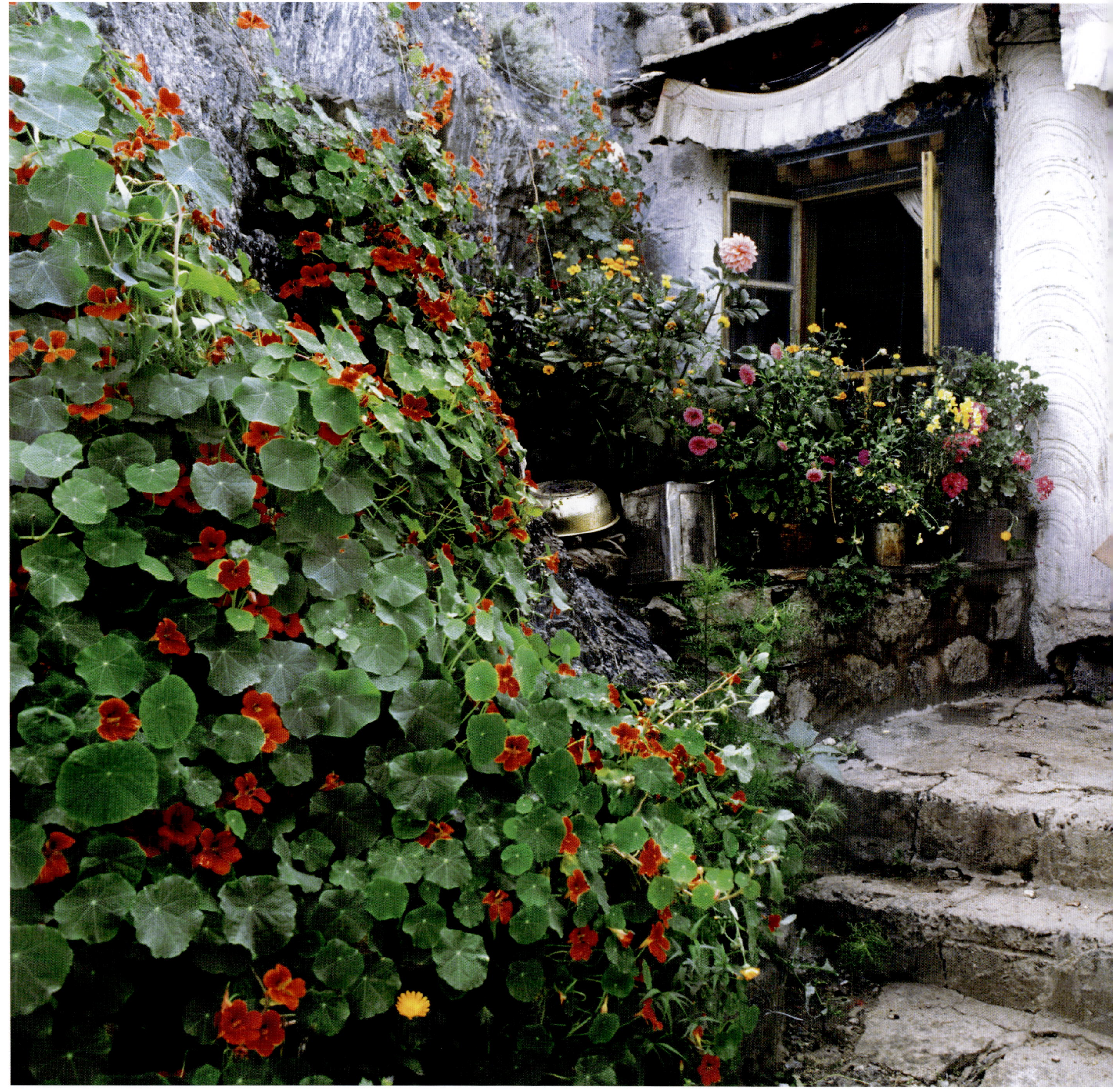

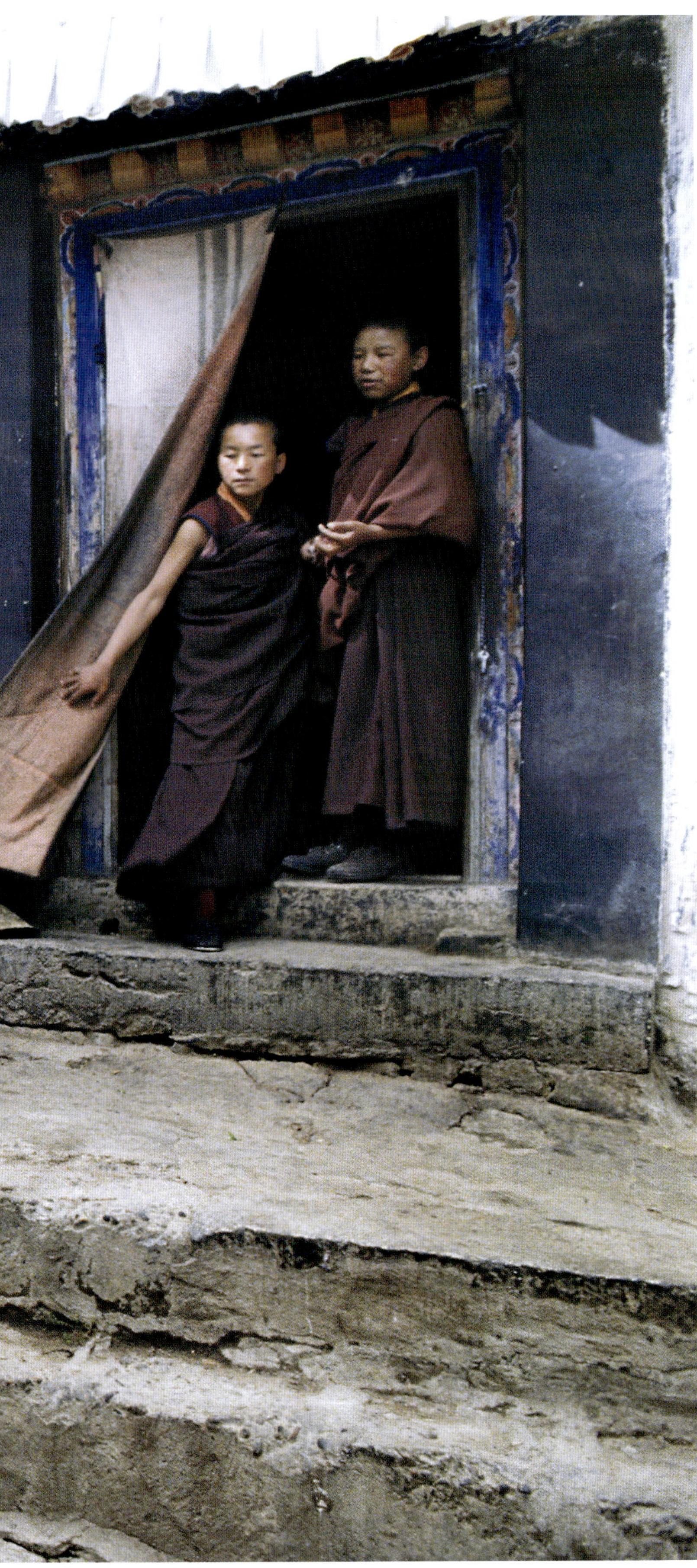

LHASA
NASTURTIUMS

DAVID THURSTON

Canon EOS 5, Canon EF 20-35mm L lens, Fuji Provia, f/8. Fortunately, although it was a sunny day, the garden was in shadow. If it had been in direct sunlight, the colour would have been desaturated and the contrast of highlight and shadow would have been too severe for a good shot.
FINALIST, 2009

Lhasa is 3,650 metres above sea level. The air is thin, winters are long and vegetation is sparse. The colours of nature are few, so it was unusual to see this bank of nasturtiums (*Tropaeolum* spp.) in full bloom. Also growing, apparently in old tin cans, are some dahlias (*Dahlia* spp.) and geraniums (*Geranium* spp.). While walking, I stopped to photograph this splash of clear colour. I was moved by the idea that the very same flowers grow in my garden in Devon. A door creaked open, the curtain was pulled back and out came two lads in monks' robes to see what I was doing. What a bonus.

GREAT DIXTER, EAST SUSSEX, ENGLAND

HEAD GARDENER FERGUS GARRETT AT GREAT DIXTER GARDENS

RICHARD BLOOM

Nikon D200.
FINALIST, 2010

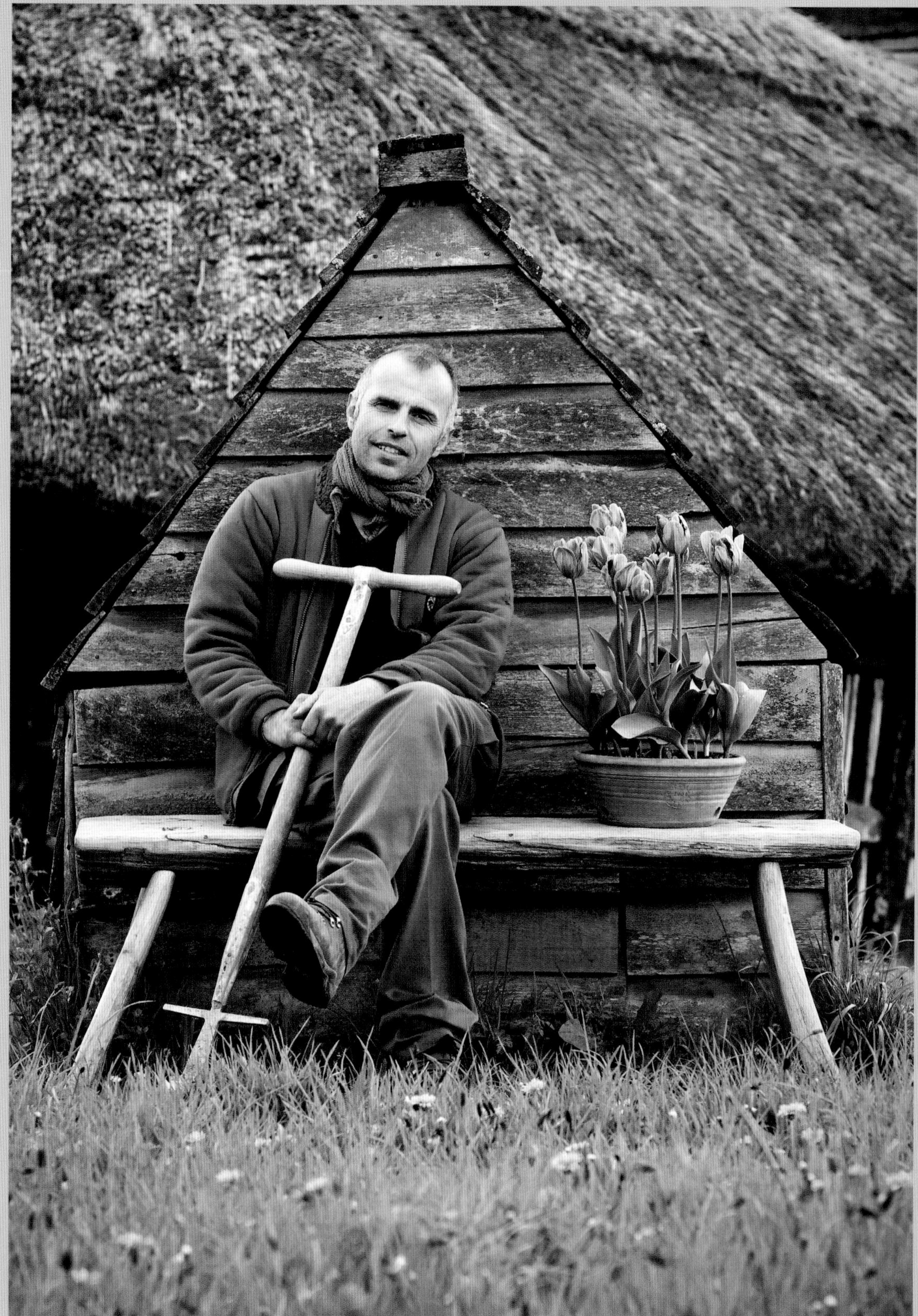

This was shot for *Country Living* magazine as part of an ongoing series entitled 'The Passionate Gardener', which focuses on gardeners, horticulturists, plants, people etc. and their individual horticultural passions. This particular feature was on Fergus Garrett and his tulips at Great Dixter.

I could see the location would work well in black and white due to the varying textures of the wooden shed, thatched roof and grass in front, which would give the image a fairly broad tonal range. The structure of the shed also frames Fergus and centres the attention on him. The pot of tulips and bulb planter were relevant props for the story.

The briefest of moments – a fleeting kiss between a mother and her little son – captured on a glorious summer day in their own garden. The main feature of my portrait work combines my passion for working outdoors using natural light with natural environments which have some emotional attachment for the subject – often their own gardens. In this case, the family was emigrating to New Zealand and they were sad to be leaving behind their beautiful English garden. I wanted to give them pictures to remember the garden and its atmosphere.

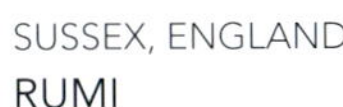

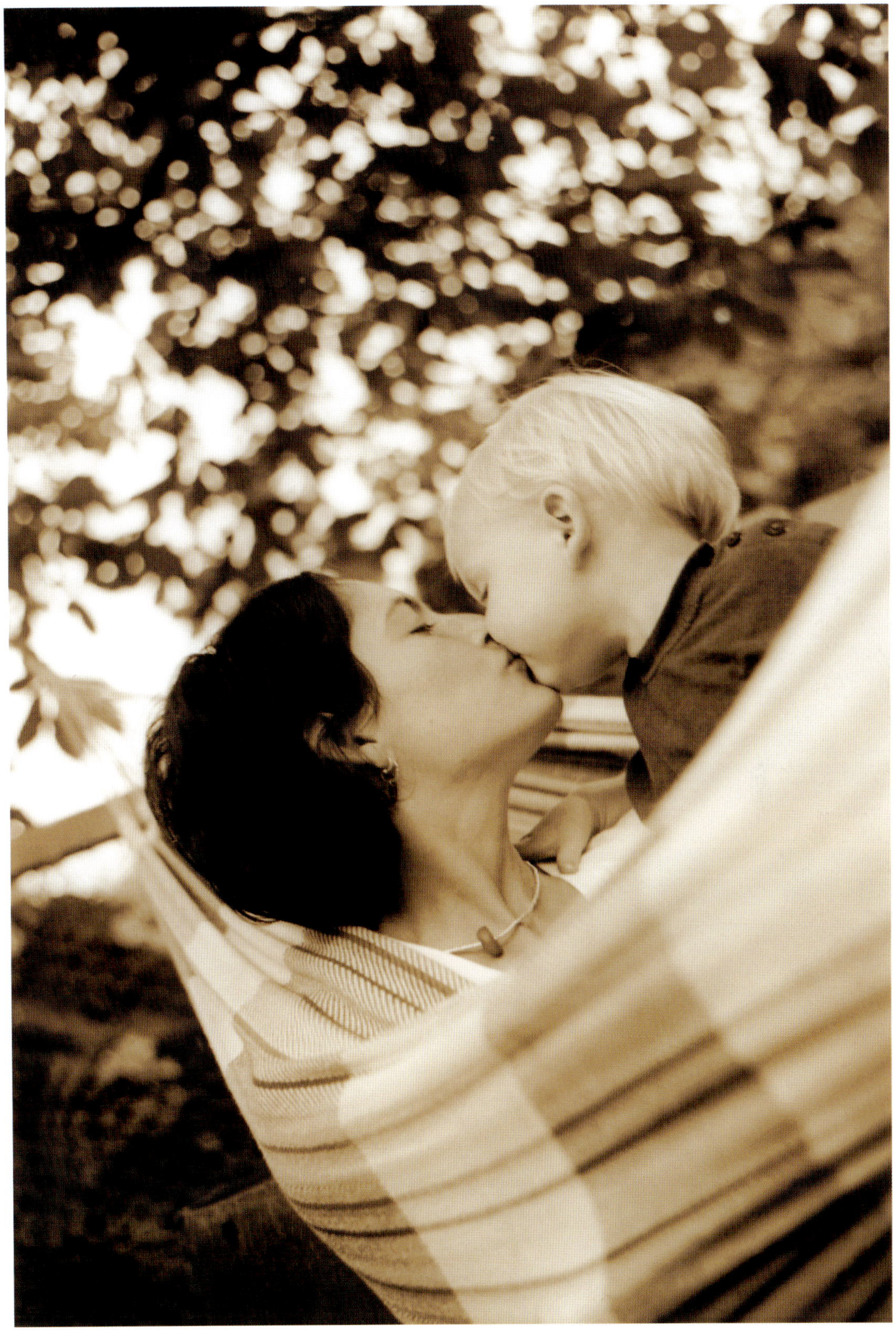

SUSSEX, ENGLAND
RUMI

SARAH WENBAN

Olympus OM2, Zuiko 50mm lens, Kodak BW 400CN, f/1.8. As this picture was taken in a fleeting second (there was no way this active toddler would keep still), I shot purely on instinct.

COMMENDED, 2009

Suddenly I saw him sitting there, tired yet relaxed, staying in the exact same position. It seemed such a striking image, so in that moment I took the photo.

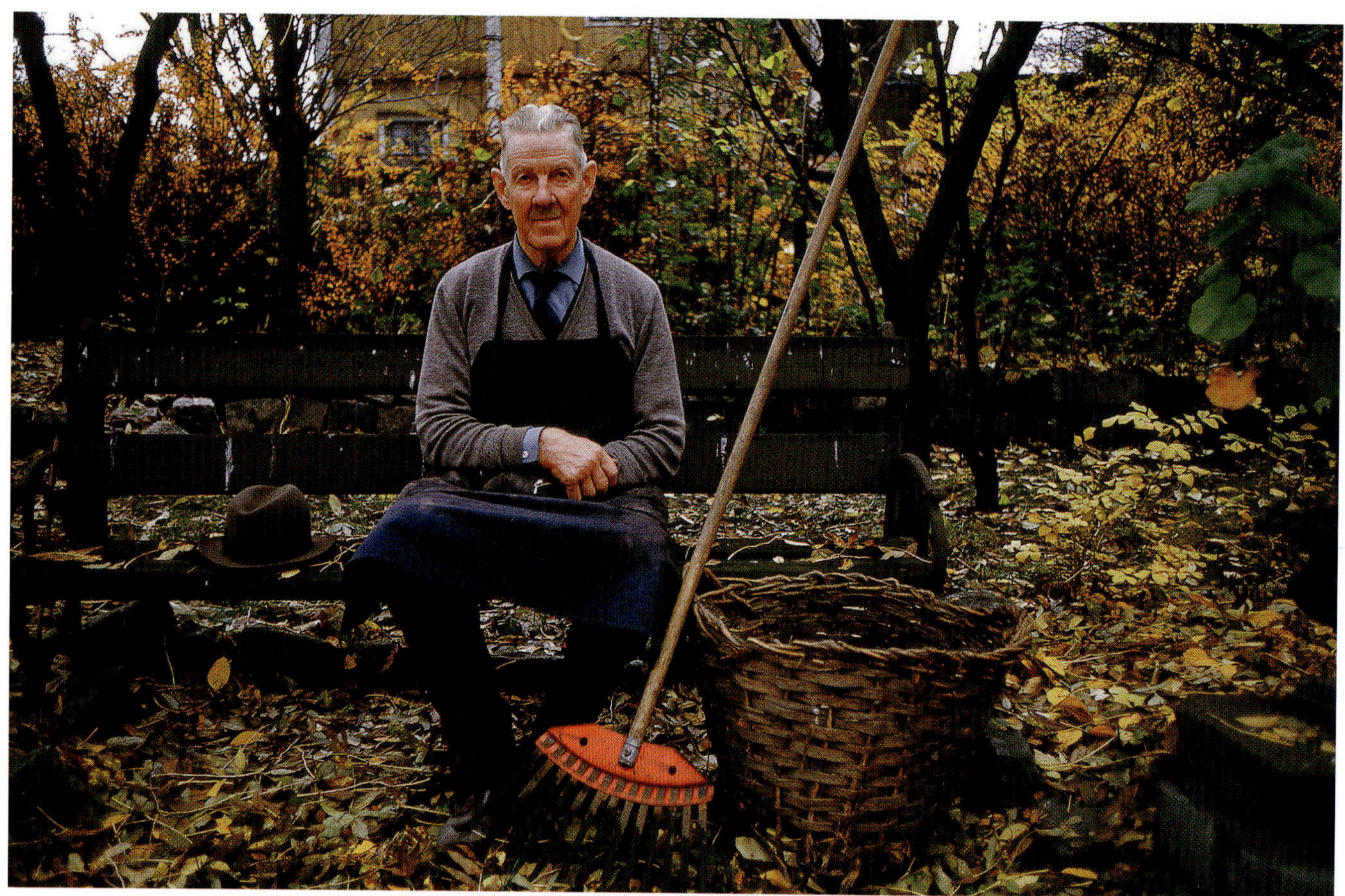

OUR GARDEN
AUTUMN TIME IN MY GARDEN

GÖSTA LINDBOM

Kodacrome, Leica M2, Summicron 35mm, 1/50 sec, f/8.
SECOND, 2010

ALF AND CHRISTINE'S GARDEN IN STROUD, GLOUCESTERSHIRE, ENGLAND
'HE WHO PLANTS A GARDEN PLANTS HAPPINESS'

LYNN KEDDIE

Canon 5D Mark II, Canon DF 200mm f/2.8L USM, f/8.
THIRD, 2010

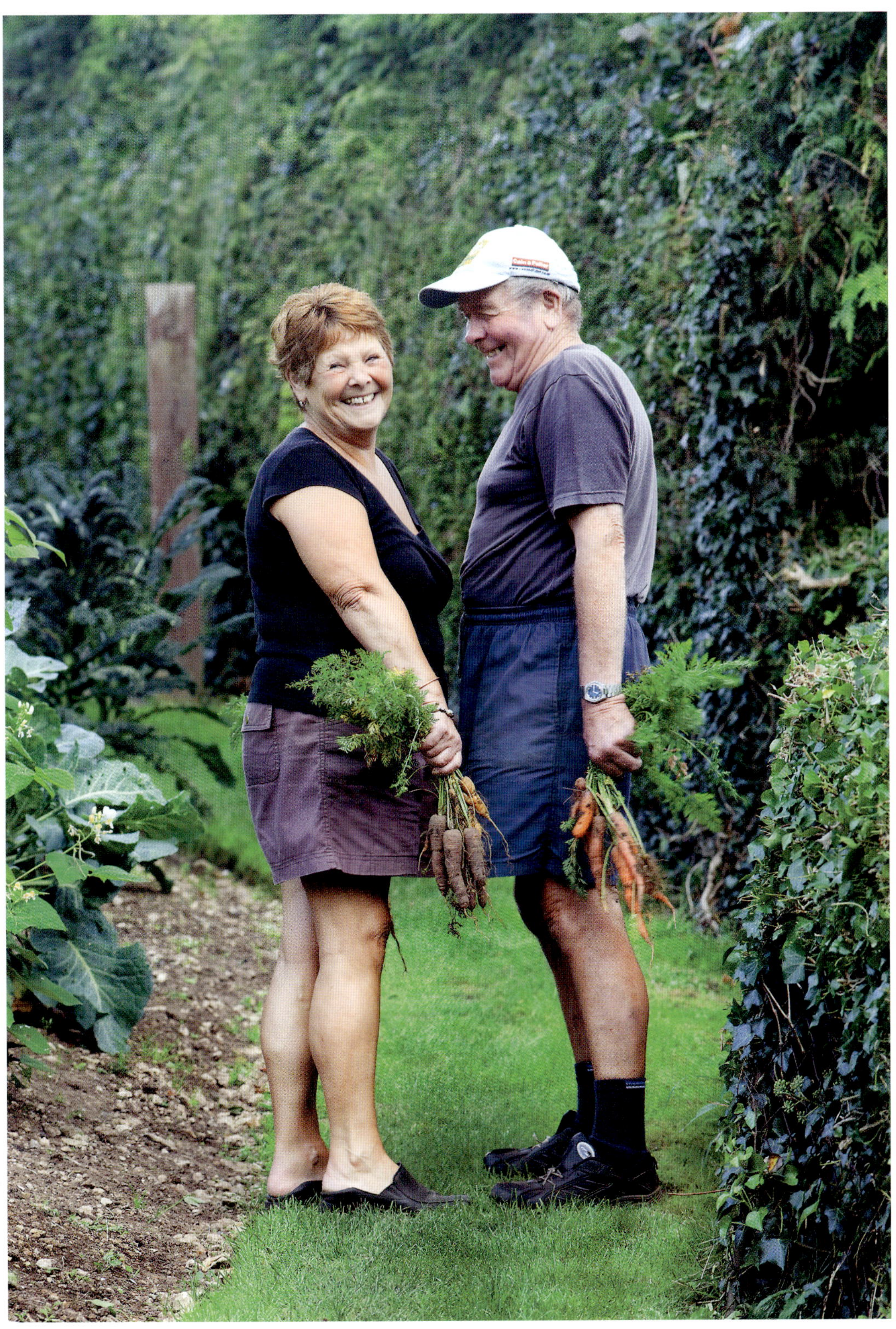

Alf had just harvested several varieties of different coloured carrots (*Daucus carota*) so that we could photograph them. Christine, his wife, came out to join us and they both walked back up the garden with their hands full of brightly coloured vegetables. They were obviously sharing a special moment, which is reflected in the cheeky grin on Christine's face. They seemed to be great friends and obviously respected and loved each other. We all worked well together, talking about their love of gardening and sharing tips. They were sharing a secret moment together when I clicked the shutter. Gardens are about people. This photograph just makes me smile.

A series of portraits of contemporary garden journalists, presenters, authors, bloggers and campaigners who all grow their own food. Usually well-known faces in the industry, the aim is to give a personal insight into the often unseen gardens or plots referred to in their public work. This is an ongoing project, currently with 30 portraits. The original inspiration for this project was a Land Girls poster from World War Two. The stylised theme and vivid colour of the poster was adopted to create a series of portraits of ladies working in the gardening industry or campaigning about green issues. The approach was to take each portrait with the same lens to keep a similar perspective, with each person a similar height within the frame for consistency.

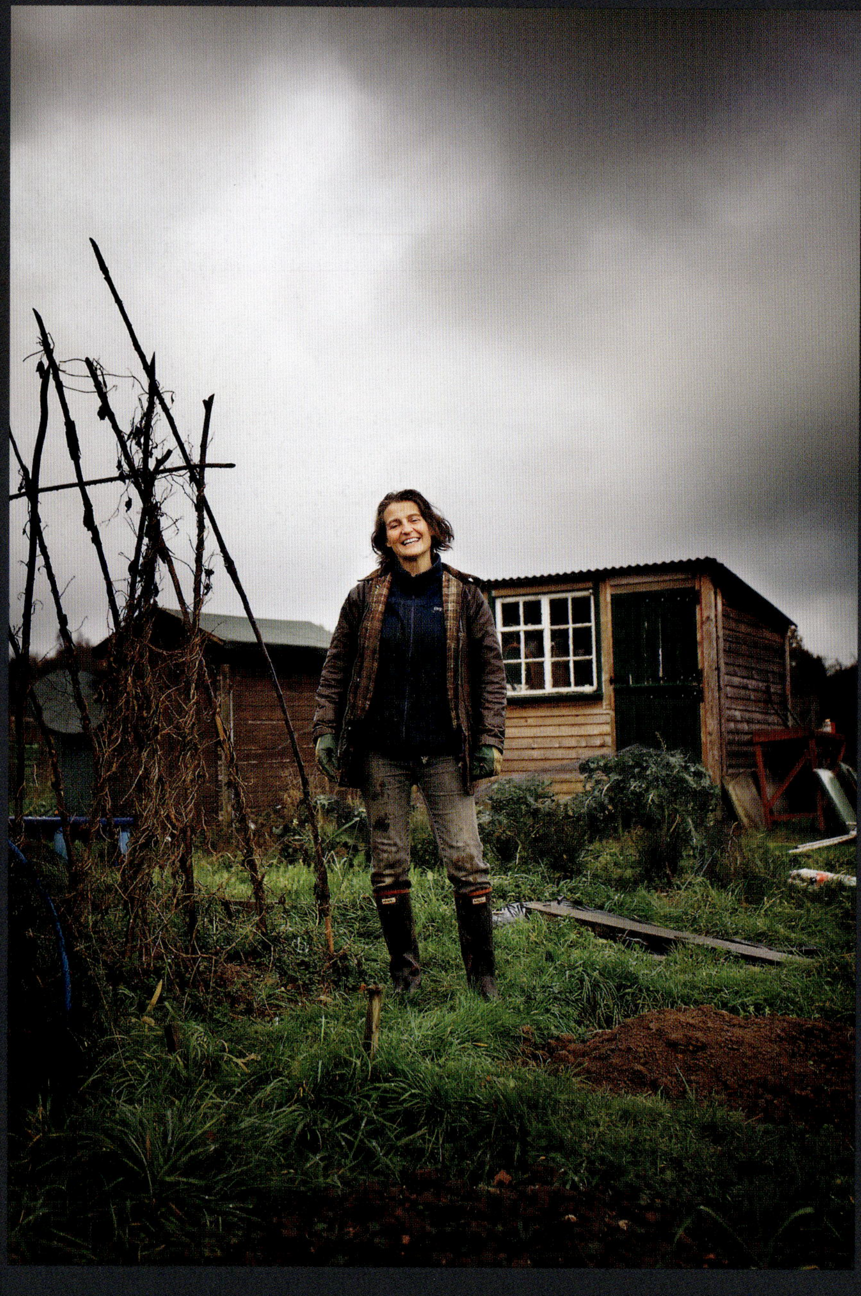

1

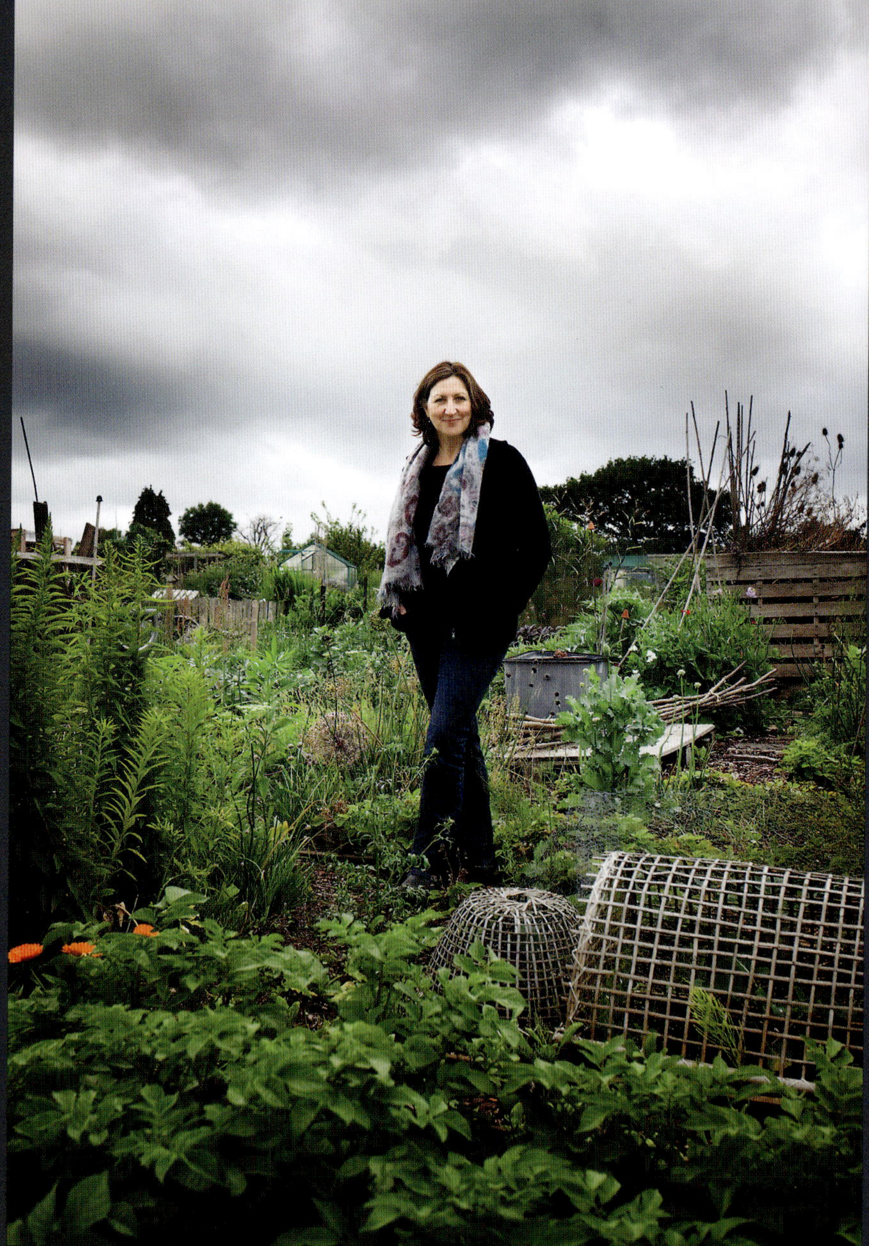

2

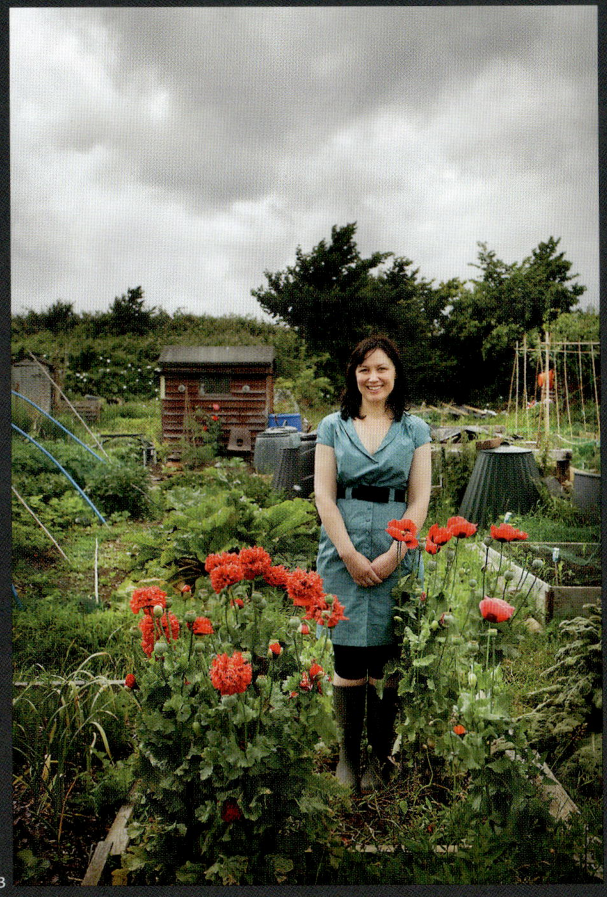
3

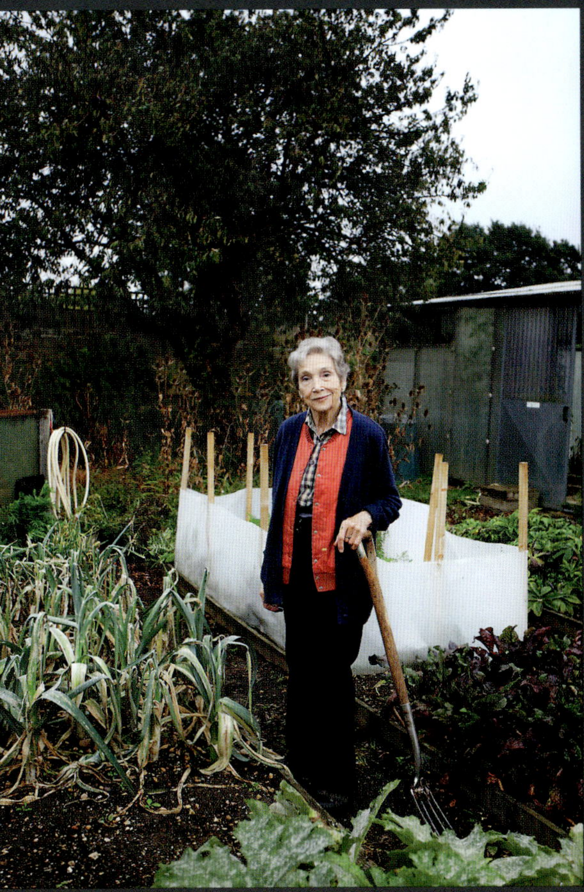
4

VARIOUS LOCATIONS IN THE MIDLANDS AND SOUTHERN ENGLAND

LAND GIRLS

PAUL DEBOIS

Canon EOS 5D, 40mm lens approximately 1/60 to 1/125sec at approximately f/5.6. Post-capture: the sky was often darkened to create a more dramatic effect, with some dodging and burning, much as I would have done when working in a darkroom.

HIGHLY COMMENDED, 2012

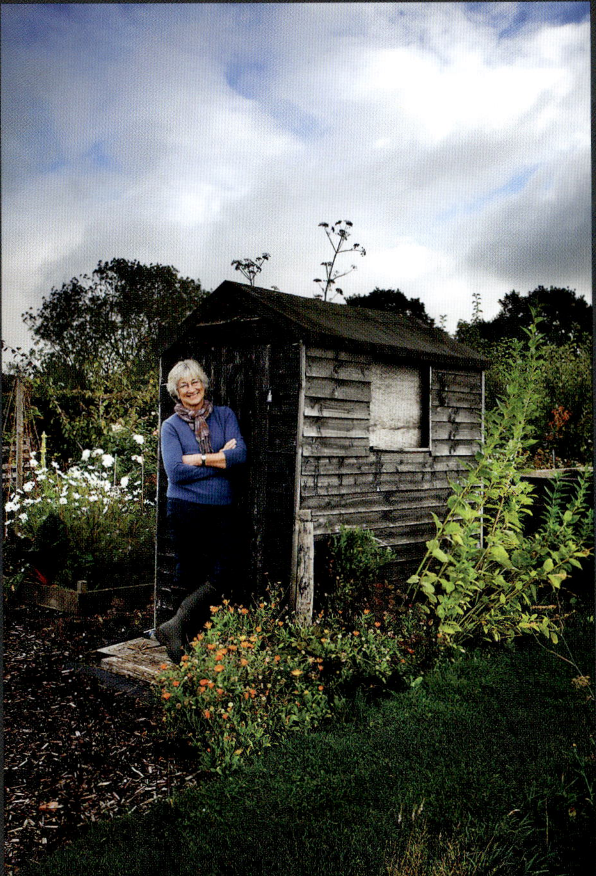
5

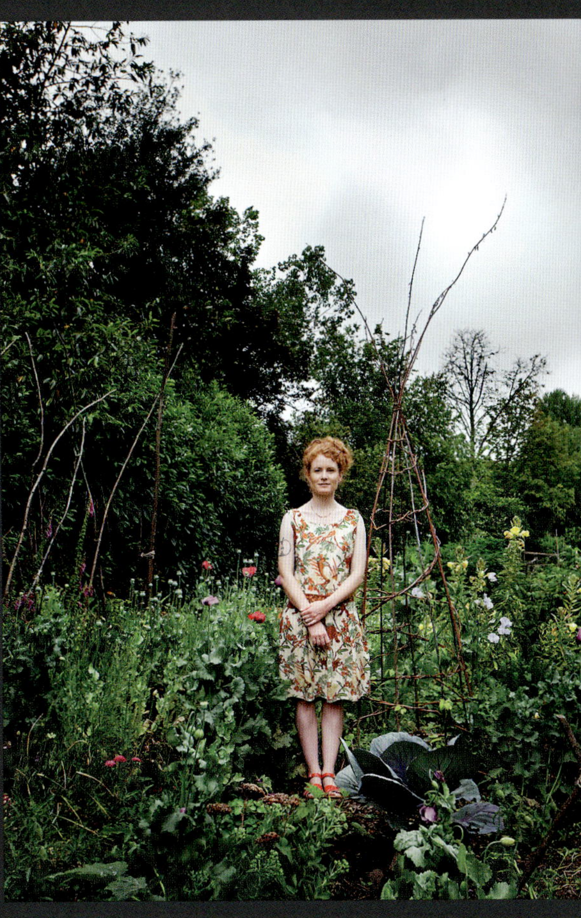
6

1–Portrait of Sally Nex on her allotment.
2–Portrait of Juliet Roberts on her allotment.
3–Portrait of Lia Leendertz on her allotment.
4–Portrait of Beth Chatto in her vegetable garden.
5–Portrait of Helen Yemm on her allotment.
6–Portrait of Alys Fowler on her allotment.

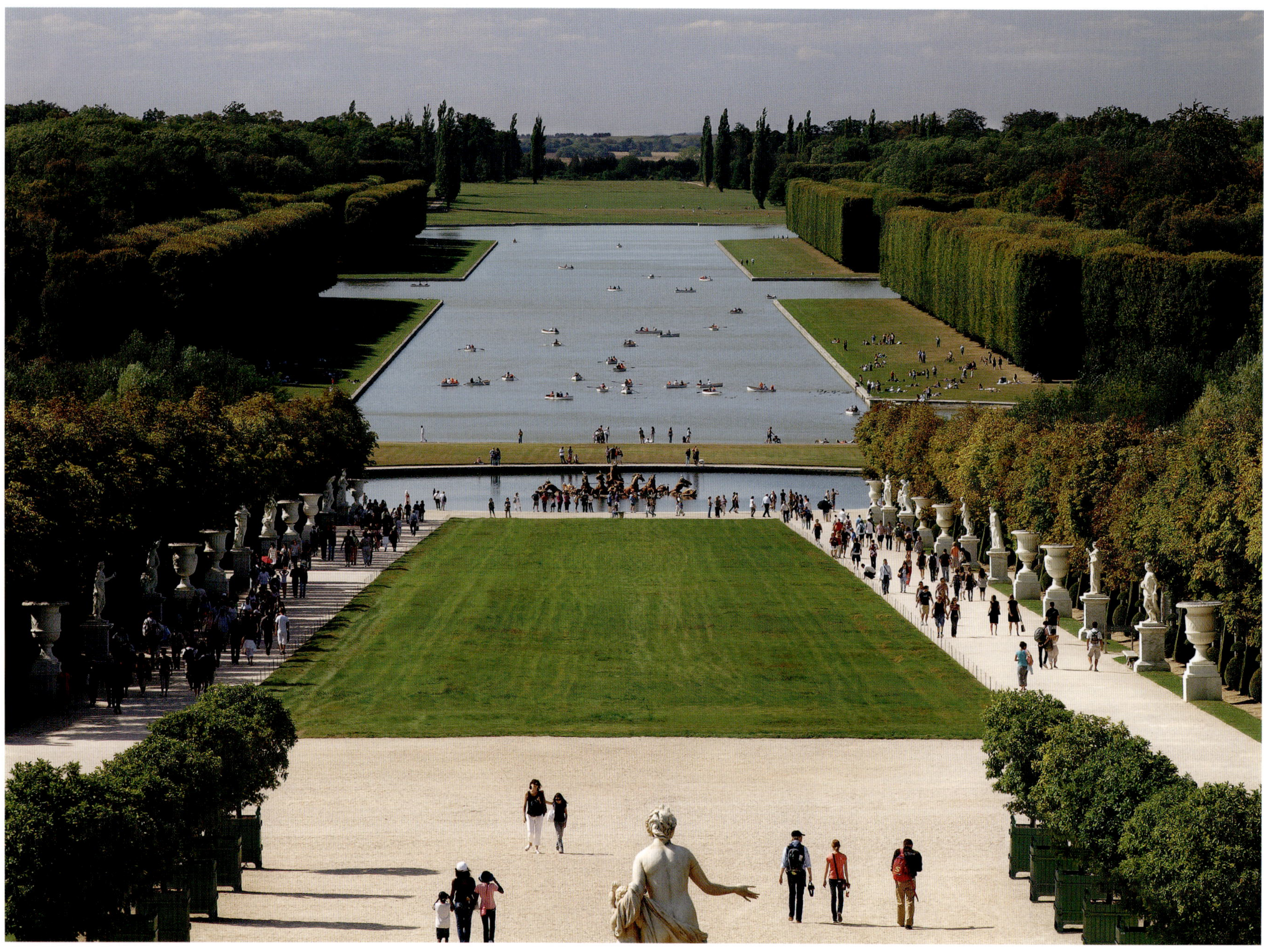

CHÂTEAU DE VERSAILLES, PARIS
VERSAILLES

JOHNNY JETSTREAM

Olympus E-3, Olympus 35–200 f/2.0, f/5.6.
HIGHLY COMMENDED, 2010

It's hard to imagine how the gardens at Versailles would have looked without people. Presumably that's why there are so many statues lining the avenues. Many landscapes and gardens are at their best without people, but Versailles thrives with the colour and bustle of its visitors.

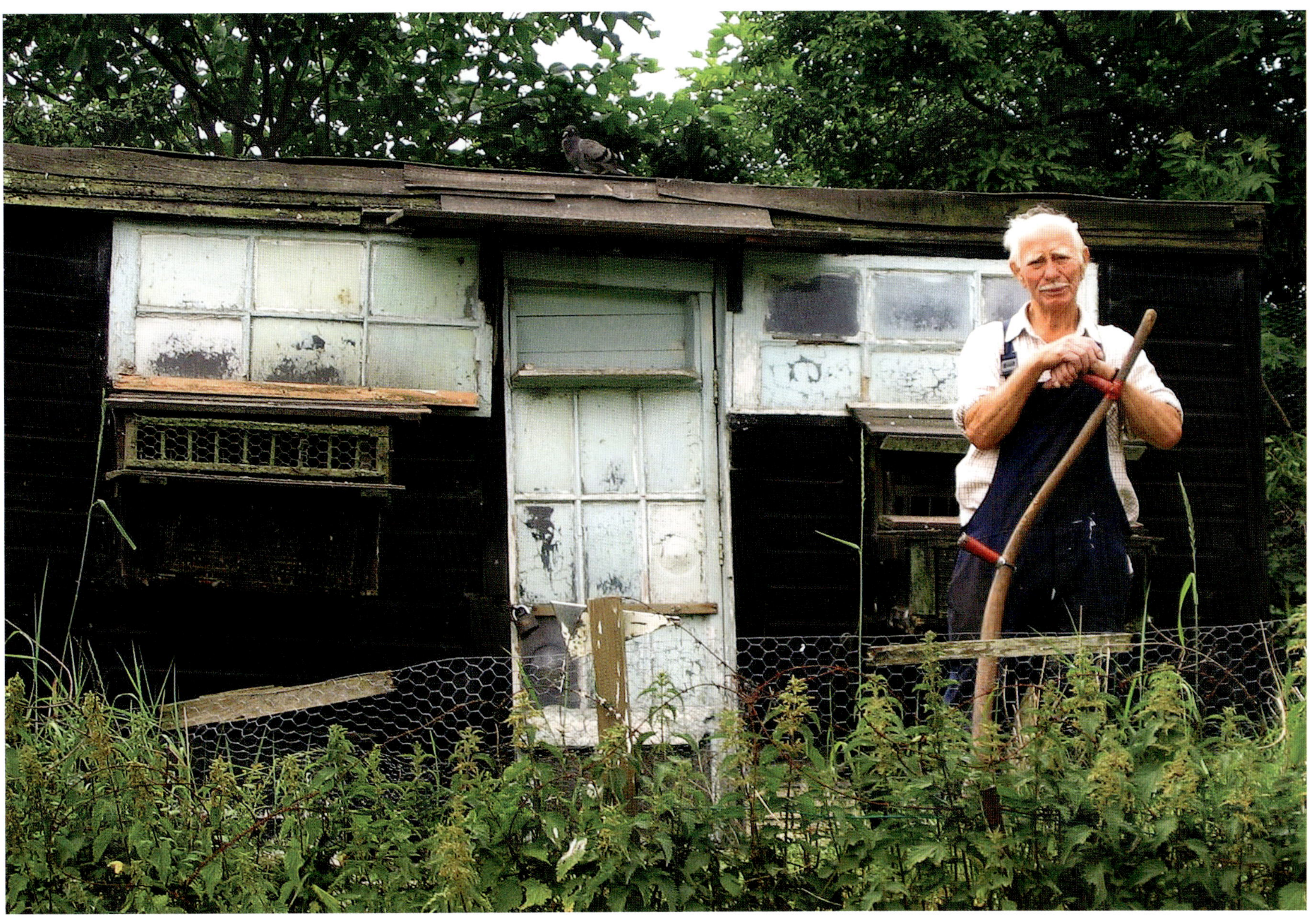

BETWEEN EYAM AND STONEY MIDDLETON IN DERBYSHIRE, ENGLAND
TENDING PIGEONS

JOHN ROGER PALMOUR

Canon PowerShot A95, 1/125sec at f/4.9. I used the camera's automatic settings with no tripod, filters or other equipment. Post-capture: slight correction/adjustments to exposure and colour saturation in Picnik on www.flickr.com.
FINALIST, 2011

I took this on a hazy July morning during a walk from Eyam to Stoney Middleton. I had not seen anyone using a scythe in years, so we stopped and admired the effortless precision with which this gentleman practiced an ancient art. He told us that he had been raising racing pigeons in these coops for over 40 years. He seemed genuinely honoured when I asked if I could take his picture. It was not until I saw the image on my computer screen that I realized that one of his pigeons had posed cooperatively above the doorway of the shed. I believe that the plants in the foreground are stinging nettles and will be all too familiar to anyone who has spent much time walking in the English countryside.

CHAPMAN VALLEY, GERALDTON, WESTERN AUSTRALIA
RUNNING GIRLS

BRAD MAILER

Cannon EOS 450D, Tamron AF 70–300, f/11.
FINALIST, 2010

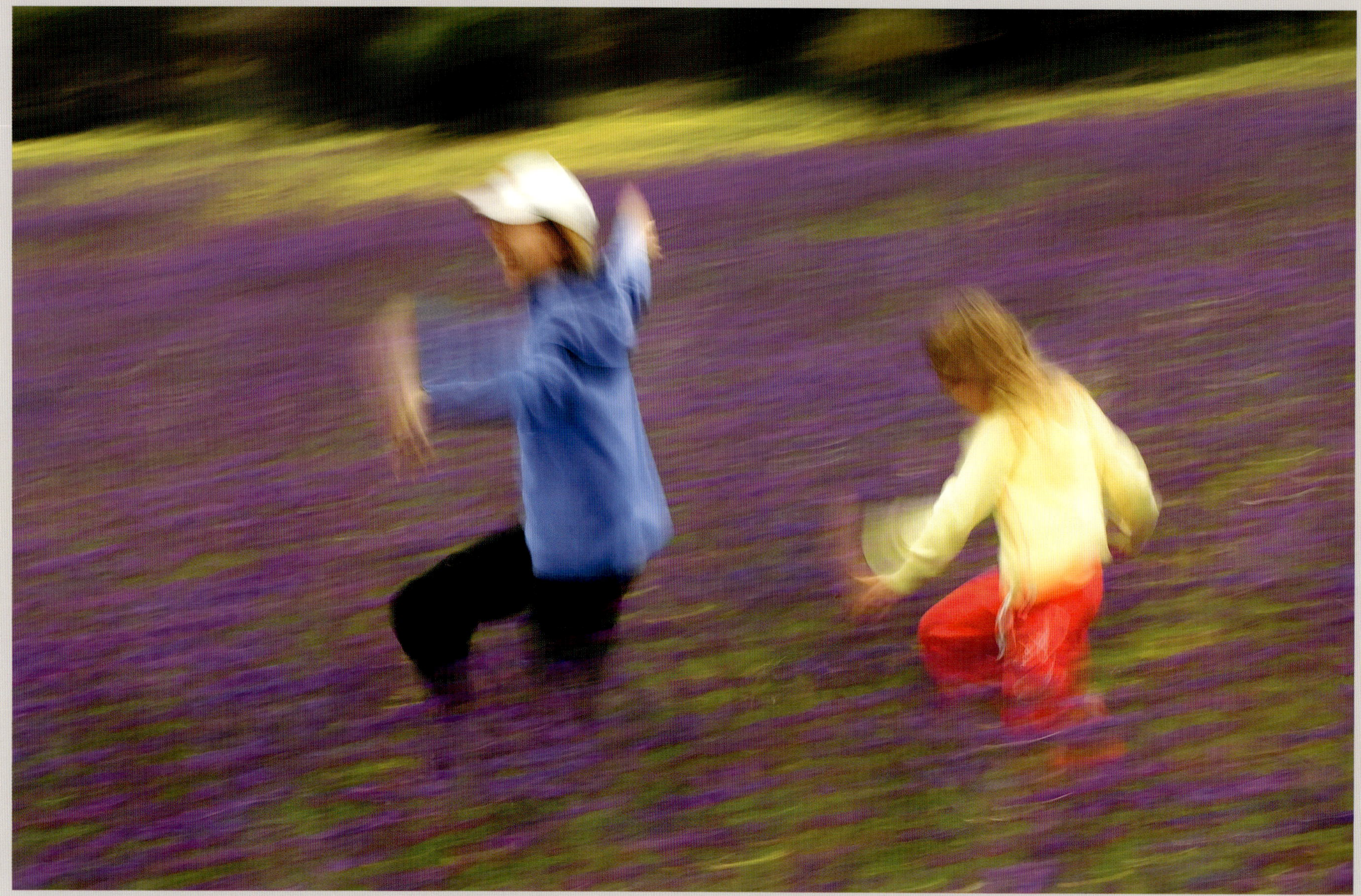

I had taken my family on a day trip to our friend's farm to take some photos. They were having such fun, laughing and running through the wildflowers, that I couldn't help but take their photo to remember what a great day we had.

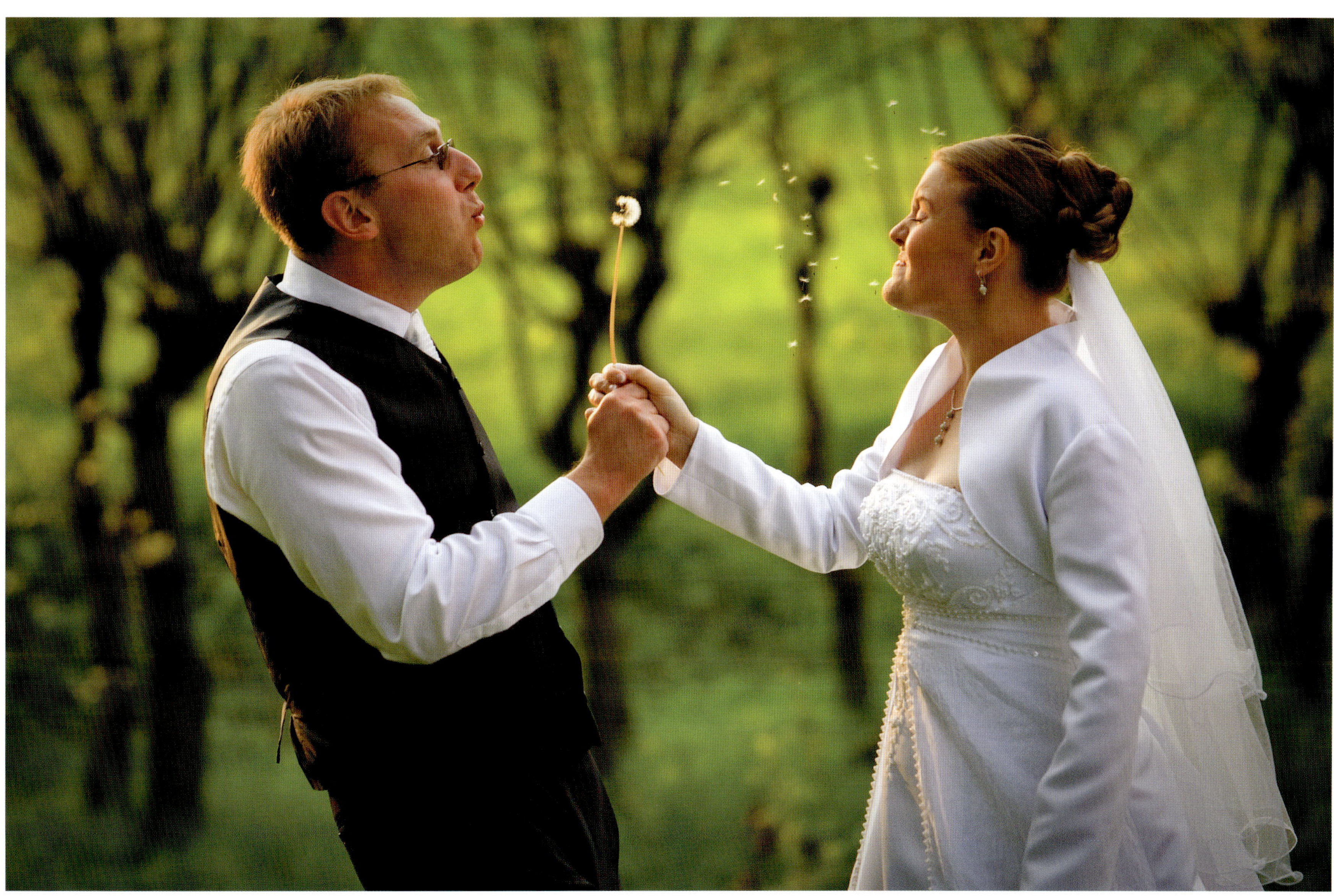

My best friend Martina and her husband are a wonderful couple, full of positive energy. They love nature, so I decided to take their wedding portrait in a public garden. There was a very nice spot with a little stream and willows and everything was backlit with evening sun. Since the bride left her bouquet at the reception, she needed a new one. But the groom couldn't resist the obvious temptation.

KRUSOVICE
MARTINA AND PETER

MAGDALENA STRAKOVA

Canon EOS-1D Mark III, Canon 70-200 lens, 1/500sec at f/3.2. Post-capture: no digital alterations.

HIGHLY COMMENDED, 2011

This image was taken in Russia, where many elderly people work really hard to grow food in their summer gardens (often because their survival still depends on it), but they also find strength and time to grow flowers just for the beauty and joy of it. This woman is very fond of her gladioli: every flower has a stick for support, enough sunshine and space to grow, and a lot of the woman's care.

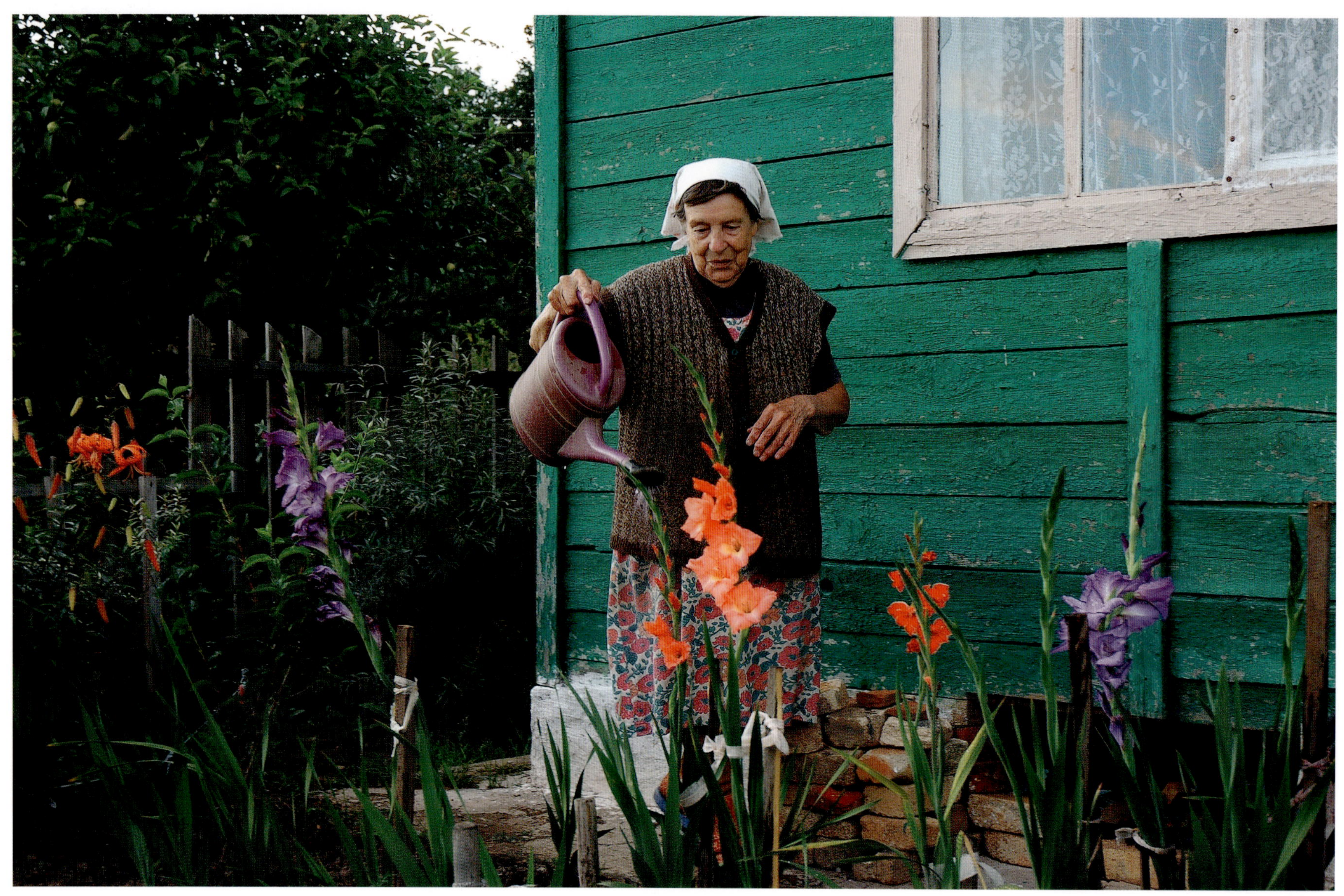

NEIGHBOUR'S DACHA NEAR THE CITY OF KAZAN, VOLGA REGION
ELDERLY WOMAN IN THE GARDEN

ZEMFIRA BAKYYEVA

Nikon D70, Nikkor 18–70mm f/3.5-4.5 G at 52mm, f/4.2.
HIGHLY COMMENDED, 2010

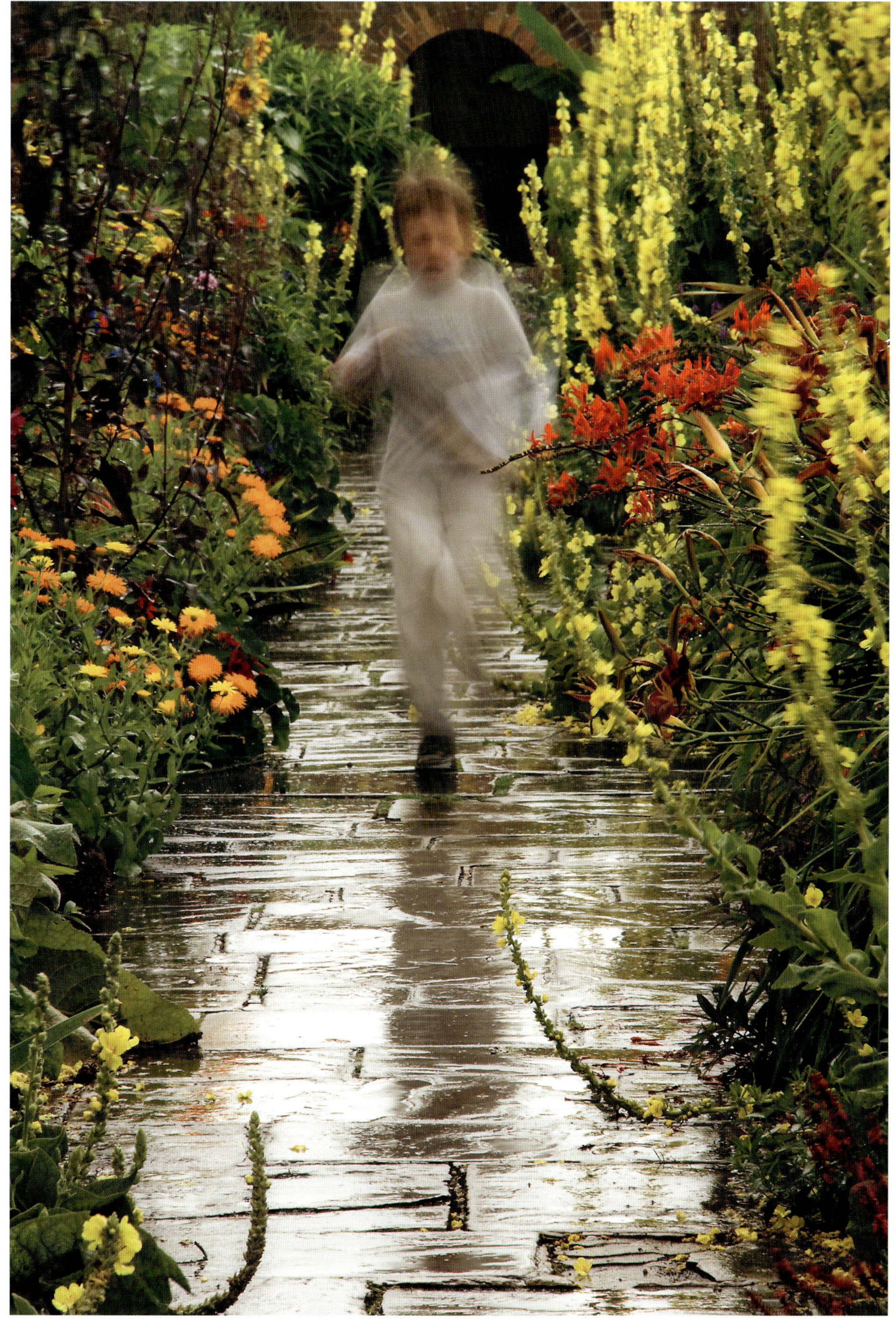

PACKWOOD HOUSE, LAPWORTH, WARWICKSHIRE, ENGLAND
By kind permission of the National Trust
RUNNING FROM THE RAIN

ANNE GILBERT

Nikon D300, Nikon 18-135mm f/3.5-5.6 AF-S lens, f/20. This shot was taken with the assistance of a tripod and a slow exposure (1/4sec) to capture motion blur.
COMMENDED, 2009

This pathway runs along the top of the walled garden at Packwood House. There are mixed flower borders along each side, planted in hot colours. While taking shelter from a heavy downpour there, I thought I'd try to capture the beauty of the gardens in the rain. Just as I pressed the shutter to capture the scene, George ran into frame – the result of which is a lovely action shot. George's mother was sheltering next to me and gave me permission to enter the photo in this competition.

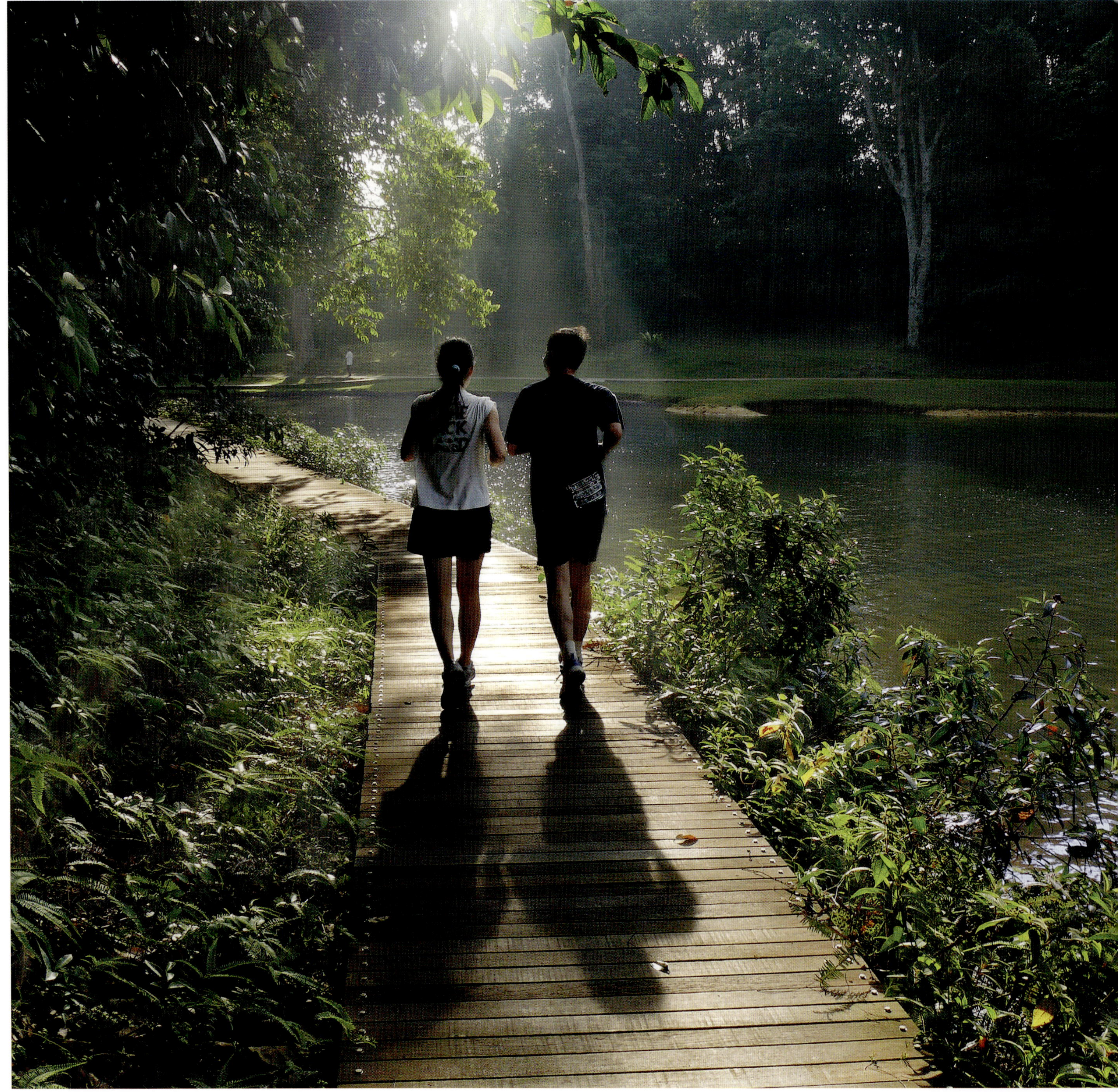

As we were strolling along the boardwalk, the morning ray caught my attention and I thought how nice it would be if there was a silhouette subject ahead of us. As there were many other strollers and joggers around, I knew that it was just a matter of time before I would capture that moment. This couple offered me that opportunity.

MACRITCHIE RESERVOIR
PATHWAY TO GLORY

DAVID LOW

Panasonic FZ-50, Kit Lens 35–420mm, f/7.1.
HIGHLY COMMENDED, 2010

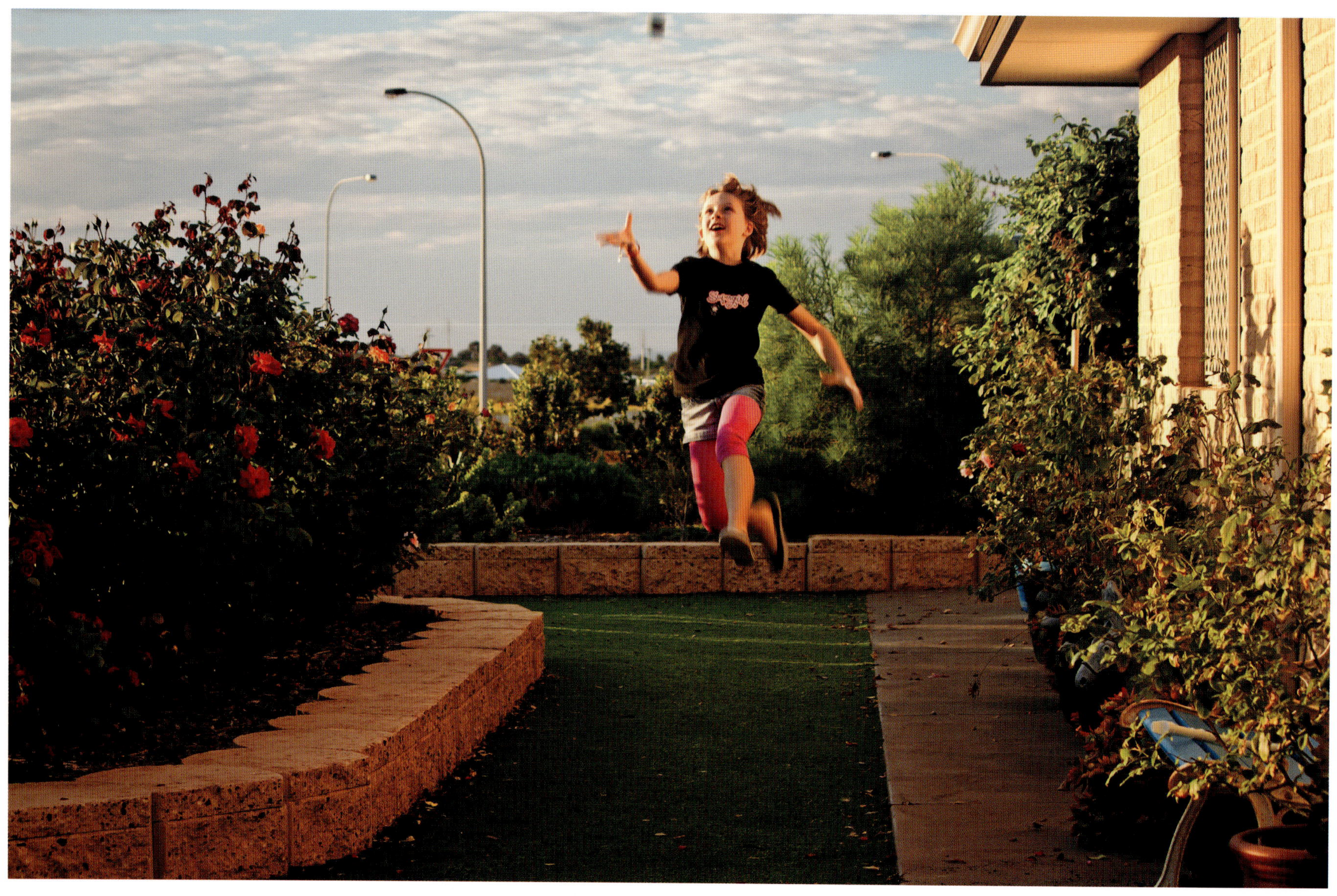

IN OUR GARDEN, AT THE FRONT OF THE PROPERTY
GARDEN JUMPER

BRAD MAILER

Canon EOS 450D, 55-250mm lens, 1/60sec at f/7.1. Post-capture: no major alterations other than basic colour management, noise control and sharpening.
FIRST, 2011

This image shows my daughter, who is jumping between a raised garden bed to the left, comprising ten various floribunda roses and flower pots, and to the right, various hybrid teas and David Austin roses. My main goal was to show how an environment that is attractive and interesting enough to be explored can encourage today's children to enjoy it the same way they did in past generations. For me, this image was easy to accomplish. I knew the light was best in the evening, so I waited until my subject was already in location at that time and I then approached her and asked her to show me some games she likes to play. It was then up to me to present them in the best way.

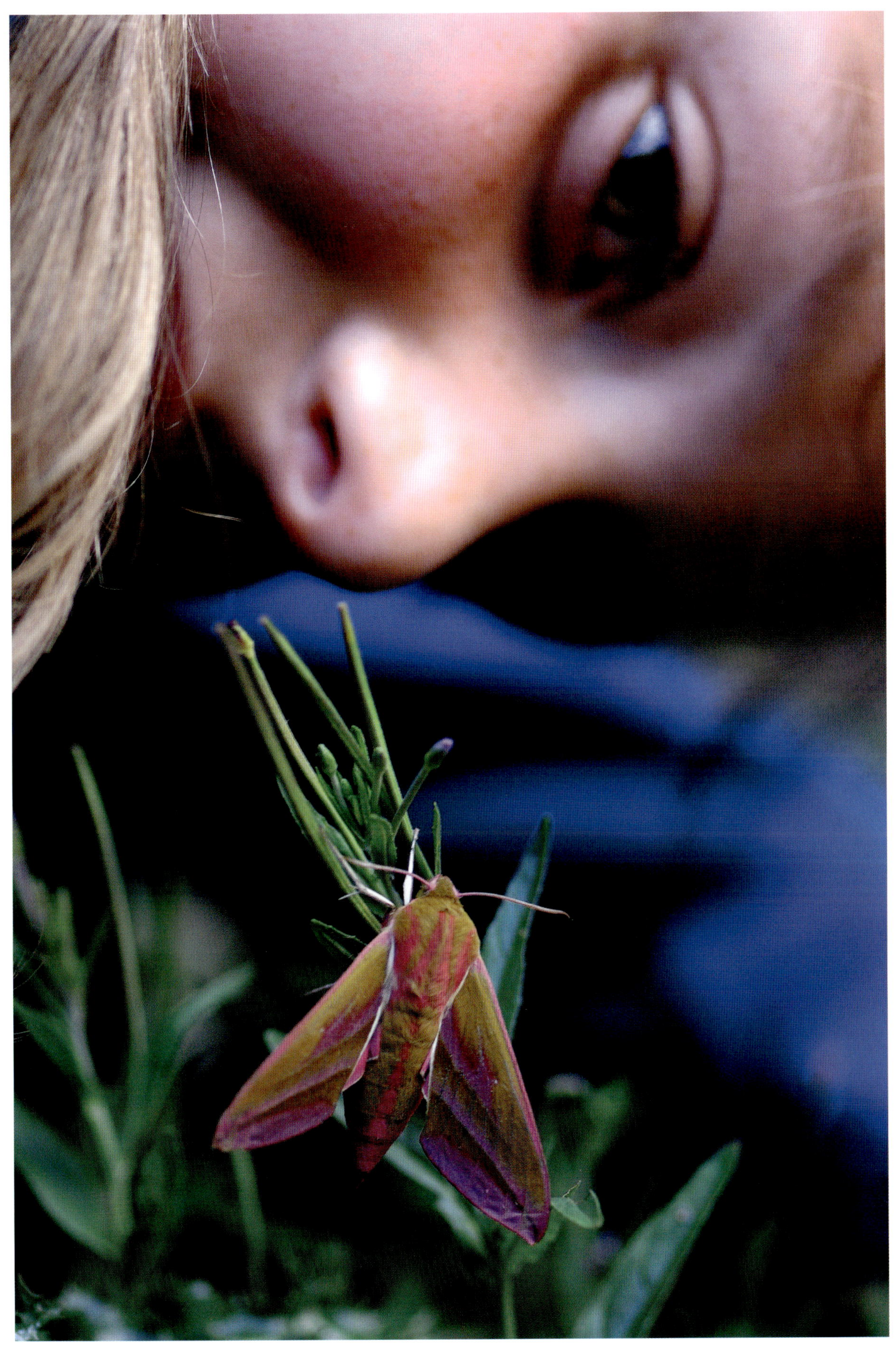

My eight-year-old daughter was admiring an elephant hawk-moth that had just hatched from its chrysalis. The moth was on some willowherb growing along the side of our house, its wings still a little crinkled. It was a very exciting moment.

OUTSIDE OUR FARMHOUSE, MORVAH, NEAR PENZANCE, CORNWALL, ENGLAND
NATURE GIRL

JOANNA CLEGG

Pentax K10D, Sigma 105mm 1:2:8 DG Macro, f/2.8.
HIGHLY COMMENDED, 2010

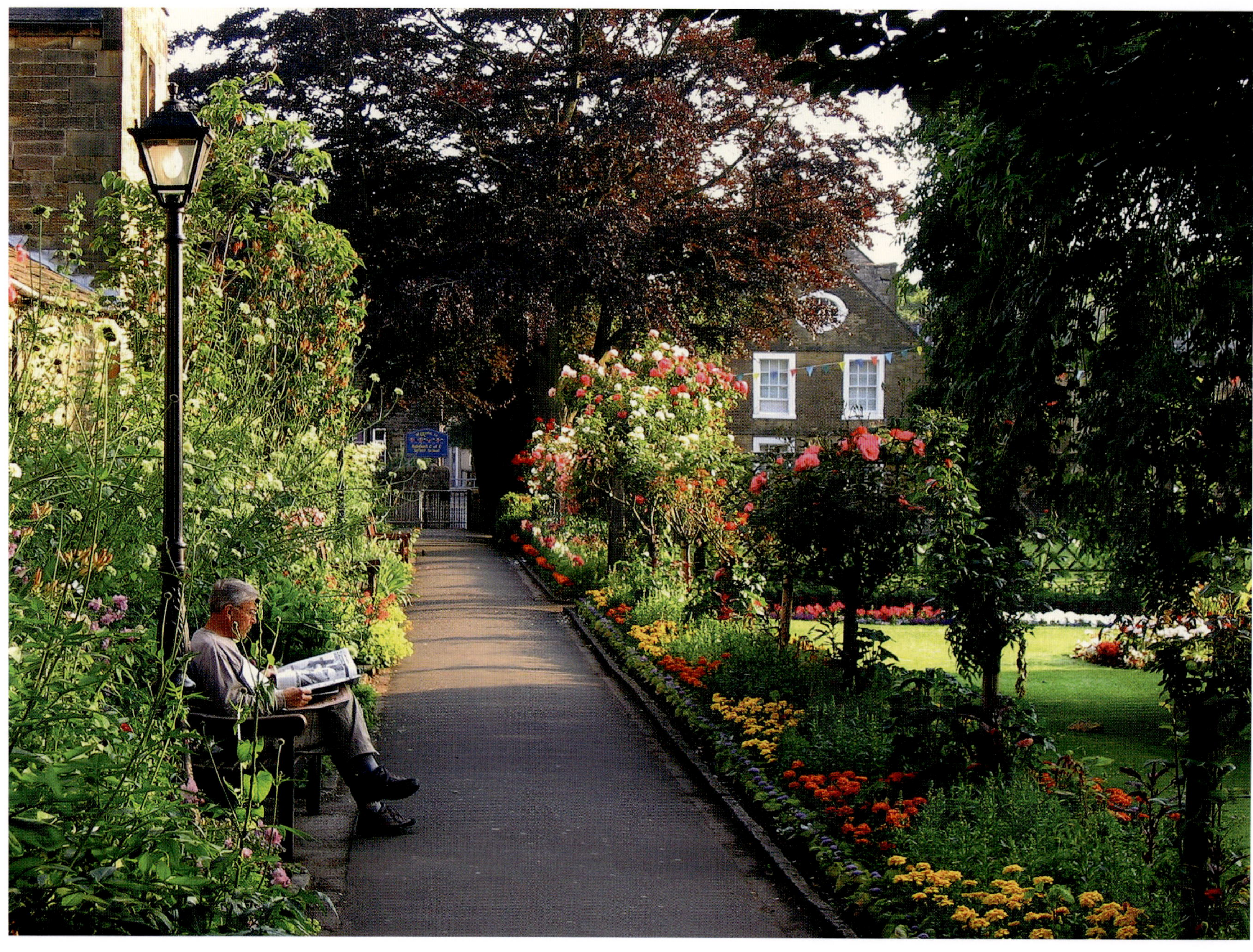

BAKEWELL, DERBYSHIRE, ENGLAND

ENJOYING THE MORNING PAPER IN AN ENGLISH PARK

JOHN ROGER PALMOUR

Canon PowerShot A95, 1/60sec at f/4.5. I used the camera's automatic settings with no tripod, filters or other equipment. Post-capture: slight correction/adjustments to exposure and colour saturation in Picnik on www.flickr.com.

HIGHLY COMMENDED, 2011

This gentleman seemed to have found the perfect spot to serenely catch up on the news of the day. The harmonious perfection of the bedding plantings is a tribute to the skill of the gardeners, and the soft light of early morning shows the fruits of their labours to their best advantage. Beneath roses pruned as standards, there is a mix of classic summer bedding plants – marigolds (*Tagetes* spp.), floss flowers (*Agertum* spp.) begonia (*Begonia* spp.) etc. The bed behind the man on the bench is planted less formally and more loosely with scabious (*Scabiosa* spp.), phlox (*Phlox* spp.), daylilies (*Hermocallis* spp.), euphorbia (*Euphorbia* spp.) etc. The copper beech (*Fagus* spp.) at the end of the pathway adds a focal point.

The many beautifully-landscaped and lovingly-tended parks and gardens of England are a constant source of inspiration for me, especially in the quiet of early morning. Whenever we are travelling, I always make a point of getting out with the camera before breakfast and move quickly, taking as many shots as possible while the light is good. I am always looking for opportunities to depict ordinary people enjoying gardens and nature. I prefer candid shots and rarely ask people to pose.

Rita Armfield's London garden is full of recycled objects that have been put to ingenious use. In this case an old bicycle, casually leaning against the fence, has a new lease of life as a quirky plant holder.

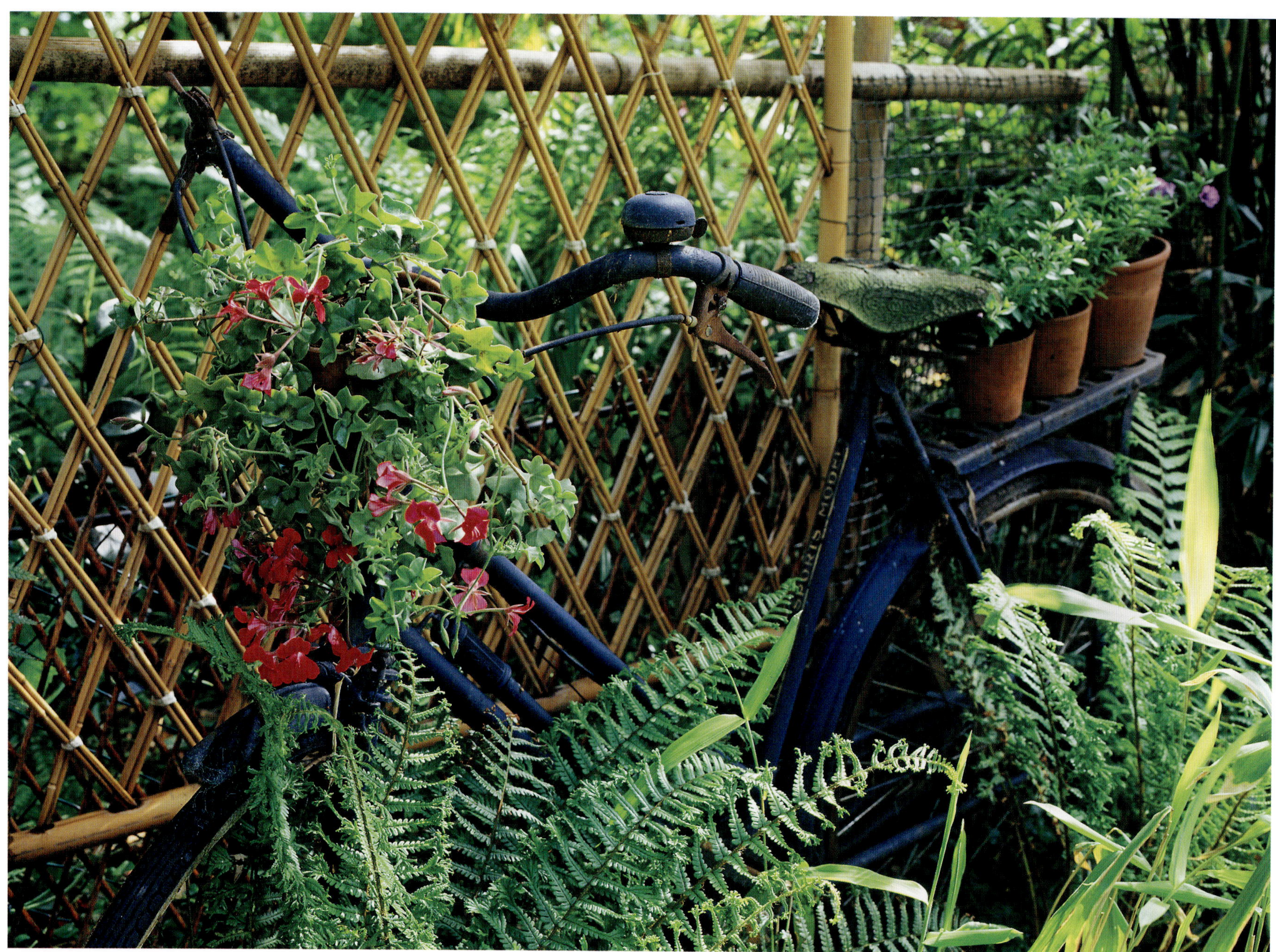

RITA ARMFIELD'S GARDEN, LONDON, ENGLAND
RITA'S BICYCLE GARDEN

SUZIE GIBBONS

Pentax 645N, 75mm lens, f/11, Velvia 50. The bike was in a shady spot at the time, but with appealing light filtering in from above. I decided on a jaunty angle to emphasise the humorous aspect of the subject.
COMMENDED, 2008

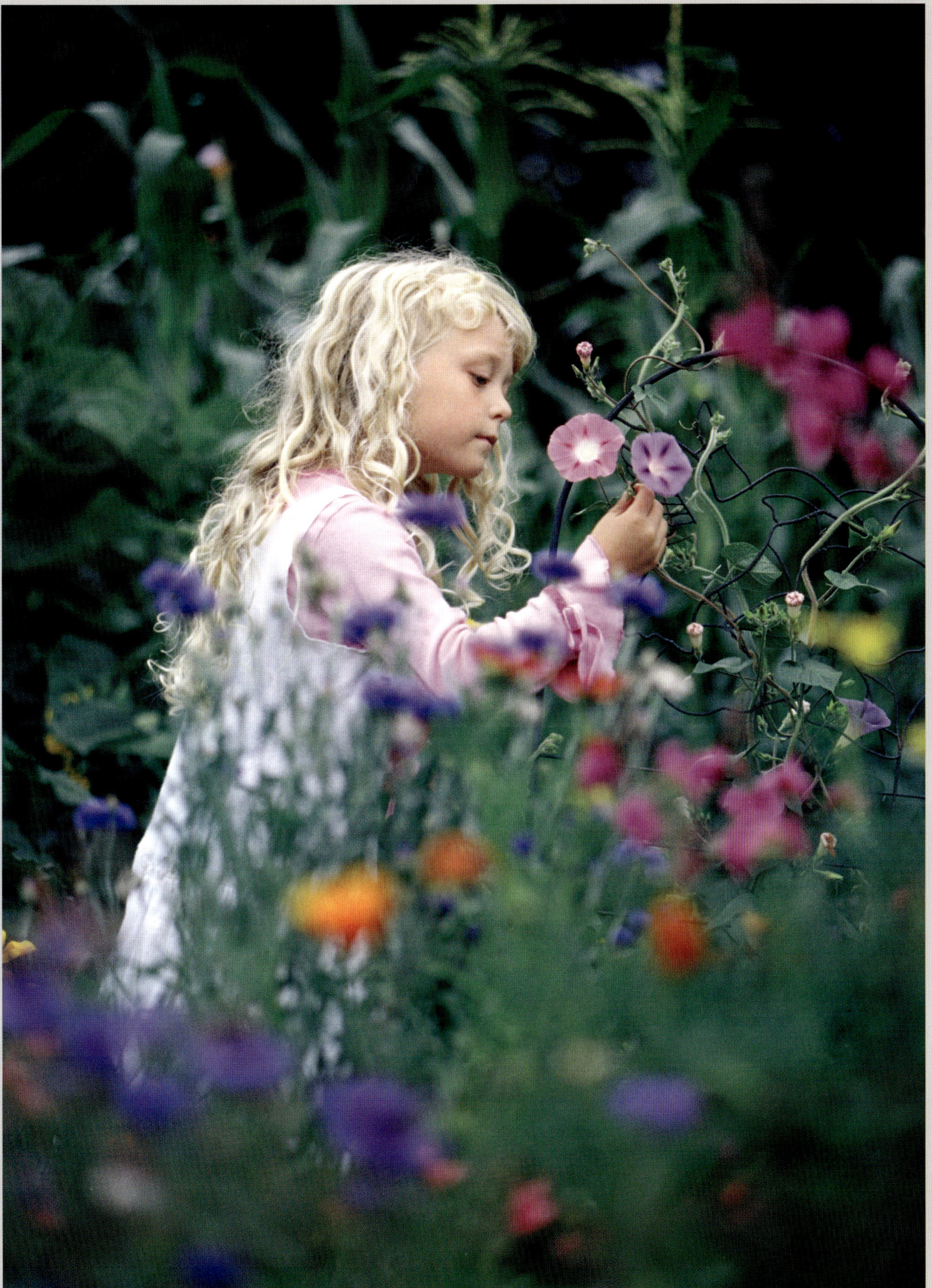

OUR GARDEN, BELLINGHAM, WASHINGTON STATE
GIRL IN HER GARDEN

STEVE SATUSHEK

Fuji Velvia, Canon EOS 1, 70–200mm, f/8.
FINALIST, 2010

My daughter Mia was out in the garden one summer morning checking on her plants. She was holding some morning glory flowers (*Ipomoea purpurea*) of the Convolvulaceae family. The out-of-focus flowers that can be seen are bachelor buttons (*Centaurea cyanus*) and sweet peas (*Lathyrus odoratus*). The vines are climbing on a wire trellis with a hummingbird outline. It is a brief moment in time, capturing the intimacy of childhood inquisitiveness and innocence.

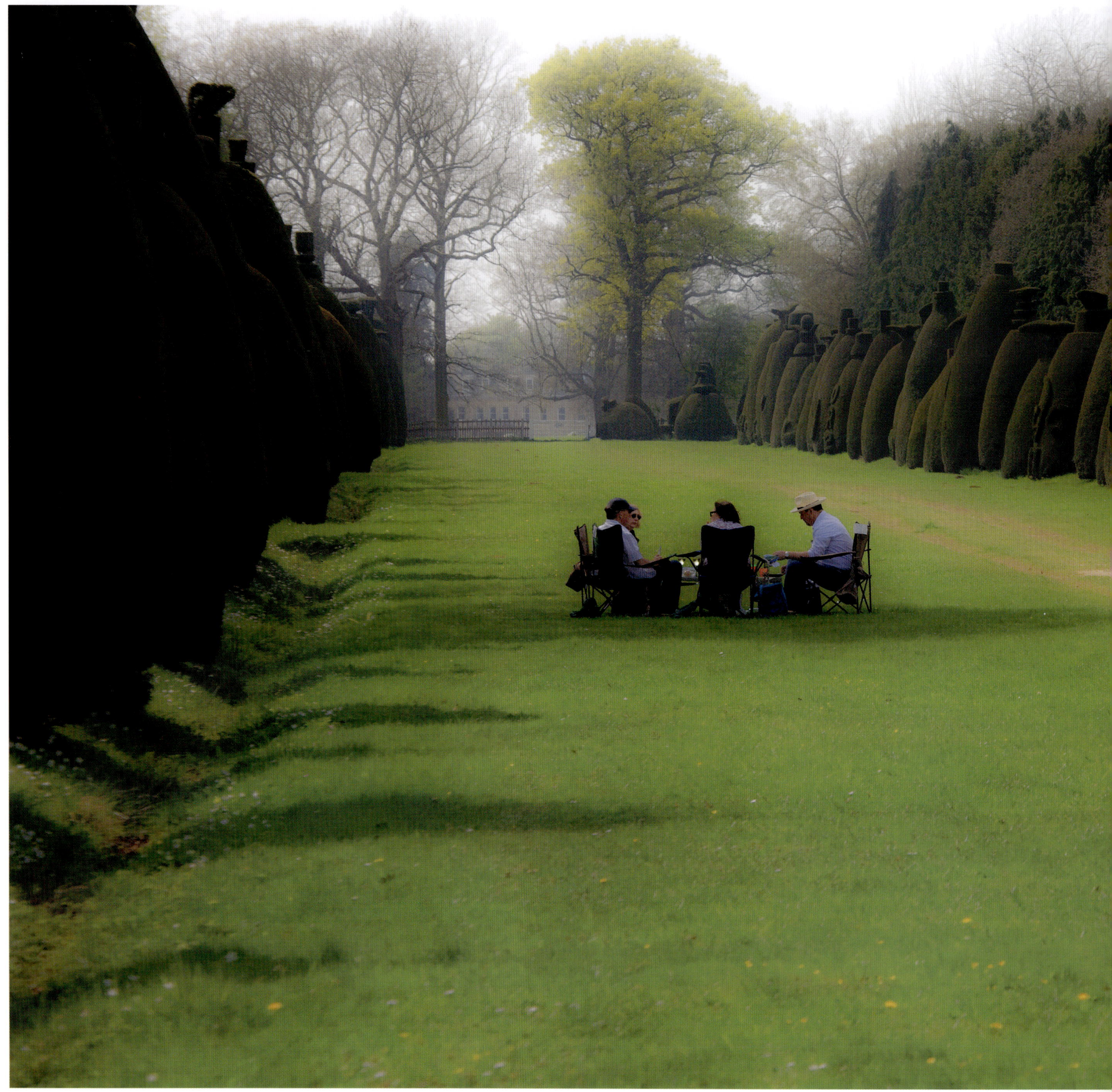

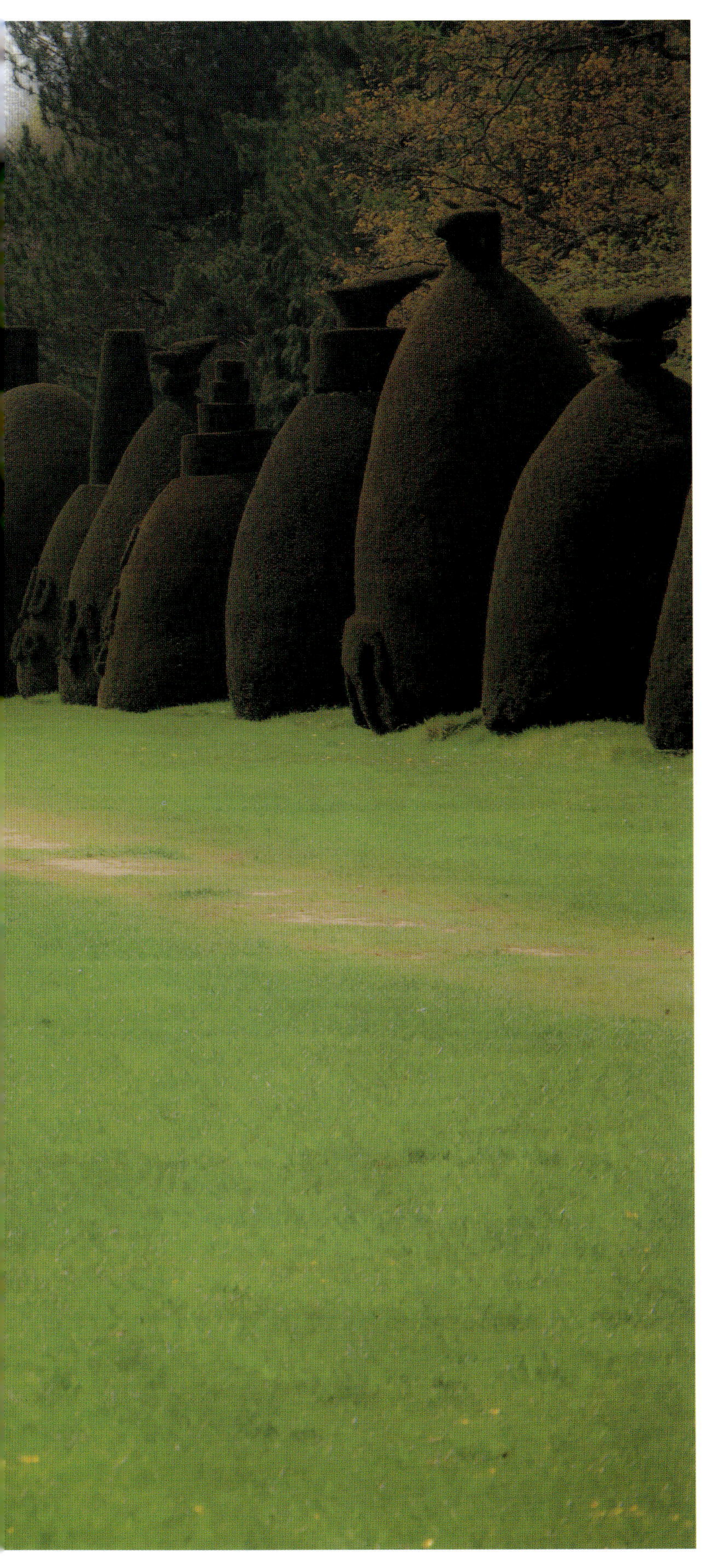

The soft spring light illuminated the scene at Clipsham Hall perfectly. Normally either a busy or empty location, the single group of people was well-placed. Even though this is in the heart of England, I had the feeling of walking into a French Impressionist picture. I used the near yews (*Taxus* spp.) on the left and the group of people to fill what would otherwise have been an empty foreground and to give the picture depth. I also used a focal length of 165mm to compress the image, making the Hall and distant yew trees more obvious. I have visited the site on several occasions and this was the best light I have seen.

THE YEW TREE AVENUE, CLIPSHAM, RUTLAND, ENGLAND
'LE PIQUE-NIQUE'

JOHN WHITAKER

Canon EOS 5D Mark II, Canon 70-300mm lens, 1/100sec at f/11. Post-capture: some small areas in the foreground that were devoid of grass have been filled.
HIGHLY COMMENDED, 2011

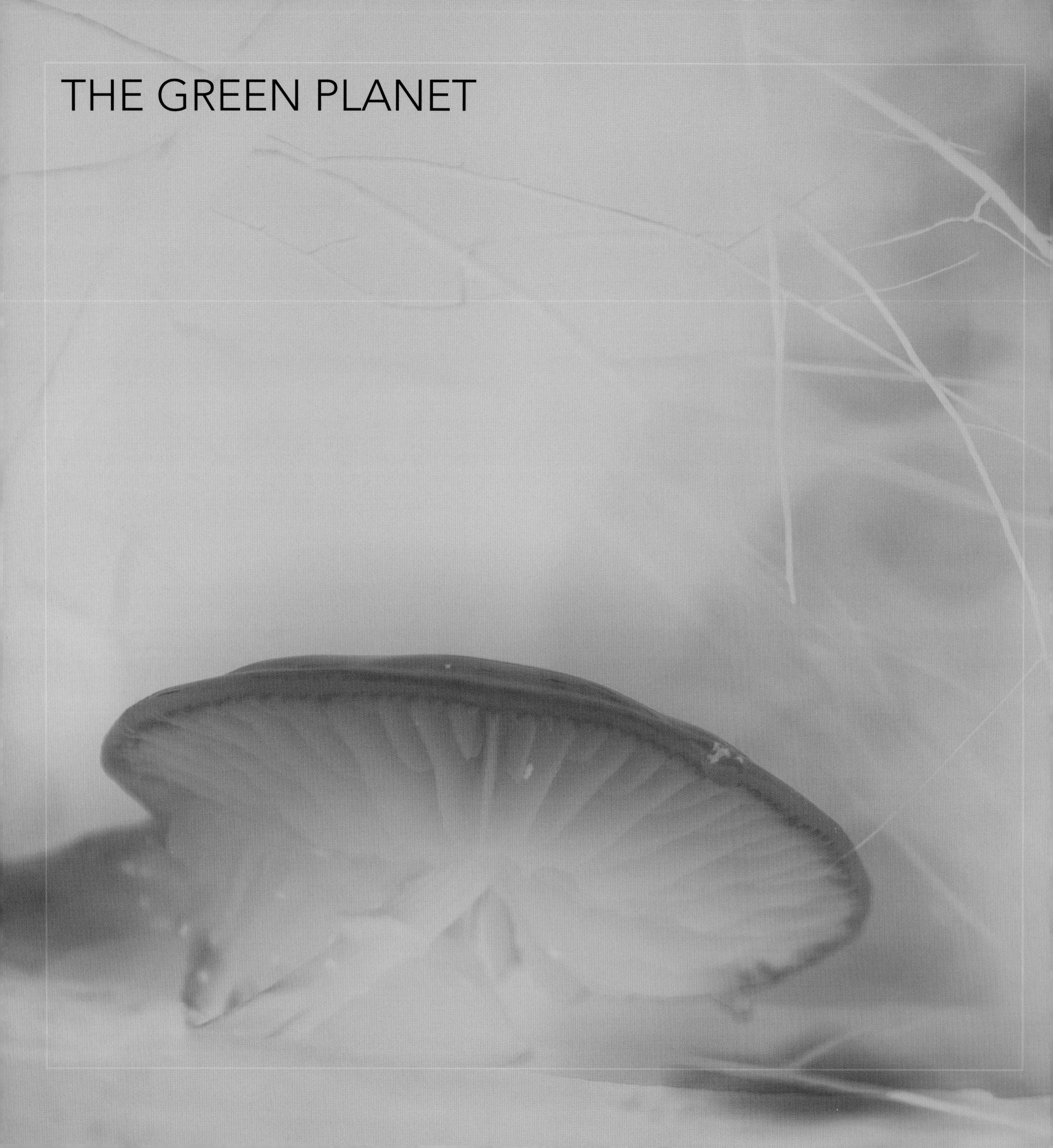

The Green Planet

Every day with my work, I have the opportunity to walk around and work in one of the greatest and most visited temperate tree collections in the world, the arboretum at Kew. The diversity, heritage and rarity of these specimen trees continues to inspire and challenge me. However, one of the more inspiring activities that I can ever do is to wander through a natural woodland or forest in the British Isles or anywhere else in the world where these plants come from. I experience and observe them growing in association with the many other species and biodiversity in their natural habitat where they belong.

This is where I am at ease, I learn and never forget what these trees need to grow comfortably. With this knowledge we can work out how to grow and display them successfully in cultivation, by studying and copying nature and transferring these attributes back to the garden environment. In a cultivated situation, whether in a garden or an urban setting, we are quick to forget where trees actually come from and ignore their needs and some of the amazing International Garden Photographer of the Year competition images are often a necessary gentle reminder to us all.

Quite often these forests are fragile environments and vulnerable to the threats from human activity, climate change and the introduction of both animal- and plant-based invasive species. But if left alone these habitats will continue to thrive and remain intact for the next generations to enjoy. We cannot preserve a single species as a part of *in situ* conservation; we can only do that by conserving the habitat that these species grow in and all the diverse species that live within it. In 1999, the loss of plants across the globe caused great concern to conservationists, and at the 16th International Botanical Congress; botanists passed a resolution urging the world to recognise plant conservation as a global priority to halt the loss of species. From this resolution came the Global Strategy for Plant Conservation with 16 targets aimed at conserving the world's flora, ranging from the creation of species checklists to the training of botanists and horticulturists who will be involved with the conservation of the world's biodiversity.

I am lucky to be involved with a team of passionate International Garden Photographer of the Year judges and since I have been a judge for the tree category in the International Garden Photography of the Year competition, I have seen many trees in both urban and natural settings in photographs which have been an inspiration to me and will help to raise awareness of the plight of trees in the landscape. They are a clear reminder of some of the many types of gardens, landscapes, woodlands or forests that are home to the many tree species and I am immediately taken back in my mind to these magical places and wish that I could be there again. I have been lucky to visit some of these places and the wonderful thing is that International Garden Photographer of the Year is giving everyone who visits the exhibitions the same opportunity that I have had.

Tony Kirkham
Head of Arboretum and Horticultural Services, Royal Botanic Gardens, Kew

I made a trip to Dartmoor in August knowing that the heather (*Calluna vulgaris*) would be in full bloom. I scouted for locations and found that the flowers were in abundance near Hay Tor. Next morning I was out before sunrise and ready for the right light when it happened. On this morning, the sun seemed to disappear under a blanket of cloud, but looking at the cloud patterns it was evident that the sun would emerge soon and the presence of clouds made exciting light all the more likely. I had my camera ready on tripod with a three-stop graduated neutral density filter in place. Sure enough, soon there was this splendid sunburst which I could make the most of as I was all set up.

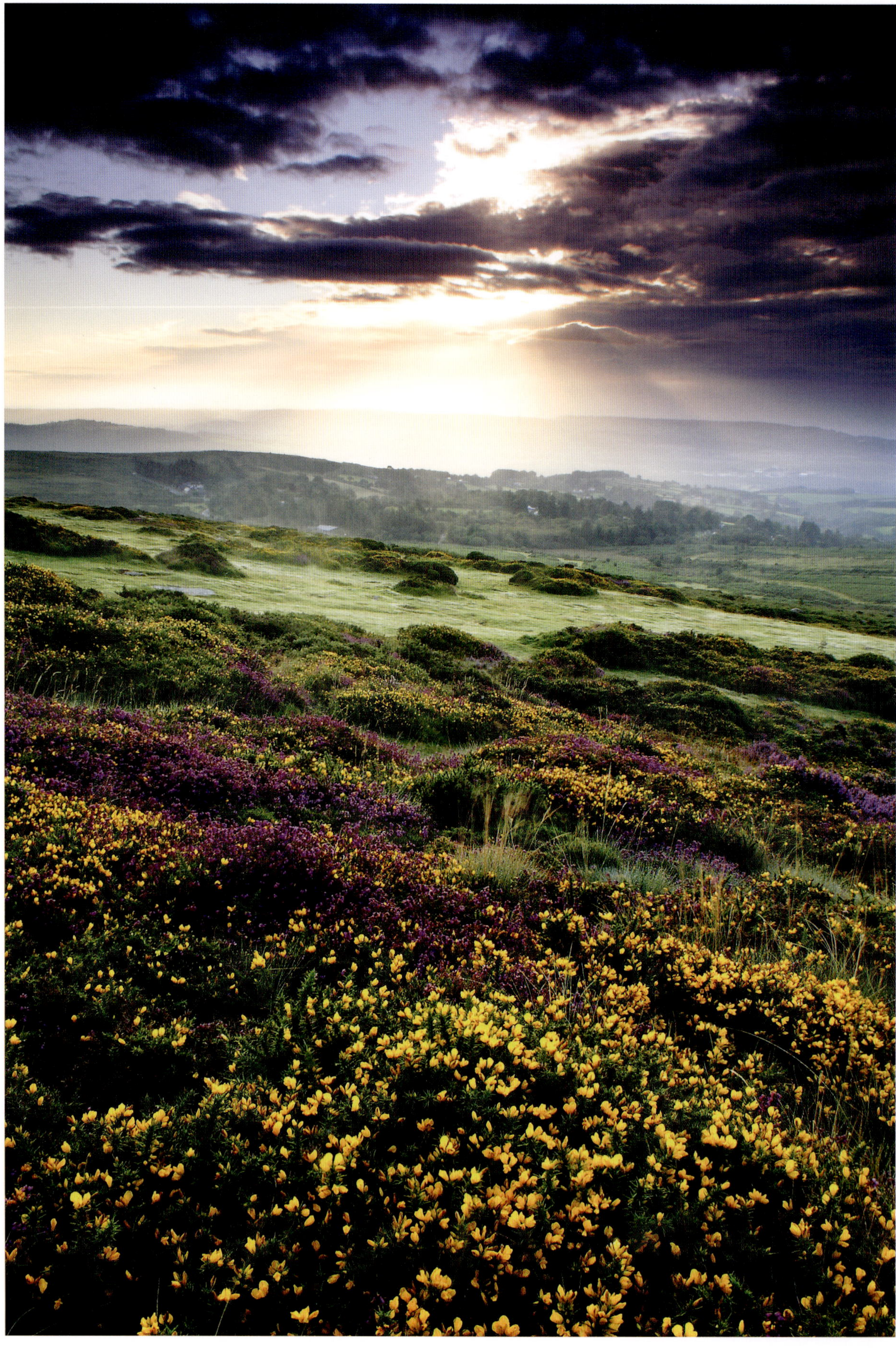

HAY TOR, DARTMOOR NATIONAL PARK, ENGLAND
A SUMMER SUNRISE

DEBASHIS BANDYOPADHYA

Canon EOS 350D, Canon 18-55mm lens. 0.6sec at f/22. Post-capture: adjustments to saturation, white balance and contrast.
SECOND, 2011

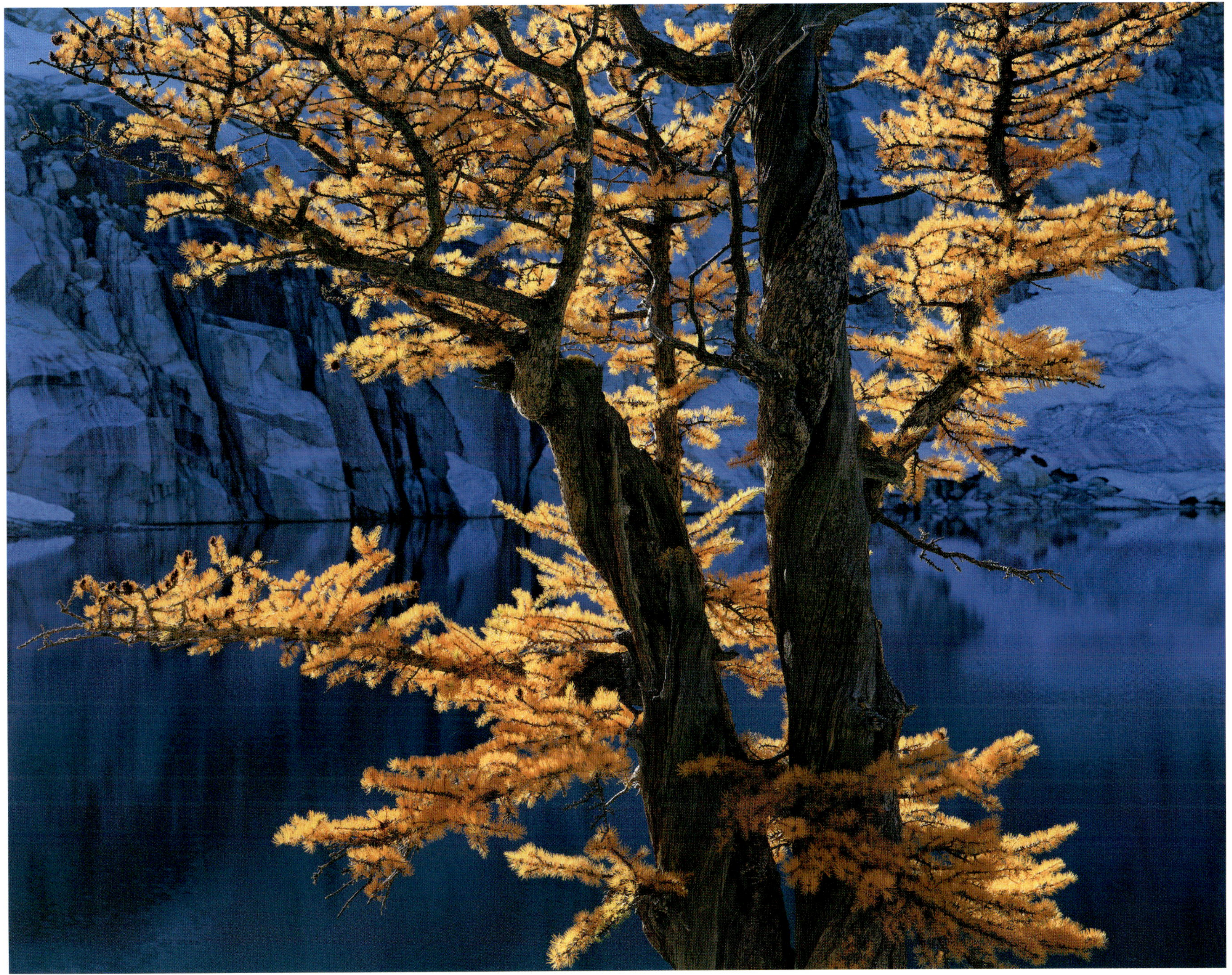

Larch needles in the fall are wonderful to photograph, especially when they are backlit. The white cliff in the background was in deep shade, and I knew from past experience that on a bright sunny day anything in shade would record the blue ambient light reflected from the sky. The larch was in direct afternoon sun, so the backlit needles stood out magnificently against the blue background.

ENCHANTMENT LAKES, ALPINE LAKES WILDERNESS, WASHINGTON STATE
ALPINE LARCH (*LARIX LYALLII*)

ADAM GIBBS

Toho-Shimo FC-45X, 300mm lens, f/45, Velvia 50. I used a relatively long lens to isolate the tree from the distracting bright sky. The sun was directly in front of me so the hardest part was trying to shade the lens from the penetrating sun.
FINALIST, 2008

KILLARNEY NATIONAL PARK,
COUNTY KERRY
AUTUMN

NOEL BROWNE

Canon EOS 30D, Canon 10-22mm lens, ISO 100, one second at f/16. I wanted to get down to the toadstools' level and exaggerate the perspective by using a very wideangle lens. It was important for them all to be in focus.
FINALIST, 2009

The previous autumn I noticed this dead tree stump, but it was too late to photograph that year as the toadstools were already dead. Going back to the same spot at the optimum time the following year, I came across this scene. There was no direct sunlight but the bright conditions were ideal for a subject like this. I was able to get down low to take the shot, and it intrigued me to think that each year, at the same time, these toadstools will spring up on this tree stump and keep on reproducing year after year.

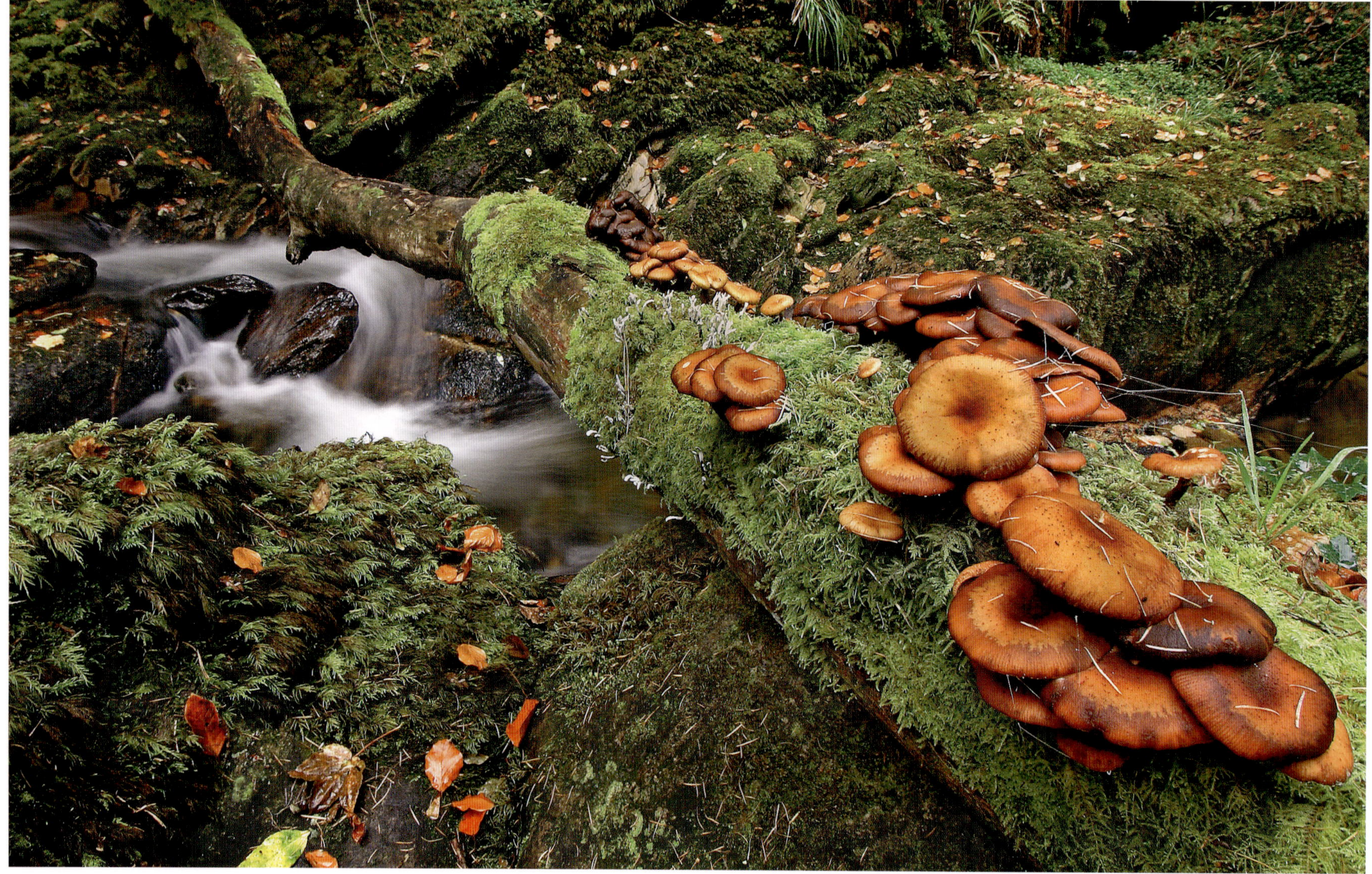

This shot was made between tropical showers just before sunset, on a trail considered one of the top hiking trails in the world. It leads to some fantastic, secluded beaches not accessible to most travellers. I hiked out with a small flashlight down some very steep slopes for two miles. By then the sun had set and the trail was almost pitch black. A couple I did not know who had passed me on their way out before sunset were worried about me and stayed at the trail's end until I came out. I was very impressed by their thoughtfulness.

THE NA PALI COAST TRAIL, KAUAI, HAWAII
NA PALI COAST AT SUNSET

DENNIS FRATES

Canon 1DS Mark III, Canon EF 16-35mm lens. 0.8sec at f/16. Post-capture: tonality and colour correction.

THIRD, 2012

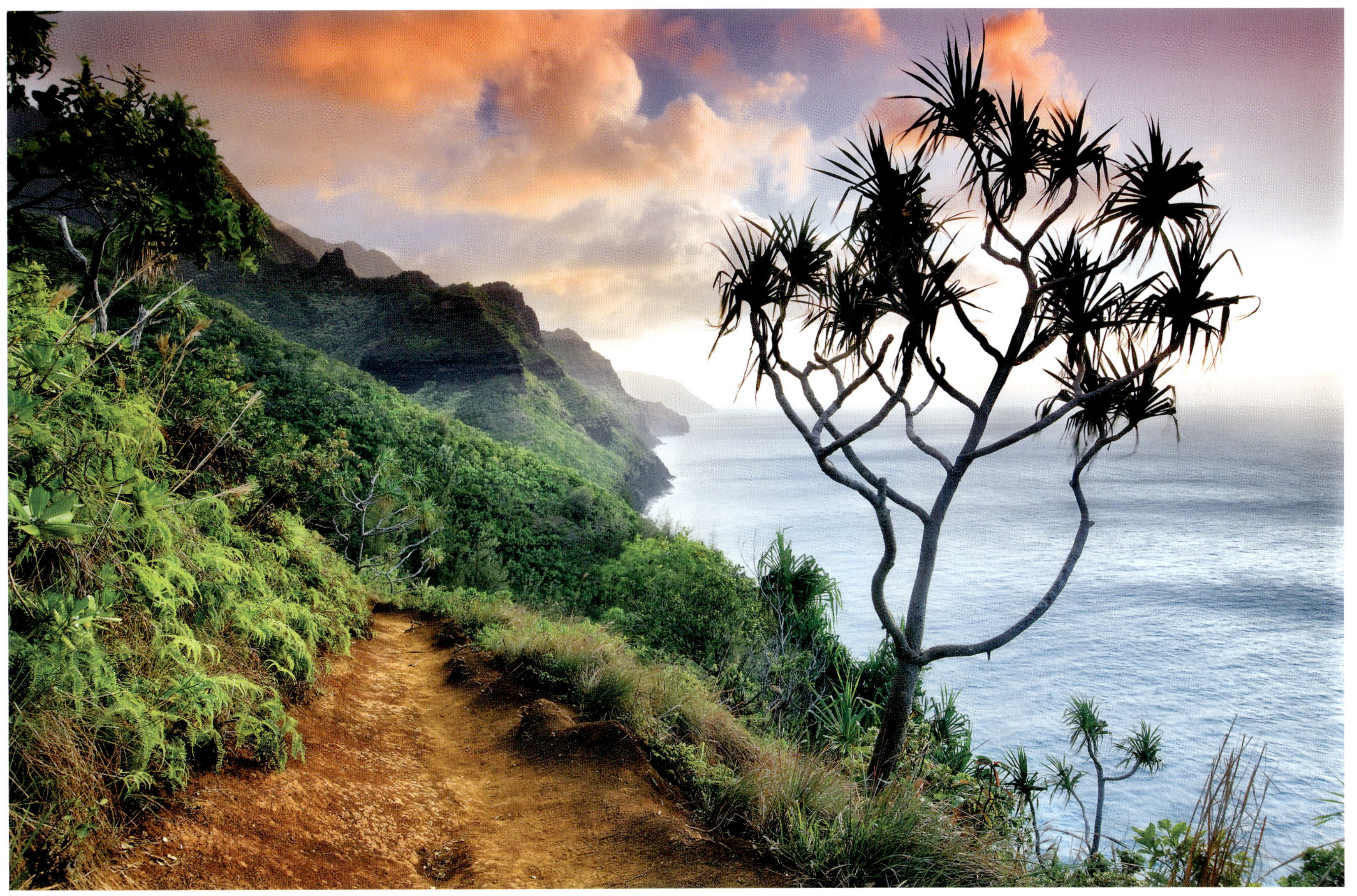

This is a rare example of an undisturbed wildflower meadow with many associated scarce flowers and insects. It is a relic from a once much larger meadow that is now situated in a clearing in Chambers Farm Wood. I sat in the meadow for several hours before I finally got this composition.

CHAMBERS FARM WOOD, LINCOLNSHIRE, ENGLAND
SCRUBS WILDFLOWER MEADOW

DANNY BEATH

Nikon D80, Sigma 70-300mm macro lens, 1/300sec at f/10, ISO 200. Post-capture: no digital alterations.
HIGHLY COMMENDED, 2012

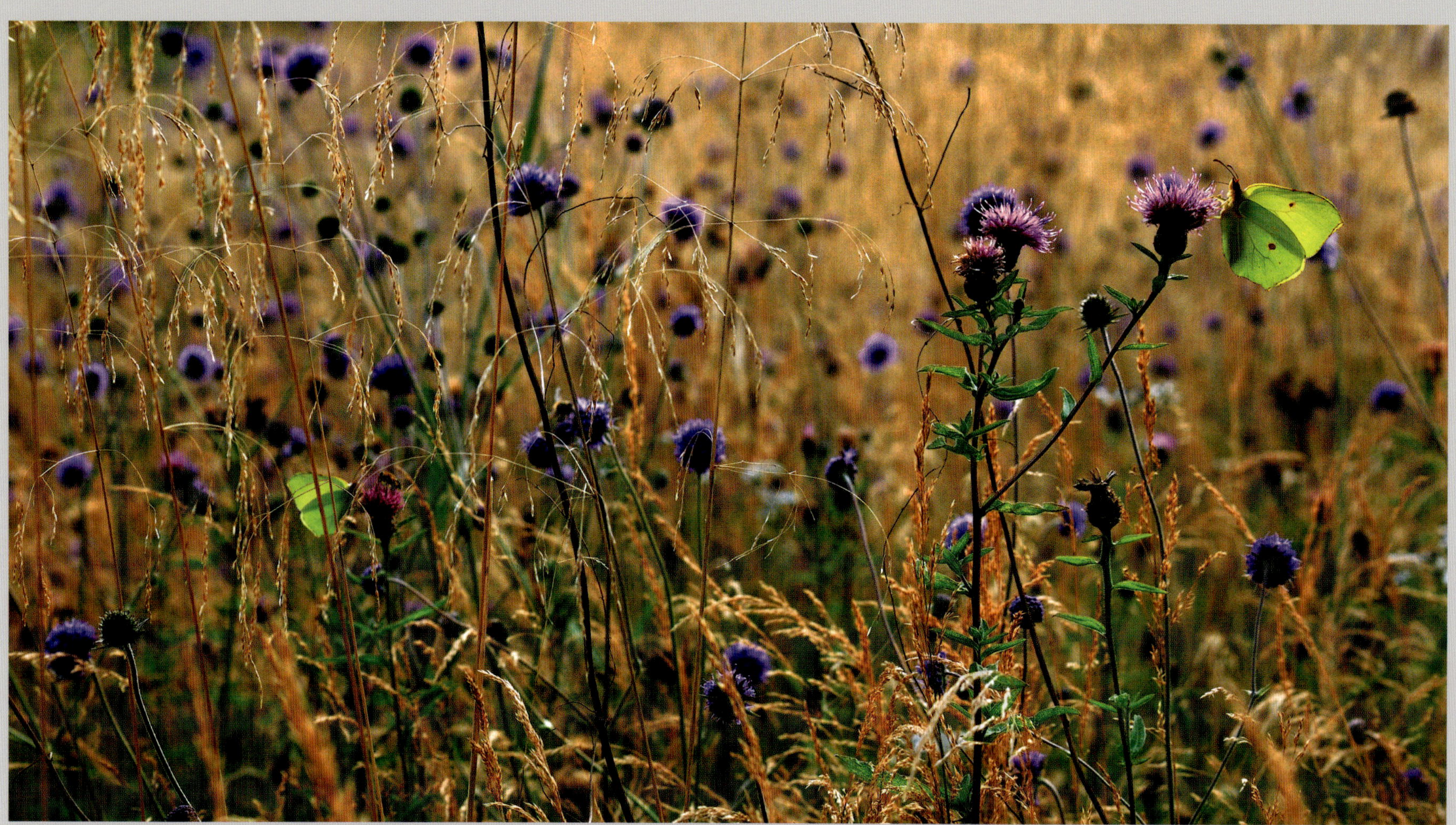

RANNOCH MOOR, HIGHLAND, SCOTLAND

LOCHAN NA H'ACHLAISE BY TORCHLIGHT

PETE BRIDGWOOD

Canon EOS-1Ds Mark III, Canon EF 17-40mm f/4 L USM lens, ISO 100, 2mins at f/10. White balancing to correct the tungsten (torch-lit) colour temperature of the island has resulted in some wonderful super-saturation of the twilight blues.

FINALIST, 2009

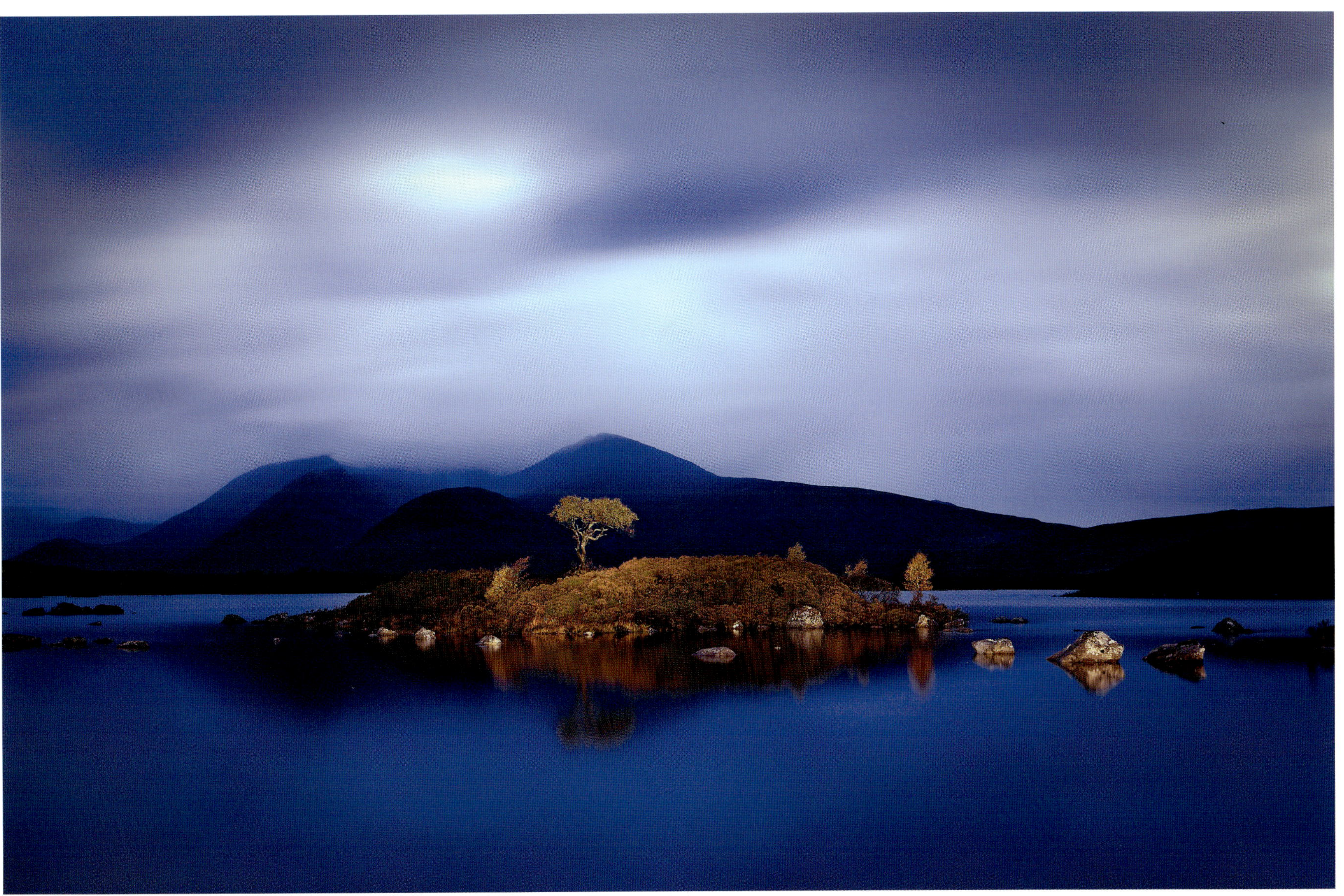

I had hoped to get to this wonderful loch before sunset, but arrived an hour too late. Not to be deterred in my quest for a magical image in the blackness of darkening twilight, I decided to create my own illumination using a large, handheld torch.

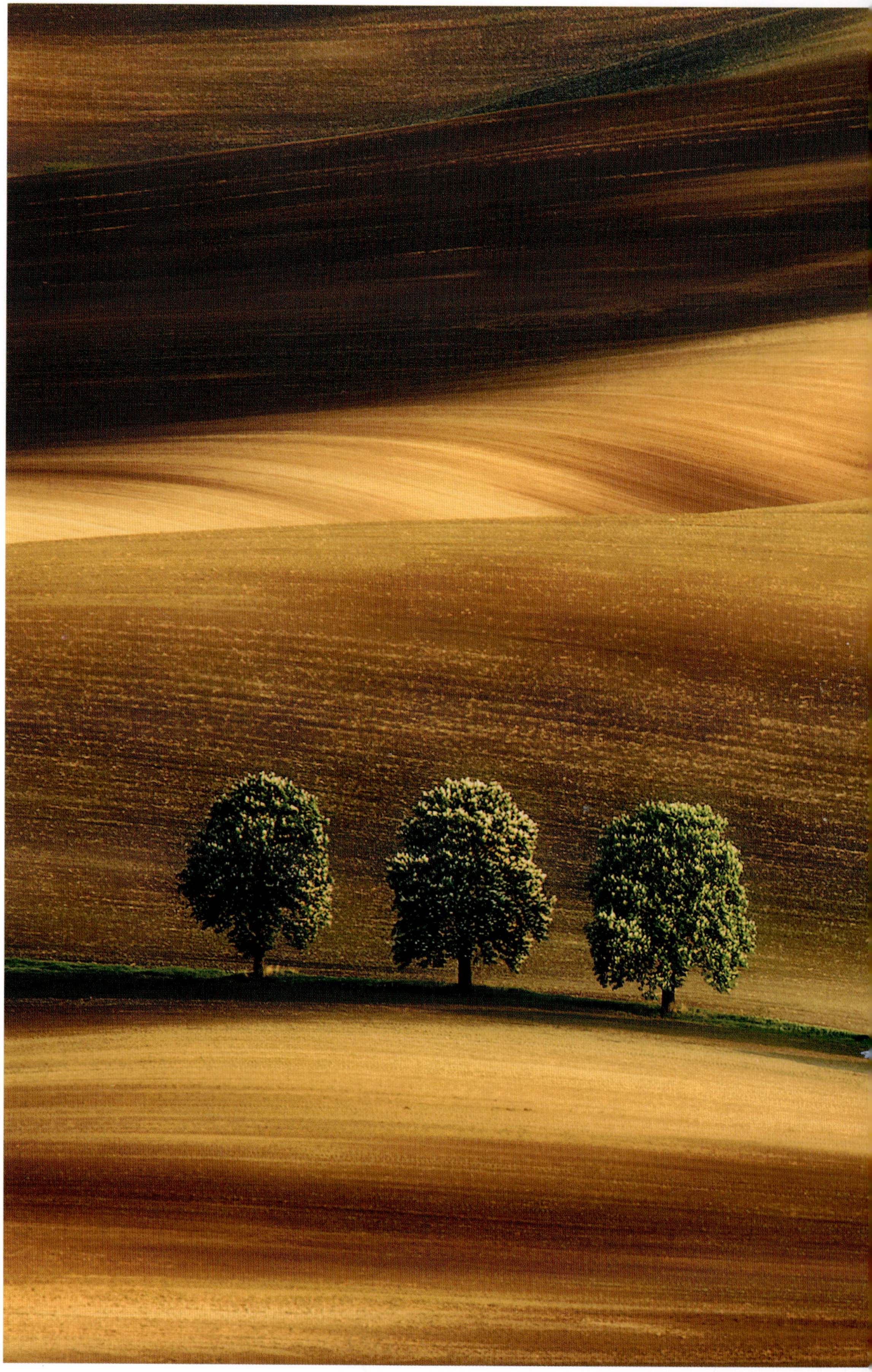

The colourful patches on the soil are caused, most probably, by erosion. This phenomenon, which is characteristic of this region, is often mistaken for shadows cast by clouds. The undulating landscape of Moravia is perfect for me to get the results I want.

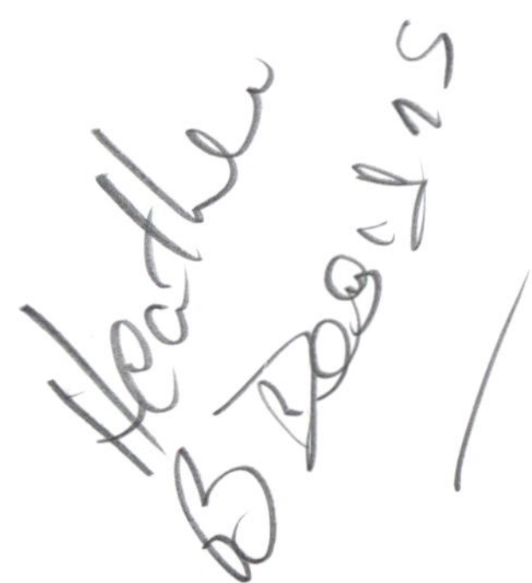

KYJOV, SOUTHERN MORAVIA
SIX...

KRZYSTOF BROWKO

Canon EOS 5D Mark II, Canon 100-400mm lens. 1/6sec at f/18. Post-capture: adjustment of crop and levels.
SECOND, 2012

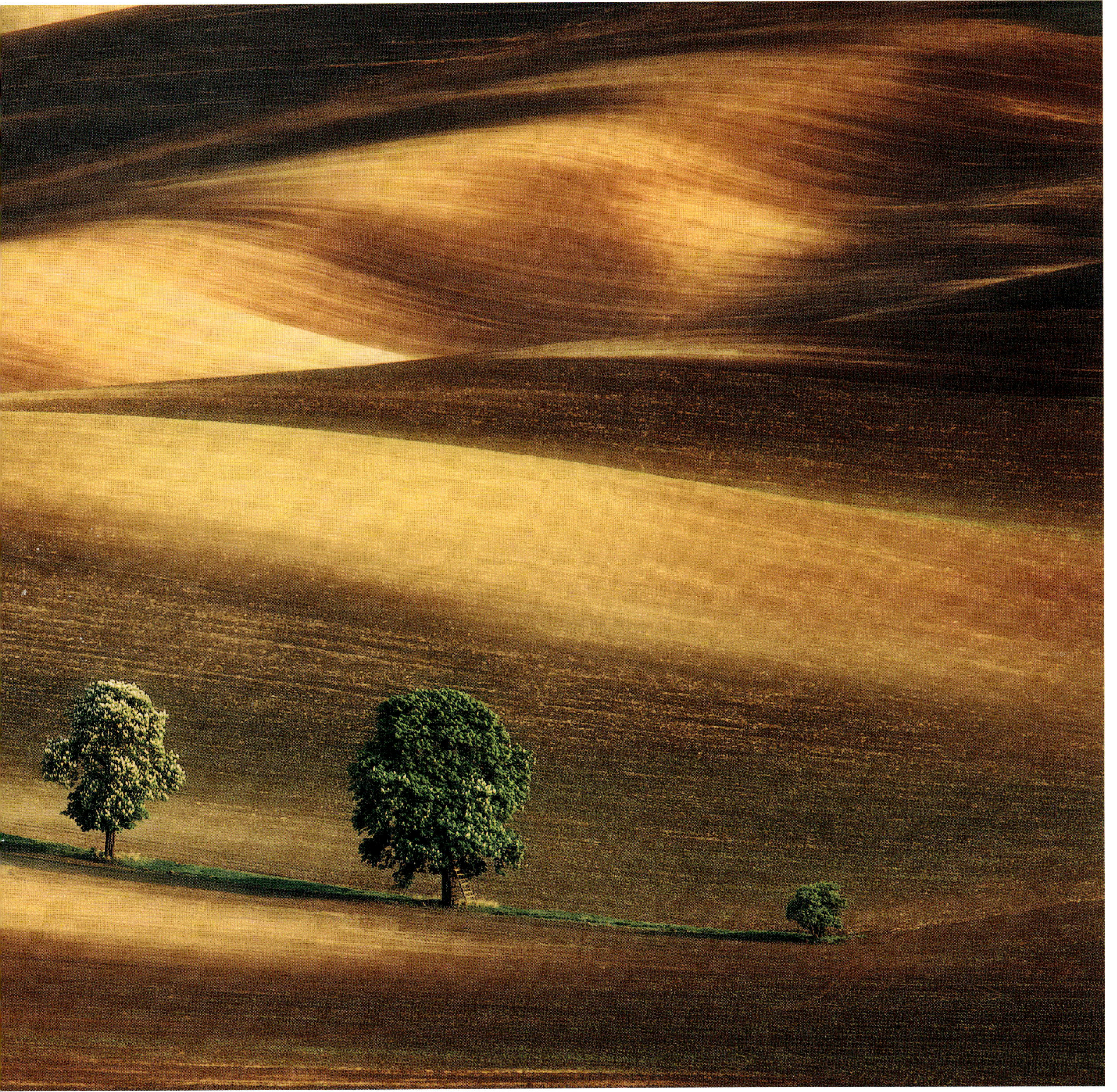

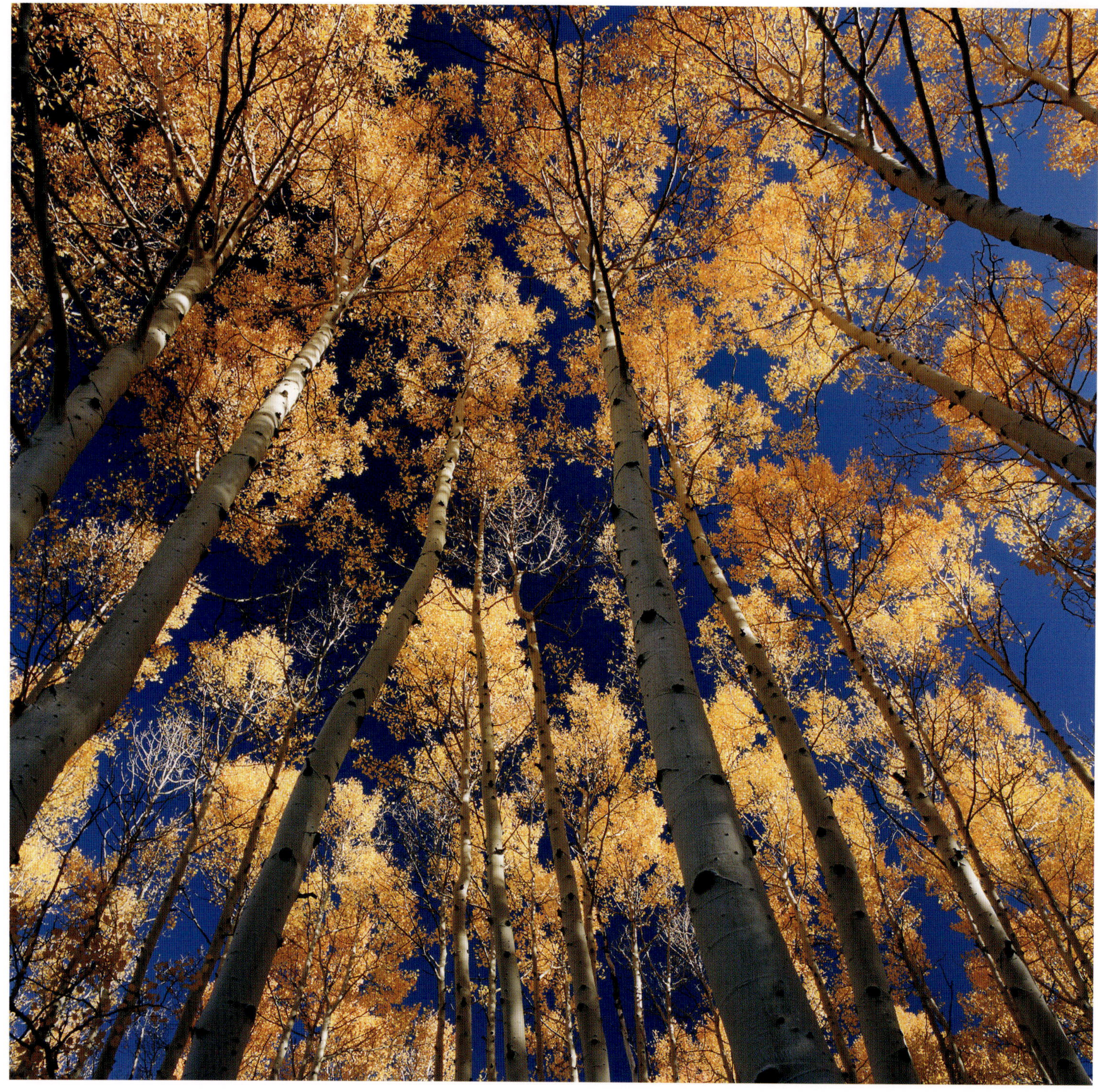

MANTI-LA SAL NATIONAL FOREST, UTAH
AMERICAN ASPEN TREES (*POPULUS TREMULOIDES*) IN FIRST LIGHT

MICHA PAWLITZKI

Rollei 6008 integral, Distagon 50mm f/4 lens, Fuji Velvia 100, 1/4sec.
COMMENDED, 2009

It was simply the incredible autumnal colours that attracted me to this scene.

FRANCONIA

AUTUMN MELODY

TOM WUNDRAK

Nikon D70, Nikkor 2.8 20–35mm, f/9.

SECOND, 2010

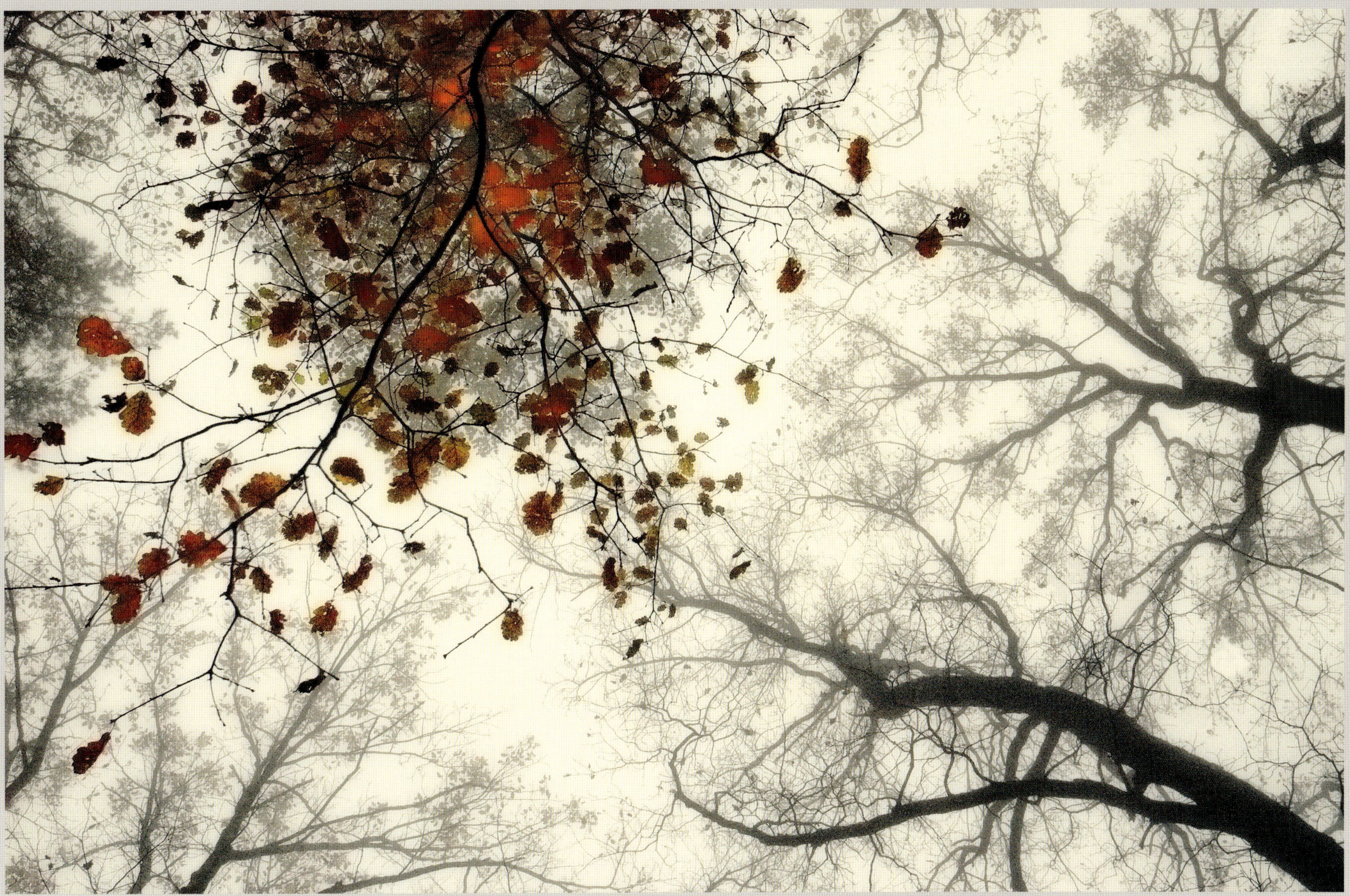

It was the poetical and abstract quality of this view up into the autumnal sky that inspired me to take this photograph. The leaves resemble a musical score writing the melody of autumn. Finding the right layout for all the elements – the close-up foliage and the distant silhouettes of the trees – was the main task here as I wanted to achieve an asymmetrical, well-balanced composition from a particular perspective.

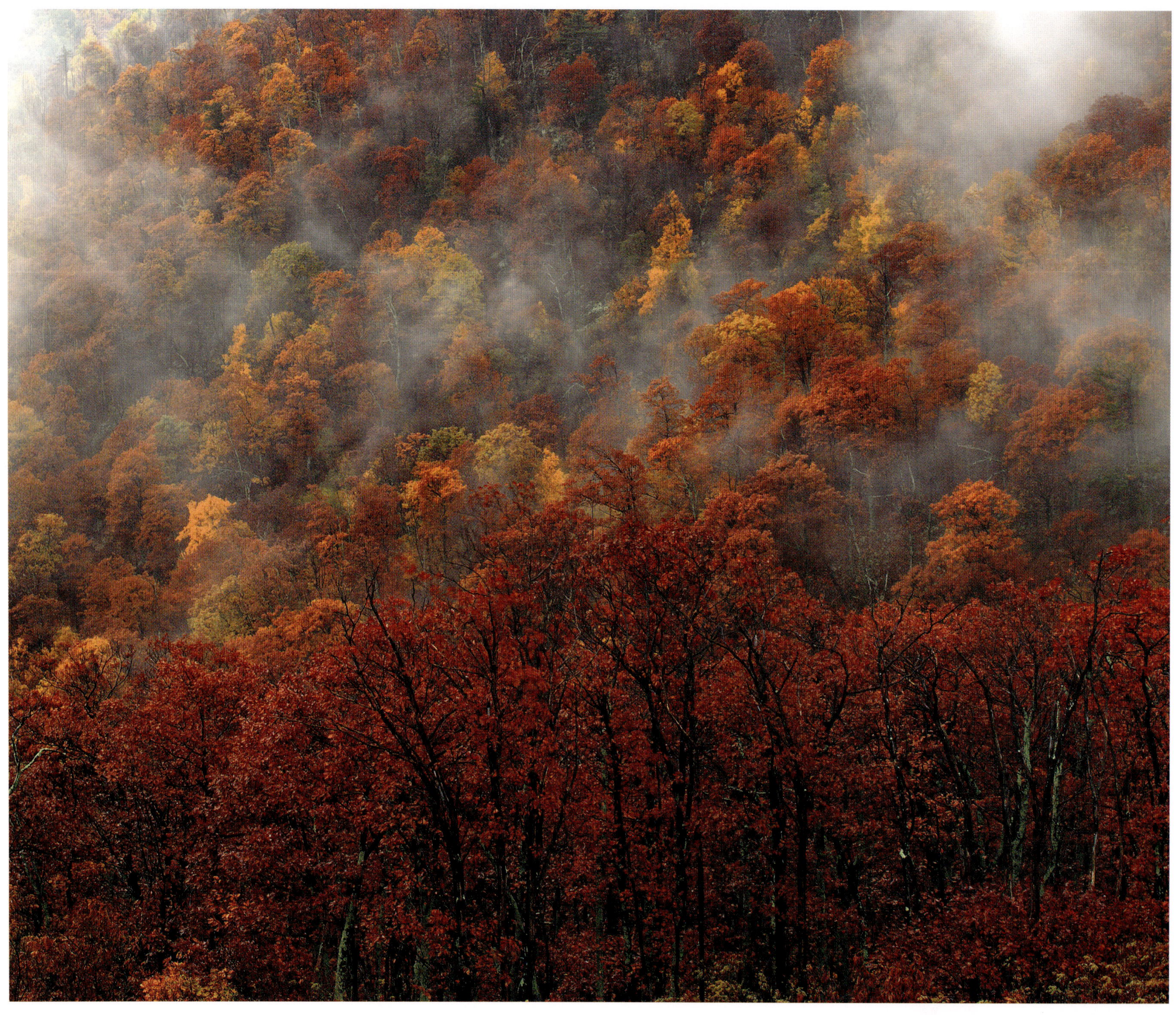

SHENANDOAH NATIONAL PARK, VIRGINIA
SMOKY MOUNTAINS

MICHAEL LOWE

Canon EOS 5D Mark II.
HIGHLY COMMENDED, 2010

Remnants of fast-moving clouds give the illusion of smoke rising from the tree-covered mountainside. This shot is actually taken looking down at the opposite mountain. Although it wasn't taken in the Great Smoky Mountains of North Carolina and Tennessee, I felt that this image gave me the feel of being there.

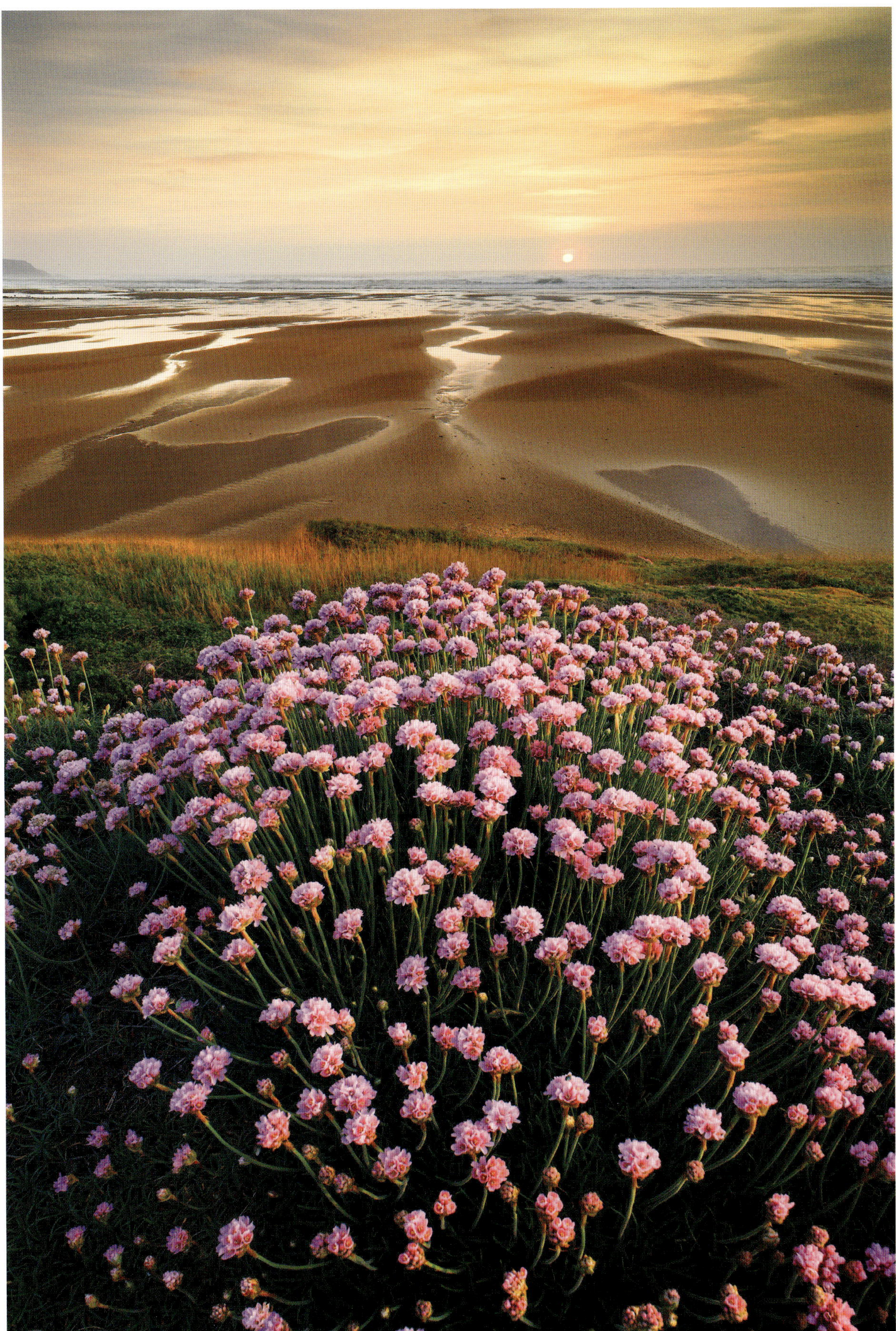

WIDEMOUTH BAY, NORTH CORNWALL, ENGLAND
SEA THRIFT FLOWERS

COLIN ROBERTS

Canon 1Ds Mark II, 20mm lens, 1/15sec at f/22. I used 2 Lee ND graduated filters in different positions to balance the lighting.

INTERNATIONAL GARDEN PHOTOGRAPHER OF THE YEAR, 2011

The tide was out and the sun-lit flowers looked beautiful against the golden sandy backdrop. I needed the perspective of a wide-angle lens to make the small cluster of flowers loom large in the foreground.

The Appian Way is the best-preserved section Rome's imperial roads. The plants were on one of the many burial mounds that are on the edge of the Way. This kind of *Ophrys* is considered very uncommon to find in the area. I had visited three times previously but this was my first visit during a sunset. The light was amazing and truly stimulating. The plant blooms early in the spring and prefers well-drained low-fertility soils and areas with partial shade.

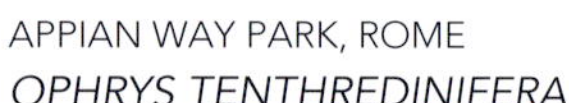

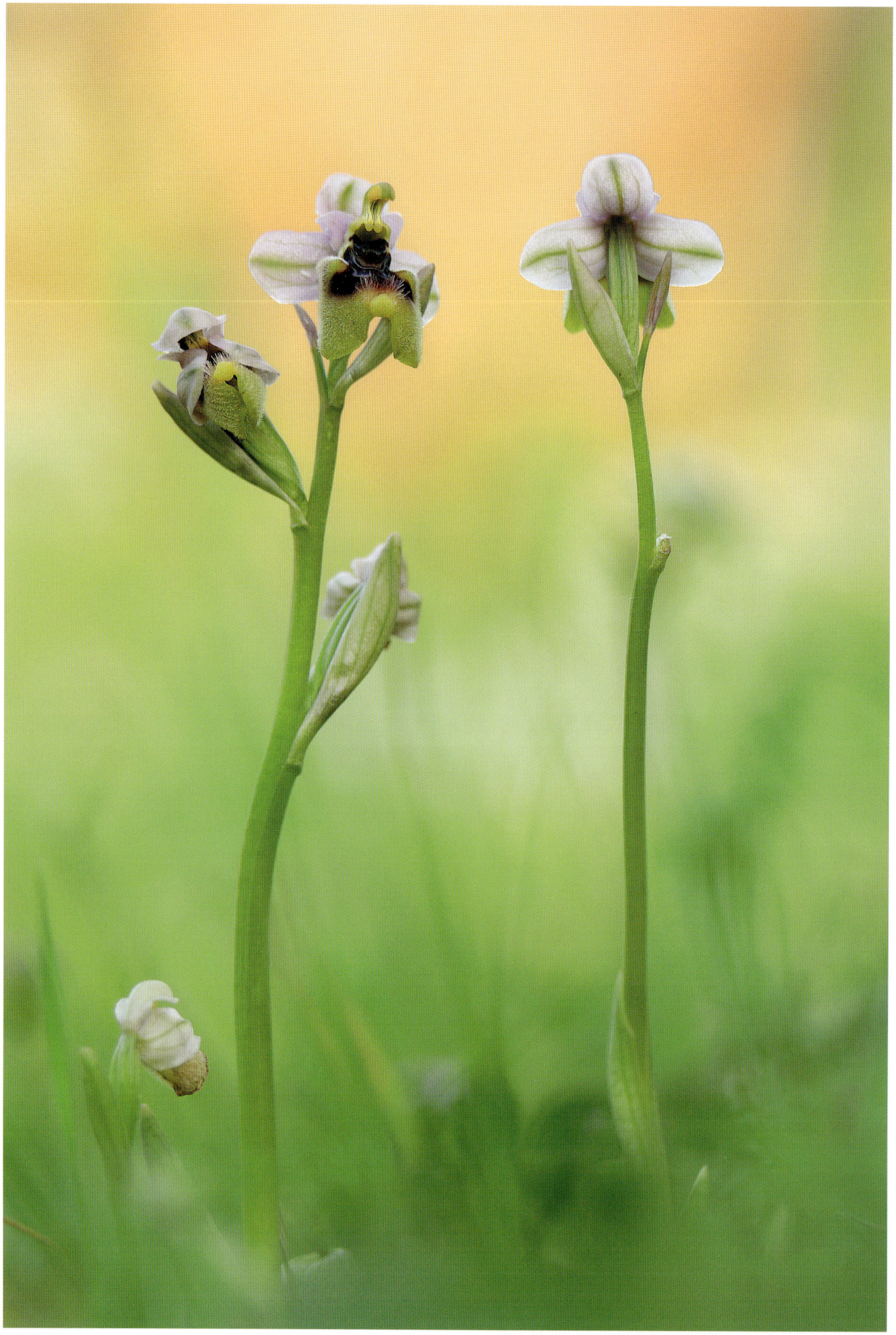

APPIAN WAY PARK, ROME
OPHRYS TENTHREDINIFERA

CLAUDIO CUGINI

Canon EOS 40D, Sigma 180mm lens, 1/8sec at f/5.6. I also used a tripod, cable release and a diffuser panel. Post-capture: I adjusted the levels, saturation and reduced noise. I also adjusted a small area of the orange zone that was a bit overexposed.
FINALIST, 2011

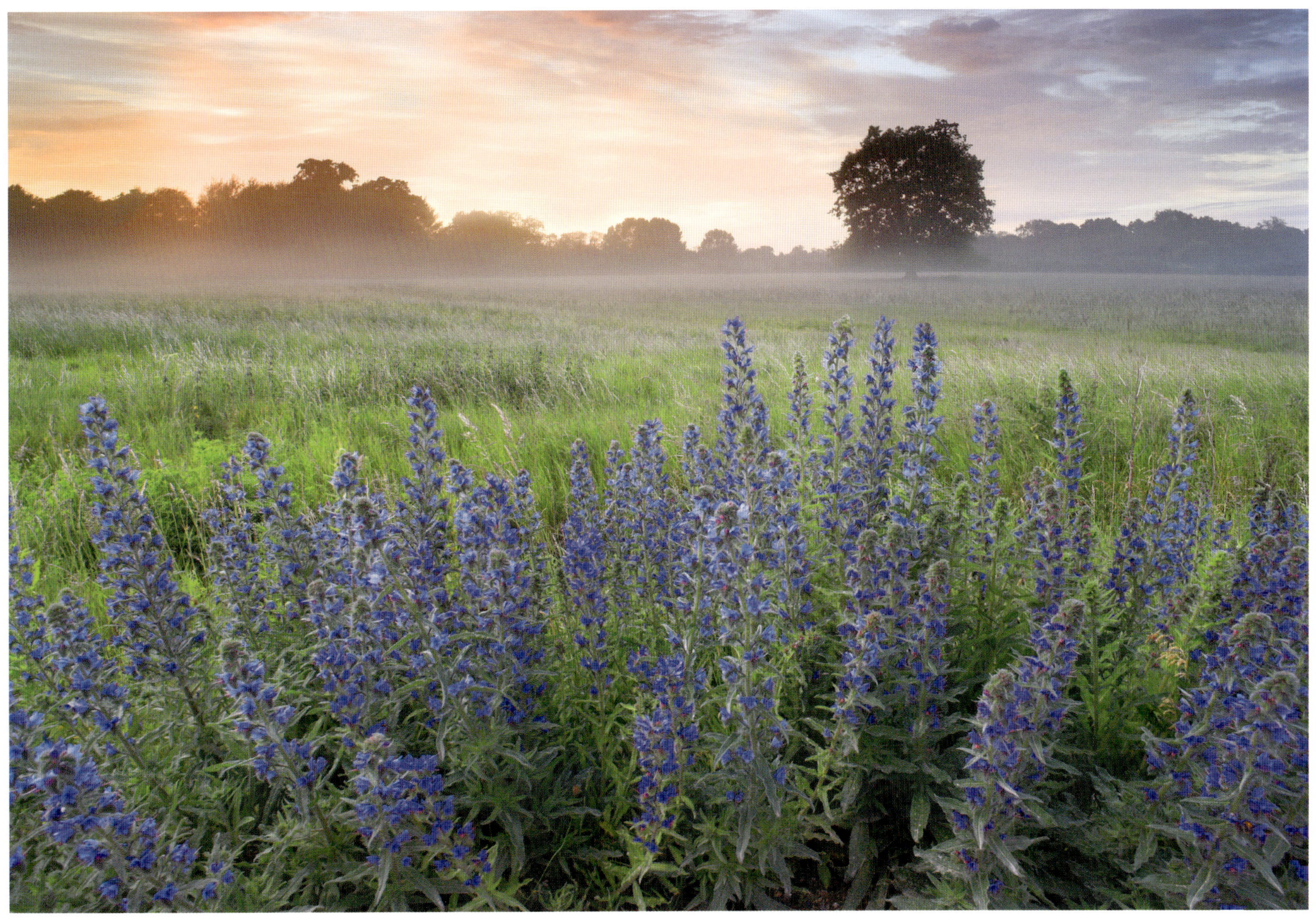

NEAR WINCHESTER IN HAMPSHIRE, ENGLAND
VIPER'S BUGLOSS

COLIN ROBERTS

Canon EOS-1Ds Mark II, 20mm lens, 1/4sec at f/16. I used two separate graduated filters to help balance the light. Post-capture: no digital alterations.
THIRD, 2011

Blue flowers of viper's bugloss (*Echium vulgare*), a localised wildflower of open grasslands, photographed around sunrise in mid-summer. I crouched very low down with a tripod so that the flowers were seen in profile against the misty landscape beyond.

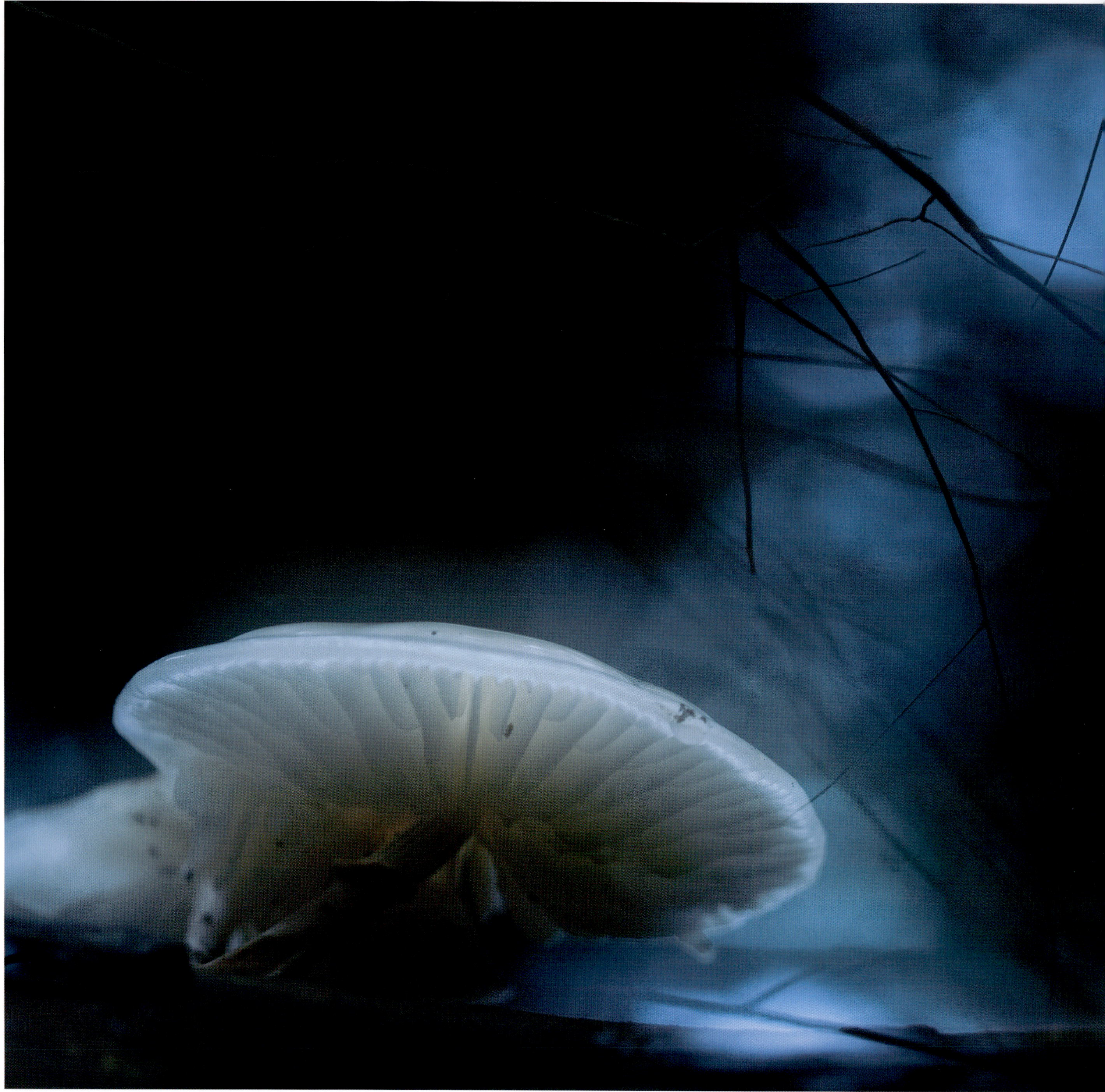

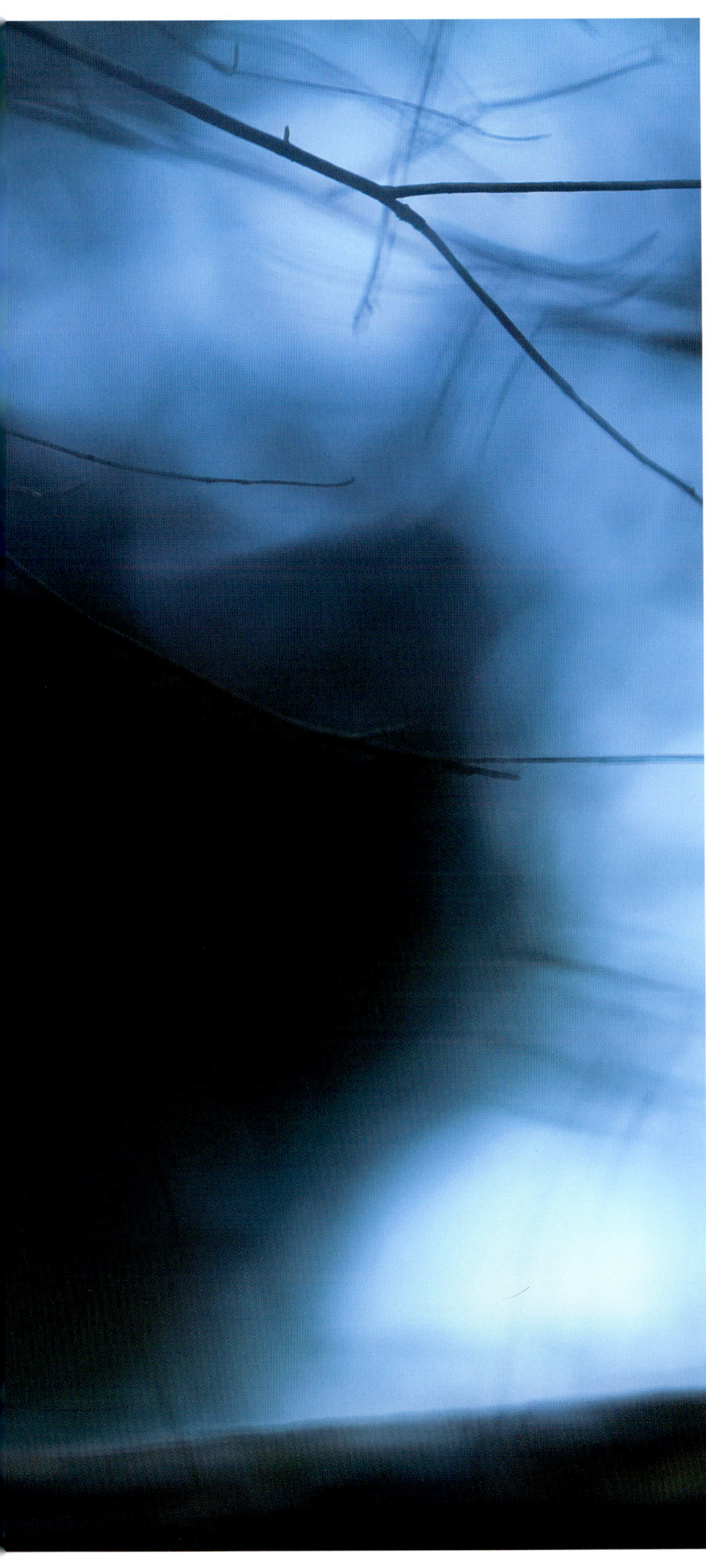

This is porcelain fungus (*Oudemansiella mucida*), usually found on beech trunks from August until November. I like fungi. I was really concentrating on them on that day and wanted to catch the bluish light. As the image needs to express autumn, I wanted the branches in the picture as well. And then I thought of the multiple exposure feature to give the image a somewhat mystical touch.

ERMELO
AUTUMN IS COMING

GERALD LEEUW

Nikon D300s, Micro-Nikkor 200mm lens, 0.4sec at f/4.2. The photograph is actually a double-exposure created in-camera. I used a tripod and a cable release. Post-capture: no digital alterations.
SECOND, 2011

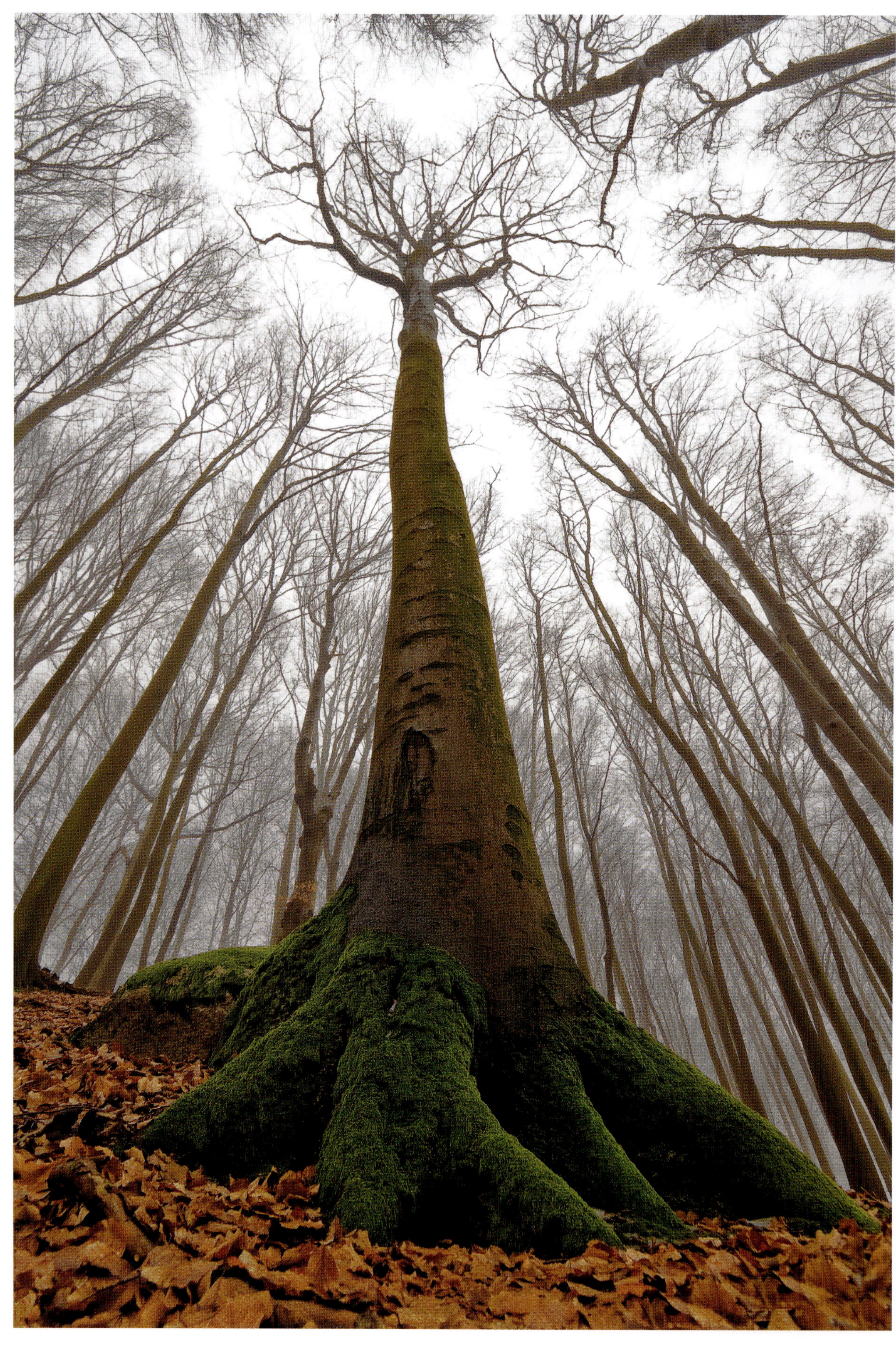

This tree is revealed in all its glory when the crown is devoid of leaves. Using a wide-angle lens and placing the camera on the ground allowed me to show the full splendor of this unique tree. After the first few frames, I noticed the unusual scratches on the bark, resembling a human face, then I stopped the session for a moment and silence fell.

SURROUNDINGS OF DRAWSKO POMORSKIE
THE BEECH WITH A HUMAN FACE

LESZEK PARADOWSKI

Canon EOS 50D, Canon 10-22mm lens, 1/30sec at f/8, ISO 100. Post-capture: no digital alterations.
FIRST, 2011

This plant is *Azorella compacta* known as yareta: the Andean cushion plant. As I drove up the rough gravel track, the terrain became more and more stony. I came to this area with an expanding mass of these cushion plants: the vivid green contrasting against the blue sky. I got down low on the ground to show the cushion nature of the plant. I took it as a landscape to see the numbers of plants and the fantastic pattern they made in the landscape.

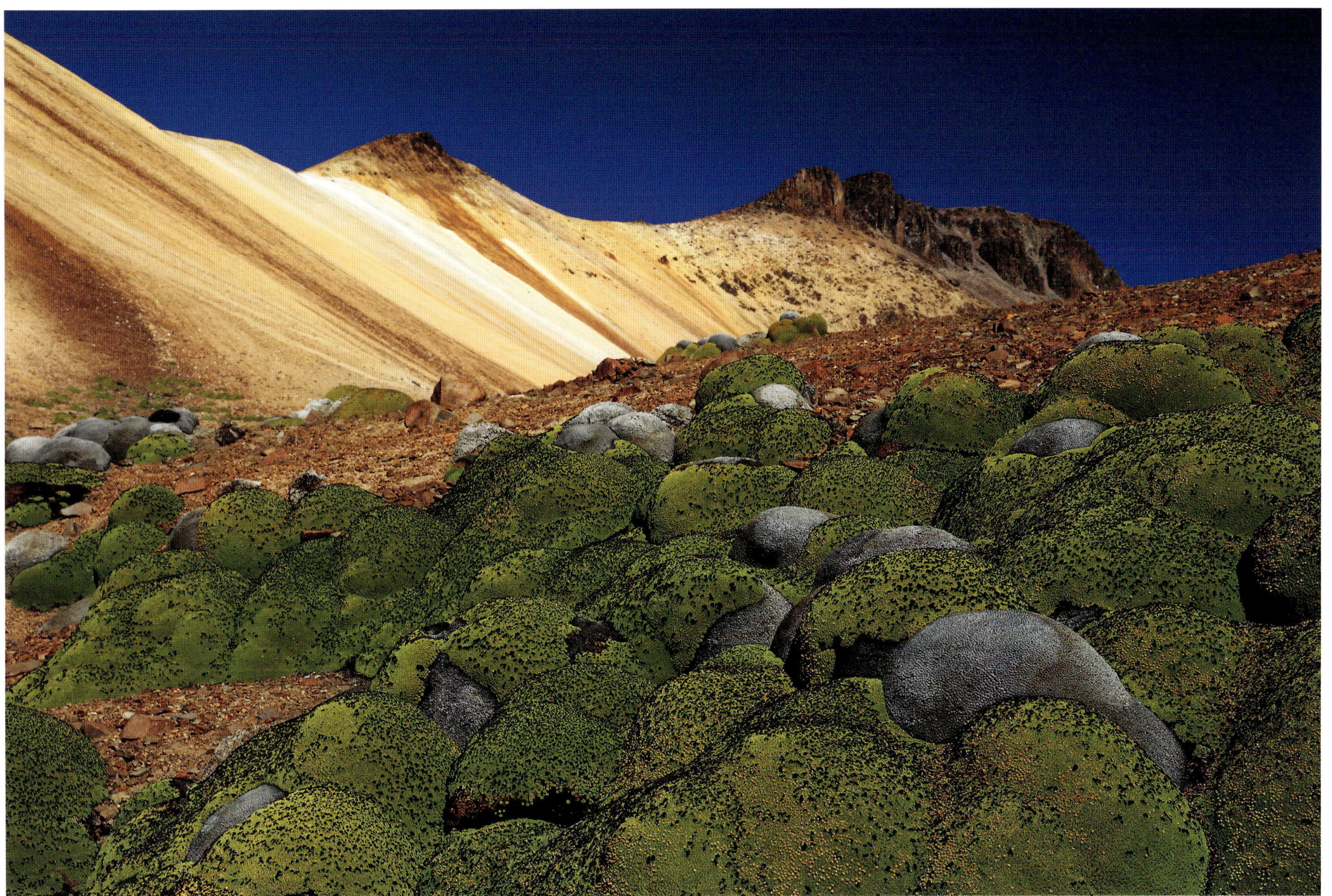

PARQUE NACIONAL LAUCA

ALTIPLANO LANDSCAPE CUSHION PLANTS

ANGELA ROWLANDS

Canon 5D Mark II 24-105 f/4 zoom lens at 58mm. 1/30 sec at f/18 ISO 100. Post-capture: basic colour management.

HIGHLY COMMENDED, 2012

The combination of low-angled sunlight, hoar frost, heavy snow and pastel skies has transformed this scene into one of defiant isolation and ordered majesty. This is a stand of mature growth beech (*Fagus* spp.) trees, surrounded by fields typically used to grow barley. I waited for winter to arrive in anticipation of improving an already interesting composition which I had envisaged in the autumn. I waited until noon for better side-lighting and I accentuated the symmetry by placing the trees in the centre. The creamy, pastel clouds however were an unexpected bonus.

Geography prevented me from getting a wide-angle horizontal shot, so I had to take several vertical frames by panning. I had to carefully time the shots between interruptions caused by road traffic passing behind the trees which would have spoiled the image. A tripod and remote shutter release were necessary to guarantee sharpness and keep the frames level.

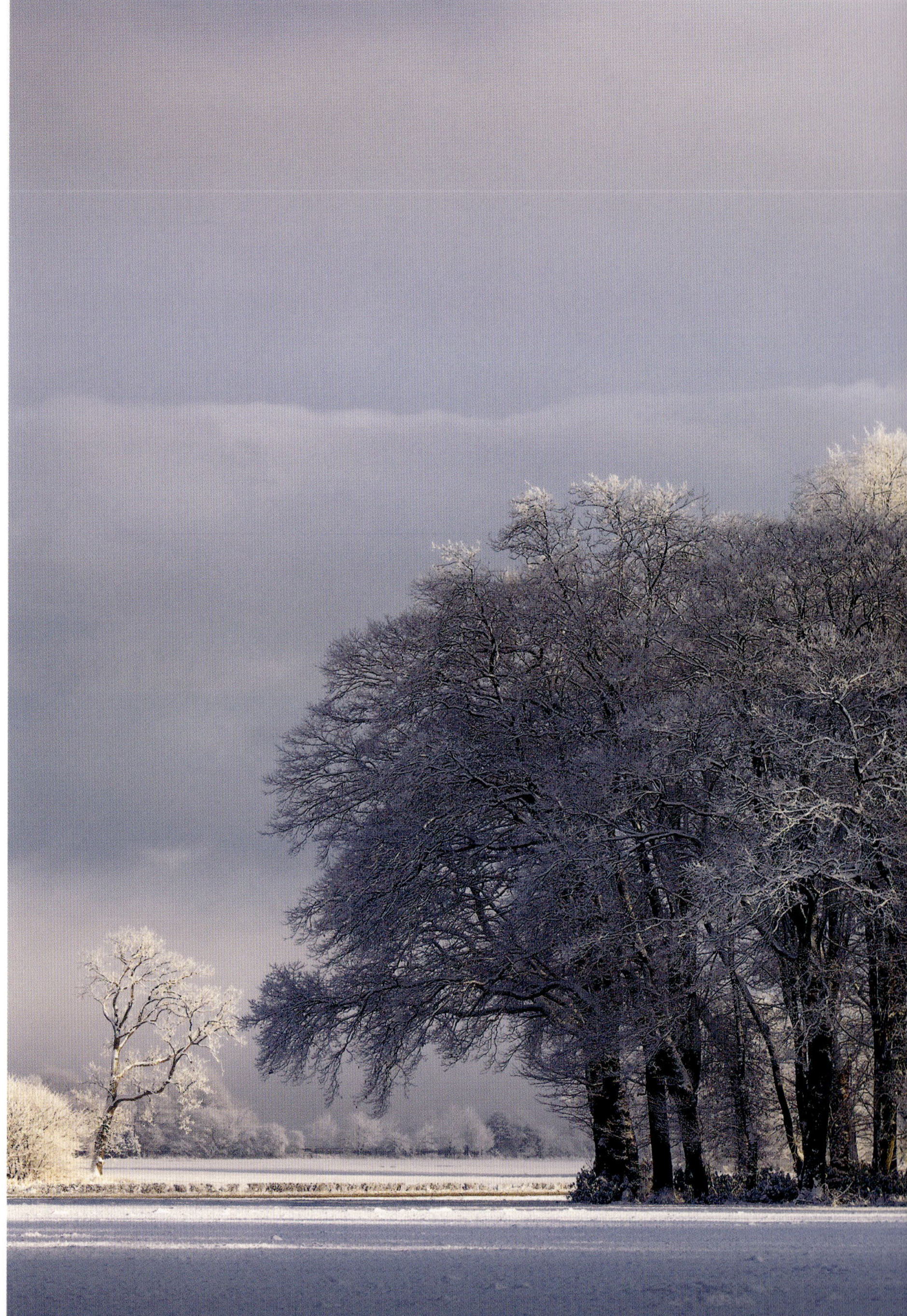

CARSE OF FORTH, NEAR THE VILLAGE OF DUNMORE, FALKIRK, SCOTLAND
ANCIENT COPPICE IN THE GRIP OF A DEEP FREEZE

GRAHAM HARRIS GRAHAM

Canon EOS 5D Mark II, 85mm lens, 1/60sec at f/11. Post-capture: this final image is a panorama constructed from several frames of the same scene and assembled using PTGui stitching software. The image was shot in RAW format which required adjustments to sharpness, saturation, contrast, brightness and RGB levels using Adobe Lightroom 2. However, the image content has not been altered and the final photograph is an accurate representation of the scene as I recall it. Other than dust spots, no elements have been artificially added or removed.
FINALIST, 2011

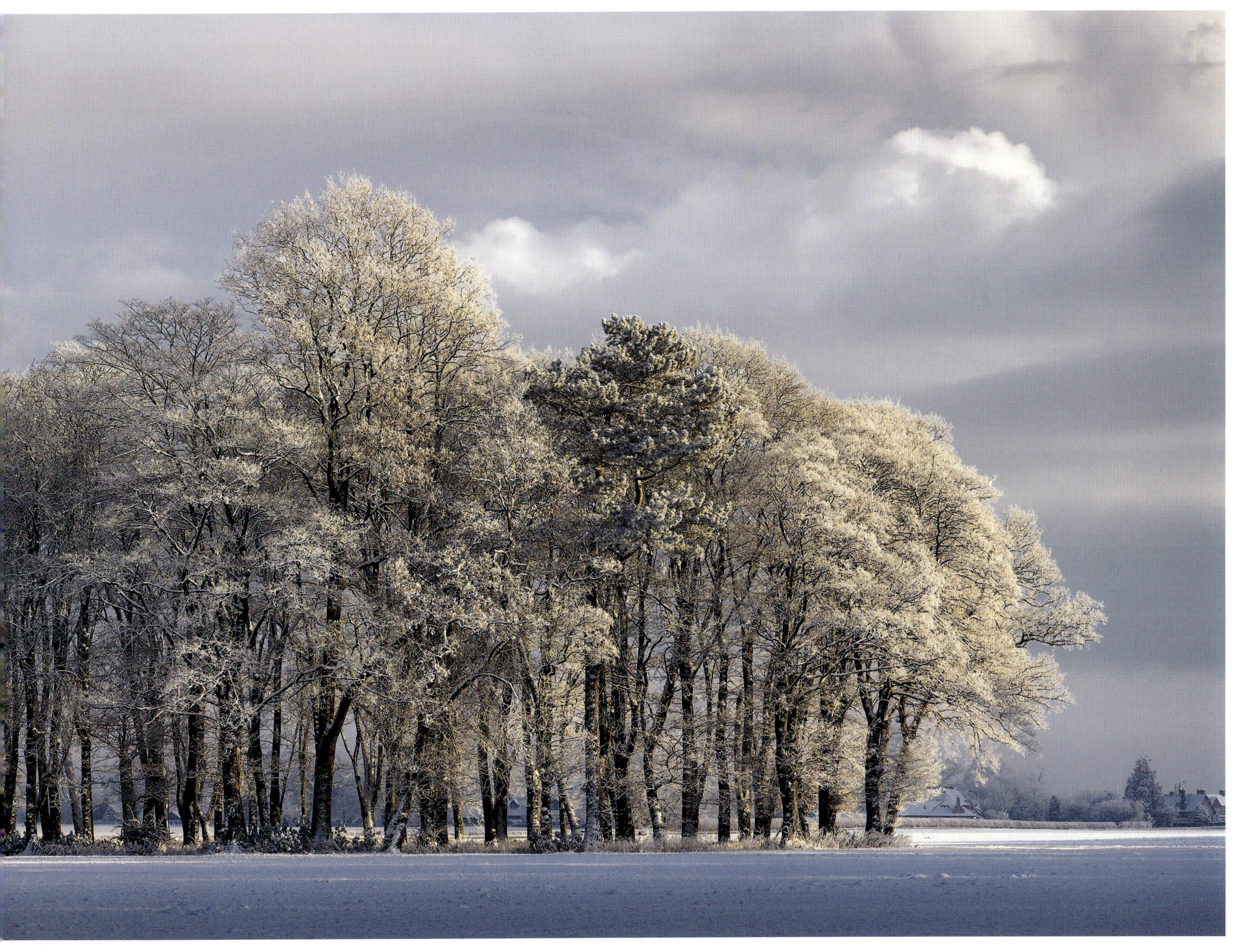

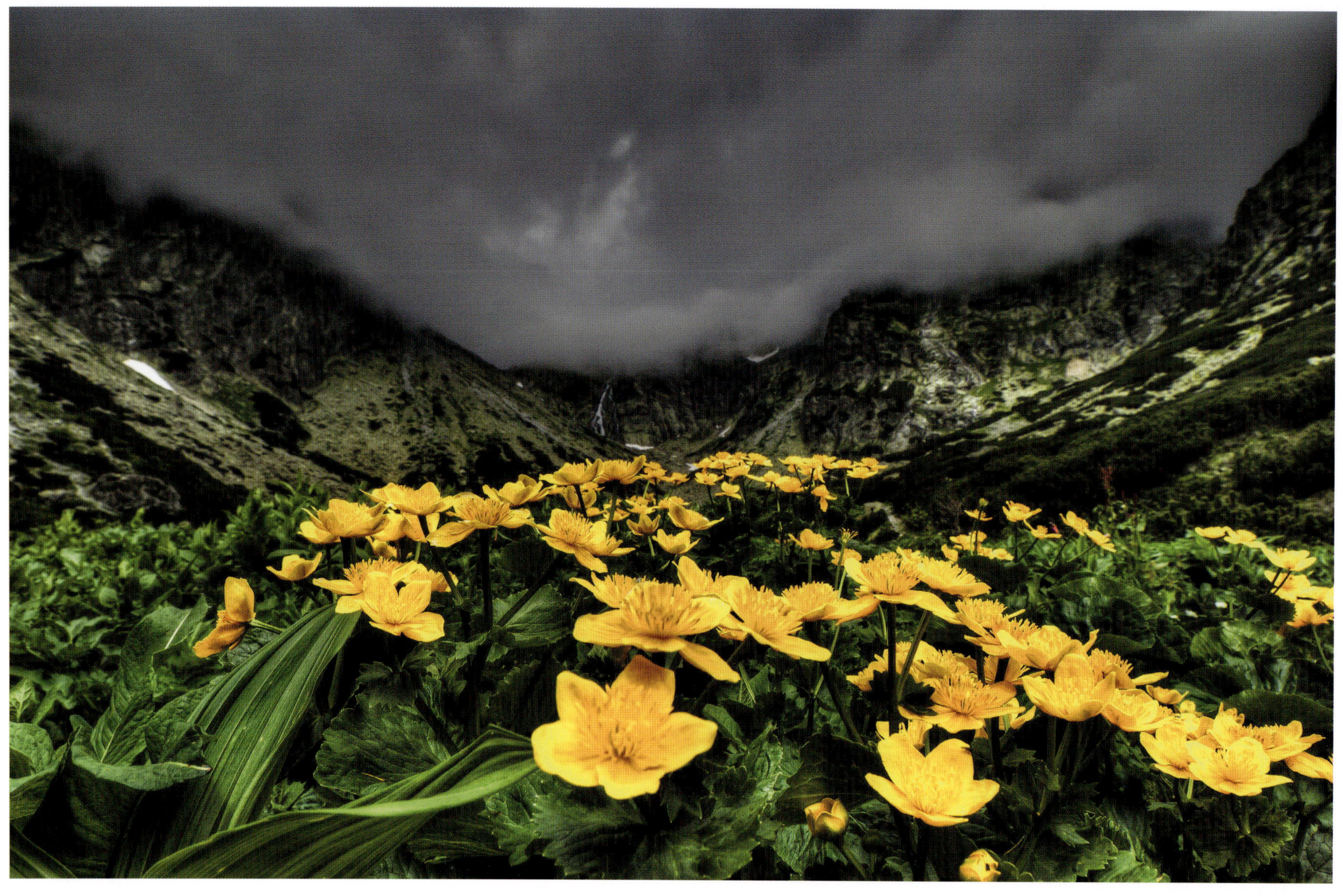

HIGH TATRA MOUNTAINS
RANUNCULUS IN FRONT OF A FOGGY WALL

THOMAS HINTZE

Nikon D2x, Nikkor 12-24mm lens and three exposures: 1/400 sec at f/11; 1/200 sec at f/11; and 1/100sec at f/11. Post-capture: the three RAW files were combined to make one HDR image.
FINALIST, 2011

The image shows a colony of kingcups (*Caltha palustris*) along a small stream located in a basin of the High Tatra Mountains, just before a massive rain storm arrived. I knew this valley from earlier hikes. I returned in June when the kingcups populate the rivers. I wanted to express the contrast of the bright yellow flowers against the large mountain wall in this valley. To achieve a maximum of visual depth, and capture the existing dramatic threatening mood, I decided to create a HDR image. The camera was handheld while I was hunched over in the small stream, to get as close to the flowers as possible.

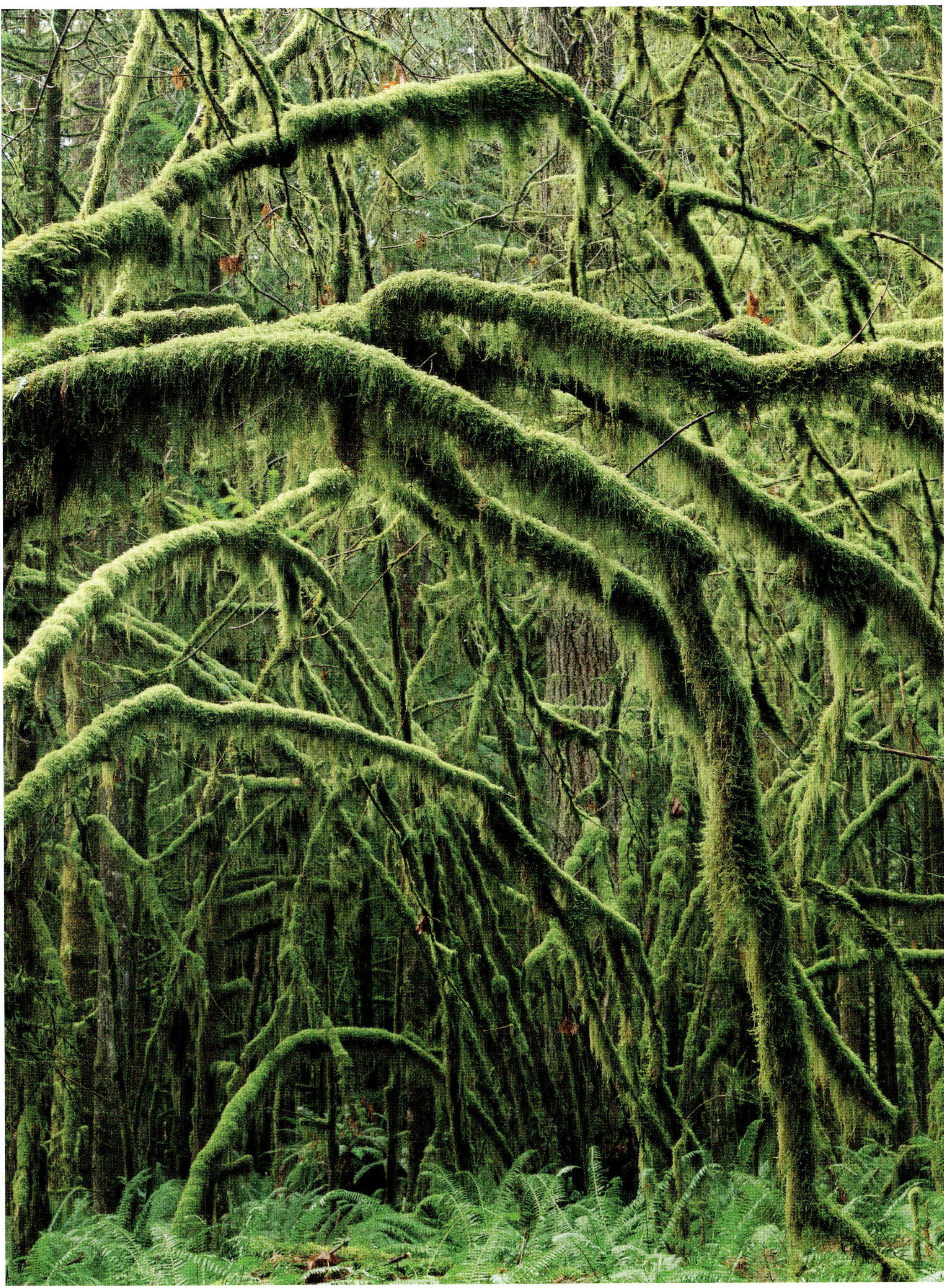

GOLDEN EARS PROVINCIAL PARK, BRITISH COLUMBIA

CATTAIL MOSS, (*ISOTHECIUM MYOSUROIDES*)

ADAM GIBBS

Toho-Shimo FC-45X, 300mm, f/64, Velvia 50, polariser. I wanted to compress the scene so that the maples would arch one beneath the other. To do this I used a relatively long lens and stopped the lens down considerably.

COMMENDED, 2008

The temperate rainforests of British Columbia are quite magical and I love their hanging mosses and vibrant greens, which make me feel as if I'm entering the world of hobbits and dragons. The arching maples (*Acer* spp.) gave the impression of looking through a tunnel.

CENTRAL AUSTRALIA, INCLUDING ULURU-KATA TJUTA NATIONAL PARK AND WEST MACDONNELL NATIONAL PARK

WILDFLOWERS AND DESERT OAK (*ALLOCASUARINA DECAISNEANA*) IN AUSTRALIA'S RED CENTRE

CLAIRE TAKACS

Canon EOS 5D Mark II, 17-40mm lens and 70-200mm lens, polarizing filter for some shots, tripod. No digital alterations.

RPS SILVER MEDAL, 2011

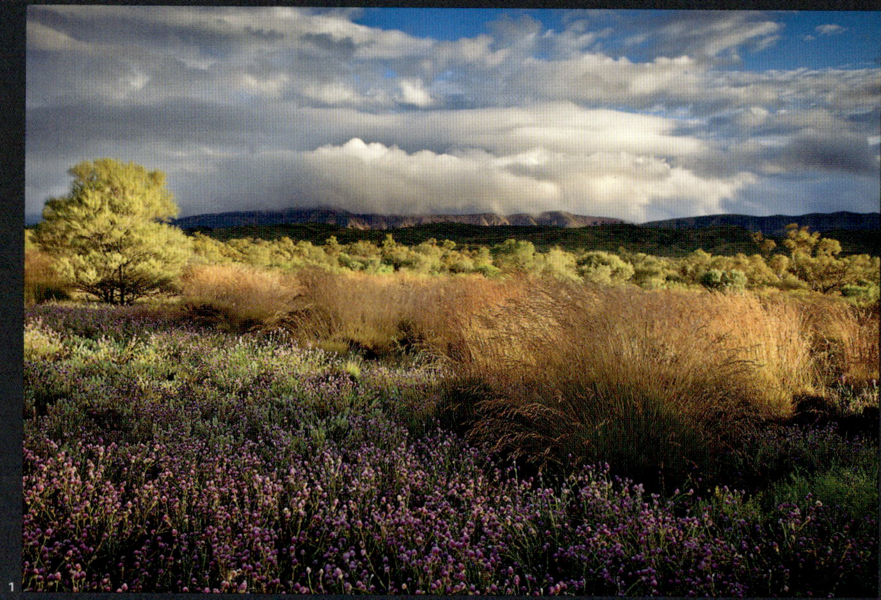

1

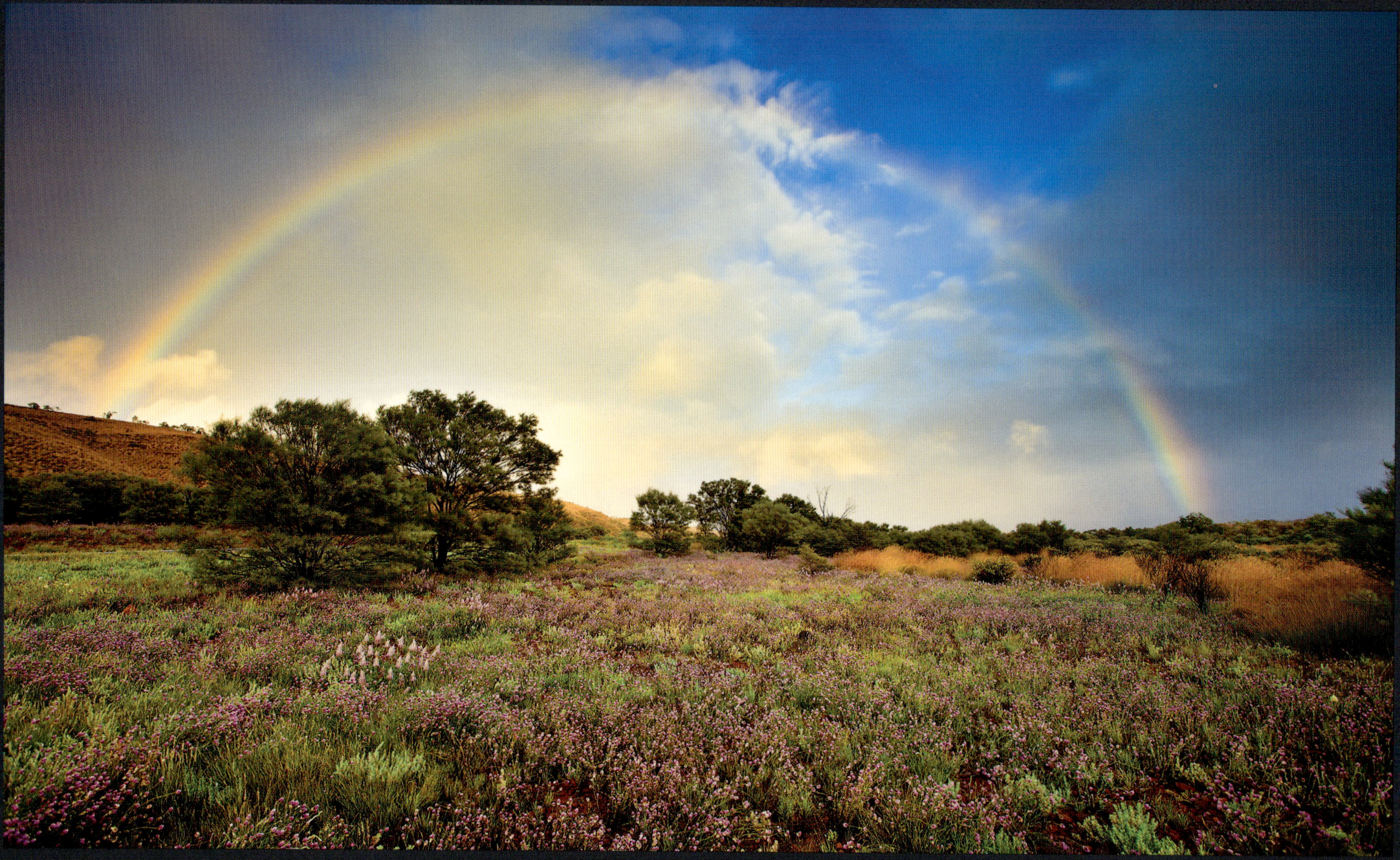

2

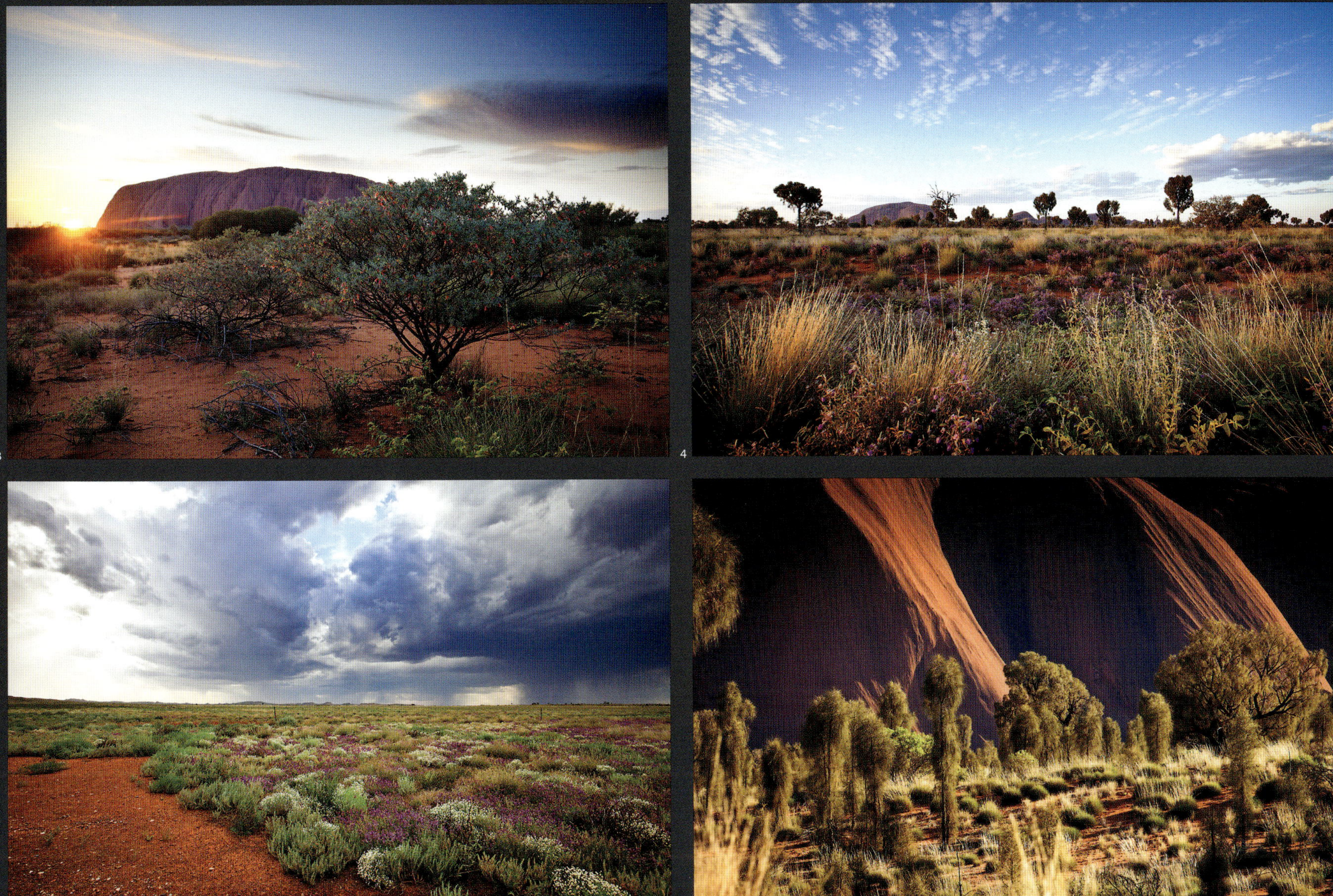
3
4
5
6

Record rainfall in Australia's red centre in 2010 brought the desert to life and wildflowers were popping up everywhere, some possibly not appearing for another ten years. I wanted to capture the wildflowers, while showing the area's beauty, vivid colours and dramatic landscape. Desert oaks in front of Uluru (Ayers Rock) were important to give the folio a sense of place. Rainfall continued during my week there, but gaps in weather resulted in interesting and dramatic skies. I photographed at sunrise and sunset and between rainfall.

1–Wildflowers (feather-heads [*Ptilotus macrocephalus*]) in West MacDonnell National Park, central Australia.
2–Rainbow over wildflowers (feather-heads [*Ptilotus macrocephalus*]) in West MacDonnell National Park, central Australia.
3–Sunrise behind Uluru, with emu bush (*Eremophilia* spp.) in foreground.
4–Desert oak (*Allocasuarina decaisneana*) in Uluru–Kata Tjuta National Park, Northern Territory, Australia. Sunrise.
5–Storm clouds and wildflowers in a desert flood plain, central Australia, south of Alice Springs.
6–Desert Oak (*Allocasuarina decaisneana*) in Uluru–Kata Tjuta National Park, Northern Territory, Australia. Sunrise.

Much of Western Canada's old-growth forest is now gone due to logging. This second-growth forest in Golden Ears Provincial Park, British Columbia is now nearly 100 years old. Stumps from earlier giants can be found throughout the area. The light on this day was quite magical. The fog was heavy but the sun was trying to push through, creating some wonderful diffused light.

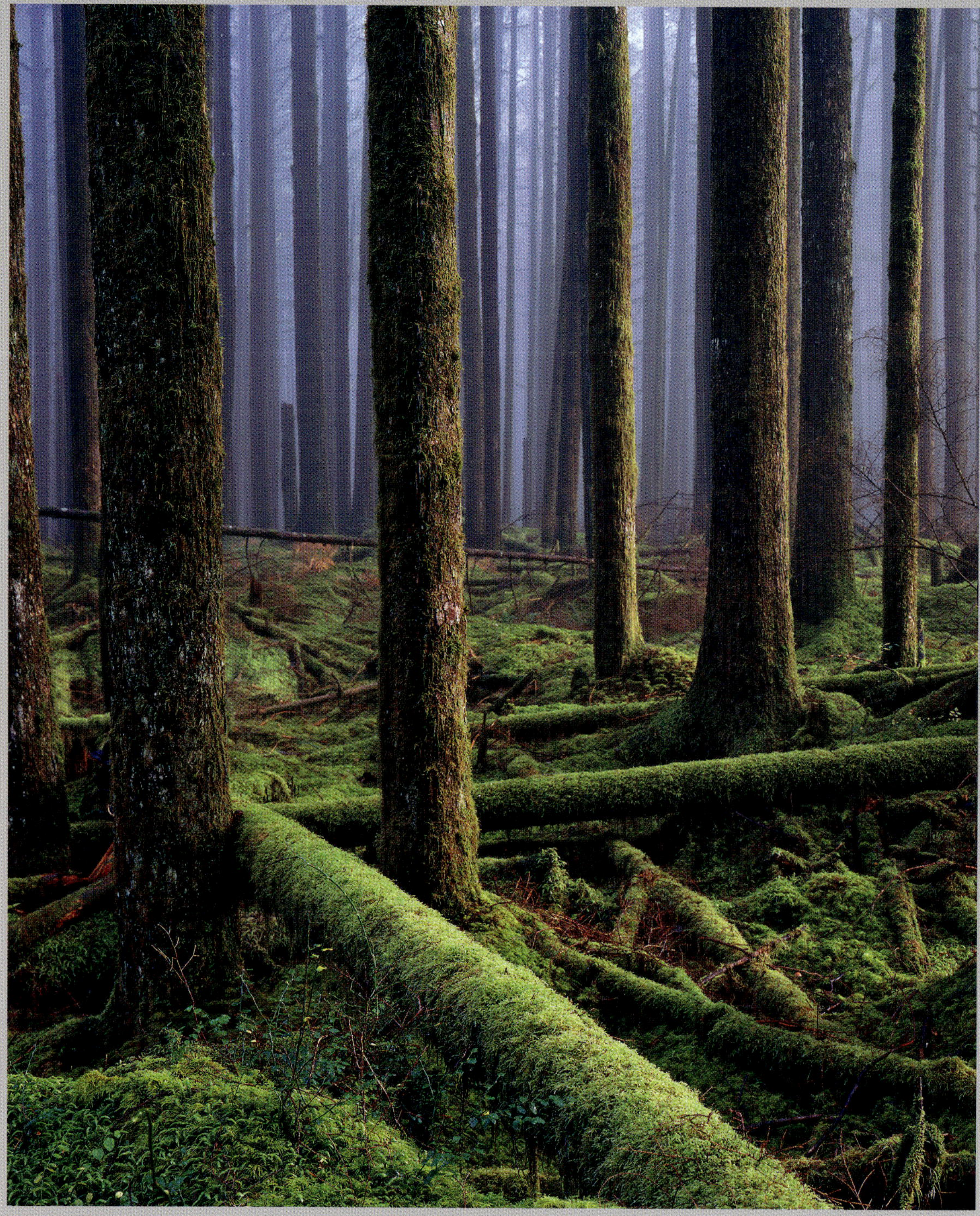

DOUGLAS FIR (*PSEUDOTSUGA MENZIESII*), WESTERN RED CEDAR (*THUJA PLICATA*). GOLDEN EARS PROVINCIAL PARK, BRITISH COLUMBIA

SECOND CHANCE

ADAM GIBBS

Toho-Shimo FC-45X, 200mm lens, f/45, Velvia 100. I wanted to find something in the foreground that would draw the viewer into the image, and the fallen timber created a zig-zag entry. It took me some time to find a group of trees that I could frame without foreground and background trees overlapping.

COMMENDED, 2008

It is very cold in midwinter and the trees are snow-covered. To the right the sky is clear, but fog is emerging. The sun is setting and the sunlit fog is getting more colourful: that is why I like this scene so much.

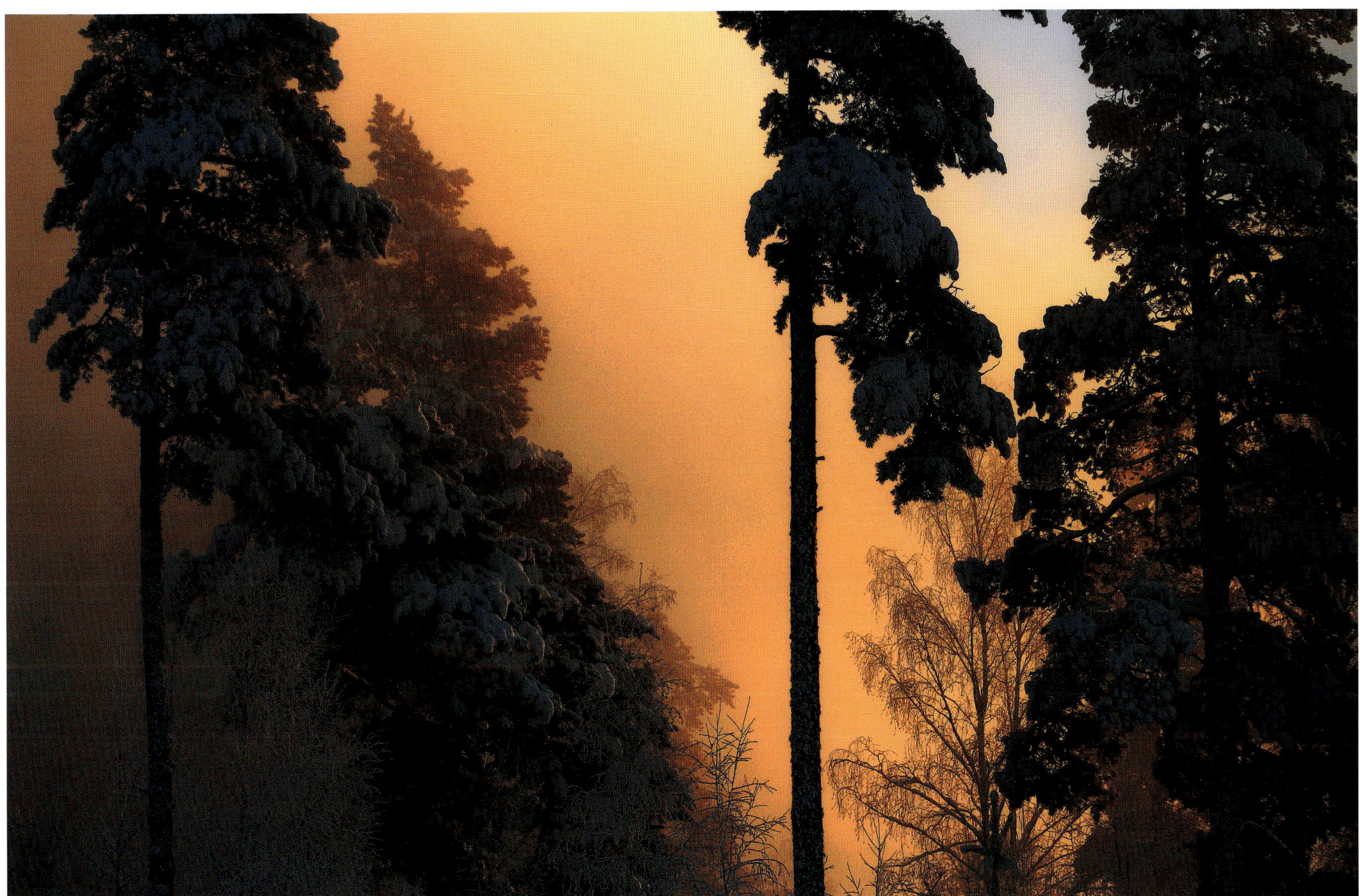

AVESTA

GOLDEN LIGHT

BROR JOHANSSON

Canon EOS 20D, Canon EF 75-300mm lens. 1/320sec at f/6.3. Post-capture: colour balance adjustment.

HIGHLY COMMENDED, 2012

THE OLYMPIC VILLAGE SITE, SEOUL

LONELY TREES IN KOREA IV

DAMIAN GILLIE

Canon EOS-1Ds, 80mm lens, f/11. Verticals corrected. This is one of a series of photographs. I wanted to show how an entire area was being transformed, with gardens and trees being created at the same time as the buildings.
FINALIST, 2008

Massive communities are being created from scratch in this part of Seoul, formerly the Olympic village. Only the mature vegetation planted during construction gives any identity to what would otherwise be a completely anonymous and repetitive environment. Great care is taken to protect the trees from the building activities, but the lifespan of these buildings is short; all will be demolished and replaced in just a few years, outlived by the trees that are planted to complement them.

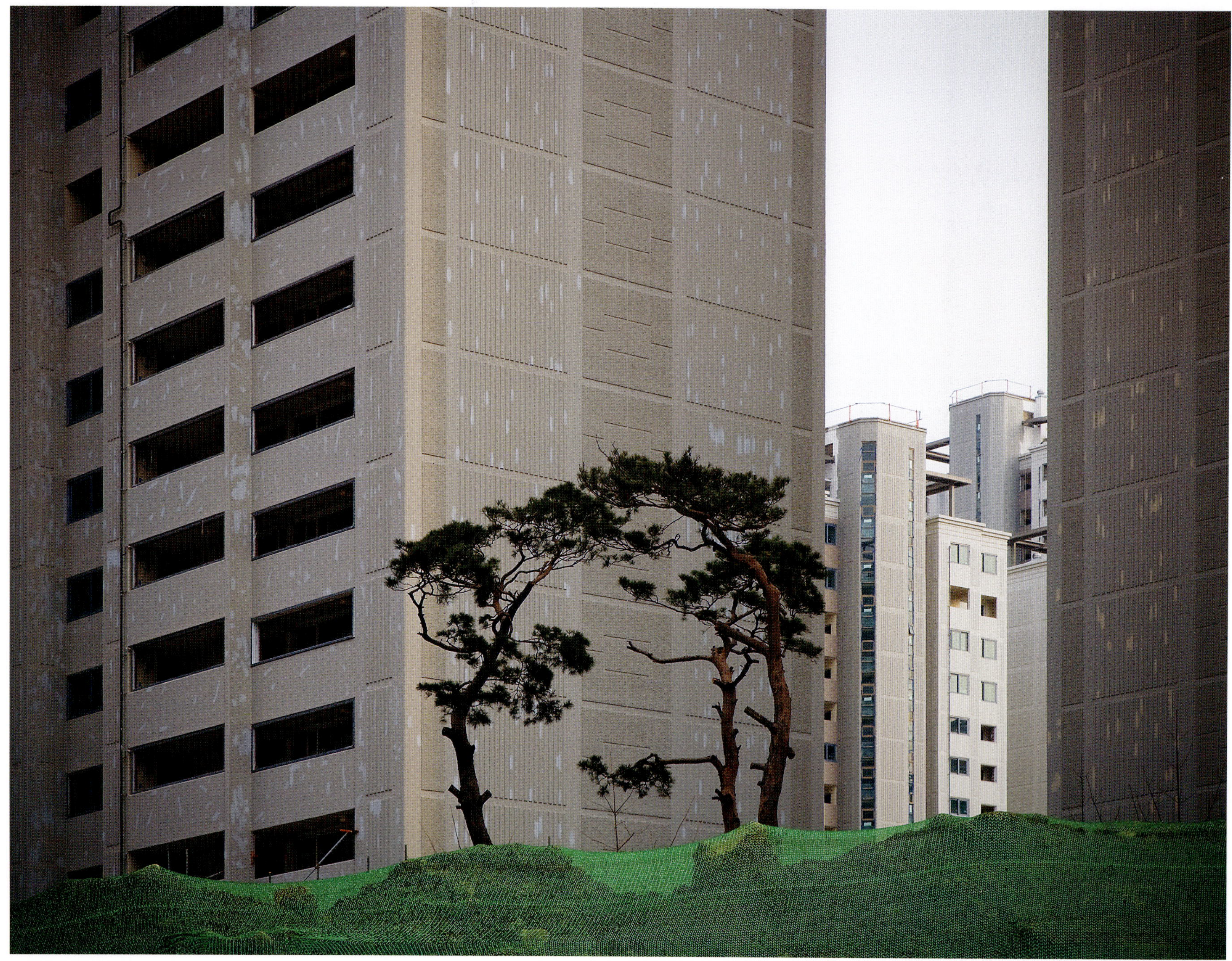

LEEUWIN-NATURALISTE NATIONAL PARK, WESTERN AUSTRALIA

ON THE EDGE

GARY STEER

Panasonic DMC – G3 Lumix, G Vario 7-14mm ASPH lens, 1/80 sec at f/18. Post-capture: small amount of cropping.
HIGHLY COMMENDED, 2012

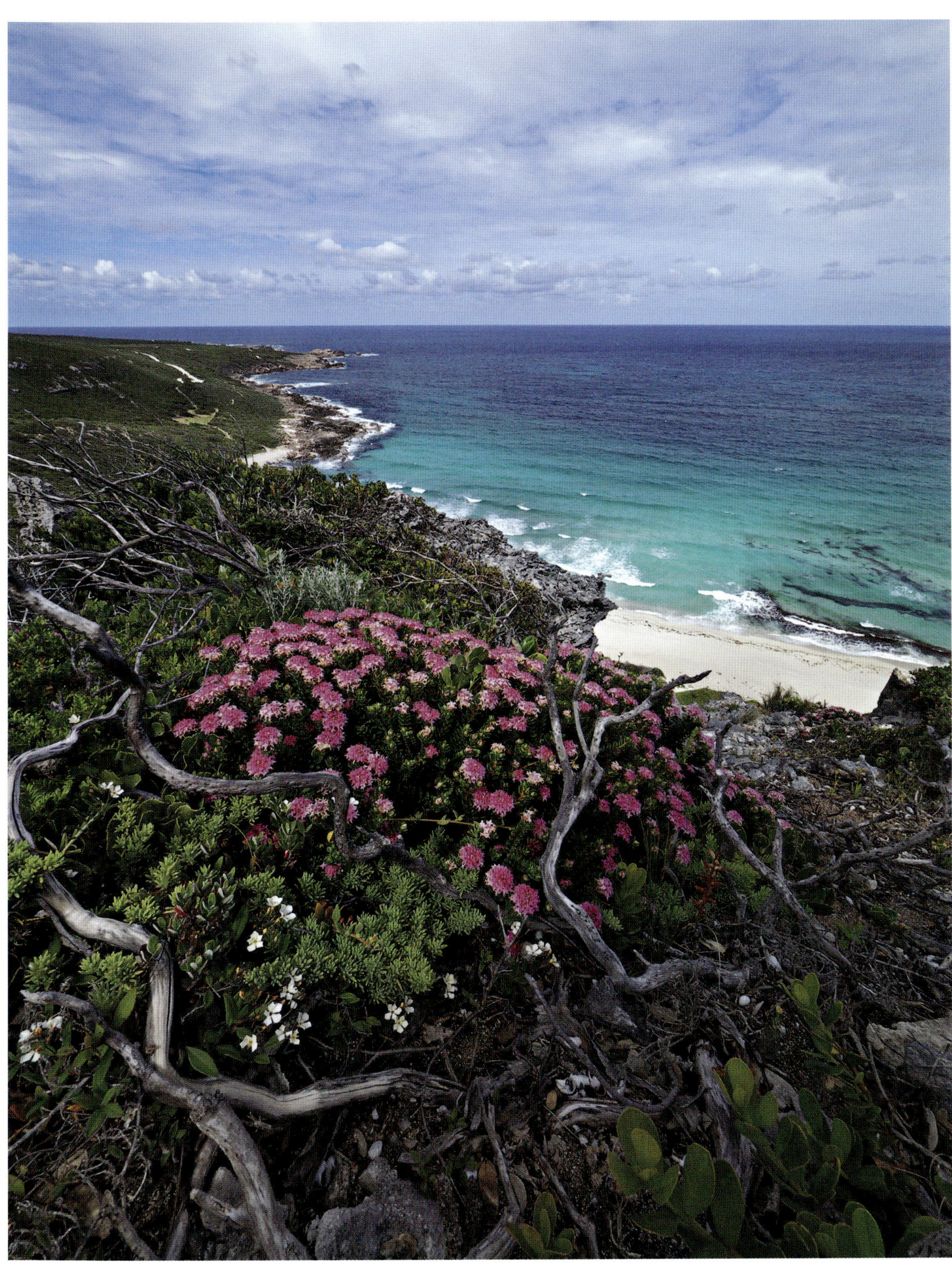

Though the coast is rugged and the seas wild, the vegetation on this edge of the continent can be fragile. One of the biggest threats is severe summer bushfire. In the foreground is the rice flower (*Pimelea ferruginea*). I had heard much about the Cape to Cape Walk, particularly the profusion of wildflowers in spring and summer, so I decided to do the walk to take photographs of the area. The concept was to get an image of a beautiful, delicate plant in its challenging habitat.

PREES HEATH RESERVE, NORTH SHROPSHIRE, ENGLAND

SILVER-STUDDED BLUE HABITAT

DANNY BEATH

Fuji Velvia 50 film. Nikon FE2, Nikkor 55mm lens, 1/60sec at f/11. Post-capture: original slide scanned. Basic cropping and cleaning.

FINALIST, 2012

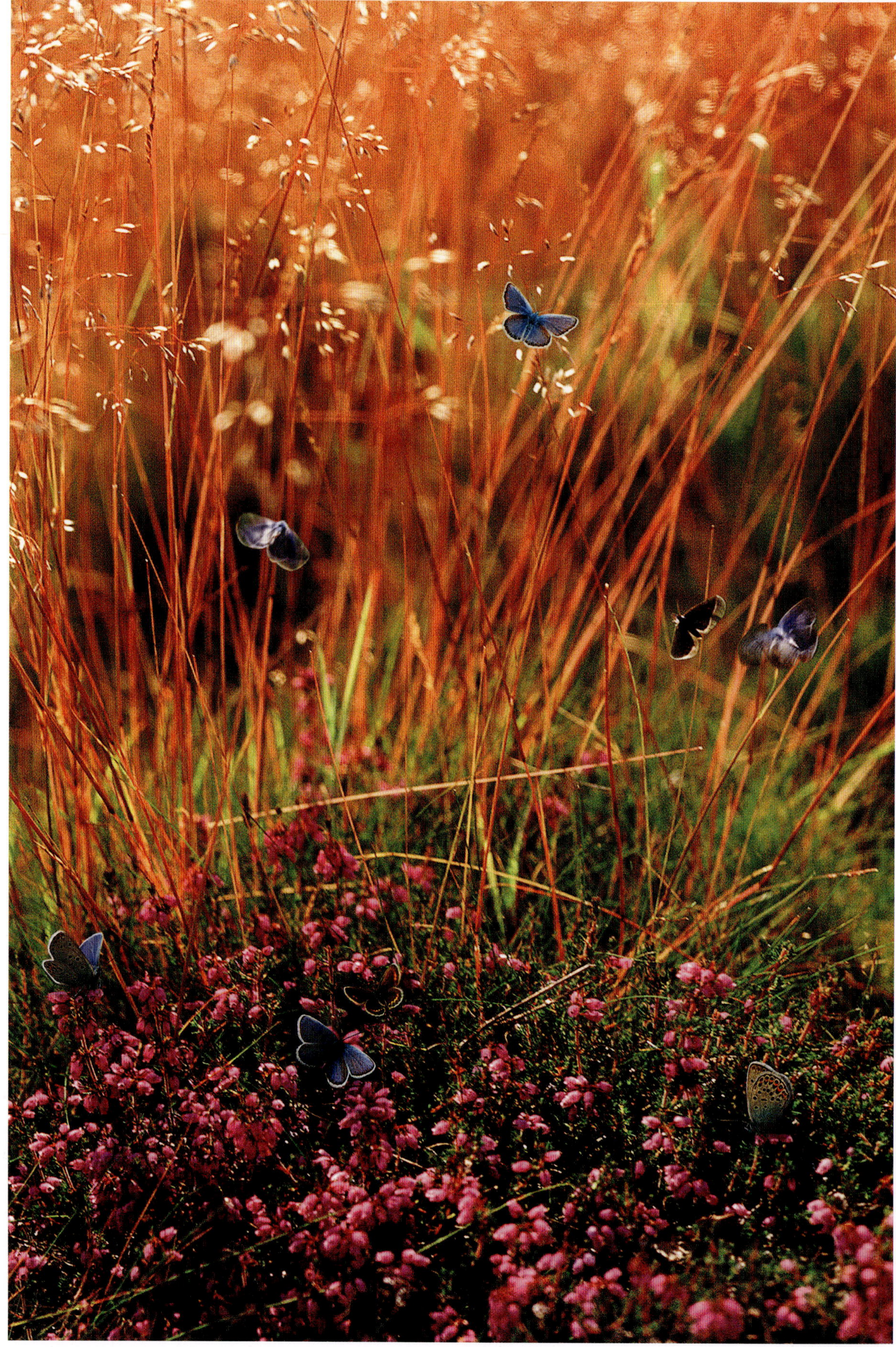

I had waited several years for the right day to take this photograph. I photographed these silver-studded blues (*Plebeius argus*) on a nature reserve specially set up for these rare butterflies. The butterflies have a symbiotic relationship with the black meadow ant, which is only found in this type of dry acid heathland. I used a slow shutter speed to convey a sense of motion. Sitting low down in the heather, I quietly clicked away all through the calm, sunny afternoon as the butterflies displayed to each other on the clump of heather.

Part one of a pair of images, Junction 6 is a 180-degree view of a motorway junction on the M40. The road has been carved through a hillside, with dense woodland planted right up to the border of the motorway. The view has always interested me. I wanted to produce an image that showed the density of traffic travelling through beautiful woodland, highlighting human intervention and the fragile nature of what remains. The image is constructed from 369 individual photographs, randomly arranged to create a sense of disorder. The only constant is the line of the motorway, which is isolated to emphasise the effect of the road through the landscape.

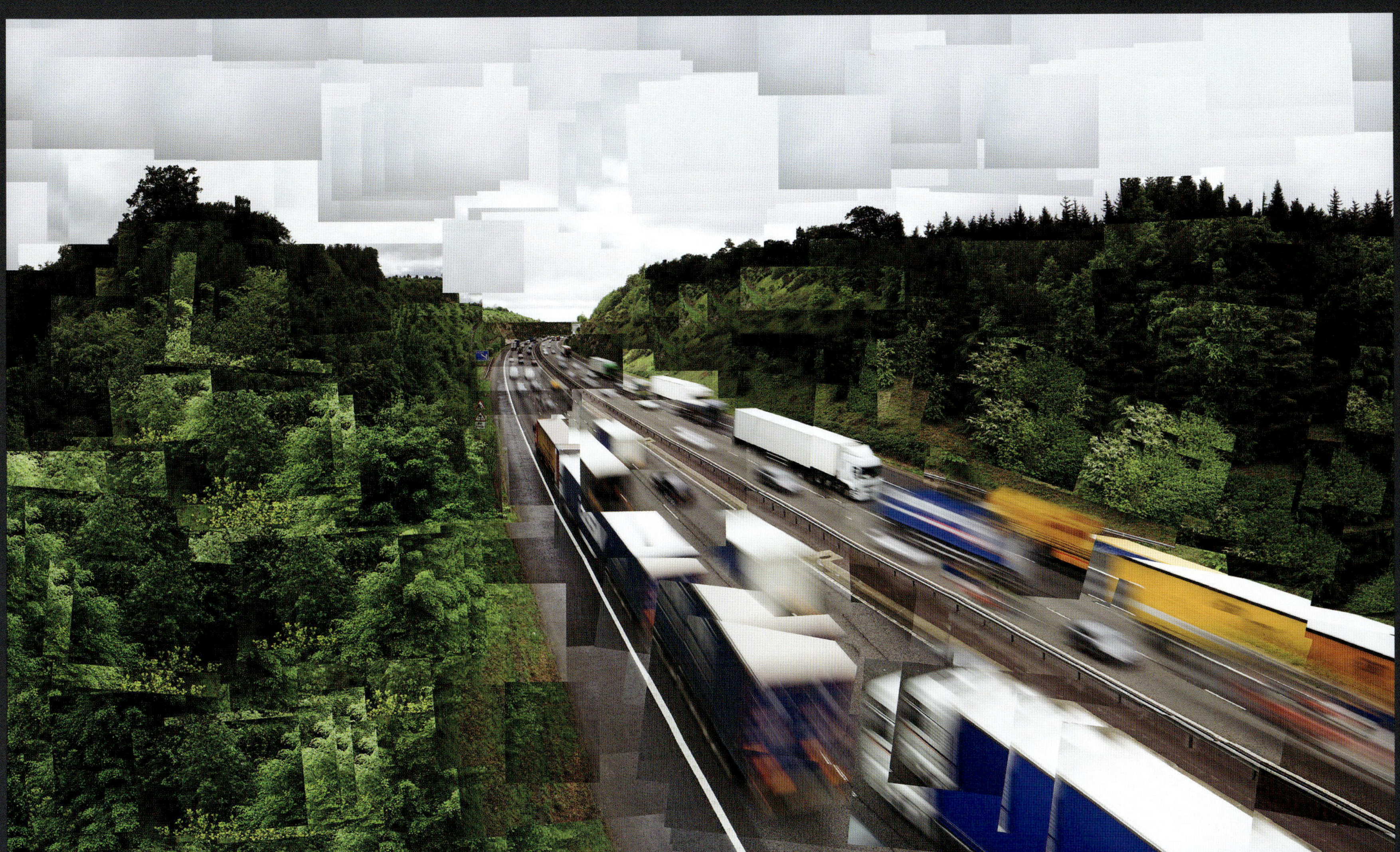

BUCKINGHAMSHIRE, ENGLAND
JUNCTION 6 NO.1. M40

PAUL DEBOIS

Kodak Pro/SLRc, 105mm Sigma macro lens, f/16-f/22. As I didn't want to create a 'perfect' panoramic, most of the shots were handheld so there would always be an overlap or random join. The traffic shots were taken on a tripod so a slower shutter speed could be used to create blur.
FINALIST, 2009

This tree was the only one around for miles in this remote area, and its stark beauty appealed to me. It just happened to be in full fall colour the day I passed by. An early fall of snow covered the mountains in the background. I waited for quite some time for the light to arrive at the tree.

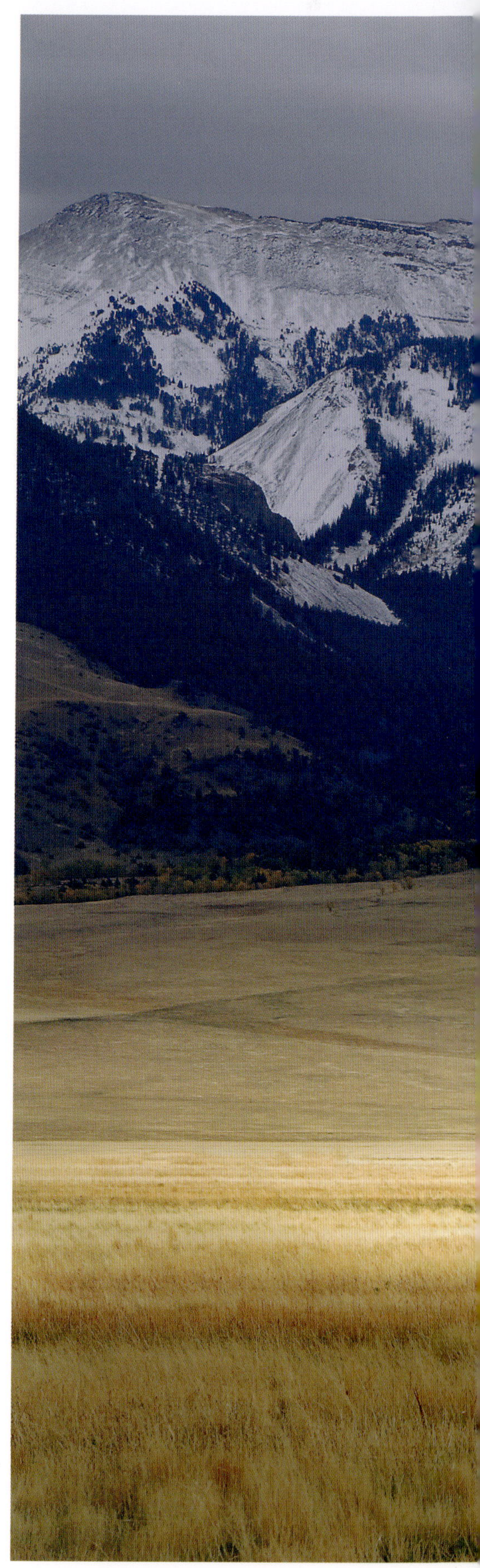

ENNIS, MONTANA
LONE FALL TREE

DENNIS FRATES

Canon EOS-1Ds Mark II, Canon 70-200mm f/2.8 L lens, f/14. The light around the tree was enhanced using levels in Photoshop.
FIRST, 2009

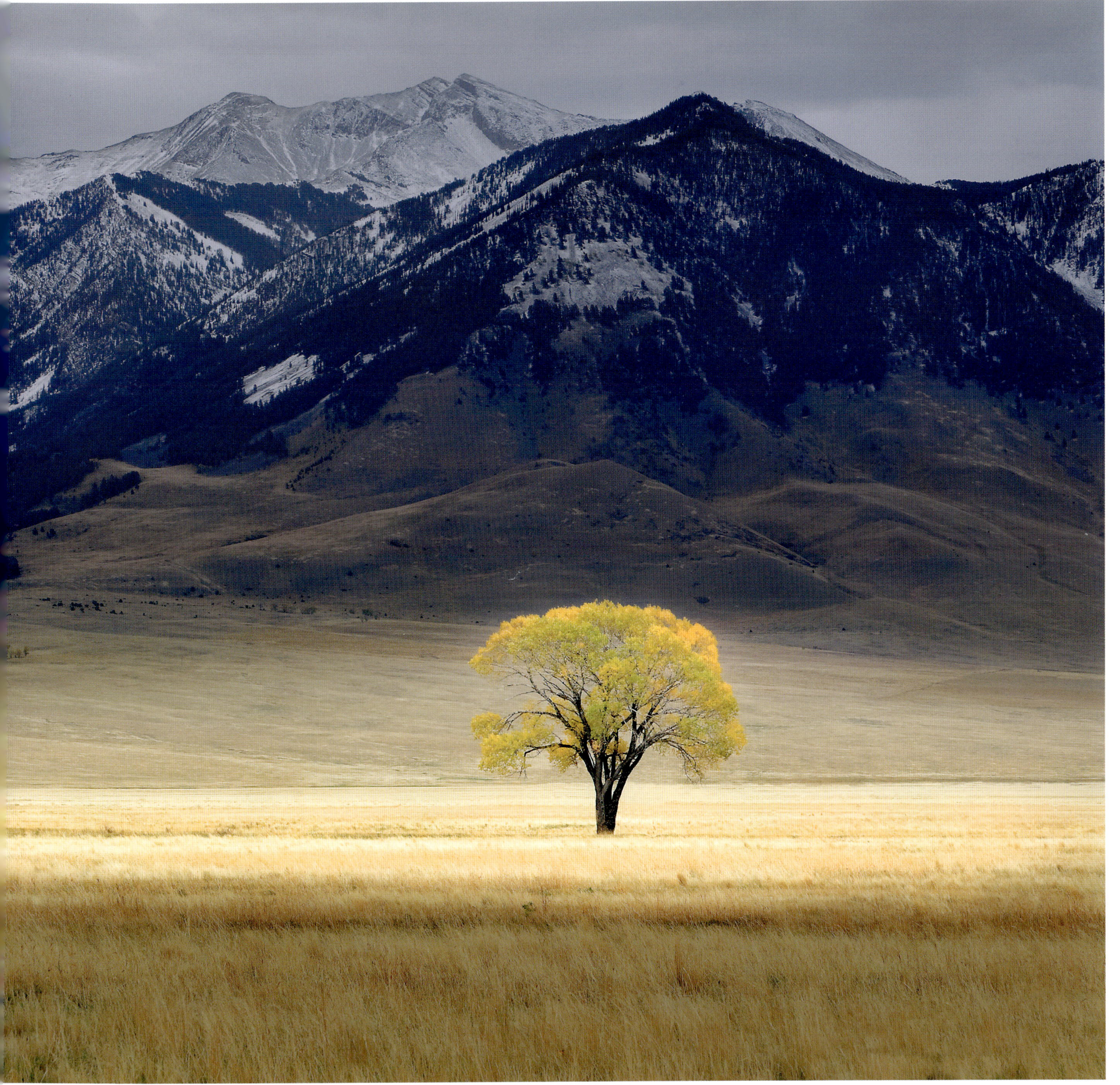

KALAPANA, BIG ISLAND, HAWAII

LAVA FERNS

STEVE NICHOLLS

Nikon D200, Nikon 18-200 zoom lens. 1/15sec at f/8. Post-capture: the black lava and bright sunset sky presented a huge tonal contrast, so I took two exposures, one to bring out details in the lava and the other to pick out the sunset colours. I combined the two images using a mask along the horizon.
FIRST, 2012

Bright green lines of the fern (*Polypodium pellucidum*) outline the patterns of cracks and crevices on a recent flow of pahoehoe lava on Hawaii's Big Island. This variety characteristically grows on windswept lava flows, and is among the first life forms to colonise newly-cooled lava flows. I particularly like the linear arrangement of these ferns as they take root in cracks in the lava. I waited until sunset so the steam plume was more softly lit and showed more contrast. The low angle of the sun made the ferns glow with an almost unnatural brightness.

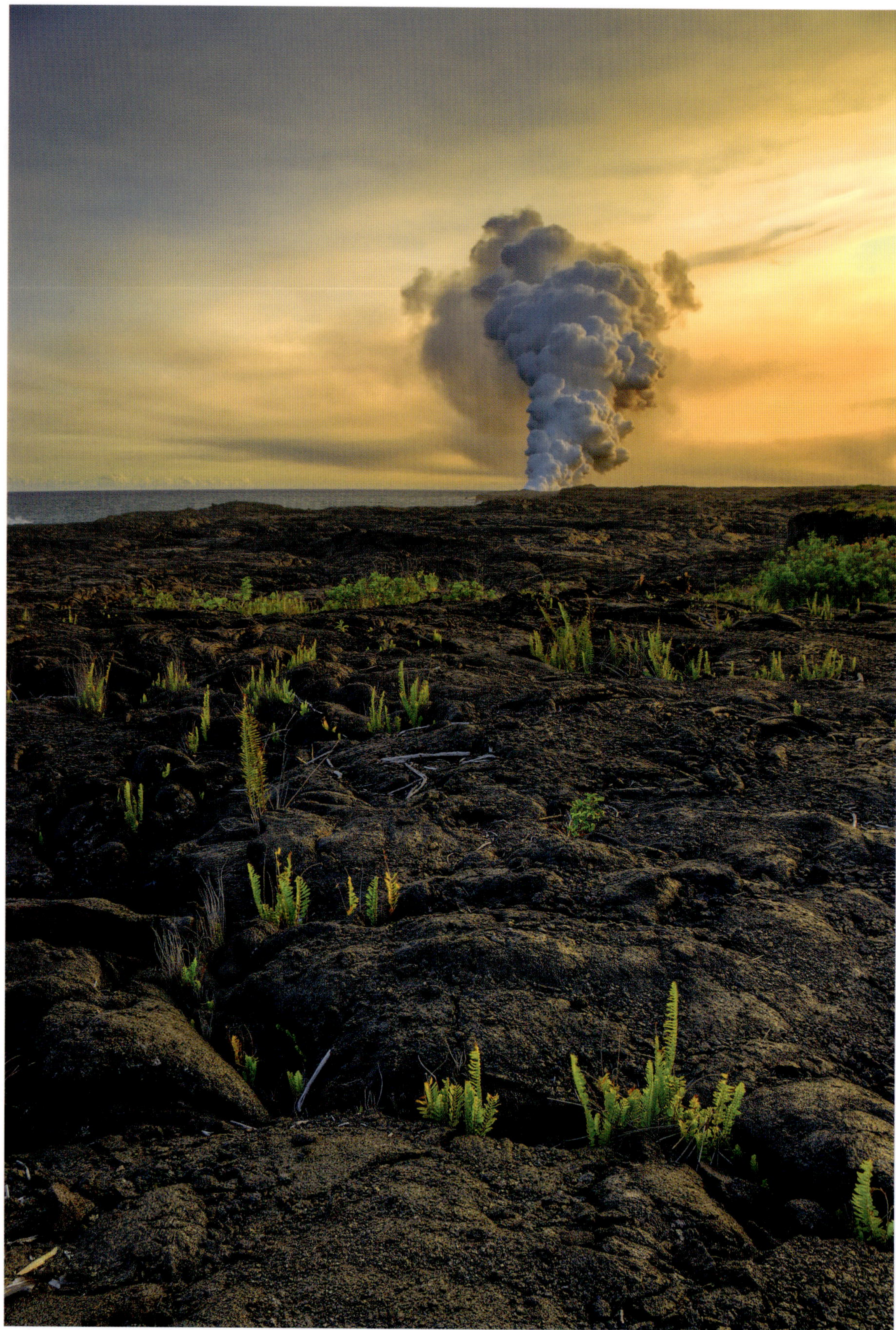

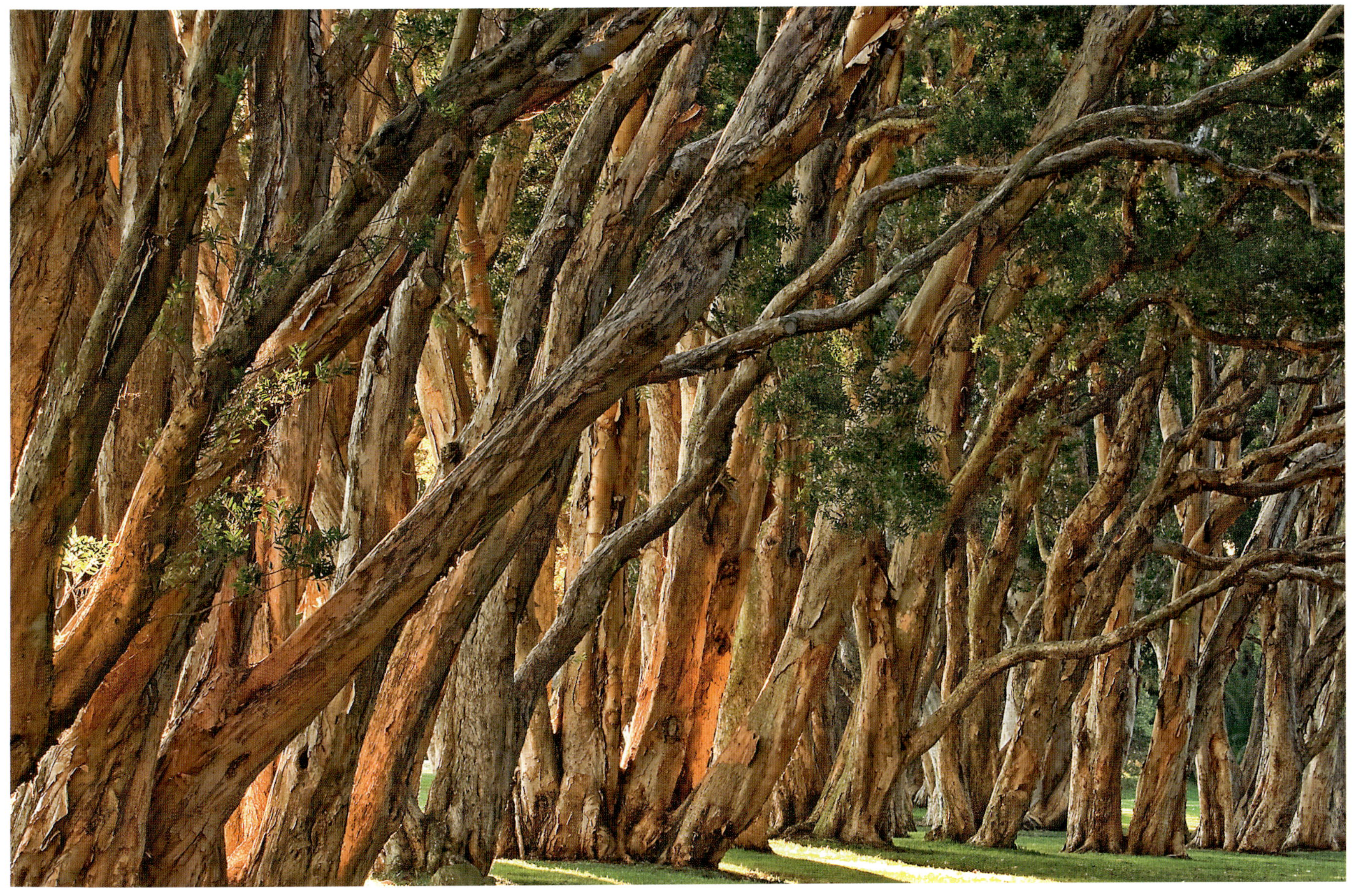

CENTENNIAL PARKLANDS,
SYDNEY, NEW SOUTH WALES
EVENING PAPERBARKS

GARY STEER

Canon EOS 10D, Canon EF 35-350mm zoom lens, 1sec at f/19. Because of the diminishing light, I set the camera on a tripod to allow a slow shutter speed, and to maintain a large depth of field.
COMMENDED, 2009

A row of broad-leaved paperbark (*Melaleuca quinquenervia*), which are native to the area, and favour moist, even swampy ground. The area was originally known as Lachlan Swamp. Water from this natural freshwater drainage area was channelled via Busby's Bore to the settlement of Sydney. In 1888, Centennial Park was established over the area. I was photographing near the end of the day with the sun behind me. I turned and looked towards the sun and was captivated by the golden backlight on the paperbark. It was irresistible to photograph them.

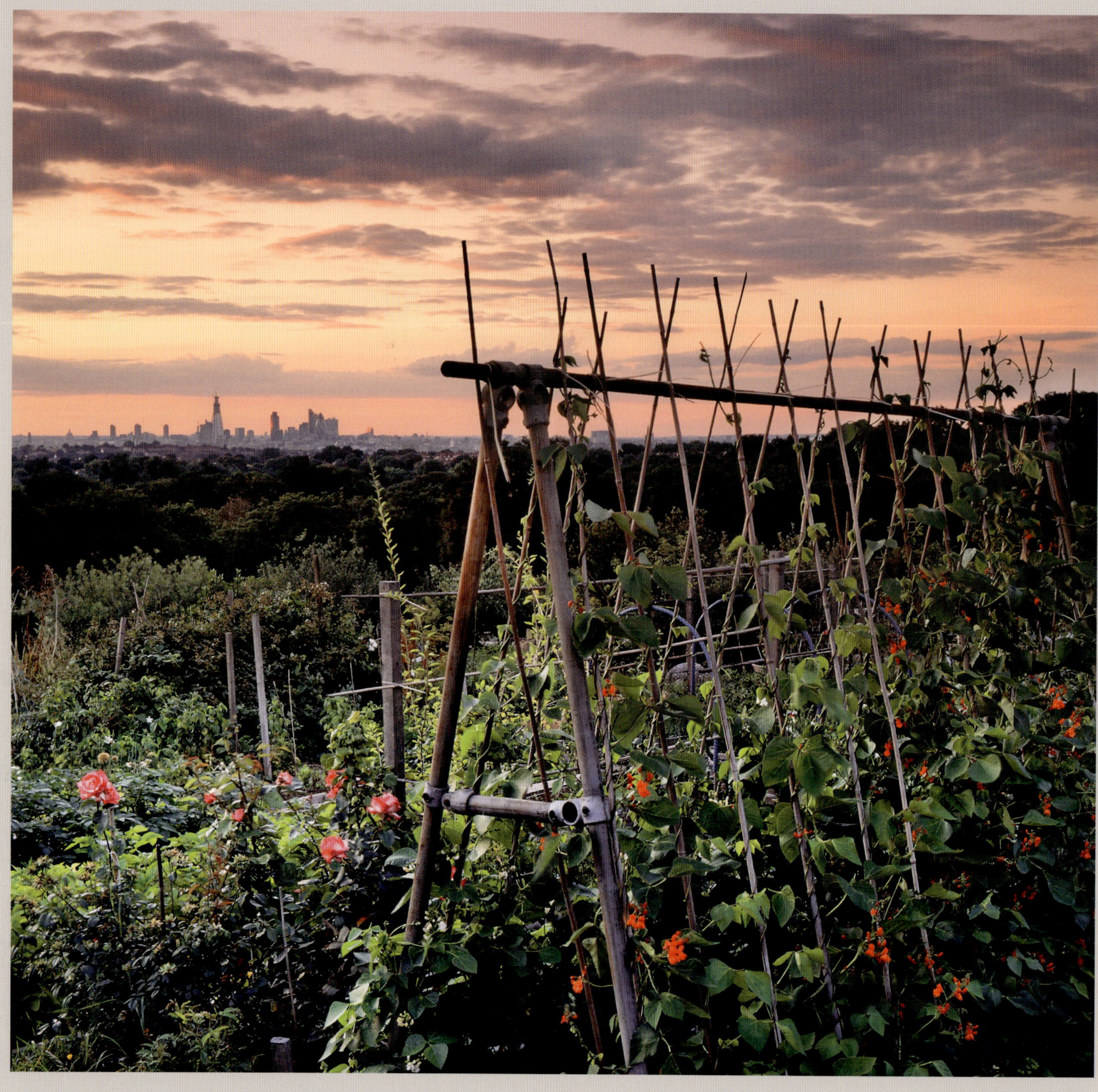

SYDENHAM HILL, LONDON, ENGLAND
BEANS AND THE CITY

MAX RUSH

Fuji Velvia 50 film, 120 Bronica SQAi, 80mm lens. 4sec at f/22, with 0.6 neutral density graduated filter to balance exposure between sky and land. Post-capture: minor tonal adjustment.
SECOND, 2012

A hillside allotment near Dulwich in late summer. This site is little-known outside the area, but its gardeners have the privilege of one of the greatest views in London. This view of climbing beans (*Phaseolus* spp.) against the backdrop of the city of London is from the first summer of a project which has already proved inspiring and exciting.

ISLE OF LEWIS, SCOTLAND

SONGS FROM THE MACHAIR

COLIN CAMPBELL

Canon EOS 40D, Tamron 11-18mm lens, 1/100sec at f/10. Post-capture: levels were tweaked with some colour management.

FINALIST, 2011

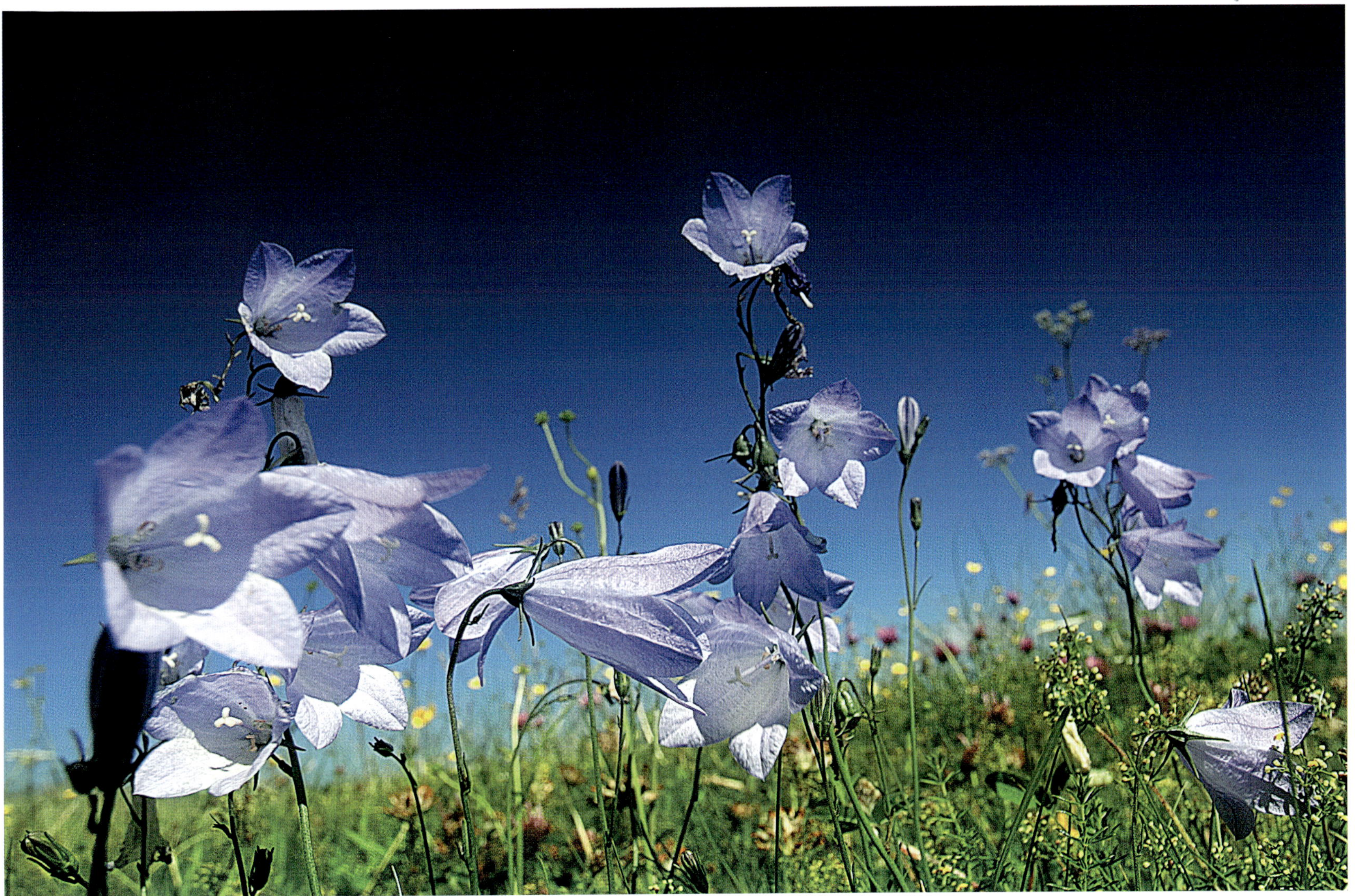

One of the rarest habitats in Europe, Machair is Scots Gaelic for 'low-lying fertile plain' and is only found between the sands and inland peats of the far northwest of Scotland and Ireland. It's a natural haven for wildlife and stunning to see. Wonderful blue harebells dominate the many flowers including daisies, buttercups, clover and orchids. This was a difficult shot to realise as the Machair itself is so large and varied in plant life. I knew a high, wide shot just wouldn't show the true nature of the beach so it was a case of getting right down amongst them. A windy day didn't help but the blur on some of the flowers expressed the movement on the day.

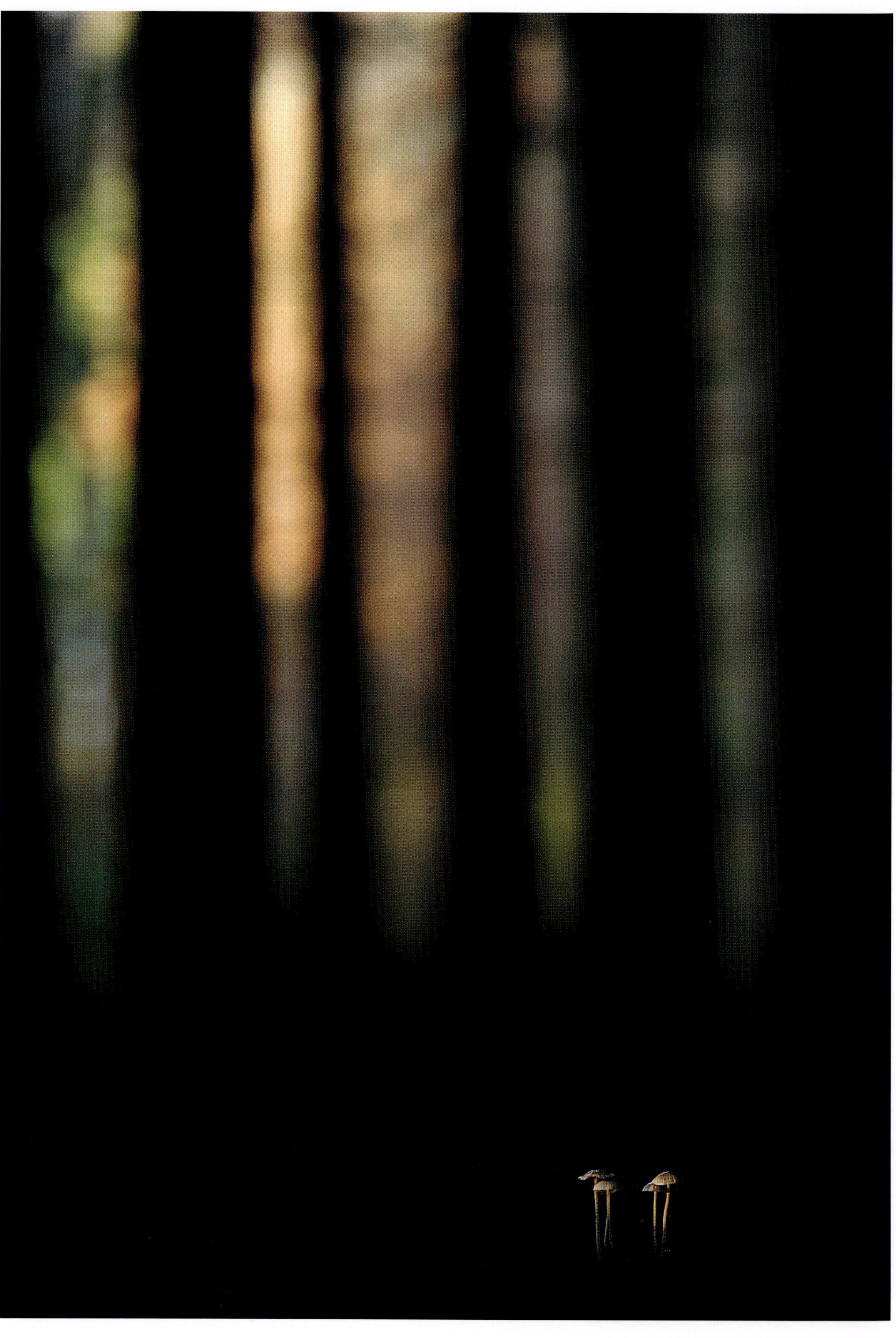

This pine forest is in the Salzkammergut region of Austria. Just as I was sitting on the ground I noticed a small group of fungus (*Mycena* spp.). I lay on my stomach and looked for a suitable composition.

SALZKAMMERGUT
FOREST DWELLERS

KEREKES ISTVÁN

Nikon D3, Nikkor 80-400mm lens. 1/100sec at f/4.8. Post-capture: sharpening, a little cropping and slight lightening.
FIRST, 2012

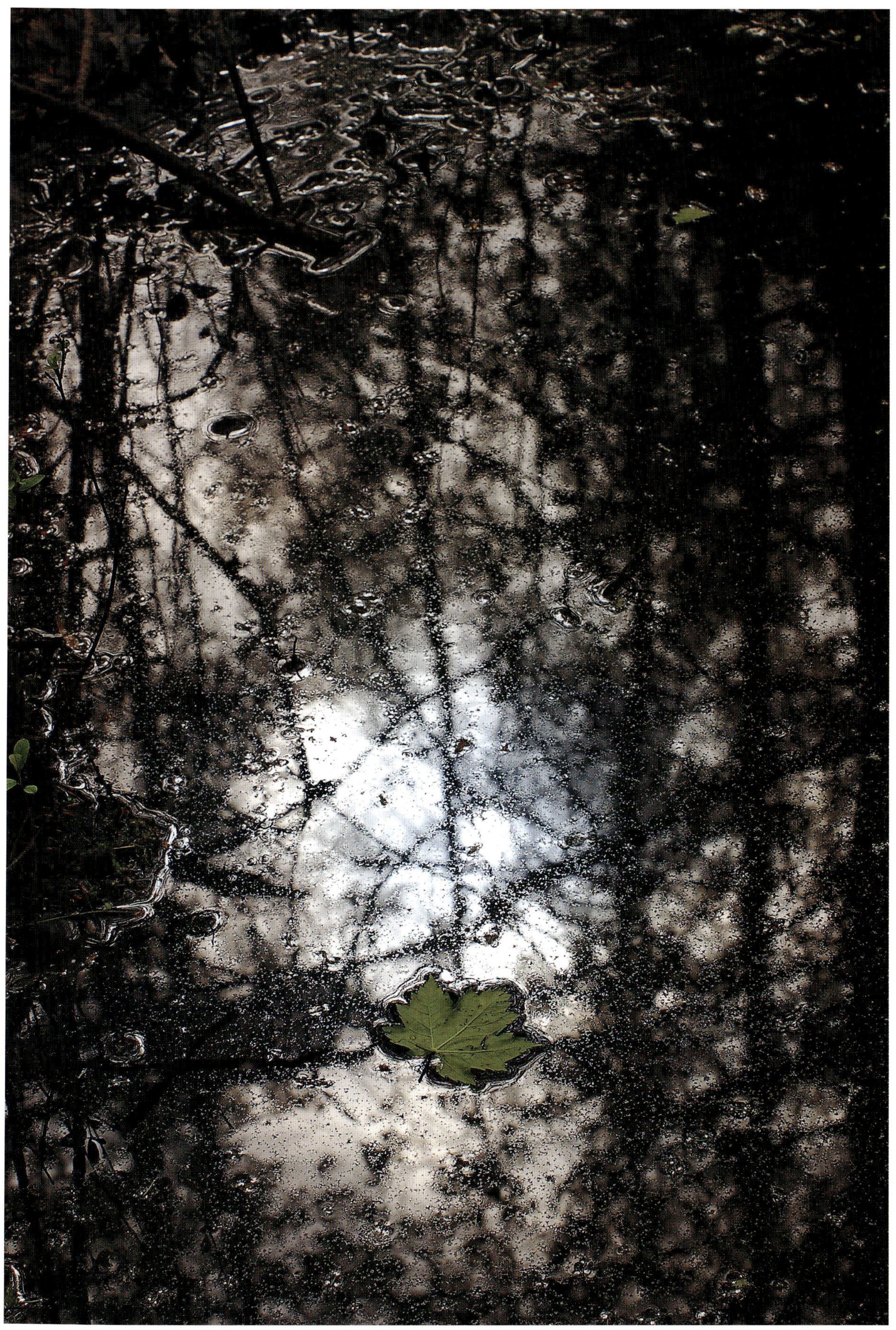

A lone maple leaf appears to float through the air as a momentary burst of light illuminates the surface of the bog to bring this surreal scene to life. I love the mystery and impermanence of this image. This matches the very nature of a bog itself, as all inevitably turn into swamps. This type of wetland is very rare in Ontario, and it is considered to be an ecological jewel in my hometown.

Bogs start out as slow-moving rivers or ponds which are gradually taken over by moss. Under this thick, floating layer of moss is a deep layer of decaying plant matter, called peat. This wetland is home to many carnivorous plants such as horned bladderwort (*Utricularia cornuta*), pitcher plants (*Sarracenia* spp.) and sundews (*Drosera* spp.).

SIFTON BOG, LONDON, ONTARIO
AFLOAT IN THE BRANCHES

KIMBERLEY BARDOEL

Nikon D50, Nikkor 70-300mm, f/11. I stood on the boardwalk observing the bog and looking for a subject. When I noticed this lone leaf there was a faint outline of the branches, but I knew if I waited for the light the reflection would brighten. I composed the picture and, when the sky opened, it created a depth to the reflection.

FINALIST, 2009

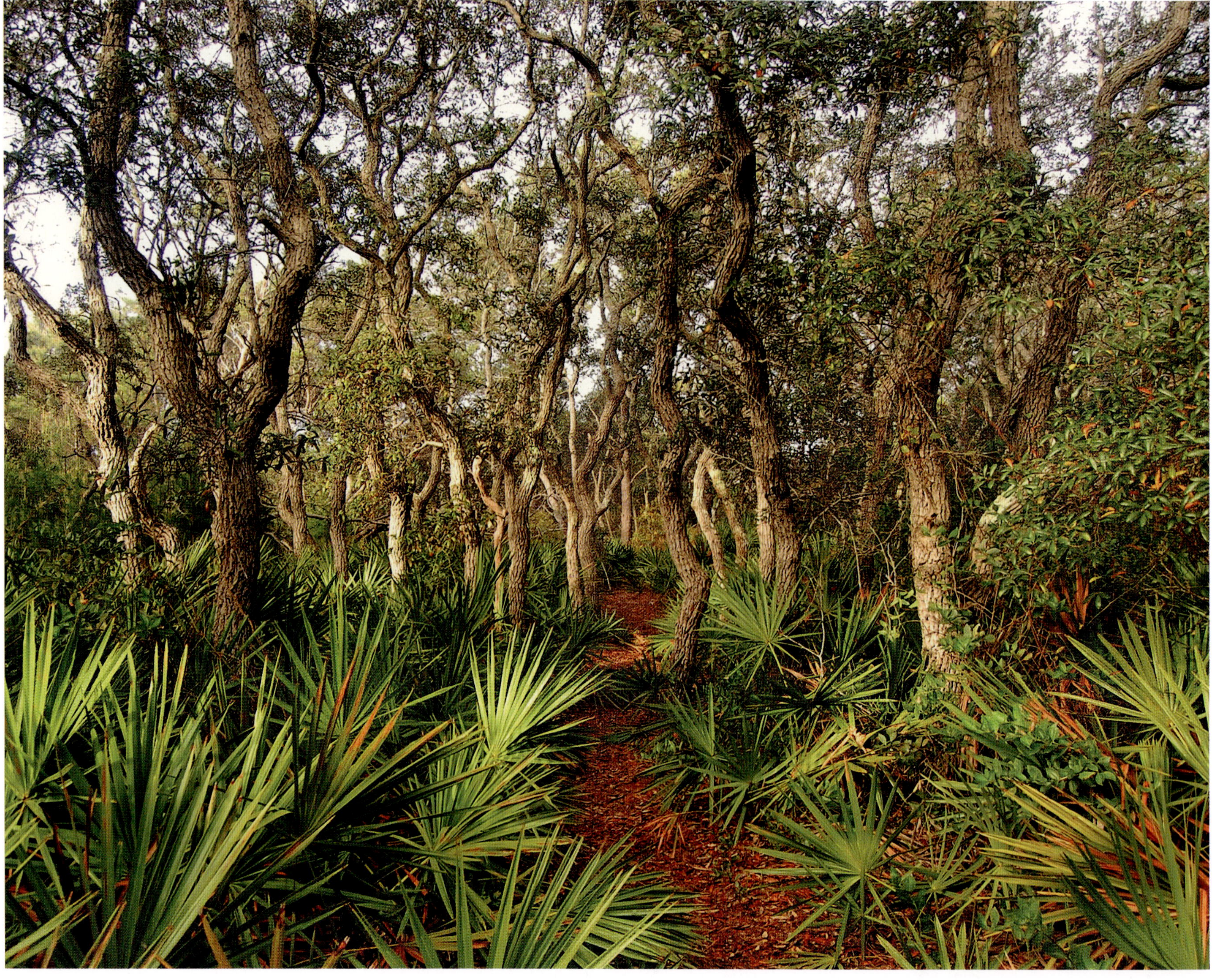

GRAYTON BEACH STATE PARK, NORTH-WEST FLORIDA

PALMETTOS AND SCRUB OAKS ON THE PATH TO THE BEACH

JOHN ROGER PALMOUR

Nikon D40, Nikkor 18-55mm lens, 1/125sec at f/5.6. Post-capture: slight correction/adjustments to exposure and colour saturation.
HIGHLY COMMENDED, 2011

I took this photograph just after dawn on an early April walk from our cabin to the white sand dunes and surf of the Gulf of Mexico. I love the way the light filters through the emerging leaves of the scrub oaks to illuminate the gnarled trunks and the palmetto leaves. I wish the picture had sound so that you could hear the mockingbirds, towhees and cardinals whose songs filled the air that morning. I'm told that this is a mixture of myrtle oak (*Quercus myrtifolia*), sandhill oak (*Quercus inopina*) and Chapman oak (*Quercus chapmanii*), with scrub palmetto (*Sabal etonia*) and saw palmetto (*Serenoa repens*) underneath a canopy of sand pines (*Pinus clausa*).

I was amazed by how totally different the sights, sounds, smells and light in this coastal ecosystem were from those in the forests of my southern Appalachian home, and hoped that when I viewed this image on my monitor it would allow me to recapture something of springtime in that special place. I took a series of shots quickly on my way to the beach that morning before the light could change, and did not use a tripod or any other special equipment. This image somehow stood out from the others.

Sponsors and Supporters

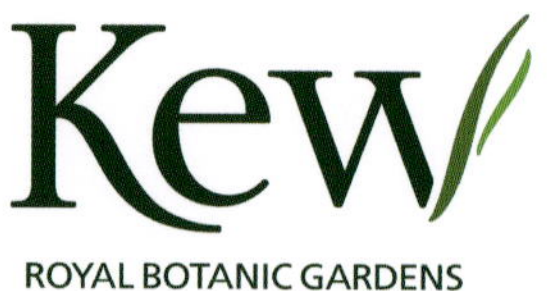

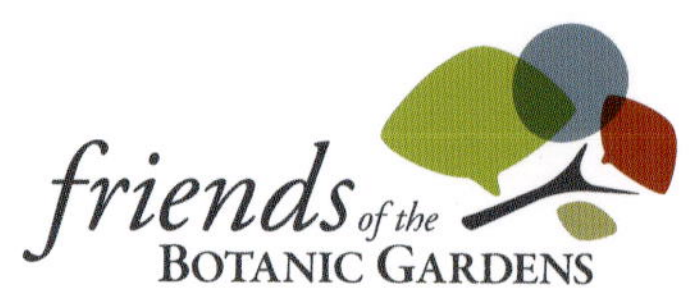

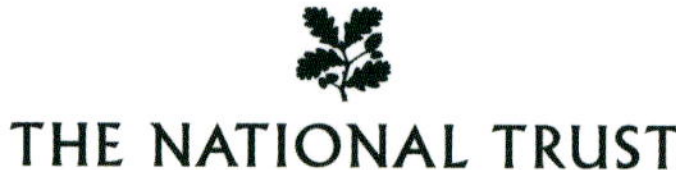

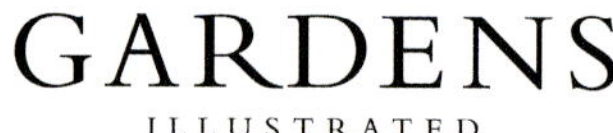

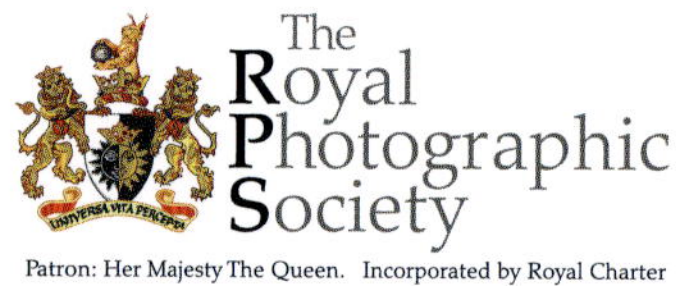

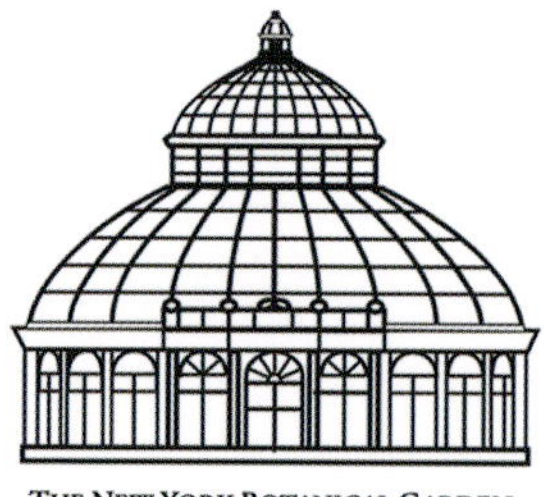

towergate camerasure